The Rare Soul Bible
A Northern Soul A - Z
The Reissue

Dave Rimmer
Visit my website at www.soulfulkindamusic.net

First Printing: June 2002
Second Printing: June 2016

Cover photo by Paul Royle

The Rare Soul Bible - The Reissue

The publication of Volume 2 of The Rare Soul Bible - A Northern Soul A - Z has prompted a huge renewal of interest in the original book from 2002.

There were a 1000 copies printed, 500 came with the box, and they all sold out many, many years ago. Occasionally copies appear on Ebay, and there are copies on Amazon right now at extortionate prices, so I decided to republish Volume 1 to cater for this demand.

The Original Introduction

So what's the point of this book? Why have I spent the time compiling the information, and why have you spent your hard earned cash buying it?

Well, over the last thirty years the Northern Soul Scene has matured. So much so that I think the breadth of Knowledge in the UK is now staggering. This book is an attempt to spread that information a little further. As a friend once said to me, we have to get this information down in writing now, to preserve the knowledge as time takes it, and sadly many of the artists themselves away from us. The artists who made those records we so revere very rarely got the recognition that they deserved back in the Sixties. Perhaps this is my way of saying Thank You, or perhaps this is my way of displaying what an anally retentive person I am. Who knows? Who cares? As long as you find this book useful

Hopefully this book will become the first place of reference for Soul fans around the world when they want a discography, or want to know who was in a group, or just something to read. It is essentially a book of information.

I'd also like to say thank you to all the artists whose names appear in the book. You have provided me with so much enjoyment over the years. I'd also like to say thank you to all the people who have shared my thirty year exploration of the music of Black America through the Northern Soul Scene. I couldn't have done it without you.

Finally I'd like to thank my long suffering wife Margie, who has for years now put up with my obsession with Sixties Soul Music.

Dave Rimmer 2002.

What's New In The Reissue ?

Essentially this is the same book that was published 14 years ago. However, there are some differences. The vast majority of the discographies have been improved upon and expanded over that period, so the ones included here are the most complete ones I can provide in 2016. This means they take up far more space in the book itself, so whilst you have the advantage of far more detailed discographies, something else had to give. Therefore I took the decision to not include any of the original photographs, and delete all the biographies that were included in the first volume. I hope you still enjoy it though

Dave Rimmer 2016

A Review by Dave Godin

The main reason Bee Cool Publishing has become the front runner in the field of specialised music publications is, in my view, due to the fact that they commission the right people to write books for them, and the results SHOW! There is no substitute for passion!

Their latest book by Dave Rimmer carries on this fine tradition and is an encyclopaedic compendium of 45rpm singles that have, at some time or another, found favour in terms of spins on the Northern Soul circuit. However, Dave hasn't just slavishly done label listings, but has arranged his entries by artist, which, as anyone who has ever compiled a discography knows, can be a mine-field with name changes, records being issued twice on the same label, or different labels, with different flipsides, and so on.

Also too, as Dave himself makes clear in the text, any such work can never hope to be "complete" since a combination of rare records surfacing and artists' amnesia lifting, will often reveal hidden assets, hidden shame, hidden naughtiness, and, sometimes, hidden gems.

Arranged alphabetically by artist surname, I was also pleased to see that some of Dave's excellent writing on the Soul scene has been included, particularly his valuable piece, the marathon titled, "Can 7-Inch 45rpm American Soul Singles Be Considered To Be Of Significant Historical Value? A Reasoned Argument". And of course, it goes without saying that they can, and Dave's reasons are compelling, sound and significant too! This essay alone is an essential read.

Some artists have biographical information, but where this work is of particular value is with those footloose artists who record all over the place! Barbara Jean English is a good example, and here we have her listed not only in her own right, but with The Clickettes, The Rinky Dinks, The Avalons and The Fashions and all label name permutations in between! Again, if you take a name like Tony Middleton, it is amazing just how many records (with various label name credits) this guy has been involved in. And Ike Turner's various involvements cover more than eight pages!

But just flipping through the book is like looking at a directory of old friends. And not just old friends who have made records, but our friends who spin them too, with club reports and various play-lists from those who have never given up on keeping the

faith.
Quite simply, this book is a must for anyone who has ever felt that thrill when the opening bars grab you, and you want to know more about whoever it was who has had the power to cast such an aesthetic spell upon you. And it proves too my oft repeat point that Black America quite simply managed to produce so many darned brilliant records that the market just couldn't absorb them all at one go. So, probably one of the most valuable services that the Northern Soul scene ever did was to get around to each and every one of them bit by bit, and spread the magic over several decades so that no worthy talent ever really got lost. Of course there is no substitute for the aesthetic rush that so many of these records deliver, but, once you've come down a bit, it's nice to know just who it was who was hitting on you so hard! And it's all here for the perusing. Great stuff.

Dave Godin 2002

Acknowledgements

In compiling these discographies the help of the following people has been invaluable.
Bosko Asanovic, who was a major contributor, both in terms of complete discographies, and corrections and additions.
Derek Pearson, who allowed me to pilfer all sorts from ***Shades Of Soul***
David Cole, who let me use discographies from ***In The Basement***
The following people have provided significant additions or corrections as well: **Graham Finch, David Flynn, Colin Dilnot, Anders Hansson, Andrew Hamilton, Keith Rylatt, and John Lester.**

There are also several hundred people, not least some of the artists themselves who have provided snippets of information that all add together to produce the bigger picture, far too many to name

I could go on forever with a list of friends who have provided me with encouragement, and inspiration, and not least lifts, but these people deserve a special mention: John Mills RIP, John Weston, Ady Croasdell, John Wilkinson, Micky Nold, Bill Randle, John Windsor RIP, Dave Godin RIP, Martyn, Tait & Lin, and all the Wolverhampton crew who adopted me when I moved to the Midlands.

And of course to Mike Ritson and Stuart Russell, from Bee Cool Publishing, who made the whole thing possible the first time round.

Group Line Ups

The Accents (Jimmy Short, Ezell 'Zeke' Johnson, Clifford Curry, Oliver Jackson, James Brown, Robert Hill)
Act One (Raeford Gerald, Reginald Ross, George Barker, Roger Terry)
The Adlibs (Mary Ann Thomas, Hugh Harris, Danny Austin, Norman Donegan, Dave Watt)
The Admirations - (Kenneth Childs, Bruce Childs, Ralph Childs)
The Adorables - (Jackie Winston, Betty Winston, Diane Lewis, Pat Lewis)

Barbara Acklin

Freddy Robinson

Checker 1143 - The Creeper / Go Go Girl - 1966 (Background Vocals Barbara Acklin)

Barbara Allen

Special Agent 203 - I'm Not Mad Anymore / Nobody Cares -1966

Barbara Acklin (born 28-February-1943 in Oakland, California. Moved to Chicago, Illinois in 1957. Died 27-November-1998 in Omaha, Nebraska. Cause: Pneumonia)

Special Agent 203 - I'm Not Mad Anymore / Nobody Cares - 1966 (rumoured to exist showing the artist's name as Barbara Acklin)

The Fantasions (members Barbara Acklin,..........................)

Thomas 308 - G.I. Joe (We Love You) / ? - 1966 (Richard "Popcorn" Wylie claims that Barbara Acklin was a member of The Fantasions)

Barbara Acklin

Brunswick 55319 - Fool, Fool, Fool (Look In The Mirror) / Your Sweet Loving - 1967
Brunswick 55355 - I've Got You Baby / Old Matchmaker - 1967

Gene Chandler & Barbara Acklin

Brunswick 55366 - Love Won't Start / Show Me The Way To Go - 1968

Barbara Acklin

Brunswick 55379 - Love Makes A Woman / Come And See My Baby - 1968

Gene Chandler & Barbara Acklin

Brunswick 55387 - From The Teacher To The Preacher / Anywhere But Nowhere - 1968

Barbara Acklin

Brunswick 55388 - Just Ain't No Love / Please Sunrise Please - 1968 (Some Copies Issued with picture sleeve)
Brunswick 55399 - Am I The Same Girl / Be By My Side - 1969

Gene Chandler & Barbara Acklin

Brunswick 55405 - Little Green Apples / Will I Find You - 1969

Barbara Acklin

Brunswick 55412 - Seven Days Of Night / Raggedy Ride - 1969
Brunswick 55421 - After You / More Ways Than One - 1969
Brunswick 55433 - Is It Me / Someone Else's Arms - 1970
Brunswick 55440 - I Did It / I'm Living With A Memory - 1970
Brunswick 55447 - I Can't Do My Thing / Make The Man Love You - 1971
Brunswick 55465 - Lady, Lady, Lady / Stop, Look And Listen - 1971
Brunswick 55486 - I Call It Trouble / Love You Are Mine Today - 1972
Brunswick 55501 - I'm Gonna Bake A Man / I Call It Trouble - 1973
Capitol 3892 - Raindrops / Here You Come Again - 1974
Capitol 4013 - Special Loving / You Gave Him Everything, But I Gave Him Love - 1974
Capitol 4061 - Give Me Some Of Your Sweet Love / First Love - 1975
Chi Sound - 1976 (No Records Released)

Barbara Acklin / Young-Holt-Unlimited

Eric 4503 - Love Makes A Woman / ?* - 1983 *Flip By Young-Holt-Unlimited.

Barbara Acklin

Krescent ? - You're The One / ? - 1990 (12" Release)

Dau 1015 - Love Makes A Woman / Come And See Me Baby - ? (A bootleg of the Brunswick release)

Adam's Apples

Brunswick 55330 - Don't Take It Out On This World / Don't You Want Me Home - 1967
Brunswick 55367 - You Are The One I Love* / A Stop Along The Way** - 1968 *also recorded in 1968 by The Leaders on Blue Rock 4060. **also recorded in 1968 by Timothy Carr on The Hot Biscuit Disc Company 1454

The Ad-Libs

The Arabians (members Hugh Harris, Danny Austin, John Alan, David Allen Watt, Jr. and James Wright)

The Creators (members Hugh Harris, James Wright (later member of The Spellbinders), John Alan, Danny Austin and Chris Coles)

T-Kay 110 - I'll Never Do It Again / Boy He's Got It - 1962
Philips 40058 - Boy He's Got It / Yeah He's Got It - 1962
Philips 40083 - I'll Stay Home (New Year's Eve) / Shoom Ba Boom - 1962

The Cheers (members

The Ad-Libs (members Mary Ann Thomas, Hugh Harris, Danny Austin, Norman Donegan and David Watt (born ? --- died 5-December-2008 in New Jersey --- cause: complications leading to pneumonia)

Blue Cat 102 - The Boy From New York City / Kicked Around - 1965
Blue Cat 114 - Ask Anybody / He Ain't No Angel - 1965
Blue Cat 119 - On The Corner / Oo-Wee Oh Me Oh My - 1965
Blue Cat 123 - Just A Down Home Girl / Johnny My Boy - 1966
Karen 1527 - Think Of Me / Every Boy And Girl - 1966
Eskee 10003 - New York In The Dark / ? - 1966
Philips 40461 - Don't Ever Leave Me / You're In Love - 1967
A. G. P. 101 - New York In The Dark / Human - 1968

The Ad Libs (members Linda Goodson, Hugh Harris, Danny Austin, Norman Donegan and David Watt)

Share 101 - You're Just A Rolling Stone / Show A Little Appreciation – 1969
Share 104 - Giving Up* / Appreciation – 1969 *also recorded in 1964 by Gladys Knight & The Pips on Maxx 326.
Share 104 - Giving Up / Appreciation - 1969
Share 106 - The Boy From New York City / Nothing Worse Than Being Alone – 1969
Share 106 - Nothing Worse Than Being Alone / If She Want's Him - 1969
Capitol 2944 - Love Me / Know All About You – 1970

The Ad-Libs / The Pastels

Owl 332 – Human* / Oo-Wee Oh Me, Oh My – 1974 *This is an acappella recording of Human by the Ad-Libs. **flip by The Pastels.

The Ad-Libs

Right-On 105 - Dance With Me, Children / Dance With Me, Children - 1977

The Ad-Libs (members David Watt (died 5-December-2008 --- cause: ?), Chris Bartley, Jimmy Hollinger, Eller Weas Little and Natalie ?) This veteran New York group are also managed by Chris Bartley's manager Bill Downs. Chris Bartley joined the group sometime around 1975

Passion 1 - I Don't Need No Fortune Teller / Spring And Summer - 1977

The Ad-Libs / The Jelly Beans

Goldisc 3058 - The Boy From New York City / I Wanna Love Him So Bad* - 1978 *flip by The Jelly Beans.

The Trade Winds / The Ad-Libs

Eric 146 - New York's A Lonely Town / The Boy From New York City - ? *flip by The Ad-Libs
Collectables Col 038797 - New York's A Lonely Town / The Boy From New York City* - ? *flip by The Ad-Libs

The Ad-Libs (members David Watt, Chris Bartley, Jimmy Hollinger, Eller Weas Little and Natalie ?) This veteran New York group are also managed by Chris Bartley's manager Bill

Downs. Chris Bartley joined the group sometime around 1975

Passion.1 - I Don't Need No Fortune Teller / Spring And Summer** - 1977 **Chris Bartley lead.

The Ad-Libs (members David Watt, Chris Bartley, Ray Block, Abby Grant and Mary Ann Thomas)

Johnnie Boy 01 - I Stayed Home (New Year's Eve) / I Stayed Home (New Year's Eve) (Acapella) – 1988
Johnnie Boy 02 – The Tide Has Turned / The Tide Has Turned (Instrumental) – 1988
Johnnie Boy 03 - Close To Me / Close To Me (Instrumental) – 1988
Johnnie Boy 04 – I Stayed Home (New Year's Eve) / Santa's On His Way – 1988

The Ad-Libs (members

Stoop Sounds 513 - Human / New York In The Dark - 1996

Jewel Akens

The Fascinators (members Albert (Jerry) Stone, Jewel Akens, Teddy Harper, and David Harris)

Dootone 441 - Teardrop Eyes / Shivers And Shakes - 1958

Jerry Stone &The Four Dots (members Jewel Akens, Albert (Jerry) Stone, Eddie Cochran, Warn Crosby and at various times Freddy Clark or Sam Dearden) Five singers but named "Four"

Freedom 44002 - It's Heaven / My Baby - 1958

The Four Dots (members Jewel Akens, Albert (Jerry) Stone, Eddie Cochran, Warn Crosby and at various times Freddy Clark or Sam Dearden)

Freedom 44005 - Pleading For Your Love / Don't Wake Up The Kids - 1959

John Ashley & Voices Of Allah

Silver 1002 - Seriously In Love / I Want To Hear It From You - 1959 (Backing vocals The Four Dots)

Jewel & Eddie (members Jewel Akens and Eddie Daniels, Eddie Cochran plays guitar)

Silver 1004 - Opportunity / Doin' The Hully Gully - 1960
Silver 1004 - Opportunity / Strollin' Guitar* - 1960 *cover of 1959 release by The Kelly Four on Silver 1001.
Silver 1008 - Sixteen Tons* / My Eyes Are Cryin' For You - 1960 *also recorded in 1955 by Ernie Tennessee Ford on Capitol F3262 and in 1963 by Eugene Church on King 5715 plus in 1967 by James & Bobby Purify on Bell 680.
Silver 1008 - Who Can I Count On / Doin' The Hully Gully - 1959
Silver 1010 - Who Can I Count On / ? - 1959

The Astro-Jets (Jewel Akens and Eddie Daniels)

Imperial 5760 - Boom-A-Lay / Hide And Seek - 1961

Jewel Akers

Capehart 5007 - (Dancing) The Mashed Potatoes / Wee Bit More Of Your Lovin' – 1962

Jewel Akens (born in 12-September-1940 in Houston, Texas)

Crest 1098 - (Dancing) The Mashed Potatoes / Wee Bit More Of Your Lovin' - 1962

The Rainbows (members Terry Evans, Jewel Akens, Jimmy Russell and Thomas Turner)

Gramo 5508 - Till Tomorrow / Mama, Take Your Daughter Back - 1963

Terry Evans

Kayo 5102 - Just 'Cause / So Nice To Be Loved - 1963

Terry & The Tyrants (members Terry Evans (from Mississippi), Jewel Akens, Jimmy Russell and Thomas Turner)

Kent 399 - Weep No More / Yea, Yea, Yea, Yea, Yea, Yea - 1964
Kent - Say It Baby - (although unissued on vinyl this was released in the U. K. on a 2005 Kent Cd "For Connoisseurs Only Volume 2" CDKEND 251)
Kent - Love Me To Death - (unissued track which was released in the U. K. on a 2007 Kent Cd "For Connoisseurs Only Volume 3" CDKEND 281)

The Turn-Arounds (members Jewel Akens, Terry Evans, Thomas Turner and Jimmy Russell)

Era 3137 - Run Away And Hide / Ain't Nothin' Shakin' - 1964

Jewel Akens

Era 3141 - The Birds And The Bees / Tic Tac Toe - 1964
Era 3142 - Georgie Porgie / Around The Corner (From My House) - 1965
Minasa 6716 - (Dancing) The Mashed Potatoes / Wee Bit More Of Your Lovin' - 1965
Dradil 01 - Doin' The Monster Mash / 13 Steps (To Room Blue) - ?
Era 3147 - You Sure Know How To Hurt A Guy / It's The Only Way To Fly - 1965
Era 3154 - You Don't Need A Crown / I've Arrived* - 1965 *also recorded in 1967 by Steve Flanagan on Era 3186.
Era 3156 - A Slice Of The Pie / You Better Believe It - 1965
Era 3164 - My First Lonely Night (Sukiyaki) / Mama Take Your Daughter Back - 1966 Colgens 1009 - Born A Loser / Little Bitty Pretty One* - 1967 *also recorded in 1957 by Thurston Harris on Aladdin 3398 and in 1960 by Frankie Lymon on Roulette 4527 plus in 1968 by The Popular Five on Minit 32050.
Colgems 1025 - It's A Sin To Tell A Lie / You Better Move On* - 1968 *originally recorded in 1962 by Arthur Alexander on Dot 16309.
Era 3207 - A Slice Of The Pie / A Land Where Animals Are People - 1969
Era 104 - Buenos Aires / Mississippi Syrup Sopper – 1969
West-One Kingdom 109 - He's Good For Me / Helplessly In Love – 1969
Paula 337 - Blue Eyed Soul Brother / Why Do You Want To Go - 1970
RTV 2005 - Music Box / Over And Over - 1972
Icepac 303 - What Would You Do / Since I Don't Have You - 1972

The Turnarounds (Jewel Akens & Terry Evans) (members Jewel Akens , Terry Evans, ...)

De Ville 155 - I Ate The Whole Thing / Live And Let Live - 197?

Jewel Akens

American International Artists 110 - When Something Is Wrong With My Baby / I Just Can't Turn My Habit Into Love - 1975

As-Wanna 2176 - I'm Goin' Back Home / Naked City - ?
Collectables Col 031667 - The Birds And The Bees / Georgie Porgie - 1980's

Jewel Akens, Mr. Birds and Bees

MDM 191 - Christine / Please God - 1988

The Feathers (members Johnny Staton, Dave Antrell, Jewel Akens and Jimmy Colbert)

Classic Artists 109 - Charlene / Irene My Darling - 1989

The Feathers / The Jaguars

Classic Artists 117 - More Than Enough For Me / Happy Holiday* - 1989 *flip by The Jaguars.

The Feathers

Classic Artists 125 - At The Altar / A Girl Like You - 1991

The Andantes

The Andantes

Dot 16495 - My Baby's Gone / No Yo Ru - 1963

LaBrenda Ben & The Andantes

Gordy 7021 - Just Be Yourself / I Can't Help It I've Got To Dance - 1963

The Andantes

V.I.P. 25006 - (Like A) Nightmare / If You Were Mine - 1964

Ruby Andrews

The Vondells (members Ruby Stackhouse,........................)

Marvello 5005 - Errand Boy / Then I Know - 1964
Marvello 5006 - Lenora / Valentino - 1964

Ruby Stackhouse & The Vondells (members: Ruby Stackhouse.................)

Kellmac - 1001 - Please Tell Me / Wishing - 1965

Ruby Andrews (born Ruby Stackhouse 12-March-1947 in Hollandale, Mississippi)

Zodiac 1001 - Let's Get A Groove Going On (Part 1) / Let's Get A Groove Going On (Part 2) - 1967
Zodiac 1003 - Johnny's Gone Away / I Just Can't Get Enough - 1967
Zodiac 1004 - Casanova (Your Playing Days Are Over)* / I Just Don't Believe It - 1967 *this backing track was also issued in 1968 by Wayne Bennett on Giant 703 (Chicago label)
Zodiac 1004 - Casonova (Your Playing Days Are Over) / I Just Don't Believe It - 1967
Zodiac 1006 - Hey Boy (Take A Chance On Me) / Come To Me - 1968
Zodiac 1007 - You Can Run / Wonderful Night - 1968

Zodiac 1010 - The Love I Need / Just Loving You - 1968
Zodiac 1012 - I Guess That Don't Make Me A Loser / I Let Him Take Me - 1968
Zodiac 1015 - You Made A Believer (Out Of Me) / Where Have You Gone - 1969
Zodiac 1016 - Help Yourself (Lover) / All The Way - 1970
Zodiac 1017 - Everybody Saw You / Can You Get Away - 1970
Zodiac 1020 - You Ole Boo Boo You / Gotta Break Away - 1970
Zodiac 1022 - Hound Dog / Away From The Crowd - 1971
Zodiac 1023 - (I Want To Be) What Ever It Takes To Please You (Part 1) / (I Want To Be) What Ever It Takes To Please You (Part 2) - 1971
Zodiac 1024 - Good 'N' Plenty / My Love Is Coming Down - 1972
Zodiac 1032 - You Gotta Do The Same Thing / Didn't I Fool You - 1973
ABC 12215 - I Got A Bone To Pick With You / I Don't Know How To Love You - 1976
ABC 12257 - Queen Of The Disco (45rpm) / Queen Of The Disco (Disco Version) (33 1/3 rpm) - 1977 (promo issue only - same song both sides and flip has same running time but label says "Disco Version")
ABC 12257 - Queen Of The Disco / A Little Fixin' Up (Will Keep Him From Messin' Up) - 1977
ABC 12286 - I Wanna Be Near You / Cinderella - 1977
Ichiban 228 -I Got What I Want At Home / To The Other Woman (I'm The Other Woman) - 1993

Ruby Andrews / The Brothers Of Soul

Collectables COL 035877 - Casanova (Your Playing Days Are Over) / I Guess That Don't Make Me A Loser*- ? *flip by The Brothers Of Soul.

Patti Austin

Patti Austin (born 10-August-1948 in New York City. God-daughter of Quincy Jones)

Coral 62455 - He's Good Enough For Me / Earl - 1965
Coral 62471 - I Wanna Be Loved / A Most Unusual Boy - 1965
Coral 62478 - Someone's Gonna Cry / You Better Know What You're Getting - 1966
Coral 62491 - Take Your Time / Take Away The Pain Stain - 1966
Coral 62500 - Leave A Little Love / My Lovelight Ain't Gonna Shine - 1966
Coral 62511 - Got To Check You Out / What A Difference A Day Makes - 1967
Coral 62518 - Only All The Time / Oh How I Need You Joe - 1967
Coral 62536 - A Tisket A Tasket / A Milion To One - 1967
Coral 62541 - I'll Keep Loving You / You're Too Much A Part Of Me - 1967
Coral 62548 - (I've Given) All My Love / Why Can't We Try It Again - 1968
ABC 11104 - Music To My Heart / Love 'Em And Leave 'Em Kind Of Love - 1968
United Artists 50520 - The Family Tree / Magical Boy - 1969
United Artists 50588 - I Will Wait For You / Big Mouth - 1969
United Artists 50640 - Your Love Made A Difference In Me / It's Easier To Laugh Than Cry - 1970
Columbia 45337 - Are We Ready For Love / Now That I Know What Loneliness Is - 1971
Columbia 45410 - Black California / All Good Gifts - Day By Day - 1971
Columbia 45499 - God Only Knows / Can't Forget The One I Love - 1971
Columbia 45592 - Day By Day / Didn't Say A Word - 1972
Columbia 45785 - Come To Him / Turn On The Music - 1973
Columbia 45906 - Being With You / Take A Closer Look - 1973

Patti Austin & Jerry Butler

CTI 7 - In My Life (Part 1) / In My Life (Part 2) - 1973

Patti Austin

CTI 33 - Say You Love Me / In My Life - 1976
CTI 41 - We're In Love / Golden Oldies - 1977

Quincy Jones

A & M 2080 - Love I Never Had It So Good / I Heard That - 1978 (Vocals By Patti Austin)

Patti Austin

CTI 51 - Love Me By Name / You Fooled Me - 1978

Patti Austin & Jerry Butler

CTI 59 - What's At The End Of The Rainbow / In My Life - 1978

Patti Austin

CTI 9600 - Body Language / People In Love - 1980
CTI 9601 - I Want You Tonight / Love Me Again - 1980

Quincy Jones featuring Patti Austin

A & M 2334 - Razzamataz / Velas - 1981
A & M 2417 - There's A Train Leavin' / Something Special - 1981

Yutaka (born Yutaka Yokokura in Tokyo, Japan. Male jazz-pop vocalist / keyboardist)

Alfa 7004 - Love Light / Evening Star - 1981 (vocals by Yutaka and Patti Austin)

Patti Austin

Qwest 49754 - Do You Love Me / Solero - 1981
Qwest 49854 - Every Home Should Have One / Solero - 1981

Patti Austin with James Ingram / Patti Austin

Qwest 50036 - Baby, Come To Me / Solero* - 1983 *flip by Patti Austin only.

Patti Austin

Qwest 29727 - Every Home Should Have One / Solero - 1983

James Ingram & Patti Austin

Qwest 29618 - How Do You Keep The Music Playing / Long Version - 1984 (theme from the film "Best Friends")

Patti Austin

Qwest 29373 - It's Gonna Be Special / Solero - 1984 (From The Film "Two Of A Kind")
Qwest 29305 - Rhythm Of The Street / Solero - 1984
Qwest 29234 - Shoot The Moon / Change Your Attitude - 1984
Qwest 29136 - All Behind Us Now / Fine Fine Fellow (Got To Have You) - 1984

Narada Michael Walden with Patti Austin

Warner Brothers 29077 - Gimme, Gimme, Gimme / Wear Your Love - 1985

Patti Austin

Qwest 28935 - Honey For The Bees / Hot In The Flames Of Love - 1985
Qwest 28788 - The Heat Of Heat / Hot In The Flames Of Love - 1986
Qwest 28573 - Only A Breath Away / Summer Is The Coldest Time Of The Year - 1986
Qwest 28659 - Gettin' Away With Murder / Anything Can Happen Here - 1986
Qwest 27718 - Smoke Gets In Your Eyes / How Long Has This Been Goin' On? - 1988 (Some Copies Issued With Picture Sleeve)
Elektra 69254 - Miles Apart / Any Other Fool - 1989

Masters At Work featuring Patti Austin

MAW 057 - Like A Butterfly (You Send Me) / Like A Butterfly (You Send Me) (Kenny Dope Dub) - 2001 (12" release)

Venue Reports January 2001

The Down Inn, Bridgnorth, 6th January, 2001
Still no bloody heating. We almost gathered a load of flyers together on a table and set fire to them. Don't let that put you off though, this is a great little venue, and this was the best attended yet. Great music ranging from old stompers to current '90s tunes.

The Lea Manor, Albrighton, 13th January, 2001
Bumpy Thumpy again. Andy Davies was the guest, and that several of the other DJs worked for free so that Albrighton could hire this Messiah of Modern, he wasn't worth it! Very safe boring spot, and that's what the Modern Soul fans thought of it. Ted Massey dug a few Sixties out for what seems like their annual airing these days, but Chris Anderton did the best spot of the night. If it was up to me I'd get the money back from Andy Davies and pay it to Chris.

The Black Horse, Wolverhampton, 19th January, 2001
Only the second night here, but about 90 through the door. It's a great venue, and it's good to see Sixties back in Wolverhampton, and by that I mean a whole night of, in effect, Non-Oldies. Kenny Onions played a set of obscure and forgotten Stafford things which elicited a mixed dance floor response, then Andy Rix played a storming set, to virtually an empty dancefloor. The problem of course being that not many people travel outside the Midlands these days, and Andy doesn't DJ here nearly often enough so nobody knew the records except for about a dozen people. Great night though. Looking forward to next month with Butch as guest.

The 100 Club, London, 20th January, 2001
Busy night, a coach load of 48 people came down to support Carl Willingham. His first set was a little too early R & B sounding for me, but some of his supporters were claiming that the 100 Club regulars deliberately played all his big records before he went on. Shame on you naughty boys (Please don't do it to me next month). Highlight of the night for me was Butch's second spot. Awesome in content, and the order he played them. I also heard Mick Smith's new acetate. Sorry I think it's a very poor copy of what - despite being played out, it's in the Alliance Premier League - was, and still is, a brilliant record. Oh by the way, it's 'do I Love You', by allegedly Frank Wilson's brother, Mickey.

The Dome, Tufnell Park, London, 26th January
Back to London again for The Dome, and what a busy night it was. There must have been well over five hundred people in! I know at one stage the door was operating on a 'one out, one in' basis. Great spots from all the DJs. Sixties all the way, and no boring Oldies in earshot. As always there were the usual suspects propping up the bar and the new record dealer's room,

but it was nice to see Roger Banks down for the first time. Thanks to Claire for the accommodation afterwards, and Andy Dyson for the comedy routine!

Group Line Ups

The Ballards (Rico Thompson, Nathan Robertson, Jon Foster, Lesley La Palma)
The Blenders (Gail Mapp, Goldie Coates, Delores Johnson, Hilliard Jones, Albert Jones)
The Blue Lights (Leroy Gordon, Carlton 'Larry' Hart, Albert Townes, Phillip Townes, Charles Williams)
Blue Magic (Theodore 'Ted' Mills, Keith Beaton, Vernon Sawyer, Wendell Sawyer, Richard Pratt)
The Bobettes (Laura Webb, Janice Pought, Emma Pought, Heather Dixon)

Vickie Baines

Parkway 957 - Losing You / Got To Run - 1965
Parkway 966 - Country Girl / Are You Kidding - 1966
Symbol 222 - We Can Find That Love / Sweeter Than Sweet Things
Loma 2078 - We Can Find That Love / Sweeter Than Sweet Things - 1967

Bessie Banks

The Turbans (members Bessie White, ...)

Three Guys & A Doll (members Bessie White, David Jones (died 1995), Jimmy McGowan and Larry Banks)

Miss Toni Banks And The Four Fellows (members Bessie White (lead), Jimmy McGowan (born James A. McGowan ?-February-1932 in Brooklyn, New York --- died ?-October-2008 --- cause: ?) and Jimmy Mobley (alternating first and second tenor on both songs), Larry Banks (baritone - later to become Bessie's husband) and Teddy Williams (bass))

Glory 263 - You're Still In My Heart / Johnny The Dreamer - 1957

The Four Fellows (members Jimmy McGowan (singing lead), David Jones (tenor), Larry Banks (baritone) and Teddy Williams (bass))

Glory 263 - You're Still In My Heart* / I Sit In My Window** - 1957 *Toni Banks sings on "A" side only. **flip by The Four Fellows.

The Companions (members Larry Banks, Bessie (White) Banks, Harriette Banks, Milton Bennett and Al Wiiliams)

Brook's 100 - Why, Oh Why Baby / I Didn't Know (You Got Married) - 1959
Federal 12397 - Why, Oh Why Baby / I Didn't Know (You Got Married) - 1960

Bessie Banks

Tiger 102 - Go Now / It Sounds Like My Baby - 1964 *session: Cissy Houston (backing vocals) -- song was covered in 1965 by The Moody Blues on London 9726.
Blue Cat 106 - Go Now / It Sounds Like My Baby - 1964
Spokane 4009 - Do It Now / (You Should Have Been A) Doctor - 1964
Wand 163 - Do It Now / (You Should Have Been A) Doctor - 1964
Verve 10519 - I Can't Make It (Without You Baby) / Need You - 1967

Linda Jones / Bessie Banks

Cotique C-177 - Fugitive From Luv * / Go Now ** - 1969 *"A" side sung by Linda Jones. **flip side sung by Bessie Banks

Bessie Banks

Volt 4112 - Ain't No Easy Way / Try To Leave Me If You Can (I Bet You Can't Do It) - 1974
Quality 503 - Don't You Worry Baby The Best Is Yet To Come* / Try To Leave Me If You Can - 1976
Quality 508 - Baby You Sure Know How To Get To Me / Do You Really Want To Be Right - 1976

Darrell Banks

The Daddy B Combo (members Darrell Banks, ...)

The Grand Prix (members Darrell Banks, ...)

Darrell Banks (born Darrell Eubanks on 25-July-1937 in Mansfield, Ohio - moved to Buffalo, New York while still an infant. Died March-1970 in Detroit, Michigan. Cause: mortally wounded in the neck by a gunshot wound)

Revilot 201 - Open The Door To Your Heart* / Our Love (Is In The Pocket)** - 1966 *covered in 1967 by Dave Banyase & Sum Guys on Solid Rock 004 and also in 1967 by Lil Murray & The Soul Exciters on Tammy 1028 Plus in 1972 by Na Leen on Janus 197 and yet again in 1973 by Sonny Munro on Epic 8-50174. . **also recorded in 1969 by J. J. Barnes on Revilot 222.
Revilot 203 - Somebody (Somewhere) Needs You* / Baby, What'cha Got (For Me) - 1966 *also recorded in 1967 by Herb & Doris on HIP 91015.
Atco 6471 - Here Come The Tears - 1967 (one-sided demo issue only)
Atco 6471 - Here Come The Tears* / I've Got That Feelin'** - 1967 *recorded 8-February-1967. -- also recorded in 1965 by Gene Chandler on Constellation 164.
Atco 6484 - Angel Baby (Don't You Leave Me)* / Look Into The Eyes Of A Fool - 1967 *recorded at Mira Sound Studios, NYC. 8-February-1967.
Cotillion 44006 - I Wanna Go Home / The Love Of My Woman – 1968
Volt 4014 - Just Because Your Love Is Gone / I'm The One Who Loves You* - 1969 *track also recorded but unreleased by Melvin Davis)
Volt 4026 - Beautiful Feelings / No One Blinder (Than A Man Who Won't See) – 1969

Darrell Banks / The Parliaments

Collectables Col 033727 - Open The Door To Your Heart / I Wanna Testify* - ? *flip by The Parliaments.

Homer Banks

The Soul Consolidators (members Homer Banks, Raymond Jackson, ...) l957 gospel group. Homer Banks was drafted into the military from 1962 ~ 1964.

Homer Banks (born 2-August-1941 in Memphis, Tennessee --- died 3-April-2003 at Saint Francis Hospital in Memphis, Tennessee - cause: cancer)

Genie 101 - Sweetie Pie / Lady Of Stone - 1965 (500 copies pressed)
Genie 1000 - Hooked By Love / Lady Of Stone - 1966
Minit 32000 - A Lot Of Love / Fighting To Win - 1966
Minit 32008 - 60 Minutes Of Your Love / Do You Know What - 1966
Minit 32020 - Lady Of Stone / Hooked By Love - 1967
Minit 32036 - Round The Clock Lover Man / Foolish Hearts Break Fast - 1968
Minit 32056 - (Who You Gonna Run To) Me Or Your Mama / I Know You Know I Know I Know - 1968
Stax - The Ghetto - 1968 (unissued at the time this was released in the U. K. on a 2007 Kent Cd "Change Is Gonna Come The Voice Of Black America 1963 - 1973" CDKEND 270 --- song was also recorded in 1968 by The Staple Singers on Stax 0019)

Banks & Hampton (Homer Banks and Carl Hampton)

Warner Bros. 8177 - Caught In The Act (Of Gettin' It On) / Make Due With What'cha Got - 1976
Warner Bros. 8199 - Wonderful / It's Got To Be This Way - 1977
Warner Bros. 8344 - I'm Gonna Have To Tell Her / We're Movin' On - 1977

Barbara & Brenda

Barbara & Brenda (members Barbara Jean Gaskins and her niece Brenda Gaskins)

Avanti 1600 - Let's Get Together / Shame – 1963
Heidi 104 - That's When You've Got Soul / Hurtin' Inside – 1964
Heidi 106 - You Don't Love Me Anymore / Special Kind Of Love - 1965
Heidi 109 - One More Chance / That's Why I Love You – 1965
Dynamo 103 - If I'm Hurt You Feel The Pain / Too Young To Be Fooled – 1967
Dynamo 108 - Sally's Party / Never Love A Robin – 1967
Dynamo - That's Enough - 1968 (recorded 23-April-1968 but unissued until released in the U. K. on a 1997 Kent CD "Kent's Magic Touch" CDKEND 146)
Dynamo 120 - Don't Wait Up For Me Mama / Who Put Out The Rumour - 1968

After the Barbara & Brenda sides Brenda left the music business to get married.

Ecstacy, Passion & Pain (members Barbara Roy (aunt of Jocelyn Brown), Althea "Cookie" Smith, Alan Tizer, Billy Gardner and Joseph Williams Jr.)

Roulette 7151 - I Wouldn't Give You Up (Stereo) / I Wouldn't Give You Up (Mono) – 1974
Roulette 7151 - I Wouldn't Give You Up / Don't Burn Your Bridges Behind You- 1974
Frankford Wayne - Good Things Don't Last Forever - 1974 (45 Rpm One Sided Acetate Has Roulette Records Handwritten On Label With Number R-7156 Plus Time 3:18)
Roulette 7156 - Good Things Don't Last Forever / Born To Lose You – 1974#
Roulette 7159 - Ask Me / I'll Take The Blame – 1974
Roulette 7163 - One Beautiful Day / Try To Believe In Me – 1975

Roulette 7178 - There's So Much Love All Around Me (Short) / There's So Much Love All Around Me (Long) - 1975
Roulette 7182 - Touch And Go / I'll Do Anything For You - 1976

Whirlwind / Ecstacy Passion & Pain

Roulette Rd-2003 - Full Time Thing (Between Dusk And Dawn) (5:36) / Touch And Go (5:07)* - 1976 *flip by Ecstacy, Passion & Pain. (12" release)

Ecstacy Passion & Pain

Roulette 7205 - There's So Much Love All Around Me / Dance The Night Away – 1977
Roulette 7205 - Passion (3:08) / Passion (3:48) - 1977 (Promo Issue Only)
Roulette 7025 - There's So Much Love All Around Me / Passion – 1977
Roulette 7209 - There's So Much Love All Around Me / Dance The Night Away – 1977
Roulette 2205 - Passion / There's So Much Love All Around Me - 1977

Barbara Roy & Ecstacy, Passion & Pain

Roy B. Rbs-4515 - If You Want Me / If You Want Me (Long Version) – 1981
Roy B. Rbs-4515 - If You Want Me / I've Got You – 1981
Roy B. Rbds 2516 - If You Want Me (6:30) / I've Got You (5:05) - 1981 (12" Release)

Barbara Roy (Barbara Gaskins using her fathers first name as a surname)

Ascot 105 - With All My Love (6:28) / ? - 1984 (12" Release)
RCA 14404 - Gotta See You Tonight / Gonna Put Up A Fight – 1986
RCA Pw 14405 - Gotta See You Tonight (Dance Version) (6:57) / Gotta See You Tonight (Single Version) (3:43) /// Gotta See You Tonight (Extended Dub Version) (10:03) - 1986 (12" release)

Ecstacy, Passion & Pain

Sunnyview Sun-33007 - Touch And Go (Danny Krivit Remix) (8:42) /// Touch And Go (Acapella) (3:15) / Touch And Go (Original Version) (4:20) - 1986

Barbara Roy

RCA 14402 - Gotta See You Tonight / Gotta See You Tonight – 1986
RCA 5097 - Gonna Put Up A Fight / Gotta See You Tonight – 1987
RCA Pd-14405 - Gotta See You Tonight (Dance) (Single) (Extended Dub) - 1987 (12"Release)
RCA 5943-1-Rd - Gonna Put Up A Fight (7:35) - 1987 (12"Release)

Billy Barnes

The Five Echoes (members in 1953 Willie Barnes, Eugene McDaniels, James Farmer, Jimmy Mimms and ? ------ Jimmy Mimms left group shortly after it was formed and was replaced by Richard Beasley, at this time Wesley Devreaux (the son of the famous blues shouter Wynonie Harris) also joined group)
The Sultans (members Richard Beasley, Wesley Devreaux, Eugene McDaniels, Willie Barnes and James Farmer)

Duke 125 - How Deep Is The Ocean / Good Thing Baby - 1954.
Duke 133 - I Cried My Heart Out / Baby Don't Put Me Down - 1954
Duke 135 - Boppin' With The Mambo / What Makes Me Feel This Way - 1954

The Admirals (members Richard Beasley, Wesley Devreaux, Eugene McDaniels, Willie Barnes and James Farmer) group name change came about because group was broke but still under contract with DUKE records. This way they could record for someone else.

King 4772 - Oh Yes / Left With A Broken Heart - 1955
King 4782 - Close Your Eyes / Give Me Your Love - 1955

Cathy Ryan with The Lucky Millinder Orchestra

King 4792 - It's A Sad, Sad Feeling*/ Ow - 1955 *Backing Vocals The Admirals.

Bubber Johnson

King 4793 - Ding Dang Doo* / Drop Me A Line* - 1955 *Backing Vocals The Admirals.
King 5068 - A Crazy Afternoon* / So Much Tonight - 1955 *Backing Vocals The Admirals.

The Sultans

Duke 178 - If I Could Tell / My Love Is So High - 1957 (in 1957 Jimmy Farmer enlisted and this was the end of the group. Willie Barnes and Wesley Devreaux recorded for a while as a duo. unsure of recordings.

Billy Barnes (Willie Barnes)

Mercury 71057 - Poor Old Me / Penalty - 1957
United Artists 148 - You'd Have To Fall In Love / If You But Knew - 1958
United Artists 157 - I'm Coming To See You / What Am I Supposed To Do - 1959
United Artists 218 - Home Again / I Wish I Didn't Love You So - 1960
United Artists 311 - C. C. Rider / Here Am I - 1961
Liberty 55421 - To Prove My Love / Until - 1962
Tahoe 2532 - Road Of Love / There's A Lion Out There - 1963

J J Barnes

The Halo Gospel Singers (members J. J. Barnes, Ortheia Barnes, Johnny Starks, Charles Sims, Calvin Southern, and Donald Southern)

The Five Seniors (members J. J. Barnes, Barry Reed, Don York, Walter Payton and Bobby ?)

J. J. Barnes & The Dell Fi's / J. J. Barnes

Kable 437 - My Love Came Tumbling Down / Won't You Let Me Know - 1960 *flip by J. J. Barnes

J. J. Barnes (born Jimmy James Barnes 30-November-1943 in Detroit, Michigan)

Rich 1005 - My Love Came Tumbling Down / Won't You Let Me Know – 1960

J. J. Barnes Orchestra Conducted by F. Brown

Rich 1737 - My Love Came Tumbling Down / Won't You Let Me Know – 1962

J. J. Barnes

Mickay's 3004 - Just One More Time / Hey Child I Love You - 1963
Scepter 1266 - Just One More Time / Hey Child I Love You – 1963
Mickay's 3114 - These Chains Of Love / Color Green - 1963
Mickay's 300 - These Chains Of Love / Color Green – 1963
Mickay's 351 - Teenage Queen / Someone – 1963
Mickay's 353 - So Far Away / Love Requires Understanding – 1964
Mickay's 4471/4472 - Lonely No More / Get A Hold Of Yourself - 1964
Ring 101 - Poor Unfortunate Me (I Ain't Got Nobody)* / She Ain't Ready - 1964 *backing vocals Ortheia Barnes. Also recorded in 1967 by Gigi & The Charmaines on Columbia 4-44246 and in 1968 by Gloria Taylor on King Soul 493-2.
Ring - It's Alright To Cry - Unreleased
Ric-Tic 106 - Please Let Me In / I Think I Found A Love – 1965
Ric-Tic 110 - Real Humdinger / I Ain't Gonna Do It – 1966
Ric-Tic 115 - Day Tripper / Don't Bring Me Bad News – 1966

The Holidays (members Eddie Anderson, Steve Mancha and J.J. Barnes, Edwin Starr's vocal overdubbed on recording - not actual member)

Golden World 36 - I'll Love You Forever / Makin' Up Time - 1966 (produced by Don Davis)

J. J. Barnes

Ric-Tic 117 - Say It / Deeper In Love - 1966
Groovesville 555 - Sweet Sherry* / ? - 1967 *unreleased as a legitimate 45 in the U. S. A. this track saw release as a bootleg on this label number. It was released in 1975 in the U. K. backed with "Chains Of Love" on Contempo 2048.
Groovesville 1006 - Baby Please Come Back Home / Chains Of Love – 1967
Groovesville 1008 - Now That I Got You Back / Forgive Me – 1967
Groovesville 1009 - Easy Living / ? – 1967 (Possibly unreleased)
Groove City 206 - Easy Living / I've Lost You - 1967 (With The Holidays)
Revilot 216 - Now She's Gone* / Hold On To It** - 1968 * an instrumental of this release was issued in 1967 by The Le Baron Strings on Solid Hit 111 and in 1969 on Revilot 225. **covered in 1971 by The Limitations on Volt 4057
Revilot 218 - Sad Day A-Coming / I'll Keep Coming Back* - 1968 *an instrumental of this release was issued in 1967 by The Le Baron Strings on Solid Hit 111 and in 1969 by The Holidays on Revilot 226.
Revilot 222 - Our Love Is In The Pocket* / All Your Goodies Are Gone (Instrumental)** - 1969 *originally recorded in 1966 by Darrell Banks on Revilot 201. **a vocal version was issued in 1967 by The Parliaments on Revilot 211.

J. J. Barnes / Le Baron Strings

Revilot 225 - So Called Friends / Now She's Gone (Instrumental)* - 1969 *flip by The LeBaron Strings.

J. J. Barnes

Buddah 120 - Evidence / I'll Keep Coming Back – 1969
Volt 4027 - Snowflakes / Got To Get Rid Of You – 1969
Invasion 1001 - My Baby / You're Still My Baby - 1970

Jay Rhythm (James Thorpe - co-owner of Leo and later Magic Touch with J. J. Barnes)

Leo Ar 884 - Wouldn't It Be A Pleasure / Soul Emotions* - ? *J. J. Barnes states he sings on flipside only

J. J. Barnes

Magic Touch 1000 - To An Early Grave / Cloudy Days – 1970
Perception 546 - You Are Just A Living Doll / I Make Believe I'm Touching You - 1973

Jimmy J. Barnes (J. J. Barnes)

Organic Cwo-1 - I Think I've Got A Good Chance (Part 1) / I Think I've Got A Good Chance (Part 2) - 1975

J. J. Barnes

Contempo 7003 - How Long / The Errol Flynn - 1977

The Halo Gospel Singers featuring J. J. Barnes

Golden Age 101 - Only Things From God (Will Last) (Part 1) / Only Things From God (Will Last) (Part 2) - 1981

J. J. Barnes

Achievement 10011 - Talk Of The Grapevine / On Top Of The World - 1988

Sidney Barnes

The Embracers (members Sidney Barnes, Marvin Gaye, Van McCoy..) unrecorded group formed by Sidney Barnes which auditioned for George Goldner of END records.

The Serenaders (members Sidney Barnes, Luke Gross, Georrge Kerr and Howard Curry)

Chock Full O' Hits 101 - I Wrote A Letter / Never Let Me Go - 1957
Chock Full O' Hits 102 - Dance Darling, Dance / Give Me A Girl - 1957
MGM 2623 - I Wrote A Letter / Never Let Me Go - 1958#
MGM 12666 - Dance Darling, Dance / Give Me A Girl - 1958
Rae Cox 101 - Gotta Go To School / My Girl Flip-Flop - 1959

Sidney Barnes (born in Welch, West Virginia 1941)

Gemini - Wait My Love / I'm Satisfied - 1961

The Serenaders (Timothy Wilson, Sidney Barnes, George Kerr and Howard Curry)

Riverside 4549 - Adios, My Love / Two Lovers Make One Fool - 1963
Motown 1046 - If Your Heart Says Yes / I'll Cry Tomorrow - 1963
V.I.P. 25002 - If Your Heart Says Yes / I'll Cry Tomorrow - 1964
Jobete Music Company Inc. - Saftety Zone - 1964? (acetate with mis-spelling should read "Safety Zone")

Sidney Barnes

Blues Tone 402 - Talkin' Bout A Shindig / New York City - 1964
Blues Tone 1267 - Talkin' 'Bout A Shindig / New York City - 1964
Red Bird 10-039 - You'll Always Be In Style / I'm So Glad - 1965
Red Bird 10-054 - I Hurt On The Other Side / Switchy Walk - 1966
Blue Cat 125 - I Hurt On The Other Side / Switchy Walk - 1966

Johnny Goode (Sidney Barnes)

Solid Hit 106 - Payback / Payback (Instrumental) - 1967

The Rotary Connection (members Sidney Barnes, Minnie Riperton -- on all her album credits with the group her last name is misspelled Ripperton, Mitch Aliotta, Judy Hauf and Bobby Sims)

Cadet Concept 7000 - Like A Rollin' Stone / Turn Me On - 1967
Cadet Concept Dj-1 - Lady Jane / Amen - 1968 (Promo Issue Only)
Cadet Concept 7002 - Ruby Tuesday / Soul Man - 1968
Cadet Concept 7007 - Paper Castle / Teach Me How To Fly - 1968
Cadet Concept 7008 - Aladdin / Magical World - 1968
Cadet Concept 7009 - Silent Night Chant / Peace At Last - 1968
Cadet Concept 7014 - The Weight / Respect - 1969
Cadet Concept 7018 - Want You To Know / Memory Band - 1969
Cadet Concept 7021 - Love Me Now / May Our Amens Be True - 1970
Cadet Concept 7027 - Stormy Monday Blues / Teach Me How To Fly - 1970

The New Rotary Connection

Cadet Concept 7028 - Hey Love / If I Sing My Song - 1971

Sidney Barnes

Chess 2094 - Baloney / Old Times - 1970

Minnie Riperton & Rotary Connection

Janus 249 - Living Alone / Magical World - 1975

Sidney Barnes

Parachute 521 - Hold On I'm Coming / Your Love Is So Good To Me - 1978
Parachute Rrd 20515 - Get On Up And Dance To The Boogie (Or The Boogie Man Will Get Cha) (5:11) / ? - 1978? (12" Release)

The Serenaders

Starfire 115 - Nite Owl / I'm Gonna Love You - 1980

Arpeggio (members Sidney Barnes

Love And Desire / ? - ?

Lee Bates

Leroy Bates

White Cliffs 270 - Bad, Bad Understanding / I'm Forever Crying 1967

Lee Bates

Instant 3304 - Bad, Bad Understanding / Simon Says - 1970
Instant 3307 - International Playboy / Look What They've Done To My Song, Ma - 1970
Instant 3310 - Why Don't You Write / Gonna Make You Mine - 1971

Instant 3313 - Mean Mistreater / Things Come Naturally - 1971
Instant 3316 - Three Trips Around The World/Running Around - 1971
Instant 3316 - Three Trips Around The World/ You Won't Do Right - 1971
Instant 3318 - Project Queen/Girl Listen To Me - 1972
Instant 3321 - Dock Of The Bay/Key To My Heart - 1972

Lee Bates & Velvet Funk

Instant 3323 - Help Me Make It through the Night / Slowly - 1972

Lee Bates

Instant 3329 - What Am I Gonna Do / Your Love Is Slipping Away - 1972
IX Chains 7011 - (What Am I Gonna Do) What Am I Gonna Say / Your Love Is Slipping Away - 1975
Sansu 1002 - Shake, Baby, Shake / Shake, Baby, Shake (Disco version) - 1976
Sansu 1003 - Dance With Me / All That Matters (Is Love) - 1976
Sansu 1005 - Something You Got / Dance With Me - 1976
Sansu 1009 - Easy, Easy / Wishing, Waiting And Hoping - 1976
Magnolia 300 - Overnight Sensation / Hooked On A Feeling - 1981
Magnolia 400 - Get 'Em And Hit 'Em / ? (12" Single) - 1983
Magnolia 500 - You Blew It / You Blew It (Instr) - 1985)
Ichiban 87-119 - Searchin' / What Am I Gonna Do - 1987

Lee Bates & Sharon Henderson / Lee Bates

Soul Sound 1988 - Does It Mean You Love Me / All That Matters 1988

William Bell

Red Saunders Band around 1954 ~ 1955 William Bell won a talent contest at Memphis' annual Mid-South fair. The first prize was $500.00 and a trip to Chicago to sing at Club Delisa for a weekend with The Red Saunders Band. It was Red Saunders who recommended William Bell to Phineas Newborn.

The Phineas Newborn Band (members William Bell, ...) was a member of the band on and off for the next five years while at the same time being a member of The Del-Rios.

The Del-Rios with Rufus Thomas' Bearcats (members Harrison Austin, Melvin Jones, David Brown and William Bell)

Meteor 5038 - Alone On A Rainy Night / Lizzie - 1955

The Del Rios

Bet T 7001 - Heavenly Angel / Dangerous Lover - 1959

William Bell (born William Yarborough on 16-July-1939 in Memphis, Tennessee)

<u>Stax</u> 116 - You Don't Miss Your Water / Formula Of Love - 1961 (copies of a 1961 release by Macy Skipper entitled "Goofin' Off / Night Rock" can also be found with this label number)

The Del-Rios (members Louis Williams (later member of The Ovations), Robert Huntley, Harrison Austin, William Bell and Tino ?) group reformed to record this 45.

Stax 125 - Just Across The Street / There's A Love* - 1962 *William Bell lead vocals -- covered in 1967 by The Gentrys on MGM 13690.

William Bell

Stax 128 - Any Other Way / Please Help Me, I'm Falling - 1962 (after this release William Bell was drafted into U.S. Army from 1962 ~ 1966. When he came back from training, he cut as much material as he could in two weeks, which was then released as singles. Stax had enough material stock-piled that they could release everything as an album "The Soul Of A Bell". When William Bell came out of the service, the first couple of releases didn't really hit so he took a hiatus and pondered over what he was doing wrong -- then he started writing - the first hit record that came out was "Everybody Loves A Winner")

Stax 132 - I Told You So / What'cha Gonna Do - 1963
Stax 135 - Just As I Thought / I'm Waiting On You - 1963
Stax 138 - Somebody Mentioned Your Name / What Can I Do To Forget - 1963
Stax 141 - I'll Show You / Monkeying Around - 1963
Stax 146 - Who Will It Be Tomorrow / Don't Make Something Out Of Nothing - 1964
Stax 174 - Crying All By Myself / Don't Stop Now - 1965
Stax 191 - Share What You Got (But Keep What You Need) / Marching Off To War - 1966
Stax 199 - Never Like This Before / Soldier's Goodbye - 1966
Stax 212 - Everybody Loves A Winner / (You're Such A) Sweet Thang - 1967
Stax 227 - Eloise (Hang On In There) / One Plus One - 1967
Stax 237 - Everyday Will Be Like A Holiday / Ain't Got No Girl - 1967
Stax 248 - A Tribute To A King* / Every Man Oughta Have A Woman - 1968 *tribute to Otis Redding, the song was written a few days after his death. William Bell not wanting to "cash in" on the tragedy, decided to send his recording to Otis Redding's widow Zelma as a keepsake. Zelma Redding loved the recording and called Stax requesting them to release it.

Judy Clay & William Bell

Stax 0005 - Private Number / Love-Eye-Tis - 1968

William Bell

Stax 0015 - I Forgot To Be Your Lover / Bring The Curtain Down - 1968

William Bell & Judy Clay

Stax 0017 - My Baby Specializes / Left Over Love - 1968

William Bell

Stax 0032 - All God's Children Got Soul / My Whole World Is Falling Down - 1969
Stax 0038 - My Kind Of Girl / Happy - 1969

Johnnie Taylor / Johnnie Taylor, Eddie Floyd, William Bell, Pervis Staples, Carla Thomas, Mavis Staples, Cleotha Staples

Stax 0040 - Soul-A-Lujah (Part 1) / Soul-A-Lujah (Part 2)* - 1969 *flip by Johnnie Taylor, Eddie Floyd, William Bell, Pervis Staples, Carla Thomas, Mavis Staples, Cleotha Staples.

William Bell & Mavis Staples

Stax 0043 - Love's Sweet Sensation / Strung Out - 1969

William Bell & Carla Thomas

Stax 0044 - I Need You Woman / I Can't Stop - 1969

William Bell

Stax 0054 - Born Under A Bad Sign / A Smile Can't Hide (A Broken Heart)* - 1969 *also recorded but unissued in 1968 by Ollie & The Nightingales on Stax until released in the U. K. on the 2008 Kent Cd Box Set "Take Me To The River A Southern Soul Story" KENTBOX 10 (Disc 2)

William Bell & Mavis Staples / William Bell & Carla Thomas

Stax 0067 - Leave The Girl Alone / All I Have To Do Is Dream* - 1970 *flip by William Bell, Carla Thomas

William Bell

Stax 0070 - Lonely Soldier / Let Me Ride - 1970
Stax 0092 - A Penny For Your Thoughts / Till My Back Ain't Got No Bone - 1971
Stax 0106 - All For The Love Of A Woman / I'll Be There - 1971
Stax 0128 - Save Us / If You Really Love Him - 1972
Stax 0157 - Lovin' On Borrowed Time* / The Man In The Street - 1973 *also recorded in 1970 by Mitty Collier on Peachtree 125 plus track was recorded at Malaco but unreleased by Anita Mitchell.
Stax 0175 - I've Got To Go On Without You / You're The Kind Of Love I Need - 1973
Stax 0198 - Gettin' What You Want (Losin' What You Got) / All I Need Is Your Love - 1974
Stax 0221 - Get It While It's Hot / Nobody Walks Away From Love Unhurt - 1974
Atlantic 13154 - Everyday Will Be Like A Holiday / Winner - 1975
Mercury 73839 - Tryin' To Love Two / If Sex Was All We Had - 1976
Mercury 73922 - Coming Back For More / You I Absolutely Positively Love - 1977
Mercury 73961 - Easy Comin' Out (Hard Going In) / Our Love Keeps Me Going – 1977
Andee 0006 - Share What You Got / March Off To War - 197?
Kat Family 03502 - Bad Time To Break Up / The Truth In Your Eyes – 1983
Kat Family 03995 - Playing Hard To Get / The Truth Is In Your Eyes - 1983
Wilbe 85-201 - Lovin' On Borrowed Time / That's What You Get – 1985

William Bell & Janice Bullock

Wilbe 86-202 - I Don't Want To Wake Up (Feelin' Guilty) / Whatever You Want You Got It – 1986

William Bell

Wilbe 86-204 - Headline News / Let Him Pay The Band – 1986
Wilbe 86- 205 - Everyday Will Be Like A Holiday / Please Come Home For Christmas – 1986

William Bell & Judy Clay

Collectables Col 710097 - Private Number / My Baby Specializes - ?

William Bell

Collectables Col 4355 - Trying To Love Two / Easy Comin' Out - ?
Collectables Col 71061 - I Forgot To Be Your Lover / My Whole World Is Falling - ?
Wilbe 89-508 - Getting Out Of Your Bed / Short Circuit – 1989
Wilbe 90-515 - I Need Your Love So Bad / I'm Ready – 1990
Wilbe 92-619 - Bedtime Story / Keep Your Body Warm – 1992
Wilbe 92-624 - Shake Hands (Come Out Lovin') / Private Number - 1992

Chuck Bernard

Chuck Bernard

Joyce 305 - Calling Your Name / Every Time I Think Of You - 1958 (could be a different singer entirely)
New Breed 501 - Can't Get You Off My Mind / Anything For You - 1961
New Breed 502 - Hall Of Soul / Yes We Got It Going – 1961

Chuck Bernard & The Satellite Band (members Chuck Bernard, ...)

Satellite 2003 - Let's Go Get Stoned / Wasted - 1965

Chuck Bernard

Satellite 2005 - Indian Giver / Dial My Number – 1965
Satellite 2008 - Funny Changes / Every Hurt Makes You Stronger - 1965
Satellite 2012 - My Baby / She's Already Married* - 1965 *also recorded in 1965 by Billy Bland (McKinley Mitchell) on St. Lawrence 1005.
Mi Boute ? - 1960's
St. Lawrence 1025 - I Can't Fight It / Send For Me – 1967
Maverick 1009 - You're An Indian Giver / Hobo Flats - 1969
Zodiac 1014 - Bessie Girl / Love Can Slip Away – 1969
Zodiac 1018 - Everything Is Alright Now / The Other Side Of My Mind – 1970
Zodiac 1019 - Deeper Than The Eyes Can See / Turn Her Loose – 1970
Zodiac 1021 - Love Bug / I'm Lonely – 1971
Zodiac 1025 - Turn Her Loose / Thank You Ma'am – 1971
Zodiac 1050 - Got To Get A Hold Of Myself / Everybody's Got Their Own Thing - 1973
Brunswick 55521 - Contract On Your Love / A Shoulder To Lean On - 1975

Cody Black

Cody Black

Pamela 7453 - Come To Me (Girl) / Stranger Than A Fairy Tale – 1961

Cody Black & The Celestials / Cody Black & His Girls

Universe 551 - The Camel Walk / Joreen (She's Soemthing Else) - 1962

Cody Black

D Town 1032 - Move On / These Chains Of Love – 1964
D Town 1057 - Mr. Blue / You Must Be In Love – 1965
D Town 1066 - Would You Let Me Know / Too Many Irons In The Fire – 1965
Wheelsville 1071 - I Will Give You Love / I Am Particular – 1966
Gig 201 - It's Our Time To Fall In Love / (Keep Your Baby Home Or) You'll Be Sorry – 1966
Groove City 960 - Because You First Loved Me / The Night A Star Was Born – 1967
Ram Brock 2002 - Somebody's Gonna End Up Lovin' / Going Going Gone – 1967
King 6148 - Keep On Keeping On / I'm Slowly Molding – 1968
Ram Brock 2003 - Life Goes On / (The Night) A Star Was Born – 1968
Ram Brock 2004 - Love Like I Never Had / Reap What You Sow – 1968
Ston-Roc 3378 - I Still Love You / Ice Cream Song – 1969

Capitol 2807 - I'm Sorry / Fool On The Wild – 1970
Capitol 2858 - Stop Trying To Do What You See Your Neighbor Do / Ain't No Love Like Your Love – 1970
Renaissance 1001 - Keep On Trying / Steppin' On Toes (You Can't Make It) – 1977
Renaissance 0002 - Sweet Love / What Goes Around - 1978

Billy Bland

The Bees (members Billy Bland ....)

Imperial 5314 - Toy Bell* / Snatchin' Back - 1954 (glossy red label is scarcer than flat red label) *a double entendre taken from David Bartholmew's "My Ding-A-Ling" a 1952 recording on King 4544 (re-written in 1972 by Chuck Berry and released on Chess 2131)
Imperial 5320 - I Want To Be Loved / Get Away Baby - 1954

The Toppers (Members Billy Bland, ...)

Jubilee 5136 - Baby Let Me Bang Your Box / You're Laughing Cause I'm Crying - 1954

Billy Bland (born 5-April-1932 in Wilmington, North Carolina)

Old Town 1016 - Chicken In The Basket / The Fat Man - 1956
Old Town 1022 - Chicken Hop / Oh You For Me - 1956
Old Town 1035 - If I Could Be Your Man / I Had A Dream - 1957
Tip Top 708 - Chicken In The Basket / Chicken Hop - 1958
Old Town 1067 - Grandmaw Gave A Party / I'm Not Your Slave - 1959
Old Town 1076 - Let The Little Girl Dance* / Sweet Thing - 1960 (there is one known copy found in Los Angeles pressed in yellow vinyl) *also recorded in 1958 by Carl Spencer & The Videos on Manhattan 507
Old Town 1082 - You Were Born To Be Loved / Pardon Me - 1960
Old Town 1088 - Make Believe Lover / Harmonys - 1960
Old Town 1093 - Everything That Shines Ain't Gold / Keep Talkin' That Sweet Talk - 1960
Old Town 1098 - I Cross My Heart / Steady Kind - 1961
Old Town 1105 - My Heart's On Fire* / Can't Stop Her From Dancing - 1961*Written By Billy Bland - also covered in 1966 by Little Bob on La Louisianne 8075.
Old Town 1109 - Do The Bug With Me / Uncle Bud - 1961
Old Town 1114 - All I Want To Do Is Cry / Busy Little Boy - 1962
Old Town 1124 - Mama Stole The Chicken / I Spent My Life Loving You - 1962
Old Town 1128 - Darling Won't You Think Of Me / How Many Hearts - 1962
Old Town 1143 - Doing The Mule / Farmer In The Dell - 1963
Old Town 1151 - A Little Touch Of Your Love / Little Boy Blue - 1963

Billy Bland (actually McKinley Mitchell)

St. Lawrence 1005 - She's Already Married* / My Divorce - 1965 *also recorded in 1965 by Chuck Bernard on Satellite 2012.
St. Lawrence 1018 - I'm Sorry About That / Booga-Loo And Silly Dog - 1966

The Earls / Billy Bland

Eric 286 - Remember Then / Let The Little Girl Dance* - ? *flip By Billy Bland

Atlantic 13114 - Remember Then / Let The Little Girl Dance* - ? *flip By Billy Bland

The Solitaires / Billy Bland

Collectables Col 010397 - The Angels Sang / Let The Little Girl Dance* **- ?** *flip by Billy Bland.

Bobby Bland

The Miniatures (members Robert Calvin Bland, ...) local gospel group

Roscoe Gordon (born 10-April-1928 in Memphis, Tennessee - died 11-July-2002 in Queens, New York - cause: heart attack)

Chess 1487 - Booted / Love You Til The Day I Die* - 1951 *with Bobby "Blue" Bland (78 rpm format)

The Beale Streeters (members at one time or another of this loose knit group were Johnny Ace (born John Marshall Alexander Jr. on the 9-June-1929 in Memphis, Tennessee --- died 25-December-1954 --- cause: playing Russian roulette) , Earle Lacy Forrest (born in Memphis - died 26-February-2003 at the Memphis Veterans Medical Center - cause: cancer), Rosco Gordon, Tuff Green, B. B. King, Bobby "Blue" Bland, Junior Parker (born 27-March-1932 in West Memphis, Arkansas --- died 18-November-1971 --- cause: after surgery for brain tumor), ...)

Modern 848 - Crying All Night Long / Dry Up Baby - 1952 (78rpm format) produced at SUN studios in Memphis with Sam Phillips at the controls --- session: Ike turner on piano.

Bobby "Blue" Bland

Modern 868 - Good Lovin' / Drifting From Town To Town - 1952 (78 RPM format)

Bobby "Blue" Bland / Roscoe Gordon

Chess 1489 - Crying / A Letter From A Trench In Korea - 1952 (78rpm format)

"Bobby Blue" Bland with The Beale Streeters (members

Duke 105 - Lovin' Blues / I.O.U. Blues - 1952

"Bobby Blue" Bland and Orchestra

Duke 115 - Army Blues / No Blow, No Show - 1953

Bobby "Blue" Bland

Duke 141 - Time Out / It's My Life Baby - 1955
Duke 146 - You Or None / Woke Up Screaming - 1955
Duke 153 - I Can't Put You Down / You've Got Bad Intentions - 1956

Bobby "Blue" Bland, Bill Harvey's Band (members Bobby Bland, Bill Harvey, ...)

Duke 160 - I Learned My Lesson / Lead Us On - 1956

Bobby "Blue" Bland

Duke 160 - I Learned My Lesson / I Don't Believe - 1956
Duke 167 - Don't Want No Woman / I Smell Trouble - 1957
Duke 170 - Farther Up The Road / Sometime Tomorrow - 1957

Duke 182 - Teach Me (How To Love You) / Bobby's Blues - 1957
Duke 185 - You Got Me Where You Want Me / Loan A Helping Hand – 1958
Duke 196 - Little Boy Blue / Last Night – 1958

Bobby "Blue" Bland And His Band

Duke 300 - You Did Me Wrong / I Lost Sight Of The World - 1959

Bobby "Blue" Bland

Duke 303 - Wishing Well / I'm Not Ashamed - 1959
Duke 310 - Is It Real / Someday - 1959

Bobby Bland

Duke 314 - I'll Take Care Of You / That's Why - 1959
Duke 318 - Lead Me On* / Hold Me Tenderly - 1960 *also recorded in 1970 by Gwen McRae on Columbia 4-45214
Duke 327 - Cry, Cry, Cry* / I've Been Wrong So Long - 1960 *also recorded in 1968 by Willie Hobbs on Le Cam 333 and in 1969 by Oscar Irvin on Hollywood 1135.
Duke 332 - I Pity The Fool / Close To You - 1961
Duke 336 - Don't Cry No More* / How Does A Cheating Woman Feel - 1961 *also recorded in 1966 by Roy Head on Back Beat 571.
Duke 338 - Ain't That Loving You / Jelly, Jelly, Jelly - 1961
Duke 340 - Don't Cry No More / Saint James Infirmary - 1961
Duke 344 - Turn On Your Love Light* / You're The One (That I Need) - 1961 *also recorded in 1968 by The Human Beinz on CAPITOL 2119.
Duke 347 - Who Will The Next Fool Be / Blue Moon - 1962

Bobby "Blue" Bland & Ike Turner And His Orchestra

Kent 378 - Love You Baby / Drifting - 1962

Bobby Bland

Duke 352 - Yield Not To Temptation / How Does A Cheating Woman Feel - 1962
Duke 355 - Stormy Monday Blues* / Your Friends – 1962 *also recorded in 1964 by Jimmy Hughes on Vee-Jay Lp 1102.
Duke 360 - That's The Way Love Is / Call On Me - 1962
Duke 366 - Sometimes You Gotta Cry A Little / You're Worth It All - 1963
Duke 369 - Ain't It A Good Thing / Queen For A Day - 1963
Duke 370 - The Feeling Is Gone / I Can't Stop Singing - 1963
Duke 375 - Ain't Nothing You Can Do (About This)* / Honey Child - 1964 *also recorded in 1971 by Gwen McRae on Columbia 4-45448
Duke 377 - Share Your Love With Me / After It's Too Late - 1964
Duke 383 - Ain't Doing Too Bad (Part 1) / Ain't Doing Too Bad (Part 2) - 1964
Duke 385 - These Hands (Small But Mighty) / Today - 1965
Duke 386 - Blind Man / Black Night - 1965
Duke 390 - Dust Got In Daddy's Eyes / Ain't No Telling - 1965
Duke 393 - I'm Too Far Gone (To Turn Around) / If You Could Read My Mind - 1965

Bob Gunner

Robey - 3rd Straight Hit - 1965 (Single Sided, No Selection Number Used) A Promotional Announcement By Duke / Peacock's
Bob Gunner, Who Is Not Credited On Label, Plugging A Bobby Bland Release. Includes A Segment Of A Bobby Bland Track. Promotional Issue Only.

Bobby Bland

Duke 402 - Good Time Charlie / Good Time Charlie (Part 2) - 1966
Duke 407 - Poverty / Building A Fire With Hair - 1966
Duke 412 - Back In The Same Old Bag Again / I Ain't Myself Anymore - 1966
Duke 416 - You're All I Need / Deep In My Soul - 1967
Duke 421 - That Did It / Getting Used To The Blues - 1967
Duke 426 - A Touch Of The Blues / Shoes - 1967
Duke 432 - Driftin' Blues / You Could Read My Mind - 1968
Duke 433 - Honey Child / A Piece Of Gold - 1968
Duke 435 - Save Your Love For Me / Share Your Love With Me - 1968
Duke 440 - Rockin' In The Same Old Boat / Would'nt You Rather Have Me - 1968
Duke 447 - Gotta Get To Know You / Baby I'm On My Way - 1969
Duke 449 - Chains Of Love / Ask Me 'Bout Nothing (But The Blues) - 1969
Duke 458 - If You've Got Heart / Sad Feeling - 1970
Duke 460 - Lover With A Reputation / If Love Ruled The World - 1970
Duke 464 - Keep On Loving Me (You'll See The Change) / I've Just Got To Forget About You - 1970
Duke 466 - I'm Sorry / Yum Yum Tree - 1971
Duke 471 - Shape Up Or Ship Out / The Love That We Share (Is True) - 1971
Duke 472 - Do What You Set Out To Do / Ain't Nothing You Can Do - 1972
Duke 477 - I'm So Tired / If You Could Read My Mind - 1972
Duke 480 - That's All There Is (There Ain't No More) / I Don't Want Another Mountain To Climb - 1973
ABC Dunhill 4369 - This Time I'm Gone For Good / Where Baby Went – 1973
Goldies 45 1480 - Turn On Your Lovelight / I Pity The Fool - 1970's
Goldies 45 1481 - Stormy Monday Blues / Gotta Get To Know You - 1970's
Goldies 45 1482 - Chains Of Love / Call On Me - 1970's
Goldies 45 1483 - That's The Way Love Is / Rocking In The Same Old Boat - 1970's
Goldies 45 1484 - These Hands (Small But Mighty) / Farther Up The Road - 1970's
Goldies 45 1485 - I'm So Tired / Ain't Nothing You Can Do - 1970's
Goldies 45 1486 - Yield Not To Temptation / Share Your Love With Me - 1970's
Goldies 45 1487 - Do What You Set Out To Do / Ain't Nothing You Can Do - 1970's
ABC Dunhill 4379 - Goin' Down Slow / Up And Down World – 1974
ABC Dunhill 15003 - Ain't No Love In The Heart Of The City / Twenty-Four Hour Blues - 1974
ABC Dunhill 15015 - I Wouldn't Treat A Dog (The Way You Treated Me) / I Ain't Gonna Be The First To Cry - 1974
ABC 12105 - Yolanda / When You Come To The End Of Your Road - 1975
ABC 12134 - I Take It On Home / You've Never Been This Far Before - 1975
ABC 12156 - Today I Started Loving You Again / Too Far Gone - 1976
ABC 12189 - It Ain't The Real Thing / Who's Foolin' Who - 1976

Bobby Bland And B. B. King

ABC / Impulse 31006 - Let The Good Times Roll / Strange Things Happening* - 1976 *also recorded in 1950 by Percy Mayfield on Speciality 375.
ABC Impulse 31009 - Everyday I Have The Blues / The Thrill Is Gone – 1976

Bobby Bland

ABC 12280 - The Soul Of A Man / If I Weren't A Gambler – 1977
ABC 12330 - Sittin' On A Poor Man's Throne / I Intend To Take Your Place – 1978

Bobby Blue Bland

Goldies 45 2644 - This Time I'm Gone For Good / Where Baby Went - 1970's
Filmways/Heider - I Love To See You Smile - 1978 (one-sided 10" 45rpm acetate - has date 2 / 22 / 78 and time 3:41 typed across label)

Bobby Bland

ABC 12360 - Love To See You Smile / I'm Just Your Man – 1978
ABC 12405 - Come Fly With Me / Ain't God Something – 1978
MCA 1835 - I Feel Good, I Feel Fine / Tit For Tat /// Come Fly With Me / Love To See You Smile - 1979 (12" release)

Bobby Blue Bland

Goldies 45 2740 - Ain't No Love In The Heart Of The City / I Wouldn't Treat A Dog - 1970's

B. B. King & Bobby Bland

Goldies 45 2816 - Slow And Easy / The Thrill Is Gone - 1970's

Bobby Bland

MCA 41140 - Tit For Tat / Come Fly With Me – 1979
MCA 41197 - Soon As The Weather Breaks / To Be Friends - 1980
MCA 51068 - You'd Be A Millionaire / Swat Vibrator - 1981
MCA 51181 - What A Difference A Day Makes / Givin' Up The Streets For Love - 1982
MCA 52085 - Recess In Heaven / Exactly, Where It's At - 1982
MCA 52136 - Here We Go Again / You're About To Win - 1982
MCA 52180 - Is This The Blues / You're About To Win - 1983
MCA 52270 - If It Ain't One Thing / Tell Mr. Bland - 1983
MCA 52436 - Looking Back / You Got Me Loving You - 1984
MCA 52482 - Get Real Clean / It's Too Bad - 1984
MCA 52508 - You Are My Christmas / New Merry Christmas Baby - 1984
Malaco 2122 - Members Only / I Just Got To Know - 1985
Malaco 2126 - Can We Make Love Tonight / In The Ghetto - 1986
Malaco 2133 - Angel - 1986 (one sided disc)
Malaco 2142 - Get Your Money Where You Spend Your Time / For The Last Time – 1988

Bobby Bland / Latimore

Collectables Col 035967 - Members Only / Bad Risk* - ? *flip by Latimore.

Bobby Bland

Collectables Col 901017 - Turn On Your Love Light / I Pity The Fool - ?
Collectables Col 902427 - Stormy Monday Blues / Gotta Get To Know You - ?
Malaco 2146 - 24 Hours A Day / I've Got A Problem – 1988
Malaco 2154 - You've Got To Hurt Before You Heal / I'm Not Ashamed To Sing The Blues – 1989
Malaco 2158 - Ain't No Sunshine / If I Don't Get Involved – 1989
Malaco 2161 - Starting All Over Again / Midnight Run – 1990
Malaco 2166 - Take Off Your Shoes / If I Don't Get Involved – 1990
Malaco 2185 - She's Putting Something In My Food - 1991 (One Sided Disc)
Malaco 2185 - She's Putting Something In My Food / Let Love Have It's Way - 1992
Malaco 2195 - Theres A Stranger In My House / Hurtin' Time Again - 1993
Malaco 2199 - I Just Tripped On A Piece Of Your Broken Heart / Hole In The Wall – 1994
Malaco 2199 - I Just Tripped On A Piece Of Your Broken Heart / Hole In The Wall - 1994 (Promo Issue Cd Single)
Malaco 2303 - Double Trouble (Radio Version) / Double Trouble (Long Version) - 1995 (promo issue Cd single)

Blinky

The Cogic Singers (members Edna Wright (sister of Darlene Love), Frankie Karl, Gloria Jones, Billy Preston, Sondra Williams and Andrea Crouch and Sandra Crouch) group name stands for Church Of God In Christ.

Simpson 273 - It's A Blessing / Since I Found Him - 1964

Sondra Williams

Vee-Jay 941 - He's Got The Whole World In His Hands / Heartaches – 1964
Spiritual Oldies 45 2287 - He's Got The Whole World In His Hands / Heartaches - 1964
Atlantic 7552 - He's Got The Whole World In His Hands / Hark! The Voice – 1967
Atlantic 2432 - God Bless The Children / Heartaches – 1967

Blinky (Sondra Williams)

Motown 1134 - I Wouldn't Change The Man He Is / I'll Always Love You* - 1968 *originally released in 1964 by Brenda Holloway on Tamla 54099.

Edwin Starr & Blinky

Gordy 7090 - Oh How Happy / Ooh Baby Baby* - 1969 (some copies issued on red vinyl) *originally released in 1965 by The Miracles on Tamla 54113.

Blinky (born 21-May-1944)

Motown 1168 - How You Gonna Keep It (After You Get It) / This Time Last Summer - 1970 (unissued) Two different records with the same number were meant to be released at the same time. The other unissued 45 with the same number was by The Ding Dongs with "Gimme Dat Ding / Everything Is Beautiful" on Motown 1168.
Soul 35089 - How You Gonna Keep It (After You Get It) / This Time Last Summer* - 1971 (unissued) *also recorded in 1965 by Danny Day (Hal Davis) on V. I. P. 25019.
Mowest 5019 - Money (That's What I Want) / Money (That's What I Want) - 1972 (promo issue only)
Mowest 5019 - Money (That's What I Want)* / For Your Precious Love - 1972 *originally recorded in 1960 by Barrett Strong on Anna 1111 and in 1960 on Tamla 54027.
Mowest 5019 - For Your Precious Love* / So Tired - 1972 *originally released in 1958 by Jerry Butler & The Impressions on Vee-Jay 280.
Mowest 5033 - T'ain't Nobody's Bizness If I Do / What More Can I Do – 1973
Motown 1233 - You Get A Tangle In Your Lifeline / This Man Of Mine - 1973

Blinky Williams

Reprise 1197 - Walk With Me Jesus / When Love Calls Your Name – 1974

Blinky Williams & The Hollywood Choir (members Blinky Williams (piano), sometime members Brenda Holloway (vocals) and Starletta DuPois (vocals)

Unreleased MOTOWN recordings.

Till The End Of Time
I'm Going Crazy
Is There A Place In His Heart For Me
You Pulled The World Right Out From Under Me
Rescue Me

Lady Sings The Blues
Sweet Joy Of Life (solo rather than a duet with Edwin Starr as released on the album 'Just We Two')
I See A Rainbow (solo rather than a duet with Edwin Starr as released on the album 'Just We Two')

The Blue Notes

Featuring recordings by both the Bernard Williams version of the group, and the Harold Melvin version of the group

The Blue Notes

Rama 25 - If You'll Be Mine / Too Hot To Handle- 1953 (Possibly not the same group)

Bernie Williams

Imperial 5360 - Don't Tease Me / Why Fool Yourself - 1955

The Blue Notes

Josie 800 - If You Love Me / There's Something In Your Eyes, Eloise - 1956

Todd Randall And The Blue Notes

Josie 814 - Letters / With This Pen - 1957

The Blue Notes

Josie 823 - Retribution Blues / Wagon Wheels - 1957

The Blue Notes (Possibly not the same group)

Gamut 1000 - My Heart Cries For You / ? - 1959
Tico 1083 - Charlotte Amalie / Make A Box- 1959

Todd Randall With The Blue Notes

Glory 298 - Monkey Chambo / ? -1959

The Blue Notes

Lost Nite 104 - She Is Mine / The Letter - 1960
Instant Action 101 - She Is Mine / The Letter - 1960
Val-Ue 213 - My Hero / A Good Woman - 1960
Val-Ue 215 - O Holy Night / Winter Wonderland - 1960
Bluco (No Number) - Rigor Mortis / ? - 1960
Jalynne 135 - My Hero / A Good Woman - 1960
Val-Ue ? - Blue Star / Pucker Your Lips - 1961
Gamut 100 - Shrimp Boats Are Coming / My Heart Cries For You - 1961
Twentieth Century 1213 - Blue Star / Pucker Your Lips - 1961
Accent 1069 - Your Tender Lips / ? - 1961
Val-Ue ? - Devoted To You / ? - 1961
Val-Ue ? - Hey Doc / ? - 1961
Last Chance 103 - If You Love Me / ? - 1961
Port 70021 - If You Love Me / There's Something In Your Eyes, Eloise - 1961

3 Sons 103 - Wplj / While I'm Away - 1962
United Artists 816 - Rags To Riches / ? - 1962
Red Top 135 - My Hero / A Good Woman - 1963

Bernard Williams & The Original Blue Notes

Harthon 136 - Needless To Say / Focused On You - 1965

The Blue Notes

Landa 703 - Get Out (And Let Me Cry) / You May Not Love Me - 1965 Lead Vocal By John Atkins

Harold Melvin & The Blue Notes

Arctic 135 - Go Away / What Can A Man Do - 1967

Eddie Holman

Parkway 157 - Why Do Fools Fall In Love / Never Let Me Go - 1967 (Bernie Williams Version Of Group Doing Back Up Vocals)

The Victors

Phillips 40475 - Not Only A Girl Knows / Hurt - 1967

The Blue Notes

Checker 1196 - I Can't Take My Eyes Off You / Goodbye My Lover Goodbye - 1968
Uni 55132 - Got Chills And Cold Thrills / Never Gonna Leave You - 1969

The Blue Notes

Uni 55201 - Lucky Me / This Time Will Be Different - 1970

Harold Melvin & The Blue Notes

Dash 5005 - Never Gonna Leave You / Hot Chills, Cold Thrills And Fever - 1972
Phil. Int. 3516 - I Miss You (Part 1) / I Miss You (Part 2) - 1972 Teddy Pendergrass Lead.
Phil. Int. 3520 - If You Don't Know Me By Now / Let Me Into Your World - 1972
Phil. Int. 3525 - Ebony Woman / Yesterday I Had The Blues - 1973
Phil. Int. 3533 - The Love I Lost (Part 1) / The Love I Lost (Part 2) - 1973
Phil. Int. 3543 - Satisfaction Guaranteed (Or Take Your Love Back) / I'm Weak For You - 1974
Phil. Int. 3552 - Where Are All My Friends / Let It Be You - 1974
Phil. Int. 3562 - Bad Luck (Part 1) / Bad Luck (Part 2) - 1975

Sharon Paige And Harold Melvin & The Blue Notes

Phil. Int. 3569 - Hope That We Can Be Together Soon / Be For Real - 1975

Harold Melvin & The Blue Notes

Phil. Int. 3579 - Wake Up Everybody (Part 1) / Wake Up Everybody (Part 2) - 1975
Phil La Of Soul 372 - Get Out / You May Not Love Me - 1975 (Possible Uk Bootleg)
Phil. Int. 3588 - Tell The World How I Feel About 'Cha Baby / You Know How To Make Me Feel So Good - 1976
Phil. Int. 3712 - Don't Leave Me This Way / Bad Luck - 1975

Phil. Int. 3768 - Where Are All My Friends / Hope That We Can Be Together Again - 1975
ABC 12240 - Reaching For The World / Stay Together - 1976

Harold Melvin & The Blue Notes Featuring Sharon Page

ABC 12268 - After You Love Me, Why Do You Leave Me / Big Singing Star - 1977
ABC 12311 - I Wanna Know Your Name / New To You - 1977

Harold Melvin And The Blue Notes

Glades 1746 - Standing By You, Girl / It's Over - 1977
Fantasy 840 - Another Summer Breeze / All I Need - 1978
ABC 12327 - Baby, You Got My Nose Open / Try To Live A Day - 1978
ABC 12368 - Now Is The Time / Power Of Love - 1978
Source 41156 - Prayin' (Part 1) / Prayin' (Part 2) - 1979

Sharon Paige And Harold Melvin & The Blue Notes

Source 41157 - Tonight's The Night / Your Love Is Taking Me On A Journey - 1979

Harold Melvin & The Blue Notes

Source 41231 - I Should Be Your Lover (Part 1) / I Should Be Your Lover (Part 2) - 1980
Fantasy 41231 - I Should Be Your Lover / X Rated Version - 1980
Fantasy 41291 - Tonight's The Night (Instrumental) / If You're Looking For Someone To Love - 1980

Sharon Paige And Harold Melvin & The Blue Notes

MCA 41291 - Tonight's The Night / If You're Looking For Someone To Love - 1980

Harold Melvin & The Blue Notes

MCA 51190 - Hang On In There / If You Love Me, Really Love Me - 1981

The Blue Notes

Collectables 1113 - Winter Wonderland / O Holy Night - 1982

Harold Melvin & The Blue Notes

Philly World 99674 - Time Be My Lover / This Is The Love - 1983
Philly World 99709 - I Really Love You / Can't Let You Go - 1984
Philly World 99735 - Today's Your Lucky Day (Long) / Today's Your Lucky Day (Short) - 1984 Featuring Nikko
Philly W. 99761 - Don't Give Me Up / Don't Give Me Up (Instrumental) - 1984

The Blue Notes / The Crystalairs

Stoop Sounds 133 - If It's Our Destiny / One Night Stand - 2007 (If It's Our Destiny was recorded in 1957 for Josie but never released)

Reader Help Needed On The Below
Allied 1001 - Yesterday / Jelly Beans - ?

Tony Borders

Delta 1902 - Counting On You / Can't Stand To See You Cry – 1961
Hall-Way 1817 - It'll Be My Song / Dreamers Prayer - 1963
Smash 1817 - It'll Be My Song / Dreamer's Prayer – 1963
Hall 1918 - Pass The Word / Soft Wind, Soft Voice - 1963
Hall 1921 - Get Yourself Another Man / Bit By Bit By Little Bit – 1964
Hall 1926 - You Are My Treasure / Can't Stand To See You Cry - 1964
TCF125 - Love's Been Good To Me / Stay By My Side – 1966
South Camp 7009 - You Better Believe It / What Kind Of Spell - 1967
Greenlite 101 - Love Is A Friend / Cheaters Never Win* - 1968 *also recorded in 1970 by Bobby Boseman On Eve Jim 1941.
Revue 11025 - Cheaters Never Win / Love And A Friend - 1968
Revue 11040 - I Met Her In Church / What Kind Of Spell – 1969
Revue 11054 - Polly Wolly / Gentle On My Mind - 1969
Uni 55180 - Lonely Weekend / You Better Believe It - 1969
Quinvy 001/002 - For My Woman's Love / Please Don't Break My Heart - 1970
Quinvy 7101 - Promise To Myself / Mix And Mingle -1970

Jan Bradley

The Passions (members Addie Bradley, Morris Spearmon, Jerry Williams, Ernest Lemon, and Roscoe Brown) an unrecorded neighbourhood group Jan Bradley started singing with in 1959.

Jan Bradley (born Addie Bradley on 6-July-1943 in Byhalia, Mississippi.)

Formal 1014 / 1015 - We Girls* / Curfew Blues - 1962 *written and produced by Curtis Mayfield.
Formal 1017 - Whole Lot Of Soul / I Am Going To Change – 1962
Night Owl 1055 - Behind The Curtains* / Pack My Things (And Go) - 1962 (backing vocals by The Impressions) *covered by The Five Stairsteps in 1967 on Windy "C" 604.
Formal 1044 - Mama Didn't Lie* / Lovers Like Me - 1962 *written by Curtis Mayfield. (also released in the U.K. on Pye International 7N25182)
Hootenanny 1 - Christmas Time / Christmas Time (Instrumental) - 1962 (subsidiary label of Stacy -Chicago)
Formal 2021 - These Tears / Baby, What Can I Do – 1962
Chess 1845 - Mama Didn't Lie* / Lovers Like Me - 1962 *also released in 1962 by The Fascinations on ABC 10387.
Formal 1048 - Dear Sears And Roebuck / ? – 1963
Chess 1851 - These Tears / Baby, What Can I Do – 1963
Chess 1884 - Pack My Things (And Go) / Curfew Blues – 1964
Chess 1897 - Please Mr. D. J. / Two Of A Kind – 1964
Chess 1919 - I'm Over You / The Brush-Off – 1964
Adanti 1051 - Back In Circulation / Love Is The Answer – 1965
Sound Spectrum 36002 - Back In Circulation / Love Is The Answer – 1965

Jan & Chuck (Jan Bradley & ?)

Night Owl 1004 - Whata Weekend / West Coast Living - 1966

Jan Bradley

Chess 1975 - Just A Summer Memory - 1966 (One Sided Disc - Promo Issue Only)
Chess 1975 - Just A Summer Memory / He'll Wait On Me – 1966
Chess 1996 - Trust Me / These Are The Things A Woman Needs – 1967
Chess 2023 - It's Just Your Way / Your Kind Of Lovin' – 1967
Chess 2043 - Nights In New York City / You Gave Me What's Missing – 1968
Doylen 001 - Tricks Of The Trade / I Kinda See The Light – 1970

Jan Bradley / Fontella Bass

Eric 0236 - Mama Didn't Lie / Rescue Me* - 1973 *Flip By Fontella Bass

Jan Bradley / Fontella Bass

Chess 91006 - Mama Didn't Lie / Rescue Me* - 1975 *Flip By Fontella Bass

Jan Bradley / Fontella Bass

Collectables Col 034067 - Mama Didn't Lie / Rescue Me* - ?*Flip By Fontella Bass

Jan Bradley / Fontella Bass

Chess 107 - Mama Didn't Lie / Rescue Me* - 1982 *flip by Fontella Bass

Jan Bradley / The Ray Bryant Combo

MCA 53322 - Mama Didn't Lie / The Madison Time - 1988 (two tracks used in the movie "Hairspray" which had amongst the stars Sonny Bono, Ruth Brown, Divine, Debbie Harry, Ricki Lake and Jerry Stiller)

Johnny Bragg

The Prisonaires (members Johnny Bragg (lead), Edward Lee Thurman (tenor), John Edward Drue Jr. (tenor), Marcel Sanders (bass) and William Stewart (baritone))

Sun 186 - Just Walkin' In The Rain (2 Complete Versions) / Just Walkin' In The Rain (2 Incomplete Versions) - 1953 (Acetate) Recorded Monday 1-June-1953.
Sun 186 - Just Walkin' In The Rain / Baby Please - 1953 (Red Vinyl Only Six Copies Known To Exist)
Sun 186 - Just Walkin' In The Rain / Baby Please - 1953 (Black Vinyl)
Sun 189 - My God Is Real / Softly And Tenderly - 1953
Sun 191 - A Prisoner's Prayer / A Prisoner's Prayer - 1953 (A Number Pressed With Same Track Both Sides)
Sun 191 - I Know / A Prisoner's Prayer - 1953
Sun 207 - There Is Love In You / What'll You Do Next - 1954

The Sunbeams (members Johnny Bragg, Edward Lee Thurmon, William Stewart, John Edward Drue (re-joined group), Hal Hebb and Willy Wilson with Henry "Dishrag" Jones on piano and L. B. McCollough on guitar)

The Marigolds (members Johnny Bragg, Edward Lee Thurmon, John Edward Drue, Henry Jones, Hal Hebb, Willie Wilson and Alfred Brooks who replaced a pardoned William Stewart (died 1959 --- cause: drug overdose))

Excello 2057 - Rollin' Stone* / Why Don't You - 1955 *also released in 1955 by The Cadets on Modern 960.

The Solotones (members Johnny Bragg, Edward Lee Thurmon, William Stewart, John Edward Drue, Henry Jones, Hal Hebb, Willie Wilson and Alfred Brooks)

Excello 2060 - Pork And Beans / Front Page Blues - 1955

The Marigolds

Excello 2061 - Two Strangers / Love You - Love You - Love You - 1955

Johnny Bragg & The Marigolds

Excello 2078 - Foolish Me / Beyond The Clouds - 1956
Excello 2091 - Juke Box Rock ' N ' Roll / It's You Darling, It's You - 1956
Excello 2091 - It's You Darling,It's You / It's You Darling, It's You - 1956 (Dj. Copy)

Johnny Bragg (Born 26-February-1925 in North Nashville, Tennesee --- died 1-September-2004 aged 79 at the Imperial Manor Convalescent Center in Madison, Tennessee - cause: cancer)

Decca 9 - 30917 - True Love Will Never Die / Just So That Someone Is Me - 1959
Decca 9 - 30972 - World Of Make Believe / Everything's Alright - 1959
El Be Jay 100 - Fools Hill / No Chance For Happiness - 1967
El Be Jay 001 - They're Talking About Me* / Is It True, Darlin' - 1967 (some copies issued with picture sleeve)
El Be Jay 104 - Walk Tall Like A man / I'm Free - 1967
El Be Jay 105 - I'm Free The Prisoner's Song / Hurt And Lonely - 1967
El Be Jay - Just Walking In The Rain - (previously unissued version which was released in Germany on a 2007 Blue Label Cd "The Bullet And Sur-Speed Records Story - The R&B And Soul Sessions" SPV 95892)
El Be Jay - Goin Over Fool Hill - (unissued track which was released in Germany on a 2007 Blue Label Cd "The Bullet And Sur-Speed Records Story - The R&B And Soul Sessions" SPV 95892)
Hollywood 1130 - Freedom Marches - Pt. 1 / Freedom Marches -Pt. 2 - 1968 (unsure if this is the same Johnny Bragg)
Bedflame 101 - Flame Of Love / Storybook Love - ?

Jimmy Breedlove

The Cues (Members Ollie Jones, Jimmy Breedlove, Abe Decosta (Born 1929 - Died 1985), Robey Kirk And Eddie Barnes)

Lamp 8007 - Forty 'Leven Dozen Ways / Scoochie Scoochie – 1954
Jubilee 5201 - Only You / I Feel For Your Loving – 1955
Capitol F3245 - Burn That Candle / Oh My Darling – 1955
Capitol F3310 - Charlie Brown / You're On My Mind – 1956
Capitol F3400 - Destination 2100 And 65 / Don't Make Believe – 1956
Capitol F3483 - The Girl I Love / Crackerjack – 1956
Capitol F3582 - Why / Prince Or Pauper – 1956

Jimmy Breedlove

Capitol 3626 - Danny Boy / The Sky - Le Ciel – 1956

The Cues (Members Ollie Jones, Jimmy Breedlove, Abe Decosta, Robey Kirk And Eddie Barnes)

Prep 104 - I Pretend / Crazy, Crazy Party – 1957

Jimmy Breedlove With Orchestra

Atco 6094 - That's My Baby / Over Somebody Else's Shoulder (I Fell In Love With You) - 1957

Jimmy Breedlove

Atco 6105 - I Can Still Hear You Say You Love Me / I Wish I Were Twins – 1957
Epic 9270 - Could This Be Love / This Too Shall Pass Away – 1958
Epic 9283 - Whirlpool / Loveable – 1958
Epic 9283 - Love Is All We Need / Loveable – 1958
Epic 9289 - Love Is All We Need / Oo-Wee Good Gosh A-Mighty – 1958
Epic 9319 - All Is Forgiven / I Say Hello – 1959
Epic 9360 - To Belong / Waiting For You – 1960
Okeh 7145 - Anytime You Want Me / My Guardian Angel – 1962
Okeh 7152 - Don't Let It Happen / Queen Bee – 1962
Diamond 144 - Jealous Fool / Lil' Ol' Me (Loves Li'l Ol' You) – 1963

J. B. Love (Jimmy Breedlove)

Congress 239 - I Am A Heart / No One Else But You – 1965
Kapp 603 - Then Only Then* / I Wouldn't Have It Any Other Way - 1964 *Also Recorded In 1963 By Walter Jackson On Columbia 42659.

Jimmy Breedlove

Alert 424 - I Ain't What I Used To Be / Why Did My Dream End - ?
Jubilee 5551 - Jealous Fool / The Greatest Love (Nothing Less, Nothing More) – 1966
Roulette 7010 - I Can't Help Lovin' You* / I Saw You - 1968 *also recorded in 1966 by Paul Anka on RCA-Victor 47-8893.

Ep's

Jim Breedlove

RCA Camden Cae-447 - Rock And Roll Music / Swanee River Rock /// The Lonesome Road / Whole Lot-Ta Shakin' Goin' On - 1958

Maxine Brown

The Manhattans (members Maxine Brown, ...) late 1950's gospel group.

The Royaltones (members Maxine Brown, ...) late 1950's gospel group.

The Treys (members Maxine Brown, Sammy Turner, Mack Starr, ...)

Maxine Brown (born 27-April-1932 in Kingstree, South Carolina)

Nomar 103 - All In My Mind* / Harry Let's Marry - 1960 *in 1961 The Harptones (later to become **The Soothers** on **Port**) recorded an "answer" record to this track entitled "All In Your Mind" on Companion 102.
Nomar 106 - Funny / Now That You're Gone – 1961

Maxine Brown / Frankie & The Flips

Nomar 107 - Heaven In Your Arms / Maxine's Place* - 1961 *Flip By Frankie & The Flips.

Maxine Brown

ABC-Paramount 10235 - Think Of Me / I Don't Need You No More - 1961
ABC-Paramount 10255 - After All We've Been Through Together / My Life* - 1961 *also recorded but unissued by Junior Lewis & Group until it was released in the U. K. on

a 2002 KentCD "The Arock & Sylvia Story" CDKEND 212.
ABC-Paramount 10290 - What I Don't Know (Won't Hurt Me) / I Got A Funny Kind Of Feeling - 1962
Wham 7036 - All In My Mind / Funny - 1962
Wham 7036 - All In My Mind / Funny - 1962
ABC-Paramount 10315 - Forget Him / A Man – 1962
ABC-Paramount 10327 - My Time For Crying / Wanting You – 1962
ABC-Paramount 10353 - I Kneel At Your Throne / If I Knew Then – 1962
ABC-Paramount 10370 - Am I Falling In Love / Promise Me Anything - 1962
ABC-Paramount 10388 - Life Goes On Just The Same / If You Have No Real Objection – 1962
Musictone 1117 - Funny / Now That You've Gone - 1963
Musictone 1118 - All In My Mind / Harry Let's Marry - 1963
Wand 135 - Ask Me / Yesterday's Kisses - 1963 (some copies issued with picture sleeve)
Oldies 45 1 - Funny / Now That You're Gone - 1964
Oldies 45 2 - All In My Mind / Harry Let's Marry - 1964
Wand 142 - Coming Back To You / Since I Found You - 1964
Wand 152 - Little Girl Lost / You Upset My Soul – 1964
Wand 158 - Put Yourself In My Place / I Cry Alone – 1964
Wand 162 - Oh No Not My Baby* / You Upset My Soul - 1964 *Backing Vocals **Dee Dee Warwick.**
Wand 173 - It's Gonna Be Alright / You Do Something To Me – 1965

Chuck Jackson & Maxine Brown

Wand 181 - Something You Got* / Baby Take Me - 1965 *originally recorded in 1961 by Chis Kenner on Instant 3237.

Maxine Brown

Wand 185 - One Step At A Time / Anything For A Laugh - 1965

Chuck Jackson & Maxine Brown

Wand 191 - Can't Let You Out Of My Sight / Don't Go – 1965
Wand 198 - I Need You So* / Cause We're In Love - 1965 *also recorded in 1950 by Ivory Joe Hunter on MGM K10663

Maxine Brown

Wand 1104 - If You Gotta Make A Fool Of Somebody* / Your In Love - 1965 *also recorded in 1961 by James Ray With the Hutch Davie Orch. on Caprice 110.

Chuck Jackson & Maxine Brown

Wand 1109 - I'm Satisfied / Please Don't Hurt Me - 1966

Maxine Brown

Wand 1117 - One In A Million* / Anything You Do Is Alright - 1966 *also recorded in 1967 by Rhetta Hughes on Columbia 44073.
Wand 1128 - Let Me Give You My Lovin' / We Can Work It Out – 1966
Wand 1145 - I Don't Need Anything / The Secret Of Livin' – 1966

Chuck Jackson & Maxine Brown

Wand 1148 - Hold On, I'm Coming* / Never Had It So Good** - 1967 *originally recorded in 1966 by Sam & Dave on Stax 189. **also recorded in 1965 by Ronnie Milsap on Scepter 12109.
Wand 1155 - Daddy's Home* / Don't Go - 1967 *originally recorded in 1961 by Shep & The

Limelites on Hull 740
Wand 1162 - Tennessee Waltz / C. C. Rider - 1967

Maxine Brown

Wand 1179 - Soul Serenade / He's The Only Guy I'll Ever Love - 1968 (Possibly unreleased)
Epic 10334 - Seems You've Forsaken My Love / Plum Outa Sight – 1969
Epic 10424 - From Loving You / Love In Them There Hills – 1969
Commonwealth United 3001 - We'll Cry Together* / Darling Be Home Soon - 1969 *also recorded in 1973 by Ellerine Harding on Mainstream 5539.
Commonwealth United 3008 - I Can't Get Along Without You / Reason To Believe – 1970
Avco Embassy 4585 - Make Love To Me / Always And Forever – 1971
Avco Embassy 4604 - Treat Me Like A Lady / I. O. U. – 1972
Avco Embassy 4612 - Picked Up, Packed And Put Away / Bella Mia – 1972

Chuck Jackson & Maxine Brown

Scepter/Wand Forever 21020 - Let's Go Get Stoned / Never Had It So Good - 1973

Maxine Brown

Scepter/Wand Forever 21023 - All In My Mind / You Do Something To Me - 1973
Gusto 2234 - If You Gotta Make A Fool Of Somebody / ? - ?
Collectables Col 012867 - All In My Mind / Harry Let's Marry – 1981
Collectables Col 012877 - Funny / Now That You're Gone – 1981

Maxine Brown / Tommy Hunt

Collectables Col 030077 - Oh No Not My Baby / Human* - 1981 Flip By Tommy Hunt.

Maxine Brown / Dionne Warwick

Eric 4013 - Oh No Not My Baby / Don't Make Me Over* - 1983 *Flip By Dionne Warwick
Gladys Knight & The Pips / Maxine Brown

Original Sound Obg-4522 - Every Beat Of My Heart / All In My Mind* - 1984 *Flip By Maxine Brown.

Lillie Bryant

Lillie Bryant (born 14-February-1940)

Cameo 122 - Good Good Morning, Baby / The Gambler - 1957

Billy & Lillie (members Billy Ford and Lillie Bryant)

Swan 4002 - La Dee Dah / The Monster* - 1957 (two label versions of this 45 were issued, one with Swan in capital letters. The other had just the letter S in Swan capitalized) *flip is by Billy Ford & The Thunderbirds.
Swan 4005 - Happiness / Creepin' Crawlin' Cryin' - 1958
Swan 4011 - The Greasy Spoon / Hanging On To You - 1958
Swan 4020 - Lucky Ladybug / I Promise You - 1958
Casino 105 - Lucky Ladybug / I Promise You - 1959

Lillie Bryant

Swan 4029 - Smokey Grey Eyes / I'll Never Be Free - 1959

Billie & Lillie

Swan 4030 - Tumbled Bown / Aloysius Horatio Thomas The Cat - 1959
Swan 4036 - Bells, Bells, Bells / Honeymoonin' - 1959
Swan 4042 - Terrific Together / Swampy - 1959
Swan 4051 - Free For All / The Ins And Outs Of Love - 1960
Swan 4058 - Over The Mountain, Across The Sea / That's The Way The Cookie Crumbles (Ah-So) - 1960
Swan 4069 - Ain't Comin' Back (To You) / Bananas - 1961
Stacy 928 - My Pledge Of Love / You Made Me Love You - 1962
ABC-Paramount 10421 - Love Me Sincerely / Whip It To Me Baby - 1963
ABC-Paramount 10489 - Carry Me Across The Threshold / Why I Love Billie (Lillie) - 1963
Ric 144 - Tic Tac Toe / Coconut Cake - 1964
Crossroad 101 - Baby You Just Don't Know / I'm In Love - 1965
Cameo 412 - Nothing Moves (Without A Little Push) / The Two Of Us - 1966
Cameo 435 - You Got Me By The Heart / Hear You Better Hear - 1966

Lillie Bryant

Monarch Record Mfg. Co. (No #) - Meet Me Halfway - ? (test pressing 45 with title / artist and label Id hand written on label)
Tay-Ster 6016 - Meet Me Half Way / Mama - 1966

Billie & Lillie

Goldies 2578 - La Dee Dah / The Monster - 1973
Goldies 2579 - Lucky Ladybug / I Promise You - 1973
Old Gold 89 - La Dee Dah / Lucky Ladybug - ?
Underground 1156 - La Dee Dah / Lucky Ladybug - ?

Billie & Lillie / Vicki Lawrence

Collectables Col 031227 - La Dee Dah / Night The Lights Went Out In Georgia* - **?** flip by Vicki Lawrence.

Solomon Burke

The Gospel Cavaliers (members Solomon Burke, ...)

Solomon Burke (born James Solomon McDonald 21-March-1940 in Philadelphia, Pensylvania --- died 10-October-2010 at Schipol airport in Amsterdam, Holland --- cause: ?)

Apollo 485 - Christmas Presents From Heaven / When I'm All Alone - 1955
Apollo 487 - I'm In Love / Why Do Me That Way – 1956
Apollo 491 - I'm All Alone / To Thee – 1956
Apollo 500 - No Man Walks Alone / Walking In A Dream – 1956
Apollo 505 - You Can Run But You Can't Hide / A Picture Of You – 1956
Apollo 511 - I Need You Tonight / This Is It – 1957
Apollo 512 - For You And You Alone / You Are My One Love - 1957
Apollo 522 - They Always Say / Don't Cry – 1958
Apollo 527 - My Heart Is A Chapel / This Is It - 1958

Singular 1314 - Doodle Dee Doo / It's All Right - 1959
Singular 1812 - This Little Ring / I'm Not Afraid - 1960
Mala 420 - This Little Ring / I'm Not Afraid - 1960

Little Vincent (Solomon Burke)

Apollo 747 - You Don't Send Me Anymore / Always Together - 1961
Apollo 748 - Honk, Honk, Honk (Part 1) / Honk, Honk, Honk (Part 2) - 1961

Solomon Burke

Atlantic 2089 - Keep The Magic Working / How Many Times - 1961
Atlantic 2114 - Just Out Of Reach (Of My Two Open Arms) / Be-Bop Grandma - 1961
Atlantic 2131 - Cry To Me* / I Almost Lost My Mind - 1961 *recorded 6-December-1961.
Atlantic 2147 - I'm Hanging Up My Heart For You / Down In The Valley* - 1962 *track recorded 4-April-1962.
Atlantic 2157 - I Really Don't Want To Know / Tonight My Heart She Is Crying (Love Is A Bird) - 1962
Atlantic 2170 - Go On Back To Him / I Said I Was Sorry - 1963
Atlantic 2180 - Words / Home In Your Heart - 1963
Atlantic 2185 - If You Need Me / You Can Make It If You Try - 1963
Atlantic 2196 - Can't Nobody Love You / Stupidity - 1963
Atlantic 2205 - You're Good For Me / Beautiful Brown Eyes - 1963
Atlantic 2218 - He'll Have To Go* / Rockin' Soul - 1964 *recorded 12-December-1963 --- song also recorded in 1959 by Billy Brown on Columbia 41380.
Atlantic 2226 - Goodbye Baby (Baby Goodbye) / Someone To Love Me - 1964
Atlantic 2241 - Everybody Needs Somebody To Love / Looking For My Baby - 1964
Atlantic 2254 - Yes I Do / Won't You Give Him (One More Chance) - 1964
Atlantic 2259 - The Price / More Rockin' Soul - 1964
Atlantic 2276 - Got To Get You Off My Mind / Peepin' - 1965
Atlantic 2288 - Tonight's The Night / Maggie's Farm* - 1965 *recorded 8-April-1965 --- written by Bob Dylan.
Atlantic 2299 - Someone Is Watching / Dance, Dance, Dance - 1965
Atlantic 2308 - Only Love (Can Save Me Now) / A Little Girl That Loves Me - 1965
Atlantic 2314 - Baby Come On Home / (No, No, No) Can't Stop Lovin' You Now - 1965
Atlantic 2327 - Mountain Of Pride / I Feel A Sin Coming On - 1966
Atlantic 2345 - Lawdy Miss Clawdy / Suddenly - 1966
Atlantic 2349 - Keep Lookin'* / Don't Want You No More - 1966 *recorded 16-June-1966.
Atlantic 2359 - When She Touches Me / Woman How Do You Make Me Love You Like I Do - 1966
Atlantic 2369 - A Tear Fell / Presents For Christmas - 1966

Lukas Lollipop

Loma 2067 - Don't Hold On To Someone (Who Don't Love You) / Hoochie-Coochie-Coo - 1967 (although the Warner Bros. / Loma record label has stated in numerous compilations that this is Solomon Burke using a pseudonym, Solomon Burke stated a few years back that this isn't him. It is widely felt by many that this is probably Israel "Popper Stopper" Tolbert)

Solomon Burke

Atlantic 2378 - Keep A Light In The Window Till I Come Home / Time Is A Thief - 1967
Atlantic 2416 - Take Me (Just As I Am)* / I Stayed Away Too Long - 1967 *also recorded in 1966 by Arthur Conley on Fame 1009 and in 1968 by Mitty Collier but unissued)
Atlantic 2459 - Detroit City / It's Been A Change - 1967
Atlantic 2483 - Party People / Need Your Love So Bad - 1968
Atlantic 2507 - I Wish I Knew (How It Would Feel To Be Free) / It's Just A Matter Of Time - 1968

The Soul Clan (members Solomon Burke, **Arthur Conley**, **Don Covay**, **Ben E. King** and **Joe Tex**)

Atlantic 2530 - Soul Meeting / That's How It Feels - 1968

Solomon Burke

Atlantic 2537 - Meet Me In Church / Save It - 1968
Atlantic 2566 - What'd I Say / Get Out Of My Life Woman - 1968
Bell 759 - Up Tight Good Woman* / I Can't Stop – 1969 *also recorded in 1967 by Spencer Wiggins on Goldwax 321.
Bell 783 - Proud Mary / What Am I Living For - 1969
Bell 806 - That Lucky Old Sun / How Big A Fool (Can A Fool Be) - 1969
Bell 829 - Generation Of Revelations / I'm Gonna Stay Right Here - 1969
Bell 891 - In The Ghetto / God Knows I Love You - 1970
MGM 14185 - All For The Love Of Sunshine / Lookin' Out My Backdoor - 1970
MGM 14221 - The Electronic Magnetism (That's Heavy, Baby) / Bridge Of Life - 1971
MGM 14279 - J. C. I Know Who You Are / The Things Love Will Make You Do - 1971
MGM 14302 - The Night They Drove Old Dixie Down / Psr 1983 - 1971
MGM 14353 - Love's Street And Fool's Road* / I Got To Tell It - 1972 *From The Film "Cool Breeze"
MGM 14402 - We're Almost Home / Fight Back - 1972
MGM 14425 - Get Up And Do Something For Yourself / Misty - 1972
MGM 14425 - Get Up And Do Something For Yourself / We're Almost Home - 1972
Pride 1017 - I Can't Stop Loving You (Part 1) / I Can't Stop Loving You (Part 2) - 1972
Pride 1022 - All I Want For Christmas / I Can't Stop Loving You (Part 1) - 1972
MGM 14571 - Shanbala / Love Thy Neighbour - 1973
MGM 14651 - Georgia Up North / Here Comes The Train - 1973
Pride 1028 - My Prayer / Ookie Bookie Man - 1973

Solomon Burke & Lady Lee

Pride 1038 - Sentimental Journey / Vaya Con Dios - 1973

Solomon Burke

ABC / Dunhill 4388 - Midnight And You / I Have A Dream – 1974
Chess 2159 - You And Your Baby Blues / I'm Leaving On That Late, Late Train – 1975
Chess 2172 - Let Me Wrap My Arm's Around You / Everlasting Love - 1975
Chess 401 - I'll Never Stop Loving You (Never Ever Song) / Do Right Song - 1976
Chess 30003 - Going Back To My Roots / Loves Paradise – 1977
Amherst 736 - Please Don't Say Goodbye To Me / See That Girl – 1978
Infinity 1023 - Sidewalks, Fences And Walls (3:39) / Sidewalks, Fences And Walls (5:15) - 1979 (12" promo issue only)
Infinity 50,046 - Sidewalks, Fences And Walls / Boo-Hoo-Hoo (Cra-Cra-Craya) – 1979
The Big One ? - Silent Night / A Christmas Prayer – 1980
Flashback 48 - Proud Mary / What Am I Living For - ?
Soultown 3001 - Bettin' On America / Cowboy Hat - 1981
Savoy 0002 - Silent Night / A Christmas Prayer –
1982

Solomon Burke & The House Of God Band (members Solomon Burke, ...)

Mother Earth 27 - My Aunt Margarite / God We Need A Miracle – 1985

Solomon Burke

Rounder 4554 - A Change Is Gonna Come / Let It Be You And Me - 1986 (Some copies issued with picture sleeve)
Rounder 4557 - Love Buys Love / What A Man Won't Do For A Woman – 1987
Rounder 332042 - Just A Matter Of Time - Truth Will Set You Free /// Tonight's The Night - I Can't Stop - ? (12" promo issue only - medley)
Outpost ? - Power / ? – 1989
Outpost Oet-30001 - Power (Club Mix) (7:51) / Power (Radio Mix) (4:57) /// Power (Paradise Mix) (5:24) / (Dub Mix) (5:22) / Radio Long Mix (5:31) - 1989 (12" red vinyl release from the Italian movie "Potere" soundtrack)

Solomon Burke / Rayne

MCI 717842 - You're All I Want For Christmas / No Place Like Home* - 199? *flip by Rayne.

Solomon Burke

Bizarre / Straight 90113 - Try A Little Tenderness - 1991 (promo issue only Cd single taken from Cd "Homeland")
Pointblank S7-19520 - Ooooooyou / Today Is Your Birthday – 1997
Odeon ?
Bell 891 - In The Ghetto / God Knows I Love You - ? (promo issue only Cd single)

Solomon Burke with The Blind Boys Of Alabama

Fat Possum 976712 - None Of Us Are Free (Radio Edit) / Don't Give Up On Me (Live) / I Need A Holiday (Previously Unreleased) - 2002 (Cd Single)

Jerry Butler

The Roosters (Members Arthur Brooks, Richard Brooks, Sam Gooden, Fred Cash And ?)

The Northern Jubilee Gospel Singers (Members Jerry Butler, Curtis Mayfield, Sam Hawkins, Tommy Hawkins, Charles Hawkins, ...)

The Quails (Members Jerry Butler, Wille Wright, James "Doolaby" Wright And Ronald Sherman) 1956 Line-Up.

The Alphatones (Members Curtis Mayfield, Al Boyce, James Weems And Dallas Nixon)

The Roosters (Members Jerry Butler, Curtis Mayfield, Arthur Brooks, Richard Brooks And Sam Gooden) Group tried to get audition for Chess Records but was refused entry by company secretary, so they went to the other side of the street to Vee-Jay Records.

The Impressions (Members Jerry Butler, Curtis Mayfield, Arthur Brooks, Richard Brooks And Sam Gooden) Name of group was changed by Calvin Carter Of Vee-Jay who gave them their audition it is said in the hallway of the company!

Jerry Butler and The Impressions (members Jerry Butler, Curtis Mayfield, Arthur Brooks, Richard Brooks and Sam Gooden)

Vee-Jay 280 - For Your Precious Love* / Sweet Was The Wine - 1958 *also recorded in 1963 by Garnett Mimms & The Enchanters on United Artists 658.
Falcon 1013 - For Your Precious Love* / Sweet Was The Wine - 1958 *also recorded in 1971 by Geater Davis on House Of Orange 2405.
Abner 1013 - For Your Precious Love / Sweet Was The Wine - 1958

The Impressions Featuring Jerry Butler (Members Jerry Butler, Curtis Mayfield, Arthur Brooks, Richard Brooks And Sam Gooden)

Abner 1017 - Love Me / Come Back My Love – 1959

Jerry Butler (Born 8-December-1939 In Sunflower, Mississippi -- Older Brother Of Billy Butler)

Abner 1024 - Lost / One By One – 1959
Abner 1028 - Rainbow Valley / Hold Me Darling – 1959
Abner 1030 - I Was Wrong / Couldn't Go To Sleep – 1959
Abner 1035 - Lonely Soldier / I Found A New Love – 1960
Vee-Jay 354 - He Will Break Your Heart / Thanks To You - 1960 (One Known Copy Has Surfaced In Los Angeles In 1999 Pressed In Silver Vinyl)
Vee-Jay 371 - Silent Night / O Holy Night – 1960
Vee-Jay 375 - Find Another Girl / When Trouble Calls – 1961
Vee-Jay 390 - I'm Telling You / I See A Fool – 1961
Vee-Jay 396 - For Your Precious Love / How Sweet Was The Wine – 1961
Vee-Jay 405 - Moon River / Aware Of Love – 1961
Vee-Jay 426 - Island Of Sirens / Chi Town – 1962
Vee-Jay 451 - Make It Easy On Yourself / It's Too Late – 1962
Vee-Jay 463 - You Can Run / I'm The One – 1962
Vee-Jay 475 - Wishing Star / You Go Right Through Me – 1962
Vee-Jay 486 - You Won't Be Sure / Whatever You Want – 1963
Vee-Jay 526 - Strawberries / Almost Lost My Head – 1963
Vee-Jay 354 - He Will Break Your Heart* / Thanks To You - 1960 (one known copy has surfaced in Los Angeles in 1999 pressed in silver vinyl) *also released in 1969 by The Groovers on A & M 1077.
Vee-Jay 556 - Just A Little Bit* / A Woman With Soul - 1963 *also recorded in 1965 by Roy Head on Scepter 12116 and in 1967 by Roscoe Robinson on Wand 1161.
Vee-Jay 567 - Need To Belong / Give Me Your Love – 1963
Vee-Jay 1971 - Aware Of Love - 1963 (white promo issue only - a compact 33 release 45rpm)

Gene & Jerry (**Gene Chandler** and Jerry Butler)

Roulette 4537 - Hootenanny Christmas / Carousel – 1963

Jerry Butler

Oldies 45 14 - He Will Break Your Heart / Thanks To You - 1964

Jerry Butler & The Impressions

Oldies 45 20 - For Your Precious Love / Sweet Was The Wine - 1964

Jerry Butler

Oldies 45 31 - Aware Of Love / Moon River - 1964
Oldies 45 70 - Make It Easy On Yourself / It's Too Late - 1964

Jerry Butler & The Impressions

Oldies 45 77 - The Gift Of Love / At The County Fair – 1964

Jerry Butler / The Shepherd Sisters

Oldies 45 108 - Chi Town / Alone* - 1964 *Flip By The Shepherd Sisters.

The Four Seasons / Jerry Butler & The Impressions

Oldies 45 116/77 - Candy Girl / At The County Fair – 1964

Jerry Butler / The Scarlets
Oldies 45 117 - Isle Of Sirens / Dear One* - 1964 *Flip By The Scarlets.

Jerry Butler

Oldies 45 134 - Find Another Girl / When Trouble Calls - 1964
Vee-Jay 588 - Giving Up On Love / I've Been Trying - 1964
Vee-Jay 598 - I Stand Accused* / I Don't Want To Hear It Anymore - 1964 *Also Recorded In 1966 By Inez & Charlie Foxx On Dynamo 104.

Betty Everett & Jerry Butler

Vee-Jay 613 - Let It Be Me / Ain't That Loving You Baby – 1964
Vee-Jay 633 - Smile / Love Is Strange - 1964

Jerry Butler

Vee-Jay 651 - Good Times / I've Grown Accustomed To Her Face – 1965

Betty Everett & Jerry Butler

Vee-Jay 676 - Since I Don't Have You / Just Be True – 1965
Vee-Jay 691 - Fever / The Way You Do The Things You Do – 1965

Jerry Butler

Vee-Jay 696 - I Can't Stand To See You Cry / Nobody Needs Your Love – 1965
Vee-Jay 707 - Just For You / Believe In Me - 1965

Betty Everett & Jerry Butler

Oldies 45 303 - Let It Be Me / Ain't That Loving You Baby - 1965

Jerry Butler

Oldies 45 318 - A Woman With Soul / Just A Little Bit – 1965
Oldies 45 321 - Giving Up On Love / I've Been Trying – 1965
Oldies 45 326 - Need To Belong / Give Me Your Love – 1965
Vee-Jay 711 - Moon River / Make It Easy On Yourself - 1966
Vee-Jay 715 - For Your Precious Love / Give It Up – 1966
Mercury 72592 - Love / Loneliness – 1966
Mercury 72625 - You Make Me Feel Like Someone / For What You Made Of Me – 1966
Mercury 72648 - I Dig You Baby / Some Kind Of Magic – 1966
Mercury 72676 - You Walked Into My Life / Why Do I Lose You – 1967
Mercury 72698 - The Way I Love You / You Don't Know What You've Got Until You Lose It – 1967
Mercury 72721 - Mr. Dream Merchant / 'Cause I Love You So – 1967
Mercury 72764 - Lost / You Don't Know What You've Got Until You Lose It – 1968
Mercury 72698 - The Way I Love You / You Don't Know What You've Got Until You Lose It* - 1967 *also recorded in 1971 by Willie Hobbs on Seventy Seven 101.
Mercury 72850 - Hey Western Union Man / Just Can't Forget About You – 1968
Mercury 72876 - Are You Happy / I Still Love You – 1969
Mercury 72898 - Only The Strong Survive / Just Because I Really Love You – 1969
Mercury 72929 - Moody Woman / Go Away Find Yourself – 1969

Mercury 72960 - What's The Use Of Breaking Up / Brand New Me – 1970
Mercury Dj 152 - Don't Let Love Hang You Up / Walking Around In Teardrops - 1970 (Promo Issue Only)
Mercury 73091 - Don't Let Love Hang You Up / Walking Around In Teardrops – 1970
Mercury Dj 177 - Got To See If I Can Get Mommy / Forgot To Remember - 1970 (Promo Issue Only)
Mercury 73015 - Got To See If I Can Get Mommy / Forgot To Remember – 1970
Mercury 73145 - I Could Write A Book / Since I Lost You Baby – 1970
Mercury 73101 - Where Are You Going / You Can Fly – 1970
Mercury 73131 - How Does It Feel / Special Memory – 1970

Jerry Butler & Gene Chandler

Mercury 73163 - You Just Can't Win (By Making The Same Mistake) / The Show Is Grooving – 1971

Jerry Butler

Mercury 73169 - If It's Real What I Feel / Why Are You Leaving Me – 1971

Jerry Butler & Gene Chandler

Mercury 73195 - Two And Two (Take This Woman Off The Corner) / Everybody Is Waiting – 1971

Jerry Butler

Mercury 73210 - How Did We Lose It Baby / Do You Finally Need A Friend – 1971
Mercury 73241 - Walk Easy My Son / Let It Be Me – 1971

Jerry Butler & Brenda Lee Eager (Lead Singer Of Jerry Butler's Back-Up Group)

Mercury 73255 - Ain't Understanding Mellow / Windy City Soul – 1971

Jerry Butler

Mercury 73290 - I Only Have Eyes For You / A Prayer - 1972

Jerry Butler Featuring Brenda Lee Eager

Mercury 73301 - (They Long To Be) Close To You / You Can't Always Tell – 1972

Jerry Butler

Mercury 73335 - One Night Affair / Life's Unfortunate Son's – 1972

Jerry Butler & Brenda Lee Eager

Mercury 73395 - Can't Understand It / How Long Will It Last – 1972
Mercury 73422 - We Were Lovers, We Were Friends / The Love We Had Stays On My Mind – 1973

Betty Everett & Jerry Butler

Eric 0169 - Let It Be Me / Smile – 1973

Jerry Butler

Mercury 73443 - Power Of Love / What Do You Do On A Sunday Afternoon – 1973
Goldies 45 02431 - Aware Of Love / He Will Break Your Heart – 1973

Jerry Butler & The Impressions

Goldies 45 02436 - For Your Precious Love / Sweet Was The Wine – 1973

Jerry Butler

Goldies 45 02441 - Make It Easy On Yourself / Find Another Girl – 1973

Betty Everett & Jerry Butler

Goldies 45 02444 - Let It Be Me / Ain't That Loving You Baby – 1973

Jerry Butler

Goldies 45 02452 - I Stand Accused / Need To Belong - 1973
Trip 37 - He Will Break Your Heart / Thanks To You - 1970's
Trip 39 - Make It Easy On Yourself / Need To Belong - 1970's

Jerry Butler / Jerry Butler & Betty Everett

Trip 40 - I Stand Accused / Let It Be Me* - 1970's *Flip By Jerry Butler & Betty Everett.

Jerry Butler & Patti Austin

Cti 7 - In My Life (Part 1) / In My Life (Part 2) – 1973

Jerry Butler

Mercury 73459 - That's How Heartaches Are Made / Too Many Danger Signs – 1974
Mercury 73495 - Take The Time To Tell Her / High Stepper – 1974
Mercury 73629 - Playing On You / Me And You Against The World – 1974
Mistletoe 803 - Silent Night / O Holy Night – 1974
Motown 1403 - The Devil In Mrs. Jones / Don't Wanna Be Reminded – 1976
Motown 1414 - I Wanna Do It To You / Don't Wanna Be Reminded – 1977
Motown 1421 - Chalk It Up / I Don't Want Nobody To Know – 1977

Smokey Robinson / Jerry Butler

Motown M00004d1 - Vitamin U / Chalk It Up - 1977 (12" Release - Some Copies Issued With Picture Sleeve)

Jerry Butler & Thelma Houston

Motown 1422 - It's A Lifetime Thing / Kiss Me Now – 1977

Jerry Butler / Marvin Gaye

W. I. A. A. 1147 - What's It All About Public Service Programme - 1978 (Radio Station Promo Only (Flip Is By Marvin Gaye))

Jerry Butler

Philadelphia International 3656 - Cooling Out / Are You Lonely Tonight – 1978
Philadelphia International 2z8 3664 - (I'm Just Thinking About) Cooling Out (7:00) / Are You Lonely Tonight (5:29) - 1978 (12" Release)

Philadelphia International 3664 - (I'm Just Thinking About) Cooling Out / Are You Lonely Tonight – 1979
Philadelphia International 3673 - Nothing Says I Love You Like I Love You / Glad To Be Back – 1979
Philadelphia International 3683 - Dream World / Let's Make Love – 1979
Philadelphia International 3746 - The Best Love I Ever Had / Would You Mind – 1980

Jerry Butler Featuring Debra Henry Of Silk

Philadelphia International 3113 - Don't Be An Island / The Best Love I Ever Had – 1980

Jerry Butler

Philadelphia International 3117 - Tell Me Girl / We've Got This Feeling Again – 1980
Lost-Nite 299 - Let It Be Me / Ain't That Lovin' You Baby – 1981
Fountain 400 - No Love Without Changes / All The Way – 1982
MCA D-2436 - For Your Precious Love / Sweet Was The Wine - ?

Jerry Butler & Stix Hooper / Stix Hooper

Mca 52177 - Let's Talk It Over / Especially You* - 1983 *Flip By Stix Hooper.

Jerry Butler & Patti Austin

Cti 59 - In My Life / What's At The End Of The Rainbow – 1983

Jerry Butler

Collectables Col 014387 - A Lonely Soldier / I Found Love - ?
Collectables Col 014397 - He Will Break Your Heart / Thanks To You - ?
Collectables Col 014407 - Moon River / Aware Of Love - ?
Collectables Col 014417 - Make It Easy On Yourself / It's Too Late - ?

Jerry Butler & Betty Everett

Collectables Col 014427 - Let It Be Me / Ain't That Loving You Baby - ?

Jerry Butler

Collectables Col 014437 - Need To Belong / Giving Up On Love - ?
Collectables Col 040517 - For Your Precious Love / I Stand Accused - ?

Jerry Butler / Brook Benton

Collectables Col 042207 - Never Gonna Give You Up / Just A Matter Of Time* - ? *Flip By Brook Benton.

Jerry Butler

Collectables Col 042217 - Mr. Dream Merchant / Only The Strong Survive - ?
Collectables Col 042227 - Hey Western Union Man / Moody Woman - ?

Jerry Butler & Brenda Lee Eager

Collectables Col 042237 - Ain't Understanding Mellow / What's The Use Of Breaking Up - ?

Jerry Butler

Mercury 872 914-7 - Only The Strong Survive / Lost – 1989
Mercury 872 916-7 - Never Give You Up / Hey Western Union Man – 1989
Mercury Celebrity 30155 - Only The Strong Survive / Lost - ?
Mercury Celebrity 30156 - Hey Western Union Man / Never Gonna Give You Up - ?

Jerry Butler & Brenda Lee Eager / Jerry Butler

Mercury Celebrity 30161 - Ain't Understanding Mellow / I Only Have Eyes For You* - ? Flip By Jerry Butler Only.

Jerry Butler

Ichiban 269 - Angel Flying Close To The Ground / You're The Only One – 1992
Ichiban 290 - Need To Belong / Sure Feels Good – 1993

Jerry Butler / Jerry Butler & The Impressions

Original Sound Obg-4510 - He Will Break Your Heart / For Your Precious Love* - ? *Flip By Jerry Butler & The Impressions.

Group Line Ups

The Cairos (Keni Lewis, Tommy Monteir, Famon Johnson, Gerald Richardson)
The Capitols (Samuel George, Donald Norman Storball, Willie Ford, Richard McDougal)
The Casualeers (Arnold Davis, Jimmy Johnson, Ollie Johnson, Isiah Love)
The Contours (Billy Gordon, Billy Hoggs, Joe Billingslea, Sylvester Potts, Hubert Johnson)
The Creators (Hugh Harris, James Wright, John Alan, Danny Austin, Chris Coles)

Candy & The Kisses

Candy & The Kisses (Members Beryl "Candy" Nelson, Suzanne Nelson (Sisters) And Jeanette Johnson) - Revived Name, Originally Called Themselves The Symphonettes - No Known Recordings - Discovered By Jerry Ross..

Cameo 336 - The 81* / Two Happy People - 1964 *Song Composed By Jerry Ross And Kenny Gamble After Watching Some Kids Do A New Dance Called The 81 To A Martha & The Vandellas 45 Titled "In My Lonely Room".
Cameo 355 - Soldier Boy (Of Mine)* / Shakin' Time - 1964 *Cover Of An Unreleased Ronettes Song.

Honey Love & The Love Notes (Members Harriet Laverne, Beryl "Candy" Nelson, Suzanne Nelson And Jeanette Johnson)

Cameo 380 - We Belong Together / Mary Ann* - 1965 *Cover Of An Unreleased Crystals Song.

Candy & The Kisses

Scepter 12106 - Keep On Searchin' / Together - 1965
Scepter 12125 - Out In The Streets Again / Sweet And Lovely - 1965

The Love Notes (Members Harriet Laverne, Beryl "Candy" Nelson, Suzanne Nelson And Jeanette Johnson)

Cameo 409 - Baby Baby You / Beg Me - 1966

Candy & The Kisses

Scepter 12136 - Tonight's The Night* / The Last Time - 1966 *Original Version By The Shirelles.
Decca 32415 - Chains Of Love / Someone Out There - 1968

Sweet Love (Members Beryl "Candy" Nelson, Suzanne Nelson And Jeanette Johnson)

Mercury 72415 - If You Love Him / Oh No, Oh No - 1969

The Capitols

The Capitols (members Samuel George (born 1-October-1942, died 17-March-1982 - cause: stabbed to death during a domestic dispute), Donald Norman Storball, Richard Mitchell McDougal,) formed in 1962 in Detroit.

Karen 16 - Dog And Cat / The Kick - 1963
Karen 1524 - Cool Jerk / Hello Stranger* - 1966 *also recorded in 1963 by Barbara Lewis on Atlantic 2184 and in 1974 by The Quickest Way Out on Karen 717.
Karen 1525 - Zig Zaggin' / I Got To Handle It - 1966 (shares same record number 1525 as the 1966 release by Sharon McMahan "Hello Stranger / Got To Find Another Guy")
Karen 1526 - We Got A Thing That's In A Groove / Tired Of Runnin' From You - 1966
Karen 1534 - Take A Chance On Me Baby / Patty Cake - 1967
Karen 1536 - Cool Pearl / Don't Say Maybe Baby - 1967
Karen 1537 - Afro Twist / Cool Jerk '68 - 1968
Karen 1543 - Ain't That Terrible* / Soul Sister, Soul Brother - 1968 *also recorded in 1967 by Roy Redmond on Loma 2071.
Karen 1546 - When You're In Trouble / Soul Soul - 1969
Karen 1549 - I Thought She Loved Me / When You're In Trouble - 1969

The Capitols / The Larks

Goldisc 3094 - Cool Jerk / The Jerk* - 1979 *flip by The Larks.

The Capitols

Collectables Col 012147 - Cool Jerk / Hello Stranger - 1981

Is there any relation to the above Capitols from these listed below?

Mickey Tolliver & The Capitols (members ?)

Cindy 3002 - Rosemary / Millie - 1957

The Capitols / The Jones Boys

Baron 103 - Honey, Honey /Alone In The Night* - 1973 *flip by The Jones Boys

James Carr

The Southern Wonders Juniors (members James Carr, . group James Carr started with at age nine.

The Sunset Travellers (members James Carr, ...)

The Jubilee Hummingbirds (members James Carr, ...)

The Harmony Echoes (members James Carr, ...) group James Carr was singing lead for in 1962.

James Carr (born James Edward Carr on 13-June-1942 in Coahoma County , near Clarksdale, Mississippi - died 7-January-2001 in a Memphis nursing home - cause: lung cancer)

Goldwax 108 - You Don't Want Me / Only Fools Run Away – 1964
Goldwax 112 - Lover's Competition / I Can't Make It – 1964
Goldwax 119 - Talk Talk / She's Better Than You – 1965
Goldwax 302 - You've Got My Mind Messed Up / That's What I Want To Know - 1966
Goldwax 309 - Love Attack / Coming Back To Me Baby – 1966
Goldwax 311 - Pouring Water On A Drowning Man / Forgetting You – 1966
Goldwax 317 - The Dark End Of The Street / Lovable Girl – 1967
Goldwax 313 - Let It Happen / A Losing Game – 1967
Goldwax 328 - I'm A Fool For You* / Gonna Send You Back To Georgia - 1967 *female vocals by an uncredited Betty Harris.
Goldwax 332 - A Man Needs A Woman / Stronger Than Love – 1968
Goldwax 335 - Life Turned Her That Way / A Message To Young Lovers – 1968
Goldwax 338 - That's The Way Love Turned Out For Me / Freedom Train – 1969
Goldwax 340 - To Love Somebody / These Ain't Raindrops – 1969
Goldwax 343 - Everybody Needs Somebody / Row Row Your Boat – 1969
Atlantic 2803 - Hold On / I'll Put To You - 1971
River City 1940 - Bring Her Back / Let Me Be Right – 1977
Flashback 26 - You've Got My Mind Messed Up / That's What I Want To Know - ?
Flashback 42 - A Man Needs A Woman / Stronger Than Love - ?
Flashback 83 - Pouring Water On A Drowning Man / The Dark End Of The Street - ?
Soul Trax 101 - Soul Survivor / Gonna Marry My Mother In Law - 1990

Chairmen Of The Board

Chairmen Of The Board (members General Norman Johnson (born 23-May-1943 in Norfolk, Virginia --- former member of The Showmen), Danny Woods (born 1944 in Atlanta, Georgia), Harrison Kennedy (born in Canada) and Eddie Custis (born Philadelphia, Pennsylvania)

Invictus 9074 - Give Me Just A Little More Time / Since The Days Of Pigtails - 1970
Invictus 9078 - You've Got Me Dangling On A String / I'll Come Crawling - 1970
Invictus 9079 - Everything's Tuesday / Patches* - 1970 *also recorded in 1970 by Clarence Carter on Atlantic 2748.
Invictus 9081 - Pay To The Piper / Bless You - 1970
Invictus 9086 - Chairmen Of The Board / When Will She Tell Me She Needs Me - 1970
Invictus 9089 - Hanging On To A Memory / Tricked And Trapped - 1970
Invictus 9093 - Savannah Lady / I'm In Love Darling - 1970

Invictus 9099 - Working On A Building Of Love* / Try My Love For Size – 1970 *lead vocals Danny Woods, session: Thelma Hopkins, Joyce Wright (backing female vocals)
Invictus 9103 - Men Are Getting Scarce / Bravo, Hooray - 1970
Invictus 9105 - Elmo James / Bittersweet – 1972

General Johnson

Invictus 9106 - All We Need Is Understanding / Savannah Lady – 1972

Chairmen Of The Board (members General Johnson, Danny Woods, Harrison Kennedy and Eddie Custis)

Invictus 9122 - Working On A Building Of Love / Everybody's Got A Song To Sing – 1972

Chairmen Of The Board (members General Johnson, Danny Woods and Harrison Kennedy)

Invictus 9126 - Let Me Down Easy / I Can't Find Myself - 1972
Invictus 1251 - Finders Keepers / Finders Keepers (Instrumental) - 1973
Invictus 1252 - Only Time Will Tell / Only Time Will Tell (Instrumental) - 1973
Invictus 1263 - Life & Death / Live With Me, Love With Me - 1974
Invictus 1268 - Everybody Party All Night / Morning Glory (Instrumental) - 1974
Invictus 1271 - Let's Have Some Fun / Love At First Sight - 1974
Invictus 1276 - Skin I'm In / Love At First Sight – 1975

Chairmen Of The Board Featuring Prince Harold (members General Johnson, Danny Woods, ...)

Invictus 1278 - Someone Just Like You / You've Got The Extra Added Power In Your Love – 1976

General Johnson

Arista 0177 – All In The Family / Ready, Willing And Able – 1976
Arista 0192 – We The People / Keep Keepin' On – 1976
Arista 0203 – Don't Walk Away / Temperature Rising (Part 2) – 1976
Arista 0234 – Only Love Can Mend A Broken Heart / Patches – 1977
Arista 0264 – Temperature Rising / Let's Fool Around – 1977
Arista 0359 – Can't Nobody Love Me Like You Do / Lies – 1978
Ica 023 - Someone Just Like You / Someone Just Like You – 1978 (Promo Issue)
Ica 023 – Come On In And Dance* / Someone Just Like You – 1979 *session: Danny Woods.

Chairmen Of The Board feat. General Norman Johnson (members General Johnson, Danny Woods and Ken Knox)

Surfside 800414 - On The Beach / Pretty Women - Hey Baby - 1980

General Johnson and The Chairmen Of The Board (members General Johnson, Danny Woods and Ken Knox)

Surfside 800902 - Carolina Girl / Down At The Beach Club - 1980
Surfside 810216 - Summer Love / Summer Love - 1981
Surfside 820215 - Beach Fever / Bird In The Hand - 1982
Surfside 830113 - Shag Your Brains Out / Shag Your Brains Out - 1983
Surfside 830117 - I'd Rather Be In Carolina / When Can I See You Again - 1983
Surfside 840229 - Lover Boy / Hi Dee Hi Dee Ho - 1984
Surfside 850401 - Love Is What You Make It / Love Is What You Make It - 1985
Surfside 870709 - Don't Walk Away / Forever Together - 1987
Surfside 880209 - A Piece Of Candy / A Piece Of Candy - 1988
Surfside 890214 - Gone Fishin' / X - Rated Love - 1989

Surfside 0401901 - I Wanna Doop Doop Doop Your Doo Wop She Doo Wop / Let The Good Times Roll – 1990

The Chairmen Of The Board (members General Johnson, Danny Woods, Harrison Kennedy and Eddie Custis)

Ripete 103 - Give Me Just A Little More Time / Everything's Tuesday – 1990

General Johnson and The Chairmen Of The Board (members General Johnson, Danny Woods and Ken Knox)

Surfside 910114 - You Don't Know What Love Is / You Don't Know What Love Is - 1991
Surfside 911119 - Christmas Time Is Here / Christmas Time Is Here - 1991
Surfside 920301 - Boy Toy / Boy Toy - 1992
Surfside 920701 - Alive And Kickin' / Alive And Kickin' – 1992

Nolan Chance

The Trinidads (members Charles Davis (lead and tenor), Hosea Brown (lead and tenor), Charles Colbert Jr. (first tenor), Norman Price (baritone) and Claude Forch (bass))

Formal 1005 - Don't Say Goodbye / On My Happy Way – 1960
Formal 1006 - One Lonely Night / When We're Together - 1960 (with The Frank Derrick Orchestra)

The Trinidads (members Charles Davis, "Kitchen" ?, Charles Colbert Jr. (later member of The Daylighters), Norman Price and Claude Forch)

Lorenzo Smith & The Turbo-Jets Band (members Lorenzo Smith, Charles Davis (lead),..)from 1960

The Dukays (members (members Charles Davis, Margaret "Cookie" Stone, James Lowe, Earl Edwards and Ben Broyles)

Vee-Jay 442 - I'm Gonna Love You So / Please Help - 1962

The Duke Of Earl (**Gene Chandler**)

Vee-Jay 450 - Daddy's Home / The Big Lie - 1962 (although uncredited The Dukays sang on this release)
Vee-Jay 455 - I'll Follow You / You Left Me - 1962 (although uncredited The Dukays sang on this release)

The Dukays (members Charles Davis, Margaret "Cookie" Stone, James Lowe, Earl Edwards and Ben Broyles)

Vee-Jay 460 - I Feel Good All Over / I Never Knew – 1962
Vee-Jay 491 - Combination / Every Step - 1963

The Artistics (members Charles Davis (lead), Larry Johnson, Jesse Bolian and Aaron Floyd) late 1963 ~ early 1964 line-up.

Nolan Chance (born Charles Davis on 11-November-1939 in Vidalia, Louisiana)

Constellation 144 - She's Gone / If He Makes You – 1965
Constellation 161 - Just Like The Weather / Don't Use Me – 1965
Bunky 161 - Just Like The Weather / Don't Use Me – 1965
Thomas 802 - I'll Never Forget You / I'm Loving Nothing – 1969
Scepter Sdj-12353 - Sara Lee / Sara Lee - 1972 (Promo Issue)
Scepter Sce-12353 - Sara Lee / I'd Like To Make It With You - 1972

Gene Chandler

The Gaytones (members Eugene Dixon, ...) 1955 group formed while at Englewood High School, Chicago, Illinois.

The Dukays (members Eugene Dixon (lead), James Lowe, Earl Edwards and Ben Broyles) 1957 line-up.

The Dukays (members Eugene Dixon (lead), Shirley Johnson (tenor), James Lowe (tenor), Earl Edwards (baritone) and Ben Broyles (bass)). Drafted in U.S. army from 1957 ~ 1960 rejoined The Dukays in 1960.

Nat 4001 - The Big Lie / The Girl's A Devil - 1961
Nat 4002 - Nite Owl / Festival Of Life - 1961
Nat 4003 - Duke Of Earl* / Kissin' In The Kitchen - 1961 *Bass Line Was Sung By Ben Broyles. (Apparently A Few Copies Have Been Found)

Gene Chandler (born Eugene Dixon on 6-July-1937 in Chicago, Illinois)

Universal Recording Corp. 61-2172 - Duke Of Earl (2:22) / Kissin In The Kitchen - 1961 (acetate --- has Vee Jay records, song titles, times and artist name typed on label)
Vee-Jay 416 - Duke Of Earl* / Kissin' In The Kitchen - 1962 *there was an "answer" record to this track released in 1962 by The Pearlettes (members Sheila Galloway (lead), Lynda Galloway, Priscilla Kennedy and Mary Meade) titled "Duchess Of Earl" on Vee-Jay 435.
Nat 4003 - Duke Of Earl / Kissin' In The Kitchen - 1962 (copies exist on this label - probably company trying to cash in on it's success)

The Duke Of Earl (Gene Chandler)

Vee-Jay 416 - Duke Of Earl / Kissin' In The Kitchen - 1962

The Dukays (Members Eugene Dixon, Shirley Johnson, James Lowe, Earl Edwards And Ben Broyles)

Vee-Jay 430 - Nite Owl / Festival Of Life - 1962

The Duke Of Earl (Gene Chandler)

Vee-Jay 440 - Walk On With The Duke / London Town - 1962
Vee-Jay 450 - Daddy's Home / The Big Lie - 1962
Vee-Jay 455 - I'll Follow You / You Left Me - 1962

Gene Chandler

Vee-Jay 455 - Forgive Me / You Left Me - 1962
Vee-Jay 461 - Tear For Tear / Miracle After Miracle - 1962
Vee-Jay 468 - You Threw A Lucky Punch / Rainbow - 1962 (background vocals by Cal Carter & Friends)

Vee-Jay 511 - Check Yourself* / Forgive Me - 1963 *also released in 1961 by The Temptations on Miracle 12.
Vee-Jay 536 - Baby, That's Love / Man's Temptation - 1963
Vee Jay 536 - Man's Temptation / Wonderful, Wonderful - 1963
Constellation 104 - From Day To Day / It's So Good For Me - 1963

Gene & Jerry (Gene Chandler And Jerry Butler)

Roulette 4537 - Hootenanny Christmas / Carousel - 1963

Gene Chandler

Constellation 110 - Pretty Little Girl / A Little Like Lovin' - 1963
Constellation 112 - Think Nothing About It / Wish You Were Here - 1964
Constellation 114 - Soul Hootenanny (Part 1) / Soul Hootenanny (Part 2) - 1964
Constellation 124 - A Song Called Soul / You Left Me - 1964
Oldies 45 21 - Duke Of Earl / Nite Owl - 1964
Constellation 130 - Just Be True / A Song Called Soul* - 1964 *written by Billy Butler.
Constellation 136 - Bless Our Love / London Town - 1964
Constellation 141 - What Now / If You Can't Be True* - 1964 *also recorded in 1965 by Marva Lee on Atco 45-6367
Oldies 45 39 - You Threw A Lucky Punch / Rainbow - 1964
Oldies 45 315 - Check Yourself / Forgive Me - 1965
Oldies 45 316 - Man's Temptation / Baby That's Love - 1965
Constellation 146 - You Can't Hurt Me No More / Everybody Let's Dance - 1965
Constellation 149 - Nothing Can Stop Me / The Big Lie - 1965
Constellation 158 - Rainbow '65 (Part 1) / Rainbow '65 (Part 2) - 1965
Constelation 160 - Good Times / No One Can Love You - 1965
Constellation 164 - Here Come The Tears* / Soul Hootenanny (Part 2) - 1965 *also recorded in 1967 by Darrell Banks on Atco 6471.
Constellation 166 - Baby, That's Love / Bet You Never Thought - 1966
Constellation 167 - (I'm Just A) Fool For You / Buddy Ain't It A Shame - 1966
Constellation 169 - I Can Take Care Of Myself* / If I Can't Save It - 1966 *also recorded in 1967 by The Spyders on Golden State 106 and MTA 128
Constellation 172 - Mr. Big Shot / I Hate To Be The One To Say - 1966
Checker 1155 - I Fooled You This Time / Such A Pretty Thing - 1966
Checker 1165 - To Be A Lover / After The Laughter (Here Comes The Tears) - 1967
Checker 1190 - I Won't Need You / No Peace, No Satisfaction - 1967
Brunswick 55312 - Girl Don't Care / My Love - 1967
Brunswick 55339 - There Goes The Lover / Tell Me What Can I Do - 1967
Checker 1199 - River Of Tears / It's Time To Settle Down - 1968

Gene Chandler & Barbara Acklin

Brunswick 55366 - Love Won't Start / Show Me The Way To Go - 1968

Gene Chandler

Brunswick 55383 - There Was A Time* / Those Were The Good Old Days - 1968 *also recorded in 197? by Six Pack on Trip Universal 15.

Gene Chandler & Barbara Acklin

Brunswick 55387 - From The Teacher To The Preacher / Anywhere But Nowhere - 1968

Gene Chandler

Brunswick 55394 - Teacher, Teacher / Pit Of Loneliness - 1968
Checker 1220 - Go Back Home / In My Baby's House - 1969

Gene Chandler & Barbara Acklin

Brunswick 55405 - Little Green Apples* / Will I Find You - 1969 *also recorded in 1968 by O. C. Smith on Columbia 4-44616.

Gene Chandler

Brunswick 55413 - Eleanor Rigby / Familiar Footsteps - 1969
Brunswick 55425 - This Bitter Earth / Suicide - 1969
Mercury 73083 - Groovy Situation / Not The Marrying Kind - 1970
Mercury 73121 - Simply Call It Love / Give Me A Chance - 1970

Gene & Jerry (Gene Chandler And Jerry Butler)

Mercury 73163 - You Just Can't Win (By Making The Same Mistake) / Sho Is Grooving - 1971
Mercury 73195 - Ten And Two (Take This Woman Off The Corner)* / Everybody Is Waiting - 1971 *also recorded in 1970 by James Spencer on Memphis 101.

Gene Chandler

Mercury 73206 - You're A Lady / Stone Cold Feeling - 1971
Mercury 73258 - Yes I'm Ready (If I Don't Get To Go) / Pillars Of Glass - 1971
Curtom 1979 - Don't Have To Be Lyin' Babe (Part 1) / Don't Have To Be Lyin' Babe (Part 2) - 1973
Curtom 1986 - Baby I Still Love You / I Understand - 1973
Curtom 1992 - Without You Here / Just Be There - 1973
Oldies 45 21 - Duke Of Earl / Nite Owl - ?
Eric 0171 - Duke Of Earl / Check Yourself - 1974
Eric 0172 - Rainbow (Original) / Man's Temptation - 1974
Eric 0173 - Bless Our Love / Just Be True - 1974
Eric 0174 - Rainbow '65 (Complete) / What Now - 1974
Lost Nite 310 - Rainbow / Duke Of Earl - ?
Goldies 45 2437 - Duke Of Earl / Nite Owl - ?
Goldies 45 2438 - Turn On Your Lovelight / Rainbow - ?

Gene Chandler / Gene Chandler Orchestra

Marsel 501 - Tell It Like It Is / Live Your Life - Pt. 2 (Instrumental)* - 1976 *flip by Gene Chandler Orchestra.

Gene Chandler

Chi-Sound 1168 - Give Me The Cue / Tomorrow I May Not Feel The Same - 1978
Chi-Sound Tcd-68 - Get Down (Special Mix) (8:14) / Get Down (Special Mix) (8:14) - 1978 (12" promo issue only)
Chi-Sound 2386 - Get Down / I'm The Travelling Kind - 1978
Chi-Sound Tcd-68 - Get Down (Special Mix) (8:14) / I'm The Traveling Kind (4:06) - 1978 (12" release)
Chi-Sound 2404 - Please Sunrise / Greatest Love Ever Known - 1979

Edwin Starr / Gene Chandler

20th Century/Chi-Sound Tcd-073 - Contact (7:21) / Get Down (8:14) - 1979 (12" release) *flip by Gene Chandler.

Gene Chandler

Chi-Sound 2411 - When You're #1 / I'll Remember You - 1979
Chi-Sound Tcd-080-Dj - When You're #1 (8:59) / Dance Fever (7:45) - 1979 (12" promo issue only)
Chi-Sound Tcd-081 - When You're #1 (8:59) / I'll Remember You (3:50) - 1979 (12" release)
20th Century 2411 - When You're #1 / I'll Remember You - 1979
20th Century 2428 - Do What Comes So Natural / That Funky Disco Rhythm - 1979
Chi-Sound Tcd-098 - That Funky Disco Rhythm / ? - 1979 (12" Release)
Chi-Sound 2451 - Does She Have A Friend? / Let Me Make Love To You - 1980
Chi-Sound Tcd-101 - Does She Have A Friend? (6:05) / Let Me Make Love To You (4:08) - 1980 (12" Release)
Chi-Sound 2468 - Lay Me Gently / You've Been So Good To Me - 1980
Chi-Sound 2480 - Rainbow '80 / I'll Be There - 1980
Chi-Sound 2494 - I'm Attracted To You / I've Got To Meet You - 1981
Chi-Sound 2507 - Love Is The Answer / Godsend - 1981
Collectables Col 014607 - Duke Of Earl / Rainbow - 1981
Chi-Sound 111 - I Keep Coming Back / Baby You're Something In The Clutch - 1982
Chi-Sound 1000 - I'll Make The Living If You Make The Loving Worthwhile / (Instrumental) - 1982
Chi-Sound 2001 - Make The Living Worthwhile (Disco Version) (6:10) / Make The Living Worthwhile (Short Version) (4:05) - 1982 (promo issue only)
Chi-Sound 1001 - I'll Make The Living If You Make The Loving Worthwhile / Time Is A Thief - 1982 Chi-Sound 2001 - I'll Make The Living If You Make The Loving Worthwhile (6:10) / Time Is A Thief (4:45) - 1982 (12" promo issue only)

Jamie Lynn & Gene Chandler

N. Y. International 1001 - You're The One / I Keep Coming Back For More - 1983
Salsoul 7051 - You're The One / I Keep Coming Back For More - 1983

Gene Chandler / Barbara Acklin

Collectables Col 030557 - The Girl Don't Care / Love Makes A Woman* - ? *Flip By Barbara Acklin.

Gene Chandler

Collectables Col 034367 - I Fooled You This Time / To Be A Lover - ?
Collectables Col 034827 - Rainbow '65 / What Now? - ?
Collectables Col 034837 - Bless Our Love / Just Be True - ?
Collectables Col 039657 - Rainbow '80 / Does She Have A Friend - ?

Johnny Bristol / Gene Chandler

Collectables Col 043607 - Hang On In There Baby / Groovy Situation* - ? *flip by Gene Chandler

Gene Chandler

Collectables Col 044867 - Get Down / When You're # 1 - ?
MCA ? - 1984
Solid Smoke ? - 1984

Gene Chandler / Dee Clark

Original Sound Obg-4507 - Duke Of Earl / Raindrops* - 1984 *Flip By Dee Clark.

Gene Chandler

Fastfire 7003 - Haven't I Heard That Line Before / You'll Never Be Free Of Me - 1985
Fastfire 7005 - Lucy / Please, You Got Tonight - 1986

Jimmy Reed / Gene Chandler

Ripete 147 - Big Boss Man Duke Of Earl* - 1990 *flip by Gene Chandler.

Gene Chandler / Stephanie Mills Featuring Teddy Pendergrass

20th Century Fox / Chi-Sound Tcd-68 - Get Down (8:14) / Two Hearts (4:40) - 2007 (12" reissue release)

Lee Charles

Lee Charles (born Lee Charles Nealy)

Dakar 601 - It's All Over Between Us / Then Would You Love Me – 1968
Revue 11007 - Standing On The Outside / If That Ain't Loving You – 1968
Revue 11022 - Wrong Number / Someone, Somewhere -1968
Brunswick 55401 - Wrong Number / I'll Never Ever Love Again – 1969
Bamboo 110 - Girl You Turned Your Back / I Never Want To Lose – 1970
Bamboo 111 - Why Do You Have To Go / I Never Want To Lose My Sweet Thing – 1970
Bamboo 117 - You Can't Get Away / Girl You Turned Your Back - 1970
Bamboo 119 - You Got To Get It For Yourself / I Get High On My Baby's Love – 1971
Wand 11242 - When The Deal Goes Down / Let's Play House – 1972
Hot Wax 7209 - Love Ain't Gonna Run Away / ? - 1972 (this was an unissued 45 - no flip side title was planned)
Hot Wax 7303 - I Just Want To Be Loved / Somebody's Gonna Hurt You, Like You Hurt Me - 1973
Invictus 1260 - Sittin' On A Time Bomb (Waitin' For The Hurt To Come) / Get Your House In Order (Instrumental) - 1974

The Charts

The Thrilltones (members Joe Grier, Glenmore Jackson, Ross Buford, Leroy Binns and Stephen Brown (born 9-January-1941 in New York City, New York --- died 20-January-1989 --- cause: ?))

The Charts (members Joe Grier, Glenmore Jackson, Ross Buford, Leroy Binns and Stephen Brown)

Everlast 5001 - Deserie* / Zoop - 1957 *written by Joe Grier. Over one million copies of this 45 are reported to have been sold over the years, but Joe Grier had sold off the writers share to a photographer of the stars named James Kriegsman.

The Charts With Rhythm Accompaniment (members Joe Grier, Glenmore Jackson, Ross Buford, Leroy Binns and Stephen Brown)

Everlast 5002 - Dance Girl / Why Do You Cry - 1957

The Charts (members Joe Grier, Glenmore Jackson, Ross Buford, Leroy Binns and Stephen Brown)

Everlast 5006 - You're The Reason / I've Been Wondering - 1957
Everlast 5008 - All Because Of Love / I Told You So - 1958
Everlast 5010 - My Diane / Baby Be Mine - 1958 (after this 45 flopped Joe Grier joined the services and the group disbanded. Joe Grier later became a member of Les Cooper & The Soul Rockers)
Guyden 2021 - For The Birds / Ooba Gooba - 1959 (an instrumental release, put out whilst the group was going through personnel changes due to the draft)
Enjoy 1000/1 - Deserie / Zoop - 1962
Everlast 5026 - Deserie / Zoop - 1963

The Charts (members Tony Harris, Frankie Pierce, Stephen Brown and Leroy Binns)

Vel-V-Tone 102 - What's Your Excuse / You Keep Dancing With Me - 1963

The Charts (members Joe Grier, Glenmore Jackson, Ross Buford, Leroy Binns and Stephen Brown)

Lost Nite 173 - Deserie / Zoop - ?
Lana 117 - Deserie* / I Wanna Take You Home** - 1965 *a re-release of Everest 5001 with overdubbed instrumentation. **bit of a mystery here, although the flip is credited to The Charts apparently it is not the group.

The Charts (members Tony Harris, Frankie Pierce, Stephen Brown and Leroy Binns)

Wand 1112 - Deserie / Fell In Love With You Baby - 1966
Wand 1124 - Livin' The Nightlife / Nobody Made You Love Me - 1966

The Original Cadillacs (members J. R. Bailey, Bobby Phillips, Bobby Spencer and Leroy Binns)

Polydor 14031 - Deep In The Heart Of The Ghetto (Part 1) / Deep In The Heart Of The Ghetto (Part 2) - 1969

The Charts / The Starlights

Trip 22 - Deserie / Valerie* - 1970 *flip by The Starlights.

The Original Cadillacs (members J. R. Bailey, Stephen Brown, Bobby Spencer and Leroy Binns)

The Charts (members Joe Grier, Glenmore Jackson, Ross Buford, Leroy Binns and Stephen Brown)

Last Chance 115 - Dance Girl / Why Do You Cry - 1972
Goldies 45 2499 - Deserie / Zoop - 1973

The Twelth Of Never (members

? -1976

The Charts (members Leroy Binns, Raymond Binns, Stephen Brown and John "Spider" Truesdale) group line-up from 1980 ~ 1983

Cleveland Still's Dubs (members Cleveland Still, Stephen Brown, John Truesdale, Bernard Jones and Leslie Anderson)

Clifton 77 - Could This Be Magic / Teddy Bear - 1986

Cleveland Still's Dubs / Lillian Leach & The Mellows

U. G. H. A (no #) - Beside My Love / If I Didn't Care* - 1986 *flip by Lillian Leach & The Mellows

The Charts (members Joe Grier, Glenmore Jackson, Ross Buford, Leroy Binns and Stephen Brown)

Collectables Col 016177 - Deserie / Zoop - ?
Collectables Col 16197 - You're The Reason / I've Been Wondering - ?
Collectables Col 016217 - All Because Of Love / I Told You So - ?

The Charts (members Joe Grier, Leroy Binns, Dickie Harmon and Butch Phillips) 2002

The Charters

Mel-O-Dy 104 - Trouble Lover / Show Me Some Sign - 1962
Tarx 1003 - My Rose / El Merengue - 1962
Alva 1001 - I Lost You / My Little Girl - 1963
Merry-Go-Round 103 - Lost In A Dream / This Makes Me Mad - 1964

Chris Clark

Chris Clark (born 1946 in Los Angeles. T.V. writer since 1969. Co-wrote the screenplay for "Lady Sings The Blues")

? - (AL?) - 7-65-F8 (H.T) (2:49) - Sweeter As The Days Go BY - 1965 (10" one sided acetate plays at 45rpm -- this is the original unreleased version of this song -- label has RECOAT written over it four times with thick black felt pen followed by MASTER written in smaller letters also in felt pen. Unfortunately the Black felt pen obscures rest of the information typed on the label hence the (AL?)) song was co-written by Frank Wilson.

Connie Clark

Joker 716 - My Sugar Baby / (Instrumental) – 1966

Chris Clark

V.I.P. 25031 - Do Right Baby, Do Right / Don't Be Too Long* - 1966 *vocal accompaniment credited to The Lewis Sisters.
Test Pressing American Record Pressing Co. - Do I Love You (Indeed I Do) / Don't Be Too Long - 1966 (unissued test pressing info on label has --- Label V.I.P. --- Artist Chris Clark --- Record No. VIP 25034 --- Master No. 187313 for "A" side and Master No. 169302 for "flip" side --- Date 4-7-66 --- also on label two X's)
V. I. P. 25034 - Do I Love You (Indeed I Do) / Don't Be Too Long - 1966 (unreleased) The Velvelettes "These Things Will Keep Me Loving You / Since You've Been Loving Me" was released on this number.
V.I.P. 25038 - Love's Gone Mad / Love's Gone Mad - 1966 (incorrect title - promo issue only)
V.I.P. 25038 - Love's Gone Mad / Put Yourself In My Place- 1966 (incorrect title - pulled shortly after release)
V.I.P. 25038 - Love's Gone Bad* / Put Yourself In My Place - 1966 *also released in 1967 by The Underdogs on V.I.P. 25040 - some copies issued on red vinyl.
Larrabee Sound Studios (No #) - I Want To Go Back There Again - 1966 (10" mono one sided

acetate - has title, Jobete Music and address (6811 Santa Monica Boulevard, Los Angeles. California 657-6750) on label)
V.I.P. 25041 - I Want To Go Back There Again / I Want To Go Back There Again - 1967 (promo issue only) also released in 1971 by Thelma Houston on Mowest 5008 and in 1983 by Charlene on Motown 1663.
V.I.P. 25041 - I Want To Go Back There Again* / I Love You - 1967 *co-written by Berry Gordy and Chris Clark.
Motown 1114 - From Head To Toe / From Head To Toe - 1967 (Promo Issue Only)
Motown 1114 - From Head To Toe / Beginning Of The End – 1967
Motown 1121 - Whisper You Love Me Boy / Whisper You Love Me Boy - 1968 (promo issue only) originally released in 1964 by Mary Wells on Motown 1065.
Motown 1121 - Whisper You Love Me Boy / The Beginning Of The End* - 1968 *also released in 1969 by Diana Ross & The Supremes on Motown 1146.

Judy Clay

The Drinkard Sisters (members Lee Drinkard (who is Dionne Warwick and Dee Dee Warwick's mother) and her sister Emily Drinkard (aka Cissy Houston -- Whitney Houston's mother) and Judy Clay (who was "adopted" by Lee Drinkard)

The Drinkard Singers (members Lee Drinkard and later Judy Clay, Ann Moss, Marie Epps, Nicholas Drinkard and Larry Drinkard)

Judy Clay (born Judy Guions 12-September-1938 in St. Paul, North Carolina - died 19-July-2001 - cause: automobile accident)

Ember 1080 - More Than You Know / I'd Thought I'd Gotten Over You - 1961
Ember 1085 - Do You Think That's Right / Stormy Weather – 1962

The Drinkard Singers (members Emily Drinkard, Judy Clay, Marie Epps, Ann Moss, Sylvia Shemwell and Nicholas Drinkard)

Choice 24 - Out Of The Depths / You Can't Make Me Doubt Him - 1962
Choice 30 - Do You Love Him / Holding The Saviours Hand - 1962
Choice 36 - Joy Unspeakable / Out Of The Depths - 1962

Little Lee & Judy

Lavette 1002 - Everyday Since You've Been Gone / My Blue Heaven – 1963

Judy Clay

Lavette 1004 - Let It Be Me / I'm Uptight - 1963
Scepter 1273 - My Arm's Aren't Strong Enough / That's All - 1964
Scepter 1281 - Lonely People Do Foolish Things / I'm Comin' Home - 1964
Scepter 12135 - Haven't Got What It Takes / The Way You Look Tonight - 1966
Scepter 12157 - You Busted My Mind / Your Kind Of Loving - 1966
Scepter 12218 - He's The Kind Of Guy / I Want You - 1966
Stax 230 - You Can't Run Away From Your Heart / It Takes A Lotta Good Love - 1967

Billy Vera & Judy Clay

Atlantic 2445 - Storybook Children / Really Together - 1967 (with The Sweet Inspirations)
Atlantic 2480 - So Good (To Be Together) / Country Girl - City Man (Just Across The Line) - 1968 (with The Sweet Inspirations)

Atlantic 2515 - When Do We Go / Ever Since – 1968

Judy Clay & William Bell

Stax 0005 - Private Number / Love-Eye-Tis - 1968

Judy Clay

Stax 0006 - Remove These Clouds / Bed Of Roses - 1968

William Bell & Judy Clay

Stax 0017 - My Baby Specializes / Left Over Love - 1968)

Judy Clay

Stax 0026 - It Ain't Long Enough / Give Love To Save Love - 1969

Billy Vera & Judy Clay

Atlantic 2654 - Tell It Like It Is / Reaching For The Moon – 1969

Judy Clay

Atlantic 2669 - Sister Pitiful / Get Together - 1970
Atlantic 2697 - The Greatest Love* / Saving All For You - 1970 *recorded 15-May-1969 written by Allen Toussaint.
LA - DCP 0912 - Stayin' Alive (Live) / Stayin' Alive (Live) – 1978

William Bell & Judy Clay

Collectables Col 710097 - Private Number / My Baby Specializes - ?

The C.O.D.'s

The C.O.D.'s (members Larry Brownlee (who wrote all their songs), Robert Lewis and Carl Washington. Session Ruby Andrews)

Kellmac 1003 - Michael / Cry No More – 1965
Kellmac 1005 - Pretty Baby / I'm A Good Guy – 1965
Kellmac 1008 - I'm Looking Out For Me / I'll Come Running Back To You – 1966
Kellmac 1010 - Fire (She's Fire) / It Must Be Love – 1966
Kellmac 1012 - Coming Back Girl / It Must Be Love – 1966

The Lost Generation (members Larry Brownlee, (brothers) Fred Simon, Lowrell Simon and Jesse Dean (both Lowrell Simon and Jesse Dean were previously with The Vondells))

Brunswick 55436 - The Sly, Slick, And The Wicked / You're So Young, But You're So True – 1970
Brunswick 55441 - Wait A Minute / Wasting Time – 1970
Brunswick 55445 - Someday / Sorry I Can't Help You – 1971
Brunswick 55453 - Talking The Teen Age Language / You're So Young But You're So True – 1971
Brunswick 55469 - Young, Tough, And The Terrible / All In The Course Of A Day – 1971
Brunswick 55492 - You Only Get Out Of Love / Pretty Little Angel Eyes - 1972

Innovation 800 - Your Mission (If You Decide To Accept It) Pt. 1 / You're Mission (If You Decide To Accept It) Pt. 2 - 1974

Mystique (members Larry Brownlee (born 18-March-1943 in Chicago, Illinois - died 1978 - cause: he was murdered), Charles Fowler, Lowrell Simon, Fred Simon and Ralph "Preacherman" Johnson who had been in The Impressions from 1973 ~ 1976)

Curtom 658 - What Would The World Be Without Music (6:37) / Keep On Playing The Music -- If You're In Need (9:01) - 1977 (12" Promo)
Curtom 0123 - What Would The World Be Without Music (Mono) / What Would The World Be Without Music (Stereo) - 1977 (Promo)
Curtom 0123 - What Would The World Be Without Music */ This Time I'll Be The Fool - 1977
*Written By Bunny Sigler And Don Covay - Produced By Curtis Mayfield.
Curtom 0126 - Is It Really You / All Of My Life – 1977
Curtom 0130 - It Took A Woman Like You (Long Version) / It Took A Woman Like You (Short version) – 1977

The C. O. D.'s (members Larry Brownlee, Robert Lewis and Carl Washington. Session Ruby Andrews)

Eric 0177 - Michael / I'm A Good Guy - ?

Lowrell (Lowrell Simon)

Avi 235 - Overdose Of Love / ? – 1978
Avi Pro-12-236-D - Overdose Of Love / Smooth And Wild - 1978 (12" Release)
Avi 300 - Mellow Mellow Right On / Overdose Of Love – 1979
Avi 314 - You're Playing Dirty / Out Of Breath – 1979
Avi 325 - Mellow Mellow Right On / Smooth And Wild – 1979
Zoo York Ae7 1324 - Love Massage (Mono) / Love Massage (Stereo) - 1981 (Promo Issue Only)
Columbia 02703 - Love Massage (Part 1) / Love Massage (Part 2) - 1982

Arthur Conley

The Evening Smiles (members Arthur Conley, ...) with the exception of Arthur Conley an all-female gospel group.

The Corvetts (member Arthur Conley, ...)

Moon 100 - I'm Going To Cry / You're Blue - 1964 (a "take off" on "My True Story" by The Jive Five on Beltone 1006 from 1961)

Arthur & The Corvets (members Arthur Conley, ...)

Na-R-Co 203 - Poor Girl / Darling I Love You – 1964
Na-R-Co 232 - Miracles / I Believe – 1964
NRC 2781 - Miracles / I Believe - 1964
Na-R-Co 2871 - Aritha / Flossie Mae - 1964

Arthur Conley (born 4-January-1946 in McIntosh, Atlanta. Discovered by Otis Redding in 1965 - Died 17-November-2003 in his house in Ruurlo, Netherlands cause: intestinal cancer)

Ru-Jac 0014 -Where You Lead Me / I'm A Lonely Stranger - 1964

Harold Holt & Band (members Harold Holt, Arthur Conley, ...)

Ru-Jac 0014 -Where You Lead Me / I'm A Lonely Stranger – 1964

Arthur Conley

Jotis 470 - I'm A Lonely Stranger / Where You Lead Me - 1965 (Re-Recorded Version)
Jotis 472 - Who's Fooling Who / There's A Place For Us – 1966
Fame 1007 - I Can't Stop (No, No, No) / In The Same Old Way – 1966
Fame 1009 - Take Me (Just As I Am) / I'm Gonna Forget About You – 1966
Atco 6463 - Sweet Soul Music */ Let's Go Steady - 1967 *tune originally written by Sam Cooke as "Yeah Man".
Atco 6494 - Shake, Rattle And Roll / You Don't Have To See Me* - 1967 *written by Roosevelt Grier and Chris Harris --- recorded 17-May-1967
Atco 6529 - Whole Lot Of Woman / Love Comes And Goes – 1967
Atco 6563 - Funky Street / Put Our Love Together – 1968
Atco 6588 - People Sure Act Funny / Burning Fire – 1968

The Soul Clan (Solomon Burke, Arthur Conley, Don Covay, Ben E. King and Joe Tex)

Atlantic 2530 - Soul Meeting / That's How It Feels – 1968

Arthur Conley

Atco 6622 - Is That You Love / Aunt Dora's Love Soul Shack – 1968
Philco-Ford Hp-15 - Sweet Soul Music / You Don't Have To See Me - 1968 (4" plastic "Hip Pocket Record" with colour sleeve)
Atco 6640 - Ob-La-Di, Ob-La-Da / Otis Sleep On – 1969
Atco 6661 - Speak Her Name / Run On – 1969
Atco 6706 - Star Review / Love Sure Is A Powerful Thing – 1969
Atco 6733 - Hurt / They Call The Wind Maria – 1970
Atco 6747 - God Bless / (Your Love Has Brought Me A) Mighty Long Way – 1970
Atco 6790 - Nobody's Fault But Mine / Day-O – 1970
Capricorn 8017 - I'm Living Good / I'm So Glad You're Here – 1971
Capricorn 0001 - More Sweet Soul Music / Walking On Eggs – 1972
Capricorn 0006 - More Sweet Soul Music / Rita – 1972
Capricorn 0047 - Bless You / It's So Nice (When It's Someone Else's Wife) - 1973

Bill Withers / Arthur Conley

Gigi 573 - Ain't No Sunshine / Sweet Soul Music* - ? *Flip By Arthur Conley.

Lee Roberts & The Sweaters (members Lee Roberts (Arthur Conley legally changed his name - Roberts was his mother's maiden name), ...) 1988 group.

The Contours

The Hi-Fidelities (members Sylvester Potts, Huey Marvin Davis (born 17-August-1938 in Columbus, Missouri --- died 23-February-2002 in Detroit, Michigan --- cause: ?), Tommy Potts and Juanita ?)

Hi-Q 5000 - Street Of Loneliness / Help, Murder, Police - 1957

The Majestics (members Cyril Clark, Johnny Mitchell, Don Storball (later member of The Capitols), Billy Gordon and Joe Billingslea))

The Blenders (members Billy Gordon, Billy Hoggs, Joe Billingslea and Billy Rollins) group formed in 1959.

The Blenders (members Billy Gordon, Billy Hoggs, Joe Billingslea and Leroy Fair) 1959.

The Blenders (members Billy Gordon, Billy Hoggs, Joe Billingslea, Leroy Fair and Hubert Johnson (born 14-January-1941 --- died 11-July-1981 - cause: shot himself)) 1959.

Jack Sucrell and The Contours (with male voices) (members……)

HOB 116 - I'm So Glad / Your's Is My Heart Alone - 1961

The Contours (members Billy Gordon, Billy Hoggs, Joe Billingslea, Leroy Fair and Hubert Johnson (cousin of Jackie Wilson))

Motown 1008 - Whole Lotta Woman / Come On And Be Mine – 1961

The Contours (members Billy Gordon, Billy Hoggs, Joe Billingslea, Bennie Reeves (Martha Reeves brother) and Hubert Johnson)

The Contours (members Billy Gordon, Billy Hoggs, Joe Billingslea, Sylvester Potts and Hubert Johnson)

Motown 1012 - Funny / The Stretch – 1961

The Contours (members Sylvester Potts, Billy Gordon, Billy Hoggs, Joe Billingslea, Hubert Johnson and Huey Davis (guitar))

Berry Gordy Jr. / B. Gordy, B. Gordon

Gordy 7005 - Do You Love Me / Move Mr. Man - 1962 (A Motown oddity - this is actually The Contours but the label credits Berry Gordy Jr. on the "A" side and B. Gordy, B. Gordon on the flip and The Contours as the writers - audition copies only)

The Contours (members Sylvester Potts, Billy Gordon, Billy Hoggs, Joe Billingslea, Hubert Johnson and Huey Davis (guitar))

Gordy 7005 - Do You Love Me / Move Mr. Man - 1962

Marvin Gaye / Supremes / Singin' Sammy Ward / Contours / Marvelettes / The Miracles

Promo - Motor Town Special Mts-1 - Individual Artists - 1962 (promo issue only - from the first Motown revue. It features the various artists on tour, all talking over their latest record to promote the tour. Of interest are The Supremes talking over their minor hit "Let Me Go The Right Way", on which Diana Ross introduces herself as Diane, her earlier name)

The Contours (members Sylvester Potts, Billy Gordon, Billy Hoggs, Joe Billingslea, Hubert Johnson and Huey Davis (guitar))

Gordy 7012 - Shake Sherry / You Better Get In Line - 1962 (the promo version is an alternate take of the commercial "Shake Sherry")
Gordy 7016 - Don't Let Her Be Your Baby / It Must Be Love – 1963
Gordy 7019 - You Get Ugly / Pa (I Need A Car) – 1963
Gordy 7029 - Can You Do It / I'll Stand By You – 1964
Hitsville U.S.A. Dm 097311 - Greetings To The Tamla Motown Appreciation Society - 1964 (this American record was limited to three hundred copies for dispersal throughout various European fan clubs as a promo for their first European tour. Each act gives an individual greeting over it's latest record. Artists involved include The Miracles, Stevie Wonder, Marvin Gaye, The

Marvelettes, The Temptations, Martha and The Vandellas, The Contours, Eddie Holland, Kim Weston and The Supremes. The record has an introduction from publicist Margaret Phelps and Berry Gordy)

The Contours (members Billy Gordon, Council Gay, Jerry Green, Alvin English and Huey Davis (guitar))

The Contours (members Billy Gordon, Sylvester Potts, Council Gay, Jerry Green and Huey Davis (guitar))

Gordy 7037 - Can You Jerk Like Me / The Day When She Needed Me* - 1964 *also recorded in 1968 by The Performers on Mirwood 5536
Gordy 7044 - First I Look At The Purse* / Searching For A Girl - 1965 *covered in 1967 by The Assortment on Sound Spot 2224. The spoken word intro to this track was provided by Bobby Rogers of The Miracles.

The Contours (members Joe Stubbs (former member of The Falcons), Sylvester Potts, Council Gay, Jerry Green and Huey Davis (guitar))

Gordy 7052 - Just A Little Misunderstanding* / Determination – 1966 *session: Stevie Wonder (drums)

Kim Weston / The Contours

Gordy 7052 – A Love Like Yours (Don't Come Knocking Everyday) / Determination – 1966 (although different artists credited the 45 plays The Contours on both sides with tracks "Just A Little Misunderstanding / Determination")

The Contours (members Dennis Edwards, Sylvester Potts, Council Gay, Jerry Green and Huey Davis (guitar))

Gordy 7059 - It's So Hard Being A Loser / Your Love Grows More Precious Every Day – 1967

The Contours (members Sylvester Potts, Billy Gordon, Billy Hoggs, Joe Billingslea, Hubert Johnson and Huey Davis (guitar))

Motown Yesteryear 448 - Do You Love Me / Shake Sherry – 1972
Motown Yesteryear 448 - Do You Love Me / Shake Sherry – 1988

The Contours (members

Solid Gold 554 - I'm A Winner* / Makes Me Wanna Come Back - ? *track was recorded twice by Michael Valvano as "For The First Time In My Life" on Jodi-Pat 2067 in 19?? and on Jodi-Pat ? in 19?? both with different mixes.

Les Cooper

The Empires (members Les Cooper (tenor), John "Buddy" Barnes (lead tenor), William Goodman (bass) and Bobby Dunn (baritone)) The first three members of group were from Norfolk, Virginia, but moved to New York in the late 1940's. It was here where they met Bobby Dunn who had come to New York from Henderson, North Carolina.

Harlem 2325 - My Baby, My Baby / Corn Whiskey - 1954

The Empires, featuring Johnny Ace, Junior (members Les Cooper, John "Buddy" Barnes, William Goodman and Bobby Dunn)

Harlem 2333 - Magic Mirror / Make Me Or Break Me - 1955

Lightnin' Junior & The Empires (members "Champion" Jack Dupree, Les Cooper, John "Buddy" Barnes, William Goodman and Bobby Dunn)

Harlem 2334 - Somebody Changed The Lock / Ragged And Hungry - 1955

The Empires (members Les Cooper, John "Buddy" Barnes, William Goodman and Bobby Dunn)

Wing 90023 - I Want To Know / Shirley - 1955

The Prestos (members Les Cooper, John "Buddy" Barnes, William Goodman and Bobby Dunn)

Mercury 70747 - Looking For Love / 'Til We Meet Again - 1955

The Empires (members Les Cooper, John "Buddy" Barnes, William Goodman and Bobby Dunn)

Wing 90050 - Tell Me Pretty Baby / By The Riverside - 1955
Wing 90080 - My First Discovery / Don't Touch My Gal
Whirlin' Disc 104 - Whispering Heart / Linda - 1956

The Whirlers (members Les Cooper, John "Buddy" Barnes, William Goodman and Bobby Dunn)

Whirlin' Disc 108 - Magic Mirror / Tonight And Forever - 1957
Port 108 - Magic Mirror / Tonight And Forever - 1961.

Les Cooper & The Soul Rockers (members Les Cooper, ...)

Everlast 5016 - Twistin' (One More Time) / Dig Yourself - 1961
Everlast 5019 - Wiggle Wobble* / Dig Yourself - 1962
Everlast 5023 - Garbage Can / Bossa Nova Dance - 1963
Dimension 1023 - Motor City / Swobblin' - 1963

Les & Gloria (Les Cooper and Gloria Ford)

Enjoy 1011 - Twisting One More Time / Peter Piper - 1963

Les Cooper & The Soul Rockers (members Les Cooper, ...)

Enjoy 2024 - Owee Baby / Let's Do The Boston Monkey - 1965
Enjoy 2029 - Stay Loose / Hallelujah - ?
Arrawak 1008 - I Can Do The Soul Jerk / At The World's Fair - 1965
Samar 114 - Skating With Bill / Wahoo - 1966

Les Cooper & The Soul Rockers featuring Guy Turner

Atco 6644 - Gonna Have A Lot Of Fun / Thank God For You - 1969

Les Cooper & The Soul Rockers

Sussex 202 - The Hawk (Part 1) / The Hawk (Part 2) - 1970

Lou Courtney

Lew Courtney

Imperial 66006 - Come On Home / The Man With The Cigar - 1963

Lou Courtney (born Louis Russell Pegues)

Imperial 66043 - Little Old Love Maker / Professional Lover - 1964
Philips 40287 - I Watched You Slowly Slip Away* / I'll Cry If I Want To - 1965 *also recorded in 1966 by Howard Guyton on Verve 10386.
Riverside 4588 - Skate Now / I Can Always Tell - 1966
Riverside 4589 - Do The Thing / Man Is Lonely - 1967
Riverside 4591 - You Ain't Ready / I've Got Just The Thing - 1967
Pop-Side 4594 - Hey Joyce / I'm Mad About You - 1967
Pop-Side 4596 - If The Shoe Fits / It's Love Now - 1968
Verve 10602 - Do The Horse / Rubber Neckin' (Chicken Checkin') - 1968
Verve 10631 - Please Stay / You Can Give Your Love To Me - 1968
Buddah 121 - Tryin' To Find My Woman / Let Me Turn You On - 1969

Lou Courtney / Mr. C. Funck Junction

Hurdy Gurdy 101 - Hot Butter 'N All (Part 1) / Hot Butter 'N All (Part 2) (Instrumental)* - 1971 *flip by Mr. C. Funck Junction.

Lou Courtney

Rags 100 - What Do You Want Me To Do* / Beware - 1973 *recorded 12-June-1973.
Epic 11062 - What Do You Want Me To Do / Beware - 1973
Epic 11088 - I Don't Need Nobody Else / Why - 1974
Epic 50046 - The Best Thing A Man Can Do For His Woman / I'm Serious About Lovin' You - 1974
Epic 50070 - Somebody New Is Lovin' You / Just To Let Him Break Your Heart - 1975

Lou Courtney & Buffalo Smoke

RCA 10644 - 911 / Call The Police - 1976

Lou Courtney / Salt

Milk 001 - Hey Joyce (You're My Choice) / Hung Up* - ? *flip by Salt.

Don Covay

The Cherry Keys (Early 1950's Family Gospel Group)

The Rainbows (Members Ronald Miles, John Berry, James Nolan?....................)

Red Robin 134 - Mary Lee / Evening - 1955 (Don Covay Possible Member Of Group At This Time)
Red Robin 141 - Shirley / Stay - 1955 Is A Bootleg, Originals Do Not Exist!

The Rainbows (Members Ronald Miles, John Berry, Chester Simmons And Don Covay)

Pilgrim 703 - Mary Lee / Evening – 1956
Pilgrim 711 - Shirley / Stay – 1956
Rama 209 - They Say / Minnie – 1956

"Pretty Boy"

Atlantic 1147 - Bip Bop Bip / Silver Dollar - 1957 (Backed By Little Richards Band The Upsetters)

Pretty Boy Lee Simms Orch.
Big 617 - Switchin' In The Kitchen / Rockin' The Mule (Back In Kansas) Swingin' Like A Young Gray Mare - 1958

Don Covay

Blaze 350 - Standing In The Doorway / I'm Lonely Too – 1958
Sue 709 - Betty Jean / Believe It Or Not – 1958

The Rainbows

Fire 1012 - Mary Lee / Evening – 1960

Don Covay

Big Top 3033 - Beauty And The Beast / Cause I Love You – 1960
Big Top 3060 - Hey There / I'm Coming Down With The Blues – 1960

The Goodtimers

Arnold 1002 - Pony Time / Love Boat - 1961 (Different Artist Titles)

Don Covay & The Goodtimers

Arnold 1002 - Pony Time / Love Boat - 1961 (Different Artist Titles)
Fleetwood 2001 - Pony Time Twist / ? - 196?

The Goodtimers

Epic 9484 - It's Twistin' Time / Twistin' Train – 1961

Don Covay

Columbia 41981 - Shake Wid The Snake / Every Which - A Way – 1961

Don Covay & The Goodtimers

Columbia 42058 - Hand Jive Workout / See About Me – 1961

Don Covay

Columbia 42197 - (Where Are You) Now That I Need You / Teen Life Swag -

The Soldier Boys

Scepter 1230 - I'm Your Soldier Boy / You Picked Me - 1962 (Don Covay Member Of Group)

The Rainbows

Argyle 1012 - Shirley / Stay – 1962

Don Covay

Cameo 239 - The Popeye Waddle / One Little Boy Had Money – 1962
Cameo 251 - Do The Bug / Wiggle Wobble – 1962
Parkway 910 - The Froog / One Little Boy Had Money – 1964
Parkway 984 - Ain't That Silly / Turn It On – 1964
Landa 704 - You're Good For Me / Truth Of The Lite – 1964

Don Covay & The Goodtimers

Rosemart 801 - Mercy Mercy / Can't Stay Away - 1964 (Session Jimi Hendrix)

Don Covay

Rosemart 802 - Take This Hurt Off Me / Please Don't Let Me Know - 1964 (Session Jimi Hendrix) Atlantic 2280 - The Boomerang / Daddy Loves Baby – 1965

Don Covay & The Goodtimers

Atlantic 2286 - Please Do Something / A Woman's Love – 1965
Atlantic 2301 - See Saw / I Never Get Enough Of Your Love – 1965 (Two different versions of 'I Never Get Enough Of Your Love' were released, one has the matrix A7077-I, the other A7077-II. Version I has female backing singers, version II doesn't.

Don Covay

Atlantic 2323 - Sookie Sookie / Watching The Late Late Show – 1966
Atlantic 2340 - You Put Something On Me / Iron Out The Rough Spots – 1966
Atlantic 2357 - Somebody's Got To Love You / Temptation Was Too Strong – 1966
Atlantic 2375 - Shing-Aling ' 67 / I Was There – 1967
Atlantic 2407 - 40 Days ---40 Nights / The Usual Place – 1967
Atlantic 2440 - You've Got Me On The Critical List / Never Had No Love – 1967
Atlantic 2481 - Chain Of Fools / Prove It* - 1968 *The Goodtimers.
Atlantic 2494 - Don't Let Go / It's In The Wind – 1968
Atlantic 2521 - Gonna Send You Back To Your Mama / House On The Corner – 1968

The Soul Clan

Atlantic 2530 - Soul Meeting / That's How It Feels - 1968 (Group Comprised Of Solomon Burke, Arthur Conley, Don Covay, Ben E. King And Joe Tex)

Don Covay

Atlantic 2565 - I Stole Some Love / Snake In The Grass – 1968

Don Covay & The Jefferson Lemon Band

Atlantic 2609 - Sweet Pea / C. C. Rider Blues – 1969

Don Covay & The Jefferson Lemon Blues Band

Atlantic 2666 -Black Woman - 1969 (One Sided White Label Promo Issue Only)
Atlantic 2666 - Ice Cream Man (The Gimme Game) / Black Woman – 1969
Atlantic 2725 - Everything I Do Goin' To Be Funky / Key To The Highway – 1970

Don Covay

Atlantic 2742 - Soul Stirrer / Sookie Sookie – 1970
Janus 164 - Sweet Thang / Standing In The Grits Line – 1971
Janus 181 - Daddy Please Don't Go Out / Shoes Under My Bed – 1972
Mercury 73311 - Overtime Man / Dungeon # 3 – 1972
Mercury 73385 - I Was Checkin' Out She Was Checkin' In* / Money (That's What I Want) - 1973
*Backing Vocal By Prince Phillip Mitchell.
Mercury 73430 - Somebody's Been Enjoying My Home / Bad Mouthing – 1973
Mercury 73469 - It's Better To Have (And Don't Need) / Leave Him (Part 1) – 1974
Mercury 73648 - Rumble In The Jungle / We Can't Make It No More – 1975
Philadelphia International 3594 - Right Time For Love / No Tell Motel – 1976
Philadelphia International 3602 - Travelin' In Heavy Traffic / Once You Have It – 1976
U - Von 102 - Back To The Roots (Part 1) / Back To The Roots (Part 2) – 1977
Newman 500 - Badd Boy / (Instrumental) – 1980
Newman N5001 - Badd Boy (Vocal) (7:44) / Badd Boy (Instrumental) (7:18) - 1980 (12" Release)

Can 7" 45rpm American Soul Singles Be Considered To Be Of Significant Historical Value ?

A Reasoned Argument.

All recorded music is pop music. Whatever the style, era, technology used to record it, it is all pop music. Simply because the aim of the person making the recording is to make it popular with others, thus the inherent design of recorded music is to be 'pop' music, and one would assume that Pop music is regarded as a disposable art form. However, several other factors are also significant in deciding whether a record can be considered of value, both monetary, and historical value.

I intend, using examples that are available in both printed and electronic media, to prove that certain records, of a certain style can be considered to be of considerable historical value, based upon their place within the socio-economic development of a culture in the United States of America during the 1960s, and their place as the basis for a whole underground culture within the United Kingdom during the 1970s, which has now spread world wide.

I have already mentioned that pop music is regarded as a disposable art form. Certainly in the late 1950s and early 1960s when the term pop music was first used, and significantly when the 7" vinyl record was introduced (as opposed to the 10" 78rpm record) the whole aim of most recording artists was to get a hit single.

Consequently, as the teenage market expanded, many thousands of groups and solo artists recorded their debut single. For most, it would be a one off attempt at stardom, the record would not sell, so they would be consigned to history without making any impact upon the charts.

Things were slightly different for the Black communities in America though.

When slavery was abolished in the United States of America it meant different things in theory and practice. The vast majority of Black Afro Americans were employed as slaves working in the South of the country on cotton plantations. Following the abolition of slavery the vast majority of Black Afro Americans were employed as employees working in the South of the country on cotton plantations. They were still poor, still had the worst living conditions, and were still discriminated against in the worst possible ways. The simple reason that they remained working on cotton plantations was that no other work was available to them as Blacks. Slavery might have been abolished, but that didn't change the political attitudes of the land owners and employers.

The first real changes came about almost Sixty years later when the industrial cities of the North needed a large influx of cheap labour to work in the factories that had greatly increased production, partly because of the war, and then throughout the 1950s as a result of consumer demand. This cheap labour came from a significant migration of Black Afro Americans from the South to the North of the States. Things didn't change that much, the Blacks still had the worst jobs, the worst pay and the worst living conditions, however, they were better off than they had been working on the plantations in the South.

By the late 1950s, things had improved considerably in the industrialised North, segregation still existed, but Blacks were able to earn a reasonable living wage. However, they still had the worst living conditions and the worst jobs. Traditionally it was regarded that the only way out of the 'ghetto' was through sports, boxing in particular never showed any racial bias against Black boxers, evidenced by the fact that there was a Black world heavyweight champion as far back as the 1940s. The 1950s though presented another route out of the ghetto; music.

The story of young Black teenagers hanging about on street corners and singing to amuse themselves is well documented elsewhere, suffice to say that Rhythm and Blues, and Doo Wop were the Black equivalent of Rock and Roll, in fact many of the Rock and Roll hit records were simply white cover versions of Black originals, re-recorded with the same tune, even the same inflection on the vocals, but by a white artist. This reflected the segregation that existed within society as a whole at this time, there was the Billboard Hot 100 chart, and the Race chart. Black American youth had found a way to express itself, admittedly within its own culture, but status and money could be earned from being a recording artist.

The 1960s heralded the first real advances for Black Americans. As a culture, Black Americans had become politically aware, the end of segregation was in sight, white politicians had realised that Black voters could significantly affect elections. Race riots tore apart some cities, Dr Martin Luther King was assassinated, the Civil Rights movement became headline news and featured on television news almost every day. Integration into mainstream society was, certainly by the early 1970s, the way that America had to proceed.

It is against this backdrop that the specific genre of Soul music developed. Soul music was the refinement of the vocal groups of the Doo Wop and Rhythm and Blues era in the '50s caused by the combination of those styles with the strong Gospel roots that most Black Americans still retained.

In order to illustrate the effect and influence of Soul music I have chosen to use the Motown Records Group based in Detroit, whilst Motown became the largest independently Black owned corporation in America I could just as easily have used Chess Records in Chicago, Atlantic Records in New York, King Records in Cincinnati, Modern Records in Los Angeles, Stax Records in Memphis, and these are just the main record companies within those cities.

Motown records was started in 1959 by Berry Gordy Jr with a loan of $800 from his family Credit Union. At it's inception Motown was no different than any other of the many hundreds of record companies within Detroit, However Berry Gordy was a remarkable business man with true vision. He surrounded himself with talented young Black performers, and experienced white business men. This combined with the songwriting talents of William 'Smokey' Robinson, and Brian and Eddie Holland with Gene Dozier almost ensured that the company would get hits. Probably even more significantly, Berry Gordy wanted his records to be hits in the white market place. This was a crucial marketing tactic. A record by a Black American could be a local hit in Detroit and sell in excess of 50,000 copies to the Black market alone, and assuming the Record company was honest, could give the artist a very healthy income (Although it was recognised that the real income from a hit record came not from the record itself, but from the monies generated by touring on the back of a hit record). However, if the same record became a national hit in the white market it could easily sell in excess of 3,000,000 copies. Consequently, the tours used bigger venues, and ran for longer thus generated far more money for the artist.

It must be remembered though, that whilst I have named several record companies in several cities, these are only the tip of the iceberg in terms of records released. For each record released by Motown, in Detroit alone there would have been five or six other releases by independent Record Companies. As with all businesses, some were successful, others disappeared without trace at the time of release. Some like Ric-Tic Records became a challenger for Motown's crown in Detroit. Berry Gordy solved this aspect of competition by buying Ric-Tic Records in 1968 for what was a huge sum in those days, a reputed million Dollars.

A whole generation of American teenagers, both Black and white grew up listening to "The Sound Of Young America" (One of Motown Records' advertising slogans). Those teenagers are now in middle age, and a large number are in considerable positions of power and influence within the large American corporations that dominate the global economy these days. It is not without significance that the music they first heard thirty five years ago is commonly used as the background music to many commercial advertising campaigns.

That wasn't the only affect upon American society. The Vietnam war saw the draft calling up what has now been proven as a disproportionate number of young Black Americans to fight in Vietnam. There wasn't a particularly strong movement amongst Black Americans to oppose the war. They felt that they had only just been accepted as Americans, so they were proud to go and fight for their country. That's why the music that accompanied the troops to Vietnam was Black music overall. Listen to the soundtrack to the Robin Williams film 'Good morning Vietnam'. Pure soul music throughout. That's also the reason why the protest songs about the war tended to come from the disenchanted white Rock and Roll music scene.

Black music though did have its own protest songs in the 1960s and 1970s. Artists such as James Brown, Marvin Gaye, Curtis Mayfield, and The Temptations all had hits which were social commentaries on the political state of America. It was recognised that great advances had been made throughout the Sixties in terms of equality in most areas, and by the mid 1970s, Black Americans wanted equality in all areas of their lives, and felt that it had been achieved.

By the mid 1970s Black Americans had moved from living entirely in the ghettos, having the worst education, and working in the worst jobs, to being able to access higher education all over the country, thus leading to better paid jobs, and better social conditions. The role models for the generation which achieved the level of integration that existed by this time were the sportsmen and women, singers, and record company owners who had become nationally known during the Sixties and early Seventies.

The style of Black music also changed during the mid Seventies, Disco records became the in-demand sound. Many artists who had previously been recognised as Soul singers made the transition to Disco records successfully. Many did not, thus the whole genre of Soul music became pressured by reducing demand and many previously successful recording artists careers ended in the mid 1970s.

It is only recently in the United States that the social and historical significance of these recordings has been recognised. As the prominence of Black Americans in business and politics has increased these people have realised that they were inspired and guided by the music of their youth, and only now, with hindsight is the value of these recordings being realised.

Several museums have been established across America to commemorate and celebrate these pioneers of the music world. Certainly Detroit has 'The Hitsville Museum' based at the original Motown building on West Grand Boulevard. Chicago similarly has the Chess recording studio Museum in their original building. Cincinnati has the King Records Museum, and Memphis, having used Graceland as it's major tourist attraction for many years is now investing nearly a million Dollars in a museum for Stax records. In addition, several books have been published over the last ten years. Some are artist biographies, some chart the history of Record Companies, and some chart the socio-economic effect of Soul music upon America.

To summarise the argument for recognising 7" 45rpm Soul records as having significant historical value in America I would direct you to the dictionary definitions contained within the Merriam-Webster Dictionary.

Main Entry: **sig·nif·i·cant**
Pronunciation: -k&nt
Function: *adjective*
Etymology: Latin *significant-, significans,* present participle of *significare* to signify
Date: 1579
1 : having meaning;
2 a : having or likely to have influence or effect **: IMPORTANT** <a *significant* piece of legislation>; *also* **:** of a noticeably or measurably large amount

Main Entry: **his·tor·i·cal**
Pronunciation: -i-k&l
Function: *adjective*
Date: 15th century
1 a : of, relating to, or having the character of history **b :** based on history **c :** used in the past and reproduced in historical presentations
2 : famous in history

Main Entry: [1]**val·ue**
Pronunciation: 'val-(")yü
Function: *noun*
Etymology: Middle English, from Middle French, from (assumed) Vulgar Latin *valuta,* from feminine of *valutus,* past participle of Latin *valEre* to be worth, be strong
Date: 14th century
1 : a fair return or equivalent in goods, services, or money for something exchanged
2 : the monetary worth of something **:** marketable price
3 : relative worth, utility, or importance

Consequently, given that the records produced in the 1960's and 1970s can be judged to have or likely to have influence or effect, based on history, they must also have relative worth, utility, or importance.

In other words: **Significant Historical Value.**

So how does this apply in the UK ?

The world record price for a 7" American 45rpm record is currently £15,000. This huge amount was paid in 1998 by Scotsman Kenny Burrell. One would not be criticised for assuming that Mr Burrell was either mad or a fool for paying this much for one single. He is neither. He is an extremely successful business man in Scotland, and he is also a Northern Soul fan.

Northern Soul music is the longest running underground cult music scene that has ever existed. The scene, it's values, it's music, it's culture, and it's adherents form a paradox that appears impenetrable to the outsider, but the basis of a lifestyle for those on the inside.

To explain this further, one would have to go back to 1964, when the Mods were doing battle with the Rockers on Brighton seafront every Bank Holiday weekend. The Mod movement was born in London from very much the same socio-economic roots as the revolution that hit American teenagers in the same period. For the first time, young people began to gain an identity which could be regarded as different from what had gone before. Throughout the 1940s and 1950s teenagers were just regarded as young adults (Or if they dared to be different were regarded as "the wrong crowd"). By the 1960s teenagers had gained an important foothold in the economic market, they had money to spend, and wanted to spend it on themselves.

Fashions came and went, both clothes, music, methods of transport. All became vitally important in the lives of teenagers, and they had the money to support their trend setting habits. The Mods, either by luck or design, decided that their choice of music was going to be American Soul music. It was 'cool and right up to the minute', both pre-requisites for any Mod. However, like most trends within four years the Mod movement in London and the South had been replaced by the latest fashion, which didn't include Soul music.

Things took a different route in the North and Midlands though. Whilst the dedication to fashion was just as strong in the North, the music played a much stronger role. Clubs like The Twisted Wheel in Manchester developed a whole scene based around Mods, and more specifically their love of Soul music. So much so that the only magazine dedicated to Soul music in the UK, but based in London, sent their star reporter, Dave Godin, to see what all the fuss was about in Manchester. The resultant article was printed in 1970, and titled "The Soul Of The North". Unbeknown to Dave Godin, his article was to establish an identity for an underground cult which still exists today, 31 years later.

Eventually the Twisted Wheel club was closed by the Police in 1971 amidst allegations of drug abuse at the allnighters that they ran on a Saturday night. The Twisted Wheel was not the only club playing all night Soul music though, clubs abounded all over the North and Midlands. Sheffield boasted the King Mojo (Owned at the time by Peter Stringfellow). Crewe had the Blue Orchid, Doncaster, The Bin Lid, Wolverhampton, The Catacombs, so the scene carried on.

At this time, all the records which were played were British releases of American records, there were significant problems with importing records up until 1972 (Mostly the fact that prior to 1972 it was actually illegal to import records !) so the dancers and DJs had to rely on British record companies releasing records made by American artists.

In the late 1960s, The Golden Torch Ballroom, in Tunstall, Stoke On Trent, was bought by a local entrepreneur called Chris Burton. It was an old cinema which had already been converted into a nightclub and was used to provide a venue for many of the 'Beat Groups' who played around the Country. Both the Beatles and The Rolling Stones are reputed to have played at the venue prior to becoming big name stars in the late Sixties. However, by 1971, and spurred on by the closure of the Twisted Wheel, Chris Burton decided to try running Northern Soul allnighters every Saturday night.

This coincided with the relaxation of the law on imported American records. Up until this time, the UK record companies had only been releasing, in the vast majority, Soul records that had been hits in America. This meant that whilst the major companies in America had an outlet in the UK, all the smaller independent releases had never been heard in this country. The relaxation of the law meant that imports flooded into the country, highly desirable, as status symbols, and as reputation builders. The best DJs had the best records, therefore got to DJ at the best clubs.

The Torch was eventually closed in 1973, again following allegations of drug abuse, but on the actual basis of overcrowding at the club and nuisance to neighbours from club goers leaving the venue on a Sunday morning. By this time though the music had established itself as a lifestyle, with its own culture, trends, to a certain degree even its own language. Collecting records had also become a very important part of this scene.

In late 1973, 23rd September to be exact, a night club in Wigan, Lancashire, called the Casino opened it's doors for its first allnighter. Over the next eight years, the Casino would become a legend in Northern Soul terms. Eventually over 25,000 people became members of the club, it was voted No 1 Night-club in the world (With the world famous Studio 54 in New York in second place.), and regularly packed in excess of 2,500 members in at every Saturday night allnighter.

The record collector culture came to the fore at Wigan, with DJs and collectors travelling to the States on a regular basis to search through the warehouses containing the abandoned Sixties Soul singles that nobody in America wanted at that time. Values of records became astronomical, the rarity of the record affected the value, but more often the popularity of the record on the dance floor determined the value. It has to be remembered that in the 1960s, a record pressing plant in America would accept a minimum order of 300 singles. Consequently, if that single failed to sell, the record company would not have any other records pressed up, meaning that only 300 would ever exist. Ten years later, in Lancashire, if that record became a really big in-demand sound, it would soar in value. Over the eight years of its allnighters the Casino DJs must have found and played in excess of 100,000 different American Soul records, sometimes, multiple copies of records would be found so the price dropped drastically, on occasions, only one or two copies of a record would be found, making them almost priceless.

That brings us back to Mr Burrell and his £15,000 single. The record itself, "Do I Love You (Indeed I Do)" by Frank Wilson became one of the biggest anthems of Wigan Casino. The story is well documented, by The Scottish Daily Mirror amongst others, suffice to say that only two copies have ever been found of the record. The second one being the copy that Mr Burrell bought in 1998. Consequently it has not only maintained its value, but has become even more of a collectors most wanted single.

Wigan Casino closed in 1981, as a result of a planned town centre development this time. Many of the scene's followers left at this time. They imagined that their youthful pastimes were over and it was time to get a career, married and have children. The Northern Soul scene still continued, but on a much smaller scale. Clubs in Stafford, Warrington, Bradford, and of all places London, took up the mantle of being 'the standard bearer for the ultimate underground music scene'.

One would have thought that eventually the reduction in numbers attending events would have killed the Northern Soul scene off. Of course, the opposite happened. As most of the people who left after Wigan Casino closed reached their late Thirties they had, generally, established themselves in their chosen careers, got married, and had children who were now growing up. They also had a greater disposable income than at any time previous in their lives. The rejuvenation of the Northern Soul scene was gradual but persistent. To the extent that there are probably now as many people attending Northern Soul nights all over the country as there ever were back in the 1970s.

Northern Soul is still an underground movement, but these days there has been a subtle change in the definition of underground. As with America, the teenagers who discovered Soul music have now reached middle age, they have quite important, powerful, well paid jobs, and are in a position to influence the media quite extensively. Remember, if all 25,000 members of Wigan Casino want to buy a CD, it will outsell everything else in the charts and become a number one album.

Furthermore, the same age group of people have now held ex patriot Northern Soul nights in the following countries: Australia, The Philippines, Japan, Hong Kong, Italy, Austria, Germany, Spain, France, Canada, and surprisingly, The United States of America. At each of these venues the records have been fond memories for the English and Scottish attendees, but brand new records for the indigenous people who attended, and were on the whole of a younger generation. So the music, and culture, will continue on for at least one more generation.

So, as with all professions, there are Northern Soul fans in the media. Several books have been written on the scene, some describing specific clubs, some the scene itself. Several television documentaries have been shown, and Radio Two has now broadcast two series of six shows specifically about Northern Soul.

There are specialist record companies dedicated to producing CDs for the Northern Soul scene. Two in particular, Kent Records, and Goldmine / Soul Supply have now released well over 100 CDs each. One would have thought that the availability of so many records on CD would have killed the market place for original vinyl 45s. Again, the paradox that is the Northern Soul scene, dumbfounds outsiders to the scene. The demand for original vinyl 45s has soared, to a level that is probably higher than at any stage over the last 40 years.

The buyers of these records are in the main middle aged men and women who wish to re-establish the record collections they had in their youth. These records were the soundtrack to their teenage years, and in many cases, were records that they owned when they were teenagers. With fairly large disposable incomes, and the dedication of the slightly obsessed collector, the record buyers have bestowed upon these records a different set of values to those in America.

They may be different values, and may well be approached from a different perspective, but it does not lessen that fact that in the UK the records have a significant historical value for a whole generation of teenagers throughout the late Sixties to early Eighties.

So, to summarise the argument for recognising 7" 45rpm Soul records as having significant historical value in the UK I would again direct you to the dictionary definitions contained within the Merriam-Webster Dictionary.

Main Entry: **sig·nif·i·cant**
Pronunciation: -k&nt
Function: *adjective*
Etymology: Latin *significant-, significans,* present participle of *significare* to signify
Date: 1579
1 : having meaning;
2 a : having or likely to have influence or effect **: IMPORTANT** <a *significant* piece of legislation>; *also* **:** of a noticeably or measurably large amount

Main Entry: **his·tor·i·cal**
Pronunciation: -i-k&l
Function: *adjective*
Date: 15th century
1 a : of, relating to, or having the character of history **b :** based on history **c :** used in the past and reproduced in historical presentations
2 : famous in history

Main Entry: [1]**val·ue**
Pronunciation: 'val-(")yü
Function: *noun*
Etymology: Middle English, from Middle French, from (assumed) Vulgar Latin *valuta,* from feminine of *valutus,* past participle of Latin *valEre* to be worth, be strong
Date: 14th century
1 : a fair return or equivalent in goods, services, or money for something exchanged
2 : the monetary worth of something **:** marketable price
3 : relative worth, utility, or importance

Consequently, given that the records produced in the 1960's and 1970s and listened to by a British audience in the 1970's up until today can be judged to have or likely to have influence or effect, based on history, they must also have relative worth, utility, or importance.

In other words: **Significant Historical Value.**

As a final point, I would return to Mr Burrell. Can you imagine anyone, especially a Scotsman, investing £15,000 of their hard earned money in buying one record if they didn't think it was of significant historical value ?

Venue Reports February 2001

Redditch Town Hall, 24th February, 2001.

The first night at this venue, and the lads who were running it were a little nervous about how it would turn out. They needn't have worried though, a full room, a full dancefloor, and lots of happy punters who didn't want to go home at the end, ensured that they now have a successful venue. The room itself is superb, a rather strange octagonal type of shape, but with bits sticking off it, in a very modern and nice town hall. The music policy tended a little towards Oldies for my liking, but if it works, it works. So, considering that Winsford allnighter was on the same night it turned out to be a really good night. Well done to the team of locals who did the organising (And the Town Hall were so impressed that they offered the lads the room for New Year's Eve as well).

The In Crowd CD Launch Party, The Pop Bar, London, Tuesday 27th February, 2001.

I'd never been to a CD launch party, so when the invitation arrived I thought this might be good fun. I'm sorry to say it was an absolute disaster. The record company had obviously decided to invest heavily in the event....they put two posters up ! and there weren't even any CDs in evidence anywhere either. The drinks prices were horrendous....£3.20 for a bottle of lager, £6.00 for a short. As you can imagine, I was less than happy about that. In fairness to Mike Ritson and Stuart Russell, the authors of the book and the guys behind the CD, they were terribly embarrassed by the pathetic efforts of the record company. There were several people off the scene there as well as several people connected with the Bee Cool company. Virtually everyone I spoke to complained about the price of drinks, but that was that. It only cost me about £60 and a days holiday !

Group Line Ups

The Delcos (Glen Msdison, Peter Woodard, Richard Green, Otis Smith, Ralph Woods)
The Del - Larks (Sammy Campbell, Mert Matthews, Ronald Taylor, Jmaes Anderson, Raymond Davis)
The Dells (Marvin Junior, Chuck Barksdale, Michael 'Mickey' McGill, Johnny Carter, Verne Allison)
The Detroit Emeralds (James Mitchell Jr, Abrim 'AC' Tilman, Ivory 'Ivy' Tilman)
The Dramatics (Ron Banks, William Howard, Larry Demps, Willie Ford, and Elbert Wilkins.)
The Dynamics (Fred Baker, Zerben R Hicks, Samuel D Stephenson, George H White, Styling Shazer)
The Delfonics (William "Poogie" Hart, Wilbert "Will Hart", Randy "The Doctor" Caine, and later Major Harris)

The Danleers

The Dandleers (members Jimmy Weston, Johnny Lee, Willie Ephraim, Nat McCune and Roosevelt Mays)

Amp 3 2115 - One Summer Night / Wheelin' And Dealin' - 1958 (first pressings have misspelled group name)

The Danleers (members Jimmy Weston, Johnny Lee, Willie Ephraim, Nat McCune and Roosevelt Mays)

Amp 3 2115 - One Summer Night / Wheelin' And Dealin' - 1958
Mercury 71322 - One Summer Night / Wheelin' And A-Dealin' - 1958

Patti Page / The Diamonds /// The Danleers / The Platters

Mercury Mep-55 - Fibbin' / Walking Along /// I Really Love You / It's Raining Outside - 1958 (promo issue 45 Shorties : abridged selections for disc jockey programming only)

The Danleers (members Jimmy Weston, Johnny Lee, Willie Ephraim, Nat McCune and Roosevelt Mays)

Mercury 71356 - I Really Love You / My Flaming Heart - 1958
Mercury 71401 - A Picture Of You / Prelude To Love - 1958

The Webtones (members Louis Williams, Terry Wilson, Frank Clemens ....)

MGM 12724 - My Lost Love / Walk, Talk And Kiss - 1958

The Danleers

Mercury 71441 - I Can't Sleep / Your Love - 1959 (after this release the group found themselves dropped by Mercury, they then broke up. Jimmy Weston resurrected the group)

The Danleers (members Jimmy Weston, Doug Ebrom, Louis Williams, Terry Wilson and Frankie Clemens)

Epic 9367 - If You Don't Care / Half A Block From An Angel - 1960
Epic 9421 - I'll Always Believe In You / Little Lover - 1960
Everest 19412 - Foolish / I'm Looking Around - 1961
Lemans 004 - Baby You've Got It / The Truth Hurts - 1963
Lemans 008 - I'm Sorry / This Thing Called Love - 1963
Smash 1872 - If / Were You There - 1964
Smash 1895 - Where Is Love / The Angels Sent You - 1964

The Dandleers (members Jimmy Weston, Johnny Lee, Willie Ephraim, Nat McCune and Roosevelt Mays)

Amp 3 1005 - One Summer Night / Wheelin' And Dealin' - 196? (Re-Issue)

The Danleers / Don & Juan

Oldies 45 91 - One Summer Night / What's Your Name* - 196? *Flip By Don & Juan.

Tyrone Davis

Tyrone (The Wonder Boy)

4 Brothers 447 - Suffer / Try Me – 1965

Tyrone 'Wonder Boy'

4 Brothers 450 - If You Don't Need Me / Good Company* - 1966 *written by Harold Burrage.

Tyrone (The Wonder Boy)

Four Brothers 453 - Please Consider Me* / You Made Me Suffer - 1967 *same backing track used on the 1968 release "What More Can I Do" by Johnny Moore on Larry-O 404.

Tyrone Davis (The Wonder Boy)

Sack 4359 - I Tried It Over (And Over Again) / I'm Running A Losing Race – 1967

Tyrone Davis (born 4-May-1938 in Greenville, Mississippi --- died 9-February-2005 in Chicago, Illinois four months after suffering from a stroke that left him in a coma)

ABC 11030 - What A Man / Bet You I Win - 1967
Dakar 1452 - Can I Change My Mind / A Woman Needs To Be Loved – 1968
Dakar 602 - Can I Change My Mind / A Woman Needs To Be Loved – 1968
Dakar 605 - Is It Something You've Got / Undying Love – 1969
Dakar 609 - All The Waiting Is Not In Vain / Need Your Loving, Everybody – 1969
Dakar 611 - If It's Love That You're After / While I'm Not Around – 1969
Dakar 615 - You Can't Keep A Good Man Down / If I Didn't Love You – 1969
Dakar 616 - Turn Back The Hands Of Time / I Keep Coming Back 1970
Hit Sound 888 - I'm Confessin' / Good Company – 1970
Hit Sound 968 - I'm Confessin' / ? - ?
Dakar 618 - I'll Be Right Here / Just Because Of You – 1970
Dakar 621 - Let Me Back In / Love Bones – 1970
Dakar 623 - Could I Forget You / Just My Way Of Loving You – 1971
Dakar 624 - One Way Ticket / We Got A Love – 1971
Dakar 626 - You Keep Me Holding On / We Got A Love No One Can Deny – 1971
Brunswick 4501 - I Had It All The Time / You Wouldn't Believe - ?
Dakar 4501 - I Had It All The Time / You Wouldn't Believe – 1972
Dakar 4507 - Was I Just A Fool / After All This Time – 1972
Dakar 4510 - Come And Get This Ring / After All This Time – 1972
Dakar 4513 - If You Had A Change Of Mind / Was It Just A Feeling – 1972

Eddie Holman / Tyrone Davis

Roulette 139 - Hey There Lonely Girl / Can I Change My Mind* - 1973 *Flip By Tyrone Davis.

Tyrone Davis

Dakar 4519 - Without You In My Life / How Could I Forget You – 1973
Dakar 4523 - There It Is / You Wouldn't Believe – 1973
Dakar 4526 - Wrapped Up In Your Warm And Tender Love / True Love Is Hard To Find – 1973
Dakar 4529 - I Wish It Was Me / You Don't Have To Beg Me To Stay – 1974
Dakar 4532 - What Goes Up (Must Come Down) / There's Got To Be An Answer – 1974
Dakar 4536 - Happiness Is Being With You / Where Lovers Meet – 1974
Dakar 4538 - I Can't Make It Without You / You Wouldn't Believe – 1974

Dakar 4541 - Homewreckers / This Time – 1975
Dakar 4545 - A Woman Needs To Be Loved / Just Because Of You – 1975
Dakar 4550 - Turning Point / Don't Let It Be Too Late – 1975
Dakar 4553 - It's So Good (To Be Home With You) / I Can't Bump – 1976
Dakar 4558 - Saving My Love For You / I Cant Bump (Part 2) – 1976
Columbia 10388 - Give It Up (Turn It Loose) / You're Too Much – 1976
Dakar 4561 - Ever Lovin' Girl / Forever – 1976
Columbia 10457 - Close To You / Wrong Doers – 1976
Dakar 4563 - Where Lovers Meet (At The Dark End Of The Street) / It's All In The Game – 1977
Perpetuate 162 - Can I Change My Mind / Turn Back The Hands Of Time - ?
Columbia 10528 - This I Swear / Givin' Myself To You – 1977
Columbia 10540 - All You Got / This I Swear – 1977
Columbia 10604 - All You Got / I Got Carried Away – 1977
Columbia 10684 - Get On Up (Disco) / It's You, It's You – 1978
Columbia 10773 - Can't Help But Say / Bunky – 1978
Columbia 10904 - In The Mood / I Can't Wait – 1979
Columbia 11035 - Ain't Nothing I Can Do / All The Love I Need – 1979
Columbia 11128 - Be With Me / Love You Forever – 1979
Columbia 11199 - Can't You Tell It's Me / I Don't Think You Heard Me – 1980
Columbia 11246 - Heart Failure / Keep On Dancin' – 1980
Columbia 11344 - How Sweet It Is (To Be Loved By You) / I Can't Wait – 1980
Columbia 11415 - I Just Can't Keep On Goin' / We Don't Need No Music – 1980
Columbia 02269 - Just My Luck / Let's Be Close Together – 1981
Columbia 02634 - Leave Well Enough Alone / I Won't Let Go – 1981
Hi C-Lo 2005 - Are You Serious / Overdue - ?
Hi C-Lo 2009 - Little Bit Of Loving (Goes A Long Way) / Where Did We Lose - ?
Highrise 2005 - Are You Serious / Overdue – 1982
Highrise 2009 - A Little Bit Of Loving (Goes A Long Way) / Where Did We Lose – 1983
Epic ? – 1983
Ocean Front 2001 - I Found Myself When I Lost You / (Instrumental) – 1983
Ocean Front 2004 - Let Me Be Your Pacifier* / Turning Point - 1984 *also recorded in 1976 by Willard Burton & The Pacifiers on Money 702
Prelude 8090 - Sexy Thing / Save Me – 1984
Future 101 - Sexy Thing / Save Me - 1987
Future 102 - I'm In Love Again / Serious Love - 1987
Future 103 - Do You Feel It / (Instrumental) – 1988
Future 104 - It's A Miracle / Wrong Doers – 1988
Future 204 - Flashin' Back / Flashin' Back (Lp Version) – 1988

Tyrone Davis / Eddie Holman

Ichiban 139 - Can I Change My Mind / Hey There Lonely Girl* - 1989 *Flip By Eddie Holman Only.

Debbie Dean

Penny Smith

Kahill 1006 - I've Got News For You* / Mad Mad Mad** - 1955 ~ 1956 *Written By Bill Haley & Frank Pingatore, arranged and conducted by Carmen Dello.** Written by Anson - Waller, arranged and conducted by Carmen Dello
Kahill 1018 - These Things We'll Share / Love Me* - 1955 ~ 1956 *Written By Leiber And Stoller.

Penny & The Ekos

Argo 5295 - Gimme What You Got / Share Your Love – 1958 (Both written by Berry Gordy Jr and R Davis)

Debbie Stevens (With The Deltones)

Roulette 4081 - Jerry / Rockin' Cha Cha – 1958
ABC-Paramount 10034 - I Sit And Cry / Billy Boy's Tune – 1959 (Writer and guitarist Fred Carter)
Apt 25027 - If You Can't Rock Me / What Will I Tell My Heart – 1959 (Troy Shondell played piano on 'If You Can't Rock Me)

Debbie Dean (Born Reba Jeanette Smith In Corbin, Kentucky On 1-February-1928, Died 17-February-2001in Ojai, California -

Motown 1007 - (Don't Let Him) Shop Around* / A New Girl** - 1961 (* Written by L Wakefield, B Gordy, W Robinson, produced by Berry Gordy Jr. ** Written by B Gordy & W Robinson, Produced by Berry Gordy) (Accompanied by The Miracles on (Don't Let Him) Shop Around.)ment
Motown 1014 - Itsy, Bitty, Pity Love* / But I'm Afraid** – 1961* Marvin Gaye on Drums **Berry Gordy on Cowbells
Motown 1025 - Everybody's Talking About My Baby* / I Cried All Night - 1962 (Some Copies Issued With Picture Sleeve* Written by B Gordy Jr)

Debbie Deane

Treva 223 - Take My Hand / Dream In A Dream - 1966

Debbie Dean

V.I.P. 25044 - Why Am I Lovin' You* / Stay My Love – 1967 (*Written by D Dean & Dennis Lussier (AKA Deke Richards)
Jobete Music Company Inc. - You Ask Me - ? (Unissued Acetate)

The Delcos

The Delcos (members Peter Woodard (first and second tenor), Pike Miller (first tenor), Richard Greene (second tenor, baritone), and Otis Smith (bass), and James Thomas (Tenor)

Tonight / Sunday Kind Of Love / Summertime /Si, Si, Pedro /September Song /Rainbow / Peace Of Mind / Lucky Old Sun / Kathleen / Just A Memory / Give Me A Chance / Crazy Baby /Come On Back / Broken Heart (All these tracks were unreleased on vinyl at the time of recording)

The Delcos (Members Glenn Madison, Ralph Woods, Otis Smith, Richard Greene And Pete Woodard)

My Guardian Angel (Unreleased on vinyl at the time of recording)
Diddy Bop (Unreleased on vinyl at the time of recording)
Cleopatra (Unreleased on vinyl at the time of recording)
Ebony 01 - Arabia / These Three Little Words - 1962 (Backed by the Buddy Kay Band)
Showcase 2501 - Arabia / Those Three Little Words - 1963 (Backed by the Boots Randolph Band) (released as white Demos, and blue, green, and red label issues)

Glenn Madison (The label credits Glenn Madison as a solo singer, but the whole group were on the recording)

Ebony 05 - When You Dance / Why Do You Have To Go - 1963

The Delcos

Showcase 2515 - Still Miss You So / Just Ask - 1964
Sound Stage 7 2501 - Arabia / Those Three Little Words - 1965 (Debatable whether this was ever released, although it does appear in the Sound Stage 7 listings)
Sound Stage 7 2515 - Still Miss You So / Just Ask - 1965 (Group disbanded in 1966)

The Dells

The Cats and The Fiddle (members Chuck Barksdale, Ernie Price, Austin Powell and Herbie Miles)

The El-Rays with Willie Dixon and Orchestra (members Johnny Funches, Marvin Junior, Verne Allison, Mickey McGill, Lucius McGill and Chuck Barksdale)

Checker 794 - Darling I Know / Christine - 1954

The Dells (Members Johnny Funches, Marvin Junior, Verne Allison, Mickey Mcgill And Chuck Barksdale)

The Dells / Count Morris

Vee-Jay 134 - Tell The World / Blues At Three*- 1955 (Red Vinyl Much Scarcer Than Black)
*Flip By Count Morris.

The Dells with Al Smith's Orchestra (members Johnny Funches, Marvin Junior, Verne Allison, Mickey McGill and Chuck Barksdale. Al Smith's Orch. members Al Smith, James "Red" Holloway, Norman Simmons, Paul "Guitar Red" Simmons, ...)

Vee-Jay 166 - Dreams Of Contentment / Zing, Zing, Zing - 1955

The Dells (Members Johnny Funches, Marvin Junior, Verne Allison And Mickey Mcgill)

Vee-Jay 204 - Oh What A Nite / Jo-Jo - 1956

The Dells (Members Johnny Funches, Marvin Junior, Verne Allison, Mickey Mcgill And Chuck Barksdale)

Vee-Jay 230 - Movin' On / I Wanna Go Home - 1956
Vee-Jay 236 - Why Do You Have To Go / Dance, Dance, Dance - 1957
Vee-Jay 251 - A Distant Lover / O-Bop She-Bop - 1957
Vee-Jay 258 - Pain In My Heart / Time Makes You Change - 1957
Vee-Jay 274 - The Springer / What You Say Baby - 1958
Vee-Jay 292 - I'm Calling / Jeepers Creepers - 1958
Vee-Jay 300 - Wedding Day / My Best Girl - 1958
Vee-Jay 324 - Dry Your Eyes / Baby Open Up Your Heart - 1959
Vee-Jay 338 - Oh What A Night / I Wanna Go Home - 1960

The Dells (Members Johnny Carter (Vocalist For The Flamingos) , Marvin Junior, Verne Allison, Mickey Mcgill And Chuck Barksdale)

The Dells (Members Dallas Taylor (From The Dandeliers), Marvin Junior, Verne Allison And Mickey Mcgill)

Vee-Jay 376 - Swingin' Teens / Hold On To What You've Got - 1961
Argo 5415 - I'm Going Home / God Bless The Child - 1962
Argo 5428 - The (Bossa Nova) Bird / Eternally - 1962
Argo 5442 - If It Ain't One Thing It's Another / Hi Diddley Dee Dum Dum (It's A Good Good Feelin')* - 1963 *also released in 1966 by Jimmy James & The Vagabonds on HBR 496.
Argo 5456 - After You / Goodbye Mary Ann - 1963
Oldies 45 13 - I Wanna Go Home / Oh What A Nite - 1964

The Dells / Ray Smith

Oldies 45 26 - Dry Your Eyes / Rockin' Little Angel* - 1964 *Flip By Ray Smith.

The Dells / Bobby Day

Oldies 45 55 - Dreams Of Contentment / Little Bitty Pretty One - 1964

The Dells / Bob & Earl

Oldies 45 57 - Zing Zing Zing / Gee Whiz* - 1964 *Flip By Bob & Earl

Ritchie Valens / The Dells

Oldies 45 94 - Donna / Pain In My Heart* - 1964 *Flip By The Dells.

The Dells

Oldies 45 98 - Times Make You Change / Pain In My Heart - 1964
Oldies 45 99 - Why Do You Have To Go / Dance, Dance, Dance -1964

The Dells / The Harptones

Oldies 45 100 - I Wanna Go Home / I Almost Lost My Mind* - 1964 Flip By The Harptones.

The Dells / Gladys Knight & The Pips

Oldies 45 112 - Times Make You Change / Letter Full Of Tears* - 1964 *Flip By Gladys Knight & The Pips.

Preston Epps / The Dells

Oldies 45 122 - Bongo Rock / Movin' On* - 1964 8 Flip by The Dells

The Dells / Harold Dorman

Oldies 45 ? - Baby Open Up Your Heart / Mountain Of Love* - 1960s * Flip by Harold Dorman

The Dells (Members Johnny Carter (Born John Edward Carter on 2 June 1934...died 21 August 2009..cause: Lung Cancer) Marvin Junior, Verne Allison, Mickey McGill and Chuck Barksdale)

Vee-Jay 595 - Shy Girl / What Do We Prove - 1964
Vee-Jay 615 - Wait Till Tomorrow / Oh What A Good Night - 1964

The Dells / The Harptones

Oldies 45 155 - I Wanna Go Home / The Shrine Of St. Cecilia* - 1965 Flip By The Harptones.

The Dells

Vee-Jay 674 - Stay In My Corner / It's Not Unusual* - 1965 *Cover Of 1965 Recording By Tom Jones On London 9737.
Vee-Jay 712 - Hey Sugar (Don't Get Serious) / Poor Little Boy - 1965
Cadet 5538 - The Change We Go Thru (For Love) / Thinkin' About You - 1966

The Players (members Herbert Butler (lead), John Thomas and Otha Givens)

Minit 32001 - He'll Be Back* / I Wanna Be Free - 1966 *with this track Player member John Thomas and his friend Colis Gordon were the song writers, but Calvin Carter and Al Smith regarded The Players as not having good enough voices for the tracks, so they were replaced by The Dells (minus Marvin Junior) leaving only The Players' lead, Herbert Butler, as the sole member of the group to sing on this particular single. Also on some later Players tracks Chuck Barksdale provided vocals.

The Dells

Cadet 5551 - Run For Cover / Over Again - 1966
Cadet 5563 - Inspiration / You Belong To Someone Else - 1967
Cadet 5574 - O-O, I Love You / There Is - 1967
Cadet 5574 - O-O, I Love You / The Changes We Go Through (For Love) - 1967
Cadet 5590 - There Is / Show Me - 1967
Philco-Ford Hp-32 - There Is / Show Me - 1968 (4" Plastic "Hip Pocket Record")
Cadet 5599 - Wear It On Our Face / Please Don't Change Me Now - 1968
Cadet 5612 - Stay In My Corner / Love Is So Simple - 1968
Cadet 5621 - Always Together / I Want My Mama - 1968
Cadet 5631 - Make Sure (You Have Someone Who Loves You) / Does Anybody Know I'm Here? - 1968
Cadet 5636 - Hallways Of My Mind / I Can't Do Enough - 1969
Cadet 5641 - I Can Sing A Rainbow / Love Is Blue /// Hallelujah Baby - 1969
Cadet 5649 - Oh What A Night / Believe Me - 1969
Cadet 5658 - Sittin' On The Dock Of The Bay / When I'm In Your Arms - 1969
Cadet 5663 - Oh What A Day / The Change We Go Thru For Love - 1969
Cadet 5667 - Open Up My Heart / Nadine - 1970
Cadet 5672 - Long Lonely Nights / A Little Understanding - 1970
Cadet 5679 - The Glory Of Love* / A Whiter Shade Of Pale** - 1970 *a hit for Benny Goodman in 1936 and also recorded in 1951 by The Five Keys on Aladdin 3099 **also recorded in 1967 by Procol Harum on Deram 7507.
Trip 60 - Oh What A Night / Pain In My Heart - 197?
Cadet 5683 - The Love We Had (Stays On My Mind) / Freedom Means - 1971
Cadet 5689 - It's All Up To You / Oh, My Dear - 1971
Cadet 5691 - Walk On By* / This Guy's In Love With You - 1972 *originally recorded in 1964 by Dionne Warwick on Scepter 1274.
Cadet 5694 - Just As Long As We're In Love / I'd Rather Be With You - 1972

The Dells / The Packers

Trip 130 - Stay In My Corner / Hole In The Wall - 1972

The Dells

Cadet 5696 - Give Your Baby A Standing Ovation / Closer - 1973
Cadet 5698 - My Pretending Days Are Over / Let's Make It Last - 1973
Chess 6006 - O-O I Love You / There Is - 1973 (Blue Chip Series)
Goldies 45 2430 - I Wanna Go Home / Oh What A Nite - 1973
Cadet 5700 - Don't Make Me A Story Teller / I Miss You - 1973
Cadet 5702 - I Wish It Was Me You Loved / Two Together Is Better Than One - 1974
Cadet 5703 - Learning To Love You Was Easy (It's So Hard Trying To Get Over You) / Bring Back The Love Of Yesterday - 1974

Cadet 5703 - Sweeter As The Days Go By / Learning To Love You Was Easy (It's So Hard Trying To Get Over You) - 1974 (the "A" sides of both CADET 5703 releases is the same song, just a different title)
Cadet 5707 - You're The Greatest / The Glory Of Love - 1975

The Dells & The Dramatics

Cadet 5710 - I'm In Love / Love Is Missing From Our Lives - 1975

The Dells (Members

Cadet 5711 - We Got To Get Our Thing Together / The Power Of Love - 1975
Mercury 73723 - Got To Get Our Thing Together / Reminiscing - 1975
Mercury 73759 - The Power Of Love / Gotta Get Home To My Baby - 1975
Mercury 73807 - Slow Motion / Ain't No Black And White In Music - 1976
Mercury 73842 - No Way Back / Too Late For Love - 1976
Mercury 73901 - Bet'cha Never Been Loved (Like This Before) / Get On Down - 1977
Mercury 73909 - Our Love / Could It Be - 1977
Mercury 73977 - Private Property / Teaser - 1978
Warner Brothers 8606 - Love Island / ? - 1978
ABC 12386 - My Life Is So Wonderful (When You're Around) / Super Woman - 1978
ABC 12422 - (I Wanna) Testify / Drowning For Your Love - 1978
ABC 12422 - (I Wanna) Testify / Don't Save Me - 1978
ABC 12440 - (You Bring Out) The Best In Me / Wrapped Up Tight - 1979
MCA 41051 - What I Could / Plastic People - 1979
20th Century 2463 - I Touched A Dream / All About The Paper - 1980
20th Century 2475 - Passionate Breezes / Your Song - 1980
Lost-Nite 297 - Pain In My Heart / Time Makes You Change - 1981
Lost-Nite 305 - Oh What A Nite / Jo-Jo - 1981
20th Century 2504 - Happy Song / Look At Us Now - 1981
20th Century 2602 - Stay In My Corner / Ain't It A Shame - 1982

The Dells / The El Dorados

Eric 306 - Oh What A Night / At My Front Door (Crazy Little Mama)* - ? *flip by The El Dorados.

The Dells / Count Morris

Collectables Col 014317 - Tell The World / Blues At Three* - 1980's *flip by Count Morris.

Jackie Ross / The Dells

Collectables Col 034207 - Selfish One / Stay In My Corner* - 1980's *Flip By The Dells.

The Dells

Collectables Col 014327 - Dreams Of Contentment / Zing Zing Zing - 1980's
Collectables Col 014337 - Why Do You Have To Go / Dance, Dance, Dance - 1980's
Collectables Col 014347 - Stay In My Corner / A Distant Love - 1980's
Collectables Col 014357 - Pain In My Heart / Time Makes You Change - 1980's
Collectables Col 014367 - Oh What A Nite / Jo Jo - 1980's

The Dells

Collectables Col 034327 - There Is / Wear It On Our Face - 1980's

The Dells / Laura Lee

Collectables Col 034357 - Always Together / Dirty Man* - 1980's *Flip By Laura Lee.

The Dells / The Vibrations

Collectables Col 034547 - The Love We Had (Stays On My Mind) / The Watusi* - 1980's *flip by The Vibrations.

The Dells

Collectables Col 034787 - Give Your Baby A Standing Ovation / My Pretending Days Are Over - 1980's
Collectables Col 034937 - Oh What A Nite (1969 Version) / Nadine - 1980's

The Dells / The Jaguars

Original Sound Obg-4521 - Oh What A Nite / Moonlight And You* - 1984 *flip by The Jaguars. (note that some labels read "Have You Heard" by The Duprees as the flip but still play "Moonlight And You" by The Jaguars)

The Dells

Private 1 04343 - You Just Can't Walk Away / Don't Want Nobody - 1984
Private 1 04448 - Come On Back To Me / One Step Closer - 1984
Private 1 04540 - Love On / Don't Want Nobody - 1984
Skylark 558 - I Can't Help Myself / She's Just An Angel - 198?
Skylark 581 - Someone To Call Me Darling / Now I Pray - 198?

John Lee Hooker / The Poets /// Harmonica Fats / The Dells

Ripete 1027 - One Bourbon, One Scotch, One Beer / So Young (And So Innocent) /// Tore Up / Run For Cover - ?

The Dells

Chess 91031 - Stay In My Corner / Always Together - 1984
Veteran 10038 - That's How Heartaches Are Made / Thought Of You Just A Little Too Much - 1988
Veteran 7-101 - Can We Skip That Part / Thought Of You Just A Little Too Much - 1988

John Lee Hooker / The Poets /// Harmonica Fats / The Dells

Ripete 1027 - One Bourbon, One Scotch, One Beer / So Young (And So Innocent) /// Tore Up / Run For Cover - 1988

The Dells

Urgent 613 - My Lady Is So Perfect / Sweetness - 1991

Virgin 98829 - A Heart Is Not A House For Love / Stay In My Corner - 1991

Etta James / The Dells

Cadet ? - I'd Rather Go Blind / There Is - ?

The Dells / Gladys Knight & The Pips

Vee-Jay 1000 - Oh What A Nite / Every Beat Of My Heart* - ? (vintage series) *flip by Gladys Knight & The Pips.

Moses & Joshua Dillard

The Golden Wings (Members Moses Dillard, ...) Gospel Quartet

Moses Dillard & The Dynamic Showmen

Mark V 20-66 - They Don't Want Us Together / I'll Pay The Price - 1964
Mark V 40-26 - Pretty As A Picture / Go Way Baby - 1964

Moses & Joshua Dillard (Moses Dillard And James Moore)

Mala 575 - My Elusive Dreams* / What's Better Than Love - 1967 *Also Recorded In 19 By Tammy Wynette And David Houston On
Mala 598 - Get Out Of My Heart / They Don't Want Us Together - 1967

The Sons Of Moses

Coral 62549 - Soul Symphony / Fatback - 1968
Bix International 102 - Deviled Egg / Alpine Winter - ?

Moses Dillard & The Tex-Town Display (Members Moses Dillard, Peabo Bryson, Bill Wilson,

Curtom 1950 - I've Got To Find A Way (To Hide My Hurt) (Part 1) / I've Got To Find A Way (To Hide My Hurt) (Part 2) 1971
Curtom 1958 - Our Love Is True / Thank God (For This Thing Called Love) - 1971

Moses Dillard & Martha Starr

Shout 248 - Cheating Teasing And Misleading / You Can't Laugh It Off - 1972

Moses Dillard & The Tex-Town Display

Shout 253 - I Promised To Love You / We Gotta Come Together - 1972

Moses Dillard & Lovejoy

1-2-3 711 - Theme From "Lovejoy" / Good Stuff - 1974

Moses Dillard (Born 30-September-1946 In Greenville, South Carolina)

1-2-3 712 - What'cha See In Me / Filet Of Fatback - 1975

Moses

Piedmont 075 - I Got My Mind Together / If You Don't Mean It, Don't Touch Me - 1977

Dillard & Johnson

Piedmont 076 - Here We Go Loving Again / (Instrumental) - 1977
Epic 8 50239 - Here We Go Loving Again / Fairytale Come True - 1977

The Saturday Night Band (Members Moses Dillard, Jesse Boyce, ...)

Prelude 71104 - Come On Dance, Dance / ? - 1978
Prelude 71118 - Keep Those Lovers Dancing / Boogie With Me - 1979

Dillard & Boyce

Mercury 76061 - Love Zone / Love Is In The Melody - 1980
Mercury 76073 - I Feel Your Love / I Should Be Loving You - 1980

Nella Dodds

Nella Dodds (born Donzella Petty-John on 25-January-1950 in Havre De Grace, Maryland)

Wand 167 - Come See About Me* / You Don't Love Me Anymore - 1964 *also recorded in 1964 by The Supremes on Motown 1068
Wand 171 - Finders Keepers, Losers Weepers / A Girl's Life - 1964
Wand 178 - Your Love Back / P's And Q's - 1965
Wand 187 - Come Back Baby / Dream Boy - 1965
Wand 1111 - Gee Whiz* / Maybe Baby - 1966 *also recorded in 1960 by Carla Thomas on Satellite 104.
Wand 1136 - Honey Boy / I Just Gotta Have You - 1966
Wand - First Date - (unissued track which was released in the U. K. on a 1996 Goldmine CD "Big City Soul Four 60 Northern Soul Classics" GSCD 65 and released in the U. K. on a 2007 Kent CD "Nella Dodds This Is A Girl's Life: The Complete Wand Recordings 1964-5" CDKEND 282)
Wand - One Love Not Two - (unissued track which was released in the U. K. on a 2007 Kent Cd "Nella Dodds This Is A Girl's Life: The Complete Wand Recordings 1964-5" CDKEND 282)
Wand - Whisper You Love Me Boy - (unissued track which was released in the U. K. on a 2007 Kent Cd "Nella Dodds This Is A Girl's Life: The Complete Wand Recordings 1964-5" CDKEND 282. Song was also recorded in 1965 by The Supremes on Motown 1075)

Don & Juan

The Genies (members Roy Hammond, Bill Gains, Alexander "Buddy" Faison, Fred Jones and Claude Johnson)

Shad 5002 - Who's That Knockin' / The First Time - 1958 (shortly after this single came out Bill Gains ran off with a girl to Canada and was never heard of again)

Hollywood 69-1 - No More Knockin' / On The Edge Of Town - 1959 (the group breaks up in 1959, Fred Jones moved back to Brooklyn, Roy Hammond became Roy C and actually records a 45 in 1961 Roy Hammond & The Genies on FORUM 701 titled "Mama Blow Your Top / It's Getting Cold (unsure of The Genies line-up), Claude met Roland Trone in a coffee shop in Long Beach in 1960 and the two began painting houses for a living. A tenant heard them singing while they were painting an apartment building and put them in touch with Peter Paul who brought them to BIG TOP records they became Don (Roland) and Juan (Claude)).

Warwick 573 - There Goes That Train / Crazy Love - 1960
Warwick 607 - Just Like The Bluebird / Twistin' Pneumonia - 1960
Warwick 643 - Crazy Feeling / Little Young Girl - 1961

Don & Juan (Roland Trone and Claude Johnson (born 24-November-1934 - died 31-October-2002 - cause: ?))

Big Top 3079 - What's Your Name / Chicken Necks - 1961
Big Top 3106 - Pot Luck / Two Fools Are We- 1962
Big Top 3121 - What I Really Meant To Say / Magic Wand - 1962
Big Top 3145 - True Love Never Runs Smooth / Is It All Right If I Love You - 1963
Lana 150 - What's Your Name / Chicken Necks - 1963
Mala 469 - Lonely Man / Could This Be Love - 1963
Mala 479 - Pledging My Love / Molinda - 1964
Mala 484 - Sincerely / Maryana Cherie - 1964
Mala 494 - I Can't Help Myself / All Thats Missing Is You - 1964
Mala 509 - Heartbreaking Truth / Thank Goodness - 1965
Twirl 2021 - Are You Putting Me On The Shelf / Because I Love You - 1966
Terrific 5002 - All That's Missing Is You / What's Your Name - 197?

The Danleers / Don & Juan

Trip Oldies 91 - One Summer Night / What's Your Name* - ? *flip by Don & Juan.

Don & Juan / Sammy Turner

Eric 0249 - What's Your Name / Lavender Blue* 197? *flip by Sammy Turner.

The Dramatics

The Sensations (members Larry Reed, Rob Davis, Elbert Wilkins, Robert Ellington, Larry "Squirrel" Demps and Ronald Banks) Detroit group 1964 line-up.

The Theatrics (members Elbert Wilkins, ...)

V. R. 4003 - I Gotcha (Where I Want You) / We Got Love - ?

The Dynamics (members Larry Reed, Rob Davis, Elbert Wilkens, Robert Ellington, Larry Demps and Ron Banks)

Wingate 018 - Bingo / Somewhere – 1966
Wingate 022 - Inky Dinky Wang Dang Do / Baby I Need You – 1966

The Dramatics (members Larry Reed, Rob Davis, Elbert Wilkins, Larry "Squirrel" Demps and Ronald Banks)

Sport 101 - If You Haven't Got Love / All Because Of You - 1967

The Dramatics (members William "Wee Gee" Howard (died ?-February-2000 in New York -- cause: ?), Willie Ford former member of The Capitols (born 10-July-1950), Elbert Wilkins (died 13-December-1992 -- cause: heart attack), Larry Demps (born 23-February-1949) and Ronald Banks (born 10-May-1951 in Detroit, Michigan died 4th March, 2010 in Detroit))

Bell 5 - Toy Soldier / Hello Summer – 1968
Crackerjack 4015 - Toy Soldier / Hello Summer – 1968
Volt 4029 - Your Love Was Strange / Since I've Been In Love - 1969
Volt 4058 - Whatcha See Is Whatcha Get* / Thankful For You Love - 1971 *an "answer" song to this track was recorded in 1972 titled "What You See You Can't Get" by Pam Kellum on A&B 7171.
Volt 4071 - Get Up And Get Down / Fall In Love, Lady Love – 1971

Volt 4075 - In The Rain / (Gimme Some) Good Soul Music - 1972
Volt 4082 - Toast To The Fool / Your Love Was Strange – 1972
Volt 4090 - Hey You! Get Off My Mountain / The Devil Is Dope - 1973

The Dramatics (members L. J. Reynolds (born 1953 in Saginaw, Michigan) former member of Chocolate Syrup, Willie Ford (born 10-July-1950), Lenny Mayes (born Leonard Cornell Mayes on 5-April-1951 in Detroit, Michigan --- died 4:30 a.m. 7-November-2004 in Southfield, Michigan --- cause: heart failure), Larry Demps and Ronald Banks)

Volt 4099 - Fell For You / Now You Got Me Loving You - 1973
Volt 4105 - And I Panicked / Beware Of The Man (With Candy In His Hand) - 1974

Ron Banks & The Dramatics

Cadet 5704 - Door To Your Heart / Choosing Up On You – 1974

The Dramatics

Volt 4108 - Highway To Heaven / I Made Myself Lonely – 1974
Cadet 5706 - Don't Make Me No Promises / Tune Up – 1974

Ron Banks & The Dramatics

ABC 12090 - Me And Mrs. Jones / I Cried All The Way Home – 1975

The Dells & The Dramatics

Cadet 5710 - Love Is Missing From Our Lives / I'm In Love – 1975

Ron Banks & The Dramatics

ABC 12125 - (I'm Going By) The Stars In Your Eyes / Trying To Get Over Losing You – 1975

The Dramatics

ABC 12150 - You're Fooling You / I'll Make It So Good - 1975
ABC 12180 - Treat Me Like A Man / I Was The Life Of The Party – 1976
ABC 12220 - Finger Fever / Say The Word – 1976
ABC 12235 - Be My Girl / The Richest Man Alive – 1976
Mainstream 5571 - No Rebate On Love / Feel It – 1976
ABC 12258 - Sundown Is Coming (Hold Back The Night) / I Can't Get Over You – 1977
ABC 12299 - Shake It Well / That Heaven Kind Of Feeling – 1977
ABC Dm-4 - Shake It Well (5:51) / Shake It Well (5:51) - 1977 (12" Release)
ABC 12331 - Ocean Of Thoughts And Dreams / Come Inside – 1978
ABC 12372 - Stop Your Weeping / California Sunshine – 1978
ABC 12400 - Do What You Want To Do / Jane - 1978
ABC12429 - Why Do You Want Me To Do Wrong / Yo' Love (Can Only Bring Me Happiness) – 1978
ABC12460 - I Just Wanna Dance With You / I've Got A Schoolboy Crush – 1979
MCA 41017 - I Just Wanna Dance With You / I've Got A Schoolboy Crush – 1979
MCA 41056 - That's My Favourite Song / Bottom Line Woman - 1979
MCA 41178 - Welcome Back Home / A Marriage On Paper Only – 1980

The Dramatics (Members Craig Jones, Willie Ford, Lenny Mayes, Larry Demps And Ronald Banks)

MCA 41241 - Be With The One You Love / If You Feel Like You Wanna Dance, Dance – 1980
MCA 51003 - Get It / Share Your Love With Me – 1980

MCA? - Get It (Long Version) / Get It (Short Version) - 1980 (12" Release)
MCA 51041 - You're The Best Thing In My Life / (We Need More) Loving Time – 1981
Capitol 5103 - Live It Up / She's My Kind Of Girl – 1982
Capitol 5140 - Treat Me Right / Nightlife – 1982

Ron Banks (Born 10-May-1951 In Detroit, Michigan)

CBS 04142 - Truly Bad / Truly Bad – 1983
CBS 4z904143 - Truly Bad (6:06) / Truly Bad (Instrumental) (6:25) - 1983 (12" Release)
CBS 04242 - Make It Easy On Yourself / You And Me – 1983
CBS 4z904243 - Make It Easy On Yourself / You And Me - 1983 (12" Release)
CBS 04401 - Let Love Flow / This Love Is For Real – 1984

The Dramatics (Members William "Wee Gee" Howard, Ron Banks, Lenny Mayes, Willie Ford, And L.J. Reynolds)

Fantasy 966 - Luv's Callin' / Dream Lady – 1986
Fantasy 967 - One Love Ago / Dream Lady – 1986
Striped Horse 1214 - Born To Be Wild / (Instrumental) – 1988
Striped Horse Sh1214 - Born To Be Wild (Extended Version) /// Born To Be Wild (Radio Edit) / Born To Be Wild (Instrumental) - 1988 (12" Release)

Thomas Hearns & The Dramatics

Round-5 100 - We Are The Champions (Part 1) / We Are The Champions (Part 2) - 1988 (With Tommy Hearns the boxer out of Detroit covering the 1977 recording by Queen On Elektra 45441)

The Dramatics (Members Ron Banks, L.J. Reynolds, William Howard, Willie Ford, And Lenny Mayes)

Volt 302 - Bridge Over Troubled Water / Please Say You'll Be Mine – 1989
Volt 1602 - Bridge Over Troubled Water / Please Say You'll Be Mine - 1989 (12" Release)
Fantasy / Volt 1612 - Ready 4 Love - 1990 (12" Release)
Bellmark 745301 - Try Love Again (Six Mixes) - 1996 (12" Release)
Bell Mark 7 - Try Love Again (Lp Version) (4:54) / Try Love Again (Short Remix Radio) (4:10) / Try Love Again (Short Instrumental) (4:10) / Try Love Again (Long Remix) - 1996 (Cd Single Release)
Fantasy ? - Golden Horn / All I Want For Christmas Is My Baby - 1997 (Cd Single Release)

The Drifters

Coral 65037 – Wine Head Woman / I'm The Caring Kind – 1950 (Possibly a different group entirely)
Coral 65040 – And I Shook / I Had To Find Out For Myself – 1951 (Possibly a different group entirely)
Rama 22 – Beasame Muncha / Summertime – 1953 (Possibly a different group entirely)

Clyde Mcphatter & The Drifters

Atlantic 1006 - Money Honey* / The Way I Feel* - 1953 *Lead Clyde Mcphatter

The Drifters Featuring Clyde Mcphatter

Atlantic 1019 - Lucille* / Such A Night* - 1954 *Lead Clyde Mcphatter

The Drifters

Atlantic 1029 - Honey Love* / Warm Your Heart* - 1954 *Lead Clyde Mcphatter
Atlantic 1043 - Someday You'll Want Me To Want You* / Bip Bam** - 1954 *Lead Clyde Mcphatter **Leads Clyde Mcphatter And Bill Pinkney.

Atlantic 1048 - White Christmas* / The Bells Of St. Mary's** - 1954 *Vocal Duet Bill Pinkney And Clyde Mcphatter, **Lead Clyde Mcphatter
Atlantic 1055 - Whatcha Gonna Do* / Gone* - 1955 *Lead Clyde Mcphatter
Atlantic 1070 - Everyone's Laughing* / Hot Ziggety* - 1955 *Lead Clyde Mcphatter
Atlantic 1078 - Adorable* / Steamboat** - 1955 * Lead Johnny Moore, **Lead Bill Pinkney.

The Drifters Featuring Clyde Mcphatter

Atlantic 1048 - White Christmas / Bell's Of St. Mary's - 1955 (Reissue Featuring The "Original" Drifters)

The Drifters

Atlantic 1089 - Ruby Ruby* / Your Promise To Be Mine** - 1956 * Lead Johnny Moore, **Lead Gerhart Thrasher.
Atlantic 1101 - I Gotta Get Myself A Woman* / Soldier Of Fortune** - 1956 *Lead Johnny Moore. **Leads Johnny Moore And Bill Pinkney.

The Drifters Featuring Clyde Mcphatter

Atlantic 1048 - White Christmas / Bell's Of St. Mary's - 1956 (Reissue Featuring The "Original" Drifters)

The Drifters

Atlantic 1123 - Fools Fall In Love* / It Was A Tear* - 1957 *Lead Johnny Moore.
Atlantic 1141 - Hypnotized* / Drifting Away From You** - 1957 *Lead Johnny Moore, **Lead Gerhart Thrasher
Atlantic 1161 - I Know* / Yodee Yakee* - 1957 Lead Johnny Moore
Atlantic 1187 - Drip Drop* / Moonlight Bay** - 1958 *Lead Bobby Hendricks. **Group Singing In Unison.
Atlantic 2025 - There Goes My Baby* / Oh My Love* - 1959 *Lead Benjamin Nelson (Aka Ben E. King)

Clyde Mcphatter

Atlantic 2028 - Since You've Been Gone / Try Try Baby * - 1959 * (Credited To Clyde Mcphatter Only, But Includes The Drifters)
Atlantic 2038 - You Went Back On Your Word / There You Go * - 1959 *Credited To Clyde Mcphatter Only, But Includes The Drifters.

The Drifters

Atlantic 2040 - (If You Cry) True Love, True Love* / Dance With Me** - 1959 * Lead Johnny Lee Williams, ** Lead Ben E. King.

The Harmony Grits (The Original Drifters Minus Clyde Mcphatter)

End 1051 - I Could Have Told You / Am I To Be The One - 1959 (David "Little David" Baughn Lead Singer)
End 1063 - Santa Claus Is Coming / Gee - 1959 (David "Little David" Baughn Lead Singer)

Clyde Mcphatter

Atlantic 2049 - Just Give Me A Ring / Don't Dog Me * - 1960 * Credited To Clyde Mcphatter Only, But Includes The Drifters.

The Drifters

Atlantic 2050 - This Magic Moment* / Baltimore** - 1960 * Lead Ben E. King.**Lead Charlie Thomas And Elsbeary Hobbs.

Clyde Mcphatter

Atlantic 2060 - Deep Sea Ball / Let The Boogie Woogie Roll * -1960 * Credited To Clyde Mcphatter Only, But Includes The Drifters.

The Drifters

Atlantic 2062 - Lonely Winds* / Hey Senorita** - 1960 *Lead Ben E. King. **Lead Charlie Thomas.
Atlantic 2071 - Save The Last Dance For Me* / Nobody But Me* - 1960 *Lead Ben E. King.

Clyde Mcphatter

Atlantic 2082 - If I Didn't Love You Like I Do* / Go! Yes Go! - 1960 * Credited To Clyde Mcphatter Only, But Includes The Drifters.

The Drifters

Atlantic 2087 - I Count The Tears* / Suddenly There's A Valley** - 1960 *Lead Ben E. King.**Leads Bobby Hendricks And Tommy Evans.

The Drifters Featuring Clyde Mcphatter

Atlantic 1048 - White Christmas / Bell's Of St. Mary's - 1960 (Reissue Featuring The "Original" Drifters)

The Drifters

Atlantic 2096 - Some Kind Of Wonderful * / Honey Bee** - 1961 *Lead Rudy Lewis, **Lead David "Little David" Baughn.
Atlantic 2105 - Please Stay* / No Sweet Lovin' ** - 1961 *Lead Rudy Lewis. **Lead David "Little David" Baughn.
Atlantic 2117 - Sweets For My Sweet* / Loneliness Or Happiness** - 1961 *Lead Charlie Thomas.**Lead Ben E. King.
Atlantic 2127 - Room Full Of Tears* / Somebody New Dancin' With You** - 1961 *Lead Charlie Thomas. **Lead Rudy Lewis.
Atlantic 2134 - When My Little Girl Is Smiling* / Mexican Divorce** - 1962 *Lead Charlie Thomas. **Lead Rudy Lewis.
Atlantic 2143 - Stranger On The Shore* / What To Do* - 1962 *Lead Rudy Lewis.
Atlantic 2151 - Sometimes I Wonder* / Jackpot** - 1962 * Lead Ben E. King. **Lead Rudy Lewis.
Atlantic 2162 - Up On The Roof* / Another Night With The Boys* - 1962 *Lead Rudy Lewis.

The Drifters / Grady K & Kuhfus Band

Quality Checkd 82592 - Cherry Chocolate Twist - 1962 (Promo Issue Only Given Out Free With A 2 Gallon Purchase Of Chocolate Milk)

The Drifters Featuring Clyde Mcphatter

Atlantic 1048 - White Christmas / The Bells Of St. Mary's - 1962 (Reissue Featuring The "Original" Drifters)

The Drifters

Atlantic 2182 - On Broadway* / Let The Music Play* - 1963 Lead Rudy Lewis.
Atlantic 2191 - If You Don't Come Back */ Rat Race** - 1963 *Lead Johnny Moore. **Lead Rudy Lewis.
Atlantic 2201 - I'll Take You Home* / I Feel Good All Over** - 1963 *Lead Johnny Moore. **Lead Charlie Thomas.
Atlantic 2216 - Vaya Con Dios */ In The Land Of Make Believe** - 1964 *Lead Rudy Lewis. **Leads Rudy Lewis And Johnny Moore.
Atlantic 2225 - One-Way Love* / Didn't It* - 1964 Lead Johnny Moore.
Atlantic 2237 - Under The Boardwalk* / I Don't Want To Go On Without You** - 1964 *Lead Johnny Moore, **Lead Charlie Thomas
Atlantic 2253 - I've Got Sand In My Shoes* / He's Just A Playboy* - 1964 *Lead Johnny Moore.
Fontana 1956 - Do The Jerk* / Don't Call Me - 1964 Recorded By The "Original" Drifters. *Lead Bobby Lee Hollis
Atlantic 2260 - Saturday Night At The Movies* / Spanish Lace* - 1964 *Lead Johnny Moore.
Atlantic 2261 - I Remember Christmas* / The Christmas Song* - 1964 *Lead Johnny Moore.
Atlantic 2268 - At The Club* / Answer The Phone* - 1965 *Lead Johnny Moore.
Atlantic 2285 - Come On Over To My Place* / Chains Of Love** - 1965 *Lead Johnny Moore. **Lead Charlie Thomas
Atlantic 2292 - Follow Me* / The Outside World** - 1965 *Lead Johnny Moore. **Lead Charlie Thomas.
Atlantic 2298 - I'll Take You Where The Music's Playing* / Far From The Maddening Crowd* - 1965 *Lead Johnny Moore.
Atlantic 2310 - Nylon Stockings* / We Gotta Sing* - 1965 *Lead Johnny Moore.
Atlantic 2325 - Memories Are Made Of This* / My Islands In The Sun* - 1966 *Lead Johnny Moore.
Atlantic 2336 - Up In The Streets Of Harlem* / You Can't Love Them All** - 1966 *Lead Johnny Moore. Lead Charlie Thomas.
Veep 1264 - I Found Some Lovin' / The Masquerade Is Over * - 1966 * Recorded By The "Original" Drifters.
Atlantic 2366 - Baby What I Mean */ Aretha* - 1966 *Lead Johnny Moore.

The Drifters / Lesley Gore / Roy Orbinson / Los Bravos

Swingers For Coke - 1966 (Promotional Record For Coca-Cola)

Bill Pinkney & The Original Drifters

S & J 800826 - (More Than A Number) In My Little Red Book / Count The Tears - 1967

The Drifters

Atlantic 2426 - Ain't It The Truth* / Up Jumped The Devil** - 1967 *Lead Johnny Moore. **Lead Bill Fredericks.
Atlantic 2471 - Still Burning In My Heart* / I Need You Now** - 1968 *Lead Johnny Moore. **Lead Bill Fredericks.
Atlantic 2624 - Steal Away* / Your Best Friend** - 1969 *Lead Bill Fredericks. **Lead Johnny Moore.
Atlantic 2746 - You Got To Pay Your Dues* / Black Silk** - 1970 *Lead Johnny Moore. **Lead Bill Fredericks.
Atlantic 2786 - A Rose By Any Other Name* / Be My Lady* - 1971 *Lead Johnny Moore.

Game 394 - Millionaire / Old Man River * - 1971 * Recorded By The "Original" Drifters.
Andee 0014 - Black Silk / You Got To Pay Your Dues - 1971

The Drifters (Johnny Moore Group)

Bell 1269 - Something Tells Me / Every Night - 1972
Bell 45,320 - You've Got Your Troubles / I'm Feeling Sad (And Oh So Lonely) - 1973
Bell 45,387 - Like Sister And Brother / The Songs We Used To Sing - 1973
Bell 45,600 - Kissin' In The Back Row Of The Movies / I'm Feelin' Sad - 1974

The Drifters (Charlie Thomas Group)

Steeltown 671 - Peace Of Mind / The Struggler - 1973

The Drifters (Johnny Moore Group)

Bell 1339 - I'm Free (For The Rest Of My Life) / Say Goodbye To Angelina - 1974
Bell 1358 - Kissin' In The Back Row Of The Movies / I'm Feelin' Sad - 1974

Charlie Thomas And The Drifters

Musicor 1498 - On A Midsummer Night In Harlem / Lonely Drifter Don't Cry -1974

The Drifters (Johnny Moore Group)

Bell 1381 - Down On The Beach Tonight / Say Goodbye To Angelina - 1974
Bell 1396 - Love Games / The Cut Is Deep - 1975
Bell 1433 - There Goes My First Love / Don't Cry On The Weekend - 1975
Bell 1462 - Can I Take You Home Little Girl / Please Help Me Down - 1975
Bell 1469 - Hello Happiness / I Can't Get Away From You - 1976
Bell 1491 - Every Night's A Saturday Night With You / I'll Get To Know Your Name Along The Way - 1976
Arista 78 - You're More Than A Number In My Little Red Book / Do You Have To Go Now - 1976

Bill Pinckney & The Drifters

Sounds South16053/4 - Plain Simple But Sweet / Just Let Your Heart Be Your Guide - 1978

Bill Pinkney Of The Original Drifters

Southern Charisma 3289 - 60 Minute Man / Broke Blues - ?

The Drifters / Little Willie John

Atlantic 89189 - Ruby Baby / Fever* - 1987 * Flip Side By Little Willie John

The Drifters Featuring Rick Sheppard

Emi-Capitol Music S7 - 19351 - Christmas Time Is Here / I'll Be Home For Christmas - 1996

The Drifters / Little Joey & The Flips

Gary's Ferry 7943809 - Honky Tonk / Bongo Stomp - ?

Dyke & The Blazers

Carl LaRue & His Crew (members Carl LaRue (piano), Alvester Jacobs (guitar), Arlester Christian (bass) and Willie Earl (drums)) 1960 line-up.

K K C ? - Please Don't Drive Me Away / Monkey Hips And Oyster Stew - 1963?

Dumas King

Ronn 4 - Loose Eel / Wish You'd Come Home - 1964 (session "Big Boy" Pete Casey (guitar) --- later member of Miles Davis group. Richard Cason (keyboards)

The Three Blazers (members Bernard Williams (saxaphone), ...)

Dyke and the Blazers (members Arlester "Dyke" Christian (vocals and bass) (born 1943 in Buffalo, New York - died 30-March-1971 in Phoenix, Arizona - cause: shot four times with a .22 calibre pistol by Clarence Daniels, the bullets striking him in the right temple, the upper chest and right thigh in a bar-room altercation, pronounced dead one hour later. Clarence Daniels was arraigned on murder charges but the case was delayed several times and then eventually dismissed on 1-December-1971, because of "evidence indicating self-defence"), Alvester "Pig" Jacobs (guitar), Bernard Williams (saxophone) (born 12-April-1944 --- died 5-July-2006 --- cause: ?), J. V. Hunt (saxophone), Richard Cason (organ) and Rodney Brown (drums))

Artco 45-101 - Funky Broadway - Part 1 / Funky Broadway - Part 2 - 1966 (written by Lester Christian - apparently recorded in under one hour at a cost of $45.00!)
Original Sound Os-64 - Funky Broadway (Part 1)* / Funky Broadway (Part 2) - 1967 *covered in 1967 by Wilson Pickett on Atlantic 2430 and in 19? by Glen Miller on Doctor Bird 1089.

Dyke And The Blazers (members Arlester Christian (Dyke) (vocals), Alvester "Pig" Jacobs (guitar), Bernard Williams (saxophone), Alvin Battle (bass)...)

Dyke And The Blazers (members Arlester Christian (Dyke) (vocals), Alvester "Pig" Jacobs (guitar), Otis Tolliver (bass), Bernard Williams (saxaphone), Maurice "Little Mo" Jones (trumpet), Ray Byrd (keyboards), Willie Earl (drums) and Wardell "Baby Wayne" Peterson (drums - died 1989 - cause: liver disease)

Original Sound Os-69 - Don't Bug Me / So Sharp – 1967
Original Sound Os-79 - Funky Walk (Part 1) / Funky Walk (Part 2) – 1968
Original Sound Os-83 - Funky Bull (Part 1) / Funky Bull (Part 2) – 1968
Original Sound Os-86 - We Got More Soul / Shotgun Slim - 1969 (both sides written by Arlester Christian)
Original Sound Os-89 - Let A Woman Be A Woman - Let A Man Be A Man* / Uuh (Edit) - 1969 *recorded in Los Angeles using the nucleus of The Watts 103rd Street Band as session players.

Dyke And The Blazers (members Arlester Christian (Dyke) (vocals), Alvester "Pig" Jacobs (guitar), Otis Tolliver (bass), Bernard Williams (saxophone), Maurice "Little Mo" Jones (trumpet), Ray Byrd (keyboards), and Wardell "Baby Wayne" Peterson (drums))

Original Sound Os-90 - City Dump / You Are My Sunshine* - 1969 *recorded in Los Angeles using the nucleus of The Watts 103rd Street Band as session players.

(After the band's equipment was stolen from a club in 1969 and not replaced The Blazers, worn down by travel and low pay fractured and broke up)

Original Sound Os-91 - My Sisters And My Brothers / Uuh - 1970 (both sides written by Arlester Christian)
Original Sound Os-96 - Runaway People* / I'm So All Alone - 1970 *recorded in Los Angeles using the nucleus of The Watts 103rd Street Band as session players.
Original Sound Os-102 - Stuff / The Wobble – 1971

The Odd Squad (members Arlester Christian, ...)

Minit 32088 - Just To See Your Face / Runaway People - 1971

Rosie & The Originals / Dyke And The Blazers

Original Sound Obg 4505 - Angel Baby / We Got More Soul* - 1984 (Oldies But Goodies Series) *flip by Dyke And The Blazers.

Dyke And The Blazers (members Arlester Christian, Alvester Jacobs, Bernard Williams, Clarence Towns, Alvin Battle, Will Earl, Richard Cason and Rodney Brown)

Original Sound Obg 4506 - Funky Broadway (Part 1) / Funky Broadway (Part 2) - 1984 (Oldies But Goodies Series)

The Kingsmen / Dyke And The Blazers

Original Sound Obg 4517 - Louie Louie / Shotgun Slim* - 1984 (Oldies But Goodies Series) *flip by Dyke And The Blazers.

Dyke & The Blazers

Collectables Col 040537 - Funky Broadway (Parts 1 & 2) / We Got More Soul - ?

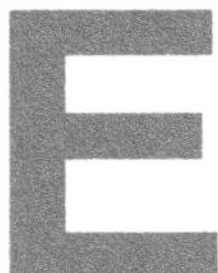

Group Line Ups

The Embers (Jackie Hamilton Gore, Bobby Tomlinson, Johnny Hopkins, Carig Woolard, Gerald Davis, Doug Strange, Johnny Barker)
Patti & The Emblems (Patty Russell, Alex Wilde, Eddie Watts, Vance Walker)
The Enjoyables (Keni Lewis, Sidney Hall, Carl 'Maxx' Kidd, James Johnson, William Britton, Gerald Richardson)
The Escorts (Robert Jones, Eugene Proctor, Herman Robinson, Leonard Hogains)
The Essex (Anita Hulmes, Walter Vickers, Rodney Taylor, Billie Hill, Rudolph Johnson)

Donnie Elbert

The Vibra-Harps (member Donnie Elbert, Danny Cannon (later to become Lenny O'Henry), Charles Hargro and Donald Simmons) Although Donnie Elbert and Danny Cannon formed the group, Danny Cannon and Donald Simmons were the basis of the group. Donnie Elbert did background vocals, as well as being the groups guitarist and arranger. He left the group in 1957 due to personnel problems)

Beech 713 - Walk Beside Me / Cosy With Rosy - 1958

Donnie Elbert (born 25-May-1936 in New Orleons, moved to Buffalo New York at the age of three. Died 26-January-1989 in Philadelphia, PA cause: stroke)

Deluxe 6125 - What Can I Do* / Hear My Plea** - 1957 *also recorded in 1970 by Val Martin on All Platinum 2304. **song originally titled "Somebody, Somewhere", but record company changed it to "Hear My Plea". Song covered in 1966 by Marvin L. Sims on Mellow 1002.
Deluxe 6143 - Believe It Or Not / Tell Me So - 1957
Deluxe 6148 - Have I Sinned / Leona - 1957
Deluxe 6156 - Let's Do The Stroll / Wild Child - 1958
Deluxe 6161 - My Confession Of Love / Peek - A - Boo - 1958
Deluxe 6164 - I Want To Be Loved But Only By You / Someone Made You For Me - 1958
Deluxe 6168 - I Want To Be Near You / Come On Sugar - 1958
Deluxe 6175 - Just A Little Bit Of Lovin' / When You're Near Me - 1958

The Vibra-Harps (unsure of Donnie Elbert's involvement with group, if any, at the time of these releases)

Fury 1022 - The Only Love Of Mine / Be My Dancing Partner - 1959
Atco 6134 - It Must Be Magic / Nosey Neighbours - 1959

Donnie Elbert

Red Top 122 - Someday (You'll Want Me To Want You) / Help Me - 1960
Vee - Jay 336 - Will You Ever Be Mine / Hey Baby - 1960
Vee - Jay 353 - Half As Old / Baby Let Me Love You Tonite - 1960
Vee - Jay 370 - I've Loved You Baby / I Beg Of You - 1961
Jot 122 - Hey Baby / Will You Ever Be Mine - 1961
Jalynne 107 - Mommie's Gone / For Sentimental Reasons - 1961
Jalynne 110 - Lucille (I've Done You No Wrong) / What You're Doing To Me - 1961
Red Top 130 - Will You Ever Be Mine / Hey Baby - 1962
P & L 316 - Nobody Knows / After All I've Done For You - 1962
Parkway 844 - Baby Cakes / Set My Heart At Ease - 1962
Red Top 6502 - Sentimental Reasons / Someday (You'll Want Me To Want You) - 1963
Cub 9125 - Love Stew / Don't Cry My Love - 1963
Up State 829 - Love Stew / Don't Cry My Love - 1963
Checker 1062 - Just A Cotton Pickin' Minute / Everything To Me - 1963
Gateway 731 - Run Little Girl / Who's It Gonna Be - 1964
Gateway 748 - Lily Lou / Do Wat'cha Wanna - 1964
Gateway 757 - A Little Piece Of Leather - 1965 (One Sided Disc --- Promo Issue Only)
Gateway 757 - A Little Piece Of Leather / Do Wat'cha Wanna - 1965
Gateway 761 - Your Red Wagon (You Can Push It Or Pull It) / Never Again - 1965
Atco 6550 - In Between Heartaches / Too Far Gone - 1968
Deram 7526 - Without You* / Baby Please Come Home - 1969 *A Number One Hit In Jamaica.
Rare Bullet 101 - I Can't Get Over Losing You / I Got To Get Myself Together - 1970
Elbert 800 - I Got To Get Myself Together / Can't Get Over Losing You - 1970
Elbert 800 - Sweet Baby / Can't Get Over Losing You - 1970
Bradley's 7501 - You're Gonna Cry When I'm Gone / Another Tear Will Take It's Place - 1970
Deluxe 133 - Have I Sinned / What Can I Do - 1971
All Platinum 2330 - Where Did Our Love Go* / That's If You Love Me - 1971 *Also recorded in 1964 by The Supremes on Motown 1060.
All Platinum 2333 - Sweet Baby / I Can't Get Over Losing You - 1972
Avco 4587 - I Can't Help Myself* / Love Is Here And Now You're Gone - 1972 *Also recorded in 1965 by The Four Tops on Motown 1076

All Platinum 2336 - If I Can't Have You / Will You Ever Be Mine - 1972
All Platinum 2336 - If I Can't Have You / Can't Get Over Losing You* - 1972 *Also recorded in 1974 by Baby Washington on Master 5 9109.
All Platinum 2337 - A Little Piece Of Leather / Sweet Baby - 1972
All Platinum 2338 - I Can't Get Over Losing You / That's If You Love Me - 1972
Avco 4598 - Ooh Baby Baby* / Tell Her For Me - 1972 *also recorded in 1965 by The Miracles on Tamla 54113. (this 45 was released without approval from Donnie Elbert --- while at Avco Donnie Elbert was arguing with Hugo and Luigi about the cost of finishing his album for the label, plus his choice of material for the album as it had nine Motown covers - he refused to finish the album without the extra money, so Avco sold the unfinished album to Trip to recoup their money. Donnie Elbert reluctantly went back to All Platinum)
Trip 175 - I Can't Help Myself / Can't Get Over Losing You - 1972
Trip 3011 - Stop In The Name Of Love / If You Were My Woman - 1972
Polydor 15048 - This Old Heart Of Mine / Be Good To Me - 1972

Jackie Milton, Morris Bailey, Donnie Elbert, Bert Keyes

De-Vel Zs7 6755 - You'll Never Know / Will You Love Me Tomorrow - 1973

Donnie Elbert

All Platinum 2346 - This Feeling Of Losing You / Can't Stand These Lonely Nights - 1973
All Platinum 2351 - Love Is Strange* / Instrumental - 1974 *cover of the 1956 record by Mickey & Sylvia on Groove 0175.
All Platinum 2367 - What Do You Do / Will You Love Me Tomorrow - 1977
All Platinum 2374 - You Should Be Dancing* / What Do You Do - 1974 *also recorded in 1976 by The Bee Gees on RSO 853.
A / O 1000 - You Keep Me Crying (With Your Lying) / Instrumental - 1975 (The A/O Label is owned by Donnie Elbert)
Up State 829 - Can't Get Over Losing You / Love Stew - 197?
Command Performance 101 - Who's It Gonna Be / Your Red Wagon (You Can Push It Or Pull It) - 197?
Goldies 45 2675 - Where Did Our Love Go / If I Can't Have You - 197?
Echo 7001 - Are You Ready (Willing And Able) / You Keep Me Crying (With Your Lying) - 1979
Gusto 2171 - Have I Sinned / What Can I Do - 198?
Gusto 2172 - Hear My Plea / My Confession Of Love - 198?
Deluxe 01 - Have I Sinned / What Can I Do - ?
Collectables Col 036467 - I Want To Be Loved But Only By You / Believe It Or Not - ?
Collectables Col 036477 - Come On Sugar / Peek-A-Boo - ?

The Enchantments

Gone 5130 - (I Love You) Sherry / Come On Home - 1962
Ritz 17003 - I Love You Baby / Pains In My Heart - 1963
Faro 620 - I'm In Love With Your Daughter / Part Two - 1964
Doyle - Why Can't We Fall In Love / ? - ? (No Label Selection Number Used)

The Enchantments Featuring Leroy. (possibly a different group)

Romac 1001 - Lonely Heart / Popeye (The Dance To Do - 1962 (With The Jim Drake Orchestra)

Barbara Jean English

The Gospelettes (members Charlotte McCartney, Trudy McCartney, ...)

The Bouquets (members Barbara English, Charlotte McCartney, Trudy McCartney and Sylvia Hammond a later member of The Loreleis on Brunswick))

The Ding Dongs (members Bobby Darin, Barbara English, Charlotte McCartney, Trudy McCartney and Sylvia Hammond)

Brunswick 55073 - Now We're One / Early In The Morning - 1958

The Rinky Dinks (members Bobby Darin, Barbara English, Charlotte McCartney, Trudy McCartney and Sylvia Hammond)

Atco 6121 - Now We're One / Early In The Morning - 1958

The Click-Etts (members Barbara English, Charlotte McCartney, Trudy McCartney and Sylvia Hammond)

Dice 100 - But, Not For Me / I Love You I Swear - 1958

The Clickettes (members Barbara English, Charlotte McCartney, Trudy McCartney and Sylvia Hammond)

Dice 83 / 84 - Jive Time Turkey / A Teenager's First Love 1958

The Avalons (members ? (a male lead), Barbara Jean English, Charlotte McCartney, Trudy McCartney and Sylvia Hammond)

Dice 90 / 91 - Louella / You Broke Our Hearts - 1958

The Clickettes (members Barbara English, Charlotte McCartney, Trudy McCartney and Sylvia Hammond)

Dice 94 / 95 - Warm, Soft And Lovely* / Why Oh Why** - 1959 *also recorded in 1958 by Johnnie & Joe on J & S 1630/1631, written by The Hearts piano player Rex Garvin. **also recorded in 1958 by Johnnie & Joe on Chess 1693.

The Clickettes (members Barbara English, Jeanne Bolden, Barbara Saunders and Sylvia Hammond) (this was the line-up for touring purposes as Charlotte and Trudy McCartney had not graduated from school, so their parents would not give them permission to perform away from home)

The Click-Ettes (members Barbara English, Charlotte McCartney, Trudy McCartney and Sylvia Hammond)

Dice 96/97 - Lover's Prayer / Grateful - 1959 (copies that have "Distribution By Memo Record Corp" on label are scarce)

The Clicketts (members Barbara English, Charlotte McCartney, Trudy McCartney and Sylvia Hammond)

Dice 92 / 93 - To Be A Part Of You / Because Of My Best Friend - 1960

Click-Etts (members Barbara English, Charlotte McCartney, Trudy McCartney and Sylvia Hammond)

Dice 92 / 93 - To Be A Part Of You / Because Of My Best Friend - 1960
Dice - That's The Way It Is - (although previously unissued this was released in 2006 in the U. K. on a Ace Cd "The Clickettes Meet The Fashions" CDCHD 1095)

Dice - Light A Candle - (although previously unissued this was released in 2006 in the U. K. on a Ace Cd "The Clickettes Meet The Fashions" CDCHD 1095)

The Clickettes (members Barbara English, Jeanne Bolden, Barbara Saunders and Sylvia Hammond)

Guyden 2043 - Where Is He* / The Lone Lover - 1960 *Written By Richard Barrett.

The Fashions (members Barbara English, Jeanne Bolden, Barbara Saunders and Helen Powell a former member of The Impacts)

Warwick 646 - Dearest One* / All I Want - 1961*Written By Richard Barrett.
Elmor 301 - Please Let It Be Me / Fairy Tales* - 1961 *also recorded in 1970 by The Spaniels on North American 001.

Barbara English and The Fashions (members Barbara English, Jeanne Bolden, Barbara Saunders and Helen Powell)

Roulette 4428 - We Need Them / Ta - Ta - Tee - Ta - Ta* - 1962 *written by Arthur Crier -- a member of The Halos, who also sang bass on the 45.

Barbara English & The Fashions (members Barbara English, Jeanne Bolden, Barbara Saunders and Helen Powell)

Barbara English & The Fashions (members Barbara English, Jeanne Bolden, Barbara Saunders and Helen Powell)

Roulette 4450 - Fever* / Bad News** - 1962 *also recorded in 1956 by Little Willie John on King 4935 and in 1976 by Esther Phillips on Kudu 929 plus in 2007 by Patti Drew on Stateside SS 2234. **written by Johnny Nash.

Barbara English (born 22-August-1946 in Sumpter, South Carolina)

Mala 488 - Easy Come, Easy Go / I Don't Deserve A Boy Like You - 1964
Reprise 290 - I've Got A Date / Shoo Fly - 1965
Reprise 349 - Small Town Girl (With Big Town Dreams) / Tell Me Like It Is - 1965
Warner Bros. 5685 - All Because I Love Somebody / All The Good Times Are Gone - 1965
Aurora 155 - (You Got Me) Sittin' In The Corner / Standin' On Tip Toe - 1966

The Clickettes (members Barbara English, Charlotte McCartney, Trudy McCartney and Sylvia Hammond)

Lost Nite 138 - Lover's Prayer / Grateful - ?
Lost Nite 139 - Because Of My Best Friend / Grateful - ?
Lost Nite 140 - To Be A Part Of You / Because Of My Best Friend - ?

Barbara Jean English

Alithia 6035 - Love's Arrangement / ? - 1971
Alithia 6040 - I'm Living A Lie / All This - 1972
Alithia 6041 - So Many Ways To Die */ Danger Signs - 1972 *from the movie The Arrangement.
Alithia 6042 - I'm Sorry* / Lil' Baby - 1972 *also recorded in 1960 by Brenda Lee on Decca 31093.
Alithia 6046 - Baby I'm-A Want You* / Don't Make Me Over** - 1973 *also recorded in 1971 by Bread on Elektra 45751. **cover of Dionne Warwick's 1962 classic on Scepter 1239.
Alithia 6053 - You're Gonna Need Somebody To Love (While You're Looking For Someone To Love) / All This - 1973
Alithia 6059 - Comin' Or Goin' / Love's Arrangement - 1973
Alithia 6064 - Breakin' Up A Happy Home / Guess Who - 1974

Tony Middleton / Barbara English

TK TKD-12 - Lady Fingers / House Of Strangers* - 1976 (12" release) *flip by Barbara English.

Barbara English

Royal Flush 101 - If This Ain't Love / If It Feels This Good - 1977
Royal Flush 103 - House Of Strangers / If It Feels This Good - 1977
Royal Flush 104 - Make Up And Make Love / If This Ain't Love - 1977
Helva 100 - I'm Dancing To Keep From Crying / (Instrumental) - 1979
Zakia Zk 100 - I'm Dancing To Keep From Crying / (Instrumental) - 1979 (12" release)

The Clickettes (members Barbara English, Charlotte McCartney, Trudy McCartney and Sylvia Hammond)

Collectables Col 012217 - Lovers Prayer / Grateful - ?
Collectables Col 012227 - To Be A Part Of You / Grateful - ?
Collectables Col 012237 - Because Of My Best Friend / Grateful - ?

The Clickettes (members Barbara English, Lorraine Joyner, Trudy McCartney and Sylvia Hammond) 1999

The Escorts

The Escorts (Robert Jones, Eugene Proctor, Herman Robinson, Leonard Hogains)

RCA Victor 47-6834 - Bad Boy / Tore Up Over You - 1957
RCA Victor 47-6963 - So Hard To Laugh, So Easy To Cry / Lonely Man - 1957
Judd 1014 - My First Year / Clap Happy - 1959
Wells 102 - One More Kiss Good Night / ? - 1959
Scarlet 4005 - I Will Be Home Again / Leaky Heart And His Red Go-Kart - 1960
RCA Victor 47-8228 - You Can't Even Be My Friend / Itchy Coo - 1963
RCA Victor 47-8327 - The Hurt / No City Folks Allowed - 1964

The Essex

The Essex (members Walter Vickers (vocals and guitar) and Rodney Taylor (drums)) 1961

The Essex (members Walter Vickers (vocals and guitar), Billie Hill (vocals), Rudolph Johnson (guitar) and Rodney Taylor (drums))

The Essex (members Anita Humes (vocals), Walter Vickers, Billie Hill, Rudolph Johnson and Rodney Taylor)

Roulette 4494 - Easier Said Than Done* / Are You Going My Way - 1963

The Essex featuring Anita Humes (members Anita Humes (vocals), Walter Vickers, Billie Hill and Rodney Taylor)

Roulette 4515 - A Walkin' Miracle / What I Don't Know Won't Hurt Me - 1963

The Essex (members Anita Humes (vocals), Walter Vickers, Billie Hill and Rodney Taylor)

Roulette 4530 - She's Got Everything* / Out Of Sight, Out Of Mind - 1963 *written by Jimmy

Radcliffe and Oramay Diamond.

Anita Humes And The Essex (members Anita Humes (vocals), Walter Vickers, Billie Hill and Rodney Taylor)

Roulette 4542 - What Did I Do / Curfew Lover – 1964
Roulette - Be My Baby - 1964 (although unissued on vinyl at the time this cover of the 1963 release by The Ronettes on Philles 116 was released in 1994 in the U. K. on a Sequel CD "The Best Of The Essex Featuring Anita Humes" NEM CD 714)

Anita Humes

Roulette 4564 - Don't Fight It Baby / When Somethin's Hard To Get – 1964
Roulette - Be Sure - 1964 (although unissued on vinyl at the time this track was released in 1994 in the U. K. on a Sequel CD "The Best Of The Essex Featuring Anita Humes" NEM CD 714)
Roulette 4575 - I'm Making It Over / Just For The Boy – 1964
Roulette - When The Music Stops - 1965 (although unissued on vinyl at the time this track was released in 1994 in the U. K. on a Sequel CD "The Best Of The Essex Featuring Anita Humes" NEM CD 714)
Roulette - Real True Lover - 1965 (although unissued on vinyl at the time this track was released in 1994 in the U. K. on a Sequel CD "The Best Of The Essex Featuring Anita Humes" NEM CD 714)

The Essex (members Anita Humes, ...)

Bang 537 - The Eagle / Moonlight, Music And You* - 1966 *also recorded in 1967 by Laura Greene on RCA 47-9164.

Anita Humes And The Essex (members Anita Humes, ...)

Roulette 4750 - Are You Going My Way / Everybody's Got You (For Their Own) - 1967

The Essex

Collectables Col 002537 - Easier Said Than Done / A Walkin' Miracle - ?

Betty Everett

Betty Everett (born 23-November-1939 in Greenwood, Mississippi - died 19-August-2001)

Cobra 5019 - My Love / My Life Depends On You - 1957
Cobra 5024 - Ain't Gonna Cry / Killer Diller - 1958

Bettie Everett & The Willie Dixon Band

Cobra 5031 - I'll Weep No More / Tell Me Darling – 1959

Bettie Everett & The Daylighters (members Betty Everett, George Wood, Dorsey Wood, Tony Gideon, Eddie Thomas and Gerald Sims)

CJ 611 - Why Did You Have To Go / Please Come Back – 1960

Betty Everett & Earl Hooker & The Ike Perkins All Stars

CJ 619 - Happy I Long To Be / Your Loving Arms – 1961

Betty Everett

Renee 102 - Your Love Is Important To Me / I've Got A Claim On You - 1962
One-Der-Ful! 4806 - Your Love Is Important To Me / I've Got A Claim On You – 1963
One-Der-Ful! 4823 - I'll Be There / Please Love Me - 1963
Vee-Jay 513 - By My Side / Prince Of Players - 1963
Vee-Jay 566 - You're No Good* / Chained To Your Love - 1963 *also recorded in 1963 by Dee Dee Warwick on Jubilee 5459 and also covered in 1968 by Barbara West on Ronn 27 and again in 1975 by Linda Ronstadt on Asylum 3990. This was Maurice White's first session as a "gig" drummer.
Vee-Jay 585 - The Shoop Shoop Song (It's In His Kiss)* / Hands Off - 1964 *also recorded in 1964 by Ramona King on Warner Bros. 5416.

Betty Everett

Dottie 1126 - Tell Me Darling / I'll Weep No More – 1964
Vee-Jay 599 - I Can't Hear You / Can I Get To Know You* - 1964 *also recorded in 1966 by The Turtles on White Whale 238.
Vee-Jay 610 - It Hurts To Be In Love* / Until You Were Gone - 1964 *also recorded in 1957 by Annie Laurie on Deluxe 6107.

Betty Everett & Jerry Butler

Vee-Jay 613 - Let It Be Me / Ain't That Loving You Baby - 1964

Betty Everett

Vee-Jay 628 - Getting Mighty Crowded / Chained To A Memory - 1964
Oldies 45 132 - Chained To Your Love / You're No Good - 1964

Betty Everett & Jerry Butler

Vee-Jay 633 - Smile / Love Is Strange – 1964
Vee-Jay 676 - Since I Don't Have You / Just Be True – 1965

Betty Everett

Vee-Jay 683 - The Real Thing / I'm Gonna Be Ready – 1965

Betty Everett & Jerry Butler

Vee-Jay 691 - Fever / The Way You Do The Things You Do – 1965
Oldies 45 303 - Let It Be Me / Ain't That Loving You Baby – 1965

Betty Everett

Oldies 45 320 - Shoop Shoop Song / Hands Off - 1965
Vee-Jay 699 - Too Hot To Hold / I Don't Hurt Anymore – 1965
Vee-Jay 716 - The Shoe Won't Fit / Trouble Over The Weekend – 1966
ABC 10829 - In Your Arms / Nothing I Wouldn't Do – 1967
ABC 10861 - Bye, Bye Baby* / Your Love Is Important To Me - 1967 *also recorded in 1960 by Mary Wells on Motown 1003.
ABC 10919 - Love Comes Tumbling Down / People Around Me – 1967
ABC 10978 - I Can't Say / My Baby Loving My Best Friend – 1967
Uni 55100 - There'll Come A Time / Take Me - 1968
Uni 55122 - I Can't Say No / Better Tomorrow Than Today – 1969
Uni 55141 - Maybe / 1900 Yesterday – 1969
Uni 55174 - It's Been A Long Time / Just A Man's Way – 1969

Uni 55189 - Sugar / Just Another Winter – 1969
Uni 55219 - Unlucky Girl / Better Tomorrow Than Today – 1970
Fantasy 652 - I Got To Tell Somebody / Why Are You Leaving Me – 1970
Fantasy 658 - Ain't Nothing Gonna Change Me / What Is It – 1970
Fantasy 667 - I'm A Woman / Prove It – 1971
Fantasy 687 - Black Girl / What Is It - 1972
Fantasy 687 - Black Girl / Innocent Bystanders – 1972
Fantasy 696 - Danger / Just A Matter Of Time Till You're Gone – 1972
Fantasy 714 - Sweet Dan / Who Will Your Next Fool Be – 1973
Fantasy 725 - Try It You'll Like It / Wondering – 1974
Fantasy 738 - Happy Endings / Keep It Up – 1975
Sound Stage 7 1520 - Hey Lucinda / My Love To Lean On – 1976
Sound Stage 7 2509 - Secrets / Prophecy – 1977
United Artists XW 1200 - True Love (You Took My Heart Away) / You Can Do It – 1977

Betty Everett & Jerry Butler

Eric 0169 - Let It Be Me / Smile - 1970's

Betty Everett

Eric 0170 - The Shoop Shoop Song (It's In His Kiss) / You're No Good - 1970's
20th Century Fox 2466 - Hungry For You / Think It Over Baby – 1980

Jerry Butler & Betty Everett

Collectables Col 014427 - Let It Be Me / Ain't That Loving You Baby - ?

Venue Reports - March 2001

Togetherness, Stoke On Trent, 3rd March, 2001.

"1500 People Can't Be Wrong". That's what the flyer said, and judging by what people I spoke to said, it was right. The only complaint I heard was that several records were repeated more than once throughout the night. Well, if you get 1500 people and that's the only complaint I have to agree. Very professional organisation, both in the main room and the smaller Modern room. My only complaint would be that the record Dealers can't hear the music at all.

Lea Manor, Albrighton 9th March, 2001.

Bumpy Thumpy heaven. Well actually, no, not this month. It was far far better this time. John Pugh started off with some Sixties and then mixed it up a bit, Kev Healey played a fabulous spot which was mostly Sixties and some quality Seventies. Ted Massey, the joker of the pack tonight. He played at least 40% Sixties, but unfortunately they were the same Sixties that he played two months ago (and in all honesty, was playing ten years ago !), and then played a couple of horrendous dance tracks that couldn't be called Soul by any stretch of the imagination. Onto the main guest, Dave Ripolles. I'd never heard him DJ before, and didn't know a lot of the records he played either. That doesn't mean they weren't any good, because this guy can actually tell the difference between Soul music, and Garage, and dance, and Soulful Garage, and House, and all the other tripe that people are insisting is good music these days. So he played a set of good Seventies Soul music in the main. He came across and introduced himself later on, and is a nice guy as well. John Pugh finished the night off in grand style with a few more Sixties and Seventies, and a few more Modern thing. So really the only downer of the night was the fact that three toerags managed to rob a couple of cars before being chased off and the Police called. All is not lost yet !

The Conference Centre, Llandudno, 17th March, 2001.

The first venture into Wales this year for me, and I was really looking forward to it. Picked up at Llandudno Junction station by John Mills, and then it was into the town for a drink, as you do. By 10 pm everything was ready to go. Dave from Crewe was the first DJ, and I felt a little sorry for him because the room was slow to fill up and nobody wanted to dance for the first hour. Sheila from Rotherham was next up, and she caused a little bit of controversy by playing bootlegs of rare records that other DJs who were on later had originals of. Never mind, she apologised later on. My spot went down well with a mixture of R & B, uptempo and midtempo Soul, then Clarence took over. Roger Banks, Pete Coulson, Bob Hinsley, Joan, and Robbo were the other DJs. Attendance was the best I've seen at Llandudno for a long time, the atmosphere was good, and everyone enjoyed themselves. Another winner for the Soul Dragon crew

Trentham Gardens, Stoke On Trent, 24th March, 2001.

Despite a very slow start it ended up quite a good night. Nige Mayfield was on much too early at 11.00 pm, but did a good spot nonetheless, Guy Hennigan played some of his old Stafford things, and some tracks that sounded suspiciously like Rock and Roll to me, but the star of the night was John Weston. Not because of what he played, but the way he did it. I'm not saying alcohol played it's part but draw your own conclusions: As usual John was dancing around behind the decks, with more enthusiasm than usual this time. So much so that he actually fell over twice ! The first time was the funniest because it happened just as the record was finishing, so he had to scramble to get up and start the next one. His cueing wasn't spot on either, playing the slip mat on at least one occasion. But the star turn of the night for me was when he announced Johnny Robinson, and had clearly forgotten the title of the record. A couple of seconds when his head went round in circles following the record, and then he announced it "Gone, But Not Forgotten". Oh yes it was !

The Dome, Tufnell Park, London, 30th March, 2001.

What a huge success this night is. Packed out completely by midnight, the whole place was rockin' by eleven O'clock. Music was excellent throughout with a 99% Sixties play list from all the DJs. Guest this month was 100 Club supremo Ady Croasdell, and he certainly did the business with an outstanding set. The big bonus for the night though was Sidney Barnes. What a nice person he is. He genuinely enjoyed chatting to people, and showed what a great performer he could be when he got on the stage for a couple of numbers. This was an added bonus because I wasn't expecting it, especially as Richard Searling was claiming a world exclusive later that weekend. All credit to Matt, David, Greg, Carl and Alan. You've got a major success, and deserve to enjoy it.

Group Line Ups

The Fantastic Four ('Sweet' James Epps, Joseph Pruitt, Robert Pruitt, Wallace 'Toby' Childs)
The Fascinations (Shirley Walker, Joanne Levell, Bernadine Boswell, Fern Bledsoe)
The Fashions (Barbara English,"Little" Frankie Brunson, Roger Andrews, Dave Thompson)
The Fiestas (Tommy Bullock, Eddie Morris, Sam Ingalls, Preston Lane, Randall Stewart)
The Five Stairsteps (Clarence Burke, Alohe Burke, James Burke, Kenneth Burke, Dennis

Burke, and later Cubie Burke)
The Formations (members Victor Drayton, Jerry Akines, Ernie Brooks, Reginald Turner and Johnny Bellman)
The Four Larks (Jackie Marshall, Weldon McDougal, Calvin Nicholls, Bill Oxedine)

The Fabulous Peps

Tom Storm & The Peps

Ge Ge 501 - That's The Way Love Is / I Love You - 1965

The Peps

Ge Ge 503 - This Love I Have For You / She's Going To Leave You - 1965

The Peps

D - Town 1049 - You Never Had It So Good / Detroit, Michigan - 1965
D - Town 1060 - Thinking About You / This I Pray - 1965

The Fabulous Peps

D - Town 1065 - My Love Looks Good On You / Speak Your Peace - 1966
Premium Stuff 1 - Why Are You Blowing My Mind / I Can't Get Right - 1967
Premium Stuff 3 - So Fine / I'll Never Be The Same Again - 1967
Premium Stuff 7 - Gypsy Woman / Why Are You Blowing My Mind - 1967
Wee-3 233 - With These Eyes / I've Been Trying - 1967
Wheelsville 109 - With These Eyes / Light Of My Life - 1968

The Falcons

The Falcons (members Bob Manardo (born Robert Manardo died 6-March-2004 in Warren, Michigan - cause: cancer), Eddie Floyd, Tom Shetler, Arnett Robinson and Willie Schofield)
Mercury 70940 - Baby That's It / This Day - 1956 (after this release Bob Manardo is drafted and Tom Shetler volunteers)
The Falcons (members Joe Stubbs, Eddie Floyd, Lance Finnie, Arnett Robinson and Willie Schofield)
The Falcons And Orchestra (members Joe Stubbs a former member of The Fabulous Four (born Joseph Stubbles in 1942 - died 19-January-1998 age 56 - cause: complications from heart disease - he was he brother of Levi Stubbs of The Four Tops), Eddie Floyd, Lance Finnie a former member of The Fabulous Four, Willie Schofield and Bonny "Mack" Rice -- a former member of The Five Scalders on Drummond)

Silhouette 521/522 - Sent Up / Can This Be Christmas* - 1957 * flip has the same number (Silhouette 521 I I 2) as a 1957 release by The Charmers "Rock, Rhythm and Blues / Letters Don't Have Arms".
The Falcons (members Joe Stubbs, Eddie Floyd, Lance Finnie, Willie Schofield and Bonny "Mack" Rice)

Kudo 661 - This Heart Of Mine / Romanita - 1958

The Falcons Musical Direction Sax Kari

Flick 001 - You're So Fine* / Goddess Of Angels - 1959 *also recorded in 1963 by Dorothy Berry on Challenge 59221.

The Falcons And Orchestra

Flick 001 - You're So Fine* / Goddess Of Angels - 1959 (red label with address 8424 Gallagher Detroit 14, Michigan)

The Falcons (members Joe Stubbs, Eddie Floyd, Lance Finnie, Willie Schofield and Bonny "Mack" Rice)

Unart 2013 - You're So Fine / Goddess Of Angels - 1959
Unart 2013-S - You're So Fine / Goddess Of Angels - 1959
Flick 008 - You Must Know I Love You / That's What I Aim To Do - 1959
Unart 2022 - You're Mine / Country Shack - 1959
United Artists 2013 - You're So Fine / Goddess Of Angels - 1959
Chess 1743 - Just For Your Love / This Heart Of Mine - 1959
Anna 110 - Just For Your Love / This Heart Of Mine - 1959
United Artists EP 10010 - The Teacher / Waiting For You //// You're So Fine / Goddess Of Angels - 1959
United Artists 229 - Waiting For You / The Teacher - 1960
United Artists 255 - I + Love + You / Wonderful Love - 1960

The Falcons (members Wilson Pickett, Eddie Floyd, Lance Finnie, Willie Schofield and Bonny "Mack" Rice)

United Artists 289 - Workin' Man's Song / Pow! You're In Love - 1960 (Joe Stubbs leaves group)

The Falcons (members Joe Stubbs, Eddie Floyd, Lance Finnie, Willie Schofield and Bonny "Mack" Rice)

United Artists 420 - You're So Fine / Goddess Of Angels - 1962

The Falcons & Band (Ohio Untouchables) (members Wilson Pickett, Eddie Floyd, Lance Finnie, Willie Schofield and Bonny "Mack" Rice)

Lupine 103 - I Found A Love* / Swim - 1962 * *released in the U. K. as "I Found Your Love" on London American HLK 9565 --- also recorded in 196? by Joe Woods on Hit-Pack 437.
Lupine 1003 - I Found A Love / Swing - 1962 (Same as the previous release but with a misspelt title)

The Newports (members Wilson Pickett, Eddie Floyd, Lance Finnie, Willie Schofield and Bonny "Mack" Rice)

Contour 301 - Hurry Arthur Murray / Chicky Chop Chop - 1959

The Falcons (members Wilson Pickett, Eddie Floyd, Lance Finnie, Ben Knight and Bonny "Mack" Rice)

Atlantic 2153 - Lah - Tee - Lah - Tah / Darling - 1962

The Falcons (members Wilson Pickett, Gene "Earl" Martin, Lance Finnie, Ben Knight and Bonny "Mack" Rice)

Atlantic 2179 - Take This Love I've Got / Let's Kiss And Make Up - 1963

The Falcons (members Carlis "Sonny" Monroe, James "Ooh Wee" Gibson, Johnny Alvin and Alton "Bart" Hollowell a former member of The Enchanters on CORAL)

Atlantic 2207 - Oh Baby / Fine Fine Girl - 1963 (after this release Willie Schofield gets drafted -- group disbands -- but Robert West refuses to let group die, he takes a group known as The Fabulous Playboys (who recorded on Daco, Apollo and Contour and were The Ramblers on Federal) and made them The Falcons)

The Falcons (members Joe Stubbs, Eddie Floyd, Lance Finnie, Willie Schofield and Bonny "Mack" Rice)

United Artists 1624 - You're So Fine / Goddess Of Angels - 1964

The Falcons (members Carlis "Sonny" Monroe, James "Ooh Wee" Gibson, Johnny Alvin and Alton "Bart" Hollowell)

Lu Pine 124 - Has It Happened To You Yet / Lonely Nights - 1964 (lead Carlis Monroe)

Wilson Pickett and The Falcons (members Wilson Pickett, Eddie Floyd, Lance Finnie, Willie Schofield and Bonny "Mack" Rice)

Lu Pine 003 - You're On My Mind / Anna - 1965

The Falcons (members Carlis "Sonny" Monroe, James "Ooh Wee" Gibson, Johnny Alvin and Alton "Bart" Hollowell)

Lu Pine 1020 - Lonely Nights / Has It Happened To You Yet - ?

The Falcons (members Wilson Pickett, Eddie Floyd, Lance Finnie, Willie Schofield and Bonny "Mack" Rice)

Lu Pine 5986 - I Found A Love / ? - ?

The Falcons (members Carlis "Sonny" Monroe, James "Ooh Wee" Gibson, Johnny Alvin and Alton "Bart" Hollowell)

Big Wheel 321 - (I'm A Fool) I Must Love You / Love, Love, Love - 1966
Big Wheel 322 - (I'm A Fool) I Must Love You / Love, Love, Love - 1966
Big Wheel 323 - I Can't Help It / Standing On Guard - 1966
Big Wheel 324 - I Can't Help It / Standing On Guard - 1966
Big Wheel 1967 - Standing On Guard / I Can't Help It - 1966

Sandy Hollis

Big Wheel 1968 - I'm Tempted / Tables Will Turn - 1967 (backing vocals by The Falcons)

The Falcons (members Carlis "Sonny" Monroe, James "Ooh Wee" Gibson, Johnny Alvin and Alton "Bart" Hollowell)

Big Wheel 1971 - Love Look In Her Eyes / In Time For The Blues - 1967
National Sound Corporation - Good Good Feeling / ? - ? (acetate with plain label showing group name handwritten --- phone number and address on label (313) 336-3800. 17610 West Warren Detroit, MI 48228)
Big Wheel 1972 - Good Good Feeling / Love Like You Never Been Loved - 1967
Rowe Ami - Play Me - Jukebox Promotional Sales Stimulator - ? (red vinyl - no number, promo only, less than sixty seconds long)
Carl 504 - My Heart Is Open / We Stopped And Thought It Over - ?
The Firestones (members Carlis "Sonny" Monroe, James "Ooh Wee" Gibson, Johnny Alvin and Alton "Bart" Hollowell)
Moira 102 - I Just Can't Wait / Buy Now Pay Later Plan - 1970
The Falcons (members

Relic 1036 - You're So Fine / ? - 1978
The Falcons & Band (Ohio Untouchables) (members Wilson Pickett, Eddie Floyd, Lance Finnie, Willie Schofield and Bonny "Mack" Rice)
Relic 1037 - I Found A Love / Swim - 1978
The Falcons & Band (Ohio Untouchables) / Chris Kenner
Atlantic Os13112 - I Found A Love / Land Of 1000 Dances* - ? *flip by Chris Kenner. (Oldies Series)

The Falcons / The Falcons & Band (Ohio Untouchables)

Collectables Col 3385 - You're So Fine / I Found A Love* - ? *flip by The Falcons & Band (Ohio Untouchables)

The Miracles / The Falcons (members Joe Stubbs, Eddie Floyd, Lance Finnie, Willie Schofield and Bonny "Mack" Rice)

Teen 2 - The Christmas Song / Can This Be Christmas* - ? *flip by The Falcons (early re-release)

The Fantastic Four

Ric-Tic 113 - Can't Stop Looking For My Baby (Part 1) / Can't Stop Looking For My Baby (Part 2) - 1966 (Only Rumoured To Exist)
Ric-Tic 119 - Girl Have Pity / (I'm Gonna) Live Up To What She Thinks - 1967
Ric-Tic 121 - Can't Stop Looking For My Baby / Just The Lonely - 1967
Ric-Tic 122 - Ain't Love Wonderful / The Whole World Is A Stage - 1967
Ric-Tic 128 - You Gave Me Something / I Don't Want To Live Without You - 1967
Ric-Tic 130 - As Long As I Live (I Live For You) / To Share Your Love - 1967
Ric-Tic 134 - As Long As The Feeling Is There / Goddess Of Love - 1968
Ric-Tic 136 - Goddesss Of Love / Love Is A Many Splendored Thing - 1968
Ric-Tic 137 - Man In Love / No Love Like Your Love - 1968
Ric-Tic 139 - I've Got To Have You / Win Or Lose (I'm Going To Love You) - 1968
Ric-Tic 144 - I Love You Madly / I Love You Madly (Instrumental) - 1968
Soul 35052 - I Love You Madly / I Love You Madly (Instrumental) - 1968
Soul 35058 - I Feel Like I'm Falling In Love Again / Pin Point It Down - 1969
Soul 35065 - Just Another Lonely Night / Don't Care Why You Want Me - 1969
Soul 35072 - On The Brighter Side Of A Blue World / I'm Gonna Caryy On - 1970
Eastbound 609 - If You Need Me, Call Me (And I'll Come Running) / I Had This Whole World To Choose From (And I Chose You) - 1973
Eastbound 620 - I'm Fallin' In Love (I Feel Good All Over) / I Believe In Miracles (I Believe In You) - 1974
Westbound 5009 - Alvin Stone (The Birth And Death Of A Gangster) / I Believe In Miracles (I Believe In You) - 1975
Westbound 5017 - Have A Little Mercy / County Line - 1975
Westbound 5030 - They Took The Show On The Road / Don't Risk Your Happiness On Foolishness - 1976
Westbound 5032 - (Meet Me At The) Hideaway / They Took The Show On The Road - 1976
Westbound 55403 - I Got To Have Your Love / Ain't I Been Good To You - 1977
Westbound 55408 - Mixed Up Moods And Attitudes / Disco Pool Blues - 1978
Westbound 55417 - Sexy Lady / If This Is Love - 1979
Westbound 55419 - B. Y. O. F. Bring Your Own Funk / If This Is Love - 1979

The Fascinations

The Sabre-Ettes (Members Martha Reeves, Shirley Walker, Maxine Wood And ?)

The Boswell Sisters (Members Bernadine Boswell, Joanne Levell and one other Sister ?)

The Sabre-Ettes (Members Martha Reeves, Shirley Walker, Bernadine Boswell, Joanne Levell and Fern Bledsoe (A former secretary at Motown)) Group survived for roughly one year (1960 Roughly) singing at The Broadway Sportman Club)

The Fasinations (Members Shilrley Walker, Joanne Levell, Bernadine Boswell And Fern Bledsoe) Group Originated From Detroit, Michigan. Shirley Walker Formed Group In 1960.

ABC-Paramount 10387 - Mama Didn't Lie / Someone Like You – 1962

The Fascinations (Members Shilrley Walker, Joanne Levell, Bernadine Boswell And Fern Bledsoe)

ABC-Paramount 10387 - Mama Didn't Lie / Someone Like You – 1962
ABC-Paramount 10443 - Tears In My Eyes / You Gonna Be Sorry – 1962

The Aprils (Members Fern Bledsoe, ...)

Ran-Dee 121/122 -I Want To Know / Precious Love - 1964

Fern & The Aprils (Members Fern Bledsoe, ...)

Ran-Dee 123/124 - Gotta Be In Love / I Want To Know - 1964

Shirley Lawson (Shirley Walker)

Enterprise 5040 - So Much To Me / Sad Sad Day – 1965
Back Beat 567 - The Star / One More Chance - 1966

The Fascinations (Members Shirley Walker, Joanne Levell, Bernadine Boswell And Fern Bledsoe)

Mayfield 7711 - Lucky (Instrumental) / I'm So Lucky - 1966 (Demo Copies Only)
Mayfield 7711 - (Say It Isn't So) Say You'd Never Go / I'm So Lucky (He Loves Me) – 1966
Mayfield 7714 - Girls Are Out To Get You* / You'll Be Sorry - 1967 *With Donny Hathaway On Piano.
Mayfield 7716 - I'm In Love / I Can't Stay Away – 1967
Mayfield 7718 - Hold On / Such A Fool – 1968
Mayfield 7719 - Just Another Reason / Ok For You - 1968

We're fairly sure that it's not the same group who released the following singles, but is there a connection

The Fascinations

Sure 106 - It's Midnight / Boom Bada Boom - 1960 (Scarcer Copy) (A white male group from Akron, Ohio)
Sure 106 - Midnight / Boom Bada Boom - 1960

The Fascinations

Paxley 750 - If I Had Your Love / Why - 1960
Dore 593 - If I Had Your Love / Why - 1961

Cecil Garrett & The Fascinations (Members

Calla 107 - Bearcat (Part 1) / Bearcat (Part 2) - ?

The Fascinations

A & G 101 - Since You Went Away / I'm Gonna Cry – 1972 (A male group from Brooklyn, NY)
Info from Tony D'Ambrosio:
The Fascinations on A & G 101 were a male group from Brooklyn, NY. Both sides of A&G 101 were recorded for Al Browne in 1959; I released them (A&G was my label) in 1972. The real name of the group was not the Fascinations. When Al Browne and I were going through his master tapes, there was no name for the group on these two sides. I named them the Fascinations, after a few other collectors told me they sounded somewhat like the Fascinators, another Brooklyn group. Less than 150 copies of the record survived a heating system flood that occurred a few years after the records were pressed. Originally 500 were pressed.

Jordon & The Fascinations (Formed from members of the Sure label group and The Boulevards from Queens, NY)

Crystal Ball 123 - Goodnight / One-Two-Three - 1978 (500 Black Vinyl And 25 Red Vinyl Copies Made Only)

The Fiestas

The Fiestas (members Tommy Bullock (lead), Eddie Morris (first tenor), Sam Ingalls (baritone) and Preston Lane (bass))

Old Town 1062 - So Fine* / Last Night I Dreamed - 1958 (versions pressed by Columbia have a piano intro not available elsewhere. Look for ZTSP on label) *written by Jesse Belvin -- cover of 1955 track by The Sheiks on Federal 12237.
Old Town 1062 - So Fine* / Last Night I Dreamed - 1958 (standard version no ZTSP on label) *also recorded in 1964 by The Santells on Courier 115.
Old Town 1069 - Our Anniversary / I'm Your Slave – 1959
Old Town 1074 - Good News / That Was Me - 1959
Old Town 1080 - Dollar Bill / It Don't Make Sense - 1960

The Fiestas (members Bobby Moore (lead),Tommy Bullock (tenor), Eddie Morris (second tenor), Sam Ingalls (baritone) and Preston Lane (bass))

Old Town 1090 - You Could Be My Girl Friend / So Nice - 1960

The Fiestas (members Bobby Moore (lead), Jimmy Jones (tenor), Wesley Lee (baritone) and Preston Lane (bass))

Strand 25046 - Come On Everybody / Julie - 1961

The Fiestas (members Tommy Bullock (lead), Jimmy Jones (tenor), Eddie Morris (second tenor), George Bullock and Randall "Randy" Stewart)

Old Town 1104 - Look At That Girl / Mr. Dillon, Mr. Dillon -1961
Old Town 1111 - She's Mine / The Hobo's Prayer - 1961

Tommy Andre (Tommy Bullock)

Old Town 1116 - I Wonder Why / I'm Wondering - 1962

The Fiestas (members Tommy Bullock, Eddie Morris, Sam Ingalls and Preston Lane (born 1939 in Statonsburg, North Carolina --- died 27-October-2006 in New Jersey --- cause: ?))

Old Town 1122 - The Railroad Song / Broken Heart - 1962

The Fiestas (members Tommy Bullock, Eddie Morris, Sam Ingalls and Preston Lane)

Old Town 1127 - I Feel Good All Over / Look At That Girl - 1962
Old Town 1134 - The Gypsy Said / Mama Put The Law Down – 1963
Old Town 1140 - The Party's Over / Try It One More Time – 1963
Old Town 1148 - Foolish Dreamer / Rock - A - Bye Baby – 1963
Old Town 1166 - All That's Good / Rock - A - Bye Baby – 1964
Old Town 1178 - Think Smart / Anna* - 1965 *also recorded in 1962 by Arthur Alexander on Dot 16387 and in 1964 by The Beatles on Vee-Jay (Spec. DJ No. 8)
Old Town 1187 - Love Is Strange / Love Is Good To Me – 1965
Old Town 1189 - I Gotta Have Your Lovin' / Ain't She Sweet - 1965

Tommy & Cleve (Tommy Bullock and Cleveland Horne (later member of The Fantastic Four))

Checker 1154 - I Don't Want To Share Your Love / Boo-Ga-Loo Baby - 1966
Checker 1177 - Bird Dog* / At The Party - 1967 *also recorded in 1958 by The Everly Brothers on Cadence 1350.

Tommy Andre (Tommy Bullock)

Broadway 406 - One More Try / Blue Print - 1967
Broadway 503 - One More Try / Blue Print - 1967

The Fabulous Fiestas (members

DHC 107 - One Hurt Deserves Another / Keep It In The Family (If It Don't Fit, Don't Force It) - 1970
RCA 74-0364 - One Hurt Deserves Another / Keep It In The Family (If It Don't Fit, Don't Force It) - 1970

The Fiestas (members

Cotillion 44117 - So Fine / Broken Heart – 1971
Vigor 712 - So Fine / Darling You've Changed - 1974 (Tommy Bullock rejoins group on this rendition of "So Fine")
Respect 2509 - Sometimes Storm / I Can't Shake Your Love (Can't Shake You Loose) - 1975
Chimneyville 10216 - Tina (The Disco Queen)* / I'm No Better Than You - 1977 *With The Chimneyville Express Rhythm Section. Track written by Mack Rice.
Chimneyville 10221 - Is That Long Enough For You / I'm Gonna Hate Myself – 1977
Arista 0369 - Esp / One More Chance – 1978
Arista 0400 - Thanks For The Sweet Memories / One More Chance – 1978

Larry Finnegan / The Fiestas

Eric 287 - Dear One / So Fine* - ? *Flip By The Fiestas.

The Fiestas / Robert & Johnny

Atlantic 13115 - So Fine / We Belong Together - ?

The Fiestas (members Tommy Bullock, Eddie Morris, Sam Ingalls and Preston Lane)

Collectables Col 010377 - So Fine / Last Night I Dreamed - ?

The Fiestas (members Bobby Moore, Tommy Bullock, Kenny Harper and Wendell Scott) 1996

The Fiestas (members Bobby Moore, Wayne Parham, Kenny Harper and Wendell Scott) 2002

First Choice

The Debronettes (Members Rochelle Fleming, Annette Guest, Joyce Jones)

The Silver Rings (Members Rochelle Fleming, Annette Guest, Joyce Jones)

First Choice (Members Rochelle Fleming, Annette Guest, Joyce Jones And Wardell Piper (Unsure when he left group)) Also Mulaney Star was an early member of the group - unsure if she was on any recordings

Scepter 12347 - This Is The House (Where Love Died) / One Step Away – 1972
Philly Groove 175 - Armed & Extremely Dangerous / Gonna Keep On Lovin' Him – 1973
Philly Groove 179 - Smarty Pants / One Step Away – 1973
Philly Groove 183 - Newsy Neighbours / This Little Woman – 1974
Philly Groove 200 - The Player (Part 1) / The Player (Part 2) – 1974
Philly Groove 202 - Guilty / Wake Up To Me – 1974
Philly Groove 204 - Love Freeze / A Boy Named Junior – 1975
Warner Bros. 8214 - Gotta Get Away (From You Baby) / Yes, Maybe Not – 1976
Warner Bros. 8251 - Let Him Go / First Choice Theme - 1976 (Around this time Joyce jones leaves group and is replaced by Ursula Herring)
Gold Mind 4004 - Doctor Love / I Love You More Than Before – 1977
Gold Mind 12g-4004 - Dr. Love (7:35) / Dr. Love (2:38) - 1977 (12" Release)
Gold Mind 4009 - Love Having You Around / Indian Giver – 1977
Gold Mind Gg 4009 - Love Having You Around / ? - 1977 (12" Release)
Gold Mind 4017 - Hold Your Horses / Now I've Thrown It All Away – 1979
Gold Mind Gg 401 - Hold Your Horses (5:50) / Hold Your Horses (2:44) - 1979 (12" Release)
Gold Mind 4019 - Double Cross / Game Of Love - 1979 (Around this time Ursula Herring leaves group and is replaced by Debbie Martin)
Gold Mind Gg 404 - Double Cross / ? - 1979 (12" Release)
Gold Mind Gg 405 - Double Cross (7:43) / Double Cross (6:59) - 1979 (12" Release)
Gold Mind 4022 - Love Thang / Great Expectations – 1980
Gold Mind Gg 502 - Love Thang (8:04) / Great Expectations - 1980 (12" Release)
Gold Mind 4023 - Breakaway / House For Sale - 1980.
Gold Mind Gg 504 - Breakaway (6:56) / (Instrumental - 6:56) - 1980 (12" Release)

Wardell Piper

Midsong Int'l Md-501 - Captain Boogie / Captain Boogie - 1979 (12" Release)
Midsong Int'l 1001 - Captain Boogie (Short Version) (3:33) / Captain Boogie (Long Version) (5:31) – 1979
Midsong Int'l Md-508 - Super Sweet / Super Sweet - 1979 (12" Release)
Midsong Int'l 1005- Super Sweet / Don't Turn Away From Me Baby -1979
Midsong Int'l 72000 - Gimme Something Real / ? - ?
Sam 12355 - Come On Back To Mama / ? - 1983 (12" Release)

First Choice

First Choice 1983 (12" Release)

Wardell Piper

Prelude Prld 413 - Nobody (Can Take You From Me) / ? - 1984 (12" Release)
Prelude Prld 686 - Nobody (Can Take You From Me) (5:57) / Sensual Trash (4:49) - ? (12" Release)

First Choice

Salsoul Sg 397 - Let No Man Put Asunder (Vocal)(7:25) Let No Man Put Asunder (Instrumental) (Remix By Shep Pettibone) / Let No Man Put Asunder (Acapella) /// Let No Man Put Asunder (Vocal) (7:00) / Let No Man Put Asunder (Instrumental) (Remix By Frankie Knuckles)- 1984 (12" Release)

Salsoul Sg 404 - Double Cross / ? - 1984 (12" Release)
Salsoul Sg 411 - Let No Man Put Asunder (Remix) (7"58) / Let Me Down Easy - 1984 912" Release)

First Choice Featuring Rochelle Fleming

Salsoul Sg 419 - Dr. Love (Special Remix - 7:47) / Dr. Love (Mega Dub Remix - 8:15) - 1984 (12" Release)

Rochelle Fleming

Prelude Prld 700 - Love Itch (7:46) / Love Itch (Instrumental - 3:32) /// Love Itch (Dub Mix - 3:58) / Love Itch (Short Version - 5:22) - 1985 (12" Release)

First Choice

Flashback 88 - Armed & Extremely Dangerous / Smarty Pants - ?
Sophie 586001/586002 - Something Called Love / Alone Again – 1986

First Choice (Group Reforms Around 1987 Members Rochelle Fleming, Laconya Fleming And Lawrence Cottel)

First Choice

Double J / New Generation Salsoul 2574-1 - (Disc One) Dr. Love (Love Mix) (12:14) / Dr. Love (Robapella Mix) (5:52) /// Dr. Love (David's Jam) (11:55) / Dr. Love (C&C Theme) (6:40)

(Disc Two) Dr. Love (Dr. Dub) (8:37) / Dr. Love (Acapella Mix) (5:54) /// Dr. Love (Lp Version) (7:25) / Dr. Love (Radio Version) (3:38) / Dr. Love (David's Theme) (4:38) - 1993 (Double 12" Single Release)

First Choice Featuring Rochelle Fleming

Double J / New Generation Salsoul 5599-1 - Double Cross (Club Mix) (6:06) / Double Cross (Swing Mix) (8:27) / Double Cross (Percapella Mix) (5:59) /// Double Cross (Flute Dub) (6:04) / Double Cross (Techno Dub) (5:55) / Double Cross (Traxx Mix) (5:50) - 1993 (12" Single Release)

First Choice

Unidisc Spec-1693 - Double Cross (Remix) (8:11) /// Love Thang (Original) (7:55) / Love Thang (Remix) (8:16) - 1994 (12" Release)
On The Beat 2291-2 - Armed & Extremely Dangerous (Full Intention Radio Edit) / Armed & Extremely Dangerous (Blow Out Soul Mix) / Armed & Extremely Dangerous (Original Version) / Armed & Extremely Dangerous (Full Intention Vocal) / Armed & Extremely Dangerous (Cevin's Classic Club) / Armed & Extremely Dangerous (Black Science Restoration Vocal) / Armed & Extremely Dangerous (The South Beach Cool Out Jazz Mix) / Armed & Extremely Dangerous

(Dj D's...) - 1997 (Cd Single)
Salsoul 20-6500-1 - Double Cross (Original Mix) (7:02) / Double Cross (Rhythm Track) (4:01) / Double Cross (Strings & Horns) (1:12) /// Double Cross (Instrumental) (6:11) / Double Cross (Bass & Drums) (1:52) / Double Cross (Acapella) (4:38) / Double Cross (Background Vocals) (0:59) - ?
Salsoul 20-6505-1 - Love Thang (Original Mix) (7:57) / Love Thang (Acapella) (6:10) /// Love Thang (Instrumental) (5:40) / Love Thang (Rhythm Track) (3:39) / Love Thang (Bass & Drums) (2:02) / Love Thang (Strings & Horns) (2:29) / Love Thang (Backgrounds) (1:07) - 2001 (12" Release)

The Five Du-Tones

The Five Du-Tones (members Robert Hopkins (group founder), LeRoy Joyce, Willie Guest, Oscar Watson and James West) 1957 line-up.

The Five Du-Tones (members Andrew Butler, Frank McCurrey, Willie Guest, LeRoy Joyce and James West)

One-Derful 4811 - Please Change Your Mind / The Flea - 1963
One-Derful 4814 - Come Back Baby / Dry Your Eyes – 1963
One-Derful 4815 - Shake A Tail Feather / Divorce Court - 1963 (the hectic pace of touring was attributed to the death of James West who died of heart failure at the end of 1963 at age 28, he was replaced by David Scott)
One-Derful 4818 - The Gouster / Monkey See - Monkey Do – 1964
One-Derful 4821 - Nobody But (My Baby) / Thats How I Love You – 1964
One-Derful 4824 - The Cool Bird / The Chicken Astronaut – 1964
One-Derful 4828 - Sweet Lips / Let Me Love You – 1965
One-Derful 4831 - We Want More / The Woodbine Twine – 1965

Tony Diamond (David Scott)

Blue Rock 4019 - Don't Turn Away / You're The Smartest Yet - 1965

The Five Du-Tones (members Andrew Butler, Frank McCurrey, Willie Guest, LeRoy Joyce and David Scott)

One-Derful 4836 - Mountain Of Love / Outside The Record Hop – 1966
Lost Nite Ln-196 - Shake A Tail Feather* / Divorce Court - ? *also recorded by The Debutantes on Standout 601.

Sidney Pinchback

Twinight 114 - Remind Me / Soul Strokes – 1969

Lucky Cordell / Sidney Pinchback & The Sisters

Cotillion 45-44052 - This Is The Woman I Love / This Is The Woman I Love* - 1969 *flip by Sidney Pinchback & The Sisters (promo issue)

South Shore Commission (members Frank McCurrey, Sheryl Henry, Sidney "Pinchback" Lennear, Eugene Rogers, David Henderson and Warren Haygood) this group was actually formed in 1960 in Washington, DC, as The Exciters. In 1965 they became a back-up band for The Five Du-Tones and were signed to the One-Derful label in Chicago. When The Five Du-Tones broke up in 1967 Frank McCurry joined The Exciters and they became The South Shore Commission.

Atlantic 2684 - Right On Brother Pt. 1 / Right On Brother Pt. 2 – 1970

Sidney Pinchback & South Shore Commission

Nickel 1003 - This Is The Woman / Shadows - 1971

South Shore Commission

Wand Wdt-11287 - Free Man - 1975 (12" One Sided Promo, Apparently As An Acetate Only)
Wand 11287 - Free Man (3:10) / Free Man (Disco Mix) (5:35) - 1975
Wand 11291 - We're On The Right Track / I'd Rather Switch Than Fight - 1976.
Wand 11294 - Train Called Freedom / Train Called Freedom (Disco Mix) – 1976
Wand Wdt-11294 - Train Called Freedom (Disco Version) (5:10) / Train Called Freedom (Disco Version) (5:10) - 1975 (12" Release)
Wave Music 500009-1 - Free Man (Francois K. Edit) / Free Man (Original Version) - 1996 (12" release)

The Five Stairsteps

The Five Stairsteps (Clarence, Alohe, James, Kenneth And Dennis Burke)

Windy "C" 601 - You Waited Too Long / Don't Waste Your Time - 1966
Windy "C" 602 - World Of Fantasy / Playgirl's Love - 1966
Windy "C" 603 - Come Back / You Don't Love Me - 1966
Windy "C" 604 - Danger, She's A Stranger / Behind Curtains - 1967
Windy "C" 605 - Ain't Gonna Rest (Till I Get You) / You Can't See - 1967
Windy "C" 607 - Oooh, Baby Baby / The Girl I Love - 1967
Windy "C" 608 - The Touch Of You / Change Of Face - 1967

The Five Stairsteps And Cubie (Cubie Joins Group At Age Two!)

Buddah 20 - Something's Missing / Tell Me Who - 1967
Buddah 26 - A Million To One / You Make Me So Mad - 1968
Buddah 35 - The Shadow Of Your Love / Bad News - 1968
Curtom 1931 - Don't Change Your Love / New Dance Craze - 1968
Curtom 1933 - Stay Close To Me / I Made A Mistake - 1968
Curtom 1936 - Baby Make Me Feel So Good / Little Young Lover - 1969
Curtom 1944 - Madame Mary / Little Boy Blue - 1969

The Five Stairsteps

Curtom 1945 - We Must Be In Love / Little Young Lover - 1969
Buddah 165 - Dear Prudence / O-O-H Child - 1970

The Stairsteps

Buddah 165 - Who Do You Belong To / O-O-H Child - 1970
Buddah 188 - Because I Love You / America Standing - 1970
Buddah 213 - Didn't It Look So Easy / Peace Is Gonna Come - 1971
Buddah 222 - Snow / Look Out - 1971
Buddah 277 - I Love You - Stop / I Feel A Song (In My Heart Again) - 1972
Buddah 291 - Hush Child / The Easy Way - 1972
Buddah 320 - Every Single Way / Two Week's Notice - 1972

Dark Horse 10005 - From Us To You / Time - 1975
Dark Horse 10009 - Tell Me Why / Salaam - 1976

The Five Stairsteps / The Stories

Eric 218 - O-O-H Child / Brother Louie* - ? *Flip By The Stories.

Keni Burke (Kenneth Burke Solo)

Dark Horse 8474 - Shuffle / From Me To You - 1977

Dark Horse 8522 -Keep On Singing / Day - 1978

The Invisible Man's Band (Clarence *Lead,* James, Kenneth And Dennis Burke)

Mango 103 - All Night Thing (Part 1) / All Night Thing (Part 2) -1980
Move 'N' Groove 451 - Sunday Afternoon / Sunday Afternoon - 198? (Promo Issue)

Keni Burke

Rca 12228 - Let Somebody Love You / (Instrumental) - 1981

Rca Pd-12229 - Let Somebody Love You (5:05) (Vocal) / Let Somebody Love You (5:18) (Instrumental) - 1981 (12"Release)

The Invisible Man's Band

Board Walk 7-11-127 - Rated X / Same Thing - 1981
Board Walk 7-11-137 - Really Wanna See You / Along The Way - 1981

Keni Burke

RCA 13271 - Risin' To The Top / Can't Get Enough - 1982
RCA Jt 13272 - Risin' To The Top / ? - 1982 (12"Release)
RCA 13090 - Shakin' / Gotta Find My Way Back - 1982
RCA ? - Shakin' / Shakin' - ? (12" Release)
RCAa ? - Gotta Find My Way Back / The Best - ? (12" Release)

The Invisible Man's Band

Move'n Ng. 004 - Sunday Afternoon / ? - 1983

Cubie Burke

Rissa Chrissa ? - 1983 (12" Single)

Keni Burke

Expansion ? - I Need Your Love - ?

Ken Burke

Quadrille Q-868 - You Are The Woman / ? - ?
Quadrille Q-878 - Dance With Who Brung You / ? - ?

Wade Flemons

The Newcomers (members Wade Flemons ....) R&B group formed by Wade Flemons in 1955

Wade Flemons and The Newcomers (members Wade Flemmons,...)

Vee Jay 295 - My Baby Likes To Rock / Here I Stand - 1958

Wade Flemons (born 25-September-1940 in Coffeyville, Kansas. Died 13-October-1993)

Vee Jay 309 - Hold Me Close / You'll Remain Forever - 1959
Vee Jay 321 - Slow Motion / Walking By The River - 1959
Vee Jay 335 - Goodnite, It's Time To Go / What's Happening - 1959
Vee Jay 344 - Easy Lovin' / Woops Now - 1960 (released in Canada on Delta D-3097x)
Vee Jay 368 - Ain't That Lovin' You Baby / I'll Come Runnin' - 1960
Vee Jay 377 - At The Party / Devil In Your Soul - 1961
Vee Jay 389 - Please Send Me Someone To Love* / Keep On Loving Me - 1961 *cover of 1950 Percy Mayfield hit on Speciality 375.
Vee Jay 427 - Half A Love / Welcome Stranger - 1962
Vee Jay 471 - Ain't These Tears / I Hope, I Think, I Wish - 1962
Vee Jay 533 - That Time Of The Year / I Came Running (Back From The Party) - 1963
Vee Jay 578 - Watch Over Her / When It Rains, It Pours - 1964 (with The Four Seasons on backup vocals)
Vee Jay 614 - That Other Place / I Knew You When - 1964

Rosie & The Originals / Wade Flemons

Oldies 45 24 - Angel Baby / Keep On Lovin' Me* - 1964 *flip by Wade Flemons

Bobby Day / Wade Flemons

Oldies 45 38 - Rockin' Robin / Keep On Lovin Me - 1964

Wade Flemons & The Newcomers / The Vocaleers

Oldies 45 118 - My Baby Likes To Rock / Be True* - 1964 *flip by The Vocaleers.

The Velvets / Wade Flemons

Oldies 45 119 - I / Woops Now* - 1964 *flip by Wade Flemons.

The Skyliners / Wade Flemons

Oldies 45 123 - Pennies From Heaven / Here I Stand* - 1964 *flip by Wade Flemons

Wade Flemons

Oldies 45 133 - Woops Now / Easy Love - 1964
Vee Jay 668 - Where Did You Go Last Night / Empty Balcony - 1965

Wade Flemons

Ramsel 1001 - Jeanette / What A Price To Pay - 1967
Ramsel 1002 - Two Of A Kind / I Knew You'd Be Mine - 1967

The Salty Peppers (members Maurice White, Verdine White, Wade Flemons and Don Whitehead)

Tec 1014 - La, La, La (Part 1) / La, La, La (Part 2) - 1969
Capitol 2433 - La La Time / La La Time - 1969
Capitol 2568 - Your Love Is Life / Uh Huh Yeah - 1969

Wade Flemons / Jimmy Hughes

Trip 47 - Here I Stand / Steal Away* - 1971 *flip by Jimmy Hughes

Bettye Swann / Wade Flemons

Collectables Col 031537 - Make Me Yours / Here I Stand* - ? *flip by Wade Flemons.

Wade Flemons

Stardust 25 - Welcome Stranger / Half A Love - ?

Wade Flemons / Foster Sylver

Stardust 130 - That Other Place / I'm Your Puppet* - ? *flip by Foster Sylver.

Darrow Fletcher

Darrow Fletcher (born 23-January-1951 in Inkster, Michigan - Rose Battiste's cousin)

Groovy 3001 - The Pain Gets A Little Deeper / My Judgement Day - 1966
Groovy 3004 - My Young Misery / I Gotta Know Why – 1966
Groovy 3007 - Gotta Draw The Line* / I Gotta Know Why - 1966 *also recorded in 1965 by The Three Degrees on Swan 4224.
Groovy 3009 - That Certain Little Something / My Judgement Day – 1966
Jacklyn 1002 - What Have I Got Now / Sitting There That Night - 1966
Jacklyn 1003 - Infatuation / Little Girl - 1967
Jacklyn 1006 - What Good Am I Without You / Little Girl - 1967
Revue 11008 - The Way Of A Man / I Like The Way I Feel – 1968
Revue 11023 - Gonna Keep Loving You / We Can't Go On This Way – 1968
Revue 11035 - Those Hanging Heartaches / Sitting There That Night - 1969
Congress 6011 - I Think I'm Gonna Write A Song / Sitting There That Night - 1970
Uni 55244 - When Love Calls / Changing By The Minute – 1970
Uni 55270 - What Is This / Dolly Baby – 1971
Genna 1002 - Now Is The Time For Love (Part 1) / Now Is The Time For Love (Part 2) - 1971
Crossover 980 - Try Something New / It's No Mistake – 1975
Crossover 983 - We've Got An Understanding / This Time I'll Be The Fool – 1976
Atco 7083 - Improve / Let's Get Together – 1978
Atlantic 3600 - Rising Cost Of Love / Honey, Can I - 1979

Phil Flowers

The Sons Of Harmony (unrecorded gospel group Phil Flowers formed)

Tops In Blue (unrecorded group Phil Flowers performed with while in the Air Force)

Phil Flowers (born 28-January-1934 in Clarendon, North Carolina -- died 22-January-2001 in Shady Grove Adventist hospital, Gaithersburg, Maryland. cause: cancer)

Empire 505 - Sadie From Haiti / Lose - 1951 (also issued on 78rpm format)

Skip Manning (rumoured to be Phil Flowers)

Empire 508 - Ham And Eggs / Devil Blues - 1951

Phil Flowers & The Batmen / Joe Lyons and His Arrows with The Bat Men

Hollywood 1065 - Honey Chile / What's New With You* - 1958 *flip by Joe Lyons and His Arrows with The Bat Men.

Phil Flowers

Hollywood 1070 - I'm Your Lover Man / I Know What It Means To Be Blue – 1958
Hollywood 1089 - You Stole My Heart / Rosa Lee * - 1958 *(Backed By The Marionettes)
Wing 2100 - No Kissin' At The Hop / Walking After Midnight – 1958
United Artists 257 - Bingo / What Did I Do – 1960

Phil & Marie (Phil Flowers and ?)

Sway 901 - Love Doctor / Thank You My Dear – 1961

Phil Flowers and TNT Tribble

Sway 903 - No More Tossin' And Turnin' / Do The Dances – 1961

Bill Haley / Phil Flowers

Kasey 7006 - Abc Boogie / Rock Around The Clock *- 1962 *flip by Phil Flowers (issued with picture sleeve)

Phil Flowers with The 'T.N.T' Tribble Combo (members Phil Flowers (vocals), T. N. T. Tribble (drums), Melvin Lee (guitar), Harold Blair (saxophone) and Willie Melvin (bass))

Domino 500 - Twistin' Beat / I Need You Baby - 1962
Domino 501 - Move On / Whole Lotta Woman - 1962

Ray Charles / Phil Flowers

Bonus 7019 - Walkin' And Talkin' / I Can't Stop Loving You *- 1962 *flip by Phil Flowers (issued with picture sleeve)

The Hollywood Argyles / Phil Flowers

Wham 7037 - Alley Oop / C. C. Rider* - 1962 *flip by Phil Flowers. (issued with picture sleeve)

Phil Flowers

Josie 909 - The Cleopatra / You Little Devil – 1963
Almanac 803 - Don't Ever Leave Me / C'mon Dance With Me - 1964
Almanac 803 - How Can I Forget Her / C'mon Dance With Me – 1964
Almanac 812 - How Can I Forget Her / If I Could Have My Way - 1965

Almanac 815 - Johnny Bom Bonney* / ? - 1965 *also recorded in 1964 by Joey Kay on Almanac 804

Phil Flower

Columbia 43397 - Comin' Home To You / Got To Have Her For My Own - 1965

Phil Flowers

Dot 17043 - One More Hurt / Where Did I Go Wrong – 1967

Phil Flowers and The Underdogs (members Phil Flowers, Johnny Snead, Joel Bond, Stu Reid and Jim James)

Loft 103 - Discontented / Cry On My Shoulder – 1967

Phil Flowers

Dot 17058 - Discontented / Cry On My Shoulder - 1967 (the V. McCoy credited on a number of the DOT releases is not Van McCoy but Velma McCoy Phil Flowers aunt)
Audio Arts 6025 - Discontented / Cry On My Shoulder – 1967
Dot 17113 - The Alligator / The Judge And The Alligator - 1968
Dot 17154 - I Saw Her Standing There / Nobody Knows – 1968
Dot 17220 - Son Of Mine / What Could I Do Girl - 1969

Phil Flowers & The Flower Shoppe

A & M 1122 - Like A Rolling Stone / Keep On Sockin' It Children – 1970
A & M 1168 - Every Day I Have To Cry* / If It Feels Good Do It - 1970 *also recorded in 1968 by Lattimore Brown on Sound Stage 7 2616 and in 1975 by Arthur Alexander on Buddah 492 plus in 1980 by Debby Boone on Warner Bros. 49652.
Bell 928 - The Man, The Wife And The Little Baby Daughter / Nothing Lasts Forever - 1970 Bell 993 - I Just Walked By* / How 'Bout A Little Hand For Jesus - 1971 *written by Tony Joe White.

Phil Flowers

Bell 993 - I Just Walked By* / How 'Bout A Little Hand For Jesus - 1971 *written by Tony Joe White.

The Flower Shoppe (members Phil Flowers (vocals), Rick Sheltra (drums), Butch White (bass guitar), Rod Phillips (saxophone), Steve Sidor (keyboards), Johnny Snead (guitar) and Tony Thomas (guitar))

Spring - Don't Turn Me On - 1971 (previously unissued track which was released in the U. K. on a 2006 Kent CD "The Soul Of Spring Volume 2" CDKEND 268)
Spring 111 - You've Come Along Way Baby / Kill The Monster - 1971

Fun House starring Phil Flowers (members Phil Flowers, In Whose Eyes..." was recorded in Baltimore with Rick Sheltra on drums, Butch White on bass, Malcolm Lukens on guitar, Bill Shipley on sax, Bill ? on trumpet, probably Tony Thomas in rhythm guitar, Gantt Kushner on lead guitar, and Craig Anderton on electronic sound fx.

"Dead Skunk" was recorded in NYC with members of King Curtis' Kingpins - Cornell Dupree on guitar for sure, Jerry Jemmott on bass, maybe Bernard Purdie on drums, but not sure)

Epic 10956 - In Whose Eyes (Areyouwhoyouwannabe!) / Dead Skunk - 1972

Fun House

Epic 11015 - In Whose Eyes / On The Beach – 1973

Jebadiah (members Phil Flowers, David Lasley, Alvin Fields, Phillip Ballou, Debbie Gurney, Billy Hocher, Tim McQueen, Jeff Mironov, Cliff Morris, Rob Mounsey, Eric Weissberg, John Gatchell, Michael Lawrence, Alan Rubin, Ronnie Cuber, David Taylor, Gerry Chamberlain, Francisco Centeno, Allen Schwarzberg, Rubens Bassini and David Carey)

Epic 8-50602 - All Together (Special Disco Version) (6:20) / Get Off My Cloud (5:30) - 1978 (12" Release)
Epic 8-50603 - All Together / Get Off My Cloud - 1978 (Arranged By Michael Zager)
Epic 8-50644 - Under My Thumb (Mono) / Under My Thumb (Stereo) - 1978 (Promo Issue Only - Released 19-November-1978)
Epic 8-50644 - Under My Thumb / Brown Sugar – 1978
Epic ? - Honky Tonk Women / ? - ?
Epic ? - The Man, The Wife And The Little Baby Daughter / ? -?

The United Family / Phil Flowers featuring Jerri Lynn

H. E. R. E. 075 - Solidarity / Inside* - 1984 *Flip By Phil Flowers Featuring Jerri Lynn

Phil Flowers

ICI Industries 1806 - Stay Awhile / If You Really Love Him - 1985 (original - without go-go beat)
Future Records & Tapes F-0020 - Stay Awhile / Stay Awhile (Instrumental) - 1986 (go-go version -- with Chuck Brown's band) (12" release --- plays at 33 1/3 rpm)
ICI Industries 1978 - Shake A Hand / Hello My Friend - 1986
ICI Industries - Danny Boy / 1986 (Unissued)
Ripete 3011 - Little Bitty Pretty One / Love Sweet Love – 1989

Phil Flowers / Poontang Perkins

Norton 864 - Chapel On The Hill / Put De Pot On Mary - 1997?

The Formations

Margie & The Formations

Coed 601 - Sad Illusion / Better Get What Goes For You - 1965

The Formations (members Victor Drayton, Jerry Akines, Ernie Brooks, Reginald Turner and Johnny Bellman)

Bank 1007 - At The Top Of The Stairs / Magic Melody - 1967
MGM 13899 - At The Top Of The Stairs / Magic Melody - 1968
MGM 13963 - Loves Not Only For The Heart / Lonely Voice Of Love - 1968
MGM 14009 - Don't Get Close / There's No Room - 1968

The Corner Boys (members Victor Drayton, Jerry Akines, Ernie Brooks, Reginald Turner and Johnny Bellman)

Neptune 13 - Gang War (Don't Make Sense) / Take It Easy Soul Brother - 1969

The Silent Majority (members Victor Drayton, Jerry Akines, Ernie Brooks, Reginald Turner and Johnny Bellman)

Hot Wax 7008 - Frightened Girl / Colours Of My Love - 1970
Hot Wax 7112 - Colours Of My Love / Something New About You - 1971
Detroit Star 774 - Good News / ? - ?

Hot Ice (members Victor Drayton, Jerry Akines, Ernie Brooks, Reginald Turner and Johnny Bellman)

Heavy Duty 4 - Isn't It Lonely / Lady - 1972
Atlantic 3023 - Streakin' And Freakin' / Part 2- 1974
Atlantic 3201 - Boogie Joogie / Part 2- 1974

Four Tops

The 4 Falcons (members Jackie Wilson, Levi Stubbs, Lawson Smith and Sonny Woods)

The Thrillers (members Joe Murphy (lead tenor), Charles Wright (first tenor), Lawrence Payton (second tenor), John Raymond Dorsey (baritone) and Roquel "Billy" Davis (bass, songwriter and manager))

Thrillers 167 - I'm Gonna Live My Life Alone / Lessy Mae - 1953
The Thrillers 170 - Mattie, Leave Me Alone / The Drunkard - 1953

The Four Aims (members Levi Stubbs (born Levi Stubbles on 6-June-1936 in Detroit, Michigan --- died 17-October-2008 in Detroit, Michigan after a long series of illnesses including cancer and a stroke), Renaldo "Obie" Benson (born 14-June-1937 in Detroit, Michigan --- died 1-July-2005 at Harper Hospital, Detroit, Michigan --- cause: suffering a heart attack after the amputation of a leg because of circulation problems. He was subsequently diagnosed with lung cancer), Lawrence Payton (born 2-March-1938 in Detroit, Michigan --- died 10-June-1997 in Southfield, Michigan --- cause: liver cancer) and Adbul "Duke" Fakir)

Grady 012 - If Only I Had Known / ? - 1956

Carolyn Hayes with Maurice King and his Wolverines (Maurice King (born 1911 in Renshaw, Mississippi -- died 18-December-1992 in Detroit, Michigan --- cause:?)

Chateau 2001 - Baby Say You Love Me / Really - 1955 (vocal by Carolyn Hayes & The Four Tops)

Dolores Carroll with Maurice King and his Wolverines

Chateau 2002 - Everybody Knows / I Just Can't Keep The Tears From Tumblin' Down - 1955 (vocal by Dolores Carroll & The Four Tops)

The Four Tops

The Four Tops

Chess 1623 - Could It Be You? / Kiss Me, Baby - 1956
Chess - Woke Up This Morning - 1956 (although unissued at the time this was released in 2001 on a HIP-O double Cd "Street Corner Essentials" 314 556 264-2)
Columbia 41755 - Ain't That Love / Lonely Summer - 1960
Riverside 4534 - Pennies From Heaven / Where Are You? - 1962
Motown 1062 - Baby I Need Your Loving* / Call On Me - 1964 *also recorded in 1970 by O. C. Smith on Columbia 4-45206 and in 1982 by Carl Carlton on RCA PB-13313 and also in 1982 by Gayle Adams on Prelude 8046.
Motown 1069 - Without The One You Love (Life's Not Worthwhile) / Love Has Gone - 1964
Motown 1073 - Ask The Lonely* / Where Did You Go - 1965 *also recorded in 1974 by John

Gary Williams on Stax 0205.
Jobete Cb I/I 1 - 0802 - Nhi - Sweeter As The Days Go By - 1965 (10" acetate plays at 45rpm)
Columbia 43356 - Ain't That Love / Lonely Summer - 1965
Motown 1076 - I Can't Help Myself (Sugar Pie, Honey Bunch)* / Sad Souvenirs - 1965 *also recorded in 1979 by Bonnie Pointer on Motown 1478.
Motown 1081 - It's The Same Old Song / Your Love Is Amazing - 1965
Motown 1084 - Something About You / Darling, I Hum Our Song - 1965
Motown 1090 - Shake Me, Wake Me (When It's Over)* / Just As Long As You Need Me - 1966 *also recorded in 1969 by Al Wilson on Soul City 773.
Motown 1096 - Loving You Is Sweeter Than Ever / I Like Everything About You - 1966
Motown 1098 - Reach Out I'll Be There* / Until You Love Someone - 1966 (some copies issued with picture sleeve) *also recorded as an instrumental in 1967 by Lee Moses on Musicor 1227.
Motown 1102 - Standing In The Shadows Of Love / Since You've Been Gone - 1966

Various Artists

Motown 2482 - Christmas Greetings From Motown - 1966 very short "Christmas greetings" radio station spots are delivered by Martha and The Vandellas, The Temptations, The Miracles, Shorty Long, The Velvelettes, The Spinners, The Four Tops, The Elgins and The Supremes. It was pressed in red vinyl.

The Four Tops

Topps/Motown 5 - I Can't Help Myself - 1967 (Cardboard Record)
Topps/Motown 9 - Baby I Need Your Loving - 1967 (Cardboard Record)
Motown 1104 - Bernadette / I Got A Feeling - 1967
Motown 1110 - 7-Rooms Of Gloom / I'll Turn To Stone - 1967
Motown 1113 - You Keep Running Away / If You Don't Want My Love - 1967
Motown 1119 - Walk Away Renee / Your Love Is Wonderful - 1968
Motown 1124 - If I Were A Carpenter* / Wonderful Baby - 1968 *also recorded in 1970 by Wayne Cochran on King 6288.
Motown 1127 - Yesterday's Dreams / For Once In My Life - 1968

Gladys Knight & The Pips / The Four Tops / Martha Reeves & The Vandellas / The Voices Of Tabernacle

Motown W4kb-4900-1a - Excerpts From Album M 642 "In Loving Memory" (Tribute To Mrs. Loucye S. Wakefield) - 1968 (promo issue only -- The Four Tops sing "Nobody Knows The Trouble I've Seen")

The Four Tops

Motown 1132 - I'm In A Different World / Remember When - 1968
Motown 1147 - What Is A Man / Don't Bring Back Memories - 1969
Motown 1159 - Don't Let Him Take Your Love From Me / The Key - 1969
Motown 1164 - It's All In The Game* / Love (Is The Answer) - 1970 *also recorded in 1951 by Tommy Edwards on MGM 11035
Motown 1170 - Still Water (Love) / Still Water (Peace) - 1970

The Supremes & Four Tops

Motown 1173 - River Deep-Mountain High / Together We Can Make Such Sweet Music - 1970

The Four Tops

Motown 1175 - Just Seven Numbers (Can Straighten Out My Life) / I Wish I Were Your Mirror - 1971

The Supremes & Four Tops

Motown 1181 - You Gotta Have Love In Your Heart / I'm Glad About It - 1971

The Four Tops

Motown 1185 - In These Changing Times / Right Before My Eyes - 1971
Motown 1189 - Macarthur Park (Part 1) / Macarthur Park (Part 2) - 1971
Motown 1196 - A Simple Game / L.A. My Town - 1972
Motown 1198 - I Can't Quit Your Love / Happy (Is A Bumpy Road) - 1972
Motown 1210 - (It's The Way) Nature Planned It / I'll Never Change - 1972
ABC Dunhill 4330 - Keeper Of The Castle / Jubilee With Soul - 1972
ABC Dunhill 4334 - Guardian De Tu Castle / Jubilee With Soul - 1972
ABC Dunhill 4339 - Ain't No Woman (Like The One I've Got) / The Good Lord Knows - 1973
Motown 1254 - Hey Man - We Gotta Get You A Woman / How Can I Forget You - 1973 (unreleased)
ABC Dunhill 4354 - Are You Man Enough* / Peace Of Mind - 1973 *from the movie "Shaft In Africa".
ABC Dunhill 4366 - Sweet Understanding Love / Main Street People - 1973
ABC Dunhill 4377 - I Just Can't Get You Out Of My Mind / Am I My Brother's Keeper? - 1973
ABC Dunhill 4386 - One Chain Don't Make No Prison / Light Of Your Love - 1974
ABC Dunhill 15005 - Midnight Flower / All My Love - 1974
ABC 12096 - Seven Lonely Nights / I Can't Hold Out Much Longer - 1975
ABC 12123 - We All Gotta Stick Together / (It Would Almost) Drive Me Out Of My Mind - 1975
ABC 12155 - I'm Glad You Walked Into My Life / Mama, You're Alright With Me - 1975
ABC 12214 - Catfish / Look At My Baby - 1976
ABC 12223 - Catfish / Look At My Baby - 1976
ABC 12236 - Feel Free / I Know You Like It - 1976
ABC 12267 - Strung Out For Your Love / You Can't Hold Back On Love - 1977
ABC 12315 - Runnin' From Your Love / The Show Must Go On - 1977
ABC 12427 - Inside A Broken Hearted Man / H.E.L.P. - 1978
ABC 12457 - Just In Time / This House - 1978
Casablanca 2338 - When She Was My Girl / Something To Remember - 1981
Casablanca 2344 - Let Me Set You Free / From A Distance - 1981
Casablanca Nbd 20239 - Let Me Set You Free / Let Me Set You Free - 1981 (12" Release)
Casablanca 2345 - Tonight I'm Gonna Love You All Over / I'll Never Leave Again - 1981
Casablanca 2353 - Sad Hearts / I Believe In You And Me - 1982
RSO 1069 - Back To School Again / Rock-A-Hula Luau* - 1982 *flip by The Cast from the movie "Grease 2"
Motown 1706 - I Just Can't Walk Away / Hang - 1983
Motown 1718 - Make Yourself Right At Home / Sing A Song Of Yesterday - 1985
Motown 1790 - Sexy Ways / Body And Soul - 1985
Motown 1811 - Don't Tell Me That It's Over / I'm Ready For Love - 1985
Motown 1854 - Hot Nights / Again - 1986
Reliant 1691 - I'm Here Again / (Instrumental) - 1988
Arista 9706 - Indestructible / Are You With Me - 1988
Arista ? - Indestructable (Extended Version) (7:48) Indestructable (Dub Version) (5:51) Are You With Me (4:43) - 1988 (12"Release)

Aretha Franklin & The Four Tops / The Four Tops

Arista 9766 - If Ever A Love There Was / Let's Jam* - 1988 *flip by The Four Tops.

The Four Tops

Arista 9801 - Change Of Heart / Loco In Acapulco - 1989

Aretha Franklin & Whitney Houston / Aretha Franklin & The Four Tops

Arista 9850 - It Isn't, It Wasn't, It Ain't Never Gonna Be / If Ever A Love There Was* - 1989 *flip by Aretha Franklin & The Four Tops. (some copies issued with picture sleeve)

The Four Tops

Probe 579 - (I Think I Must Be) Dreaming / ? - ?
Collectables Col 043467 - When She Was My Girl / I Believe In You And Me - ?
Collectables Col 902257 - Ain't No Woman (Like The One I've Got) / The Good Lord Knows - ?
Collectables Col 902057 - Catfish / One Chain Don't Make No Prison - ?
Collectables Col 901247 - Keeper Of The Castle / Are You Man Enough - ?
Goldies 45 2616 - Ain't No Woman (Like The One I've Got) / The Good Lord Knows - ?

The Four Tops / Rockin' Louie & The Mamma Jammers /// Buster Benton / Johnnie & Joe

Ripete 1004 - Could It Be You / Don't Buy Me No Beer /// Lonesome For A Dime / I Feel Alright - ? (some copies issued in blue vinyl)

Inez & Charlie Foxx

The Gospel Tide Chorus (members Inez Foxx, ...)

Chuck Johnston & The Jaycees (members Charlie Foxx (born 23-October-1939 in Greensboro', North Carolina --- died 19-September-1998 --- cause: Leukemia), ...)

Brunswick 55154 - Stop, Baby / Sweet Baby - 1959

Inez Johnston

Brunswick 55169 - A Feeling (That I Can't Explain) / Big Bad Betsy* - 1960 *backed by The Florios.
Brunswick 55218 - Change Of Heart / Why Did Ya – 1961

Inez Foxx (born 9-September-1942 in Greensboro', North Carolina)

Symbol 919 - Mockingbird / Jaybirds – 1963

Chuck Johnson vocal acc. Inez Foxx

Symbol 921 - Here We Go 'Round The Mulberry Bush / Competition – 1963

Inez Foxx

Symbol 922 - He's The One You Love / Broken Hearted Fool – 1963
Symbol 924 - Hi Diddle Diddle / Talk With Me – 1963
Symbol 926 - Ask Me / I See You My Love – 1963
Symbol 20-001 - Hurt By Love / Confusion - 1964
Symbol 201 - La De Da I Love You / Yankee Doodle Dandy - 1964

Inez & Charlie Foxx

Symbol 204 - I Fancy You / Don't Do It No More – 1964
Symbol 206 - My Momma Told Me / I Feel Alright – 1965
Symbol 208 - I've Come To One Conclusion / Down By The Seashore – 1965
Symbol 213 - Hummingbird / If I Need Anyone (Let It Be You) - 1966

Musicor 1201 - No Stranger To Love / Come By Here* - 1966 *backing by The Sweet Inspirations.
Dynamo 102 - Tightrope* / Baby Take It All - 1967 *there exists an unissued at the time instrumental version of this by Bobby Martin which was recorded 19-July-1968 at Groove Sound Studios
Dynamo 104 - I Stand Accused* / Guilty - 1967 *also recorded in 1964 by Jerry Butler on Vee-Jay 598.
Dynamo 109 - You Are The Man / Hard To Get – 1967
Dynamo 112 - (1-2-3-4-5-6-7) Count The Days / A Stranger I Don't Know (Wish It Was You) – 1967
Dynamo 117 - I Ain't Going For That / Undecided – 1968
Dynamo 119 - Vaya Con Dios* / Fellows In Vietnam - 1968 *also recorded in 1968 by H. B. Barnum on Capitol 2139.
Dynamo 126 - Come On In / Baby Drop A Dime – 1968
Lana ? - 1960's
Dynamo 127 - Baby Give It To Me / You Fixed My Heartache – 1969

Inez & Charlie Foxx & Their Mockin' Band (members Inez Foxx, Charlie Foxx,..)

Dynamo 134 - We Got A Chance To Be Free / Speed Ticket – 1969

Inez Foxx

Dynamo 138 - North Carolina (South Carolina)* / I Got It - 1969 *A-side written by Bickerton & Waddington, formerly of The Pete Best Group.Also recorded in 1969 by The Flirtations on Deram 85048.
Dynamo 144 - You Shouldn't Have Set My Soul On Fire / Live For Today – 1970
Volt 4087 - You Hurt Me For The Last Time / Watch The Dog (That Brings The Bone) - 1972
Volt 4093 - The Time* / One Woman's Man - 1973 *originally recorded in 1958 by Baby Washington on Neptune 101.
Volt 4096 - Crossing Over The Bridge / You're Saving Me For A Rainy Day - 1973
Volt 4101 - I Had A Talk With My Man* / The Lady, The Doctor, And The Prescription - 1973 *originally recorded in 1964 by Mitty Collier on Chess 1907.
Volt 4107 - Circuit's Overloaded / There's A Hand That's Reaching Out - 1974

Barbara George / Inez Foxx

Trip 7 - I Know / Mockingbird* - ? *flip by Inez Foxx.

Charles & Inez Foxx / Barbara George

United Artists Xw516 - Mocking Bird / I Know (You Don't Love Me No More)* - 1974 *flip by Barbara George.

The Poets / Charlie & Inez Foxx

Collectables 03147 - She Blew A Good Thing / Mockingbird* - ? *flip by Charlie & Inez Foxx.

Harvey Fuqua

The Crazy Sounds (members Bobby Lester, Harvey Fuqua, Prentiss Barnes and Danny Coggins (born in Tennessee))

The Crazy Sounds (members Bobby Lester (born Robert L. Dallas on 13-January-1930 in Louisville, Kentucky), Alexander Graves, Harvey Fuqua (born 17-July-1929 in Louisville, Kentucky) and Prentiss Barnes (born 12-April-1925 in Magnolia, Mississippi)) - name was changed by Alan Freed.

The Moonglows (members Bobby Lester (lead), Alexander "Pete" Graves, Harvey Fuqua and Prentiss Barnes -- who was "Pookie" Hudson's brother)

Champagne 7500 - I Just Can't Tell You No Lie / I've Been Your Dog (Ever Since I've Been Your Man) - 1952 (Dj. Alan Freed's record label)
Chance 1147 - Baby Please / Whistle My Love – 1953
Chance 1150 - Just A Lonely Christmas / Hey, Santa Claus – 1953
Chance 1152 - Secret Love / Real Gone Mama – 1954
Chance 1156 - I Was Wrong / Ooh Rockin' Daddy – 1954
Chance 1161 - My Gal / 219 Train – 1954
Chess 1581 - Sincerely / Tempting - 1954

Bobby Lester & The Moonlighters (Duet of Bobby Lester and Harvey Fuqua)

Checker 806 - So All Alone / Shoo Doo-Be Doo – 1954
Checker 813 - Hug And Kiss / New Gal – 1954

The Moonglows

Chess 1589 - Most Of All / She's Gone - 1955
Chess 1605 - Starlite / In Love – 1955
Chess 1611 - In My Diary / Lover, Love Me – 1955
Chess 1619 - We Go Together / Chickie Um Bah - 1956 (One known copy has surfaced in Los Angeles In 1999 pressed in red vinyl)
Chess 1629 - See Saw / When I'm With You – 1956
Chess 1646 - Over And Over Again / I Knew From The Start - 1957 (8189a in the run off area -- slower version of "A" side)
Chess 1646 - Over And Over Again / I Knew From The Start - 1957 (Normal version of "A" side)
Chess 1651 - I'm Afraid The Masquerade Is Over / Don't Say Goodbye – 1957
Chess 1661 - Please Send Me Someone To Love / Mr. Engineer (Bring Her Back To Me) – 1957
Chess 1669 - The Beating Of My Heart / Confess It To Your Heart - 1957
Chess 1681 - Too Late / Here I Am – 1958
Chess 1689 - In The Middle Of The Night / Soda Pop - 1958 Written By Berry Gordy.
Chess 1701 - This Love / Sweeter Than Words – 1958

Harvey & The Moonglows

Chess 1705 - Ten Commandments Of Love* / Mean Old Blues - 1958 *Written By M. Paul (Turned out to be the nine year old son of one of the Chess brothers --- when a number of legal matters were cleared up it turned out that Harvey Fuqua had written the song)

Harvey (Harvey Fuqua)

Chess 1713 - I Want Somebody / Da Da Goo Goo – 1959

Betty & Dupree (Etta James And Harvey Fuqua)

Kent 318 - I Hope You're Satisfied / If It Ain't One Thing – 1959

The Moonglows

Chess 1717 - Love Is A River / I'll Never Stop Wanting You - 1959

After this recording Harvey Fuqua folded The Moonglows -- He met up with The Marquees whose members were Marvin Gaye (Baritone), Reese Palmer (First Tenor), James

Nolan (First Tenor) and Chester Simmons (First Tenor / Baritone) and instead of going to Baltimore to complete a Moonglows tour, he and The Marquees went to Chicago . In Chicago they added Chuck Barksdale (Bass) of The Dells to the group and proceeded to cut the next "Moonglows" single.

Harvey

Chess 1725 - Twelve Months Of The Year / Don't Be Afraid Of Love - 1959

Harvey & The Moonglows

Chess 1738 - Mama Loochie* / Unemployment - 1959 *Lead Marvin Gaye. By 1960 the "New" Moonglows dispersed and Harvey Fuqua and Marvin Gaye make their way to Detroit . While in Detroit Harvey marries Gwen Gordy.

Harvey

Chess 1749 - Blue Skies / Ooh, Ouch, Stop! – 1960

Etta And Harvey (Etta James and Harvey Fuqua)

Chess 1760 - If I Can't Have You / My Heart Cries – 1960

The Moonglows

Chess 1770 - Beatnick / Junior – 1960

Etta And Harvey (Etta James and Harvey Fuqua)

Chess 1771 - Spoonful / It's A Crying Shame – 1960

The Spinners (Originally called The Domingoes, discovered by Harvey Fuqua who sings on all their Tri-Phi recordings)

Tri-Phi 1001 - That's What Girls Are Made For / Heebie-Jeebies - 1961
Tri-Phi 1004 - Love (I'm So Glad I Found You) / Sudbuster - 1961 (Harvey Fuqua Lead)
Tri-Phi 1007 - What Did She Use / Itching For My Baby, I Know Where To Scratch - 1962

Bobby Lester & The Moonglows

Chess 1811 - Blue Velvet / Penny Arcade – 1962

The Five Quails (Members Harvey Fuqua, Billy Strawbridge, Harold Sudbury, Curtis Robinson, Art Kirpatrick and James Williams)

Harvey 114 - Been A Long Time / Get To School On Time - 1962

Harvey And Ann (Harvey Fuqua And Ann Bogan)

Harvey 121 - What Can You Do Now / Will I Do - 1962 (This was the last release on the Harvey Label)

The Moonglows

Vee Jay 423 - Secret Love / Real Gone Mama – 1962

Harvey (Formerly Of The Moonglows And The Spinners)

Tri-Phi 1010 - She Loves Me So / Whistling About You – 1962

The Spinners

Tri-Phi 1013 - I've Been Hurt / I Got Your Water Boiling Baby (I'm Gonna Cook Your Goose) – 1962

Harvey

Tri-Phi 1017 - She Loves Me So / (Dance) Any Way You Wanta – 1962

The Spinners

Tri-Phi 1018 - She Don't Love Me / Too Young, Too Much, Too Soon – 1962

Harvey (Formerly Of The Moonglows And The Spinners)

Tri-Phi 1024 - Memories Of You / Come On And Answer Me - 1963 (Around this period Harvey Fuqua links his Tri-Phi operation with that of his Brother In-Law Berry Gordy and takes The Spinners along with him)

The Moonglows

(All the singles listed here from 1964 were from another set of Moonglows formed by Alexander "Pete" Graves including Doc Green (from The Five Crowns on Rainbow Records), George Thorpe and Bearle Easton (Both from The Velvets on Red Robin Records) these are new recordings trying to recreate the old sound)

Lana 130 - Sincerely / Time After Time - 1964
Lana 131 - Most Of All / What A Difference A Day Makes – 1964
Lana 133 - See Saw / Love Is A River – 1964
Lana 134 - We Go Together / Shoo Doo-Be Doo – 1954
Lana 135 - Ten Commandments Of Love / Half A Heart – 1964
Times Square 30 - Baby, Please / I've Got The Right – 1964
Crimson 1003 - My Imagination / Gee – 1964
Lost Nite 275 - Just A Lonely Christmas / Baby Please - 196?

The Nite-Liters (Band formed in 1963 by Harvey Fuqua and Tony Churchill, later expanded to seventeen members with two vocal groups and band. Renamed New Birth Inc. --- of which Ann Bogan (Vocals) and Charlie Hearndon (Guitarist) were members)

RCA Victor 74-0374 - Con-Funk-Shun / Down And Dirty – 1970
RCA Victor 74-0591 - K-Jee / Tanga Boo Gonk – 1971
RCA Victor 74-0591 - Afro-Strut / (We've Got To) Pull Together – 1971
RCA Victor 71-0714 - Cherish Every Precious Moment / I've Got Dreams To Remember – 1972

The Moonglows (Members Harvey Fuqua, Bobby Lester, Alexander "Pete" Graves, Chuck Lewis and Doc Williams)

Big P 101 - Sincerely ' 72 / You've Chosen Me - 1972
RCA Victor 74-0759 - Sincerely / I Was Wrong – 1972
RCA Victor 74-0839 - When I'm With You / You've Chosen Me – 1972

Harvey & The Moonglows

Chess/Protein 21 P21-01 - Ten Commandments Of Love / Ten Commandments Of Beautiful Hair - 197? (promo issue for Protein 21 Shampoo)

The Moonglows

Mello 69 - Just A Lonely Christmas / Hey, Santa Claus - 19??

Harvey & The Moonglows / Bunker Hill

Intermission 584 - Ten Commandments Of Love / Hide And Go Seek (Parts 1 & 2)* - ? *flip by Bunker Hill.

The Fuzz

The Passionettes (members Sheila Young (born 16-August-1951), Barbara Gilliam (born 16-August-1952 --- died 4-August-2008 in Alexandria, Virginia --- cause: ?) and Val Williams (born 26-March-1952)) No recordings were made under this name.

The Fuzz (members Sheila Young, Barbara Gilliam and Val Williams)

Calla 174 - I Love You For All Seasons / I Love You For All Seasons (Part 2) - 1970 (bass player on this 45 was Ronald Campbell)
Calla 177 - Like An Open Door / Leave It All Behind Me - 1971
Calla 179 - I'm So Glad / All About Love - 1971 (some copies issued with picture sleeve)
Calla 183 - Mr. Heartache And Miss Tears / Do Just What You Can - 1971
Roulette Golden Great 147 - I Love You For All Seasons / Mr. Heartaches And Miss Tears - 197?

Roberta Gilliam (Barbara Gilliam)

Buddah 603 - Magic In The Music / Let's Not Rush It - 1979
Sutra 146 - All I Want Is My Baby / All I Want Is My Baby - 1985

Group Line Ups

The G-Clefs (Theodore 'Teddy Scott, Chris Scott, Tim Scott, Arnold Scott, Raymond Gipson)
The Glories (Betty Stokes, J R Bailey, Kenny Williams)

The G-Clefs

The Bob-O-Links (members Teddy Scott, Timmy Scott, Chris Scott, Joe Jordan and Ray Gipson)

The G-Clefs (members Teddy Scott, Timmy Scott, Chris Scott, Joe Jordan and Ray Gipson)

Pilgrim 715 - Ka-Ding-Dong* / Darla My Darlin' - 1956 *guitar by Fred Picarielo (aka Freddie "Boom Boom" Cannon)
Pilgrim 720 - 'Cause Your Mine / Please Write While I'm Away – 1956
Paris 502 - Symbol Of Love / Love Her In The Mornin' – 1957
Paris 506 - Zing Zang Zoo / Is This The Way – 1957
Pilgrim 24971 - Ka-Ding-Dong / ? - ?

The G-Clefs (members Teddy Scott, Timmy Scott, Chris Scott, Arnold Scott and Ray Gipson)

Terrace 7500 - I Understand (Just How You Feel)* / Little Girl I Love You - 1961 *cover of a 1954 record by The Four Tunes on Jubilee 5132
Terrace 7503 - A Girl Has To Know / (There Never Was A Dog Like) Lad - 1962
Terrace 7507 - Make Up Your Mind / They'll Call Me Away This Is My Country - 1962
Terrace 7510 - A Lover's Prayer (All Through The Night) / Sitting In The Moonlight – 1962
Ditto 503 - I'll Remember All Your Kisses* / Ka-Ding-Dong -1962 *also recorded as "I Remember Your Kisses" in 1952 by Rosco Gordon on RPM 358.
Terrace 7514 - All My Trials / The Big Rain - 1963
Regina 1314 - To The Winner Goes The Prize / I Believe In All I Feel – 1964
Regina 1319 - Angel Listen To Me / Nobody But Betty – 1964
Veep 1218 - I Have / On The Other Side Of Town – 1965
Veep 1226 - This Time (I Know We're Gonna Make It) / On The Other Side Of Town – 1965
Loma 2034 - Party ' 66 / Little Lonely Boy – 1966
Loma 2048 - The Whirlwind / I Can't Stand It - 1966
Roulette Gg1 - Cause You're Mine / Symbol Of Love - 197?
Cheap Ch-1002 - Ka-Ding-Dong / Cause You're Mine - ? (issued on red vinyl)
Rock 'N' Mania Rmg-001 - I Understand / A Girl Has To Know - ?

The G-Clefs / Gloria Mann

Goldisc 3128 - I Understand / Teenage Prayer* - ? *flip by Gloria Mann only.

The G-Clefs

Relic 7105 - Ka-Ding-Dong / ? – 1995

Earl Gaines

Earl Gaines with Louis Brooks & His Hi-Toppers (members Earl Gaines (vocals), Louis Brooks (tenor saxophone), Ali Brown (upright bass), Lovell Phillips (piano) and Andy Davis (drums))

Excello 2056 - It's Love Baby (24 Hours A Day)* / Chicken Huffle - 1955 *also recorded in 1955 by The Midnighters on Federal 12227 and also in 1955 by Ruth Brown on Atlantic 1072.
Excello 2056 - It's Love Baby (24 Hours A Day) / Chicken Shuffle - 1955
Excello 2063 - Can't Keep From Cryin' / Baby, Baby, What's Wrong - 1955

Earl Gaines (born Earl Gaines on 19-August-1935 in Mt. Nebo near Decatur, Alabama. Moved to Nashville in 1951 - recorded solo both as Earl Gains or Earl Gaines --- died 30-December-2009 at St.. Thomas Hospital, Nashville, Tennessee)

Excello 2072 - Long Time Ago / It's Drivin' Me Mad - 1955

Earl Gaines with Louis Brooks & His Hi-Toppers (members Earl Gaines, ...)

Excello 2088 - Please Understand / I Don't Need You Now - 1956

Earl Gaines With Freddy Robinson Orchestra (members Earl Gaines, Gene Allison, Freddy Robinson, ...)

Athens 706 - White Rose (Theme) / White Rose (Commercial) - 1957

Earl Gaines

Champion 1001 - Now Do You Hear / Best Of Luck Baby - 1958 (with Jimmy Beck and his Orchestra (members Johnny Jones (guitar), Larry Taylor (guitar), Big Mac (bass), Jimmy Beck (tenor saxophone), Red McMillan (tenor saxophone), Ira Wilson (tenor saxophone), Melvin Jackson (trumpet), Wilson Jenkins (piano) and Little Willie Mitchell (drums))
Champion 1004 - Love You So / Sittin' Here Drinkin' - 1960 (with Jimmy Beck and his Orchestra)
Champion 1017 - Three Times Seven / Hold Back My Tears - 1960 (with Jimmy Beck and his Orchestra)
Poncello 712 - Let Me Down Easy / Show Me Something - 1961
Excello 2217 - It's Love Baby / Please Love Me - 1962

Earl Gaines with Lucille Johns

Spar - You Are My Sunshine - (track can be found on a German Blue Label Cd released in 2007 "The Poncello Records Story - Tennessee R&B" SPV 95822)

Earl Gains

HBR 481 - It's Worth Anything / The Best Of Luck To You* - 1966 *also recorded in 1964 by Sam Baker on Athens 213.
HBR 510 - I Have Loved And I Have Lived / Don't Take My Kindness For A Weakness - 1966

Earl Gaines

Hollywood 1117 - Fruit From Another Man's Tree / My Woman - 1967 (recorded in Nashville 5-May-1967)
Hollywood 1120 - Have Faith (In Me) / The Things I Used To Do - 1967 (recorded in Nashville 5-May-1967 / 20-July-1967)

A Friend (Earl Gaines)

Hollywood 1123 - We're Gonna Miss You Otis / Macon - 1968

Earl Gaines

Hollywood 1128 - Our Friend Is Gone / He Went To The Mountain - 1968
Hollywood 1128 - Our Friend Is Gone (Part 1) / Our Friend Is Gone (Part 2) - 1968 !
Hollywood 1131 - Tell Me Tonight / Three Wishes For A Fool - 1968 (recorded in Nashville 20-July-1967 / 5-May-1967)
Deluxe 102 - The Door Is Still Open / My Pillow Stays Wet - 1968
Deluxe 111 - Good, Good Lovin' / The Meaning Of A Sad Song (Medley) - 1969
Deluxe 117 - Don't Deceive Me (Please Don't Go) / It's Love Baby (24 Hours A Day) - 1969
Deluxe 125 - You Belong To Me / From Warm To Cool To Cold - 1970
Deluxe 131 - Let's Go, Let's Go, Let's Go (Thrill On The Hill) / What In The World Can I Call My Own - 1970
Seventy-Seven 77-103 - Yearning And Burning / Loving Her Was Easier* - 1972 *also recorded in 1971 by Kris Kristofferson on Monument 8525.
Seventy-Seven 77-110 - That's How Strong My Love Is / Keep Your Mind On Me - 1972
King 6408 - Don't Deceive Me (Please Don't Go) / My Pillow Stays Wet* - 1973 *also recorded in 1964 by James Duncan And The Duncan Trio on King 5887 and in 1968 by Oscar Irving on Boblo 211.

Seventy-Seven 77-128 - You're The One / Turn On Your Love Light - 1973
Seventy-Seven 77-131 - Hymn Number Five* / If You Want What I Got - 1973 *also recorded in 1966 by Mighty Hannibal on Shurfine 021.
Seventy-Seven 77-135 - I Can't Face It / Soul Children - 1973
Ace 3010 - Drowning On Dry Land / Nine-Pound Steel* - 1975 *also recorded in 1967 by Joe Simon on Sound Stage 7 2589.
Ace - Don't Take My Kindness For Weakness - (this unreleased rehearsal recording was released in the U. K. on a 2000 WESTSIDE Cd "Curiosities - The Ace (MS.) 70's Singles & Sessions" WESCD 208)
Dough Boy 001 – Fruit From Another Man's Tree / Warm To Cool To Cold – 1986

Marvin Gaye

The Embracers (members Sidney Barnes, Marvin Gaye, Van McCoy.......................................) unrecorded group formed by Sidney Barnes which auditioned for George Goldner of End records.

The Marquees (members Marvin Gay, Reese Palmer, Chester Simmons and James Nolan)

Billy Stewart

Okeh 7095 - Baby, You're My Only Love / Billy's Heartache - 1957 (with The Marquees on background vocals)

The Marquees (members Marvin Gay, Reese Palmer, Bob Hawkins, Chester Simmons and Nolan Ellison)

Okeh 7096 - Hey Little Schoolgirl / Wyatt Earp - 1957 (lead Reese Palmer - produced by Bo Diddley)

Chuck Berry

Chess 1722 - Almost Grown* / Little Queenie - 1959 *background vocals Harvey and The Moonglows

Harvey

Chess 1725 - Twelve Months Of The Year* / Don't Be Afraid To Love - 1959 *lead Harvey Fuqua and Marvin Gaye. (although uncredited The Moonglows sang on this release)

Chuck Berry

Chess 1729 - Back In The U.S.A.* / Memphis Tennessee - 1959 *background vocals Harvey and The Moonglows

Harvey and The Moonglows

Chess 1738 - Mama Loochie* / Unemployment - 1959 *lead Marvin Gaye.

Marvin Gaye

Tamla 54041 - Let Your Conscience Be Your Guide / Never Let You Go (Sha-Lu-Bop) – 1961
Tamla 54055 - Sandman / I'm Yours, You're Mine – 1962

Marvin Gay

This is one of many Motown mysteries! These 45's have been placed here as this is where many collectors feel they belong -------- but please read on.

Tamla - Masquerade (Is Over) / Witchcraft - 1962 no selection number issued, 45 states "single not available extracted from album (TM-221)".

Tamla 54062 - Masquerade (Is Over) / Witchcraft - 1962 it seems Motown skipped over this number altogether. Many collectors feel that this 45 was scheduled to be released on this selection number, but this has been disproven since a found promo un-numbered disc has a "stripes" label (the "stripes" label design had long been discontinued around selection number 54044 - The Miracles -Broken Hearted / Mighty Good Loving - 1961 release, almost two years earlier).

Marvin Gaye

Tamla 54063 - Soldier's Plea / Taking My Time – 1962

Marvin Gaye Love Tones

Tamla 54063 - Soldier's Plea / Taking My Time – 1962

Marvin Gaye

Tamla 54068 - Stubborn Kind Of Fellow* / It Hurts Me Too - 1962 *vocal accompaniment by The Vandellas

Marvin Gaye / Supremes / Singin' Sammy Ward / Contours / Marvelettes / The Miracles

Promo - Motor Town Special Mts-1 - Individual Artists - 1962 (promo issue only --- features the various artists on tour all talking over their latest record to promote the tour)

The Marvelettes / Mary Wells / Miracles / Marvin Gaye

Tamla/Motown - Album Excerpts - 1963 (though from Tamla / Motown, no label name is shown, nor is there a title. Promo issue only)

Marvin Gaye

Tamla 54075 - Hitch Hike / Hello There Angel – 1963
Tamla 54079 - Pride And Joy / One Of These Days – 1963
Tamla 54087 - Can I Get A Witness */ I'm Crazy 'Bout My Baby - 1963 *The Supremes on backing vocals.
Tamla 54093 - You're A Wonderful One / When I'm Alone I Cry – 1964

Marvin Gaye & Mary Wells

Motown 1057 - Once Upon A Time / What's The Matter With You Baby – 1964

Marvin Gaye

? 080210 - Try It Baby - 1964 (One Sided Acetate)
Tamla 54095 - Try It Baby / If My Heart Could Sing – 1964
Tamla 54101 - Baby Don't You Do It / Walk On The Wild Side – 1964

Marvin Gaye & Kim Weston

Tamla 54104 - What Good Am I Without You / I Want You 'Round – 1964

Marvin Gaye

Tamla 54107 - How Sweet It Is To Be Loved By You / Forever* - 1964 *originally recorded in 1957 as "Darling Forever" by The Four Chevelles on Delft 357 the flip is "This Is Our Wedding". The song was also recorded in 1963 by The Marvelettes on Tamla 54077.

Hitsville U.S.A.

Greetings To Tamla Motown Appreciation Society DM 097311 - 1964 this Amerian 45 was limited to 300 copies for dispersal throughout various European fan clubs as a promo for their first tour. Each act gives an individual greeting over it's latest record. Artist's involved are The Miracles, Stevie Wonder, Marvin Gaye, The Marvelettes, The Temptations, Martha and The Vandellas, The Contours, Eddie Holland, Kim Weston and The Supremes.

Marvin Gaye

Tamla 54110 - I'll Be Doggone / You've Been A Long Time Coming – 1965
Tamla 54110 - I'll Be Doggone - 1965 (One Sided Promo Issue Only)
Hitsville Sound Studio Oli-120116 Cbmn-0482-Nh1 - Talk About A Good Feeling - 1965 (10" acetate plays at 45rpm - has date (March 2nd 1965) on label also has REJECT and RECOAT daubed all over it)
Tamla S4km 0741/2- My Way / This Is The Life - 1965 (No Selection Number Used -- Promo Issue Only)
Tamla 54117 - Pretty Little Baby / Pretty Little Baby - 1965 (White Label Dj Copy)
Tamla 54117 - Pretty Little Baby / Now That You've Won Me – 1965
Tamla 54122 - Ain't That Peculiar* / She's Got To Be Real - 1965 *note U.S.A. "A" sides running time 2:50. Canadian "A" sides running time 2:57.
Tamla 54122 - Ain't That Peculiar / Ain't That Peculiar - 1965 (rare same flip side stock copy)
Transco ? - One More Heartache - 1965 (10" acetate recorded 10-November-1965 - unreleased alternate studio version (2:41))

Detroit Free Press The Action Paper - The Teen Beat Song / Loraine Alterman Interviews Marvin Gaye For Teen Beat Readers - 1966 no selection number issued Dj copy only. This is a very thinly disguised version of ""Pride And Joy", Marvin praises the teenage column of one of Detroit's daily newspapers. The Detroit Free Press.

Jobete Music Inc. Ccmn-0770-Nhdd (+7.6) - Take This Heart Of Mine - 1966 (10" acetate plays at 45rpm - has date (4 / 27 / 66) on label -- alternate take of song)
Tamla 54129 - One More Heartache / When I Had Your Love – 1966
Tamla 54132 - Take This Heart Of Mine* / Need Your Lovin' (Want You Back) - 1966 * first pressing in mono - back up chorus more prominent.
Tamla 54132 - Take This Heart Of Mine* / Need You Lovin' (Want You Back) - 1966 *second pressing in stereo - back up chorus less prominent.
Tamla 54138 - Little Darling, I Need You / Hey Diddle Diddle – 1966
Tamla 54138 - Little Darling (I Need You) / Hey Diddle Diddle – 1966

Marvin Gaye & Kim Weston

Jobete Music Company Inc. (No #) - Baby Say Yes - ? (one sided acetate of unreleased track by the duet)
Tamla 54141 - It Takes Two / It's Got To Be A Miracle – 1966

Marvin Gaye & Tammi Terrell

Tamla 54149 - Ain't No Mountain High Enough / Give A Little Love – 1967

Marvin Gaye

Tamla 54153 - Your Unchanging Love / I'll Take Care Of You – 1967
U-334m10 - At Last (I Found Love) - 1967 (10" 45rpm acetate containing unreleased track has time of 2:36 and date 10-13-67)
Jobete Music Company Inc. (No #) - No Good Without You - ? (one sided acetate of unreleased track)
Topps/Motown 6 - How Sweet It Is - 1967 (cardboard record)

Marvin Gaye & Tammi Terrell

Tamla 54156 - Your Precious Love / Hold Me Oh My Darling – 1967

Marvin Gaye

Tamla 54160 - You / Change What You Can – 1967

Marvin Gaye & Tammi Terrell

Tamla 54161 - If I Could Build My Whole World Around You / If This World Were Mine – 1967
Tamla 54163 - Ain't Nothing Like The Real Thing / Little Ole Boy, Little Ole Girl* - 1968 *cover of 1961 record by Loe & Joe (Lorrie Rudolph and Joe Charles) on HARVEY 112.
Tamla 54169 - Two Can Have A Party / You're All I Need To Get By – 1968

Marvin Gaye

Tamla 54170 - Chained* / At Last (I Found A Love) - 1968 *also released in 1967 by Paul Peterson on Motown 1108 and in 1974 by Rare Earth on Rare Earth 5057.

Marvin Gaye & Tammi Terrell

Tamla 54173 - You Ain't Livin' Till You're Lovin' / Keep On Lovin' Me Honey – 1968

Marvin Gaye / Gladys Knight & The Pips

Motown 1128 - His Eye Is On The Sparrow* / Just A Closer Walk With Thee** - 1968 *Marvin Gaye only. **Gladys Knight & The Pips only.

Marvin Gaye

Tamla 54176 - I Heard It Through The Grapevine / You're What's Happening (In The World Today) – 1968

Marvin Gaye & Tammi Terrell

Tamla 54179 - Good Lovin' Ain't Easy To Come By */ Satisfied Feelin' - 1969 (*Originally title "It Ain't Easy")

Marvin Gaye

Tamla 54181 - Too Busy Thinking About My Baby / Wherever I Lay My Hat (That's My Home) – 1969
Tamla 54185 - That's The Way Love Is / Gonna Keep On Tryin' Till I Win Your Love – 1969

Marvin Gaye & Tammi Terrell

Tamla 54187 - What You Gave Me / How You Gonna Keep It – 1969

Marvin Gaye

Tamla 54190 - Gonna Give Her All The Love I've Got / How Can I Forget You* - 1970 (promo copies on red vinyl - *originally titled "Where Is My Baby" and "How Can I forget You").

Marvin Gaye & Tammi Terrell

Tamla 54192 - The Onion Song / California Soul - 1970 (Promo Copies On Red Vinyl)

Marvin Gaye

Monarch (No #) - The End Of Our Road / Me And My Lonely Room - 1970 (Test Pressing)
Tamla 54195 - The End Of Our Road / Me And My Lonely Room – 1970
Tamla Pr-62a - What's Going On - 1971 (One Sided Promo Copy With Same Running Time As Commercial
Issue (3:40))
Tamla 54201 - What's Going On / God Is Love – 1971
Jobete 1 - Save The Children / ? – 1971
Tamla 54207 - Mercy Mercy Me (The Ecology) / Sad Tomorrows – 1971
Tamla 54209 - Inner City Blues (Make Me Wanna Holler) / Wholly Holy – 1971
Tamla 54221 - You're The Man (Part 1) / You're The Man (Part 2) - 1972 (Promo Copies On Red Vinyl)
Tamla T-54228 F - Trouble Man (Stereo) / Trouble Man (Mono) - 1972 (White Label Promo Issue Only)
Tamla 54228 - Trouble Man* / Don't Mess With Mister "T" - 1972 (*From The Film Of The Same Name)
Tamla 54229 - Christmas In The City / I Want To Come Home For Christmas - 1972 (45 Cancelled)
Tamla 54234 - Let's Get It On / I Wish It Would Rain – 1973

Diana Ross & Marvin Gaye

Motown 1269 - My Mistake (Was To Love You) / Include Me In Your Life – 1973
Motown 1280 - You're A Special Part Of Me / I'm Falling In Love With You – 1973

Marvin Gaye

Tamla 54241 - Come Get To This / Distant Lover – 1973
Tamla T-5244 F - You Sure Love To Ball (Stereo) / You Sure Love To Ball (Mono) - 1973 (White Label Promo Issue Only)
Tamla 54244 - You Sure Love To Ball / Just To Keep You Satisfied – 1974

Diana Ross & Marvin Gaye

Motown 1296 - Don't Knock My Love / Just Say Just Say – 1974

Marvin Gaye

Tamla T 54253f - Distant Lover (Live Version) (Mono) / Distant Lover (Live Version) (Stereo) - 1974 (Promo Copy Only - Has Date Oct-26-1974 Stamped Across Label)
Tamla 54253 - Trouble Man */ Distant Lover (Live Edit) - 1974 (Some Promos Contain Longer Versions) *From Film Of Same Title
Tamla 54264 - I Want You / I Want You - 1975 (Promo) Both Sides Are Edited Versions Of The Vocal. Limited Numbers Of The Promo Are In Yellow Vinyl.
Tamla 54264 - I Want You / I Want You (Instrumental) – 1975

Diana Ross / Marvin Gaye

Motown Pr 16 - Love Hangover / I Want You * - 1976 (12" Promo Issue) *Flip By Marvin Gaye

Marvin Gaye

Tamla 54273 - After The Dance / Feel All My Love Inside – 1976
Tamla 54280 - Got To Give It Up --- Pt. 1 / Got To Give It Up --- Pt. 2 – 1977
Motown 00014 - A Funky Space Reincarnation / (Instrumental) - 1978 (12" Release)

Jerry Butler / Marvin Gaye

W.I.A.A. 1147 - What's It All About Public Service Program - 1978 (Radio Station Promo Issue Only - Flip Is By Marvin Gaye)

Diana Ross, Marvin Gaye, Smokey Robinson & Stevie Wonder

Motown 1455 - Pops, We Love You (A Tribute To Father) / (Instrumental) - 1979 Song written for Berry Gordy Sr.'s 90th birthday. Limited numbers of promo copies pressed on heart shaped vinyl in a special sleeve. Some also issued on green vinyl.

Marvin Gaye

Tamla Pr-62b - Mercy Mercy Me (The Ecology) - 1979 (one sided promo copy with same running time as the 1971 commercial issue (2:39))
Tamla 54298 - Funky Space Reincarnation --- Pt. 1 / Funky Space Reincarnation --- Pt. 2 – 1979
Tamla 54300 - Time To Get It Together / Anger - 1979 (Canadian Release Only)
Tamla 54305 - Ego Tripping Out / (Instrumental) – 1979

Marvin Gaye / Meatloaf

W.I.A.A. 530 - What's It All About (July 80) Public Service Show - 1980 (Radio Station Promo issue only - flip is by Meatloaf)

Marvin Gaye

Tamla 54322 - Funk Me / Praise – 1981
Tamla 54326 - Heavy Love Affair / Far Cry - 1981
Columbia 03302 - Sexual Healing / (Instrumental) – 1982
Columbia 03344 - Sexual Healing - 1982 (One Sided Budget Release 45)
Columbia 03585 - Sexual Healing / (Instrumental) - 1983 (Reissue)
Columbia 03589 - 'Til Tomorrow / Rockin' After Midnight – 1983
Columbia 03860 - Joy / (Instrumental) – 1983
Columbia 03870 - Star Spangled Banner / Turn On Some Music – 1983
Columbia 03935 - Joy / Turn On Some Music – 1983
Columbia 04861 - Sanctified Lady / (Instrumental) – 1985
Columbia 05188 - Sanctified Lady / (Instrumental) - 1985 (12"Release)
Columbia 05442 - It's Madness / Ain't It Funny (How Things Turn Around) – 1985
Columbia 13-05474 - Sexual Healing / (Instrumental) – 1985
Columbia Cas 2124 - Masochistic Beauty / (Instrumental) - 1985 (12" Promo Issue)
Tamla 1836tf-Re1 - The World Is Rated X (New Mix) / The World Is Rated X (New Mix) - 1986 (promo issue only)
Columbia 05791 - Just Like / More - 1986
Tamla 1836 - The World Is Rated X / The World Is Rated X (Instrumental) – 1986
Tamla 1836 - The World Is Rated X / No Greater Love – 1986
Motown Pr233mf - His Eye Is On The Sparrow / His Eye Is On The Sparrow - 1988 (Promo issue only)

Marvin Gaye / Marvin Gaye & Mary Wells

Motown Mots7-2083 - My Last Chance (Radio Edit) / Once Upon A Time* - 1990 *Flip By Marvin

Gaye & Mary Wells.

Marvin Gaye

Motown 2086 - 5, 10, 15, 20 Years Of Love / (no "B" side) - 1990 (cancelled release)

Freddie Gorman

Sax Kari & The Quailtones

Josie 779 - Tears Of Love / Roxanna - 1955

The Fideltones:

Aladdin 3442 - Pretty Girl / Game Of Love - 1959
Poop Deck 101 - For Your Love / Whispering Words Of Love - 1960

Freddie Gorman:

Miracle 11 - The Day Will Come / Just For You - 1961
Ric-Tic 101 - In A Bad Way / There Can Be Too Much (Of Everything I Do) - 1965
Ric-Tic 102 - Take Me Back / Can't Get It Out Of My Mind - 1965

The Originals

Soul 35029 - Goodnight Irene / Need Your Lovin' (Want You Back) - 1966
Soul 35056 - You're The One / We've Got A Way Out Love - 1969
Soul 35061 - Green Grow The Lilacs / You're The One - 1969
Soul 35066 - Baby, I'm For Real / Moment Of Truth - 1969
Soul 35069 - The Bells / I'll Wait For You - 1970
Soul 35074 - We Can Make It Baby / I Like Your Style - 1970
Soul 35079 - God Bless Whoever Sent You / Desperate Young Man - 1971
Soul 35085 - Keep Me / A Man Without Love - 1971
Soul 35093 - I'm Someone Who Cares / Once I Have You - 1972
Soul 35102 - Be My Love / Endlessly Love - 1973
Soul 35109 - First Lady (Sweet Mother's Love) / There's A Chance When You Love, You Lose - 1973
Motown PR-1 - Young Train / Young Train - 1973
Soul 35112 - Supernatural Voodoo Woman Part 1 / Part 2 - 1974
Soul 35113 - Game Called Love / Ooh You (Put A Crush On Me) 0 1974
Soul 35115 - You're My Only World / So Near And Yet So Far - 1975
Motown 1355 - Good Lovin' Is Just A Dime Away / Nothing Can Take The Place (Of Your Love) - 1975
Motown 1370 - Fifty Years / Financial Affair - 1975
Motown 1379 - Everybody's Got To Do Something / Instrumental - 1975
Soul 35117 - Touch / Ooh You (Put A Crush On Me) - 1976
Soul 35119 - Down To Love Town / Just To Be Closer To You - 1976
Soul 35121 - (Call On Your) Six Million Dollar Man / Mother Nature's Best - 1977
Fantasy 820 - Ladies (We Need You) / Take This Love - 1978
Fantasy 847 - Blue Moon / Ladies (We Need You) - 1979
Fantasy 856 - J-E-A-L-O-U-S (Means Is Love You) / Jezebel (You've Got Under Your Spell) - 1979

Freddie Gorman

Rene 70061 - Alive Again / Love Has Seen Us Through - 1980
LA 70061 - Love Has Seen Us Through / Same - 1980

The Originals

Phase II 5653 - Waitin' On A Letter - Mr. Postman / The Magic Is You - 1981
Phase II 02061 - Baby, I'm For Real / Share Your Love With Me - 1981
Phase II 02147 - The Magic Is You / Let Me Dance- 1982
Phase II 02724 - Baby, I'm For Real '82 / The Magic Is You - 1982 (Featuring Hank Dixon)
Suspension 1001 - Ain't No Sun / Ain't No Sun - ?

Freddie Gorman

Airwave 1167 - Get Up Off The Funk / It's Over Now - 1983

Delia Renee & The Originals

Airwave ? Please Mr Postman / ? - 1984

The Originals

Motorcity - I Just Keep Falling In Love (on Dancin' and Romancin') - 1990

The Originals with Jean, Scherrie & Lynda

Motorcity - Back By Popular Demand / Please Mr. Postman - 1990

Dobie Gray

Dobie Gray (born Leonard Victor Ainsworth on 26-July-1942 in Brookshire, Texas)

Stripe 826 - To Be Wanted / I Can Hardly Wait - 1960
Stripe 827 - To Be Wanted / Hearts Are Wild - 1960
Stripe 828 - Rags To Riches / I Can Hardly Wait - 1960
Stripe 829 - Love Has A Way / Delia - 1960
Stripe 831 - Love Has A Way / Young Boy - 1961
Stripe 832 - Kissin' Doll / A Boy And A Girl In Love - 1961
Real Fine 835 - Love Has A Way / Tears Keep Falling On My Tears - 1962
Cordak 1602 - Look At Me / Walkin' And Whistlin' - 1962
Cordak 1605 - Feelin' In My Heart / That's How You Treat A Cheater - 1963
Jaf 2504 - Be A Man / Inka-Dinka-Doo - 1963
Cordak 1701 - My Shoes Keep Walkin' Back To You / Funky Funky Feelin' - 1964
Charger 105 - The "In" Crowd* / Be A Man - 1964 (backing vocals The Extremes (members Bobby Sanders, Charles Ingersol, Robert Rozelle and Melvin Isley)) *also recorded in 1966 by Jean King on HBR 463
Charger 107 - See You At The "Go-Go" / Walk With Love - 1965 (backing vocals The Extremes)
Charger 109 - In Hollywood / Mr. Engineer - 1965
Charger 113 - My Baby / My Baby - 1965 (Promo Issue Only)
Charger 113 - Monkey Jerk / My Baby - 1965
Lana 138 - The "In" Crowd / Be A Man - 1965
Charger 115 - Out On The Floor / No Room To Cry - 1966
Capitol 5853 - River Deep, Mountain High / Tennessee Waltz - 1967
Thunderbird 549 - Out On The Floor / My Baby - 1968
Capitol 2241 - We The People / Funky And Groovy - 1968
White Whale 300 - Rose Garden / Where's The Girl Gone - 1969
White Whale 330 - Do You Really Have A Heart? / Do You Really Have A Heart? - 1969 (Promo)
White Whale 342 - Honey, You Can't Take It Back / Guess Who? - 1970

Pollution (Dobie Gray, Carmen "Tata" Vega (co-lead singers), James Quill Smith "Smitty" (guitars), Dennis Kenmore (drummer), Christaan Mostert (saxophone / piano) along with former members of Beethoven Soul - Otis Hale (woodwind), John Lambert (bassist) and Richard Lewis (trumpet / piano))

Capitol 2458 - Getting Together / Angela Jerome – 1970
Prophecy 55001 - Do You Really Have A Heart? (Mono)* / Do You Really Have A Heart? (Stereo) - 1971 *Re-Recorded version of White Whale 330 track.
Prophecy 55003 - The River (Mono) / The River (Stereo) - 1972 All Dobie's Prophecy 45 releases were mono / stereo

Dobie Gray

Anthem 200 - Guess Who? / Bits And Pieces – 1972
Decca 33057 - Drift Away* / City Stars - 1973 *also recorded in 1972 by John Kurtz on ABC 11341.
MCA 40100 - Loving Arms / Now That I'm Without You – 1973
MCA 40153 - Good Old Song / Reachin' For The Feelin' – 1973
MCA 40188 - Rose / Lovin' The Easy Way – 1974
MCA 40201 - There's A Honky Tonk Angel (Who'll Take Me Back In) / Lovin' The Easy Way – 1974
MCA 40268 - Watch Out For Lucy* / Turning On You - 1974 *written by Lonnie Mack.
MCA 40315 - The Music's Real / Roll On Sweet Mississippi – 1974
Capricorn 0249 - If Love Must Go / Lover's Sweat – 1975
Capricorn 0259 - Find 'Em, Fool 'Em & Forget 'Em / Mellow Man – 1976
CCapricorn Pro 646 - Find 'Em, Fool 'Em & Forget 'Em (Disco Mix) (4:48) / Find 'Em, Fool 'Em & Forget 'Em (Disco Mix) (4:48) - 1976 (12" Promo Issue Only)
Capricorn 0267 - Let Go / Mellow Man - 1976

Dobie Gray / Hot Chocolate

Infinity L33-1001 - You Can Do It (6:15) / Every One's A Winner (7:17)* - 1978 (promo issue only) *flip by Hot Chocolate only.

Dobie Gray

Infinity Inf-16001 - You Can Do It (6:15) / Thank You For Tonight (7:58) - 1978 (12" release)
Infinity 50003 - You Can Do It / Sharing The Night Together – 1978
Infinity 50010 - Who's Lovin' You / Thank You For Tonight – 1979
Infinity Inf-16001 - You Can Do It / Thank You For Tonight - 1979 (12" Release)
Infinity 50020 - Spending Time, Making Love, And Going Crazy / Let This Man Take Hold Of Your Life -1979
Infinity 50043 - The "In" Crowd (Long Version) (6:40) / The "In" Crowd (Short Version) (3:38) - 1979 (Promo Issue Only)
Infinity 50043 - The "In" Crowd / Let This Man Take Hold Of Your Life - 1979

Dobie Grey / The Reflections

Eric 277 - The "In" Crowd / Just Like Romeo And Juliet* - 1979 *Flip By The Reflections

Dobie Grey

Collectables Col 012927 - The "In" Crowd / Be A Man - 1981
Robox Rrs-117 - Decorate The Night / Decorate The Night - 1981 (some copies issued with picture sleeve)
Robox 1806 - Decorate The Night / Ave Maria - 1981
Arista 1047 - One Can Fake It / Stranger In The Mirror - 1983
Gusto 2007 - Drift Away / Lovin' Arms - 1985

Collectables Col 900117 - Drift Away / City Stars - ?
Capitol B-5562 - Gonna Be A Long Night / That's One To Grow On - 1986
Capitol B-5596 - The Dark Side Of Life / A Night In The Life Of A Country Boy - 1986
Capitol B-5647 - From Where I Stand / So Far So Good - 1986
Capitol B-44087 - Take It Real Easy / You Must Have Been Reading My Heart - 1987
Capitol B-44126 - Love Letters / Steady As She Goes - 1988
MCA 60160 - Drift Away / City Stars - ?

Uncle Kracker featuring Dobie Gray (members Matthew Shafer (born 6-June-1974) and Dobie Gray)

Lava ? - Drift Away / ? - 2003

Garland Green

Garland Green (born Garfield Green Jr. on the 24-June-1942 in Dunleath - Leland, Mississippi - discovered by Jo Armstead)

Gamma 103 - Girl I Love You / It Rained Forty Days And Nights - 1967
Revue 11001 - Girl I Love You / It Rained Forty Days And Nights* - 1968 *also recorded in 1967 by Jimmy Scott on Giant 708.
Revue 11020 - You Played On A Player / Mr. Misery – 1968
Revue 11030 - Ain't That Good Enough / Love Now, Pay Later - 1968
Uni 55143 - Jealous Kind Of Fella / I Can't Believe You Quit Me - 1969 (Backing vocals by Joshie Jo Armstead)
Uni 55188 - Don't Think That I'm A Violent Guy / All She Did – 1969
Uni 55213 - Angel Baby / You Played On A Player – 1970
Cotillion 44098 - Plain And Simple Girl / Hey Cloud – 1970
Cotillion 44126 - Just My Way Of Loving You* / Always Be My Baby - 1971 *also recorded in 1967 by Johnny Moore on Date 2-1562 and in 1971 by Tyrone Davis on Dakar 623.
Cotillion 44146 - You Can't Get Away That Easy / Get Rich Quick - 1971
Cotillion 44159 - 80 - 90 - 100 Mph. / If A Dream Goes By - 1972
Cotillion 44162 - Love Is What We Came Here For / Running Scared - 1972
Spring 142 - He Didn't Know (He Kept On Talking) / Please Come Home - 1973
Spring 146 - Sweet Lovin' Woman / Sending My Best Wishes - 1974
Spring 151 - Let The Good Times Roll / You And I Go Good Together - 1974
Spring 158 - Bumpin' And Stompin' / Nothing Can Take Me From You - 1975
Spring 160 - Just Loving You / Nothing Can Take You From Me - 1975
Spring - Come Through Me - (unissued at the time, released in the U. K. on a 1997 Kent Cd "The Soul Of Spring" CDKEND 151 plus on a 2003 Kent Cd "Masterpieces Of Modern Soul" CDKEND 222)
Spring - Just What The Doctor Ordered (Unissued At The Time)
Spring - Since You've Been Gone (Unissued At The Time)
Casino 056 - It's A Backdoor World (When The Front Money Is Gone) / I. O. U. - 1975
RCA 10889 - Don't Let Love Walk Out On Us / Ask Me For What You Want* - 1977 *also recorded in 1972 by Millie Jackson on Spring 123.
RCA 11023 - Shake Your Shaker / Lovin' You Baby - 1977
RCA 11126 - Let's Celebrate / Let Me Be Your Pacifier* - 1978 *also recorded in 1976 by Willard Burton & The Pacifiers on Money 702 and Money 2031 plus in 1984 by Tyrone Davis on Ocean-Front 2004.
Ocean-Front 2000 - Tryin' To Hold On / Love's Calling - 1983
Love L.A. Music ? - Let's Keep It Simple / You Color My World - 1987
Love L.A. Music 101 - When You've Got It At Home / Let's Keep It Simple / You Color My World - 1987 (12" Release)
Love L.A. Music 101 - By My Side / Let's Make A Better Place / If You Stand Beside Me / You Came Along - 1987 (Backing Vocals By Johnny Baker)

Roosevelt Grier

Roosevelt Grier (born 14-July-1932 in Cuthbert, Georgia)

A 105 - Sincerely / Why Don't You Do Right – 1959
A 110 - Moonlight In Vermont / Smoky Morning - 1960
Spindle Top 102 - I'm Going Home / Jinny - 1961
Liberty 55413 - Struttin' 'N Twistin' / Let The Cool Wind Blow - 1962
Liberty 55453 - The Mail Must Go Thru / Your Has Been – 1962
Battle 45911 - Why / Lover Set Me Free - 1963
R I C 102 - Fool, Fool, Fool / Since You've Been Gone – 1964
R I C 112 - In My Tenement* / Down So Long - 1964 *also recorded in 1963 by Jackie Shane on Sue 788.
R I C 132 - I (Who Have Nothing) / ? - 1964

The New Yorkers (members Jimmy Gresham, Rosie Grier, Ben Wilson, Larry Johnson, Ben ? and Willie ? (two brothers))

Tac-Ful 101 - Don't Want To Be Your Fool / You Should Have Told Me - 1965 (Label co-owned by Rosey Grier)

The Royal Knights (members Jimmy Gresham, Rosie Grier, Ben Wilson, Larry Johnson, Ben ? and Willie ?)

Radio City 1001 - Don't Want To Be Your Fool / You Should Have Told Me - 1965

The New Yorkers (members

Tac-Ful 102 - There's Going To Be A Wedding / Ain't That News - 1965

Roosevelt Grier

Youngstown 609 - Deputy Dog / High Society Woman – 1966
D - Town 1058 - Pizza Pie Man / Welcome To The Club - 1966
M-G-M 13698 - Slow Drag / Yesterday - 1967
M-G-M 13840 - Spanish Harlem / I'm Living Good* - 1967 *also recorded in 1965 by The Ovations featuring Louis Williams on Goldwax 117 and in 1971 by Arthur Conley on Capricorn 8017.

Rosie Grier & The Fearsome Foursome (members Roosevelt Grier, Merlin Olsen, Roger Brown, David Jones and Lamar Lundy) all LA Rams football stars

Amy 11,004 - Who's Got The Ball (Y'all) - 1967 (one sided promo issue)
Amy 11,004 - Who's Got The Ball (Y'all) / Halftime - 1967

Roosevelt Grier

Amy 11,015 - High Society Woman / C'mon Cupid – 1968
Amy 11,029 - People Make The World - 1968 (one sided promo issue)
Amy 11,029 - Hard To Forget / People Make The World* - 1968 *written by Bobby Womack.
AGP 109 - Bad News / Ring Around The World – 1969

Rosey Grier

ABC 11275 - Rat Race / I Don't Want Nobody (To Lead Me On) - 1970

United Artists 50893 - Bring Back The Time / Oh How I Miss You Baby – 1972

Rosie Grier

A & M 1457 - Beautiful People / I'll Be Back Tomorrow – 1973 (promo issue)

Rosey Grier

A & M 1457 - Beautiful People / I'll Be Back Tomorrow – 1973
A & M 1500 - If You Hit On A Good Lick, Lay On It / You're The Violin – 1974
Bell 45,459 - It's Alright To Cry / It's Alright To Cry - 1974 (Promo Issue Only)
Bell 45,459 - It's Alright To Cry / ? – 1974
20th Century 2212 - Take The Time To Love Somebody / Your Love Is Right Up My Alley – 1975

The Gypsies

The Gypsies (members Lestine Johnson and sisters Betty Pearce, Ernestine Pearce and Shirley Pearce)

Old Town 1168 - Hey There, Hey There / Blue Bird - 1964
Old Town 1180 - Jerk It* / Diamonds, Rubies, Gold And Fame - 1965 *written by Sidney Barnes, J.J. Jackson and Randy Stewart a former member of The Fiestas.

The Gypsies (members Viola Billups, Betty Pearce, Ernestine Pearce and Shirley Pearce)

Old Town 1184 - It's A Woman's World (You Better Believe It) / They're Having A Party - 1965
Old Town 1193 - Oh I Wonder Why / Diamonds, Rubies, Gold And Fame - 1966
Caprice 8442 - Look For The One Who Loves You / Oh Girl - 1966

The Flirtations (members Viola Billups and sisters Betty Pearce, Ernestine Pearce and Shirley Pearce)

Josie 956 - Change My Darkness Into Light / Natural Born Lover - 1966 (J.J. Jackson and Sidney Barnes arranged and wrote the songs on this release --- Betty Pearce leaves group)

The Flirtations (members

Festival 705 - Stronger Than Her Love / Settle Down - 1967

The Flirtations (members Viola Billups, Ernestine Pearce and Shirley Pearce)

Parrot 40028 - How Can You Tell Me*/ Someone Out There - 1968 *produced by Arthur "Wayne" Bickerton who previously had sung lead on the 1965 release "Boys / Kansas City" on Cameo 391 by Peter Best - former drummer for The Beatles. Bickerton had later success with the groups The Rubettes and Mac & Katie Kissoon.
Deram 85036 - Nothing But A Heartache / Christmas Time Is Here Again - 1968
Deram 85038 - Nothing But A Heartache / How Can You Tell Me - 1968
Deram 85048 - Need Your Loving / South Carolina* - 1969 *also recorded in 1969 by Inez & Charlie Foxx on Dynamo 138.
Deram 85057 - Keep On Searchin' / I Wanna Be There - 1969
Deram 85062 - Can't Stop Lovin' You */ Everybody Needs Somebody - 1969 *covered by Tom Jones in 1970 on Parrot 40056
Deram 7531 - Give Me Love, Love, Love / This Must Be The End Of The Line - 1970
Polydor 15047 - Hold On To Me Baby / Love A Little Longer - 1972

The Flirtations (members Loretta Noble, Ernestine Pearce and Shirley Pearce)

D & D 5501 - Earthquake / Earthquake (Long Version) - 1977
D & D 103 - Earthquake (8:50) /// Earthquake (Original Version) (6:57) / Earthquake (Instrumental Version) (6:57) - 1983 (12" Release)
Passion 1267 - Read All About It / Read All About It (Remix) - 1986
Megatone Mt-169 - Back On My Feet Again (7:05) / Back On My Feet Again (Reunion Instrumental Mix) (7:05) - 1989 (12" Release)

White Plains / The Flirtations
Collectables Col 043397 - My Baby Loves Lovin' / Nothing But A Heartache* - 1992 *flip by The Flirtations.

Venue Reports April 2001

Scenesville, Notre Dame Hall, London, 6th April, 2001.

So, two weeks in a row, I'm in London to listen to 'Northern Soul'. What's gone wrong in the Midlands and the North ? That aside this was a great night. I travelled down with John Pugh who was one of the guest DJs for the night. When we arrived Frank Giacobbe was doing the business with some Stafford rarities and disappointingly not getting much dancefloor reaction. Then a guy whose name I never discovered played some really nice stuff, but again failed to fill the floor. In fact his last record was really downtempo and virtually emptied the dancefloor for John Pugh. Never mind, John started off with The Vondells followed by Little John. Full dancefloor ensued for the rest of the set. The busiest it got was for the vocal to 'Six By Six', although people hadn't realised it was the vocal when they started dancing. It was also nice to hear John play the Chris Bartley track as well. Andy Rix followed on: Keni Lewis, Jimmy Radcliffe, Phonetics, Jesse James, Cindy Scott, all unreleased acetates (Does the lad have any real records ?). Awesome spot though. It was left to Nick 'The Driveller' Brown to finish the night off. Not to be outdone, he started off with the Doc & The Interns unreleased acetate. Overall, the quality of music was top notch throughout the night, and I think you would struggle to hear so many great records in one night anywhere else. The venue itself is rather special as well. An underground dance hall, just off Leicester Square in Central London, the main dance floor room is actually an oval in shape. Well done to Nick Brown who is the promoter, another top night to rival The Dome in London.

The Lea Manor, Albrighton, 13th April, 2001.

The best of the year so far for me, again though on a social side rather than a musical side. Michael & Silke from Germany were over on their Easter tour, so rather a large amount of beer was consumed. Musically Keith Williams played the best spot of the night. The 'star guest', Dave Fleming was so remarkable that I can't remember a single record he played ! Sorry, I'd never heard of him before tonight, and I doubt if I'll travel to hear him DJ again.

The Ritz, Manchester, 15th April, 2001.

It's been quite a while since I went to the Ritz for one reason or another so I was looking forward to it. Quite a busy night in terms of bodies through the door. Music policy was advertised as an Easter Extravaganza, and with the line up of DJs would clearly be predominately Oldies based. Good spots from Soul Sam, Ginger, and Ian Levine early on, led up to what must have been the worst spot I have ever heard at an allnighter. I know the guy runs a successful Soul night, but the stuff he was playing was youth club standard ! Wearing a shiny gold jacket does not excuse playing a load of tripe. It was clearly discernible that people left in quite large numbers during this spot. Terry Davies pulled what was left round nicely though, and

Kenny Burrell was doing his spot as I decided that I'd also had enough and would catch the 6.30 train home.

Valatone, St Aloysius Church Social Club, London, 21st April, 2001

Johnny Timlin's new 100 Club warm up venue, and it's walking distance from Euston Station ! It's also a great venue, with a fairly large dancefloor with tables around it and a separate bar area, with cheap beer (For London anyway). There weren't many there this time, I suspect mostly because there were two other warm ups on in London that night (Including trickster's 40th birthday). I spoke to Jonny though and he says he is determined to keep it going, even if he makes a loss on the first couple. One interesting thing which demonstrates the friendliness of the Northern scene. The table I sat at contained a Lancastrian, a Yorkshire man, a Midlander, a Scotswoman, a Welshman, and an Essex bloke, how's that for diversity.

100 Club, London, 21st April, 2001.

This was one of the 'all guest' allnighters that Ady runs a couple of times a year. This time the guests were Kenny Burrell, Keith Money, Ion, and Rob Messer. A good mixture there, and Keith Money is one of my favourite DJs anyway. Kenny Burrell played a couple of good strong spots, Keith Money was on blinding form, but the real surprise for me was Rob Messer's spot really does have some good records ! Fairly quiet night by 100 Club standards, but there was heavy competition in the form of King Georges Hall in Blackburn, and Keele University, so that was to be expected.

Black Horse, Wolverhampton, 27th April, 2001.

A very strange night. Musically it was very good with Carl Fortnum laying some absolutely outstanding records, but virtually no dancefloor reaction. Partly I think because one half of the room were collectors rather than dancers and the other half were, in the majority oldies fans, and we weren't playing oldies ! The best dancefloor fillers for me were R & B things like Lonnie Lester and A C Reed, The Magnetics got a total of three people dancing ! Des Parker eventually got quite a few dancing with the last spot of the night, but although numbers were respectable, I feel it needs a little more support from the 'collectors who dance' side of the scene.

Students Union, Loughborough University, 28th April, 2001.

This was originally planned as an allnighter in the University itself, however, they pulled out, at a considerable cost to the promoters I might add. The Students Union came to the rescue, so it became a Soul night running until 2 am. Two rooms were set up, a smaller one playing Modern, and a huge room playing Northern Oldies, Rarities and R & B. As it turned out the the Modern room was virtually deserted all night, and the bigger Northern room had about 300 through the door. Music policy was oldies overall, and certainly during my DJ spot I played some records that I haven't played in a long time, but I was also able to get some of the rarer stuff in as a result of some requests (Thanks to the Capitol Soul Club people who were there), the result, a busy dancefloor. As the first one this was a good result for the promoters, everyone enjoyed it, the room has capacity for probably five hundred people, so get yourself along there on the 7th July, or even the 15th September. Strangest requests to the DJs: Chris Anderton was asked near the end of his spot "Can you play some Soul music now", and someone asked me "Are you going to play some Motown or just that obscure Northern Soul Music.

Winsford Allnighter, 28th April, 2001.

Straight onto Winsford from Loughborough, and I must thank John Mills for doing all the driving. I arrived just as Ginger was starting his set, he was followed by Terry Davies. Both of them did good spots of quality rare Soul music. Rob Smith also turned in a good performance as well. Things slipped a little then, but overall I had a good night. Congratulation to Gary Beattie of Llandudno who was celebrating his Birthday, and congratulations to Jack McDougal, who told us the sickest joke I've heard in a long time, Scotland is proud of you !

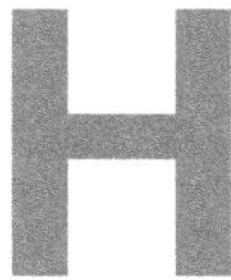

Groups Line Ups

The Hesitations (George 'King' Scott, Charles Scott, Leonard Veal, Robert Sheppard, Arthur Blakely, Phillip Dorroh, Fred Deal
The High Keys (Troy Keyes, Jimmy Williams, Bobby Haggard, Cliff Rice)
Honey Cone (Edna Wright(aka Sandy Wynns), Carolyn Wills, Sharon Cash, Shellie Clark)

Roy Hamilton

Roy Hamilton (born 16-April-1929 in Leesburg, Georgia --- died 20-July-1969 in New Rochelle, New York --- cause: hospitalised for hypertension, pneumonia and a stroke, he died a few weeks later

Epic 9015 - You'll Never Walk Alone / I'm Gonna Sit Right Down And Cry (Over You) - 1954
Epic 9047 - So Let There Be Love / If I Loved You - 1954 Orchestra Directed By O. B. Masingill
Epic 9068 - Ebb Tide / Beware - 1954 Orchestra Directed By O. B. Masingill
Epic 9086 - Hurt / Star Of Love - 1954 Orchestra Directed By O. B. Masingill
Epic 9092 - I Believe / If You Are But A Dream - 1955
Epic 9102 - Unchained Melody / From Here To Eternity - 1955 *also recorded in 1963 by The Diplomats on Arock 1000 and also in 1963 by Vito & The Salutations on Herald 583.
Epic 9111 - Forgive This Fool / You Wanted To Change Me - 1955
Epic ? - Fascination / Cacaquinho - 195?
Epic 9118 - A Little Voice / All This Is Mine - 1955
Epic 9125 - Without A Song / Cuban Love Song - 1955
Epic 9132 - Everybody's Got A Home / Take Me With You - 1955
Epic 9147 - There Goes My Heart / Walk Along With Kings - 1956
Epic 9160 - Somebody, Somewhere / Since I Fell For You - 1956
Epic 9180 - I Took My Grief To Him / Chained - 1956
Epic 9203 - The Simple Prayer / A Mother's Love - 1957
Epic 9212 - My Faith, My Hope, My Love / So Long - 1957
Epic 9224 - The Aisle / That Old Feeling - 1957
Epic 9232 - (All Of A Sudden) My Heart Sings / I'm Gonna Lock You In My Heart - 1957
Epic 9257 - Don't Let Go / The Night To Love - 1957 With The Jesse Stone Orchestra
Epic 9268 - Crazy Feelin' / In A Dream - 1958
Epic 9274 - Lips / Jungle Fever - 1958
Epic 9282 - Wait For Me / Everything - 1958
Epic 9294 - Pledging My Love / My One And Only Love - 1958
Epic 9301 - It's Never Too Late / Somewhere Along The Way - 1959
Epic 9307 - I Need Your Lovin' / Blue Prelude - 1959
Epic 9323 - Time Marches On / Take It Easy, Joe - 1959
Epic 9342 - Great Romance / On My Way Back Home - 1959

Epic 9354 - The Ten Commandments / Nobody Knows The Trouble I've Seen - 1959
Epic 9354 - The Ten Commandments / Down By The Riverside - 1959 (Alternate Flip Side)
Epic 9372 - Nobody Knows The Trouble I've Seen / Down By The Riverside - 1960
Epic 9373 - I Let A Song Go Out Of My Heart / I Get The Blues When It Rains - 1960
Epic 9374 - My Story / Please Send Me Someone To Love - 1960
Epic 9375 - Something's Gotta Give / Cheek To Cheek - 1960 (Unreleased)
Epic 9376 - Sing You Sinners / Blow, Gabriel, Blow - 1960
Epic 9386 - Having Myself A Ball / Slowly* - 1960 *Flip By Bobby Sykes
Epic 9388 - Never Let Me Go / I Get The Blues When It Rains - 1960 (Unreleased)
Epic 9390 - The Clock / I Get The Blues When It Rains - 1960
Epic 9398 - A Lover's Prayer / Never Let Me Go - 1960
Epic 9407 - Lonely Hands / Your Love - 1960
Epic 9434 - You Can Have Her / Abide With Me - 1961
Epic 9443 - You're Gonna Need Magic / To The One I Love - 1961
Epic 9449 - No Substitute For Love / Please Louise - 1961
Epic 9460 - Excerpts From "You Can Have Her" - 1961
Epic 9461 - Excerpts From "You Can Have Her" - 1961
Epic 9462 - Excerpts From "You Can Have Her" - 1961
Epic 9463 - Excerpts From "You Can Have Her" - 1961
Epic 9464 - Excerpts From "You Can Have Her" - 1961
Epic 9466 - There We Were / If - 1961
Epic 9492 - Don't Come Cryin' To Me / If Only I Had Known - 1962
Epic 9520 - Climb Ev'ry Mountain / I'll Come Running Back To You - 1962
Epic 9538 - Earthquake / I Am - 1962 (some copies issued with picture sleeve)
MGM 13138 - Let Go / You Still Love Him - 1963
MGM 13157 - Midnight Town ----- Daybreak City / Intermezzo - 1963
Memory Lane / Epic I 5-2201 - Don't Let Go / You'll Never walk Alone - 1963
Memory Lane / Epic I 5-2213 - You Can Have Her / Ebb Tide -1963
MGM 13175 - Theme From "The V.I.P.'S" (The Willow) / The Sinner (El Pecador) - 1963
MGM 13217 - The Panic Is On / There She Is - 1964
MGM 13247 - Answer Me, My Love / Unchained Melody - 1964
MGM 13291 - You Can Count On Me / She Makes Me Wanna Dance - 1964
MGM 13315 - Sweet Violets / A Thousand Years Ago - 1965
RCA Victor 47 - 8641 - Heartache / Ain't It The Truth - 1965
RCA Victor 47 - 8705 - And I Love Her / Tore Up Over You - 1965
RCA Victor 47 - 8813 - The Impossible Dream / She's Got A Heart - 1966
RCA Victor 47 - 8960 - Crackin' Up Over You / Walk Hand In Hand - 1966
RCA Victor - Let The Music Play - (recorded 2-November-1966 but unissued until it appeared on a 1997 Kent Cd "Rare Collectable And Soulful" Cdkend 141)
RCA Victor 47 - 9061 - I Taught Her Everything She Knows / Lament - 1967
RCA Victor 47 - 9171 - You Shook Me Up / So High My Love – 1967
Capitol 2057 - Let This World Be Free / Wait Until Dark - 1967
AGP 113 - The Dark End Of The Street / 100 Years - 1969
AGP 116 - Angelica / Hang Ups - 1969
AGP 25 - It's Only Make Believe / It's Only Make Believe - 1969 (Promo release only)
AGP 125 - It's Only Make Believe / 100 Years - 1969
Epic 10559 - You'll Never Walk Alone / The Golden Boy - 1969
RCA Victor 48 - 1034 - Crackin' Up Over You / Walk Hand In Hand - 1972
Epic 2773044 - Don't Come Cryin' To Me / If Only I Had Known - ????
CBS 02201 - You'll Never Walk Alone / Don't Let Go - ?
CBS 02213 - Ebb Tide / You Can Have Her - **?**
Stardust ? - Reach out for Me / All Time - ?
Stardust ? - Reach out for Me / Island in the Sun - ?
Stardust ORS 021- Panic is On / You Can Count on Me - ?

Slim Harpo

Slim Harpo (born James Isaac Moore on 11-February-1924 in Baton Rouge, Louisiana, died 31-January-1970 in London U.K., cause: heart attack)

Excello 2113 - I'm A King Bee / I Got Love If You Want It - 1957 (orange and blue label, company address at top)
Excello 2138 - Wonderin' And Worryin' / Strange Love -1958 (orange and blue label, company address at top)
Excello 2162 - You'll Be Sorry One Day / One More Day – 1959
Excello 2113 - I'm A King Bee / I Got Love If You Want It - 1960 (Orange And Blue Label, Company Address At Bottom)
Excello 2138 - Wonderin' And Worryin' / Strange Love -1960 (Orange And Blue Label, Company Address At Bottom)
Excello 2171 - Buzz Me Baby / Late Last Night - 1960 (Counterfeits Have Hole Off-Centre)
Excello 2184 - Blues Hang-Over / What A Dream – 1960
Excello 2194 - Rainin' In My Heart / Don't Start Cryin' Now – 1961
Excello 2113 - I'm A King Bee / I Got Love If You Want It - 1963 (Red, White And Blue Label)
Excello 2239 - I Love The Life I'm Livin' / Buzzin' – 1963
Excello 2246 - Little Queen Bee (Got A Brand New King) / I Need Money (Keep Your Alibis) – 1964
Excello 2253 - Still Rainin' In My Heart / We're Two Of A Kind – 1964
Excello 2261 - Sittin' Here Wondering / What's Goin' On Baby – 1964
Excello 2265 - Harpo's Blues / Please Don't Turn Me Down – 1965
Excello 2273 - Baby, Scratch My Back / I'm Gonna Miss You (Like The Devil) – 1966
Excello 2278 - Shake Your Hips / Midnight Blues – 1966
Excello 2282 - I'm Your Breadmaker, Baby / Loving You – 1967
Excello 2285 - Tip On In (Part 1) / Tip On In (Part 2) – 1967
Excello 2289 - I'm Gonna Keep What I've Got / I've Got To Be With You Tonight – 1967
Excello 2294 - Te-Ni-Nee-Ni-Nu / Mailbox Blues – 1968
Excello 2301 - Mohair Sam* / I Just Can't Leave You – 1969 *also recorded in 1965 by Charlie Rich on Smash 1993
Excello 2305 - That's Why I Love You / Just For You – 1969
Excello 2306 - Folsom Prison Blues / Mutual Friend – 1969
Excello 2309 - The Price Is Too High / I've Got My Finger On Your Triger - 1969
Excello 2316 - Jody Man / Raining In My Heart* - 1970 *re-mixed, overdubbed version.

(ALL Slim Harpo 45's with a yellow and blue Excello label are counterfeits)

Goldies 45 2606 - Baby Scratch My Back / I'm Gonna Miss You - 1973
Blues Unlimited 2015 - Wild About My Baby / Raining In My Heart - ?
Zirkon 1063 - Don't Start Cryin' Now / Rainin' In My Heart - ?

Slim Harpo / Chris Kenner

Collectables Col 030447 - Baby Scratch My Back / I Like It Like That* - ? *flip by Chris Kenner.

Betty Harris

The Hearts (Members Theresa Chatman, Mandy Hopper, Lezli Green, Mary Green, Betty Crews And Ann King)

J&S 1626/1627 - I Want Your Love Tonight / Like, Later Baby - 1958

Betty Harris (born in 1939 in Orlando, Florida)

Douglas 104 - Taking Care Of Business / Yesterday's Kisses - 1962
Jubilee 5456 - Cry To Me* / I'll Be A Liar - 1963 *cover of 1961 version by Solomon Burke on

Atlantic 2131. Also released in the U. K. on London American HL 9796.
Jubilee 5465 - His Kiss / It's Dark Outside - 1963
Jubilee 5480 - Mo Jo Hannah* / Now Is The Hour - 1964 *also recorded in 1962 by Henry Lumpkin on Motown 1029.
Jubilee - Everybody's Love A.K.A. Just Like Mine - (unissued track originally titled "Just Like Mine" when recorded in 1961 by The Renaults on Wand 114. This cut was recorded 13-November-1963 at Bell Sound Studio A in New York this was released in the U. K. on a 1998 Westside CD " Betty Harris - Soul Perfection Plus - Complete Jubilee - Sansu - SSS International Masters - 1963-1969" WESA 807)
Jubilee - Why Don't You Tell Him (Take 37) - (unissued track recorded 25-May-1964 at Bell Sound Studio B in New York this was released in the U. K. on a 1998 Westside CD " Betty Harris - Soul Perfection Plus - Complete Jubilee - Sansu - SSS International Masters - 1963-1969" WESA 807)
Sansu 450 - I'm Evil Tonight / What A Sad Feeling - 1965
Sansu 452 - Sometime / I Don't Want To Hear It - 1966
Sansu 455 - 12 Red Roses / Show It - 1966
Sansu 461 - Bad Luck / Lonely Hearts - 1967
Sansu 466 - I'm Evil Tonight / Nearer To You - 1967

James Carr

Goldwax 328 - I'm A Fool For You* / Gonna Send You Back To Georgia - 1967 *female vocals by an uncredited Betty Harris.

Betty Harris

Sansu 471 - Can't Last Much Longer / I'm Gonna Git Ya - 1967

Lee Dorsey & Betty Harris

Sansu 474 - Love Lot's Of Lovin' / Take Care Of Our Love - 1967

Betty Harris

Sansu 478 - Mean Man / What'd I Do Wrong - 1968
Sansu 479 - Hook, Line N' Sinker / Show It - 1968
Sansu 480 - Ride Your Pony / Trouble With My Lover - 1968
Sss Int'l 766 - There's A Break In The Road / All I Want Is You - 1969
Jubilee 5658 - Cry To Me / I'll Be A Liar - 1969

Betty Harris / Joe Henderson

Virgo 6014 - Cry To Me / Snap Your Fingers* - 1973 *flip by Joe Henderson.

Betty Harris

Vigor 6035 - His Kiss / It's Dark Outside - 1975
Cash 1721 - Cry To Me / ? - ?
Flashback 43 - Nearer To You / I'm Evil Tonight - ?

Kurt Harris

The Charmers (members Nathaniel Epps (lead --- later member of The Chips on Josie), Jose Harris (first tenor) with brothers Kenny Scott (baritone) and Kurtis Scott (bass)) 1955.

The Capitols (members Nathaniel Epps (lead), Billy Hall (first tenor), Eddie Jacobs (second tenor), Clarence Collins (baritone --- later member of **The Imperials** on End) and Kurtis Scott (bass))

Pet 807 - Angel Of Love* / Cause I Love You** - 1958 *leads Nathaniel Epps and Kurtis Scott. **lead Nathaniel Epps.

Kurt Harris

Josie 898 - Let Her Dance / I Can't Love Nobody Else - 1962 (With Group)
Josie 902 - Uh-Huh / You Better Shut Your Mouth – 1962
Diamond 158 - Emperor Of My Baby's Heart / Go On - 1964
Apex 76903 - Emperor Of My Baby's Heart* / Go On - 1964 (Canadian release) *co-writer Mark Barkan also wrote "Pretty Flamingo" for Manfred Mann.

Kurtis Scott (Kurt Harris)

Sure Shot 5020 - No, No Baby / No Place Like Home - 1966
Marky Ho 100 - Moon River (Vocal) / Moon River (Instrumental) - 1975
Cherokee 101/102 - Teach Me To Love Again / Lonely Singer - ?
Apache 100 - Brother / Black Child

The Hesitations

The Metrotones (members Charles "Sonny" Turner (aka Sonny Dinks) later of The Platters fame, Melvin Smith, James Frierson, Leonard Veal and Leuvenia Eaton)

Reserve 114 - More And More / ? - 1957 (Same Number Also Used For A Tracey Twins Release)
Reserve 116 - Please Come Back / Skitter Skatter - 1957

The El Pollos (members Tommy Hobbs, George Scott, Robert Manley, Walter Jones and Robert Chalmers)

Studio 999 - High School Dance / These Four Letters - 1958 (Lead Robert Chalmers)
Neptune 1001 - School Girl / Why Treat Me This Way - 1958 (Lead Robert Chalmers)

The Hesitations (members George "King" Scott (lead) Fred Deal (tenor), and Leonard Veal (tenor))

Kapp 790 - I'm Not Built That Way / Soul Superman - 1966
Kapp 810 - Soul Kind Of Love / Wait A Minute - 1967
Kapp 822 - I'll Be Right There / She Won't Come Back - 1967
Kapp 848 - You Can't Bypass Love / You'll Never Know - 1967
Kapp 878 - Born Free* / Love Is Everywhere - 1967 *From The Film Of The Same Title.
Kapp 899 - The Impossible Dream* / Nobody Knows You When You're Down And Out - 1968 *From The Broadway Musical "Man Of La Manche".
Kapp 911 - Climb Every Mountain / My World - 1968
Kapp 926 - Who Will Answer / If You Ever Need A Hand - 1968
Kapp 948 - A Whiter Shade Of Pale / With Pen In Hand - 1968
GWP 504 - Is This The Way To Treat A Girl / Yes I'm Ready - 1969

The Hesitations & Debbie Taylor

GWP 512 - No Bag Just Fact / Momma, Look Sharp - 1969

Holland / Dozier / Holland

Eddie Holland

Mercury 71290 - You / Little Miss Ruby - 1958
Tamla 102 - Merry-Go-Round / It Moves Me - 1959
United Artists 172 - Merry-Go-Round / It Moves Me - 1959
United Artists 191 - Because I Love Her / Everybody's Going - 1959
United Artists 207 - Magic Mirror / Will You Love Me - 1960
United Artists 280 - The Last Laugh / Why Do You Want To Let Me Go - 1960
Motown 1021 - Jamie - 1961 (one sided promo)
Motown 1021 - Jamie / Take A Chance On Me - 1961
Motown 1026 - You Deserve What You Got / Last Night I Had A Vision - 1962
Motown 1030 - If Cleopatra Took A Chance / What About Me - 1962
Motown 1031 - If It's Love (It's All Right) / It's Not Too Late - 1962
Motown 1036 - Darling I Hum Our Song / Just A Few Memories - 1963
Motown 1043 - Brenda / Baby Shake - 1963
Motown 1049 - I'm On The Outside Looking In / I Couldn't Cry If I Wanted To - 1963
Motown 1052 - Leaving Here / Brenda - 1964
Motown 1058 - Just Ain't Enough Love / Last Night I Had A Vision - 1964
Motown 1063 - Candy To Me / If You Don't Want My Love - 1964

Hitsville U.S.A. Dm 097311 - Greetings To Tamla Motown Appreciation Society - 1964 (This American 45 Was Limited To 300 Copies For Dispersal Throughout Various Fan Clubs Within Europe As A Promo For Their First European Tour. Each Act Gives A Greeting Over It's Latest Record. Artists Involved Include The Miracles, Stevie Wonder, Marvin Gaye, The Marvelettes, The Temptations, Martha And The Vandellas, The Contours, Kim Weston, The Supremes.and Eddie Holland The Record Has An Introduction From Publicist Margaret Phelps And Berry Gordy)

Holland - Dozier (Eddie Holland And Lamont Dozier)

Motown 1045 - What Goes Up Must Come Down / Come On Home - 1963
Invictus 9110 - Don't Leave Me (Part 1) / Don't Leave Me (Part 2) - 1972
Invictus 9125 - Why Can't We Be Lovers / Don't Leave Me - 1972
Invictus 9133 - Don't Leave Me Starvin' For Your Love (Part 1) / Don't Leave Me Starvin' For Your Love (Part 2) - 1972
Invictus 1253 - Slipping Away / Can't Get Enough - 1973
Invictus 1254 - If You Don't Wanta Be In My Life / New Breed Kinda Woman - 1973
Invictus 1258 - You Took Me From A World Outside / I'm Gonna Hijack Ya, Kidnap Ya, Take What I Want - 1973

The Romeos (Members Lamont Dozier, Tyrone Hunter, Gene Dyer, Ken Johnson, Leon Ware And Don Davenport
-- From Larados)

Fox 749 - Gone, Gone, Get Away / Let's Be Partners - 1957 (Cream Label Scarcer Than Yellow Label)
Fox 846 - Moments To Remember You By / Fine, Fine Baby - 1957 (Cream Label Scarcer Than Yellow Label)
Atco 6107 - Momemts To Remember You By / Fine, Fine Baby - 1958

The Voice Masters (Members Ty Hunter, C.P. Spencer, Lamont Dozier, David Ruffin And Freddie Gorman)

Anna 101 - Hope And Pray / Oop's I'm Sorry - 1959
Anna 102 - Needed / Needed (For Lovers Only) - 1959

Frisco 15235 - In Love In Vain / Two Lovers - 1960 (Identification Number Shown Since No Selection
Number Is Used)

Lamont Anthony

Anna 1125 - Let's Talk It Over / Benny The Skinny Man - 1960
Anna 1125 - Let's Talk It Over / Popeye - 1960
Checkmate 1001 - Just To Be Loved / I Didn't Know - 1961

Lamont Dozier

ABC 11407 - Trying To Hold On To My Woman / We Don't Want Nobody To Come Between Us - 1973
ABC 11438 - Fish Ain't Bitin' / Breaking Out All Over - 1974
ABC 12012 - Fish Ain't Bitin' / Breaking Out All Over - 1974
ABC 12044 - Let Me Start Tonite / I Wanna Be With You - 1974
ABC 12076 - All Cried Out / Rose - 1975
ABC 12234 - Out Here On My Own / Take Off Your Make-Up - 1976
Warner Brothers 8432 - Sight For Sore Eyes / Tear Down The Walls - 1977
Warner Brothers 8792 - Boogie Business / True Love Is Bittersweet - 1979
Warner Brothers 8802 - Boogie Business / True Love Is Bittersweet - 1979 (12" Release)
Columbia 02035 - Cool Me Out / Starting Over (We've Made The Necessary Changes) - 1981
Columbia 02238 - Too Little Too Long / Chained (To Your Love) - 1981
M & M 502 - Shout About It / (Instrumental) - 1982

Briant Holland

Kudo 667 - (Where's The Joy?) In Nature Boy / Shock - 1958

The Satintones (Members Charles "Chico" Leverette, Freddie Gorman, Brian Holland, James Ellis,
Sonny Sanders, Robert Bateman, Vernon Williams, Sammy Mack And Joe Charles)

Tamla 54026 - Motor City / Going To The Hop - 1960
Motown 1000 - Sugar Daddy / My Beloved - 1960 (Without Strings On "A" Side -- Matrix Number Is Mnt 12345)
Motown 1000 - Sugar Daddy / My Beloved - 1960 (With Strings On "A" Side --- Matrix Number Is 1000 G-3)
Motown 1006 - Tomorrow And Always / A Love That Can Never Be - 1961 (Without Strings)
Motown 1006 - Angel / A Love That Can Never Be - 1961
Motown 1006 - Tomorrow And Always / A Love That Can Never Be - 1961 (With Strings)
Motown 1010 - I Know How It Feels / My Kind Of Love - 1961
Motown 1020 - Zing Went The Strings Of My Heart / Faded Letter - 1962

Brian Holland

Invictus 1265 - I'm So Glad (Part 1) / I'm So Glad (Part 2) - 1974
Invictus 1272 - Super Woman / Let's Get Together - 1974

Brenda Holloway

Brenda Holloway (born 21-June-1946 in Atascadero, California, moved to L.A. at age two. Whilst in High school Brenda Holloway was a member of a school group with Walter and Wallace Scott, later of The Whispers. Also a member of a group called The Watesians who backed Johnny Rivers and Ike & Tina Turner when they performed in their region -- she is also a classically trained violinist)

Donna 1358 - Hey Fool / Echo- 1962
Donna 1366 - Game Of Love / Echo-Echo-Echo – 1962
Donna 1370 - I'll Give My Life / More Echo - 1962 (The Above Three Flip Sides Are Identical Versions Of The Same Song)

The Watesians (Members Of This Girl Group Brenda Holloway, Patrice Holloway, Pat Hunt And Priscilla Kennedy (Who Later Became Known As Eleanore Rigby And Had A 1969 Release On Amsterdam 85004 - "Father Mackenzie"))

Donna 1371 - I'll Find Myself A Guy / I Told You Baby – 1962

The Four J's (Members Brenda Holloway, Patrice Holloway, Pat Hunt And Priscilla Kennedy)

4-J 506 - Will You Be My Love / Nursery - 1963

Freddie Romain (Former Member Of The Native Boys)

Spindletop ? - Be My Girl / Be My Girl (Instrumental) - 1963 (With Backing Vocals By Brenda Holloway, Patrice Holloway And Their Cousin Pat Hunt)
Spindletop ? - Be My Girl* / I've Got A Feeling - 1963 *With Backing Vocals By Brenda Holloway, Patrice Holloway And Pat Hunt)

Patrice Holloway

Taste 125 - Do The Del-Viking (Pt. 1) / Do The Del-Viking (Pt. 2) - 1963 (Backing Vocals Brenda Holloway -- Co-Written By Brenda And Her Sister Patrice Holloway)

The Sisters (Members Rosella Arvizu, Ersi Arvizu And Mary Arvizu, A Chicano girl group with whom Brenda Holloway claims she sang backing vocals)

Del-Fi 4300 - Gee Baby Gee / All Grown Up - 1963
Del-Fi 4302 - Ooh Poo Pa Do / Happy New Year Baby – 1963
Del-Fi 4306 - Wait 'Til My Bobby Comes Home / For Sentimental Reasons - 1963

Brenda Holloway

Del-Fi - Every Little Bit Hurts* / I'll Give My Life - ? *Original Version Of Song Later To Be Released In 1964 On Tamla 54094. Both of these tracks can be found on a DEL-FI Cd released in the U. S. A. in 1999 "Del-Fi Girl Groups: Gee Baby Gee" DFCD 71266)

Hal And Brenda (Hal Davis And Brenda Holloway)

Minasa 6714 - It's You / Unless I Have You – 1963
Snap 6714 - It's You / Unless I Have You – 1963

Brenda Holloway & Jess Harris

Brevit 641 - I Never Knew You Loooked So Good Until I Quit You / Gonna Make You Mine - 1963

Bonnie & Clyde (Brenda Holloway & Robert Jackson (Brother Of Gloria Jones))

In-Sound 405 - I Get A Feeling / I Want A Boyfriend (Girlfriend) – 1963

The Soul-Mates (Brenda Holloway & Robert Jackson (Brother Of Gloria Jones))

Era 3109 - I Get A Feeling / I Want A Boyfriend – 1963

Brenda Holloway & The Carrolls

Catch 109 - I Ain't Gonna Take You Back / You're My Only Love* - 1964 *The Verdict Is Still Out Whether This Is Brenda Holloway Or Not Singing This Track.

Brenda Holloway

Tamla 54094 - Every Little Bit Hurts* / Land Of A Thousand Boys** - 1964 *Written By Ed Cobb And Featuring The Piano Of Lincoln Mayorga And Backing Vocals By Patrice Holloway And Gloria Jones. Covered In 1973 By Stacie Johnson On Motown 1236. **Written By Brenda And Her Sister Patrice Holloway. Both Tracks Are On Her Only Album Released In May 1964 "Every Little Bit Hurts" On Tamla T-257. This Was Motown's First West Coast Produced Hit.

Brenda & Patrice Holloway

? - Come Into My Palace - 1964 (Unreleased Demo Of Song Previously Recorded In 1962 By Lee & The Leopards On Gordy 7002, Also Recorded By The Supremes -- Apparently Only Track Recorded By The Two Sisters As A Duet)

Brenda Holloway

Tamla 54099 - I'll Always Love You - 1964 (One Sided Disc -- Promo Issue Only)
Tamla 54099 - I'll Always Love You* / Sad Song** - 1964 *Written By Ed Cobb - Covered By Blinky In 1968 On Motown 1134 Also Released By The Spinners In 1965 On Motown 1078. **Written By Frank Wilson.
Tamla 54111 - When I'm Gone* / I've Been Good To You - 1965 (Also Issued With Picture Sleeve) *Originally Recorded By Mary Wells In 1964 On Motown 1061.
Tamla 54115 - Operator* / I'll Be Available - 1965 *Originally Recorded By Mary Wells In 1962 On Motown 1035.
Tamla 54121 - You Can Cry On My Shoulder* / How Many Times Did You Mean It - 1965 *Written By Berry Gordy. Slated To Be Released On The Cancelled Album "Hurtin' & Cryin' ". The Promo Copies Have A Different Mix To The Released Version. This Was Covered In 1972 By Michael Jackson On Motown 1207.
Tamla 54125 - Together 'Til The End Of Time* / Sad Song* - 1965 *Written By Frank Wilson.
Tamla 54137 - Hurt A Little Every Day / Where Were You – 1966
Q-lcm Kxxx ? - Keep Me - 1966 (10" 45rpm One Sided Acetate, Label Has Rundown Stamped On It And With Thick Felt Pen Has Recoat Handwritten On It, Plus Two Signatures?)
Tamla Zt1l-206312 - Play It Cool, Stay In School - 1966 (One Sided Promo Issue -- Recorded In Co-Operation With The Women's Ad Club Of Detroit. It Was Composed By The Writer Of The Miracles Promo "I Care About Detroit", Jimmy Clark)

The Ikettes (members rumoured to be Pat Arnold, **Brenda Holloway** and Patrice Holloway) after The Ikettes split with Ike Turner over royalties, Ike Turner retained the rights to the group name and he continued to record the group with ever changing personnel.

Phi-Dan 5009 - Down Down / What'cha Gonna Do - 1966

The Belles (members Sherlie Matthews, Brenda Holloway and Patrice Holloway) on all recordings this was group line-up.While the Mirwood contract lists the members as Sherlie Matthews, Debra Dion, Rose Mary Bailey and Patricia McElroy.

Mirwood 5505 - Don't Pretend / Word's Can't Explain - 1966
Mirwood - Cupid's Got A Hold On Me - 1966 (lead vocals by Patrice Holloway this track can be found on a U. K. 2006 Kent CD "The Mirwood Soul Story Volume 2" CDKEND 264)

Brenda Holloway

Tamla 54144 - 'Til Johnny Comes / Where Were You - 1967 (Unissued) It Was Long Believed That The Miracles "I Care About Detroit" Was To Have Been Assigned This Number. But The Motown Listings For Recording Sessions Have Brenda Holloway Assigned This Number)
Tamla 54148 - Just Look What You've Done* / Starting The Hurt All Over Again - 1967 *Written By Frank Wilson And R. Dean Taylor.
Tamla 54155 - You've Made Me So Very Happy* / I've Got To Find It - 1967 *Written By Berry Gordy, Frank Wilson, Brenda Holloway And Patrice Holloway, Slated To Be Released On The Cancelled Album "Hurtin' & Cryin' ". Song Covered By Blood, Sweat & Tears In 1969 On Columbia 44776.
Tk4m-0401 - I Don't Want Nobody's Gonna Make Me Cry - 1968 (Unreleased Track Scheduled For An Album Release)

Brendetta Davis (Rumoured To Be Brenda Holloway)

Liberty 56056 - I Can't Make It Without Him* / Until You Were Gone - 1968 *Written By Barry White And Vernon Jones.

Brenda Holloway

Bronco / Mustang ? - Under Construction - 19?? (Unreleased Track Found In Company Vaults)
Music Merchant 1001 - Let Love Grow / Some Quiet Place - 1972 (The First 45 Issued By Hdh On This Label)
All For U 2 - I'm So Happy / Baby Don't Waste My Time - ?
All For U 3 - On The Real Side / Make Me Believe In You - ?
Mare 53 - Give Me A Little Inspiration - 1987 (One Sided Disc)

Brenda Holloway retired in the late sixties, returning only for occasional sessions with Joe Cocker

The Honey Bees

Vee Jay 611 - One Girl, One Boy / No Guy - 1964
Fontana 1939 - One Wonderful Night / She Don't Deserve You - 1964
Fontana 1505 - You Turn Me On / Some Of Your Lovin' - 1965
Garrison 3005 - Let's Get Back Together */ Never In A Million Years - 1966 *Co-Written By Edwin Starr
Wand 1141 - Let's Get Back Together / Never In A Million Years - 1966

Pookie Hudson

The Four Bees (members Thornton James "Pookie" Hudson, Billy Shelton, Gerald Gregory and Calvin Fossett)

"**Pookie Hudson & The Hudsonnaires** (members Thornton James "Pookie" Hudson, Billy Shelton, Gerald Gregory and Calvin Fossett)

The Spaniels (members Thornton James "Pookie" Hudson, Gerald Gregory, Opal Courtney (born Opal Leverte Courtney Jr on 22-November-1936 in Gery, Indiana --- died 18-September-2008 --- cause: heart attack), Willie C. Jackson and Earnest Warren)

Vee Jay 101 - Baby It's You / Bounce - 1953

The Spaniels with Rhythm Acc.

Chance 1141 - Baby It's You / Bounce – 1953

The Spaniels

Vee Jay 103 - The Bells Ring Out / House Cleaning – 1953

The Spanials (members Thornton James "Pookie" Hudson, Gerald Gregory, Opal Courtney, Willie C. Jackson and Earnest Warren)

Vee Jay 107 - Goodnight, Sweetheart, Goodnight* / You Don't Move Me - 1953 *also recorded in 1954 by Gloria Mann with The Carter Rays on S-L-S 102.

The Spaniels (members Thornton James "Pookie" Hudson, Gerald Gregory, Opal Courtney, Willie C. Jackson and Earnest Warren)

Vee Jay 107 - Goodnight, Sweet Heart, Goodnight / You Don't Move Me - 1953
Vee Jay 116 - Play It Cool / Let's Make Up - 1954
Vee Jay 131 - Do-Wah / Don'cha Go - 1955 (After This Release Opal Courtney Was Drafted For A Few months, then replaced by James Cochran)

The Spanials

Vee Jay 154 - You Painted Pictures / Hey, Sister Lizzie - 1955

The Spaniels

Vee Jay 154 - You Painted Pictures / Hey, Sister Lizzie - 1955 (after this release Ernest Warren was drafted and the group carried on with four members)
Vee Jay 178 - False Love / Do You Really - 1956
Vee Jay 189 - Dear Heart / Why Won't You Dance - 1956 (after this release Pookie Hudson and Willie C. Jackson leave group)

The Spaniels (members Carl Rainge, Gerald Gregory, James Cochran and Don Porter)

Vee Jay 202 - Since I Fell For You / Baby Come Along With Me - 1956

The Spaniels (members Pookie Hudson, Carl Rainge, Gerald Gregory, James Cochran and Don Porter)

Vee Jay 229 - Please Don't Tease / You Gave Me Peace Of Mind - 1956
Vee Jay 246 - Everyone's Laughing / I.O.U. - 1957
Vee Jay 257 You're Gonna Cry / I Need Your Kisses - 1957
Vee Jay 264 - I Love You / Crazee Babee - 1958
Vee Jay 278 - Tina / Great Googley Moo - 1958
Vee Jay 290 - Stormy Weather / Here Is Why I Love You - 1958
Vee Jay 301 - Baby It's You / Heart And Soul - 1958
Vee Jay 310 - Trees / I Like It Like That - 1959
Vee Jay 328 - These Three Words / 100 Years From Today - 1959
Vee Jay 342 - People Will Say We' Re In Love / The Bells Ring Out - 1960

The Spaniels (members Pookie Hudson, Ernest Warren, Gerald Gregory, Bill Carey and Andy McGruder (former member of The 5 Blue Notes on Sabre and later member of The Carltons on Chess)

Vee Jay 350 - I Know / Bus Fare Home – 1960
Vee Jay 101 - Baby It's You / Bounce – 1961

Pookie Hudson and The Spaniels (members Pookie Hudson, Bill Carey and Ricky Burden)

Neptune 124 - I Love You For Sentimental Reasons / Meek Man – 1961

Pookie Hudson (born James Hudson on 11-June-1934 in Des Moines, Iowa --- died 16-January-2006 at his home in Capital Heights, Maryland --- cause: metastatic lung cancer)

Parkway 839 - John Brown / Turn Out The Lights – 1962
Double L 711 - Jealous Heart / I Know, I Know* - 1963 *flip side backed by The Imperials minus Little Anthony.
Double L 720 - Miracles / (I Love You) For Sentimental Reasons – 1963

The Spaniels

Oldies 45 52 - Stormy Weather / Here Is Why I Love You – 1964
Oldies 45 64 - Play It Cool / Let's Make Up – 1964
Oldies 45 97 - Baby It's You / The Bounce – 1964

The Spaniels / Sandy Nelson

Oldies 45 121 - Baby Come Along With Me / Teen Beat* - 1964 *flip by Sandy Nelson.

The Spaniels / Johnny Bond

Oldies 45 140 - You Don't Move Me / Hot Rod Lincoln* - 1964 *flip by Johnny Bond.

The Spaniels / Little Caesar & The Romans

Oldies 45 148 - Let's Make Up / Those Oldies But Goodies Remind Me Of You* - 1964 *flip by Little Caesar & The Romans.

The Spaniels

Oldies 45 304 - You Painted Pictures / Do Wah – 1965

Pookie Hudson

Jamie 1319 - This Gets To Me / All The Places I've Been - 1966
Chess ? – 1966

The Spaniels (members Pookie Hudson, Alvin Wheeler, Alvin Lloyd, Peter Simmons and Andrew Lawyer (a former member of The Truetones)

Buddah 153 - Goodnight Sweetheart / Maybe – 1969

The Spaniels

North American 001 - Fairy Tales* / Jealous Heart - 1970 (Pookie backed by The Imperials minus Little Anthony) *also recorded in 1961 by The Fashions on Elmor 301.
Calla 172 - Jealous Heart / Fairy Tales - 1970

The Spaniels (members Pookie Hudson, Charles Douglas, Alvin Wheeler, Alvin Lloyd and Peter Simmons)

North American 002 - Stand In Line / Lonely Man - 1970
North American 1114 - Come Back To These Arms / Money Blues - 1970

The Spaniels

Lost Nite 262 - Baby It's You / Bounce - 197?
Lost Nite 265 - The Bells Ring Out / House Cleaning - 197?
Lost Nite 268 - Goodnight, Sweetheart, Goodnight / You Don't Move Me - 197?
Lost Nite 271 - Do-Wah / Don ' Cha Go - 1970
Lost Nite 274 - Play It Cool / Let's Make Up - 197?
Lost Nite 277 - False Love / Do You Really - 197?
Lost Nite 280 - You Painted Pictures / Hey, Sister Lizzie - 197?
Lost Nite 283 - Dear Heart / Why Won't You Dance - 197?
Lost Nite 286 - Everyone's Laughing / I.O.U. - 197?
Lost Nite 289 - I Lost You / Crazy Baby - 197?
Lost Nite 292 - You Gave Me Peace Of Mind / Please Don't Tease - 197?
Lost Nite 295 - You're Gonna Cry / I Like It Like That - 197?
Lost Nite 298 - Stormy Weather / Here Is Why I Love You - 197?
Lost Nite 301 - Tina / Great Googley Moo - 197?

The Spaniels (members Carl Rainge (cousin of Mel Britt of "She'll Come Running Back" on FIP fame), Gerald Gregory, James Cochran and Don Porter)

Lost Nite 304 - Since I Fell For You / Baby Come Along With Me - 197?

The Spaniels

Lost Nite 307 - This Is A Lovely Way To Spend An Evening / Red Sails In The Sunset - 1970
Lost Nite 446 - I Know / Bus Fare Home - 197?
Trip 103 - I Know I Know -- I Love You / For Sentimental Reasons - 1972
Owl 328 - Little Joe / The Posse - 1973

The Spaniels (members Pookie Hudson, Carl Rainge, James Cochran and Don Porter)

Canterbury 101 - Peace Of Mind / She Sang To Me ..... Danny Boy - 1974

The Spaniels

Eric 0162 - Stormy Weather / Goodnight, Sweetheart Goodnight - 1970's

The Sandpebbles / The Spaniels

Collectables Col 001617 - Love Power / Fairy Tales* - 198? *Flip By The Spaniels

The Spaniels

Collectables Col 014117 - Trees / 100 Years From Today - 198?
Collectables Col 014157 - Baby It's You / Bounce - 198?
Collectables Col 014167 - The Bells Ring Out / House Cleaning - 198?
Collectables Col 014177 - Goodnight, Sweetheart Goodnight / You Don't Move Me - 198?
Collectables Col 014197 - Play It Cool / Let's Make Up - 198?
Collectables Col 014207 - False Love / Do You Really - 198?
Collectables Col 014217 - You Painted Pictures / Sister Lizzie - 198?
Collectables Col 014227 - Dear Heart / Why Won't You Dance - 198?
Collectables Col 014257 - You Gave Me Peace Of Mind / Please Don't Tease - 198?
Collectables Col 014267 - You're Gonna Cry / I Need Your Kisses - 198?
Collectables Col 014277 - Stormy Weather / Here Is Why I Love You - 198?
Collectables Col 014287 - Tina / Great Googley Moo - 198?
Collectables Col 014297 - Since I Fell For You / Baby Come Along With Me - 198?
Collectables Col 014307 - This Is A Lovely Way To Spend An Evening / Red Sails In The Sunset - 198?
Vee Jay 107 - Goodnite Sweetheart, Goodnite / You Don't Move Me - 1993 Commemorative

Issue.
Classic Artists 138 - All The Places I've Been / Sloppy Drunk - 1995 (including 100 promos only 400 copies made total)

Fred Hughes

Vee-Jay 684 - Oo Wee Baby, I Love You* / Love Me Baby - 1965 *also recorded in 1969 by Roscoe Robinson on Atlantic 2637.
Vee-Jay 703 - My Heart Cries Oh / You Can't Take It Away - 1965
Vee-Jay 718 - Don't Let Me Down / My Heart Cries Oh – 1966
Exodus 1036 - As Long As We Are Together / Walk On Back To You – 1966
Exodus 2006 - We've Got Love / I Keep Tryin' – 1966
Exodus 2009 - As Long As We Are Together / Walk On Back To You – 1967
Cadet 5579 - Come Home Little Darlin' / Can't Make It Without You – 1967
Cadet 5616 - Baby Don't Go / Love Is Ending – 1968
Brunswick 55419 - Baby Boy / Who You Really Are – 1969
Brunswick 55439 - Oo Wee Baby I Love You / I Understand – 1970
Brunswick 55446 - Don't Let This Happen To Us / In My Time Of Need - 1971
Hip Star 1013 - Take Me As I Am / (Instrumental) - ?

Jimmy Hughes

The Singing Clouds (members Jimmy Hughes, Carl Bailey, ...) member of group till 1962.

Jimmy Hughes (born 3-February-1938 in Leighton, Alabama --- died 1-April-1997 --- cause: cancer)

Guyden 2075 - I'm Qualified / My Loving Time - 1962
Fame 1002 – Everybody Let's Dance / You Might As Well Forget Him* – 1963 *also recorded in 1964 by The Tams on ABC-Paramount Lp 481.
Jamie 1280 I'm Qualified / My Loving Time – 1964
Fame 6401 - Steal Away* / Lolly Pops, Lace And Lipstick - 1964 *also recorded in 1969 by Johnnie Taylor on Stax 0068 and in 1969 by The Sheppards on Bunky 7764 plus in 1970 by Leon Austin on King 6291. (black label scarcer than red)
Fame 6403 - Try Me* / Lovely Ladies** - 1964 *also recorded in 1958 by James Brown on Federal 12337. **also released in 1965 by the British group The Adlibs on Interphon 7717.
Fame 6404 - I'm Getting Better* / I Want Justice – 1965 *written by Ed Bruce.
Fame 6407 - Goodbye My Lover Goodbye* / It Was Nice - 1965 *also recorded in 1963 by Robert Mosley on Capitol 4961.
Fame 6410 - You Really Know How To Hurt A Guy (You Really Know How To Make Him Cry)* / The Loving Physician – 1965
Oldies 45 184 - Steal Away / Lolly Pops, Lace And Lipstick – 1965
Fame 1000 - Midnight Affair / When It Comes To Dancing - 1965
Fame 1002 - Everybody Let's Dance / You Might As Well Forget Him - 1966 (another Fame 45 was also assigned this number "Gonna Make You Say Yeah / Hit The Ground" by Terry Woodford)
Fame 1003 - Neighbor, Neighbor* / It's A Good Thing - 1966 *the 45 is a different version to the Lp track.
Fame 1006 - A Shot Of Rhythm & Blues* / I Worship The Ground You Walk On – 1966 *also recorded in 1962 by Arthur Alexander on Dot 16309.
Fame 1011 - Why Not Tonight / I'm A Man Of Action - 1966
Fame 1014 - Don't Lose Your Good Thing / You Can't Believe Everything You Hear - 1967
Fame 1015 - Hi-Heel Sneakers / Time Will Bring You Back - 1967
Atlantic 2454 - It Ain't What You Got / Uncle Sam - 1967
Volt 4002 - I Like Everything You Do / What Side Of The Door - 1968

Volt 4008 - Sweet Things You Do / Let 'Em Down Baby - 1968
Volt 4017 - Chains Of Love / I'm Not Ashamed To Beg Or Plead - 1969
Volt 4024 - I'm So Glad / Lay It On The Line - 1970
Volt 4060 - Just Ain't Strong As I Used To Be (You Done Fed Me Sumpin') / Did You Forget - 1971

Wade Flemons / Jimmy Hughes

Trip 47 - Here I Stand / Steal Away* - 1971 *flip by Jimmy Hughes.

Fred Hughes / Jimmy Hughes

Collectables Col 030737 – Oo-Wee Baby I Love You / Steal Away* - 1981 *flip by Jimmy Hughes.

Jimmy Hughes

Atlantic Oldies Series 13108 - Neighbor, Neighbor / Why Not Tonight - ?

Group Line Ups

The Incredibles (Cal Waymon, Carl Gilbert, Alda Denise Edwards, Jean Smith)
The Intrigues (Alfred Brown, James Lee, James Harris, Ronald Hamilton)
The Intruders (Sam 'Little Sonny' Brown, Eugene Daughtery, Phillip Terry, Robert 'Big Sonny' Edwards)
The Invitations (Herman Colefield, Gary Grant, Bill Morris, Bobby Rivers)
The Isley Brothers (Ronald Isley, Rudolph Isley, O'kelly Isley, later members Ernie Isley And Marvin Isley)

The Ideals

Johnny Brantley & The Ideals (members Johnny Brantley, Reggie Jackson, Leonard Mitchell, Wes Spraggins, Robert Tharp, Sam Stewart and (possibly) Major Lance)

Checker 979 - Knee Socks / Mary's Lamb - 1961

The Ideals (members Reggie Jackson, Leonard Mitchell, Robert Tharp, Sam Stewart and Major Lance)

Paso 6401 - Together / What's The Matter With You Sam - 1961
Paso 6402 - Magic / Teens - 1961 (Major Lance Departs)
Concord ? - Gorilla / Do Juan - 1963 (Eddie Williams Joins Group)
Cortland 110 - Gorilla / Do Juan - 1963
Cortland 113 - Mo Joe Hanna / Simple Simon - 1964
Cortland 115 - Feeling Of A Kiss / You Came A Long Way From St. Louis - 1964

Cortland 117 - Local Boy / L.A. - 1964
Daisy 04 - Thunder Drums / ? - 1964
St. Lawrence 1001 - Cathy's Clown / Go Get A Wig - 1965
Satellite 2007 - You Lost And I Won / You Hurt Me - 1965
Satellite 2009 - Kissing / I Had A Dream - 1966
Satellite 2011 - Go Go Gorilla / Kissing Won't Go Out Of Style - 1966
St. Lawrence 1020 - I Got Lucky (When I Found You) / Tell Her I Apologize - 1966
Boo-Ga-Loo 108 -The Mighty Lover / Dancing In U S A.

The Impressions

The Roosters (Members Arthur Brooks, Richard Brooks, Sam Gooden, Fred Cash And ?)

The Northern Jubilee Gospel Singers (Members Jerry Butler, Curtis Mayfield,...)

The Quails (On And Off Member Jerry Butler (Born 8-December-1939 In Sunflower, Mississippi -- older brother of **Billy Butler**), ...)

The Alphatones (On and off member Curtis Mayfield (Born 3-June-1942 In Chicago Illinois. Paralysed from the neck down after a freak accident in which part of a public address system collapsed on top of him during a concert on the 14-August-1990 In Brooklyn, New York - Died 26-December-1999 At North Fulton Regional Hospital in Roswell,
Georgia), ...)

The Roosters (Members Jerry Butler, Curtis Mayfield, Arthur Brooks, Richard Brooks And Sam Gooden) Group tried to get audition for Chess Records but was refused entry by Company Secretary, So they went to the other side of the street To Vee-Jay Records.

Jerry Butler & The Impressions (members Jerry Butler, Curtis Mayfield, Arthur Brooks, Richard Brooks and Sam Gooden) name of group was changed by Calvin Carter of Vee-Jay who gave them their audition it is said in the hallway of the company!

Vee-Jay 280 - For Your Precious Love* / Sweet Was The Wine - 1958 *also recorded in 1963 by Garnett Mimms & The Enchanters on United Artists 658.
Falcon 1013 - For Your Precious Love* / Sweet Was The Wine - 1958 *also recorded in 1971 by Geater Davis on House Of Orange 2405.
Abner 1013 - For Your Precious Love / Sweet Was The Wine – 1958

The Impressions Featuring Jerry Butler (Members Jerry Butler, Curtis Mayfield, Arthur Brooks, Richard Brooks And Sam Gooden)

Abner 1017 - Come Back My Love / Love Me – 1958

The Impressions (Members Jerry Butler, Curtis Mayfield, Arthur Brooks, Richard Brooks And Sam Gooden)

Abner 1023 - The Gift Of Love / At The County Fair* - 1958 *Lead Curtis Mayfield.

The Impressions (Members Curtis Mayfield, Fred Cash, Arthur Brooks, Richard Brooks And Sam Gooden)

Swirl 107 - I Need Your Love / Don't Leave Me – 1958
Bandera 2504 - Listen To Me / Shorty's Got To Go – 1958

The Impressions (Members Jerry Butler, Curtis Mayfield, Arthur Brooks, Richard Brooks And Sam Gooden)

Abner 1025 - Lonely One / Senorita I Love You – 1959

The Impressions (Members Curtis Mayfield, Fred Cash, Arthur Brooks, Richard Brooks And Sam Gooden)

20th Century Fox 172 - All Through The Night / Meanwhile Back In My Heart – 1959
Abner 1034 - Say That You Love Me / A New Love – 1960
Adore 901 - Popcorn Willie / I Dreamed Last Night - 1961 (Can Anyone Verify If This Is The Same Set Of Impressions?)
ABC-Paramount 10241 - Gypsy Woman / As Long As You Love Me – 1961
Port 70031 - Listen / Shorty's Got To Go – 1962
Vee-Jay 424 - Say That You Love Me / Senorita I Love You – 1962
ABC-Paramount 10289 - Can't You See / Grow Closer Together - 1962
ABC-Paramount 10328 - Never Let Me Go / Little Young Lover – 1962
ABC-Paramount 10357 - Minstrel And Queen / You've Come Home – 1962
Vee-Jay 574 - The Gift Of Love / At The County Fair – 1963
ABC-Paramount 10386 - I'm The One Who Loves You / I Need Your Love – 1963

The Impressions (Members Curtis Mayfield, Fred Cash And Sam Gooden)

ABC-Paramount 10431 - Sad Sad Girl And Boy / Twist And Limbo – 1963
ABC-Paramount 10487 - It's All Right / You'll Want Me Back – 1963
ABC-Paramount 10511 - Talking About My Baby / Never Took Such Love – 1963

Jerry Butler & The Impressions (Members Jerry Butler, Curtis Mayfield, Arthur Brooks, Richard Brooks And Sam Gooden)

Oldies 45 77 - The Gift Of Love / At The County Fair – 1964

The Impressions (Members Curtis Mayfield, Fred Cash, Arthur Brooks, Richard Brooks And Sam Gooden)

Vee-Jay 621 - Say That You Love Me / Senorita I Love You – 1964

The Impressions (Members Curtis Mayfield, Fred Cash And Sam Gooden)

ABC-Paramount 10537 - Girl You Don't Know Me / A Woman Who Loves Me – 1964
ABC-Paramount 10544 - I'm So Proud / I Made A Mistake – 1964
ABC-Paramount 10554 - Keep On Pushing / I Love You – 1964
ABC-Paramount 10581 - You Must Believe Me / See The Real Me – 1964
ABC-Paramount 10602 - Amen / Long Long Winter – 1964
ABC-Paramount 10622 - I've Been Trying / People Get Ready – 1965
ABC-Paramount 10647 - Woman's Got Soul / Get Up And Move – 1965
ABC-Paramount 10670 - Meeting Over Yonder / I've Found That I've Lost – 1965
ABC-Paramount 10710 - I Need You / Never Could You Be Me – 1965
ABC-Paramount 10725 - Twilight Time / Just One Kiss – 1965
ABC-Paramount 10750 - You've Been Cheatin' / Man Oh Man – 1965
ABC-Paramount10761 - Falling In Love With You / Since I Lost The One I Love – 1966
ABC-Paramount 10789 - Too Slow / No One Else – 1966
ABC 10831 - Can't Satisfy / This Must End – 1966
ABC 10869 - Love's A Coming / Wade In The Water – 1966
ABC 10900 - You Always Hurt Me / Little Girl – 1967
ABC 10932 - It's Hard To Believe / Got Me Runnin' – 1967
ABC 10964 - You Ought To Be In Heaven / I Can't Stay Away From You – 1967
ABC 11022 - We're A Winner / It's All Over – 1967
ABC 11071 - We're Rolling On (Part 1) / We're Rolling On (Part 2) – 1968
ABC 11103 - I Loved And I Lost / Up Up And Away – 1968

ABC 11135 - Sometimes I Wonder / Don't Cry My Love – 1968
Curtom Sp 3 - Merry Xmas Happy New Year – 1968
ABC 11188 - East Of Java / Just Before Sunrise – 1969
Curtom 1932 - Fool For You / I'm Loving Nothing – 1968
Curtom 1934 - This Is My Country / My Woman's Love – 1968
Curtom 1937 - My Deceiving Heart / You Want Somebody Else – 1969
Curtom 1940 - Seven Years / The Girl I Find – 1969
Curtom 1943 - Choice Of Colours / Mighty Mighty Spade And Whitey – 1969
Curtom 1946 - Say You Love Me / You'll Always Be Mine – 1969
Curtom 1948 - Amen / Wherever She Leadeth Me – 1970
Curtom 1951 - Can't You See / Check Out Your Mind – 1970

The Impressions (Members Leroy Hutson, Fred Cash And Sam Gooden)

Curtom 1954 - Turn To Me / Soulful Love – 1970
Curtom 1957 - Ain't Got Time / I'm So Proud – 1971
Curtom 1959 - Love Me / Do You Wanna Win – 1971
Curtom 1964 - We Must Be In Love / Inner City Blues – 1971
Curtom 1970 - This Love's For Real / Times Have Changed – 1972
Curtom 1973 - I Need To Belong To Someone / Love Me – 1972

The Impressions (Members Fred Cash And Sam Gooden)

Curtom 1982 - Times Have Changed / Preacher Man – 1973
Curtom 1985 - Thin Line / I'm Loving You – 1973

The Impressions (Members Ralph Johnson, Fred Cash, Sam Gooden And Reggie Torian)

Curtom 1994 - If It's In You To Do Wrong / Times Have Changed – 1973

The Impressions (Members Curtis Mayfield, Fred Cash And Sam Gooden)

Roulette 113 - Amen / People Get Ready – 1973
Roulette 112 - Keep On Pushing / We're A Winner – 1973
Roulette 115 - You Must Believe Me / See The Real Me -1973

The Impressions (Members Ralph Johnson, Fred Cash, Sam Gooden And Reggie Torian)

Curtom 1997 - I'll Always Be There / Finally Got Myself Together (I'm A Changed Man) - 1974
Curtom 2003 - Three The Hard Way / Something's Mighty Mighty Wrong – 1974

The Impressions (Members - as above for original releases)

Curtom 0101 - Fool For You / This Is My Country – 1975
Curtom 0102 - Choice Of Colors / Seven Years – 1975
Curtom 0103 - Sooner Or Later / Miracle Woman – 1975
Curtom 0104 - Check Out Your Mind / Turn On To Me (Baby) – 1975
Curtom 0105 - Ain't Got Time / I'm So Proud – 1975
Curtom 0106 - The Same Thing It Took / I'm So Glad – 1975
Curtom 0108 - Thin Line / But If It's In You To Do Wrong – 1975

The Impressions (Members Ralph Johnson, Fred Cash, Sam Gooden And Reggie Torian)

Curtom 0110 - Loving Power / First Impressions – 1976
Curtom 0116 - Sunshine / I Wish I'd Stayed In Bed – 1976

The Impressions (Members Nate Evans, Fred Cash, Sam Gooden And Reggie Torian)

Cotillion 44210 - This Time / I'm A Fool For Love – 1976
Cotillion 44211 - I Saw Mama Kissing Santa Claus / Silent Night – 1976
Cotillion 44214 - You'll Never Find / Stardust – 1977
Cotillion 44222 - Can't Get Along / You're So Right For Me – 1977
Cotillion Dsko 103 - Dance (6:19) / Dance (6:19) - 1977 (12" - 33 1/3 Rpm Release)
Chi-Sound 2418 - All I Want To Do Is Make Love To You / Sorry – 1979
Chi-Sound 2435 - All I Want To Do Is Make Love To You / Maybe I'm Mistaken – 1979
Chi-Sound 2438 - Maybe I'm Mistaken / ? – 1979
Chi-Sound 2491 - You're Mine / For Your Precious Love – 1981
Chi-Sound 2499 - Fan The Fire / Love, Love, Love – 1981
MCA 52995 - Can't Wait Til Tomorrow / Love Workin' On Me – 1987
MCA 52995 - Can't Wait Til Tomorrow (Long Version) / Can't Wait Til Tomorrow (Radio Version) - 1986 (7" Promo Issue Only
Ripete 3001 - Something Said Love / ? – 1989
Radio 024 - Seven Years / The Girl I Find - ?

The Impressions (Members Jerry Butler, Curtis Mayfield, Arthur Brooks, Richard Brooks And Sam Gooden)

Collectables Col 0336 6 - At The Country Fair / Young Lover - ?
Collectables Col 03367 - The Gift Of Love / Senorita I Love You - ?

The Impressions (Members Curtis Mayfield, Fred Cash And Sam Gooden)

Collectables Col 03713 - We're A Winner / You Must Believe Me - ?
Collectables Col 03725 - You've Been Cheating / Never Let Me Go - ?
Collectables Col 90089 - Amen / People Get Ready - ?

The Impressions

Collectables Col 90105 - Gypsy Woman* / It's All Right** - ? *Members Curtis Mayfield, Fred Cash, Arthur Brooks, Richard Brooks And Sam Gooden. ** Members Curtis Mayfield, Fred Cash And Sam Gooden

The Impressions (Members Curtis Mayfield, Fred Cash And Sam Gooden)

Collectables Col 90129 - I'm So Proud / Woman's Got Soul - ?

Jerry Butler / Jerry Butler & The Impressions (Members Jerry Butler, Curtis Mayfield, Arthur Brooks, Richard Brooks And Sam Gooden)

Original Sound Obg-4510 - He Will Break Your Heart / For Your Precious Love* - ? *Flip By Jerry Butler & The Impressions.

The Impressions (Members

Ichiban 633 - First Impressions / Sooner Or Later - 1994
Robin Hood 139 - Believe In Me / Long Time Ago - ?
Robin Hood 140 - Young Lover / Don't Send Me Away - ?
Robin Hood 147 - Lover's Lane / Let Me Know - ?

The Intrigues

The Intrigues (members James "Bubba" Thomas (lead), William Parks (first tenor), Lee Quarles (second tenor) and Cornelius "Neil" Dargan (bass / baritone)) Boston Mass. group

Port 3018 - Don't Refuse My Love / Girl Let's Stay Together - 1966 (songs written by Ben and Reggie Boyce)

The Parkteers (members

? - Zap! Pow! E-Yow! (Here Comes My Baby Batman Style) / ? - ? (backed by The Intigues (PORT)) The Parkteers were a group of dancers who worked for "Mama Lou" Parks who provided the dancers for The James Brown Revue. "Mama Lou" was William Parks sister.

Thanks to Lee Quarles for above information.

The Intrigues

The Intrigues (members Alfred Brown, James Lee, James Harris and Ronald Hamilton)

Toot 609 - Soul Brother (Part 1) / Soul Brother (Part 2) – 1968
Bullet 1001 - In A Moment / Scotchman Rock – 1969
Yew 1001 - In A Moment / Scotchman Rock – 1969
Yew 1002 - I'm Gonna Love You / I Gotta Find Out For Myself – 1969
Yew 1007 - Just A Little Bit More / Let's Dance – 1970
Yew 1010 - Tuck A Little Love Away / I Know There's Love – 1970
Yew 1012 - The Language Of Love / I Got Love – 1971
Yew 1013 - Mojo Hannah / To Make A World – 1971
Janus 175 - Mojo Hannah / To Make A World – 1972
Janus 185 - I Wanna Know / Fly Now - Pay Later – 1972
World Trade 1000 - Fly Girl / ? - 1985

The Intrigues / Shirley Ellis

Rocky Mountain Productions R. M. 1100 - In A Moment / Shy One* - ? *Flip By Shirley Ellis

The Invitations

The Champlains (members Gary Gant (born in Marion, South Carolina), ...)

The Tip Toppers (members Roy Jolly, Gary Gant (baritone), Bill Morris (died 2004 -- cause: cancer) and Robert "Bobby" Rivers)

The Invitations (members Roy Jolly (lead vocals), Gary Gant, Bill Morris and Robert Rivers)

Dyno Voice 206 - Written On The Wall / Hallelujah – 1965
Dyno Voice 210 - What's Wrong With Me Baby* / Why Did My Baby Turn Bad - 1965 *also recorded in 1966 by The Toys and released on their Lp "The Toys Sing "A Lover's Concerto" And "Attack!" on Dyno Voice 9002.
Dyno Voice 215 - Skiing In The Snow* / Why Did My Baby Turn Bad – 1966 * recorded 25-November-1964, lead vocals by Billy Morris. --- Song also recorded in 1965 by The Beach Girls on Dynovox 202.

The Invitations (members Herman Colefield (lead vocals), Gary Gant, Bill Morris and Robert Rivers)

M-G-M 13574 - Girl I'm Leavin' You / The Skate - 1966
M-G-M 13666 - Watch Out Little Girl / You're Like A Mystery* – 1967 *also recorded in 1966 by The Belmonts on United Artists 50007.
Diamond 253 - Got To Have It Now / Swingin' On The Love Vine – 1968
Big Tree 121 - Franks Folly (Carogina's Noice) / A Wednesday In Your Garden - 1971 (possibly

an entirely different group)

The Invitations (members Lew Kirton (lead vocals --- former drummer for Sam & Dave), Gary Gant, Bill Morris and Robert Rivers)

Silver Blue 801 - They Say The Girl's Crazy / For Your Precious Love – 1973
Silver Blue 804 - Love Has To Grow / Let's Love (And Find Together) – 1973
Silver Blue 809 - Living Together Is Keeping Us Apart / I Didn't Know - 1974
Silver Blue 818 - Look On The Good Side / Look On The Good Side (Part 2) – 1974

Lew Jiggs Kirton

Verdith 005 – Hold On What You Got (Part 1) / Hold On What You Got (Part 2) – 1976

The Invitations (members Lew Kirton, Gary Gant, Bill Morris and Robert Rivers)

Red Greg 211 - We Don't Allow (No Sitting Down In Here) / Funky Road – 1977
Red Greg Rg 213/4 - We Don't Allow (No Sitting Down In Here) (6:16) / Funky Road (6:32) – 1977 (12" Release)

Lew Kirton

Marlin 3311 - Do What You Want, Be What You Want / Come On With It* - 1977 *also recorded in 1976 by Clarence Reid on Alston 3720.
Alston 3739 - New York City / Let Me Off My Knees - 197?
Alston 3743 - Heaven In The Afternoon (4:00) / Heaven In The Afternoon (4:00) – 1978 (promo issue only)
Alston 3743 - Heaven In The Afternoon (3:37) / Heaven In The Afternoon (Instrumental) (4:00) - 1978
T. K. Disco 103 – Heaven In The Afternoon (5:40) / Heaven In The Afternoon (Instrumental) (5:40) – 1978 (12" Release)
Marlin 3347 - Island Girl / Time To Get With It - 1981
Believe In A Dream Zs4 04058 – Talk To Me / Talk To Me (Instrumental) – 1983
Believe In A Dream 4z9 04072 – Talk To Me (5:22) / Talk To Me (Instrumental) (5:24) – 1983 (12" Release)
Believe In A Dream Zs4 04380 – Always Will (3:59) / Always Will (3:59) – 1983 (Promo Issue Only)
Believe In A Dream As 1782 – Don't Give Up Your Dream (Hang On In There) (4:35) / Don't Give Up Your Dream (Hang On In There) (4:35) – 1983 (12" Release)
Tweeside Lk 001 – Don't Wanna Wait (5:19) / Stuck In The Middle (Between Two) (4:07) – 1986 (12" Release)

Lew Kirton / Charles Johnson

Alston 3743 – Heaven In The Afternoon / Never Had A Love So Good - ? (reissue) *flip by Charles Johnson.

The Invitations (members Lew Kirton, Gary Gant, Bill Morris and Robert Rivers)

Red Greg Rg 214 - We Don't Allow (No Sitting Down In Here) (6:16) / Funky Road (6:32) – 2005 (12" Release)

The Invitations (members Alvin Ham, Richie Pitts (former member of The Velours), Gary Gant and Robert Blanding) 2004

The Isley Brothers

The Isley Brothers (members Ronald Isley, Rudolph Isley, O'Kelly Isley (born 25-December-1937 -- died 31-March-1986, cause: heart attack) and Vernon Isley (born in Cincinnati, Ohio - died 1955 (bike accident), later members Ernie Isley and Marvin Isley)

Teenage 1004 - Angels Cried / The Cow Jumped Over The Moon – 1957
Mark-X 7003 - The Drag / Rockin' Macdonald – 1957
Cindy 3009 - Don't Be Jealous / This Is The End - 1958 (the "shadow" print writing on label is scarcer than "regular" print)
Gone 5022 - I Wanna Know / Everybody's Gonna Rock And Roll – 1958
Gone 5048 - My Love / The Drag – 1958
Mark-X 8000 - The Drag / Rockin' Macdonald – 1959
RCA Victor 47-7537 - I'm Gonna Knock On Your Door / Turn To Me – 1959
RCA Victor 47-7588 - Shout (Part1) / Shout (Part 2) – 1959
RCA Victor 61-7588 - Shout (Part 1) / Shout (Part 2) - 1959 (Stereo)
RCA Victor 47-7657 - Respectable* / Without A Song - 1959 *also recorded in 1961 by The Chants on Tru-Eko 3567 and in 1963 by Jimmy Soul & The Chants on 20th Century Fox 413.
RCA Victor 47-7718 - He's Got The Whole World In His Hands / How Deep Is The Ocean – 1960
RCA Victor 47-7746 - Gypsy Love Song / Open Up Your Heart – 1960
RCA Victor 47-7787 - Say You Love Me Too / Tell Me Who - 1960
Atlantic 2092 - Jeepers Creepers / Teach Me How To Shimmy – 1961
Atlantic 2100 - Shine On Harvest Moon / Standing On The Dance Floor – 1961
Atlantic 2110 - Your Old Lady / Write To Me – 1961
Atlantic 2122 - A Fool For You / Just One More Time – 1961
Wand 118 - Right Now / The Snake – 1962
Wand 124 - Twist And Shout* / Spanish Twist - 1962 *session: Eric Gale (guitar), Trade Martin (guitar), Cornell Dupree (guitar), Chuck Rainey (bass), Paul Griffin (keyboards)

The Isley Brothers / The Discotays

Wand 124 - Twist And Shout / Wa-Watusi* - ? *Flip By The Discotays

The Isley Brothers

RCA Victor 447-0589 - Shout (Part 1) / Shout (Part 2) - 1962 (gold standard series - dog on top)

Wand 127 - Twistin' With Linda / You Better Come Home* - 1962 *also recorded in 1966 by The Exciters on Bang 518.
Wand 131 - Nobody But Me / I'm Laughing To Keep From Crying – 1963
Wand 137 - I Say Love / Hold On Baby – 1963
United Artists 605 - She's Gone / Tango – 1963
United Artists 638 - Surf And Shout / Whatcha Gonna Do – 1963
United Artists 659 - Please, Please, Please / You'll Never Leave Him – 1963
United Artists 714 - Who's That Lady / My Little Girl – 1964

The Isley Brothers / The Go-Go's

RCA/Wurlitzer ? - 1964 (Promo Issue Only)

The Isley Brothers

T-Neck 501 - Testify (Part 1) / Testify (Part 2) - 1964 (Session Jimi Hendrix)
Atlantic 2263 - Looking For A Love / The Last Girl - 1964 (Session Jimi Hendrix)
United Artists 798 - Love Is A Wonderful Thing / Open Up Her Eyes - 1964 (Unreleased)
Atlantic 2277 - Simon Says / Wild As A Tiger – 1965
Atlantic 2303 - Move Over And Let Me Dance / Have You Ever Been Disappointed - 1965 (Session Jimi Hendrix)
RCA Victor 447-0589 - Shout (Part 1) / Shout (Part 2) - 1965 (Gold Standard Series - Dog On

Side)
United Artists 923 - Love Is A Wonderful Thing / Open Up Her Eyes - 1965 (Unreleased)
V.I.P. 25020 - I Hear A Symphony / Who Could Ever Doubt My Love – 1965
Veep 1230 - Love Is A Wonderful Thing / Open Up Her Eyes – 1966
Tamla 54128 - This Old Heart Of Mine (Is Weak For You) / There's No Love Left – 1966
Tamla 54133 - Take Some Time Out For Love / Who Could Ever Doubt My Love – 1966
Tamla 54135 - I Guess I'll Always Love You / I Hear A Symphony – 1966
Tamla 54146 - Got To Have You Back / Got To Have You Back - 1967 (Promo Issue Only -- White Label)
Tamla 54146 - Got To Have You Back / Just Ain't Enough Love – 1967
Tamla 54154 - One Too Many Heartaches / That's The Way Love Is – 1967
Tamla 54164 - Take Me In Your Arms (Rock Me A Little While)* / Why When Love Is Gone - 1968 *originally released in 1965 by Kim Weston on Gordy 7046 - also released in 1972 by Jermaine Jackson on Motown 1216.
Tamla 54175 - Behind A Painted Smile / All Because I Love You – 1968
RCA Victor 447-0589 - Shout (Part 1) / Shout (Part 2) - 1969 (gold standard series - red label)
Philco-Ford Hp-41 - Twist And Shout / Rubberleg Twist - 1969 (4"Plastic "Hip Pocket Record" With Colour Sleeve)
Tamla 54182 - Take Some Time Out For Love / Just Ain't Enough Love – 1969
T-Neck 901 - It's Your Thing / Don't Give It Away - 1969 (Session Alva Martin (Former Member Of The Beltones) On Saxophone)
T-Neck 902 - I Turned You On / I Know Who You Been Socking It To – 1969
T-Neck 906 - Black Berries ---Pt.1 / Black Berries ---Pt. 2 – 1969
T-Neck 908 - Was It Good To You / I Got To Get Myself Together – 1969
T-Neck 912 - Bless Your Heart / Give The Women What They Want – 1969
T-Neck 914 - Keep On Doin' / Save Me – 1970
T-Neck 919 - If He Can, You Can / Holdin' On – 1970
T-Neck 921 - Girls Will Be Girls, Boys Will Be Boys / Get Down Off Of The Train – 1970
T-Neck 924 - Get Into Something / Get Into Something (Part 2) – 1970
T-Neck 927 - Freedom / I Need You So – 1970
T-Neck 929 - Warpath / I Got To Find Me One – 1971
T-Neck 930 - Love The One You're With / He's Got Your Love – 1971
T-Neck 932 - Spill The Wine / Take Inventory – 1971
T-Neck 933 - Lay Lady Lay / Vacuum Cleaner – 1971
T-Neck 934 - Lay-Away / Feel Like The World – 1972
T-Neck 935 - Pop That Thang / I Got To Find Me One – 1972
T-Neck 936 - Work To Do / Beautiful – 1972
T-Neck 937 - It's Too Late / Nothing To Do But Today – 1973
T-Neck 2251 - That Lady (Part 1) / That Lady (Part 2) – 1973
T-Neck 2252 - What It Comes Down To / Highways Of My Life – 1973
T-Neck 2253 - Summer Breeze (Part 1) / Summer Breeze (Part 2) – 1974
Radio Active Gold 31 - It's Your Thing / Don't Give It Away - 197?
Radio Active Gold 91 - Get Into Something (Part 1) / Get Into Something (Part 2) - 197?
Radio Active Gold 92 - Love The One You're With / Spill The Wine - 197?
T-Neck 2254 - Live It Up (Part 1) / Live It Up (Part 2) – 1974
T-Neck 2255 - Midnight Sky (Part 1) / Midnight Sky (Part 2) – 1974
T-Neck 2256 - Fight The Power Part 1 (5:05) / Fight The Power Part 2 (3:17) – 1975
T-Neck 2259 - For The Love Of You (Part 1 & 2) / You Walk Your Way – 1975
T-Neck 2260 - Who Loves You Better-Part 1 / Who Loves You Better-Part 2 – 1976
T-Neck 2261 - Harvest For The World / Harvest For The World (Part 2) – 1976
RCA 447-0589 - Shout (Part 1) / Shout (Part 2) - 1976 (Gold Standard Series -- Black Label -- Dog Near Top)
T-Neck 2262 - The Pride (Part 1) / The Pride (Part 2) – 1977
T-Neck 2264 - Livin' In The Life / Go For Your Guns – 1977
T-Neck 2267 - Livin' In The Life / Go For Your Guns - 1977 (12" Release)
T-Neck 2270 - Voyage To Atlantis / Do You Wanna Stay Down – 1977
T-Neck 2272 - Take Me To The Next Phase (Part 1) / Take Me To The Next Phase (Part 2) – 1978

T-Neck 2276 - Tell Me When You Need It Again (Part 1 & 2) / Take Me To The Next Phase (Part 1 & 2) - 1978 (12" Release)
T-Neck 2277 - Groove With You / Footsteps In The Dark – 1978
T-Neck 2278 - Showdown (Part 1) / Showdown (Part 2) – 1978
T-Neck 2279 - I Wanna Be With You (Part 1) / I Wanna Be With You (Part 2) – 1979
T-Neck 2283 - I Wanna Be With You (6:20) / Rockin' With Fire (5:57) - 1979 (12" Release)
T-Neck 2284 - Winner Takes All / Fun And Games – 1979
T-Neck 2287 - It's A Disco Night (Rock Don't Stop) / Ain't Giving Up On Love – 1979
T-Neck 2289 - It's A Disco Night (Rock Don't Stop) / Ain't Givin' Up On Love - 1979 (12" Release)
T-Neck 2290 - Don't Say Goodnight (It's Time For Love) (Part 1) / Don't Say Goodnight (It's Time For Love) (Part 2) – 1980
T-Neck 2291 - Here We Go Again (Part 1) / Here We Go Again (Part 2) – 1980
T-Neck 2292 - Say You Will (Part 1) / Say You Will (Part 2) 1980
T-Neck 2293 - Who Said? / (Can't You See) What You Do To Me – 1980
T- Neck 02033 - Hurry Up And Wait / (Instrumental) – 1981
T-Neck As 947 - Hurry Up And Wait (3:54) / Hurry Up And Wait (4:09) - 1981 (12" Promo Issue)

The Isley Brothers / The Kingsmen

Eric 4007 - Twist And Shout / Louie Louie* - 1981 *Flip By The Kingsmen.

The Isley Brothers

T-Neck 02151 - Don't Say Goodnight (It's Time For Love) (Parts 1 & 2) - 1981 (Reissue)
T-Neck 02179 - I Once Had Your Love (And I Can't Let Go) / (Instrumental) – 1981
T-Neck 02270 - Voyage To Atlantis / Do You Wanna Stay Down - 1981 (Reissue)
T-Neck 02293 - Who Said? / (Can't You See) What You Do To Me - 1981 (Reissue)
T-Neck 02531 - Inside You (Part 1) / Inside You (Part 2) – 1981
T-Neck 02705 - Party Night / Welcome Into My Night – 1982
T-Neck 02985 - The Real Deal / (Instrumental) – 1982
T-Neck 03281 - It's Alright With Me / (Instrumental) – 1982
T-Neck 03282 - It's Alright With Me (Vocal) (5:32) / It's Alright With Me (Instrumental) (4:16) - 1982 (12" Release)
T-Neck 03798 - Between The Sheets / (Instrumental) – 1983
T-Neck 03994 - Choosey Lover / (Instrumental) – 1983
T-Neck 04148 - I Need Your Body / (Instrumental) – 1983
T-Neck 04320 - Let's Make Love Tonight / (Instrumental) – 1984

The Isley Brothers / The Larks

Original Sound 4512 - Twist And Shout / The Jerk* - 1984 (Oldies But Goodies Series) *flip by The Larks.

The Isley Brothers

Magic Sound Productions 04642 - Look The Other Way / Look The Other Way - 1984
Warner Brothers 28860 - Colder Are My Nights / (Instrumental) – 1985
Warner Brothers Pro-A-2378 - Colder Are My Nights (Edit Version) (Lp Version) - 1985 (12" Promo Issue)
Warner Brothers 28764 - May I? / (Instrumental) – 1986
Warner Brothers 28385 - Smooth Sailin' Tonight / (Instrumental) – 1987
Warner Brothers 28241 - Come My Way / (Instrumental) – 1987
Warner Brothers 20827 - I Wish (Vocal) / I Wish (Instrumental) - 1987 (12"Release)
Gusto 2229 - Twist And Shout / Wa Watusi - 198?
Warner Brothers 28129 - I Wish / (Instrumental) – 1988
Warner Brothers 27954 - It Takes A Good Woman / (Instrumental) - 1988

The Isley Brothers / Chuck Jackson

Collectables 03013 - Twist And Shout / I Wake Up Crying* - 1988 *Flip By Chuck Jackson.

The Isley Brothers

Warner Brothers 22900 - Spend The Night (Ce Soir) / (Instrumental) – 1989
Warner Brothers Pro-A-4511 - Spend The Night (Edit) / Colder Are My Nights (Edit) / Smooth Sailin' Tonight (Edit) - 1989 (12" Promo)
Warner Brothers 22748 - One Of A Kind / You'll Never Walk Alone – 1989
Warner Brothers 21415 - One Of A Kind / You'll Never Walk Alone (4 Versions) - 1989 (12"Release)
Warner Brothers Pro-A-5417 - Sensitive Lover (4 Versions) - 1992 (12" Promo Issue)
Early Bird 1007 - Don't Be Jealous / This Is The End - 1996 (Copies Were Pressed In Pink Vinyl)
Underground 1124 - It's Your Thing / Who's That Lady - ?

"I went to a great allnighter last night !"

It all started in London, at clubs like The Flamingo and The Scene, then it moved North to The Twisted Wheel, Vs Va's, The Torch, Wigan, and Stafford. We've all seen the long lists of legendary allnighters before, and I'm not going to repeat the list again. My question is, why were these legendary allnighters ? What makes an allnighter successful ? In fact why do we have allnighters at all, why can't we get some sleep on a Saturday night like normal people ?

In trying to answer my own questions I'm going to examine the different aspects of allnighters, from all the different perspectives, because it's clear that people attend allnighters for different reasons.

The Dancers: These days I don't dance, partly because I'm too unfit, but mostly because I have a dodgy knee, but in the past I was a dancer, and I had only one concern really. That the music was fast enough, and with a good enough beat to dance to. All I needed for this was a good wooden dance floor, and believe me, I've been to places where the dancefloor (If you could call it that !) has been concrete, or sheets of hardboard nailed down, or vinyl floor tiles covered in spilt beer and sticky. It all affects how much the dancer enjoys his, or her, night out.

One other thing which has become more of an issue these days is that the dance floor is big enough for the venue. Back in the Seventies this wasn't a problem, the old ball rooms and clubs had big dancefloors, but by the Eighties clubs had realised that if people were dancing, they weren't drinking, and that's where the money was made. So a lot of clubs reduced the size of the dancefloor, and a lot of the old ball rooms became Bingo Halls. Think about how often you have been in a venue with a small dancefloor that is absolutely packed. It spoils the night doesn't it.

The dancer though is probably the most pure form of Northern Soul person that attends venues, they arrive, they drop their bag and dance until they need a change of clothes, they're not bothered what label the record is on, and generally just come to have a good time.

The Promoter: The hero or the villain, who can't get it right for everyone, no matter what he does. There are two distinctly different types of promoter these days, the first type promote to make money and reputation, and tend to be businessmen. The second type promote because they love the music, and can frequently be heard saying "We're not in it for the money.". Surprisingly, I think both types of promoter are vital for the continued future of the scene. The businessmen put on large promotions using big venues, and sometimes live acts, the promotion is large scale and professional. They might have an interest in the music on a personal basis, but in reality it is a way of earning their living, it's business. There is nothing wrong with that. What you end up with is a good venue, run professionally, promoted well, and usually very well attended.

The second type of promoter tends to run a smaller, locally based allnighter, and they do so because that's what they want to do. As already noted, the favourite phrase is "We're not in it for the money.". In part this is true, I co-promoted the Pigeon Club allnighters last year with John Mills, our aim was to play something different in the North West. We deliberately picked a small venue though, because we knew that we could fill a small venue, but would struggle with a large one. So even though we planned the allnighter for musical reasons and principles, we also used realism to ensure that we didn't lose money. That's what the second type of promoter means, they don't want to lose money, but are happy breaking even. There are very, very few venues that run allnighters at loss for any length of time, no matter what the avowed aims of the promoters are. Again this type of promoter is vital to the future of the scene because they are prepared to take a risk, and often when one venue fails they are prepared to put time and money into finding a new one, thus ensuring the continued future of the scene.

But as I said, they can be hero or villain. How many times have you heard people say "the music was crap/great, it was too dark/light, the dance floor was too busy, there weren't enough there, the sound system was crap, etc etc etc." All the criticism is aimed at the promoter, rightly so, but he is in an impossible situation, trying to please everyone, so remember that when you have a criticism, by all means make your point, but accept that others have a view.

From any promoter's point of view though it's easy to say what makes a good allnighter: Plenty of people through the door, a full dancefloor, no hassles about the equipment or venue, and all the DJ's turning up on time. Simple isn't it

The Record Dealer: Another essential part of an allnighter, but again, divided into probably three different groups. The first clear grouping is that of the professional record dealer. They make their living from selling records, and are usually quite successful at it. Their needs for a good allnighter are simple, a good 'pitch', enough light to see by, and enough customers, who have money in their pockets to spend on records. That's not asking for much is it ?

The second type of record dealer is much like myself, I have a normal 9 - 5 job, and sell records at allnighters to fund my own record buying. These days the price of records has escalated beyond belief and as a married man I cannot justify spending huge amounts of money on records out of my normal wages, so I fund my record buying by buying and selling records. As such, my requirements are the same as the professional dealers, and because there always seems to be another record to buy, another CD to buy, and these days, another book to buy, I need people to spend money just as much as the next man.

The Record Collector: Aha, I mentioned three types of record collector, and then only described two. That's because the third type is the guy who walks round with a small box of records. Sometimes it's someone selling off the remnants of a collection, but more usually it's a record collector ! A very unusual species, and there have been lots of articles written about the different types of record collector so I\'m not going to reproduce those here. Suffice to say, the record collector needs other people there selling records. Without them he has nowhere to spend his night, he will move from one sales box to the next, bent over, trawling through box after box of records. Sometimes he will find something he wants, and will immediately offer "trades, mate". Sometime he will be lucky, others he has to put his hand in his pocket. A good allnighter to the record collector means leaving in the morning with as many records as possible for the least possible outlay.

The DJ: So, how do people become allnighter DJ's ? Why do people become allnighter DJ's ? and how do they contribute to a good allnighter ? In many respects the DJ is the one person who can make or break an allnighter, if he gets it right everyone is happy, if he gets it wrong, everyone complains. In reality a DJ can never satisfy everyone at an allnighter, he can just attempt to satisfy most of the people, most of the time and that in itself is a very difficult job. So why do people do it ? For some it's a desire to share discoveries they have made with as many people as possible, for others it's a desire to see people dancing to the records they have chosen, for some it\'s a big ego trip, "Look what records I've got" type of thing. Certainly back in the Seventies it was a way of making money, it wasn't unknown for some DJs to make a record big, and then all of a sudden the pressings would appear.

In terms of making money these days the vast majority of allnighter DJs actually spend far more on the records they play than they ever get in wages, although stories of big names from 20 years ago getting £500 a spot now keep surfacing. Are they worth it ? Of course not, but good luck to them if they can command that sort of payment.

As to how people become successful allnighter DJs, that's a whole article on it's own. In the ideal world people would become allnighter DJs after serving an apprenticeship as such in smaller Soul nights. Then based on their reputation from what other people say about them they should be given a chance at an allnighter. In the majority of cases this happens. Sometimes, just sometimes, people come along and have a wonderful record collection, and get spots based on the records they own. It doesn't work though unless they are actually good DJs as well. If they aren't word will eventually get round and people will stop booking them.

The fans : Everyone of the above fit into this category. Or at least they would all claim to, but there are people as well who don't fall into any of the above categories. They are the people who don' t dance all night, don' t collect records, don't promote venues, but just go for a night out. Their social life revolves around the scene, and the people they meet there, it\'s just as important that they have a good night out as any of the above categories.

The atmosphere: An intangible thing, some venues have it all the time, some never have it, and even more confusingly some venues have it some of the time, but not at others. Of all the things that contribute to a great allnighter, the one thing that is always mentioned is a great atmosphere. You can't define it, you can't use a set formula for it (otherwise you could bottle it and sell it !), and you can't know until you arrive at a venue what the atmosphere will be like. But I'm sure, like me, sometimes you have walked into a venue and an absolutely electric feeling has hit you as you've walked in, that' s atmosphere ! I'm also sure you've walked into a venue where all the signs are right, all the DJs are right, and all the other variable factors are right, and yet it's still a very flat and dull night. Why ? That is in the hands of the God's.

So far I've avoided mentioning venues and names, because what I've written above can be applied across the board, to any venue, whether it be Togetherness, The Ritz, The Wilton, The 100 Club, or Albrighton. It's even more difficult to apply what I've said to specific DJs, because everyone who has DJ'ed at allnighters on a regular basis will know that sometimes everything goes right and people dance to whatever you play, and other times whatever you play leads to the DJ'd nightmare: vast areas of visible wood !

In fact, I've had good nights at all the current allnighters, for different reasons sometimes, but still good nights at allnighters. I've also had bad ones at allnighters that are usually good, and I can't tell you why ! So perhaps I 've failed to answer the questions I set myself at the beginning of this article. By the same token, perhaps what I've written will encourage you to form your own opinions as to what makes a good allnighter. In reality that's all anyone can hope for from a written piece of work, that it informs, and makes people think.

The one question I can answer is why allnighters ? Why not Soul nights ? Where we can all go home to get some sleep. The answer......because that's boring ! Long may the concept and reality of a good allnighter continue, thats where the Northern Rare Soul scene was born, and the end of allnighters will, to me, signify the end of the Rare Soul scene.

(Published in Togetherness Magazine. March 2000)

Venue Reports - May 2001

The Ritz, Manchester, 6th May, 2001.

The Rarest Of The Rare allnighter, certainly in my opinion the best of the year, and this one didn't let me down. DJs for the night were: Soul Sam, Shifty, Butch, Carl Willingham, Ady Croasdell, Ginger. Richard Searling, Ian Levine, Kenny Burrell, Andy Rix, and Bob Hinsley. Well with that lot spinning records you know what to expect, quality rare Soul music. Just two spots which disappointed me, but we won't go into that. Numbers were up on the last Ritz as well. Great night out.

The Lea Manor, Albrighton, 12th May, 2001

Numbers well down on previous allnighters, but it is only a month to go to Cleethorpes so that might explain it. Strangely people started to leave early, and by 5 am the place was almost deserted. A shame really because I really enjoy the allnighters at Lea Manor. Next one in September.

Group Line Ups

The Jelly Beans (Elyse Herbert, Maxine Herbert, Alma Brewer, Diane Taylor, Charles Thomas)
The Jive Five (Eugene Pitt, Richard C Harris, Casy Spencer, Beatrice Best, Norman Johnson)

Chuck Jackson

The Ray Raspberry Gospel Singers (members Chuck Jackson, Doris Willingham,... 1955 ~ 1956

The Original Del-Vikings (members Kripp Johnson (born Corinthian Johnson 16-May-1933, died 22-June-1990 at his home in Pontiac, Michigan - cause: prostate cancer)
Kripp Johnson was also a member of The Black Eyed Peas who had a 1970 release on Ultra-City 70-317 "Go Thru The Motions / Smallest Man Alive"), Chuck Jackson, Eddie Everette, Don Jackson and Arthur Budd) this was the second set of Del-Vikings which was formed after the group's new manager Al Berman took the group minus Kripp Johnson to Mercury records after the success in 1956 of "Come Go With Me" on Fee Bee 205, apparently all the members with the exception of Kripp Johnson were under age when they signed their contracts. So Kripp Johnson had to stay with Fee Bee as he was still under contractual obligations, so he formed a new group also called The Del-Vikings.

Fee Bee 902 - True Love / Baby Let Me Be – 1956

The Del-Vikings (members Kripp Johnson, Chuck Jackson, Eddie Everette, Don Jackson and Arthur Budd)

Fee Bee 218 - I'm Spinning / You Say You Love Me - 1957

The Dell-Vikings (members Kripp Johnson, Chuck Jackson, Eddie Everette, Don Jackson and

Arthur Budd)

Fee Bee 218 - I'm Spinning / You Say You Love Me - 1957 (to avoid confusion with the record buyers the group became The Dell-Vikings, eventually Mercury records started legal proceedings over the name and Fee Bee began releasing what they had left in the can as by The Versatiles. Kripp Johnson ended up back with his original group once his contract with Fee Bee expired)

Fee Bee 221 - Willette / I Want To Marry - 1957 (Lead Chuck Jackson)
Fee Bee 227 - Finger Poppin' Woman / Tell Me – 1957

Kripp Johnson with The Dell-Vikings / Kripp Johnson lead singer of 'Whispering Bells' (members Kripp Johnson, Chuck Jackson, Eddie Everette, Don Jackson and Arthur Budd)

Dot 15636 - When I Come Home / I'm Spinning - 1957

Kripp Johnson (Del-Vikings) and Charles Jackson

Dot 15673 - Willette / Woke Up This Morning – 1957

Charles Jackson and Kripp Johnson's Versatiles (Chuck Jackson)

Petite 502 - Willette / Cold Feet – 1959
Petite 503 - Watching The Moon / A Little Man Cried – 1959

Charles Jackson

Clock 1015 - Come On And Love Me / Ooh Baby – 1959
Clock 1022 - I'm Yours / Hula-Hula – 1960
Clock 1027 - This Is It / Mr. Pride – 1960

Chuck Flamingo (Chuck Jackson)

Belltone 1004 - Peeping Tom / Tonight Is Gone (Tomorrow Is Here) – 1960

Chuck Jackson (born Winston Salem, South Carolina 27-July-1937) between 1959 ~ 1960 Chuck Jackson was part of The Jackie Wilson Revue.

Belltone 1005 - Mr. Pride / Hula-Hula – 1961
Wand 106 - I Don't Want To Cry* / Just Once - 1961 *session: Mickey Baker (guitar) and Jimmy Lewis (bass) --- also recorded in 1965 by Big Maybelle on Scepter 1288.
Wand 108 - (It Never Happens) In Real Life / The Same Old Story – 1961
Wand 110 - I Wake Up Crying* / Everybody Needs Love - 1961 *singing harmony were Dionne Warwick, Dee Dee Warwick and Myrna Smith.
Wand 115 - The Breaking Point / Willow Tree – 1961
Atco 6197 - Never Let Me Go / I Want To Marry You – 1961
Amy 849 - Come On And Love Me / Ooh Baby – 1961
Wand 119 - What'cha Gonna Say Tomorrow / Angel Of Angels – 1962
Wand 122 - Any Day Now (My Wild Beautiful Bird)* / The Prophet - 1962 *Chuck Jackson's label mate Tommy Hunt using the same rhythm track recorded "Lover".
Wand 126 - I Keep Forgettin' / Who's Gonna Pick Up The Pieces – 1962
Wand 128 - Gettin' Ready For The Heartbreak / In-Between Tears – 1962
Amy 868 - I'm Yours / Hula-Hula – 1962
Logo 7004 - Come On And Love Me / Hula-Hula - 1962
Lescay ? - Watching The Rainbow / Miss Frankenstein – 1962
Wand 132 - Tell Him I'm Not Home* / Lonely Am I - 1963 *covered in 1965 by Ike & Tina Turner on Loma 2011. The response to Chuck Jackson's release is sung by Doris Troy.
Wand 138 - I Will Never Turn My Back On You / Tears Of Joy – 1963

Wand 141 - Any Other Way* / Big New York - 1963 *originally recorded in 1962 by William Bell on Stax 128 also covered in 1962 by Jackie Shane on Sue 776.
Alcar 209 - Little Man / Ooh Wee Baby – 1963
Alcar 210 - Never Let Me Go / Come On And Love Me – 1963
Gateway 738 - Forever Is A Long Long Time / Goodnight Irene – 1964
Wand 149 - Hand It Over / Look Over Your Shoulder – 1964
Wand 154 - Beg Me* / This Broken Heart - 1964 *backing vocals Cissy Houston and Doris Troy. Track also released in 196? by The Entertainers on Bowmar 1001 and in 1967 by Five Card Stud on Smash 2080
Wand 161 - Somebody New / Stand By Me – 1964
Wand 169 - Since I Don't Have You* / Hand It Over - 1964 *originally recorded in 1959 by The Skyliners on Calico 103/4.
Wand 179 - I Need You / Soul Brother Twist – 1964
Wand - Since I Don't Have You - 1964 (this previously unissued version was recorded in concert December-1964 at Murray "The K" Kaufman's Christmas Show, Brooklyn Fox Theatre, Brooklyn, New York. Track was released in the U. S. A. in 1992 on Capricorn Records three Cd box set "The Scepter Records Story" 9 42003-2 (disc 2))

Chuck Jackson & Maxine Brown

Wand 181 - Something You Got* / Baby Take Me - 1965 *originally recorded in 1961 by Chis Kenner on Instant 3237.

Chuck Jackson

Wand 188 - If I Didn't Love You / Just A Little Bit Of Your Soul – 1965

Chuck Jackson & Maxine Brown

Wand 191 - Can't Let You Out Of My Sight / Don't Go – 1965
Wand 198 - I Need You So* / Cause We're In Love - 1965 *also recorded in 1950 **by Ivory Joe Hunter** on MGM K10663.

Chuck Jackson

Wand 1105 - Good Things Come To Those Who Wait* / Yah - 1966 *also recorded in 1967 by Willie Hatcher on Columbia 4-44259.

Chuck Jackson & Maxine Brown

Wand 1109 - Please Don't Hurt Me / I'm Satisfied – 1966

Chuck Jackson

Wand 1119 - All In My Mind* / And That's Saying A Lot - 1966 *originally recorded in 1960 by Maxine Brown on Nomar 103.
Wand 1129 - These Chains Of Love / Theme To The Blues – 1966
Wand 1142 - Where Did She Stay / I've Got To Be Strong – 1967

Chuck Jackson & Maxine Brown

Wand 1148 - Hold On, I'm Coming* / Never Had It So Good** - 1967 *originally recorded in 1966 by Sam & Dave on Stax 189. **also recorded in 1967 by Ronnie Milsap on Scepter 12109.

Chuck Jackson

Wand 1151 - Every Man Needs A Down Home Girl / Need You There – 1967

Chuck Jackson & Maxine Brown

Wand 1155 - Daddy's Home* / Don't Go - 1967 *originally recorded in 1961 by Shep & The Limelites on Hull 740.

Chuck Jackson

Wand 1159 - Hound Dog* / Love Me Tender** - 1967 *originally recorded in 1953 by Big Mama Thornton on Peacock 1612. **originally recorded in 1956 by Elvis Presley on RCA 47-6643.

Chuck Jackson & Maxine Brown

Wand 1162 - C. C. Rider / Tennessee Waltz - 1967

Chuck Jackson

Wand 1166 - Shame On Me / Candy - 1967
Wand 1178 - My Child's Child / Theme To The Blues – 1968
Motown 1118 - (You Can't Let The Boy Overpower) The Man In You / Girls, Girls, Girls – 1968
1144 - Chuck Jackson - Are You Lonely For Me (2:58) / Your Wonderful Love - 1969
1144 - Chuck Jackson - Are You Lonely For Me Baby (3:19) / Your Wonderful Love - 1969
Motown 1152 - Honey Come Back / What Am I Going To Do Without You – 1969
Motown 1160 - Baby, I'll Get It / The Day My World Stood Still - 1969 (Unissued)
V. I. P. 25052 - Baby, I'll Get It / The Day My World Stood Still – 1969
V. I. P. 25056 - Let Someone Love Me / Two Feet From Happiness – 1970
V. I. P. 25059 - Pet Names / Is There Anything Love Can't Do – 1971
V. I. P. 25067 - Who You Gonna Run To* / Forgive My Jealousy - 1971 (unissued) *Also recorded in 1964 by Mickey McCullers on V. I. P. 25009.
Dakar 4512 - I Forgot To Tell You / The Man And The Woman, The Boy And The Girl* - 1972 (both sides written by Eugene Record. *Also recorded in 1972 by The Chi-Lites on Brunswick 55483)
Scepter/Wand Forever 21013 - I Don't Want To Cry / Where Did She Stay – 1973
Scepter/Wand Forever 21014 - I Wake Up Crying / Every Man Needs A Down Home Girl - 1973
Scepter/Wand Forever 21019 - Something You Got / Baby Take Me – 1973

Chuck Jackson & Maxine Brown

Scepter/Wand Forever 21020 - Let's Go Get Stoned / Never Had It So Good - 1973

Chuck Jackson

Scepter/Wand Forever 21073 - I Don't Want To Cry / Beg Me – 1973

Chuck Jackson & The Del-Vikings (members

Bim Bam Boom 111- Cold Feet / A Little Man Cried - 197?

Chuck Jackson

ABC 11368 - I Only Get This Feeling / Slowly But Surely – 1973
ABC 11398 - I Can't Break Away / Just A Little Tear – 1973
ABC 11423 - If Only You Will Believe / Maybe This Will Be The Morning – 1974
ABC 12024 - Talk A Little Less / Take Off Your Makeup – 1974
All Platinum 2357 - Love Lights / (Instrumental Version) – 1975
All Platinum 2360 - I'm Needing You, Wanting You / Shine, Shine, Shine – 1975
All Platinum 2363 - If You Were My Woman / (Instrumental Version) – 1976
All Platinum 2370 - One Of Those Yesterdays / Love Lights - 1977
All Platinum 2373 - I Fell Asleep / One Of Those Yesterdays – 1977

All Platinum 2384 - I Got The Need* / Beautiful Woman - 1977 *also released in 1975 in Belgium by Spooky & Sue on Decca 105-26,465Y.

Chuck Jackson & Sylvia (Chuck Jackson and Sylvia Vanderpool)

Vibration 569 - We Can't Hide It Anymore / I'm Needing You, Wanting You - 1977

Chuck Jackson

Channel 103 - When The Fuel Runs Out* / Good Love - 1979 *also recorded in 1973 by Executive Suite on Babylon 1111.
Channel Cd103d - When The Fuel Runs Out (7:28) / Good Love (3:58) - 1979 (12" release)
Emi America 8042 - I Wanna Give You Some Love / Waiting In Vain - 1980
EMI America 8056 - Let's Get Together / After You – 1981
Sugar Hill 764 - Sometimes When We Touch / Sometimes When We Touch - 1981
Forever Oldies ? - I Don't Want To Cry / ? - ?
Ripete 192 - Any Day Now / I Don't Want To Cry - ?

Chuck Jackson / Mel & Tim

Eric 4008 - Any Day Now / Backfield In Motion* - 198? *Flip By Mel & Tim.

The Isley Brothers / Chuck Jackson

Collectables 03013 - Twist And Shout / I Wake Up Crying* - 1988 *Flip By Chuck Jackson.

Chuck Jackson

Carolina 489 - How Long Have You Been Loving Me / How Long Have You Been Loving Me (Instrumental) - ?
Ripete 192 - Any Day Now / I Don't Want To Cry - 1990

Chuck Jackson / Robert Knight

Ripete 196 - For All Time / Everlasting Love* - 1990 *flip by Robert Knight.

Chuck Jackson / The Dixie Belles

Ripete 197 - My Willow Tree / Down At Papa Joe's* - 1990 *flip by The Dixie Belles.

Deon Jackson

Deon Jackson (born 26-January-1946 in Ann Arbor, Michigan. Singer / clarinetist / drummer. Discovered by producer Ollie McLaughlin)

Atlantic 2213 - Hush, Little Baby / You Said You Loved Me - 1964
Atlantic 2252 - Come Back Baby / Nursery Rhymes - 1964
Atlantic Test Pressing - Someday The Sun Will Shine - (Unreleased, currently owned by Keith Money)
Carla 803k 2526 - Love Makes The World Go 'Round* / Hello Stranger (Instrumental) - 1964 *Session Edwin Starr, Thelma Hopkins And Joyce Vincent.
Carla 2526 - Love Makes The World Go 'Round / You Said You Loved Me - 1965
Carla 2527 - Love Takes A Long Time Growing / Hush Little Baby - 1966
Carla 2530 - I Can't Do Without You / That's What You Do To Me - 1966
Carla 2533 - When Your Love Has Gone / Hard To Get A Thing Called Love - 1966
Carla 2537 - Ooh Baby / On A Sunny Day - 1967

Carla - Still Remember The Feeling - (Unreleased)
Carla - The Reason Why - (Unreleased)
Carla 1900 - I Can't Go On / I Need A Love Like Yours - 1968
Carla 1903 - You'll Wake Up Wiser, Baby / You Gotta Love - 1968
Shout 254 - I'll Always Love You / Life Can Be That Way - 1969
ABC - 1975
Contempo Raries 9031 - Love Makes The World Go Round / I Can't Go On - 1975 (UK release with alternative versions)

Deon Jackson / Rose Marie McCoy

Goldies 45 D-2726 - Love Makes The World Go Round / I Remember The Feeling* - ? *flip by Rose Marie McCoy.

Deon Jackson / Barbara Lewis

Stardust Urs 129 - I Remember The Feeling / I Remember The Feeling* - ? *flip by Barbara Lewis.

Deon Jackson

Collectables Col 1215 - Love Makes The World Go Round / You Said You Loved Me - ?

Etta James

The Echoes Of Eden (members Jamesetta Hawkins,.....) church gospel group.

The Creolettes (members Jamesetta Hawkins, ? and ?)

Etta James and The Peaches

Modern 947 - The Wallflower (Roll With Me Henry) / Hold Me, Squeeze Me - 1955 (male voice is Richard Berry)
Modern 947 - The Wallflower (Dance With Me Henry)* / Hold Me, Squeeze Me - 1955 (male voice is Richard Berry) *a pop hit in 1955 for Georgia Gibbs on Mercury 70572.

Etta James (born Jamesetta Hawkins on 25-January-1938 in Los Angeles, California) Frequent bouts with Heroin addiction

Modern 957 - Hey Henry / Be Mine – 1955
Modern 962 - Good Rockin' Daddy / Crazy Feeling - 1955 (with The Dreamers (vocal group), including Jesse Belvin)
Modern 972 - W-O-M-A-N / That's All – 1955
Modern 984 - Number One / I'm A Fool – 1956

Etta "Miss Peaches" James

Modern 988 - Shortnin' Bread Rock / Tears Of Joy – 1956

Etta James

Modern 998 - Tough Lover / What Fools We Mortals Be - 1956 (with Lee Allen on saxophone)
Modern 1007 - Good Loookin' / Then I'll Care - 1956
Modern 1016 - The Pick-Up / Market Place – 1957
Modern 1022 - Come What May / By The Light Of The Silvery Moon – 1957
Kent 304 - Sunshine Of Love / Baby Baby Every Night - 1958

Betty & Dupree (Etta James and Harvey Fuqua)

Kent 318 - I Hope You're Satisfied / If It Ain't One Thing – 1959

Etta James

Kent 345 - Dance With Me Henry / Hey Henry - 1960
Kent 352 - How Big A Fool / Good Rockin' Daddy - 1960
Kent 370 - Do Something Crazy / Good Rockin' Daddy - 1960

Etta & Harvey (Etta James and Harvey Fuqua)

Chess 1760 - If I Can't Have You / My Heart Cries – 1960
Chess 1771 - Spoonful / It's A Crying Shame – 1960

Etta James

Argo 5359 - All I Could Do Was Cry / Girl Of My Dreams (Boy Of My Dreams) - 1960
Argo 5368 - My Dearest Darling / Tough Mary - 1960 (one known copy found in Los Angeles in 1999 pressed in blue vinyl)
Argo 5380 - At Last* / I Just Want To Make Love To You - 1961 *popularized in 1942 by Glenn Miller.
Argo 5385 - Trust In Me* / Anything To Say You're Mine - 1961 *both Wayne King and Mildred Bailey had top 5 versions of this song in 1937.
Argo 5390 - Fool That I Am / Dream – 1961
Argo 5393 - Don't Cry Baby / A Sunday Kind Of Love – 1961
Argo 5402 - Seven Day Fool / It's Too Soon To Know – 1961
Argo 5409 - Something's Got A Hold On Me / Waiting For Charlie (To Come Home)* - 1962 *recorded 14-July-1961.
Argo 5418 - Stop The Wedding* / Street Of Tears - 1962 *Recorded 27~29-July-1962.
Argo 5424 - Fools Rush In / Next Door To The Blues* - 1962 *written by Pearl Woods and Leroy Kirkland.
Argo 5430 - Would It Make Any Difference To You* / How Do You Speak To An Angel - 1962 *recorded 15-November-1962.
Argo 5437 - Pushover* / I Can't Hold It Anymore - 1963 *recorded 14-November-1962 --- written by Tony Clarke and Billy Davis.
Argo 5445 - Pay Back / Be Honest With Me – 1963
Argo 5452 - Two Sides (To Every Story) / I Worry 'Bout You – 1963
Argo 5459 - Baby What You Want Me To Do / What I Say – 1964
Argo 5465 - Loving You More Each Day / Look Who's Blue – 1964
Argo 5477 - Breaking Point / That Man Belongs Back Here With Me – 1964
Argo 5485 - Bobby Is His Name / Mellow Fellow – 1964
Oldies 45 84 - Dance With Me Henry / I'm A Fool - 1964

Etta James & Sugar Pie DeSanto

Argo 5519 - Do I Make Myself Clear / Somewhere Down The Line - 1965 (both tracks written by Shena DeMell and Peylia Parham who also wrote The Knight Brothers 1965 release "I'm Never Gonna Live It Down" on Checker 1124)

Cadet 5519 - Do I Make Myself Clear / Somewhere Down The Line - 1965

Billy Preston / Etta James

Oldies 45 309 - Billy's Bag / Good Rockin' Daddy* - 1965 *Flip By Etta James.

Etta James

Cadet 5526 - Only Time Will Tell / I'm Sorry For You - 1966
Cadet 5526 - Only Time Will Tell - 1966 (One Sided Stock Issue)

Etta James & Sugar Pie DeSanto

Cadet 5539 - In The Basement (Part 1) / In The Basement (Part 2) - 1966

Etta James

Cadet 5552 - I Prefer You* / I'm So Glad (I Found Love In You) - 1967 *Recorded 16-October-1966.
Cadet 5564 - Don't Pick Me For Your Fool / It Must Be Your Love – 1967
Cadet 5568 - 842-3089 (Call My Name) / Happiness – 1967
Cadet 5578 - Tell Mama* / I'd Rather Go Blind** - 1967 *recorded 24-August-1967 at Muscle Shoals, Alabama. **recorded 23-August-1967 at Muscle Shoals, Alabama.
Cadet - Do Right Woman, Do Right Man - 1967 (recorded 30-November-1967at Muscle Shoals, Alabama. Although unreleased on vinyl at the time this was released in 1993 on the MCA Chess double Cd "The Essential Etta James" CHD2-9341)
Cadet 5594 - Security* / I'm Gonna Take What He's Got - 1968 *Recorded 6-December-1967.
Cadet 5606 - I Got You Babe / I Worship The Ground You Walk On – 1968
Cadet 5620 - You Got It / Fire – 1968
Philco-Ford Hp 31 - Tell Mama / Security - 1968 (4" Plastic "Hip Pocket Record")
Cadet 5630 - Almost Persuaded / Steal Away – 1969
Cadet 5655 - Miss Pitiful* / Bobby Is His Name - 1969 *Recorded 10-June-1969.
Cadet 5664 - Tighten Up Your Own Thing / What Fools We Mortals Be – 1969
Cadet 5671 - Sound Of Love / When I Stop Dreaming – 1970
Cadet 5676 - Losers Weepers (Part 1) / Losers Weepers (Part 2) - 1970 (Recorded 19-June-1970)
Chess 2100 - Nothing From Nothing Leaves Nothing / Love Of My Man – 1970
Chess 2112 - Take Out Some Insurance / I Think It's You – 1971
Chess 2125 - I Found A Love / Nothing From Nothing Leaves Nothing – 1972
Chess 2128 - Tell It Like It Is / W. O. M. A. N. - 1972
Chess 2144 - All The Way Down / Lay Back Daddy – 1973
Chess - I Never Meant To Love Him - 1973 (recorded January / March - 1973 in Philadelphia. Although unreleased on vinyl at the time this was released in 1993 on the MCA Chess double Cd "The Essential Etta James" CHD2-9341)
Chess 2148 - You Can Leave Your Hat On / Only A Fool - 1974
Chess 2153 - Out On The Street Again / Feeling Uneasy - 1974 (session: Ken Marco (guitar), Danny Kortchmar (guitar), "Wah Wah" Watson (guitar), Lowell George (guitar), Chuck Rainey (bass), Louie Spears (upright bass), William Smith (keyboards), Larry Nash (keyboards), Gabriel Mekler (keyboards), Gary Coleman (percussion), Mailto Correa (percussion) and Ken "Spider" Rice (drums))
Chess 2171 - Take Out Some Insurance / Lovin' Arms – 1975
Chess 30001 - Jump Into Love / I've Been A Fool – 1976
Modern Oldies 6 - Roll With Me Henry / Good Rockin' Daddy - ?

Etta James

Warner Brothers 8545 - Piece Of My Heart / Lovesick Blues – 1978
Warner Brothers 8611 - Sugar On The Floor / Lovesick Blues – 1978

Tony Orlando / Tony Orlando & Etta James

Elektra 45501 - Don't Let Go / Bring It On Home To Me* - 1978 *flip by Tony Orlando and Etta James.

Etta James

T-Electric 41264 - Mean Mother* / It Takes Love To Keep A Woman - 1980 *written by Willie Hutch.
Epic 68593 - Baby What You Want Me To Do / Max's Theme - 1989
Capitol 15453 - Roof Tops / ? - ? (12" release)

Etta James & David A. Stewart

Capitol B44333 - Avenue D / My Head Is A City - 1989 (some copies issued with picture sleeve)

Etta James

Collectables Col 034177 - Tell Mama / Pushover - ?
Collectables Col 034467 - At Last / My Dearest Darling - ?
Collectables Col 034477 - Stop The Wedding / Fool That I Am - ?
Collectables Col 034767 - I'd Rather Go Blind / A Sunday Kind Of Love - ?
Collectables Col 034777 - All The Way Down / Out On The Street Again - ?
Collectables Col 039337 - Wallflower (Dance With Me Henry) / Good Rockin' Daddy - ?

Etta James / The Dells

Cadet ? - I'd Rather Go Blind / There Is - ?

Def Jef

Delicious Vinyl Dv1008dj - Droppin' Rhymes On Drums (Vocal) (4:23)* / Etta Droppin' Science On Drums (3:01)* / Drums (2:00) /// God Made Me Funky (Lp Version) (5:00) / God Made Me Funky (Instrumental) (4:58) - 1989 *vocals by Etta James - 12" release.

Etta James

BMG WDAB-11593-1 - Miss You (Illicit Remix) (7:22) / Miss You (Ivan's X-Mix) (6:46) /// Miss You (Popular Beat Combo Remix) (4:44) / Miss You (Giuseppe's D.'S Groovin' Mix) (6:54) - 2001 (12" promo issue only)

Etta James / Mandrill

Ugly Edits Uget09 - In The Basement (Theo Parrish Re-Edit) / Feeling Good (Theo Parrish Re-Edit)* - 2004 *flip by Mandrill. (12" release)

Etta James

RCA 82876 85243 2 - Strung Out (Quentin's Rehab Reproduction) (8:35) / Strung Out (Quentin's Rehab Instrumental) (8:35) - 2006 (Cd single)

Jay And The Techniques

The Sinceres (members Jay Proctor ....)

Jordan 117 - You're Too Young / Forbidden Love – 1960
Sigma 1003/4 - Darling / Do You Remember – 1960
Richie 545 - Please Don't Cheat On Me / If You Should Leave - 1961 (no mention of Roulette records on label --- this is the scarcer version)
Richie 545 - Please Don't Cheat On Me / If You Should Leave - 1961 (With Roulette records distribution mentioned on label)

Jay And The Techniques (members Jay Proctor, George "Lucky" Lloyd, Dante Dancho,

Chuck Crowl, Ronnie Goosley, John Walsh and Karl Lippowitsch (also known as Karl Landis)) group hails from Allentown PA.

Smash 2086 - Apples, Peaches, Pumkin Pie / Stronger Than Dirt - 1967 (this 45 was meant to be by The Techniques but the record company released it as by Jay And The Techniques, the name then stuck)
Smash 2124 - Keep The Ball Rollin' */ Here We Go Again - 1967 *track written by Linzer and Randell. (also came with picture sleeve)
Smash Djs-13 - Strawberry Shortcake (Mono) / Strawberry Shortcake (Stereo) - 1967 (promo issue only)
Smash 2142 - Strawberry Shortcake / Still (In Love With You) - 1967 (also came with picture sleeve)
Philco-Ford Hp-22 - Apples, Peaches, Pumkin Pie / Loving For Money - 1968 (4" plastic "Hip Pocket Record" with colour sleeve)
Smash 2154 - Baby Make Your Own Sweet Music / Help Yourself (To All Of My Lovin') - 1968 *track written by Linzer and Randell. (also came with picture sleeve)
Smash Djs-18 - The Singles Game (Mono) / The Singles Game (Stereo) - 1968 (promo issue only)
Smash 2171 - The Singles Game / Baby How Easy Your Heart Forgets Me - 1968 (also came in picture sleeve) (by the time of this release Karl Lippowitsch left the group and was replaced by Paul Coles Jr., John Walsh was replaced by Danny Altieri and Jack Truett joined the group as an organ player)
Smash / Mercury Djs-19 - Hey Diddle Diddle (Mono) / Hey Diddle Diddle (Stereo) - 1968 (promo issue only)
Smash 2185 - Hey Diddle Diddle* / If I Should Lose You - 1968 *track written by Marvin Gaye, Harvey Fuqua and Johnny Bristol.
Smash 2217 - Are You Ready For This / Change Your Mind – 1969
Smash 2237 - Dancin' Mood* / If I Should Lose You - 1969 *originally recorded by The Tams on their debut Lp for ABC-Paramount. (on all the above Smash releases The Techniques never actually played any instruments or provided background vocals. The Smash material was recorded in New York's Bell Sound studio "A" with Jay Proctor the only group member in attendance. Session musicians such as Al Gorgoni (guitar), Joe Macho (bass) and Bernard Purdie (drums) were on many of those records and were 'The Techniques'............ and Nicholas Ashford, Valerie Simpson and Melba Moore provided background vocals) After this release the group dissolved -- a number of the members were drafted, spelling the end of the group. The following releases are with different 'Techniques' member lineups.
Gordy 7123 - Robot Man / I'll Be There - 1972 (Jay Proctor wasn't the lead on this release ----
Silver Blue 812 - I Feel Love Coming On* / This World Of Mine - 1974 *the Barry White composition also recorded in 1967 by Felice Taylor on U. K. President PT 155.
Event 222 - I Feel Love Coming On / This World Of Mine - 1975
Event 228 - Number Onederful / Don't Ask Me To Forget – 1976
Pro 001 - "Keep The Ball Rollin'" Eagles - 1981 (one sided promo issue only with picture cover containing lyrics cut for the Philadelphia Eagles --- original song written by Linzer / Randell)

The Jelly Beans

The Jelly Beans (members (sisters) Elyse Herbert, Maxine Herbert, Alma Brewer, Diane Taylor and Charles Thomas)

Red Bird 10-003 - I Wanna Love Him So Bad / So Long - 1964
Red Bird 10-011 - Baby Be Mine / The Kind Of Boy You Can't Forget - 1964
Eskee 10001 - You Don't Mean Me No Good / I'm Hip To You - 1965
SSS International GTS-435 - Baby Be Mine / I Wanna Love Him So Bad - 1977 (Golden Treasure Series)

The Ad-Libs / The Jelly Beans

Goldisc 3058 - The Boy From New York City / I Wanna Love Him So Bad* - 1978 *flip by The Jelly Beans.

The Jelly Beans

Collectables Col 013747 - I Wanna Love Him So Bad / So Long - ?

The Dixie Cups / The Jelly Beans

Collectables Col 038817 - Iko Iko / I Wanna Love Him So Bad* - ? *Flip By The Jelly Beans.

The Jewels

The Impalas (members Sandra Peoples, Margie Clarke, Carrie Mingo and Grace Ruffin (cousin to Billy Stewart))

Checker 999 - For The Love Of Mike* / I Need You So Much - 1961 (recorded in Bo Diddley's basement studio) *written by Chester Simmons member of The Rainbows and The Marquees.

The Four Jewels (members Sandra Peoples, Margie Clarke, Carrie Mingo and Grace Ruffin)

Start 638 - Loaded With Goodies / Fire – 1962

Billy Stewart

Chess 1820 - Reap What You Sow* / Fat Boy - 1962 *Backing Vocals The Four Jewels

The Four Jewels

Start 638 - Johnny Jealousy / Someone Special – 1963
Start 641 - All That's Good / I Love Me Some You – 1963

Jimmy "D" & The "D"-Lites (members Jimmy D., Sandra Peoples, Margie Clarke, Carrie Mingo and Grace Ruffin)

Checker 1039 - Loaded With Goodies / Dapper Dan – 1963

The Four Jewels

Checker 1069 - Time For Love / That's What They Put Erasers On Pencils For - 1964 (Carrie Mingo leaves group and is replaced with Martha Harvin at time of this release, the flip of this 45 was also given to the female group The Gems)

Tec 3007 - Baby It's You* / She's Wrong For You Baby - 1964 *Original By The Spaniels.

The Jewels (members Sandra (Peoples) Bears, Margie Clarke, Martha Harvin and Grace Ruffin -- name change came about because Margie Clarke could no longer tour with group although she still recorded with group)

Dimension 1034 - Opportunity / Gotta Find A Way - 1964
Federal 12541 - This Is My Story* / My Song - 1964 *originally recorded in 1954 by Gene and Eunice with Johnny's Combo on Aladdin 3282, this 45 was produced by James Brown.
Dimension 1048 - Smokey Joe* / But I Do** - 1965 *written by Nicholas Ashford and Valerie Simpson. **original by Clarence Henry.

Dimension 1048 - Looky Looky / But I Do – 1965
Dynamite 2000 - Papas Left Mama Holdin' The Bag / This Is My Story - 1966

The Brownettes (members

King 6153 - Never Find A Love Like Mine / Baby, Don't You Know – 1968

Little Eva / The Jewels

Collectables Col 003007 - The Loco-Motion / Opportunity* - ? *flip by The Jewels.

The Jive Five

The Top Notes (Members Eugene Pitt,................................) No Recordings.

The Zip-Tones (Members Eugene Pitt,...............................) No Recordings.

The Akrons (Members Eugene Pitt, ? Murphy, ? Murphy (The Father And Uncle Of Eddie Murphy) ....) No Recordings.

The Genies (Members -- Said To Be Eugene Pitt --, Estelle Williams, Fred Jones, Claude Johnson And Haskell Cleveland)

Shad 5002 - Who's That Knockin' / The First Time - 1958 (Group formed by Fred Jones -- Both Fred Jones and Eugene Pitt state that Eugene Pitt was never a member of The Genies -- Others state that the group was called The Genies as a take on Eu (Gene's) name and that he was a member -- these are the group's five releases -- Estelle Williams and Haskell Cleveland went on to form Jeannie & Her Boyfriends who had an answer record in 1959 to "Who's That Knockin'" entitled "It's Me Knockin' / Baby" on Warwick 508)
Hollywood 69 - No More Knockin' / On The Edge Of Town – 1959
Warwick 573 - Crazy Love / There Goes That Rain – 1960
Warwick 607 - Just Like The Bluebird / Twistin' Pneumonia – 1960
Warwick 643 - Little Young Girl / Crazy Feeling - 1961

The Jive Five (Members Eugene Pitt, Jerome Hanna, Thurmon "Billy" Prophet, Richard Harris And Norman Johnson (Born 1935 - Died ?-February-1970 - Cause?)

Beltone 1006 - My True Story* / When I Was Single - 1961 *Written By Eugene Pitt.
Beltone 1014 - Never, Never / People From Another World – 1961

The Jive Five with Eugene Pitt (members Eugene Pitt, Jerome Hanna, Thurmon "Billy" Prophet, Richard Harris and Norman Johnson)

Beltone 2019 - Hully Gully Callin' Time / No Not Again - 1962

The Jive Five with Eugene Pitt (members Eugene Pitt, Andre Coles, Casey Spencer, Beatrice Best and Norman Johnson)

Beltone 2024 - What Time Is It / Beggin' You Please - 1962 (before the group recorded this 45 there were some personnel changes Jerome Hanna died and was replaced by Andre Coles, Casey Spencer replaced Thurmon "Billy" Prophet and Beatrice Best subbed for Richard Harris)

Eugene Pitt (Lead Singer Of The Jive Five)

Beltone 2027 - She's My Girl / Every Day Is Like A Year – 1962

The Jive Five With Eugene Pitt (Members Eugene Pitt, Andre Coles, Casey Spencer, Beatrice

Best and Norman Johnson)

Beltone 2029 - Do You Hear Wedding Bells / These Golden Rings – 1962
Beltone 2030 - Johnny Never Knew / Lily Marlene – 1963
Beltone 2034 - Rain / She's My Girl - 1963 (More Personnel changes came with this release, Thurmon "Billy" Prophet returned to join Eugene Pitt -- They then teamed up with three former members of The Cadillacs, they were:- J. R. Bailey, Bobby Phillips and Buddy Brooks)
Sketch 219 - United / Prove Every Word You Say - 1964 (On this release Eugene Pitt brought back the old group of Casey Spencer, Beatrice Best And Richard Harris -- They still called themselves The Jive Five even though there were only four members.
Sketch 219 - Hey Baby You Think You're So Smart / Prove Every Word You Say - 1964
United Artists 807 - United / Prove Every Word You Say - 1964

The Jive Five (members Eugene Pitt, Andre Coles, Casey Spencer, Beatrice Best and Norman Johnson)

Oldies 45 173 - What Time Is It / Beggin' You Please - 1964

The Jive Five (members Eugene Pitt, Jerome Hanna, Thurmon "Billy" Prophet, Richard Harris and Norman Johnson)

Oldies 45 175 - My True Story / When I Was Single - 1964

The Jive Five featuring Eugene Pitt

United Artists 853 - I'm A Happy Man / Kiss, Kiss, Kiss - 1965
United Artists 936 - A Bench In The Park / Please, Baby, Please Come On Back To Me- 1965
United Artists 50004 - Goin' Wild / Main Street -1966
United Artists 50033 - In My Neighbourhood / Then Came Heartbreak – 1966
United Artists 50069 - You're A Puzzle / Ha Ha – 1966
United Artists 50107 - You / You Promised Me Great Things – 1966

The Four Havens / The Jive Five

Veep 1214 - Let's Have A Good Time Baby / What Time Is It* – 1966 Flip by The Jive Five

Eugene Pitt

Veep 1229 - Why, Why, Why / Another Rainy Day - 1966 (Backed By The Jive Five)

George Jackson

Double R 248 - When I Stop Lovin' You / That Lonely Night - 1966 (Backed By The Jive Five)
Cameo 460 - When I Stop Lovin' You / That Lonely Night - 1967 (Backed By The Jive Five)

The Jive Five With Eugene Pitt

Musicor 1250 - Crying Like A Baby / You'll Fall In Love – 1967
Musicor 1270 - No More Tears / You'll Fall In Love – 1967

The Jive Five Featuring Eugene Pitt

Musicor 1305 - Sugar (Don't Take Away My Candy) / Blues In The Ghetto - 1968

The Jyve Fyve (Members in the early 1970's Eugene Pitt, Casey Spencer, Richard Fisher (whose brother is Jesse Fisher on Way-Out Records) and Webster Harris (Former member of The Persians and Richard's brother)

Decca 32671 - You Showed Me The Light Of Love / (If You Let Me Make Love To You) Why Can't I Touch You - 1970
Decca 32736 - I Want You To Be My Baby / Give Me Just A Chance – 1970

Eugene Pitt & The Jyve Five

Avco 4568 - Come Down In Time / Love Is Pain – 1971
Avco 4589 - Follow The Lamb / Let The Feeling Belong – 1972
Avco 4589 - Follow The Lamb / Lay, Lady, Lay – 1972

The Jyve Five

Brut 814 - All I Ever Do (Is Dream About You) / Super Woman (Part 2)- 1974

The Jive Five

Beltone 3001 - Hurry Back / You Know What I Would Do – 1974
Beltone 3002 - The Girl With The Wind In Her Hair / I Don't Want To Be Without You Baby - 1974

Shadow

Chess 2162 - Sad Faces / People Don't Know What Love Is – 1974

Ebony, Ivory & Jade

Columbia 10196 - Samson / Sad Faces - 1975

The Jive Five (members in the 1979 lineup was Eugene Pitt, Casey Spencer, Richard Harris and Beatrice Best)

Relic 1026 - My True Story / When I Was Single - 1975 ~ 1978
Relic 1027 - No Not Again / ? - 1975 ~ 1978
Relic 1028 - Beggin' You Please / What Time Is It? - 1975 ~ 1978
Relic 1029 - These Golden Rings / Do You Hear Wedding Bells - 1975 ~ 1978
Relic 1030 - People From Another World / Never, Never - 1975 ~ 1978
Relic 1034 - She's My Girl / Rain – 1978

The Jive Five

Goldisc 3036 - My True Story / Rain (Makes My Baby Cry) – 1978
Goldisc 3037 - What Time Is It / Never, Never – 1978

The Jive Five (Members In The 1982 Lineup Was Eugene Pitt And His Brothers Herbert And Frank Pitt, Charles Mitchell And Beatrice Best)

Ambient Sound 2742 - Magic Maker, Music Maker / Oh Baby - 1982 (With Special Guests Arlene Smith's Chantels)
Ambient Sound 3053 - Don't Believe Him Donna / Hey Sam – 1982
Ambient Sound 452 - You Lonesome Tonight / ? - ?

Later Member Additions - (1990 To Present), Eugene Pitt, Beatress Best, Harold Gil, Maurice, Unthank, Artie Loria, Danny Loria

Sir Render 007 - Falling Tears / I Remember When - ?
Stoop Sounds 101 - Where Do We Go From Here / ? - 1996 (Limited Edition. Estimates Range From Less Than Ten, To A Few Dozen Made)
Lana 105 - My True Story / When I Was Single - ?

The Jive Five / The Showmen

United Artists 1001 - I'm A Happy Man / It Will Stand* - ? *Flip By The Showmen.

The Jive Five

Eric 142 - What Time Is It / My True Story - ?

Bertha Tillman / The Genies

Eric 148 - Oh My Angel / Who's That Knocking* - ? *Flip By The Genies.

The Jive Five

Collectables Col 013397 - What Time Is It / Beggin' You Please - ?
Collectables Col 013367 - My True Story / When I Was Single - ?
Collectables Col 013407 - Never Never / These Golden Rings - ?
Collectables Col 013397 - What Time Is It / Beggin' You Please - ?

Bertha Tillman / The Genies

Collectables Col 031947 - Oh My Angel / Who's That Knocking* - ? *Flip By The Genies.

The Jive Five / Lil' Julian Herrera

Original Sound Os-45337 - My True Story / I Remember Linda* - ? *Flip By Lil' Julian Herrera

The Jive Five / The Majors

Collectables Col 060207 - I'm A Happy Man / A Wonderful Dream* - ? *Flip By The Majors.

Eugene Pitt & The Jive Five (Eugene Pitt, Beatress Best, Harold Gil, Maurice, Unthank, Artie Loria, Danny Loria)

Doesn't Matter Music DMM57A - It's Christmas - 2003 (Cd Single)

Mable John

The United Five (members William John, Mabel John, ...)

Mable John (born 3-November-1930 in Bastrop, Louisiana --- sister of Little Willie John)

Tamla 54031 - Who Would'nt Love A Man Like That / You Made A Fool Out Of Me - 1960 (with The Supremes on uncredited backing vocals)
Tamla 54040 - (I Guess There's) No Love / Looking For A Man – 1960
Above single "A" side issued with strings matrix number H667 and without strings, matrix number H632.
Tamla 54050 - Actions Speak Louder Than Words / Take Me – 1961
Tamla 54081 - Who Wouldn't Love A Man Like That / Say You'll Never Let Me Go – 1963
Stax 192 - Your Good Thing (Is About To End) / It's Catching - 1966
Stax 205 - You're Taking Up Another Man's Place/ If You Give Up What You Got (You'll See What You Lost) -1966
Stax 215 - Same Time, Same Place / Bigger And Better – 1967
Stax 225 - I'm A Big Girl Now / Wait You Dog – 1967
Stax 234 - Don't Hit Me No More / Left Over Love – 1967

Stax 249 - Able Mable / Don't Get Caught – 1968
Stax Sta-0016 - Running Out / Shouldn't I Love Him - 1968

Mable John then went on to make numerous recordings as one of Ray Charles Raelettes.

Ruby Johnson

V-Tone 222 – Calling All Boys / Pleadin' Heart – 1960
Pledge 108 - I Received Your Message / Stop Wasting Your Tears - 1961
NEB's 3 – Come Back To Me / Reach Out And Touch Me – between 1960 – 1965
Neb's 101 - Let Me Apologise / Don't Start Nothing - 1963
NEB's 502 - I'm Hooked / Worried Mind - 1964
NEB's 503 – I Want A Real Man / What Goes Up Must Come Down - 1965
NEB's 505 – Here I Go Again / Jerk Shout – 1965
Volt 133 – I'll Run Your Hurt Away / Weak Spot – 1966
Volt 140 – Come To Me My Darling / When My Love Comes Down – 1966
Volt 147 – If I Ever Needed Love / Keep On Keeping On – 1967
NEB's 508 - Come Back To Me / Reach Out And Touch - 1968
NEB's 509 – I've Been Hurt (So Many Times Before) / Through Dealing – 1968
NEB's 600 – Why Do You Want To Leave Me / Nobody Care - 1968
Capcity 511 – I Can't Do It / Why You Want To Leave Me - 1968

Syl Johnson

Syl Johnson (born Sylvester Thompson on the 1-July-1939 in Holly Springs, Mississippi)

Federal 12358 - Teardrops / They Who Love – 1959
Federal 12374 - I've Got Love / Lonely Man – 1960
Federal 12435 - I've Got To Find My Baby / (She's So Fine) I Just Gotta Make Her Mine - 1961(Recorded 27-June-1961)
Federal 12454 - Little Sally Walker / I Resign From Your Love - 1962 (Recorded 27-June-1961)
Federal 12474 - I Wanna Know / Well Oh Well* - 1962 *Also Recorded In 1950 By Tiny Bradshaw On King 4357.
Federal 12476 - Please, Please, Please / I'm Looking For My Baby – 1962
Cha Cha 728 - She's All Right / I Know - 196?
T. M. P. - Ting 115 - I've Got To Get Over / Falling In Love Again – 1965
Zachron 600 - Straight Love, No Chaser / Surrounded – 1966

Syl Johnson and Orchestra

Zachron 600 - Try Me / Surrounded - 1966

Syl Johnson

Tag Ltd. 1 - Straight Love, No Chaser / Surrounded – 1966
Special Agent 200 - Do You Know What Love Is / The Love I Found In You - 1967 (red label)
Special Agent 201 - Do You Know What Love Is / That Ain't Right - 1967 (Released again by same record company with different mix and yellow label - scarce)
Twilight 100 - Come On Sock It To Me / Try Me - 1967
Twilight 103 - Different Strokes / Sorry Bout Dat – 1967
Twinight 106 - Ode To Soul Man / I'll Take Those Skinny Legs – 1968
Twinight 107 - Send Me Some Loving / I'll Resign – 1968
Twinight 108 - I Feel An Urge / Try Me* - 1968 *Different To Twilight 100.
Twinight 110 - Dresses Too Short / I Can Take Care Of Business – 1968

Twinight 116 - I Can Take Care Of Homework / Take Me Back – 1969
Twinight 118 - Don't Give It Away / Going To The Shack – 1969
Twinight 125 - Is It Because I'm Black* / Let Them Hang High - 1969 *also recorded in 1974 by Oscar Toney Jr. on Contempo 7702.

Syl Johnson & The Pieces Of Peace (members Syl Johnson (vocals), Harold "Hal" Nesbit (drums), Bernard Reed (bass), John Bishop (guitar), Jerry Wilson (saxaphone) and Michael Davis (trumpet))

Twinight 129 - Concrete Reservation / Together, Forever – 1970

Syl Johnson

Twinight 134 - One Way Ticket To Nowhere / Kiss By Kiss – 1970
Twinight 144 - Thank You Baby* / We Do It Together - 1971 *also recorded in 1969 by Johnny Moore on Mercury 72908
Twinight 149 - Get Ready / Same Kind Of Thing – 1971
Twinight 151 - Annie's Got Hot Pants Power (Part 1) / Annie's Got Hot Pants Power (Part 2) (Instrumental) - 1971
Hi 2201 - The Love You Left Behind / Anyone But You – 1971
Twinight 155 - That's Why / Everybody Needs Love – 1972
Hi 2215 - I Wanna Satisfy Your Every Need / Age Ain't Nothing But A Number - 1972
Hi 2229 - We Did It / Anyway The Wind Blows - 1972 (Released 15-October-1972)
Hi 2250 - Back For A Taste Of Your Love / Wind Blow Her Back My Way - 1973 (released 3-July-1973)
Hi 2260 - I'm Yours / Anyone But You – 1974
Hi 2269 - Let Yourself Go / Please Don't Give Up On Me – 1974
Hi 2275 - I Want To Take You Home (To See Mama) / I Hear The Love Chimes – 1974
Hi 2285 - Take Me To The River / Could I Be Falling In Love – 1975
Hi 2295 - I Only Have Love / Come On Home – 1975
Hi 2304 - Star Bright, Star Lite / That's Just My Luck – 1976
Hi 2308 - 'Bout To Make Me Leave Home / It Ain't Easy – 1976
E. P. I. 101 - Goodie-Goodie-Good Times / Love Baby - 1976
Shama 1235 - Goodie-Goodie-Good Times / Love Baby – 1977
Shama 1236 - Can't Nobody Stop Me Now / Let Me Love You – 1977
Hi 77507 - Fonk You / That Wiggle – 1977
Hi 77517 - Stand By Me / Main Squeeze – 1978
Hi 79529 - Mystery Lady / Let's Dance For Love – 1978
Shama 1237 - Bring Out The Blues In Me / How You Need To Be Loved – 1980
Shama 1239 - Dream Of A Lifetime / All The Way To The Top – 1981
Shama 1241 - Ms. Fine Brown Frame / You Don't Have To Go – 1981
Boardwalk 7-11-165 - Ms. Fine Brown Frame / You Don't Have To Go – 1982
Boardwalk 99904 - Ms. Fine Brown Frame / You Don't Have To Go - 1982 (12" Release)

Sil Johnson & Co.

Shama 1242 - Steppin' / Suicide Blues – 1983

Syl Johnson

Boardwalk 1242 - Steppin' / Suicide Blues - 1983
Shama 1244 - I Got Your Beef / John, Muddy, Bob And Marvin - 1983

Syl Johnson With James Cotton's Blues Band (Members Syl Johnson, James Cotton, ...)

Shama 800 - Ms. Fine Brown Frame / Ms. Fine Brown Frame - 198? (12" Release)

Syl Johnson & Company (Members

Shama 801 - Gimme Some / Gimme Some (Instrumental) - 1983? (12" Release)
Erect 112 - Ms. Fine Brown Frame / You Don't Have To Go - 1988
Star Lite ? - That's Just My Luck / Star Bright - ?
Epic ?
BGP 010 - Different Strokes / Is It Because I'm Black - ?

The Notations / Syl Johnson

Collectables Col 033717 - I'm Still Here / Come On Sock It To Me* - ? *Flip By Syl Johnson.

Linda Jones

The Jones Singers (members Linda Jones, ...) gospel group comprised of her entire family.

Linda Lane (It has long been suspected that this is Linda Jones)

Cub 9124 - Cancel The Celebration / Lonely Teardrops -1963

Linda Jones (born 14-December-1944 in Newark, New Jersey - died 14-March-1972 in New York hospital - cause: diabetic shock)

Atco 6344 - Take This Boy Out Of The Country / I'll Take Back My Love - 1964
Blue Cat 128 - Fugitive From Love / You Hit Me Like T. N. T. - 1965
Loma 2070 - Hypnotized / I Can't Stop Loving My Baby - 1967
Loma 2077 - What've I Done (To Make You Mad) / Make Me Surrender (Baby, Baby Please) - 1967
Loma 2085 - Give My Love A Try / I Can't Stand It - 1967
Loma 2091 - My Heart Needs A Break* / The Things I've Been Through (Loving You) - 1968
*this was originally recorded as a demo by Sammy Turner but unissued on vinyl it can be found on the 1993 U. K. Goldmine Cd "Detroit Soul From The Vaults Volume One" GSCD 19.
Loma 2099 - What Can I Do (Without You) / Yesterday - 1968
Loma 2105 - I (Who Have Nothing) / It Won't Take Much (To Bring Me Back) - 1968
Warner 7 Arts 7278 - I Just Can't Live My Life (Without You Babe) / My Heart (Will Understand) - 1969
Neptune 17 - I'll Be Sweeter Tomorrow / That's When I'll Stop Loving You - 1969

Linda Jones / Bessie Banks

Cotique 177 - Fugitive From Luv / Go Now* - 1969 *flip by Bessie Banks.

Linda Jones

Neptune 26 - Ooh Baby You Move Me / Can You Blame Me - 1970
Turbo 012 - Stay With Me Forever / I've Given You The Best Years Of My Life - 1971
Turbo 017 - I Can't Make It Alone / Don't Go On - 1971
Turbo 021 - (For) Your Precious Love / Don't Go (I Can't Bear To Be Alone) - 1972
Turbo 024 - Not On The Outside / Things I've Been Through - 1972

Linda Jones & The Whatnauts / The Whatnauts

Stang 5039 - I'm So Glad I Found You / World Solution* - 1972 *flip by The Whatnauts only

Linda Jones

Turbo 028 - Let It Be Me / Don't Go (I Can't Stand To Be Alone) - 1972
Turbo 032 - Fugitive From Love / Things I've Been Through - 1973
Warner Bros. Gwb 0323 - Hypnotized / My Heart Needs A Break - ? (Back to Back hits series)

Linda Jones / ?

Teen 1a - Hypnotized / ?* - ? *flip not by Linda Jones.

Linda Jones

Hot Groove 300 - Hypnotized / You've Got The Makings Of A Lover - ?

Roddie Joy

Roddie Joy (Rita Coleman)

Red Bird 10-021 - Come Back Baby* / Love Hit Me With A Wallop - 1965 *Also Recorded In 1966 By The Stoppers On Jubilee 5528.
Red Bird 10-031 - He's So Easy To Love / The La La Song – 1965
Red Bird 10-037 - If There's Anything Else You Want (Let Me Know) / Stop – 1965
Parkway 101 - Stop / Something Strange Is Going On – 1966
Parkway 134 - Every Breath I Take / Walkin' Back* - 1967 *Also Recorded In 1966 By Jackie Taylor On Jubilee 5530.
Parkway 151 - I Want You Back / Let's Start All Over – 1967
Parkway 991 - Stop / A Boy Is Just A Toy - 1967

Group Line Ups

The Kittens (Bernice Willis, Laurel Ross, Thelma Mack)
The Knight Brothers (Richard Dunbar, Jerry Diggs)

Paul Kelly

The Spades (members Paul Kelly, ...)

The Valadeers (members Paul Kelly, ...)

Paul Kelly

TK ? - 1960

Clarence Reed & The Delmiros (members

Selma 4002 - Sooner Or Later / Down With It, Can't Quit It - 1963
(Not only is Clarence Reid's name misspelled in the credits – he's not even singing lead here! He had laryngitis, and at the last minute his buddy Paul Kelly stepped in! This predates Kelly's singles on the Lloyd label)

Paul Kelly

Lloyd (No #) - The Upset / It's My Baby - 1965 (inspired by Cassius Clay's victory over Sonny Liston)
Lloyd 7 - Chills And Fever / Only Your Love - 1965
Dial 4021 - Chills And Fever / Only Your Love - 1965

Paul Kelly & The Rocketeers

Dial 4025 - Since I Found You / Can't Help It - 1966 (with Frank Williams' Rocketeers)

Paul Kelly

Philips 40409 - Nine Out Of Ten Times / I Need Your Love So Bad - 1966
Philips 40457 - Cryin' For My Baby / Sweet Sweet Lovin' - 1967
Philips 40480 - If This Old House Could Talk / You Don't Know, You Just Don't Know - 1967
Dial 4088 - Call Another Doctor / We're Gonna Make It - 1968
Philips 40513 - My Love Is Growing Stronger / Glad To Be Sad - 1968

Annetta (Duet between Paul Kelly & Annette Snell. Slightly different titles, but the same recording)

Love Hill 001 - Since There's No More You / Get Away Boy - 1969
Juggy 404 - Since There Is No More You / Get Away Boy - 1970

Paul Kelly

Happy Tiger 541 - Stealing In The Name Of The Lord / The Day After Forever - 1970
Happy Tiger 555 - 509 / Sailing - 1970
Happy Tiger 568 - Poor But Proud / Hot Runnin' Soul - 1970
Happy Tiger 573 - Hangin' On In There / Soul Flow - 1971
A & M 2320 - Been To The Well Before / I Love The Way You Love - 1981
Warner 7558 - Dirt / Poor But Proud - 1972
Warner 7614 - Here Comes Ole Jezebel / Travelin' Man - 1972
Warner 7657 - Don't Burn Me / Love Me Now* - 1972 *Covered In 1974 By Ruby Winters On Polydor 14249.
Warner 7707 - Come By Here / Come Lay Some Lovin' On Me - 1973
Warner 7765 - (You Bring Me) Joy / I'm Into Something I Can't Shake Loose - 1974
Warner 7823 - Hooked, Hogtied And Collared / I Wanna Be Close To You - 1974
Warner 8040 - I Wanna Be Close To You / Let Your Love Come Down (Let It Fall On Me) - 1974
Warner 8067 - Take It Away From Him (Put It On Me) / Try My Love - 1975
Warner 8120 - Get Sexy / I Believe I Can - 1975
Warner 8187 - Play Me A Love Song / Stealin' Love On The Side - 1976
Warner 8347 - To The Bone, Get It On / Stand On The Positive Side Of Life - 1977
Warner 8421 - Hallelujah, Glory Hallelujah / To The Bone, Get It On - 1977
Epic 50555 - Everybody's Got A Jonese / Shake Your Mind (Like You Shake Your Butt) - 1978
A & M 2320 - Been To The Wall Before / I Love The Way You Love - 1981

Paul Kelly

Laurence 112883 - Livin' In A Dream / Makin' Love In The Night - ?
Laurence ? - Change To Me / Tell Me - 1989
Laurence 81788 - Children Are Listening / ? - ?

Curtis Knight

Curtis Knight (Curtis McNear)

Horton 0001 - Baby That's Where It's At / You Don't Have To Tell Me - 1960
Gulf 031 - That's Why / Voodoo Woman - 1961
Shell 45-310 - You're Gonna Be Sorry / Little Doe-Doe - 1962
Shell 45-312 - Gotta Have A New Dress* / When You've Got Love - 1963
RSVP 1111 - Ain't Gonna Be No Next Time / More Love - 1965
RSVP 1120 - How Would You Feel / Welcome Home - 1966 (With Jimi Hendrix On Guitar)

Curtis Knight & The Squires

RSVP 1124 - Hornet's Nest / Knock Yourself Out - 1966 (With Jimi Hendrix On Guitar)

Curtis Knight

Bell 45457 - Devil Made Me Do It / Oh, Rainbow - 1974

Gladys Knight

The Cashmeres (members Dodd Hicks, Henry Boyd, plus cousins Langston George and Edward Patten)

The Pips (members (sisters and brother) Gladys Knight, Brenda Knight, Merald "Bubba" Knight, (and cousins) Eleanor O. Guest (born 1940 --- died 23-August-1997 at Southwest Hospital in Atlanta --- cause: heart failure) and William Guest)

Brunswick 55048 - Whistle My Love / Ching Ching - 1958 (promo copies issued on yellow label)

The Pips (members Gladys Knight, Merald "Bubba" Knight, William Guest, Edward Patten and Langston George (also cousins))

Huntom 2510 - Every Beat Of My Heart / Room In Your Heart - 1961
Vee Jay 386 - Every Beat Of My Heart / Room In Your Heart - 1961
Vee Jay 386 - Every Beat Of My Heart / Ain'tcha Got Some Room (In Your Heart For Me) - 1961 (same song as above flip, different title)

Gladys Knight & The Pips

Fury 1050 - Every Beat Of My Heart / Room In Your Heart - 1961
Fury 1052 - Guess Who / Stop Running Around - 1961
Fury 1054 - Letter Full Of Tears / You Broke Your Promise - 1961
Fury 1064 - Operator / I'll Trust In You - 1962

The Pips (Merald "Bubba" Knight, William Guest and Edward Patten (born 2-August-1939 in Atlanta, Georgia --- died 25-February-2005 in Livonia, Michigan --- cause: stroke))

Fury 1067 – Darling / Linda - 1962

Gladys Knight & The Pips

Fury 1073 - Come See About Me / I Want That Kind Of Love - 1963

The Pips

Everlast 5025 - Happiness / I Had A Dream Last Night - 1963

Gladys Knight & The Pips

Vee Jay 545 - A Love Like Mine / Queen Of Tears - 1963
Maxx 326 - Giving Up* / Maybe, Maybe Baby - 1964 from this release the membership stayed the same. *Written by Van McCoy.
Enjoy 2012 - What Shall I Do / Love Call (Really Didn't Mean It) - 1964 (some promo issues only)
Enjoy 2012 - What Shall I Do / Love Call - 1964
Oldies 45 17 - Every Beat Of My Heart / Room In Your Heart - 1964

The Dells / Gladys Knight & The Pips

Oldies 45 112 - Times Make You Change / Letter Full Of Tears* - 1964 *Flip By Gladys Knight & The Pips.

Dee Clark / Gladys Knight & The Pips

Oldies 45 113 - You Are Like The Wind / Operator* - 1964 *Flip By Gladys Knight & The Pips.

Gladys Knight & The Pips

Maxx 329 - Lovers Always Forgive / Another Love - 1964
Maxx 331 - Either Way I Lose / Go Away, Stay Away - 1964
Maxx 334 - Stop And Get A Hold Of Myself */ Who Knows - 1965 *also recorded in 1967 by Carole Waller on U. S. A. 863.
Maxx 335 - Tell Her You're Mine / If I Should Ever Be In Love - 1965
Soul 35023 - Just Walk In My Shoes / Stepping Closer To Your Heart - 1966
Soul 35033 - Take Me In Your Arms And Love Me / Do You Love Me Just A Little More? - 1967
Soul 35034 - Everybody Needs Love* / Since I've Lost You - 1967 *Also Recorded In The U. K. in 1968 by Bobby Hanna on DeccaF 12783.
Soul 35039 - I Heard It Through The Grapevine* / It's Time To Go Now - 1967 *Also recorded in 1969 by Lloyd Price on Turntable 502.
Soul 35042 - The End Of Our Road / Don't Let Her Take Your Love From Me – 1968
Soul 35045 - It Should Have Been Me* / You Don't Love Me No More - 1968 *Also recorded in 1963 by Kim Weston on Tamla 54076 and in 1974 by Yvonne Fair on Motown 1323.
Soul 35094 - Help Me Make It Through The Night* / If You're Gonna Leave (Just Leave) - 1972 *also recorded in 1971 by O. C. Smith on Columbia 4-45435 and in the same year by Joe Simon on Spring 113.

Gladys Knight & The Pips / The Four Tops / Martha Reeves & The Vandellas / The Voices Of Tabernacle

Motown W4kb-4900-1a - Excerpts From The Album M-462 "In Loving Memory" (Tribute To Mrs. Loucye S. Wakefield) - 1968 (Promo Issue Only -- Gladys Knight & The Pips Sing "How Great Thou Art")

Gladys Knight & The Pips

Soul 35047 - I Wish It Would Rain / It's Summer - 1968

Marvin Gaye / Gladys Knight & The Pips

Motown 1128 - His Eye Is On The Sparrow* /Just A Closer Walk With Thee** - 1968 *"A" Side Marvin Gaye, ** Flip Gladys Knight & The Pips.

Gladys Knight & The Pips

Soul 35057 - Didn't You Know (You'd Have To Cry Sometime) / Keep An Eye - 1969
Soul 35063 - The Nitty Gritty / Got Myself A Good Man - 1969
Soul 35068 - Friendship Train / Cloud Nine - 1969
Soul 35071 - You Need Love Like I Do (Don't You) / You're My Everything - 1970
Soul 35078 - If I Were Your Woman / The Tracks Of My Tears - 1970
Soul 35083 - I Don't Want To Do Wrong / Is There A Place In His Heart For Me - 1971
Soul 35091 - Make Me The Woman You Come Home To / If You're Gonna Leave (Just Leave) - 1972
Soul 35094 - Help Me Make It Through The Night / If You're Gonna Leave (Just Leave) - 1972
Soul 35098 - Neither One Of Us (Wants To Be The First To Say Goodbye)* / Can't Give It Up No More - 1972 *Received "Grammy" Award For "Best Pop Vocal Performance By A Group".
Soul 35105 - Daddy Could Swear I Declare / For Once In My Life - 1973
Soul 35107 - All I Need Is Time / The Only Time You Love Me (Is When You're Losing Me) - 1973
Trip 3004 - It Hurt Me So Bad / What Will Become Of Us - 1973 (Some Copies Came With Picture Sleeve)
Buddah 363 - Where Peaceful Waters Flow / Perfect Love - 1973
Buddah 383 - Midnight Train To Georgia / (Instrumental) - 1973
Buddah 383 - Midnight Train To Georgia* / Window Raising - 1973 *Received "Grammy" Award For "Best R&B Vocal Performance By A Group".
Buddah 393 - I've Got To Use My Imagination / I Can See Clearly Now - 1973
Buddah 403 - Best Thing That Ever Happened To Me / Once In A Lifetime - 1974
Buddah 423 - On And On */ The Makings Of You - 1974 *From The Film "Claudine".
Soul 35111 - Between Her Goodbye And My Hello / This Child Needs It's Father - 1974
Buddah 433 - I Feel A Song (In My Heart) / Don't Burn Down The Bridge - 1974
Buddah 1974 - Do You Hear What I Hear / Silent Night - 1974 (Promo Issue)
Buddah 453 - Love Find's It's Own Way / Better You Go Your Way - 1975
Buddah 463 - The Way We Were-Try To Remember / The Need To Be - 1975

Gladys Knight / Alice Cooper

W.I.A.A. 280 - What's It All About (Aug 75) Public Service Show - 1975 (Radio Station Promo Issue Only -- Flip Alice Cooper)

Gladys Knight & The Pips

Buddah 487 - Money / Street Brothers - 1975
Buddah 513 - Part Time Love / Where Did I Put His Memory - 1975
Buddah 523 - Make Yours A Happy Home / The Going Up And The Coming Down - 1976
Buddah 544 - So Sad The Song* / (Instrumental) - 1976 *From The Film "Pipe Dreams" Starring Gladys Knight.
Buddah 569 - Baby Don't Change Your Mind / I Love To Feel That Feelin' - 1977
Buddah Dsc 115 - Love Is Always On Your Mind / (Instrumental) - 1977 (12" Release)
Buddah 584 - Sorry Doesn't Always Make It Right / You Put A New Life In My Body - 1977
Buddah 592 - The One And Only / Pipe Dreams - 1978
Buddah 598 - It's Better Than Good Time / Everybody's Got To Find A Way - 1978
Buddah Dsc 126 - It's Better Than A Good Time / (Instrumental) - 1978 (12" Release)

Gladys Knight (born 28-May-1944)

Buddah 601 - I'm Coming Home Again / Love Gives You The Power - 1978

The Pips

Casablanca 912 - If I Could Bring Back Yesterday / Since I Found Love - 1978
Casablanca 949 - Baby I'm Your Fool / Lights Of The City - 1978

Gladys Knight

Buddah 605 - Sail Away / I'm Still Caught Up With You - 1979
Columbia 10922 - Am I Too Late / It's The Same Old Song - 1979
Columbia 10996 - You Bring Out The Best In Me / You Loved Away The Pain - 1979 (12" Release)
Columbia 10997 - You Bring Out The Best In Me / You Loved Away The Pain - 1979
Columbia 11088 - The Best Thing We Can Do Is Say Goodbye / You Don't Have To Say I Love You - 1979

Gladys Knight & The Pips

Columbia 11239 - Landlord / We Need Hearts - 1980
Columbia 11330 - Taste Of Bitter Love / Add It Up - 1980
Columbia As 803 - Taste Of Bitter Love / Bourgie, Bourgie - 1980 (12" Promo Issue)
Columbia 11375 - Bourgie, Bourgie / Get The Love - 1980

Gladys Knight & Johnny Mathis

Columbia 11409 - When A Child Is Born / The Lord's Prayer - 1980

Gladys Knight & The Pips

Columbia 02113 - Forever Yesterday (For The Children) / (Instrumental) - 1981
Columbia 02413 - If That'll Make You Happy / Love Was Made For Two - 1981
Columbia 02549 - I Will Fight / God Is - 1981
Columbia As 1307 - I Will Fight / God Is - 1981 (12" Promo Issue)

Rupert Holmes / Gladys Knight & The Pips

W.I.A.A. 520 - What's It All About (Feb 82) Public Service Show - 1982 (Radio Station Promo Issue Only)

Gladys Knight & The Pips

Columbia 02706 - Friend Of Mine / Reach High - 1982
Columbia 03418 - That Special Time Of Year / Santa Claus Is Comin' To Town - 1982
Columbia 03761 - Save The Overtime (For Me) / Ain't No Greater Love - 1983
Columbia 03969 - Save The Overtime (For Me) / (Instrumental) - 1983 (12" Release)
Columbia 04033 - You're Number 1 In My Book / Oh La De Dah - 1983
Columbia 04219 - Hero (The Wind Beneath My Wings) / Seconds - 1983
Columbia 04965 - When You're Far Away / (Instrumental) - 1983 (12" Release)

Gladys Knight & The Pips / Maxine Brown

Original Sound Obg-4522 - Every Beat Of My Heart / All In My Mind* - 1984 *flip by Maxine Brown.

Gladys Knight & The Pips

Gusto 2118 - You're The Best Thing That Ever Happened To Me / Midnight Train To Georgia - ?
Columbia 04333 - Here's That Sunny Day / Oh La De Dah - 1984
Columbia 04369 - When You're Far Away / Seconds - 1984

Columbia 05161 - My Time (2 Versions) - 1984 (12" Release)
Columbia 04761 - My Time / (Instrumental) - 1985
Columbia 04873 - Keep Givin' Me Love / Do You Wanna Have Some Fun - 1985

Dionne & Friends (Dionne Warwick, Elton John, Gladys Knight And Stevie Wonder)

Arista 9422 - That's What Friends Are For / Two Ships Passing In The Night - 1985

Gladys Knight & The Pips

Columbia 05679 - Till I See You Again / Strivin' - 1985

Gladys Knight & Bill Medley

Scotti Bros. 06267 - Loving On Borrowed Time (Love Theme From Cobra) / Angel Of The City* - 1986 *Flip By Robert Tepper

Gladys Knight

B V 8000 - March Of Dimes - 12 Public Service Spots - 198? (Promo Issue Only -- Gladys Knight Does One 30 Second And One 60 Second Ad)

Gladys Knight & The Pips

MCA 23713 - Send It To Me / When You Love Somebody - 1986 (12" Release)
MCA 53002 - Send It To Me / When You Love Somebody (It's Christmas Every Day) - 1987
MCA 23803 - Love Overboard (6:00) / (Instrumental) - 1987 (12" Release)
MCA 53210 - Love Overboard / (Instrumental) - 1987
MCA L33-17429 - Lovin' On Next To Nothin' (4 Versions) - 1987 (12" Promo Issue)
MCA 23804 - Lovin' On Next To Nothin' / (Instrumental) - 1987 (12" Release)
MCA L33-17431 - Love Overboard (4 Versions) - 1987 (12" Promo Issue)
MCA L33-17444 - Love Overboard (6:10) / Love Overboard (5:44) - 1987 (12" Promo Issue)
MCA 53211 - Lovin' On Next To Nothin' / (Instrumental) - 1988
MCA L33-17561 - It's Gonna Take All Our Love / It's Gonna Take All Our Love - 1988 (12" Promo Issue)
MCA 23871 - It's Gonna Take All Our Love / (Instrumental) - 1988 (12" Release)
MCA 53351 - It's Gonna Take All Our Love / (Instrumental) - 1988
MCA 53657 - Licence To Kill / You - 1989
MCA 53676 - Licence To Kill / Pam* - 1989 *Flip By The National Philarmonic Orchestra.

Gladys Knight

MCA 1456 - Men (5 Versions) - 1990 (12" Promo Issue)
MCA 54130 - Men / (Instrumental) - 1990 (12" Release)
MCA 54117 - Men / (Instrumental) - 1991
MCA 1621 - Where Would I Be (3 Versions) - 1991 (12"Promo Issue)

Gladys Knight With Dionne Warwick And Patti Labelle

MCA 1694 - Superwoman (4 Versions) - 1991 (12" Promo Issue)

Gladys Knight

MCA 2080 - Meet Me In The Middle (6 Versions) - 1991 (12" Promo Issue)
MCA 3311 - This Time (4 Versions) - 1994 (12"Promo Issue)

The Dells / Gladys Knight & The Pips

Vee-Jay 1000 - Oh What A Nite / Every Beat Of My Heart* - ? (Vintage Series) *Flip By Gladys Knight & The Pips.

Gladys Knight & The Pips

Collectables Col 016297 - Letter Full Of Tears / You Broke Your Promise - ?
Lost Nite 386 - Letter Full Of Tears / You Broke Your Promise - ?

Robert Knight

Paramounts (Robert Knight, Clarence Holland, Richard Sammonds, Neil Hooper and Kenneth Buttrick)

Dot 16175 - Congratulations / Why Do You Have To Go – 1961
Dot 16201 - When You Dance / Year 17 – 1961

Robert Knight (born 21 - April - 1945 in Franklin, Tennessee.)

Dot 16256 - Because / Dance Only With Me – 1961
Dot 16303 - Free Me / The Other Half Of Man - 1962 (both Jimmy Breedlove tracks)

The Fairlanes (members Robert Knight (lead), Danny Boone (guitar), Lehman Keith (bass), Jack Jackson (tenor sax), Tommy Smith (trumpet) and Jim Tate (drums)) 1964 ~ 1967

Robert Knight

Rising Sons 705 - Everlasting Love* / Somebody's Baby - 1967 *also recorded in 1974 by Carl Carlton on Backbeat 630.
Rising Sons 707 - Blessed Are The Lonely / It's Been Worth It All – 1967
Rising Sons 708 - Love On A Mountain Top / Power Of Love – 1968
Rising Sons 709 - My Rainbow Valley / Sandy – 1968
Bell - Isn't It Lonely Together - 1969 (Test Pressing)
Eastway - Isn't It Lonely Together - 1969 (Test Pressing)
Elf 90019 - Isn't It Lonely Together / We'd Better Stop – 1968
Elf 90030 - Smokey / If I Had My Way – 1969
Elf 90037 - I Only Have Eyes For You / I'm Sticking With You – 1969
Monument 8612 - Better Get Ready For Love / Somebody's Baby – 1974
Monument 8629 - Dynamite / The Outsider – 1974
Private Stock 45,038 - I'm Coming Home To You / Glitter Lady – 1975
Private Stock 45,069 - Second Chance / Glitter Lady – 1976
Private Stock 45,118 - I've Got News For You / Honey Bun – 1976

Robert Knight / Arthur Smith

Collectables Col 04672 - Everlasting Love / Guitar Boogie* - 19?? *flip side by Arthur Smith

Chuck Jackson / Robert Knight

Ripete 196 - For All Time / Everlasting Love* - 1990 *flip by Robert Knight.

Venue Reports - June 2001

Cleethorpes Weekender 8th, 9th, 10th June, 2001.

Alcohol has a devastating effect on the ability to remember things in any sort of coherent order. If you don't believe me, ask Derek Pearson !

John Weston picked us up at 11.00 am, and we arrived just after 2.00 pm on the Friday afternoon, booked in, left my wife to unpack and went to the bar. Ostensibly to drop all my sales stuff off, in reality to and get the first beers in and say hello to people. I eventually went back with fish and chips about 5.00 pm. John Weston didn't, but more of that later.

Back out at 8.00, opened up the stall, and then started drinking. John Mills, my partner in crime for most of the weekender was spending money on records like they were going to be in short supply. I must admit he did buy some rather nice things though. I've no idea who DJ'ed when really because I couldn't see the decks from where we were sitting. I do know there were a lot of oldies played early on, no problem with that though, it filled the floor and got the place warmed up nicely.

By 10.30 pm John Weston turned up, so drunk he was totally incoherent and swaying. We got him propped up in a corner, where he promptly slumped to the floor. Viv Mills took him back to our caravan where Margie my wife took over. Apparently when he leaned forward to untie his shoes he fell off the settee ! We also thought he's lost the key to the caravan. When I realised this I shot off to retrieve my DJ box to find the sink full of a rather obnoxious mixture deposited by John sometime earlier. Lovely jubbly. The following morning John had no recollection of anything after about 9.00 pm. He was also missing two records from his sales box that he couldn't remember selling (Although he had got over £300 in his pocket from records that he couldn't remember selling either !). You've got to hand it to him, it was a classy way to start the weekender !

Following some confusion over what time I was supposed to be DJing, my inability to read the DJ rota by this time was a contributory factor ! I eventually did my spot at 4.45 am. I have very little recollection of what I played, but I know the dancefloor was full, so it must have been ok ! I know I got quite a few requests, and played them if I could. Then it was off to bed.

Saturday morning, the groans of pain and loud farts coming from John Weston's bedroom had us in stitches laughing for a good half an hour before he eventually surfaced. This made us laugh even longer, he looked as though he had died in the night.

Saturday lunchtime was spent listening to the international line up. Unfortunately Ady hadn't put any names in the programme so I don't know who most of the DJs were. I do know the standard of the international guys has increased dramatically over the last few years. Certainly the people who DJed on the Saturday would be able to hold their own at a good quality niter these days.

Satuday night. Numbers up, and the place was heaving. Hoagy Lands, when you could hear him, was ok. Sidney Barnes was great, A wonderful show by a wonderful performer. Again alcohol took over, and my recollections are vague, I do remember seeing Derek Pearson in a worse state than me, complaing that Louis had forced him to drink to excess before he even left the chalet. Butch caused a bit of a stir in the record bar by shaking a bottle of champagne and spraying it over every one. Fortunately most of it went into his record box, so if you buy a record from him, check it's not sticky ! He eventually passed out and was left outside asleep. All credit to the guy though, he spent a long time Sunday going round apologising to people.

Sunday afternoon. Well the only record I'd bought all weekend was a copy of the Lowton anniversary 12". Unfortunately, it stayed that way. There were things I would have liked, but non at the right price, so I didn't want to spend money just for the sake of it. Quiz time. Janine was in charge of the organising the KTF team. When the actual quiz finished she came over to where Chalky was standing chatting to me and we filled in nearly all the answers they had missed between us. It must have worked because KTF came second. I did the last three quarters of an hour DJIng. I had intended to play a whole spot of midtempo stuff. In the end I played 35 minutes of uptempo Soul and R & B, and ten minutes of midtempo. The simple reason for that is the dancefloor was up for it, and I was getting tons of requests. In fact before I went on stage I had requests for about ten records already. This goes back to the playing of originals. People asked me for those records because they know I have them because they have heard me play them before. End of sermon. I finished the Sunday afternoon session with Ray Pollard's Drifter (A request I had at 4.00 pm on the Friday afternoon !).

Sunday night. Party night. The night when all those forty somethings magically morph back to 1975. The fancy dress this year was a sensation with so much effort put into some of the costumes. Well done everyone. I love the Sunday night because I can get really drunk and then make a fool of myself, and nobody cares. Onto the ritual DJ humiliation. Roger Banks has a lot to answer for !!!!! Musical Chairs. The line up: Roger, me, Shifty, Bob Hinsley, Ady, Rob Messer, Dave Evison, Jodie, Jo Wallace, and Andy Rix. When I think about it, it was perfect, all these supposedly serious collectors and DJ's, ranging from Jodie at 23 to Dave Evison at 50, playing musical chairs in front of probably 800 drunks. You can imagine the response. What made it even funnier was how seriously we all took it. I was knocked out fairly early on, and managed to avoid all the pushing and cheating that followed. Roger eventually beat Ady in the final, so I wonder how long he had been practicing at home !

Then it was more beer, more beer, and more beer. Then a dance or two, then time to say goodbye, then bed.

Overall I thought the music was better this year, one live act was good, one wasn't. It was the best weekend of the year though, and the laughs we had will last a long time. Well done and congratulations to Ady and Sylvia. I suspect most people who were there will have already booked for next year (There was a booking slip on the programme) so I'd advise anyone wanting to go to book as soon as you see an advert.

The Lea Manor, Albrighton, 16th June, 2001

This was the annual 4 am finish in memory of T.C.. Unfortunately given the current musical policy in place at Albrighton there was very little played that T.C. would have recognised, most of it having not been played when he was alive. Good spots from Chris Anderton, Kenny Onions, and John Mills were the only high spots of a rather poorly attended night that featured no DJs from the Shropshire area where T.C. came from other than Len Cook.

The Black Horse, Wolverhampton, 22nd June, 2001

The best attended one yet, this place really is building rather a good reputation. Dave Welding was the local guest DJ, and he played an excellent spot mixing the rarities, both Oldies and Newies well in a balanced spot that got people up dancing very early on. Carl Willingham brought about a dozen supporters with him and started off quite well. Unfortunately he then decided to play some 1950's Cowboy themes, and the dancefloor cleared rather abruptly. In all fairness to Carl though he soon realised and quickly came back strong with some rare Soul. Result: a full floor again. Des and Martyn played the other spots between them, and there were no complaints there either.

100 Club, London, 30th June, 2001

Yet another John Weston classic ! He missed the train he was supposed to meet me on, catches the next train to London, and still beat me to the 100 Club. In the process he paid £30.00 for another train ticket, and found a brand new coat that fitted him ! Unbelievable. This was the quietest I've seen the 100 Club for a long time, and in all honesty it was a good job. The place was unbearably hot when you were DJing because of the heat rising from the dancefloor. Russ Vickers was the other guest DJ and he is one of the few DJ's that I admire because they can truly play across the board. Most 'across the board' DJs tend to ignore the Sixties side of things but Russ went at the whole lot like a champion. Well done that man. My first spot was slightly hampered by the equipment playing up, but that was sorted by the second spot, so here's the playlist for the second spot in roughly the correct order: 5 am to 5.45 am

Brooks O'Dell - Standing Tall - Columbia
Blue Jays - Point Of View - Jay

Marion James - That's My Man - Excello
Joanne Courcy - I Got The Power - Twirl
Gordon Keith - Look Ahead - Calumet
Vondells - Hey Girl - Airtown
Troy Dodds - Try My Love - El Camino
Sam Fletcher - I'd Think It Over - Tollie
Sparkels - Try Love - Old Town
Jimmey Soul Clark - I'll Be Your Winner - Soul Hawk
Magnetics - I Have A Girl - Ra Sel
Doc & The Interns - Baby I Know - Now
Bud Harper - Wherever You Were - Peacock
Patience Valentine - If You Don't Come - SAR
Lee Shot Williams - I'm Hurt - Sharma
Don Gardner - My Baby Likes To Boogaloo - Tru Glo Town.

Butch, Ady, and Mick also did the business with their spots, so all in all a very good night out.

Group Line Ups

The Larks (Don Julien, Charles Morrison, Ted Walters)
The Lovetones (Carl Jones, Stan Bracely, William 'Mickey' Stephenson, Joe Miles)

Buddy Lamp

Gone 5104 – What More Can I Do / Good News – 1961
Peanut 1001 – Have Mercy Baby / I'm Coming Home – 1961
Peanut 1003 – Insanity / Too Late – 1962
ABC-Paramount 10398 - I'm Coming Home / Promised Land - 1963
Double L 716 – My Tears / Thank You Love – 1963
Top Hat 4519 – Can You Stand It / Sad Music – 1964
D-Town 1064 – Just A Little Bit Of Lovin' / Next Best Thing – 1966
Wheelsville 113 – You've Got The Loving touch / I Wanna Go Home – 1966
Wheelsville 120 – Confusion / I Wanna Go Home – 1967
Wheelsville 122 - Save Your Love* / I Wanna Go Home - 1967 *written by Don Bryant this is the same song as the 1970 recording "I Love The Way You Love" by O. V. Wright on Backbeat 611 and has the same backing track as the 1967 recording by Lee Rogers "Sock Some Lover Power To Me" on Premium Stuff 6.
Wee 3 1002 – Confusion / I Wanna Go Home – 1967
Duke 438 – I'm Coming Home / Where Have You Been – 1968
Duke 461 – Devil's Gonna Get You / Wall Around Your Heart – 1969
Duke 468 – If You See Kate / Henpecked – 1971
MSK 790 – Shoo Shoo Disco / Get It All – 1979
MSK 798 – Pump Me Up / Part 2 – 1980
Meda 101 – Keep On Moving / Land Of Plenty – 1980

Major Lance

The Floats (members Major Lance, **Otis Leavill**, Barbara Tyson and ? (female))

? - When Johnny Comes Marching Home* / Lover - 1958 ~ 1959 (apparently a demo exists of this recording) *lead Major Lance. **lead Otis Leavill.

Major Lance (born 4-April-1939 or 1942 in Winterville, Mississippi, died 3-September-1994 at his home in Decatur, Georgia. Cause: He died in his sleep, he suffered a heart attack in 1987 and was nearly blind from glaucoma)

Mercury 71582 - I Got A Girl / Phyllis - 1959 (backed by The Impressions)

The Ideals (members Reggie Jackson, Leonard Mitchell, Wes Spraggins, Robert Tharp, Sam Stewart and (possibly) Major Lance)

Checker 920 - Knee Socks / Mary's Lamb - 1959

Johnny Brantley & The Ideals (members Johnny Brantley, Reggie Jackson, Leonard Mitchell, Wes Spraggins, Robert Tharp, Sam Stewart and (possibly) Major Lance)

Checker 979 - Knee Socks / Mary's Lamb – 1961

The Ideals (members Reggie Jackson, Leonard Mitchell, Robert Tharp, Sam Stewart and Major Lance?)

Paso 6401 - Together / What's The Matter With You Sam – 1961
Paso 6402 - Magic / Teens - 1961 (Major Lance departs)

Major Lance

Okeh 7168 - Delilah* / Everytime - 1962 *Recorded 14-September-1962.
Okeh 7175 - Monkey Time* / Mama Didn't Know - 1963 *Recorded 5-August-1963.
Okeh 7181 - Hey Little Girl* / Crying In The Rain - 1963 *Recorded 14-August-1963.
Okeh 7187 - Um, Um, Um, Um, Um, Um* / Sweet Music - 1964 *Recorded 14-August-1963.
Okeh 7191 - The Matador* / Gonna Get Married - 1964 (backing vocals by Billy Butler & The Chanters) *recorded 6-February-1964.
Okeh 7197 - It Ain't No Use / Girls - 1964
Okeh 7200 - Think Nothing About It* / It's Alright - 1964 *Recorded 18-October-1963.
Okeh 7203 - Rhythm* / Please Don't Say No More - 1964 *Recorded 11-June-1964.
Okeh 7209 - Sometimes I Wonder / I'm So Lost – 1964
Okeh 7216 - Come See / You Belong To Me My Love - 1965 (in 1965 Major Lance did a U.K. tour -- his backing band was Bluesology, whose pianist was Reg Dwight a.k.a Elton John!)
Okeh 7223 - Ain't It A Shame / Gotta Get Away* - 1965 *also recorded in 1964 by Billy Butler & The Chanters on
Okeh 7226 - Too Hot To Hold / Dark And Lonely – 1965
Okeh 7233 - I Just Can't Help It / Everybody Loves A Good Time – 1965
Okeh 7250 - Investigate / Little Young Lover – 1966
Epic / Memory Lane 5-2221 - The Monkey Time / Um Um Um Um Um Um - 1966
Epic / Memory Lane 5-2242 - Hey Little Girl / The Matador – 1966
Okeh 7255 - The Beat / You'll Want Me Back – 1966
Okeh 7266 - I /Ain't No Soul (In These Old Shoes)* - 1967 (Some Copies Issued With A Picture Cover)
Okeh 7284 - You Don't Want Me No More / Wait 'Til I Get You In My Arms - 1967
Okeh 7298 - Without A Doubt / Forever – 1968

Dakar 1450 - Do The Tighten Up / I Have No One – 1968
Dakar 608 - Follow The Leader / Since You've Been Gone – 1969
Dakar 612 - Sweeter As The Days Go By / Shadows Of A Memory – 1969
Curtom 1953 - Stay Away From Me (I Love You Too Much) / Gypsy Woman - 1970
Curtom 1956 - Must Be Love Coming Down / Little Young Lover – 1971
Volt 4069 - Girl Come On Home / Since I Lost My Baby's Love – 1971
Volt 4079 - I Wanna Make Up / That's The Story Of My Life – 1972
Volt 4085 - Ain't No Sweat / Since I Lost My Baby's Love – 1972
Playboy 6017 - Um Um Um Um Um Um* / Last Of The Red Hot Lovers - 1974 *New Version.
Playboy 6020 - Sweeter As The Days Go By / Wild And Free – 1975
Osiris 001 - You're Everything I Need / (Instrumental) - 1975 (the record label Osiris was a joint venture by Major Lance and Booker T. & The MG's drummer Al Jackson, after Al Jackson was murdered on 1-October-1975 (he was shot to death by two burglers at his Memphis home after returning from a telecast of the third Mohammad Ali / Joe Frazier boxing match) Major Lance folded the company)
Osiris 002 - I've Got A Right To Cry / You Keep Coming To Me – 1975
Columbia 10488 - Come On Have Yourself A Good Time / Come What May* - 1977 *also recorded in 1975 by John Gary Williams on Truth 3227.
Soul 35123f - I Never Thought I'd Be Losing You / I Never Thought I'd Be Losing You - 1978 (promo issue only)
Soul 35123 - I Never Thought I'd Be Losing You / Chicago Disco - 1978 (Major Lance was arrested for cocaine possesion in 1978 and had to serve a three-year prison sentence)
Kat Family 03024 - I Wanna Go Home / (Instrumental) - 1982 (back-up vocals by Freddie Grace & The Rhinestones)
Kat Family 04182 - Are You Leaving Me / Are You Leaving Me - 1982 (12" Single)
Kat Family 04185 - I Wanna Go Home / Are You Leaving Me – 1982
Gusto 2042 - Um, Um, Um, Um, Um, Um / The Monkey Time - ?

The Ideals / The Sonics

Collectables Col 034647 - Knee Socks / This Broken Heart* - ? *flip by The Sonics.

Hoagy Lands

The Dynaflows (Members Victor I.Hoagland Sr., Billy Terrell, Major Williams, Leroy Pitman And Robert Grant) - High School Group.

The New Brunswick Heart Throbs (Members Victor I. Hoagland Sr., Bobby Thomas, Harvey Drayton, Charles Gregory, Mayola Gregory, George Gregory And Lorenzo Howell)

Hoagy Lands (Born Victor I. Hoagland Sr.,On The 4-May-1936 In New Brunswick, New Jersey. Died Saturday 12-January-2002 In Orange, New Jersey - Cause: Fall At Home)

Ivory ? - Oo-Be-Do / You're Only Young Once - 195?
Judi 054 - (I'm Gonna) Cry Some Tears / Lighted Windows - 1960
ABC-Paramount 10171 - (I'm Gonna) Cry Some Tears / Lighted Windows - 1960
MGM K-13041 - My Tears Are Dry / It's Gonna Be Morning - 1961
MGM K-13062 - Goodnight Irene / It Ain't Easy As That* - 1962 *also recorded in 1963 by The Elektras (members Yolanda Robinson, Estelle McEwan, Yvonne DeMunn and Madelyn Moore) on United Artists 594.
ABC-Paramount 10392 - Tender Years / I'm Yours* - 1963 *released in the UK on Stateside SS 2085.
Atlantic 2217 - Baby Come On Home / Baby Let Me Hold Your Hand - 1964 (backing vocals Cissy Houston, Dee Dee Warwick and possibly Judy Clay - Eric Gale on guitar)
Laurie 3349 - Theme From The Other Side / Friends And Lovers Don't Go Together - 1966
Laurie 3361 - Theme From The Other Side / September - 1967

Laurie 3372 - Yesterday / Forever In My Heart- 1967
Laurie 3381 - The Next In Line / Please Don't Talk About Me When I'm Gone - 1967 (Backing Vocals The Chiffons)
Laurie 3463 - Two Years And A Thousand Tears (Since I Left Augusta) / White Gardenia - 1968

Lily Field & Hoagy Lands

Spectrum 116 - Beautiful Music / Crying Candle - 1969
Spectrum 118 - Sweet Soul (Brother) / A Boy In A Man's World - 1970

Hoagy Lands

Spectrum 122 - Do You Know What Life Is All About / Why Didn't You Let Me Know - 1971
Spectrum 129 - Reminisce / Why Didn't You Let Me Know - 1971
Spectrum 130 - A Man Ain't No Stronger Than His Heart / Do It Twice - 1972
Spectrum 140 - The Bell Ringer / (Instrumental) - 1972
Paramount 0232 - Mary Ann / Pledging My Love - 1973
Stardust 028 - I'm Yours / The Tender Years - ?

Liz Lands

Liz Lands (Born 1939 in The Georgia Sea Islands, grew up in New York City . Married Tommy Brown in the early 1950's)

Divinity 99008 - Trouble In The Land / We Shall Overcome - 1963 (This Was Issued On Motown's Short Lived Gospel Label)

Liz Lands / Rev. Martin Luther King

Gordy 7023 - We Shall Overcome / I Have A Dream - 1963
Gordy 7026 - May What He Lived For Live - 1963 (One-Sided Promo - White Label)
Gordy 7026 - May What He Lived For Live / He's Got The Whole World In His Hands – 1963

Liz Lands & The Temptations

Gordy 7030 - Midnight Johnny* / Keep Me - 1964
*Originally Titled "Midnight Lover." A slightly faster version with different lyrics in some places does exist on a Motown Acetate.

Liz Lands

One-Derful 4847 - One Man's Poison / Don't Shut Me Out – 1967
T & L 50 - Come In The Room / Someone Bigger Than You And I - ? (the T & L label was named after Liz and her husbands initials)

Liz Lands Paul Mitchell - Trio

T & L 201 - Silent Night (Part 1) / Silent Night (Part 2) (Instrumental) - 1967

Liz Lands

T & L 1001 - Echo In The Background (Of My Broken Heart) / Qualify For My Love - 1968
T & L 1002 - Cotton Fields / Let It Be Me – 1968

Ep's

T & L 118-68 - Let It Be Me / Cotton Fields /// Echo In The Background / Since I Met You Baby* - 1968 *duet with un-named vocalist.

Emmanuel Laskey

Emanuel Laskey (born 20-June-1945 in Detroit, Michigan --- died 23-June-2006 in Detroit, Michigan --- cause: cancer)

Thelma 100 - The Monkey / Welfare Cheese – 1963
Thelma 42282 - I Need Somebody / Tomorrow – 1964

Emanuel Lasky

Thelma 94494/ 94495 - Tomorrow / I Need Somebody – 1964
NPC 1003 - I Need Somebody / Tomorrow – 1964
Thelma 101 - Crazy / Welfare Cheese – 1964

Emanuel Laskey

Thelma 103 - Lucky To Be Loved (By You) / Our World - 1965 (Unissued)

Emanuel Lasky

Wild Deuce 1003 - Lucky To Be Loved (By You) / Our World - 1965

Emanuel Laskey

Thelma 106 - Don't Lead Me On Baby / What Did I Do Wrong – 1965
Thelma 108 - I'm A Peace Loving Man / Sweet Lies – 1965
Thelma 110 - (I've Got To) Run For My Life / You Better Be Sure - 1965

Emanuel Lasky

Westbound 143 - More Love (Where This Came From) / A Letter From Vietnam – 1969

Emanuel Laskey

Westbound 151 - Never My Love / A Letter From Vietnam - 1969
Music Now 2880 - Just The Way (I Want Her To Be) / Right On (Wit' It) - 1970

Emanuel Laskey

Stag 1008 - Remember Me Always (Part 1) / Remember Me Always (Part 2) - 1973 (also released in ? by Emanuel Taylor on Bernard 077)
D. T. 10008 - Remember Me Always (Part 1) / Remember Me Always (Part 2) - 1973
D. T. 100 - I'd Rather Leave On My Feet* / I'd Rather Leave On My Feet (Disco Version) - 1980
*also released in ? by Clyde Milton on Disco Tac 101.

Thelma 115 - You Better Quit It / Don't Lead Me On Baby - 1990's (unreleased versions pressed on a white demo look-alike label using the correct consecutive catalogue numbers, allegedly by a U. K. record dealer)

Bettye Lavette

Betty LaVett (born Betty Haskin on 29-January-1946 in Muskegon, Michigan)

Atlantic 2160 - My Man - He's A Lovin' Man / Shut Your Mouth – 1962
Atlantic 2198 - You'll Never Change* / Here I Am - 1962 *recorded 7-November-1962.
Lu Pine 123 - Witchcraft In The Air / You Killed The Love - 1963

Betty LaVette (after the above releases Bettye moved to New York where she became a featured vocalist with The Don Gardner Band)

Scepter 12103 - (Happiness Will Cost You) One Thin Dime - 1965 Unreleased as a 45, but available on the Kent CD 'New York Soul Serenade' (Bettye confirmed that this was just a one song demo done as a favor to Luther Dixon for Florence Greenberg to hear)
Calla 102 - Let Me Down Easy* / What I Don't Know (Won't Hurt Me) - 1965 *written by Wreich-Holloway an alias for Dee Dee Ford.
Calla - Let Me Down Easy - 1965 (slightly longer take unissued as a 45, but released in the U. K. in 2005 on a Emi/Stateside Cd "Betty Lavette / Carol Fran : The Complete Calla, Port & Roulette Recordings" 7243 860967 2 2)
Calla 104 - Only Your Love Can Save Me / I Feel Good (All Over) - 1965
Calla 106 - Stand Up Like A Man / I'm Just A Fool For You - 1965

Betty LaVett

Lu Pine 1021 - Witchcraft In The Air / You Killed The Love - 1965

Betty LaVette

Calla - Cry Me A River (Take 1) - 1966 (recorded 26-January-1966, unissued at the time, this was released in the U. K. in 2005 on a Emi/Stateside Cd "Betty Lavette / Carol Fran : The Complete Calla, Port & Roulette Recordings" 7243 860967 2 2)
Calla - Cry Me A River - 1966 (unissued at the time this was released in the U. K. on a 1998 Westside Cd "Doctor Good Soul : A Rhythm 'N' Soul Compendium 1963-74" WESM 525)
Calla - She Don't Love You Like I Love You (Take 5) - 1966 (recorded 26-January-1966, unissued at the time, this was released in the U. K. in 2005 on a Emi/Stateside Cd "Betty Lavette / Carol Fran : The Complete Calla, Port & Roulette Recordings" 7243 860967 2 2)

Betty La Vette

Big Wheel 1969 - I'm Holding On* / Tears In Vain - 1966 *with a "moonlighting" Marvin Gaye on piano.

Betty LaVette

Karen 1540 - Almost / Love Makes The World Go Round (Instrumental) - 1968
Karen 1544 - Get Away / Just Dropped In (To See What Condition My Condition Is In)* - 1969 *also recorded in 1967 by The First Edition on Reprise 0655.
Karen 1545 - With A Little Help From My Friends / Hey Love* - 1969 *also recorded in 1967 by Stevie Wonder on Tamla 54147.
Karen 1548- Let Me Down Easy / Ticket To The Moon - 1969
Silver Fox 17 - He Made A Woman Out Of Me* / Nearer To You - 1969 *Covered In 1970 By Bobbie Gentry On Capitol 2788.
Silver Fox 21 - Do Your Duty* / Love's Made A Fool Out Of Me - 1970 *Recorded 4-November-1969
Silver Fox 24 - Games People Play* / My Train's Comin' In - 1970 *Recorded 9-January-1970 --- Also Released In 1968 By Joe South On Capitol 2248

SSS Int. 839 - Take Another Little Piece Of My Heart* / At The Mercy Of A Man - 1970 *originally recorded in 1967 by Erma Franklin on Shout 221.
SSS Int. 933 - He Made A Woman Out Of Me / My Train's Coming In – 1970

Betty LaVette & Hank Ballard

SSS Int 946 - Let's Go, Let's Go, Let's Go* / ? - 1970 (unreleased as a 45 in the U. S. A. this track was released on a 2006 Varese Sarabande Cd "Bettye LaVette - Take Another Little Piece Of My Heart" 502 066 708 2) *also recorded in 1960 by Hank Ballard and The Midnighters on King 5400 and in 1966 by East Bay Soul Brass on Rampart 661.

Betty LaVette

TCA 001/002 - Never My Love* / Stormy** - 1971 *also recorded in 1967 by The Association on Warner Bros. 7074. **also recorded in 1968 by The Classics IV on Imperial 66328.
Atco 6891 - Heart Of Gold* / You'll Wake Up Wiser - 1972 *cover of a 1971 recording by Neil Young on Reprise 1065.
Atco 6913 - Your Turn To Cry* / Soul Tambourine - 1973 * a re-titled version of "Your Time To Cry" recorded in 1970 by Joe Simon on Spring 108.
Ripete 3018 - Please Don't Go / Games People Play* - 1989 *flip by Betty LaVette.
Epic 8-50143 - Thank You For Loving Me / You Made A Believer Out Of Me - 1975
Epic 8-50177 - Behind Closed Doors / You're A Man Of Words, I'm A Woman Of Action - 1975

Bettye LaVette

West End 1213 - Doin' The Best That I Can (Part 1) / Doin' The Best That I Can (Part 2) (Instrumental) – 1978
West End 22113-X/22113 - Doin' The Best That I Can (A Special New Mix) (7:43) / Doin' The Best That I Can (3:10) - 1978 (12" Release)
Motown 1532 - Right In The Middle (Of Falling In Love) / If I Were Your Woman - 1982 (unissued - this was the planned flip)
Motown 1532 - Right In The Middle (Of Falling In Love) / You Seen One You Seen 'Em All – 1982

Smokey Robinson / Bettye LaVette

Motown Pr92 - Tell Me Tomorrow / Right In The Middle (Of Falling In Love)* - 1982 (12" promo issue only) *flip by Bettye LaVette

The Temptations featuring Rick James / Bettye LaVette

Motown Pr96 - Standing On The Top (9:50) / I Can't Stop (5:36)* - 1982 (12" promo issue only) *flip by Bettye LaVette.

Bettye LaVette

Motown 1614 - Either Way We Lose / I Can't Stop - 1982
Street King Skds 1122 - Trance Dance (Vocal) (4:27) / Trance Dance (Dub Version) (4:07) - 1984 (12" release)

Kellie Evans, Don Albert, Betty Lavett, Sandra Feva

Get Down 5484 - The Rhythm And The Blues, Have You Tried Jesus / The Rhythm And The Blues - 1984

Willie Tee / Betty LaVette

Gold Coast 8001 - Please Don't Go / Games People Play* - ? *Flip By Betty Lavette.
Ripete 3018 - Please Don't Go / Games People Play* - 1989 *Flip By Betty Lavette.

Bettye LaVette

Bar None ? - Damn Your Eyes / Out Cold - 1997 (Cassette Single Only)

Andy Lewis featuring Bettye Lavette (

Ajx 159s - Laughter Ever After / Billion Pound Project (Instrumental) - 2005 (Possibly U.K. issue only)

12" Singles

Motorcity 39 - Surrender / Time Won't Change This Love - 1990 (Possibly U.K. Issue Only)
Motorcity 83 - Good Luck / (Instrumental) - 1991 (Possibly U.K. Issue Only)

Otis Leavill

The Cobb Quartet (family gospel / spiritual group Otis Leavill toured with at roughly age eight)

The Floats (members Major Lance, Otis Leavill, Barbara Tyson and ? (female))

? - When Johnny Comes Marching Home* / Lover** - 1958 ~ 1959 (demo) *lead Major Lance. **lead Otis Leavill.

Otis Leavill (born Otis Leavill Cobb on 8-February-1937, in Dewey Rose, Georgia... Died 17-July-2002 in Chicago, Illinois - cause: heart attack)

Lucky 1004 - Rise Sally Rise / I Gotta Right To Cry - 1963 (backed by (uncredited) The Opals (members Rose Addison (lead), Myra Tillison, Betty ? and Rose "Tootsie" Jackson) .
Limelight 3020 - I Am Amazed / Just A Memory – 1964
Limelight 3037 - Don't Let Me Down / Jane Girl – 1964
Blue Rock 4002 - Let Her Love Me / When The Music Grooves – 1964
Blue Rock 4015 - To Be Or Not To Be / Boomerang - 1965
Blue Rock 4031 - A Reason To Be Lonely / Because Of You – 1965
Columbia 43661 - Right Back In Love / Keep On Loving – 1966
Brunswick 55337 - Can't Stop Loving You / Baby Why Can't You Hear Me – 1967
Smash 2141 - Nobody But You / Charlotte – 1967
Blue Rock 4063 - It's The Same Old Me / Let Me Live – 1968
Dakar 614 - I Love You / I Need You – 1969
Dakar 617 - Glad I Met You* / Why Why Why** - 1970 *also recorded in 1967 by The Artistics on Brunswick 55315. **also recorded in 1967 by Mill Evans on King 6083.
Dakar 620 - Love Uprising / I Need You - 1970 (issued in Canada on Atco 620 as by Otis Leaville)
Dakar 622 - I'm So Jealous* / You Brought Out The Good In Me - 1971 *Also Recorded In 1965 By The Chi-Lites On Blue Rock 4007.
Dakar 625 - There's Nothing Better / Glad I Met You – 1971
Dakar 4511 - It Must Be Love / I Still Love You - 1972

Ketty Lester

Ketty Lester (born Revoyda Frierson 16-Aug-1934)

Everest 20007 - Queen For A Day / I Said Goodbye To My Love - 1962
Era 3068 - Love Letters* / I'm A Fool To Want You - 1962 *with Earl Palmer on drums. Also recorded in 1972 by Melba Moore on Mercury 73289
Era 3080 - But Not For Me / Once Upon A Time - 1962
Era 3088 - You Can't Lie To A Liar / River Of Salt - 1962
Era 3094 - This Land Is Your Land / Love Is For Everyone - 1962
Era 3103 - Fallen Angel / Lullaby For Lovers - 1963
RCA Victor 47-8331 - Some Things Are Better Left Unsaid / The House Is Haunted (By The Echo Of Your Last Good-Bye) - 1964
RCA Victor 47-8371 - Please Don't Cry Anymore / Roses Grow With Thorns - 1964
RCA Victor 47-8424 - I Trust You Baby / Theme From The Luck Of Ginger Coffey (Watching The World Go By) - 1964
RCA Victor 47-8471 - You Go Your Way (And I'll Go Crazy) / Variations On A Theme By "Bird"- 1964
RCA Victor 47-8573 - (Looking For A) Better World / Pretty Lies, Pretty Make Believes - 1965
Tower 166 - I'll Be Looking Back / West Coast - 1965
Tower 208 - Secret Love / Love Me Just A Little Bit - 1966
Tower 236 - When A Woman Loves A Man / We'll Be Together Again - 1966
Pete 706 - I Will Lead You / Now That I Need Him - 1968
Pete 710 - Measure Of A Man / Cracker Box Living - 1968
Pete 714 - Show Me* / Since I Fell For You - 1969 * *also recorded in 1967 by Joe Tex on Dial 4055
Mega 101 - One Day At A Time / Jesus Laid His Hands On Me - 1984
Mega 103 - Have You Heard? / She'd Never Heard Of Anyone Called Jesus - 1984

Barbara Lewis

Karen 313 – My Heart Went Do Dat Da / The Longest Night Of The Year – 1961
Atlantic 2141 – My Heart Went Do Dat Da / The Longest Night Of The Year – 1962
Atlantic 2159 – My Mama Told Me / Gonna Love You Till The End Of Time – 1962
Atlantic 2184 – Hello Stranger / Think A Little Sugar – 1963 (With The Dells)
Atlantic 2200 – Straighten Up Your Heart / If You Love Her – 1963
Atlantic 2214 – Puppy Love / Snap Your Fingers – 1963
Atlantic 2227 – Someday We're Gonna Love Again / Spend A Little Time – 1964
Atlantic 2255 – Pushin' A Good Thing To Far / Come Home – 1964
Atlantic 2283 – Baby I'm Yours / Say Love – 1965
Atlantic 2300 – Make Me Your Baby / Love To Be Loved – 1965
Atlantic 2316 – Don't Forget About Me / It's Magic – 1965
Atlantic 2346 – Make Me Belong To You / Girls Need Loving Care – 1966
Atlantic 2361 – Baby What Do You Want Me To Do / I Remember The Feeling – 1966
Atlantic 2400 – I'll Make Him Love Me / Love Makes The World Go Round – 1967
Atlantic 2413 – Fool Fool Fool / Only All The Time – 1967
Atlantic 2482 – Sho Nuff / Thankful For What I Got – 1968
Atlantic 2514 – I'll Keep Believing / On Bended Knees – 1968
Atlantic 2550 – I'm All You've Got / You're A Dream Maker – 1968
Enterprise 9012 – Just The Way You Are Today / You Made Me A Woman – 1969
Enterprise 9027 – Ask The Lonely / Why Did It Take You So Long – 1970
Enterprise 9029 – That's The Way I Like It / Anyway – 1970
Reprise 1146 – Rock & Roll Lullaby / I'm So Thankful - 1972

Little Anthony & The Imperials

The Duponts (members Anthony Gourdine (tenor), Edward Dockerty, Jr. (tenor), William

Christopher Delk (baritone) and Richard Bracey (bass))

Winley 212 - You / Must Be Falling In Love - 1956 (lead Anthony Gourdine)
Royal Roost 627 - Prove It Tonight* / Somebody* - 1957 *lead Anthony Gourdine.

The Chesters (members Anthony Gourdine (tenor), Tracy Lord (tenor), Ernest Wright, Jr. (second tenor), Clarence Collins (baritone) and Glouster "Nate" Rogers (bass))

The Chesters (members Anthony Gourdine (tenor), Tracy Lord (tenor), Ernest Wright, Jr. (second tenor), Keith Williams (baritone) and Glouster "Nate" Rogers (bass))

Apollo 521 - Lift Up Your Head* / The Fires Burn No More* - 1958 *lead Ernest Wright, Jr

The Duponts (members Willie ? (tenor), Edward Dockerty, Jr. (tenor), William Christopher Delk (baritone) and Richard Bracey (bass))

Roulette 4060 - Screamin' Ball (At Dracula Hall)* / Half Past Nothing** - 1958 *lead Richard Bracey. **lead Christopher Delk.

The Imperials (members Anthony Gourdine (lead), Tracy Lord (tenor), Ernest Wright, Jr. (second tenor), Clarence Collins (baritone --- former member of The Capitols on PET) and Glouster Rogers (bass))

End 1027 - Tears On My Pillow / Two People In The World - 1958

Little Anthony and The Imperials (members Anthony Gourdine, Tracy Lord, Ernest Wright, Jr., Clarence Collins and Glouster Rogers)

End 1027 - Tears On My Pillow / Two People World - 1958

Little Anthony Guardine and The Duponts (members Anthony Gourdine (tenor), Edward Dockerty, Jr. (tenor), William Christopher Delk (baritone) and Richard Bracey (bass))

Savoy 1552 - You / Must Be Falling In Love - 1958

Little Anthony and The Imperials (members Anthony Gourdine, Tracy Lord, Ernest Wright, Jr., Clarence Collins and Glouster Rogers)

End 1036 - So Much / Oh Yeah - 1958
End 1038 - The Diary* / Cha Cha Henry - 1959 *also recorded in 1958 by Neil Sedaka on RCA Victor 47-7408.
End 1039 - Wishful Thinking / When You Wish Upon A Star - 1959
End 1047- A Prayer And A Juke Box / River Path - 1959
End 1053 - So Near And Yet So Far / I'm Alright - 1959
End 1060 - Shimmy, Shimmy, Ko-Ko-Bop / I'm Still In Love With You - 1959
End 1067 - My Empty Room / Bayou, Bayou, Baby - 1960
End 1074 - I'm Taking A Vacation From Love / Only Sympathy - 1960
End 1080 - Limbo (Part 1) / Limbo (Part 2) - 1960
End 1083 - Formula Of Love / Dream - 1960
End 1086 - Please Say You Want Me / So Near Yet So Far - 1961
End 1091 - Traveling Stranger / Say Yeah - 1961
End 1104 - A Lovely Way To Spend An Evening / Dream - 1961

The Imperials (members George Kerr, Ernest Wright, Jr., Clarence Collins and Sammy Strain)

Carlton 566 - Faithfully Yours / Vut Vut - 1961

Little Anthony (born Anthony Gourdine on 8-January-1940 in Brooklyn, New York)

Roulette 4379 - That Lil' Ole Lovemaker Me / It Just Ain't Fair - 1961
Roulette 4477 - Lonesome Romeo / I've Got A Lot To Offer Darling - 1963

The Imperials (members George Kerr, Ernest Wright, Jr., Clarence Collins and Sammy Strain)

Newtime 503 - A Short Prayer / Where Will You Be - 1962
Newtime 505 - The Letter / Go And Get Your Heart Broken - 1962
Capitol 4291 - I'm Still Dancing / Bermuda Wonderful - 1963

Pookie Hudson (born James Hudson on 11-June-1934 in Des Moines, Iowa --- died 16-January-2006 at his home in Capital Heights, Maryland --- cause: metastatic lung cancer)

Double L 711 - Jealous Heart / I Know, I Know* - 1963 *flip side backed by The Imperials (members George Kerr, Ernest Wright, Jr., Clarence Collins and Sammy Strain)

Little Anthony and The Imperials (members Anthony Gourdine (lead), Sammy Strain (first tenor), Ernest Wright, Jr. (second tenor) and Clarence Collins (baritone/bass))

DCP 1104 - I'm On The Outside (Looking In)* / Please Go - 1964 *also recorded in 1968 by The Combinations on RCA 47-9482.
DCP 1119 - Goin' Out Of My Head* / Make It Easy On Yourself - 1964 *also recorded in 1966 by The Dotti Dunn Quartet on Scope 03137.
DCP 1128 - Hurt So Bad / Reputation - 1965
DCP 1136 - Take Me Back / Our Song - 1965
DCP 1149 - I Miss You So / Get Out Of My Life - 1965
DCP 1154 - Hurt / Never Again - 1965
Veep 1228 - Better Use Your Head* / The Wonder Of It All - 1966 *also recorded and released in the U. K. in 1967 by Dennis D'Ell on CBS 202605 upon which it was then quickly withdrawn on 22-March-1967.
Veep 1233 - Gonna Fix You Good (Every Time You're Bad) / You Better Take It Easy Baby - 1966
Veep 1239 - Tears On My Pillow / Who's Sorry Now - 1966
Veep 1240 - I'm On The Outside Looking In / Please Go - 1966
Veep 1241 - Goin' Out Of My Head / Make It Easy On Yourself - 1966
Veep 1243 - Our Song / Take Me Back - 1966
Veep 1244 - I Miss You So / Get Out Of My Life - 1966
Veep 1245 - Hurt / Never Again - 1966

Anthony and The Imperials (members Anthony Gourdine, Sammy Strain, Ernest Wright, Jr. and Clarence Collins)

Veep 1248 - It's Not The Same / Down On Love - 1966
Veep 1255 - Where There's A Will There's A Way To Forget You / Don't Tie Me Down - 1967
Veep 1262 - Hold On To Someone / Lost In Love - 1967
Veep 1269 - You Only Live Twice / My Love Is A Rainbow - 1967
Veep 1275 - If I Remember To Forget / Beautiful People - 1967
Veep 1278 - I'm Hypnotized / Hungry Heart - 1967
Veep 1283 - What Greater Love* / In The Back Of My Heart - 1968 *also recorded in the U. K. in 1969 by Jack Hammer on United Artists 35029.
Veep 1285 - Yesterday Has Gone / My Love Is A Rainbow - 1968
Veep 1293 - The Gentle Rain / The Flesh Failures - 1968
Veep 1303 - Anthem / Goodbye Goodtimes - 1969

Little Anthony and The Imperials (members Anthony Gourdine, Sammy Strain, Ernest Wright, Jr.. and Clarence Collins)

United Artists 50552 - Out Of Sight, Out Of Mind* / Summer's Comin' In - 1969 *also recorded in

1956 by The 5 Keys on Capitol 3502.
United Artists 50598 - The Ten Commandments Of Love* / Let The Sunshine In (The Flesh Failures)** - 1969 *also recorded in 1958 by Harvey & The Moonglows on Chess 1705. **also recorded in 1969 by The 5th Dimension on Soul City 772.
United Artists 50625 - It'll Never Be The Same Again / Don't Get Close - 1970
United Artists 50677 - World Of Darkness / The Change - 1970
United Artists 50720 - Help Me Find A Way (To Say I Love You) / If I Love You - 1970

The Spaniels (members James "Pookie" Hudson, backed by The Imperials minus Little Anthony)

North American 001 - Fairy Tales* / Jealous Heart - 1970 *also recorded in 1961 by The Fashions on Elmor 301.
Calla 172 - Jealous Heart / Fairy Tales - 1970

Little Anthony and The Imperials (members Anthony Gourdine, Sammy Strain, Kenny Seymour and Clarence Collins)

Janus 160 - Father, Father / Each One, Teach One - 1971
Janus 166 - Madeline / Universe - 1971
Janus 178 - Love Story / There's An Island - 1972

Little Anthony and The Imperials (members Anthony Gourdine, Sammy Strain, Robert Wade and Clarence Collins)

Avco 4614 - La La La At The End / Lazy Susan - 1973
Avco 4635 - I'm Falling In Love With You / What Good Am I Without You - 1974
Avco 4645 - I Don't Have To Worry / Loneliest House On The Block - 1974

Anthony & The Imperials (Members Anthony Gourdine, Sammy Strain, Robert Wade And Clarence Collins)

Avco 4651 - Hold On (Just A Little Bit Longer) / I've Got To Let You Go (Part 1) - 1975
Avco 4655 - I'll Be Loving You Sooner Or Later / Young Girl - 1975

Anthony & The Imperials (members Anthony Gourdine, ...)

Pure Gold 101 - Nothing From Nothing / Running With The Wrong Crowd - 1976

The Imperials (members

Power Exchange 266 - Who's Gonna Love Me / Can You Imagine - 1977
Power Exchange 271110 - Where You Gonna Find Somebody Like Me / Another Star - 1978
Omni 5501 - Who's Gonna Love Me / You Better Take Time To Love - 1978

Little Anthony

Day Spring 613 - Living Without Your Love / Closer Than Ever - 1979
MCA 41258 - Daylight / Your Love - 1980
PCM 202 - This Time We're Winning / Your Love - 1983

Little Anthony and The Imperials (members members Anthony Gourdine, ...)

Collectables Col 001497 - Tears On My Pillow / A Prayer And A Jukebox - ?
Collectables Col 001507 - Two People In The World / The Diary - ?

Little Anthony and The Imperials (members Anthony Gourdine, Tracy Lord, Ernest Wright, Jr., Clarence Collins and Glouster Rogers)

Collectables Col 001517 - So Much / Please Say You Want Me - ?
Collectables Col 001537 - Shimmy Shimmy Ko-Ko-Bop / I'm Still In Love With You - ?
Collectables Col 001547 - Travelling Stranger / So Near And Yet So Far - ?

Little Anthony and The Imperials (members Anthony Gourdine, Sammy Strain, Ernest Wright, Jr. and Clarence Collins)

Collectables Col 060187 - Goin' Out Of My Head / Take Me Back - ?
Collectables Col 060197 - Hurt So Bad / I'm On The Outside (Looking In) - ?

Little Anthony and The Imperials (members Anthony Gourdine, Tracy Lord, Ernest Wright, Jr., Clarence Collins and Glouster Rogers)

Old Hit 5001 - Tears On My Pillow / Two People In The World - ?

Little Tommy & The Elgins

The Six Teens (Members Trudy Williams, Louise Williams, Ed Wells, Beverly Pecot, Kenneth Sinclair (D.16th March 2003) And Darryl Lewis)

Flip 315 - A Casual Look / Teenage Promise - 1956
Flip 317 - Send Me Flowers / Afar Into The Night - 1956
Flip 320 - My Special Guy / Only Jim - 1956
Flip 322 - Arrow Of Love / Was It A Dream Of Mine - 1957
Flip 326 - My Surprise / Baby, You're Dynamite - 1957 (Around This Time Kenneth Wiliams Leaves The Group)

The Passions (Members Kenneth Williams, Earl Williams, Sammy Hardy, Harold Garcia And William Devase)

Era 1063 - Jackie Brown / My Aching Heart - 1957
Capitol F-3963 - Jackie Brown / My Aching Heart - 1958
Dore 505 - Nervous About Sally / Tango Of Love - 1958

The Colognes (Members Kenneth Sinclair, Earl Williams, Sammy Hardy, Harold Garcia And William Devase)

Lummtone 102 - A River Flows / A Bird And A Bee - 1959

The Elements (Members William Devase, Carl Williams, Kenneth Sinclair, Darryl Lewis And Jimmy Smith)

Titan 1708 - Lonely Hearts Club / Bad Man - 1959

Jimmy Smith

Wonder 110 - Pinch Me Quick / I Have No Sweetheart - 1959
Flip 347 - I Cry And Cry Every Night / Night Time Is The Time - 1959 (Backed By The Locketts)

The Elgins (Members Kenneth Sinclair, Jimmy Smith, William Devase, Daryl Lewis And Oscar Mcdonald)

Flip 353 - Uncle Sam's Call / Casey's Cop - 1960
Titan 1724 - Extra, Extra / My Illness* - 1961 *This Was An Unreleased Track By The Elements)
Titan 1724 - Extra, Extra / Heartache, Heartbreak - 1961 (Second Release - Same As Above

Flip Just Different Title)

Little Tommy & The Elgins

Elmar 1084 - I Walk On / Never Love Again - 1962
ABC-Paramount 10358 - I Walk On / Never Love Again - 1962

The Elgins

Lummtone 109 - A Winner Quits / Johnny, I'm Sorry - 1962
Lummtone 110 - You Got Your Magnet On Me / Johnny, I'm Sorry - 1962
Lummtone 112 - Finally / I Lost My Love - 1963
Lummtone 113 - Your Lovely Ways / Finding A Sweetheart - 1963
Valiant 712 - Street Scene / Find Yourself Another Fool - 1965

The Daniels

Lantam 01 - (I Lost My Love In) The Big City / Finally* - 1966 *Same As Track On Lummtone 112

The Bagdads (Members William Devase, Oscar Mcdonald, Kenneth Sinclair And Barry Little)

Double Shot 128 - Living In Fear / Let's Talk About The Bad Times - 1968
Double Shot 133 - Bring Back Those Doo-Wops / Green Power - 1968
Double Shot 140 - Love Has Two Faces / Jelly - 1969
Double Shot 151 - Keep Those Mini Skirts Up / Let's Talk About The Bad Times - 1970

Cold Water Flat

Outburst ? - Prestige Symbol / ? - 1971 (Rumoured To Be The Elgins)

Kenneth Sinclair Joined The Olympics In 1971

The Lollipops

RCA Victor 47-8344 - Peggy Got Engaged / I'll Set My Love To The Music - 1964
RCA Victor 47-8390 - Don't Monkey With Me / Love Is The Only Answer - 1964
RCA Victor 47-8430 - Billy, Billy Baby / Big Brother - 1964
RCA Victor 47-8494 - Busy Signal / I Want You Back Again - 1965
Smash 2057 - He's The Boy / Gee Whiz Baby - 1966
Vault 926 - Words Ain't Enough / ? - 1966
Impact 1021 - Lovin' Good Feelin' / Step Aside Baby - 1967
V.I.P. 25051 - Cheating Is Telling On You / Need Your Love - 1968
Gordy 7089 - Cheating Is Telling On You / Need Your Love - 1969
Atco 6787 - Nothing's Gonna Stop Our Love / I Believe In Love - 1970

Donna Loren

Donna Zukor / Jesse Hodges

Fable 603 - I Think It's Almost Christmas Time / My Christmas Prayer* - 1957 *flip by Jesse Hodges.

Donna Zukor

Skylark 106 - Honey Buggie / Keeping Company - 1960
Ramada 501 - The More I See Him / (Oo-Wee) Can't You See - 1960

Donna Loren

Crest 1095 - Hands Off / I'm So Lonely - 1962
Crest 1106 - Sailor Sailor / Tony - 1962
Challenge 9173 - I'm In Love With The Ticket Taker At The Bijou Movie* / I'm Gonna Be Alright - 1962 *Written By Dave Burgess leader of The Champs who had a hit in 1958 with "Tequila" On Challenge 1016.
Challenge 9190 - On The Good Ship Lollipop / If You Loved Me ... (Really Love Me) - 1963 (In 1963 Donna Loren was on The Caravan Of Stars Tour along with The Supremes, The Shirelles, Brenda Holloway, Gene Pitney and The Dixie Cups)
Challenge 9203 - I'm The One Who Loves You / Dream World - 1963
Challenge 9213 - I'm Gonna Be Alright / Johnny's Got Something - 1963
Challenge 9222 - Danny / I Can't Make My Heart Say Goodbye - 1963
Challenge 9237 - Muscle Bustle* / How Can I Face The World - 1963 *In her first movie "Muscle Beach Party" Donna Loren sings this track along with Dick Dale & The Deltones.
Capitol 5250 - Blowing Out The Candles* / Just A Little Girl - 1964 (Arranged and conducted by H. B. Barnum - Some copies issued with picture sleeve) *Also released In 1965 by Joy Holden on Magnum 725.
Capitol 5337 - Ten Good Reasons / Ninety Day Guarantee - 1964
Capitol 5409 - So, Do The Zonk / New Love* - 1965 *Arranged and conducted by H. B. Barnum, Donna Loren sang this in the movie "Beach Blanket Bingo".
Capitol 5548 - Call Me* / Smokey Joe's - 1965 *Written by Tony Hatch.
Capitol 5659 - Play Little Music Box, Play / I Believe* - 1966 *Produced by Al de Lory.
Reprise 586 - Let's Pretend / Once Before I Die - 1967 (This 45 actually seen release in Italy with Donna Loren singing in Italian)
Reprise 634 - As Long As I'm Holding You / It's Such A Shame* - 1967 *Produced by Mike Post.
Royalty 1 - Sedona / Simply Loving You - 1982
Warner Brothers 729326 - Wishin' And Hopin'* / Somewhere Down The Road - 1984 *Country version of the 1963 Dionne Warwick record on Scepter 1247.

Mary Love

Mary Love (born Mary Ann Varney on 27-July-1943 in Sacramento, California)

Modern 1006 - You Turned My Bitter Into Sweet / I'm In Your Hands - 1965 Missed A Letter
Modern 1010 - I've Got To Get You Back / Hey Stoney Face – 1965
Modern 1020 - Let Me Know* / Move A Little Closer - 1966 *co-written by Marc Gordon and Frank Wilson.
Modern 1029 - Lay This Burden Down / Think It Over Baby – 1966
Modern 1033 - Baby I'll Come* / Satisfied Feeling - 1967 *there exists an unissued demo of this track by Valerie Simpson.
Modern 1039 - Talking About My Man / Dance Children Dance* - 1967 *written by Nicholas Ashford and Valerie Simpson.

Arthur & Mary (Arthur Adams and said to be Mary Love)

Modern 1042 - Is That You / Let's Get Together* - 1967*flip by Mary Love only. Many thought it was Mary Love dueting with Arthur Adams, but according to Adams, it was a completely different female voice: "Modern records had an idea for me to do it with Mary Love, but that's Edna Wright," a well regarded session singer with various female groups and later member of The Honey Cone, better known on the scene as Sandy Wynns.

Mary Love

Josie 999 - The Hurt Is Just Beginning / If You Change Your Mind – 1968
Josie 630 - The Hurt Is Just Beginning / If You Change Your Mind – 1968
Josie 631 - If You Change Your Mind / ? - ?
Elco 444 - Born To Live With A Heartache / There's Someone For Me -

Mary Love / Santa's Disco Band

Magic Disc 215 - Joy / Santa Claus Is Coming To Town* - 1977 *Flip By Santa's Disco Band.

Mary Love

T. K. Disco Tkd-154 - Turn Me, Turn Me, Turn Me (Extended Disco Mix) (7:30) / Dance To My Music (3:00) - 1979 (12" Release)
Inphasion 7204 - Turn Me, Turn Me, Turn Me / Dance To My Music - 1979
U-Tone 2 - Tit For Tat / Liquid Fire - 198?
Mirage 7-99720 - Save Me / (Instrumental) – 1984
Mirage Dmd-767 - Save Me (3:58) / Save Me (Instrumental) (5:53) / Save Me (Club Mix) (5:54) - 1984 (12" Release)

Mary Love Comer

Co Love 1001 - Come Out Of The Sandbox / (Instrumental) - 1987
Co Love 1002 - Caught Up / Caught Up (Instrumental) /// Standing On The Edge Of Time / Standing On The Edge Of Time (Instrumental) - 1988 (12"Release)
Co Love 1004 - Understanding / In My Life (Mary Love Comer Solo) /// More Than Enough Love / More Than Enough Love (Rap Added) - 1990 (12"Release)

Matt Lucas

The Mark Twain Rhythm Band (members Matt Lucas, ...) school band

Ray Chilton Band (members Ray Chilton, Don Chilton, Glenn Chilton, Bill Chilton and Matt Lucas) local bar band.

The Narvel Felts Trio (members Narvel Felts (vocals and lead guitar), Matt Lucas (vocals and drums) and J. W. Grubbs (stand-up bass)) group Narvel Felts put together after the breakup of Narvel Felts & The Rockets.

Matt Lucas (born 19-July-1935 in Memphis, Tennessee - adopted at birth - grew up in Poplar Bluff, Missouri)

Good 003 - Tradin' Kisses / Sweetest One - 1962
Renay 304 - I'm Movin' On* / My Heavenly Angel - 1963 *Original Version By Hank Snow.
Smash 183 - I'm Movin' On / My Heavenly Angel - 1963
Smash 1840 - Ooby Dooby / No One Like You - 1963
Dot 16564 - Maybellene / Put Me Down - 1963
Dot 16614 - Turn On Your Lovelight / Water Moccasin - 1964
Karen 321 - The M. C. Twine (Part 1) / The M. C. Twine (Part 2) - 1965 (Recorded at United Sound in Detroit)
Karen 2524 - Baby You Better Go-Go / My Tune - 1965 (also recorded at United Sound in Detroit)
Kanata 1008 - I'm Movin' On / The Old Man - 1972
Kanata Kan9 - I'm Movin' On / The Old Man / Bathtub Blues - 1972

Quality 2129 - You Gotta Love / I'm So Thankful - 1975 (although released on a Canadian label this 45 was cut in Detroit and finished in Toronto, Canada under the auspices of Ollie McLaughlin. Minnie Ripperton sang background vocals and Deon Jackson was in on the session)
Celebration 1002 - You Gotta Love / I'm So Thankful (Instrumental) - 1975
Quality 2159 - I Need Your Lovin' / Zoo Blues - 1975
Celebration 1004 - I Need Your Lovin' / Zoo Blues - 1976
CJC 504 - Put Me Down / Tom Cat Blues - 1977
Underground 3001 - I'm Movin' On / Maybellene - 1981
Underground 3002 - Peepin' Tom Blues / Newsman Blues - 1982

Barbara Lynn

Bobby Lynn & The Idols (members Barbara Lynn, ...) all female band.

Barbara Lynn (born Barbara Lynn Ozen on 16-January-1942 in Beaumont, Texas)

Eric 7004 - Give Me A Break / Dina And Patrina - 1961
Jamie 1220 - You'll Lose A Good Thing / Lonely Heartaches - 1962
Jamie 1233 - Letter To Mommy And Daddy / Second Fiddle Girl - 1962
Jamie 1240 - You're Gonna Need Me / I'm Sorry I Met You - 1962
Jamie 1244 - Don't Be Cruel / You Can't Be Satisfied - 1963
Jamie 1251 - To Love Or Not To Love / Promises - 1963
Jamie 1260 - I Cried At Laura's Wedding / You Better Stop - 1963
Jamie 1265 - Everybody Loves Somebody / Dedicate The Blues To Me - 1963
Jamie 1269 - Money / Jealous Love - 1964
Jamie 1277 - Oh! Baby (We Got A Good Thing Going) / Unfair - 1964
Jamie 1277 - Oh! Baby (We Got A Good Thing Going) / Lonely Heartache - 1964
Jamie 1286 - Let Her Knock Herself Out / Don't Spread It Around - 1964
Jamie 1292 - It's Better To Have It / People Gonna Talk - 1965

Barbara Lynn & Lee Maye

Jamie 1295 (Don't Pretend) Just Lay It On The Line / Careless Hands - 1965

Barbara Lynn

Jamie 1297 - I've Taken All I'm Gonna Take / Keep On Pushing Your Luck - 1965
Jamie 1301 - You Can't Buy My Love / That's What A Friend Will Do - 1965
Jamie 1304 - You're Gonna Be Sorry / All I Need Is Your Love - 1965
Tribe 8316 - I'm A Good Woman / Running Back - 1966
Tribe 8319 - You Left The Water Running / Until I'm Free - 1966
Tribe 8324 - New Kind Of Love / I Don't Want A Playboy - 1967 (Released Three Months Before 8322)
Tribe 8322 - Watch The One That Brings You Bad News / Club A Go-Go - 1967
Atlantic 2450 - This Is The Thanks I Get / Ring Telephone Ring - 1967
Atlantic 2513 - You're Losing Me / Why Can't You Love Me - 1968
Atlantic 2553 - You're Gonna See A Lot More / Love Ain't Never Hurt Nobody - 1968
Atlantic 2585 - He Ain't Gonna Do Right / People Like Me - 1968
Atlantic 2812 - (Until Then) I'll Suffer / Take Your Love And Run - 1971
Atlantic 2853 - I'm A One Man Woman / Nice And Easy - 1971
Atlantic 2880 - You Better Quit / (Daddy Hot Stuff) You're Too Hot To Hold - 1972
Atlantic 2931 - You Make Me So Hot / It Ain't Good To Be Too Good - 1973
Copyright 2319 - Sugar Coated Love / Nice And Easy - 1974
Starflite 1001 - Give Him His Freedom / Take Your Time - 1975
Jetstream 804 - (Until Then) I'll Suffer / Take Your Love And Run - 1976

Jetstream 811 - Nice And Easy / You Better Quit It - 1976
Jetstream 828 - Takin' His Love Away / How You Think I Can Live Without Love - 1976
Jetstream 829 - Disco Music / Movin' On A Groove - 1976
Jetstream 726 - Give Me A Break / Dina & Patrina - ?
Love 111 - Mellow Feeling (Part 1) / Mellow Feeling (Part 2) - 1979

Barbara Lynn / Rockstarr

Jamstone 104 - I'm Still The Same / I'm Still The Same (Instrumental)* - 1983 *Flip By Rockstarr.

Barbara Lynn

Ichiban 88-142 - Trying To Love Two / Sugar Coated Love - 1988
Deluxe 1181 - You Can't Buy Me Happiness / Too Many Kisses - ?

The Chantels / Barbara Lynn

Collectables Col 3037 - Look In My Eyes / You'll Lose A Good Thing* - 1980's *Flip by Barbara Lynn

Milk and Northern Soul.

Do you remember when you were a kid, and the only milk you could get was pasteurised or sterilised ? Now you can get all sorts, pasteurised, sterilised, low fat, semi skimmed, skimmed, UHT long life, goat's milk, and I even bet you could get elephant milk if you looked in the right places ! Well that's what the Northern Soul scene is like these days. Back in the '70s there was Wigan and Blackpool Mecca, now.....A quote that is always attributed to Ian Levine (although I'm not sure he ever said it) is "Northern Soul is dead", well perhaps that is now the case. Twenty five years ago you knew where you were with Northern Soul, it has always been hard to define, but when you heard a track you just knew if it was, or wasn't, Northern Soul. So why, and how have things changed so much that 'Love Stormy Weather' can, and does get played at venues on a regular basis. Or how about 'I'm A Big Man' , out and out R & B, hardly Soul music, but still a very in demand record. Neither of them fall within the expected definition of Northern Soul.

The rare Soul scene is so splintered now it really is just like the milk scenario. A combination of customer demand, and manufacturer (read promoter for the scene) desire for new custom, has introduced new varieties through the years. So let's have a look at what is around:

I suppose the closest we come to the old style description of Northern Soul are the big Oldies allnighters like Togetherness. Still playing the same records, still attracting (these days) huge numbers of people, and no pretence to be anything else other than good time Soul music. Highly criticised by a certain hardcore, for not being progressive, this is really unfair. They don't claim to be progressive, they don't claim to be an allnighter for the regular week in week out niter goer. They are playing Soul music for the thousands of people who used to attend regularly back in the Seventies but now only want to go out four times a year for a massive blast of nostalgia. There is nothing wrong with that ! There can't be, or 1500 people wouldn't regularly turn out. So Togetherness have a great reputation amongst the people on the periphery of the regular scene, an awful reputation amongst the hardcore, and just to confuse matters there is the Modern room at Togetherness.

Now I'm not into the type of music being played in the Modern Rooms at Allnighters, so can't honestly pass an opinion because I don't venture in there. But I'm told by people who do that the Togetherness Modern room is superb with some of the best DJs in the country playing some of the best music in the country. How progressive do you want people to be ? And you think you're confused !

Another example might be The Ritz at Bank Holidays. But is it ? In the last year The Ritz have had an Oldies special, a rarest of the Rare, a Detroit & Chicago special, and I've attended them all, and I can't honestly claim to notice any difference in the people who attended them all either. Yet The Ritz seems to be another venue which attracts criticism for no apparent reason. Another example might have been Keele, but there again the last Keele allnighter included three 100 Club resident DJs, and three others who have been guest DJs there as well. Hardly an Oldies line up !

Let's go to the other extreme, in the majority perception anyway. The 100 Club. To me it is the leading Northern Soul Allnighter in the country. The best DJs playing the best music. A wicked combination of rare oldies, semi knowns, mega rarities, and new discoveries, and nearly all Sixties (I'll come onto the Sixties verses Seventies debate later !). This is a distinctly different crowd to those who attend Oldies venues. Around half are Northerners who travel down to London, but the other half tend to be people from the South, under thirty five, and very enthusiastic for all types of Soul music. The 100 Club's reputation though was built on playing Sixties Newies.

A strange term really, Sixties Newies, especially as it's now been in use since the Stafford Top Of The World days, and so many of those classic records that were played at Stafford are now referred to as Stafford Oldies, just like records played at Wigan are now referred to as Wigan Oldies. Still confused ? I haven't even mentioned 'Crossover' and 'Across The Board' yet !!!!

The main point about the 100 Club though is that the records move on. Playlists change, regulars don't hear the same records month in month out. This is partly due to the choice of guest DJs by Ady Croasdell, and due to the music policy he has stuck with over the years. Don't forget when the 100 Club started, it was a Rhythm & Soul club, not a Northern Soul club and had distinctly different playlists twenty years ago from the other big allnighters back in 1979. Did you notice how I just slipped another descriptive term in there, 'Rhythm & Soul\' ! The plot gets deeper.

To include the other allnighters which have Sixties Newies tags, you would have to include The Wilton Ballroom, and the Pigeon Club in Bolton.

I haven't touched on the R & B side of the scene either yet. Rhythm & Blues has always been there, right back to the Twisted Wheel days, and long may it stay. But the emphasis of the R & B has changed over the few years. I can remember when tunes like Big Daddy Rogers, 'I'm A Big Man' or ' Can't Live Without You' by Dusty Wilson would have been dismissed out of hand as too raw, too early to be played. Both records have been regular plays now for a couple of years, and fill dance floors at all sorts of venues. There have even been a few all R & B allnighters recently, particularly at the Princess Suite in Stoke, so where do they fit into the Northern SOUL scene ?

I must admit, from what I hear, because I don't attend these days, Blackburn combines a mixture of R & B to good effect with Oldies, which produces a fairly unique music policy which attracts a regular clientele up in the North West.

'Crossover'. Now what on earth does that mean, and where does it fit in amongst the Northern Soul scene ? Well it means records that were recorded during the late Sixties and early Seventies, records that don't fit the old style stomper beat, but don't fit comfortably into the Modern scene. The difficulty with Crossover is just that though, because it doesn't fit into either scene entirely it gets played on both, so just blurs the descriptions even more. I would hazard a guess that there are no allnighters that play just Crossover, but I'm sure someone will prove me wrong !

The Lea Manor at Albrighton, another of my favourite venues comes probably closest to being a venue that plays Crossover, but in reality this isn't true. Lea Manor play 'Across The Board' . Simple isn't it ! What it means is that you are likely to hear anything from the Sixties through to the Nineties at any allnighter at Albrighton. Certainly Sixties Newies get their fair share of plays there, as do Modern things, (bearing in mind that 'Modern' can mean anything from the '70s, '80s, or even '90s). Almost my home turf, Albrighton, and I know I've been associated with the club since the beginning, but I'm not actually involved in running it. That job goes to Martyn, Tate & Lin, and they more than anyone else have done more to promote an Across The Board music policy. The difficulty is that in attempting to attract supporters of everything from Newies, to Crossover, to Modern, to R & B, to Midtempo, to Beat Ballads, and all rare as well, whilst excluding played out Oldies is that it is such a difficult balancing act. Sometimes Albrighton is far too Seventies biased for me, as a Sixties fan and DJ, yet friends who attend love it.

Aha ! I mentioned Midtempo and Beat Ballads there for the first time. Originally introduced in a big way during the Stafford era, there is no denying that they are here to stay, and not just as enders.

Taking it one step further are the Colony Club allnighters at Newbury, where the emphasis changed from being Sixties based to being Seventies and Eighties based, with Sixties playing a subsidiary role. Oh dear, I'm even more confused now !

Wait a minute, I've missed out the Winsford allnighters here, but then again they don't really fit any of the descriptions I've already discussed. Winsford come closest to satisfying everyone. The Oldies fans are catered for by the inclusion of guest DJs who play oldies, the Newies fans are catered for in the regular spots by people like Butch and other guest DJs. Roger Banks covers the R & B side usually, and regular guests like Bob Hinsley cover the Crossover sounds, and there's a Modern room as well.

The final debate is one which has gone on for over twenty years, Sixties or Seventies ? My own views are quite clear on this, around a year ago I decided that I would drop all the Seventies items from my DJ playlist because I felt that the balance was swinging away from Sixties Soul. I made the announcement that I was only playing Sixties Soul from then on, and wondered whether my bookings as a DJ would drop off considerably. In fact they went up, which to mind mind shows that the average paying punter still prefers Sixties to Seventies. And that's all I'm going to say on that subject !

Do you see though, why I used the original analogy of milk. Currently running we have allnighters which play: Oldies, Newies, Crossover, Rhythm & Blues, Midtempo, Beat Ballads, Modern, Across The Board, Sixties, Seventies, and Uncle Tom Cobbly and all ! All of which have their place within the Northern Soul Scene, and the funny thing is, with the exception of Togetherness, The Ritz, and the Colony Club (Although I was asked to do the last one but was already booked elsewhere that night) I have DJ'd at all these venues. So maybe the Northern Soul scene is alive and well, just more varied than it used to be, and that has to be a good thing.

Group Line Ups

The Majors (Ricky Cordo, Eugene Glass, Idella Morris, Frank Tout, Ronald Gathers)
The Matadors (William "Smokey" Robinson, Warren "Pete" Moore, Ronnie White, Bobby Rogers, Emerson Rogers)
The Metros (Arthur Mitchell, Paul Williams, Robert Suttles, James Buckman, Gordon Dunn)

The Miracles (William "Smokey" Robinson, Warren "Pete" Moore, Ronnie White, Bobby Rogers, Claudette Rogers)
The Moonglows (Bobby Lester, Alexander "Pete" Graves, Harvey Fuqua, Prentiss Barnes

Gene McDaniels

The Echoes Of Joy - a gospel quartet formed by Eugene McDaniels at the age of eleven.

The Five Echoes (members in 1953 Willie Barnes, Eugene McDaniels, James Farmer, Jimmy Mimms and ? ------ Jimmy Mimms left group shortly after it was formed and was replaced by Richard Beasley, at this time Wesley Devreaux (the son of the famous blues shouter Wynonie Harris) also joined group)

The Sultans (members Richard Beasley, Wesley Devreaux, Eugene McDaniels, Willie Barnes and James Farmer)
Duke 125 - How Deep Is The Ocean / Good Thing Baby - 1954
Duke 133 - I Cried My Heart Out / Baby Don't Put Me Down - 1954
Duke 135 - Boppin' With The Mambo / What Makes Me Feel This Way - 1954

The Admirals (members Richard Beasley, Wesley Devreaux, Eugene McDaniels, Willie Barnes and James Farmer) group name change came about because group was broke but still under contract with DUKE records. This way they could record for someone else.

King 4772 - Oh Yes / Left With A Broken Heart - 1955
King 4782 - Close Your Eyes / Give Me Your Love - 1955

Cathy Ryan with The Lucky Millinder Orchestra

King 4792 - It's A Sad, Sad Feeling/ Ow - 1955 Backing Vocals The Admirals.

Bubber Johnson

King 4793 - Ding Dang Doo / Drop Me A Line - 1955 Backing Vocals The Admirals.
King 5068 - A Crazy Afternoon / So Much Tonight - 1955 Backing Vocals The Admirals.

The Sultans

Duke 178 - If I Could Tell / My Love Is So High - 1957

Gene McDaniels (Born Eugene Booker McDaniels 12-February-1935 In Kansas City, Kansas)

Liberty 55231 - In Times Like These / Once Before – 1959
Liberty 55265 - The Green Door / Facts Of Life – 1960
Liberty 55308 - A Hundred Pounds Of Clay* / Come On Take A Chance (Take A Chance On Love) - 1961 (with The Johnny Mann Singers) (one known copy has surfaced in Los Angeles in 1999 pressed in blue vinyl) *also recorded in 1966 by Jesse Johnson on Old Town 1195.
Liberty 55344 - A Tear / She's Come Back - 1961
Liberty 55371 - Tower Of Strength* / The Secret - 1961 (with The Johnny Mann Singers) *in 1961 Gloria Lynne had an "answer" record to this track titled "You Don't Have To Be A Tower Of Strength" released on Everest 19428
Liberty 55405 - Chip Chip / Another Tear Falls* - 1962 *Performed By Gene McDaniels In The Film "It's Trad, Dad". (One known copy has surfaced in Los Angeles In 1999 Pressed In Silver Vinyl)
Liberty 55444 - Funny / Chapel Of Tears – 1962
Liberty 55480 - Point Of No Return / Warmer Than A Whisper - 1962 (With The Johnny Mann Singers)
Liberty 55510 - Spanish Lace / Somebody's Waiting – 1962

Liberty 55541 - The Puzzle / Cry Baby Cry – 1963
Liberty 55597 - It's A Lonely Town (Lonely Without You) / False Friends – 1963
Liberty 55637 - Old Country / Anyone Else – 1963
Liberty 55723 - Make Me A Present Of You / In Times Like These – 1964
Liberty 55752 - (There Goes) The Forgotten Man / Emily – 1964
Liberty 55805 - Walk With A Winner / A Miracle – 1965
Liberty 55834 - Hang On (Just A Little Bit Longer) / Will It Last Forever – 1965
Columbia 43800 - Something Blue / Cause I Love You So – 1966
Columbia 44010 - Touch Of Your Lips / Sweet Lover No More – 1967

Eugene McDaniels

Atlantic 2805 - The Lord Is Back / Tell Me Mr. President – 1971

Universal-Jones (Members Gene McDaniels ....)

MGM / Verve 10677 - Feeling That Glow / River – 1972
MGM / Verve 10697 - Tuesday Morning / We All Know A Lot Of Things, But I Don't Know - 1972

Gene McDaniels

MGM 14613 - Ol' Heartbreak Top Ten / River – 1973
United Artists 0053 - A Hundred Pounds Of Clay / Tower Of Strength - 1973 (Silver Spotlight Series)
United Artists 0054 - Chip Chip / Point Of No Return - 1973 (Silver Spotlight Series)
Ode 66107 - Lady Fair / Natural Juices – 1975
Ode 66107 - Lady Fair / River – 1975
Collectables Col 062077 - Tower Of Strenght / Chip Chip - ?

Tennessee Ernie Ford / Gene McDaniels

Collectables Col 063007 - Sixteen Tons / A Hundred Pounds Of Clay - ?

Fats Domino / Gene McDaniels

Amp 91147 - Blue Monday / A Hundred Pounds Of Clay* - **?** *Flip By Gene McDaniels.

Barbara McNair

Barbara McNair Vocal With Chorus And Orchestra Directed By Dick Jacobs

Coral 61923 - Till There Was You / Bobby - 1958

Barbara McNair

Coral 61972 - He's Got The Whole World In His Hands / Flipped Over You - 1958
Coral 61996 - Indiscreet / Waltz Me Around - 1958
Coral 62020 - Too Late This Spring / See If I Care - 1958
Coral 62071 - Goin' Steady With The Moon / I Feel A Feeling - 1959
Coral 62116 - Lover's Prayer / Old Devil Moon - 1959

Billy Williams and Barbara McNair

Coral 62131 - Telephone Conversation / Go To Sleep - 1959

Barbara McNair

Signature 12024 - He's A King / Murray, What's Your Hurry - 1960
Signature 12033 - All About Love / You Done Me Wrong - 1960
Signature 12049 - Kansas City / Love Talk - 1960
Roulette 4346 - That's All I Want From You / (We'll be Doin') The Things We Love to Do - 1961
Roulette 4372 - Honeymoonin' / Big Shot Nothin' Bringer - 1962
KC 109 - Cross Over The Bridge / Gloryland - 1962
KC 112 - A Little Bird Told Me / Nobody Rings My Bell - 1963
Warner Bros. 5633 - Wanted Me / It Was Never Like This - 1965
Motown 1087 - You're Gonna Love My Baby / Touch Of Time - 1965
Motown 1099 - Everything Is Good About You / What A Day - 1966
Motown 1106 - My World Is Empty Without You* / Here I Am Baby** - 1966 *originally released in 1965 by The Supremes on Motown 1089. **also released in 1968 by The Marvelettes on Tamla 54166. (some copies issued in red vinyl)

Barbara

American Record Pressing Co. - Steal Away Tonight / For Once In My Life - 1967 (acetate - has Master No. 204301 for "A" side and QQK-240-M11 for "flip" side plus date 7-17-67 written on label plus label designation and number same as below)

Barbara McNair

Motown 1112 - Steal Away Tonight / For Once In My Life - 1967 (Unissued)
Motown 1123 - Where Would I Be Without You / For Once In My Life - 1968
Motown 1133 - You Could Never Love Him / Fancy Passes - 1968
Audio Fidelity 153 - Love Has A Way / ? - 1969 (Possibly promo only)
Audio Fidelity 162 - I Can Tell / After St. Francis - 1969
Marina MR606 - I Mean To Shine / I Mean To Shine - 1972 (Possibly promo only)
TEC 39 - Because Of You / I'll Never Make It Easy - 1976

Barbara McNair / Kay Starr

USAF 6 - He's Got The Whole World In His Hands / Stroll Me (Flip By Kay Starr)

The Magnetics

Rather a mish mash of a discography this one. There are at least six different groups using the name The Magnetics, so all are listed below.

The Magnetics (From Detroit. Members: Bobby Peterson, Sharon Peterson, Tony Johnson (lead singer), Jackie Perkins and Candi Bell). When Tony Johnson left the group he teamed up with Tyrone Pickens to record as the duo Tony & Tyrone

Allrite 620 - Where Are You / The Train - 1962

The Magnetics (From Detroit. Members: Gerald Mathis (lead singer), Bobby Peterson (the same singer who was in the Magnetics on Allrite), Elijah Davis, Ernest Newsome & William 'Pete' Crawford) This group was in fact The Volumes who were at the time in between contracts.

Bonnie 107374 - Lady In Green / Heart You're Made Of Stone - 1965

The Magnetics (From Detroit. The third Detroit Magnetics are definitely a white sounding girl group, which according to Andy Rix, are not particularly good, which would account for the tracks never gaining an actual release.)

Hitsville Acetate - Father Time
Histville Acetate - Please Don't Go Away

The Magnetics (From Philadelphia) (The Philadelphia Magnetics have as far as I know only the one release, although other releases on the Ra Sel label exist. John Anderson at Soul Bowl is rumoured to have several unreleased acetates by the group.)

Ra-Sel R7-104 - I Have A Girl / Love And Devotion - 1967

The Magnetics (From Chicago The Chicago Magnetics releases have Lee McKinney as the lead singer, so are all the same group.)

Sable 102 - When I'm With My Baby / Count The Days - 196?
J-V 2501 - Oh Love / Wasting Time - 1969

Lee McKinney & The Magnetics (Same group from Chicago)

Sable 104 - I'll Keep Holding On / Jackie Baby - 196?

(M.F.Williams) "featuring" THE MAGNETICS vocal with instrumental accompaniment BY: The Sounds Unlimited. (From Richmond)

Sound Trap 30391/2 - Let Me Comfort You / Good By My Love - ?

The Magnificent Men

The Possessions (members Dave Bupp, ...) 1956 all white group.

The Argons (members Dave Bupp, Buck Generette, ?, ? and ?) late 1950's intergrated group

Del - Chords (Dave Bupp and Buddy King members)

Mr. Genius 401 - Everybody's Gotta Lose Someday / Your Mommy Lied To Your Daddy - 1962
Impala 215 - Everybody's Gotta Lose Someday / Your Mommy Lied To Your Daddy - 1963
Mr. Genius 1028 - Everybody's Gotta Lose Someday / Your Mommy Lied To Your Daddy - 196?

Delcords / The Dogs

Treasure 001 - I'm So Sorry / Soul Step* - 196? *instrumental to "A" side.

The Dogs (members

Treasure 007 - Don't Try To Help Me / Soul Step - 196?

The Magnificent 7 (group was formed by the merging of The Del-Chords (Dave Bupp, Buddy King) and the instrumental players of The Endells (an all white band with black singers))

The Magnificent Men (members Dave Bupp - born 5-April-1942 in York, Philadelphia. (lead vocals), Terry Crousore (guitar), Jimmy Seville (bass), Tommy Hoover (organ), Bob "Puff" Angelucci (drums, organ, piano), Tom Pane (saxaphone) and Buddy King (trumpet))

Capitol 5608 - All Your Lovin's Gone To My Head / Peace Of Mind - 1966
Capitol 5732 - Maybe, Maybe Baby / I've Got News For You – 1967
Capitol 5812 - Stormy Weather / Much Much More Of Your Love – 1967
Capitol 5905 - I Could Be So Happy / You Changed My Life – 1967
Capitol 5976 - Sweet Soul Medley (Part 1) (Sweet Soul Music / Ain't To Proud To Beg / Ooh Baby Baby / I Can't Help Myself (Sugar Pie Honey Bunch) / Sweet Soul Medley (Part 2) (Sweet Soul Music / People Get Ready) - 1967
Capitol 2062 - Forever Together / Babe, I'm Crazy 'Bout You – 1967
Capitol 2134 - By The Time I Get To Phoenix / Tired Of Pushing – 1967
Capitol - Keep On Climbing - ? (Acetate)
Capitol 2202 - I Found What I Wanted In You / Almost Persuaded – 1968
Capitol 2319 - So Much Love Waiting / Save The Country – 1968
? - Almost Persuaded / I Found What I Wanted In You - ?
Mercury 72988 - Holly Go Softly / Open Up And Get Richer – 1969
Mercury 72988 - Holly Go Softly / Whatever It Takes – 1970
Mercury 73028 - Lay Lady Lay / What Ever It Takes – 1970
Major League 4411 - I Wanna Know / There's Something On Your Mind – 1987
Major League ? - I Wanna Know / Old Man River – 1987
Major League Mlr-4411 - I Wanna Know / There's Something On Your Mind /// Since I Lost My Baby / Old Man River - 1987 (12" Special "Souvenir" Release)

The Maggs / Big Jay Mcneeley

Spinning 5 - Misty / Mulewalk And Nervous Man Nervous* - 1991 *Flip By Big Jay Mcneeley.

The Magnificent Men / The Classics

Collectables Col 062987 - I Could Be So Happy / Pollyana* - ? *Flip By The Classics.

The Magnificent Men

Collectables Col 062997 - Peace Of Mind / Sweet Soul Medley - ?

The Majestics

The Majestics (Johnny Mitchell, Breeze Hatcher, Alvin English & Cyril Clark)

Contour 501 - Hard Time / Teenage Gossip - 1959
Jordan 123 - Angel Of Love / Searching For A New Love - 1961
Nu - Tone 123 - Angel Of Love / Searching For A New Love - 1961
Pixie 6901 - Angel Of Love / Searching For A New Love - 1961
Jordan 1057 - Angel Of Love / Searching For A New Love - 1961 (Some Copies Also Pressed In Yellow Vinyl)

The Majestics (Johnny Mitchell, Thomas Mealy, Maurice Fagan, Pedro Mancha, Warren Harris)

Chex 1000 - Give Me A Cigarette / Shoppin' And Hoppin' - 1962
Chex 1000 - Give Me A Cigarette / So I Can Forget - 1962
Chex 1004 - Give Me A Cigarette / So I Can Forget - 1962
Chex 1004 - Unhappy And Blue / Treat Me Like You Want - 1962
Chex 1006 - Lonely Heart / Gwendolyn - 1962
Chex 1009 - Baby / Teach Me How To Limbo - 1963
Linda 111 - Strange World / Everything Is Gonna Be Alright - 1963
Linda 121 - Girl Of My Dreams / (I Love Her So Much) It Hurts Me - 1965
V.I.P. 25028 - Say You / All For Someone - 1965 (Promo Only -- Stock Copies Credited To The Monitors)

The Majors

The Premiers (members Robert Morris, Eugene Glass, Frank Troutt, Rick Cordo and Ron Gathers)

The Versatiles (members Idella Morris, Eugene Glass, Frank Troutt, Rick Cordo and Ron Gathers)

Atlantic 2004 - Passing By / Crying – 1958

Sonny Day / The Versatiles

Checker 886 - Speedillac / Half Moon* - 1958 *Flip By The Versatiles.

The Versatiles (members Idella Morris, Eugene Glass, Frank Troutt, Rick Cordo and Ron Gathers)

Rocal 1002 - Lundee Dundee / I'll Whisper In Your Ear – 1960
Peacock 1910 - White Cliffs Of Dover / Just Words – 1962

The Majors (members Ricky Cordo, Eugene Glass, Idella Morris, Frank Troutt & Ronald Gathers)

Imperial 5855 - A Wonderful Dream* / Time Will Tell - 1962 *recorded at Sound Plus studios in North East Philadelphia on Harbison Avenue.
Imperial 5879 - She's A Troublemaker / A Little Bit Now – 1962
Imperial 5914 - Anything You Can Do / What In The World – 1963
Imperial 5936 - Tra La La / What Have You Been Doin' – 1963
Imperial 5968 - Get Up Now / One Happy Ending – 1963
Imperial 5991 - Your Life Begins / Which Way Did She Go – 1963
Imperial 66009 - Ooh Wee Baby / I'll Be There – 1963

The Majors / Ernie K. Doe

United Artists 0110 - A Wonderful Dream / Mother In-Law* - 1973 *flip by Ernie K. Doe

The Majors

Psycho 2601 - Spookey Stomp / Dance, Dance, Dance – 1978

The Jive Five / The Majors

Collectables Col 060207 - I'm A Happy Man / A Wonderful Dream* - ? *Flip By The Majors.

Steve Mancha

The Jaywalkers (members Melvin Davis, Clyde Wilson, David Ruffin and Tony Newton)

Two Friends (Wilburt Jackson (later member of Two Plus Two on VELGO) and Clyde Wilson)

HPC 100 - Just Too Much To Hope For / Family Reunion - 1959

Laurence Faulkon & The Stars (members Laurence Faulkon, Clyde Wilson (Steve Mancha), ...)

MRC 1202 - I'll Marry You / I Dream - 1962

Larence Faulkcon & The Sounds (members Laurence Faulkon, Clyde Wilson (Steve Mancha), ...)

Mah's 000.7 - My Girl And My Friend / Why Should We Hide Our Love - 1962

Steve Mancha (born Clyde Wilson on 25-December-1945 in Walhalla, South Carolina)

Wheelsville_102 - Did My Baby Call / Whirlpool - 1965
Groovesville 1001 - You're Still In My Heart / She's So Good – 1965
Groovesville 1002 - I Don't Want To Lose You / Need To Be Needed – 1966

The Holidays (members Eddie Anderson, Steve Mancha and J.J. Barnes, Edwin Starr's vocal overdubbed on recording - not actual member)

Golden World 36 - I'll Love You Forever / Makin' Up Time - 1966

Steve Mancha

Groovesville 1004 - Friday Night / Monday Through Thursday - 1966 Groovesville 1005 - Don't Make Me A Storyteller / I Won't Love And Leave You – 1967
Groovesville 1007 - Just Keep On Loving Me / Sweet Baby Don't Ever Be Untrue – 1967
Groove City 204 - A Love Like Yours / Hate Yourself In The Morning – 1969
Groove City - Deeper In Love - ? (although unissued as a 45 this was released 1995 in the U. K. on a Goldmine Cd "The Solid Hitbound Collection" GSCD 53 and released in 2000 in the U. K. on a VSOP Cd "Detroit Soulman - The Best Of Steve Mancha" VSOP CD 287)

The New Holidays (members

Groove City 206 - Easy Living / I've Lost You - 1969

Aged In Soul (members

Hot Wax 6904 - Too Many Cooks (Spoil The Soup) / Not Enough Love To Satisfy - 1969

100 Proof (Aged In Soul) (members Steve Mancha, Joe Stubbs, Don Hatcher and Eddie

Anderson)

Hot Wax 6904 - Too Many Cooks (Spoil The Soup) / Not Enough Love To Satisfy – 1969
Hot Wax 7004 - Somebody's Been Sleeping / I've Come To Save You – 1970
Hot Wax 7009 - One Man's Leftovers (Is Another Man's Feast) / If I Could See The Light In The Window* - 1970 *also issued in 1971 by 8th Day on Invictus 9107.

The 8th Day (members

Invictus 9087 - She's Not Just Another Woman* / I Can't Fool Myself - 1971* Steve Mancha and some "moonlighting" Motowners completed this track prior to the formation of Invictus / Hot Wax.

Freda Payne

Invictus 9092 - Bring The Boys Home* / I Shall Not Be Moved** - 1971*Steve Mancha on male vocals. **also released by The Barrino Brothers on in 1972 on Invictus 9084 and Invictus 9104 in 1971.

100 Proof (Aged In Soul) (members Steve Mancha, Joe Stubbs, Don Hatcher and Eddie Anderson)

Hot Wax 7104 - Driveway / Love Is Sweeter (The Second Time Around) – 1971

Parliament A Parliafunkadelicment Thang (members George Clinton, ...)

Invictus 9095 - Breakdown* / Little Ole Country Boy** - 1971*Steve Mancha lead vocal. **previously released in 1970 by A Parliament Thang on Invictus 9077 and also released in 1971 by Parliament on Invictus 9091

100 Proof (Aged In Soul) (members Steve Mancha, Joe Stubbs, Don Hatcher and Eddie Anderson)

Hot Wax 7108 - 90 Day Freeze (On Her Love) / Not Enough Love To Satisfy – 1971

Clyde Wilson (Steve Mancha)

SMC 111/112 - Open Up / If You'll Be My Girl - 1971

Parliament (members

Invictus 9123 - Come In Out Of The Rain* / Little Ole Country Boy - 1972 * Steve Mancha lead vocal.

100 Proof (Aged In Soul) (members Steve Mancha, Joe Stubbs, Don Hatcher and Eddie Anderson)

Hot Wax 7202 - Everything Good Is Bad / I'd Rather Fight Than Switch – 1972
Hot Wax 7206 - Don't Scratch Where It Don't Itch / If I Could See The Light In The Window - 1972
Hot Wax 7211 - Nothing Sweeter Than Love / Since You've Been Gone – 1972
Hot Wax 9254 - My Piece Of The Rock (Vocal) / My Piece Of The Rock (Instrumental) – 1976
Hot Wax 9256 - I'm Mad As Hell (Ain't Gonna Take No More) - Part 1 / I'm Mad As Hell (Ain't Gonna Take No More) - Part 2 - 1977 (with The New York Port Authority, this was the last issue on the Hot Wax label distributed by CBS records)

The Honey Cone / 100 Proof (Aged In Soul)

Collectables Col 033337 - One Monkey Don't Stop The Show / Somebody's Been Sleeping* - ?
*flip by 100 Proof (Aged In Soul).

The Manhattans

The Statesmen (members Winfred 'Blue' Lovett, Richard Taylor) late 1950's group the pair were members of while serving in the US Air force in Germany.

The Dulcets (members Sonny Bivins, Richard Taylor, ...)

The Dorsets (members, Winfred Lovett, George Smith, Edward 'Sonny' Bivens, Ethel Sanders, Buddy Bell............................)

Asnes 101 - Pork Chops / Cool It - 1961 (Released In 1965 In The UK On Sue Wi-391)

The Manhattans (Members George "Smitty" Smith (Born 18 December 1939 in Florida - Died 16 December 1970, Cause: cerebral haemorrage), Winfred "Blue" Lovett (Born 16-November-1943), Richard Taylor (Born 1940 - Died 7-December-1987 In Kansas City, Kansas. After attempting solo career, he converted to Islam taking the name Abdul Rashid Talhah), Kenneth Kelley (Born 9-January-1943) And Edward "Sonny" Bivins (Born 15-January-1942))

Piney 107 - Live It Up / Go Baby Go - 1962
Piney 108 - Crazy Love / The Hawk And The Crow - 1962
Avanti 1401 - What Should I Do / Later For You - 1963

The Manhattans

Carnival 504 - I've Got Everything But You / For The Very First Time - 1964
Carnival 506 - There Goes A Fool* / Call Somebody Please - 1964 (Identification Number Is Ca-1010. Credits "A Joe Evans Production" Is The Scarcer Copy) *Joe Evans On Flute.
Carnival 506 - There Goes A Fool / Call Somebody Please - 1964 (Identification Number Is Ca-1010x. Credits "A Joe Evans - Bob Mcghee Production" Is The Common Copy)
Carnival 507 - I Wanna Be (Your Everything)* / What's It Gonna Be - 1965
Carnival 509 - Searchin' For My Baby / I'm The One That Love Forgot - 1965
Carnival 512 - Follow Your Heart / The Boston Monkey - 1965
Carnival 514 - Baby I Need You / Teach Me The Philly Dog - 1966
Carnival 517 - Can I / That New Girl - 1966
Carnival 522 - I Bet'cha (Couldn't Love Me) / Sweet Little Girl - 1966
Carnival 524 - It's That Time Of Year / Alone On New Year's Eve - 1966
Carnival 526 - All I Need Is Your Love / Our Love Will Never Die - 1967
Carnival 529 - When We're Made As One / Baby I'm Sorry - 1967
Carnival 533 - I Call It Love* / Manhattan Stomp - 1967 *Covered In 1970 By The Pretenders On Carnival 550.
Carnival 542 - I Don't Wanna Go / Love Is Breaking Out (All Over) - 1968
Carnival 545 - 'Til You Come Back To Me / Call Somebody Please - 1968
Deluxe 109 - The Picture Became Quite Clear / Oh Lord, How I Wish I Could Sleep - 1969
Deluxe 115 - It's Gonna Take A Lot To Bring Me Back / Give Him Up - 1969
Deluxe 122 - If My Heart Could Speak / Loneliness - 1970 (George Smith Becomes Ill In 1970 And Phil Terrell Stepped In As Temporary Lead Singer)
Deluxe 129 - From Atlanta To Goodbye / Fantastic Journey - 1970
Deluxe 132 - Let Them Talk / Straight To My Heart - 1970
Deluxe 136 - Do You Ever / I Can't Stand For You To Leave Me - 1971
Deluxe 137 - A Million To One / Cry If You Wanna Cry - 1971 (Gerald Alston Former Member Of The New Imperials (Not Little Anthony's Group) And Nephew Of Shirley Alston Of The Shirelles Takes Over As Lead Singer For The Group)
Deluxe 139 - One Life To Live / It's The Only One - 1972

Deluxe 144 - Back Up / Fever - 1972
Deluxe 146 - Rainbow Week / Loneliness - 1973
Columbia 45838 - There's No Me Without You / I'm Not A Run-Around - 1973
Deluxe 152 - Do You Ever / If My Heart Could Speak - 1973
Columbia 45927 - You'd Better Believe It / Soul Train - 1973
Columbia 45971 - Wish That You Were Mine / It's So Hard Loving You - 1973
Columbia 46081 - Summertime In The City / The Other Side Of Me - 1974
Columbia 10045 - Don't Take Your Love / The Day The Robins Sang To Me - 1974
Columbia 10140 - Hurt / Nursery Rhymes - 1975
Columbia 10310 - Kiss And Say Goodbye / Wonderful World Of Love - 1976 (This Became The Second 45 To Be Certified Riaa Platinum Under The New Two Million Sales Standard. "Disco Lady" By Johnnie Taylor Was The First)
Columbia 10430 - I Kinda Miss You / Gypsy Man – 1976
Columbia As 263 - Kiss And Say Goodbye / I Kinda Missed You - 1976 (mono - both tracks "X" rated - promo issue only - came with "Warning. Not Recommended For Airplay" on label)
Columbia 10506 - Kiss And Say Goodbye / ? - 1977 (12" Release)
Columbia 10495 - It Feels So Good To Be Loved By You / On The Street (Where I Live) – 1977

The Manhattans / Willie Nelson

W.I.A.A. 366 - What's It All About (April 77) Public Service Show - 1977 (public service radio spots - promo issue only)

The Manhattans

Columbia 10586 - We Never Danced To A Love Song / Let's Start It All Over Again – 1977
Columbia 10674 - Am I Losing You / Movin' – 1978
Columbia 10766 - Everybody Has A Dream / Happiness – 1978
Columbia 10921 - Here Comes The Hurt Again / Don't Say Goodbye – 1979
Columbia 11024 - The Way We Were -- Memories / New York City – 1979
Starfire 121 - It's That Time Of Year / Alone On New Year's Eve - 1979 (some copies came in coloured vinyl and picture sleeve)
Columbia 11222 - Shining Star / I'll Never Run Away From Love Again – 1980
Columbia 11321 - Girl Of My Dreams / The Closer You Are – 1980
Columbia 11398 - I'll Never Find Another (Another Just Like You) / Rendezvous – 1980
Columbia 60511 - Do You Really Mean Goodbye / Rendezvous – 1981
Columbia 02164 - Shining Star / Summertime In The City – 1981
Columbia 855168639 - Just One Moment Away - 1981 (acetate showing time of 3:22. The size of the disc is about 9 inches, with the 45 grooves/music starting about 2 inches in from the edge. All the above info is handwritten with a red pen. It comes in a blank manila inner sleeve with 2 names written on it "McEwen" & "Armand")
Columbia 02191 - Just One Moment Away / When I Leave Tomorrow – 1981
Columbia As 1316 - Let Your Love Come Down / Let Your Love Come Down - 1981 (12" single - promo issue only)
Columbia 02548 - Let Your Love Come Down / I Gotta Thank You – 1981
Columbia 02666 - Money, Money / I Wanta Thank You – 1982
Columbia 03939 - Crazy / Gonna Find You – 1983
Columbia 44-03940 - Crazy (5:00) / Crazy (Instrumental) (5:00) - 1983 (12" Remix Single)
Columbia 04110 - Forever By Your Side / Locked Up In Your Love – 1983
Columbia 04754 - You Send Me* / You're Gonna Love Being Loved By Me - 1985 (some copies came with picture sleeve) *cover of 1957 recording by Sam Cooke on Keen 34013.
Columbia 04930 - Don't Say No* / Dreamin' - 1985 *featured female vocalist B. J. Nelson.

The Manhattans vocal by Regina Belle

Columbia 06376 - Where Did We Go Wrong? / Maybe Tomorrow – 1986

The Manhattans

Columbia 07010 - Mr. D. J. / All I Need - 1987 (Gerald Alston leaves group to pursue solo career at Motown)
Valley Vue 75303 - Sweet Talk (5 Mixes - Radio, Dub, Bonus, Extended, Single) - 1988 (12" Release)
Valley Vue 75330 - I Won't Stop / Just A Matter Of Time - 1989 (12" Release)
Valley Vue 75723 - Sweet Talk (Edit Version) / Sweet Talk (Radio Version) – 1989
Valley Vue 75749 - Why You Wanna Love Me Like That / ? – 1989
Toc / Orchard 3680148020 - Nites Like This - 2001 (Cd single release)

Updates provided by Edward 'Sonny' Bivins of The Manhattans

Bobby Marchan

The Powder Box Revue (member Bobby Marchan - a 1953 troupe of female impersonators who performed in local theatres organized by Bobby Marchan)

Bobby Marchan And His Band (members Bobby Marchan, ...)

Aladdin 3189 - Have Mercy / Just A Little Walk - 1953

Bobby Marchon

Dot 1203 - Just A Little Ol' Wine / You Made A Fool Of Me - 1954

Bobby Fields

Ace 504 - Give A Helping Hand / Pity Poor Me - 1955

Bobby Marchan (born Oscar James Gibson on 30-April-1930 in Youngstown, Ohio -- died 5-December-1999 after a lengthy illness)

Ace 523 - Chickee Wah-Wah / Don't Take Your Love From Me - 1956 (signed by Johnny Vincent who kept thinking Bobby Marchan was a woman)
Gale 4m-101 - Chickee Wah-Wah / Give A Helping Hand – 1957

Huey "Piano" Smith & The Clowns (members Huey Smith (piano) - born 26-January-1964 in New Orleons - a former member of The Blue Diamonds (James Booker while band was on the road), Bobby Marchan (vocals) later replaced by Curley Moore, John "Scarface" Williams (vocals), Lee Allen (saxaphone), Alvin "Red" Tyler (trumpet), ...)

Ace 530 - Rockin' Pneumonia And The Boogie Woogie Flu (Part 1) / Rockin' Pneumonia And The Boogie Woogie Flu (Part 2) – 1957

Bobby Marchan

Ace 532 - I'll Never Let You Go / I Can't Stop Loving You – 1957

Huey "Piano" Smith & The Clowns

Ace 538 - Free, Single And Disengaged / Just A Lonely Clown – 1957
Ace 545 - Don't You Just Know It / High Blood Pressure – 1958
Ace 548 - Havin' A Good Time / We Like Birdland – 1958
Ace 553 - Don't You Know Yockomo / Well, I'll Be John Brown – 1958

Bobby Marchan

Ace 557 - Rockin' Behind The Iron Curtain / You Can't Stop Her – 1959

Bobby Marchan & The Tick Tocks (members Bobby Marchan, John "Scarface" Williams, ..)

Fire 1014 - Snoopin' And Accusin' / This Is The Life – 1959

Bobby Marchan

Fire 1022 - There's Something On Your Mind (Part 1)* / There's Something On Your Mind (Part 2) - 1960 *Cover Of The Big Jay Mcneely Song On Swingin' 614..
Ace 595 - Hush Your Mouth / Quit My Job – 1960
Fire 1027 - Booty Green / It Hurt's Me To My Heart – 1960
Fire 1028 - You're Still My Baby (Part 1) / You're Still My Baby (Part 2) – 1960
Fire 1035 - All In My Mind / I Miss You So – 1961
Fire 1037 - What You Don't Know Don't Hurt You / I Need Someone (I Need You) – 1961
Fire 510 - Yes It's Written All Over Your Face / Look At My Heart – 1962
Volt 108 - What Can I Do (Part 1)* / What Can I Do (Part 2) - 1963 (Bobby Marchan was part of group used by Otis Redding in his warmup act for live shows, this was how Bobby Marchan was recommended to Jim Stewart by Otis Redding) *cover of the 1957 recording by Donnie Elbert on Deluxe 6125.
Volt 113 - You Won't Do Right / That's The Way It Goes - 1964 (this record number can also be found on some copies of The Drapels 1964 release "Wondering (When My Love Is Coming Home)" this is a misprint and should have read Volt 114)
Volt 114 - That's The Way It Goes / Mary Had A Little Lamb - 1964 (this record should be The Drapels 1964 release "Wondering (When My Love Is Coming Home)" but I have found mention of it in many record collecting papers and magazines in the for sale columns as this by Bobby Marchan)
Dial 3022 - I Gotta Sit Down And Cry* / I've Got A Thing Going On - 1964
Dial 4002 - Get Down With It* / Half A Mind - 1964 *covered in 1971 by Slade on Cotillion 44128.
Dial - Half A Mind - 1964 (although unissued on vinyl this alternate version was released in the U. K. on a 2003 Kent double CD "The Dial Records Southern Soul Story" CDKEN2 223)
Oldies 146 - There's Something On Your Mind (Part 1) / There's Something On Your Mind (Part 2) - 1964
Dial 4007 - Hello Happiness / Funny Style - 1965
Dial 4020 - I Feel It Coming / Gimme Your Love – 1965
Dial - Just Be Yourself - (although unissued on vinyl at the time this was released in the U. K. on a 2003 Kent double CD "The Dial Records Southern Soul Story" CDKEN2 223)
Sphere Sound 706 - Snoopin' And Accusin' / All In My Mind - 1965
Sphere Sound 709 - Things I Used To Do (Part 1) / Things I Used To Do (Part 2) – 1965
Flashback 12 - There's Something On Your Mind (Part 1) / There's Something On Your Mind (Part 2) - 1965
Cameo 405 - There's Something About You Baby / Everything A Poor Fool Needs – 1966
Cameo 429 - Shake Your Tambourine / Just Be Yourself – 1966
Cameo 489 - Rockin' Pneumonia / Someone To Take Your Place – 1967
Dial 4065 - I Just Want What Belongs To Me / Sad Sack – 1967
Cameo 453 - Meet Me In Church / Hooked – 1967
Cameo 469 - You Better Hold On / Help Yourself – 1967
Cameo 489 - Rockin' Pneumonia (And The Boogaloo Flu) / Someone To Take Your Place – 1967
Gamble 216 - (Ain't No Reason) For Girls To Be Lonely -- Pt. 1 / (Ain't No Reason) For Girls To Be Lonely -- Pt. 2 – 1968
River City 727 - Anyway You Want It / What Can I Do - 1972
Bobby Robinson 101 - There's Something On Your Mind (Part 1) / I Need Someone (I Need You) – 1973
Goldies 45 2514 - There's Something On Your Mind (Part 1) / I Need Someone (I Need You) - 1973

Ace 3004 - Push The Button / My Day Is Coming - 1974

Bobby Marchan & Willie Dixon / Willie Dixon

Ace 3008 - My Day Is Comin' / God Blessed Our Love - 1975 *flip is Willie Dixon solo recording.

Lattimore Brown

Ace 3012 - Warm And Tender Love* / You Don't Know Like I Know** - 1975 *also recorded in 1964 by Joe Haywood on Enjoy 2013. **a Lattimore Brown and uncredited Bobby Marchan duet which was also recorded in 1965 by Sam & Dave on Stax 180.

Bobby Marchan

Ace 3016 - Baby Get Your Yo-Yo (Wind It Up) / What Can I Do - 1975
Mss 16699 - Love Is So Good (Part 1) / Love Is So Good (Part 2) - 1975
Dial 1152 - Bump Your Bootie / Ain't Nothin' Wrong With Whitey - 1975
Sansu 1011 - Shake It Don't Break It / Do You Wanna Dance - 1976
Mercury 73908 - I Wanna Bump With The Big Fat Woman / Disco Rabbit - 1977
Mercury 30 - Disco Rabbit / ? - 1977 (12"Release)
Retta's 002 - There's Something On Your Mind (Part 1) / There's Something On Your Mind (Part 2) - 1978
Lost Nite 390 - There's Something On Your Mind (Part 1) / There's Something On Your Mind (Part 2) - 197?
Mass 16699 - Love Is So Good (When You're Stealin' It) (Part 1) / Love Is So Good (When You're Stealin' It) (Part 2) - 1982
B & B 1001 - Love Is So Good When You Steal It (Part 1) / Love Is So Good When You Steal It (Part 2) - 1984
Maniqure 1001 - Strokin' (Part 1) / Strokin' (Part 2) - 1987
Edge 7-010 - There's Something On Your Mind '87 / Bobby Marchan's Rap - 1987
Edge 12-010 - There's Something On Your Mind '87 / Bobby Marchan's Rap - 1987 (12" Release)
Collectables Col 016357 - There's Something On Your Mind (Part 1) / There's Something On Your Mind (Part 2) - ?

The Marvelettes

The Del-Rythmetts (members Gladys Horton (born 1944 in Detroit, Michigan --- died 26-January-2011 in a Sherman Oaks nursing home in Los Angeles, California --- cause: complications following a stroke) , Jeanette McClafin, Juanita McClafin and Rosemary Wells)

JVB 5000 - Chic-A-Boomer / I Need Your Love - 1959

The Marvelettes (members Gladys Horton, Georgeanna Marie Tillman (born 1944 --- died 6-January-1980 in Detroit, Michigan, she was stricken with sickle cell anaemia and lupus), Wanda Young, Katherine Anderson and Juanita Cowart)

Tamla 54046 - Please Mr. Postman / So Long Baby - 1961
Tamla 54054 - Twistin' Postman / I Want A Guy – 1962
Tamla 54060 - Playboy* / All The Love I've Got - 1962 *covered in 1962 by Peggy Gaines on Hit 17.

Marvin Gaye / Supremes / Singin' Sammy Ward / Contours / Marvelettes / Miracles

Promo - Motor Town Special Mts-1 - Individual Artists - 1962 (promo issue only -- features the various artists on tour, all talking over their latest record to promote the tour, of interest are The

Supremes talking over their minor hit "Let Me Go The Right Way", on which Diana Ross introduces herself as Diane her earlier name)

The Marvelettes

Tamla 54065 - Beechwood 4-5789 / Someday, Someway - 1962
Tamla 54072 - Strange I Know - 1962 (One sided promo)
Tamla 54072 - Strange I Know / Too Strong To Be Strung Along - 1962

The Marvelettes / Mary Wells / Miracles / Marvin Gaye

Tamla/Motown - Album Excerpts - 1963 (Though From Tamla / Motown, No Label Name Is Shown, Nor Is There A Title -- Promo Issue Only)

The Marvelettes

Hi-Fi (No #) - The Mashed Potato Playboy / All The Love I've Got - ?
Tamla / Dyna 2016 - Silly Boy / Way Over There - 1963/4 (Of significance because this, and the 'Mashed Potato Playboy' release listed above are both Philippines 78 rpm releases, and are potentially the only Motown releases at 78 rpm.)
Tamla 54077 - Forever* / Locking Up My Heart - 1963 *also recorded in 1957 as "Darling Forever" by The Four Chevelles on Delft 357 and as "Forever" in 1973 by Baby Washington & Don Gardner on Master 5 9103.
Tamla 54082 - Tie A String Around My Finger / My Daddy Knows Best - 1963
Tamla 54088 - As Long As I Know He's Mine / Little Girl Blue - 1963
Dub # 115 - Grass Seems Greener - 1963 (one sided acetate of unreleased track has LEAD VOICE written in pen on label but group name is not on label although it has been verified as The Marvelettes)

The Darnells (The Marvelettes)

Gordy 7024 - Too Hurt To Cry, Too Much In Love To Say Goodbye / Come On Home* - 1963 *originally released in 1963 by Holland - Dozier on Motown 1045.

The Marvelettes

Tamla 54091 - He's A Good Guy (Yes He Is) / Goddess Of Love - 1964 (Flip Side U.S.A. Copies Show Writers (Holland-Dozier-Gorman) And A Running Time Of 2:30. Canadian Copies Show Writers As (Holland-Dozier-Holland) And List An Incorrect Time Of 2:39.
Tamla 54091 - Yes He Is - 1964 (One Sided Promo Issue With Different Title Than Released Copy)
Jobete Music Company Inc. (No #) - Knock On My Door - 1964 (one sided acetate of an unreleased track)

Hitsville U.S.A. Dm 097311 - Greetings To Tamla Motown Appreciation Society - 1964 (This American 45 Was Limited To 300 Copies For Dispersal Throughout Various Fan Clubs Within Europe As A Promo For Their First European Tour. Each Act Gives A Greeting Over It's Latest Record. Artists Involved Include The Miracles, Stevie Wonder, Marvin Gaye, The Marvelettes, The Temptations, Martha And The Vandellas, The Contours, Eddie Holland, Kim Weston And The Supremes. The Record Has An Introduction From Publicist Margaret Phelps And Berry Gordy)

The Marvelettes

Tamla 54097 - You're My Remedy / A Little Bit Of Sympathy, A Little Bit Of Love - 1964
Tamla 54105 - Too Many Fish In The Sea / A Need For Love - 1964
Tamla 54116 - I'll Keep Holding On / No Time For Tears - 1965 (Marie Tillman And Juanita Cowart Leave Group In 1965)

Tamla 54116 - I'll Keep Holding On - 1965 (One Sided Promo Issue)
Tamla 54120 - Danger, Heartbreak Dead Ahead / Your Cheating Ways - 1965
Tamla 54126 - Don't Mess With Bill* / Anything You Wanna Do - 1965 *covered in 1984 by Monalisa Young on Motown 1709.
Jobete Music Company Inc - On The Other Side Of Town - 1965 (Unreleased acetate)
Tamla 54131 - You're The One / Paper Boy - 1966
Topps/Motown 12 - Please Mr. Postman - 1967 (Cardboard Record)
Tamla 54143 - The Hunter Gets Captured By The Game / I Think I Can Change You - 1967 (Gladys Horton Leaves Group In 1967 Replaced By Anne Bogan)
Tamla 54150 - When You're Young And In Love / The Day You Take One, You Have To Take The Other - 1967
Tamla 54158 - My Baby Must Be A Magician / My Baby Must Be A Magician - 1967 (white label promo issue only)
Tamla 54158 - My Baby Must Be A Magician / I Need Someone - 1967
Tamla 54166 - Here I Am Baby / Here I Am Baby - 1968 (white label promo issue only)
Tamla 54166 - Here I Am Baby / Keep Off, No Trespassing - 1968
Tamla 54171 - Destination: Anywhere / What's So Easy For Two Is So Hard For One - 1968
Tamla 54177 - I'm Gonna Hold On As Long As I Can / Don't Make Hurting Me A Habit - 1968
Tamla 54177 - I'm Gonna Hold On Long As I Can / Don't Make Hurting Me A Habit - 1968
Tamla 54186 - That's How Heartaches Are Made / Rainy Mourning - 1969
Tamla 54198 - Marionette / After All - 1970
Tamla 54213 - A Breath Taking Guy / You're The One For Me Baby - 1972

Kim Weston / The Marvelettes

Tamla/Motown 1000 - Do I Like It / Finders Keepers Losers Weepers* - 1980 *Flip Side By The Marvelettes.

The Marvelettes / Them

A & M 1201 - Danger Heartbreak Dead Ahead / Baby Please Don't Go* - 1988 *Flip Side By Them.

Maskman & The Agents

The Progressive Four (members Harmon Bethea ... - group managed by Lillian Claiborne)

DC ? - 1947 ~ 1948 (Unsure Of Recordings)
Savoy ? - 1949 (Unsure Of Recordings)

The Buddies (members Sherman Buckner (lead), Floyd Bennet (first tenor), Alfred Slaughter (lead) and Lester Fountain (baritone) - group managed by Lillian Claiborne - unsure if group made any recordings)

Paul Chapman & The Cap-Tans (members Sherman Buckner, Floyd Bennet, Alfred Slaughter, Lester Fountain and Harmon Bethea)

DC 8054 - You'll Always Be My Sweetheart / Coo-Coo Jug-Jug - 1950
DC 8064 Goodnight Mother / Let's Put Our Cards On The Table - 1950

The Cap-Tans

Dot 1009 - I'm So Crazy For Love / Crazy 'Bout My Honey Dip - 1950
Dot 1018 - With All My Love / Chief Turn The Hose On Me - 1950
Gotham 233 - My, My, Ain't She Pretty / Never Be Lonely - 1951
Gotham 268 - I Thought I Could Forget You / Waiting At The Station - 1951 (after this release

Lester Fountain is drafted he is replaced by Ray Reader)
Coral 65071 - Asking / Who Can I Turn To - 1951 (after this release the group disbands and Harmon Bethea returns to gospel music and joins The Progessivaires who in 1954 became The Octaves)
Dot 15114 - With All My Love / I'm So Crazy For Love - 1953

L'Cap-Tans (members Harmon Bethea, Lester Britton, Richard Stewart, Elmo Anderson and Francis Henry (on guitar))

Hollywood 1092 - The Bells Ring Out / Call A Doctor - 1958

L'Cap-Tans with The Go Boys (members "Baby" Jim Belt, Lester Britton, Richard Stewart, Elmo Anderson, Harmon Bethea and Francis Henry)

DC 0416 - Homework / Say Yes - 1959

L'Cap-Tans

Savoy 1567 - Homework / Say Yes - 1959

Cap-Tans (members Roosevelt "Tippie" Hubbard, Jerome "Toy" Walton, "Baby" Jim Belt and Harmon Bethea)

Anna 1122 - I'm Afraid / Tight Skirts And Crazy Sweaters - 1960

Bob Marshall's Crystals (record included Jerry Holland with The Cap-Tans)

Dc 0433 - Big Bite Of The Blues / Ain't No Big Thing (Instrumental) - 1962

Wailing Bethea & The Cap-Tans

Hawkeye 0430 - Rockin' In The Jungle / Annie Penguin - 1962

Bethea & The Cap-Tans

Loop 100 - Crazy About The Woman / Revenue Man - 1963
Sabu 501 - You Better Mind / I Wanna Make Love - 1963
Sabu 103 - Whenever I Look At You / Round The Rocket - 1963

Mask Man & The Cap-Tans

Ru-Jac 220 - Love Can Do Wonders / Chicken Wings - 1964

The Maskman & The Agents (members Harmon Bethea, John Hood, Paul Williams and Tyrone Grey)

Gama 674 - There'll Be Some Changes / Never Would Have Made It - 1968 (inspired by 'The Lone Ranger' and the group being desperate for attention Harmon Bethea started wearing a mask)
Dynamo 118 - There'll Be Some Changes / Never Would Have Made It - 1968
Dynamo 125 - One Eye Open / Y'all - 1968 (With The Billy Clark Orchestra)
Dynamo 131 - My Wife, My Dog, My Cat / Love Bandito - 1969 (With The Billy Clark Orchestra)

Bethea The Masked Man & The Agents

Dynamo 136 - Get Away Dreams / I Would'nt Come Back - 1969

Bethea (The Masked Man & The Agents)

Dynamo 139 - Moon Dream / When You Got Money - ?

The Maskman & The Agents

Dynamo 141 - One Eyed Dog In A Meat House / Never Would Have Made It - 1970
Dynamo 143 - It's The Thing / I Would'nt Come Back - 1970
Dynamo 145 - Put On Your Shoes And Walk / There'll Be Some Changes - 1970
Dynamo 148 - Ain't That Some Shame / Ain't That Some Shame - 1970

Harmon Bethea

Musicor 1393 - It Could Happen To You / She's My Meat - 1970

The Maskman & The Agents

Vigor 707 - Stand Up/ Part 2 (Instrumental) - 1970
Loop 701 - In A Crowded Station / It's The Thing 1972
Loop 711 - Roaches / I Wouldn't Come Back - 1972
Hitbound 2921 - In My Diary / Hard To Get Along - ?
Mask 901 - The World Is A Cafeteria / Wigs - ?
Cap City 104 - Wigs / The World Is A Cafeteria - ?

Harmon Bethea (died 18-December-2009 in Washington, DC --- cause: ?)

Musicor 1483 - Talking About The Boss And I / Roaches - 1973
Musicor 1493 - Roaches / Talking About The Boss And I - 1973

Harmon Bethea (The Maskman)

Musicor 1494 - Over The Hill / There'll Be Some Changes - 1974

The Cap-Tans

Roadhouse 1016 - I Love You So / I Thought I Could Forget You - 1974

The Cap-Tans / The Heartbreakers

Roadhouse 1023 - I'm Seeking Revenge / Feel Like Balling Some More* - 1974 *flip by The Heartbreakers.

The Maskman

Lebby 7967 - Ratty Ratty / Sitting On Your Doorstep - 1972
Lebby 7968 - Ratty Ratty / Sitting On Your Doorstep - 1972

The Masked Man & The Agents (members

B.B.C. 294 - Stand Up / Stand Up (Part 2 & 3) - ?

The Maskman

B.B.C. 296 - You'll Never Make It Alone / Over The Hill Gang - ?
B.B.C. 297 - Stand Up / Ghetto Love - ?

Bethea The Maskman

B.B.C. 679 - Stand Up / Ghetto Love - ?

Harmon Bethea

Smiths 205 - Funky Donkey Monkey Walk / Movin' And Groovin - 70s

The Maskman (H. Bethea Sr.) and The Agents

Jan Jan 804 - Prices And Crises / Prices And Crises (The Maskman's Band) - 1974

Harmon Bethea

Creole 62x76 - The Plainsman / Anonymous - 1975

The Cap-Tans

Gotham 261 - Grateful / Don't Believe What They Say About Me - 1975 (bootleg of 1951 recordings by The Cap-Tans using the same label numbers as a 1951 release by Camille Howard)

Harmon Bethea, The Masked Man & The Agents (members

Dynamo 602 - That's Your Roots / Don't Play A Game - 1977

The Maskman (H. Bethea Sr.) and The Agents (members

Jan Jan 805 - That's Women Lib / That's Women Lib (Instrumental) - 1985

The Masqueraders

The Stairs (members - Charlie Moore (lead), Robert Wrightsil (tenor), Johnny Davis (second tenor), Lawrence Davis (third tenor) and "Little" Charlie Gibson (bass))

South Town ? - Brown Eyed Handsome Man / ? - 1958 ~ 1959
South Town ? - Cave-Man Love / ? - 1958 ~ 1959
South Town ? - Flossy Mae* / ? - 1958 ~ 1959 *this was a cover of the 1958 recording of "Flossie Mae" by The Saucers on KICK 516 -- The Stairs were together roughly two years when Johnny and Lawrence Davis left the group and "Little" Charlie Gibson was drafted into the army. So the remaining pair began to recruit new members who included Willie Charles Gray (who later joined Les Watson & The Panthers). After a few personnel changes Lee Jones, Harold Thomas and David Sanders were added to the line-up.

The Masqueraders (members Lee Jones (lead), Harold Thomas (first tenor), Robert Wrightsil (second tenor), Charlie Moore (baritone) and David Sanders (baritone, bass))

MK 101 - Man's Temptation / Dancing Doll - 1963

The Masquaders (members Lee Jones, Harold Thomas, Robert Wrightsil, Charlie Moore and David Sanders)

Soultown 201 - Talk About A Woman / That's The Same Thing - 1965? (recorded in Dallas, Texas -- written by Harold Thomas, Lee Jones and Charlie Moore)

The Masqueraders (members Lee Jones, Harold Thomas, Robert Wrightsil, Charlie Moore and David Sanders)

La Beat 6605 - The Family (Part 1) / The Family (Part 2) - 1966
Tower 281 - The Family (Part 1) / The Family (Part 2) – 1966
La Beat 6606 - I'm Gonna Make It / How (Can I Go On?) – 1966
La Beat 6701 - Together That's The Only Way / Be Happy For Me – 1967

The Masqueraders / The L. P. T.'s

La Beat 6701 - Be Happy For Me / Be Happy For Me (Instrumental)* - 1967 (same 45 as above just different flip title) *flip by The L. P. T.'s.

The L. P. T.'s / The L. P. T. Orchestra (The La Beat Production Team)

La Beat 6701 - Together That's The Only Way (Vocal) / Together That's The Only Way (Instrumental)* - 1967 (copies exist of this 45 which is the same 45 as the first La Beat listed, this should actually be credited as The Masqueraders) *this is a bit of an oddity as the track is actually the vocal entitled "Be Happy For Me".

The Masqueraders (Lee Jones, Harold Thomas, Robert Wrightsil, Charlie Moore, David Sanders)

La Beat 6702 - (Work) Together That's The Only Way / One More Chance – 1967
La Beat 6704/5 - I Got The Power / (Work) Together That's The Only Way – 1967
Wand 1168 - I Don't Want Nobody To Lead Me On* / Let's Face Facts - 1967 (recorded in Memphis Tennessee and then leased / sold to Wand in New York) *also recorded in 1970 by Roosevelt Grier on ABC 11275 and in 197 by The Gentlemen Four on Dionne Warwick's label Sonday 6003)

Lee Jones & The Sounds Of Soul (members Lee Jones, Harold Thomas, Robert Wrightsil, Charlie Moore and David Sanders)

Amy 11008 - This Heart Is Haunted / On The Other Side - 1968 (recorded under this name to avoid contractual problems)

The Masqueraders (members Lee Jones, Harold Thomas, Robert Wrightsil, Charlie Moore and David Sanders)

Wand 1172 - Do You Love Me Baby / Sweet Loving Woman - 1968 (during this period the group also sang back-up for Alex Chilton & The Box Tops early recordings)
Bell 733 - I Ain't Got To Love Nobody Else / I Got It - 1968
Bell 847 - How Big Is Big / Please Take Me Back - 1968
Bell 932 - Steamroller / Brotherhood - 1968

The Masquerader (Members Lee Jones, Harold Thomas, Robert Wrightsil, Charlie Moore, David Sanders)

Bell Test Pressing - I'm Just An Average Guy - 1968 (One-Sided Test Pressing, the hand-written information on the label gives a time of 3:20 with AGP and the number 100 crossed out and replaced with 108, song title, plus the group name is mis-spelled)

The Masqueraders (Members Lee Jones, Harold Thomas, Robert Wrightsil, Charlie Moore, David Sanders)

Bell AGP 108 - I'm Just An Average Guy / I Ain't Gonna Stop - 1968
AGP 114 - The Grass Was Green / Say It - 1968

The Whispers / The Masqueraders

AGP 115 - I Only Ment To Wet My Feet / I'm Just An Average Guy* - 1968 (the "A" side by The Whipers has a mis-spelling and reads "Ment") *flip by The Masqueraders. This 45 is an advanced DJ pressing.

The Masqueraders

AGP 122 - Love Peace And Understanding / Tell Me You Love Me - 1969 (around this time the group started having personnel problems and began using Sam Hutchins as an alternate lead vocalist in place of Lee Jones and sometimes performed as a six man group)
Stairway 71a - Let Me Show The World I Love You / Masquerader's Theme - 1971 (Note Stairway Was The Masqueraders Own Label)
Stairway 72a - Let Me Show The World I Love You / The Truth Is Here – 1972
Stairway 72b - The Truth Is Free / The Truth Is Free (Part 2) - 1972

The Masqueraders / The Larks

Cobra 4500 - I'm Just An Average Guy / I Want You Back* - 1972 *flip is by The Larks.

The Masqueraders (members Sam Hutchins (lead), Harold Thomas (first tenor), Robert Wrightsil (second tenor), Charlie Moore (baritone) and David Sanders (baritone, bass)

Hi 2251 - Let The Love Bells Ring / Now That I've Found You – 1973
Hi 2264 - Wake Up Fool / Now That I've Found You – 1973
H. B. S. / Abc 12141 - Baby It's You / Listen - 1975 (note H. B. S. is Hot Buttered Soul -- Isaac Hayes label) Sam Hutchins replaced Charlie Moore in the group when Charlie left just prior to signing with H. B. S.
H. B. S. / ABC 12157 - Sweet Sweetening / (Call Me) The Traveling Man - 1975 (while at H. B. S. Harold Thomas although he sang on all the recordings was replaced by a friend of the group Oberdean "Deano" Deloney as Harold had a disagreement with Isaac Hayes people about publishing rights - this is why Oberdean Deloney is mentioned in the credits of their first album "Everybody Wanna Live On" and not Harold Thomas)
H. B. S. / ABC 12190 - Please Don't Try / Your Love Is A Sweet Blessing – 1975
Bang 4806 - Desire / Into Your Soul – 1980
Bang 4812 - Starry Love / It's So Nice – 1980
T. N. T. ? - Merry Christmas / (Instrumental) – 1990
T. N. T. ? - When Old Man Trouble Calls / (Instrumental) - 1992

Johnnie Mae Matthews

The Five Dapps (members James Bennett, Johnnie Mae Matthews and probably George Wooden, Emry Franklin and Albert Williams)

Brax 207/8 - Do Wop A Do / You're So Unfaithful* - 1958 *lead Johnnie Mae Matthews.

Johnnie Mae Matthews And Her Dapps (members James Bennett, Johnnie Mae Matthews,)

Northern 3727 - Dreamer / Indian Joe - 1959

Johnnie Mae Matthews and Her Dapps / Chet Oliver

Northern 3729 - Mr. Fine / Someday - 1959 *Flip By Chet Oliver.

Johnnie Mae Matthews (born 31-December-1922 in Bessemer, Alabama, at an early age her family moved to Newark, New Jersey then while a teen Johnnie Mae moved to Detroit, Michigan in 1950 - died 6-January-2002 --- cause: cancer)

Northern 3732 - So Lonely / Help Me - 1960 (This Label number was also assigned to The Distants with "Come On / Always" and also Pop Corn & His Mohawks with "Pretty Girl / You're The One")

Joannie Mae Matthews

Northern 3736 - Ooh Wee / Give Me True Love – 1960

Johnnie Mae Matthews

Northern 3742 - So Lonely / Help Me – 1960
Reel 3743 - Oh Baby / You Worry Me - ?
Glodis 1004 - Oh, Baby / You Worry Me - 1961
Reel 3745 - No One Can Love Me The Way You Do / No More Tears - ?
Northern 3746 - Nobody Business **(What I Do)** / My Destination - ?
Reel 112 - The Headshrinker / My Little Angel – 1961
Sue 755 - My Little Angel / The Headshrinker - 1962
Reel 119 - Come Home / Oh Mother – 1962

Johnnie Mae Matthews - Timmy Shaw

Reel 120 - I Don't Want Your Loving (Part 1) / I Don't Want Your Loving (Part 2) – 1963

Johnnie Mae Matthews

Reel 122 - Lonely Road / I Won't Cry Anymore – 1963
Northern 4736 - Nobody Business (What I Do) / My Destination (It True Love) **–** 1963
Spokane 4008 - Worried About You / Itty Bitty Heart – 1964
Blue Rock 4001 - Baby What's Wrong* / Here Comes My Baby - 1964 (some copies issued with picture sleeve) *also recorded in 1962 by Jimmy Reed on Vee Jay 425 and in 1963 by Lonnie Mack on Fraternity 918. Blue Rock 4011 - My Man (Sweetest Man In The World) / I Can't Live Without You – 1965
Big D 855 - Don't Talk About My Man / He Really Loves Me - 1966
Audrey 100 - Luck Walked Through My Door / Love Hides All Faults - ?

Joe L. Carter / Joe L. Carter & Johnnie M. Matthews

Audrey 112 - My Life Story (Instrumental) / Don't Cry Baby* - ? *Flip By Joe L. Carter & Johnnie M. Matthews. (yellow label - the maroon and silver Audrey 112 is by Joe L. and entitled "My Life Story (Vocal) / Don't Cry Baby")

Johnnie Mae Matthews

Jam 103 - Lonely You'll Be / That's What My Man (Is For) – 1967
Art 002 - Cut Me Loose / Lonely You'll Be* - 1967 (with The Wonderettes)*recorded 25-September-1967

Johnnie Mae Matthews And The Wonderettes (Members

Atco 6528 - Cut Me Loose / Lonely You'll Be – 1967

Johnnie Mae Matthews

Art 003 - Got To Be On (Your Case) / You're The One – 1967

Johnny Mae Matthews

Big Hit 104 - Two-Sided Thing / You Make Me Feel Good - ? (Two different label designs)
Big Hit 105 - I Have No Choice* / That's When It Hurts - ? *an acetate exists of this track by Audrey Matthews, who is the daughter of Johnnie Mae, although when it was recorded remains a matter of conjecture. Audrey and her brother formed the nucleus of the 1970's Group Black Nasty.

Johnnie Mae Matthews

Big Hit 108 - My Momma Didn't Lie / You're The One - ?
Big Hit 111 - Don't Be Discouraged / Don't Be Discouraged - ?
Northern 10039 - It's Good / Come On Back - 1979
Cotillion 45010 - It's Good / Come On Back - 1979 (Music By The ADC Band)
Northern 10040 - I Can Feel It / Crazy About You - 1980

Shirley Matthews & The Big Town Girls

Shirley Matthews & The Big Town Girls (members Shirley Matthews, ...)

Atlantic 2210 - Big-Town Boy* / (You) Can Count On That - 1963 *written by Eddie Rambeau and Bud Rehak and produced by Bob Crewe. Although Shirley was born and from Harrow, Ontario, this is the original release coming out one week before it's Canadian release.
Tamarac 602 - Big-Town Boy / (You) Can Count On That - 1963 (Canadian release)
Tamarac 603 - Private Property / Wise Guys - 1964 (Canadian release)
Atlantic 2224 - Private Property / Wise Guys - 1964 (after this release Shirley Matthews gave up her day job at Bell Telephone to concentrate on her singing career)

Shirley Matthews

Amy 910 - (He Makes Me) Feel So Pretty / Is He Really Mine – 1964
Amy 921 - Stop The Clock! / If I Had It All To Do Again – 1965
Red Leaf 611 - Stop The Clock / If I Had It All To Do Again - 1965 (Canadian Release)
Underground 1010 - Big Town Boy / ? - ? (Canadian Release)

Arthur Lee Maye

The Carmels (Members Eugene Taylor, Arthur Lee Maye, Delmar Wilburn (Who Later Became A Member Of The Turks), Norman Manley And Charles Holmes) - High School Vocal Group.

The "5" Hearts (There Were Only Three Members In The Group:- Arthur Lee Maye, Johnny Coleman And Richard Berry)

Flair 1026 - The Fine One / Please Baby Please - 1954

Arthur Lee Maye & The Crowns (Members Richard Berry, Arthur Lee Maye, Charles Colbert, Johnny Morris, Joe Moore And Johnny Coleman)

Modern 944 - Set My Heart Free / I Wanna Love* - 1954

The Rams (Members Arthur Lee Maye, Johnny Coleman And Richard Berry)

Flair 1066 - Sweet Thing / Rock Bottom - 1955

Richard Berry (Actually The Crowns Minus Johnny Morris But Label Only Credits Richard Berry)

Flair 1064 - Please Tell Me / Oh Oh Get Out Of The Car - 1955

.

Arthur Lee Maye & The Crowns (Members Arthur Lee Maye, Richard Berry, Charles Colbert, Joe Moore And Johnny Coleman)

RPM 424 -Truly / Oochie Pachie* - 1955

Arthur Lee Maye (Group Comprising Of Arthur Lee Maye, Richard Berry, Charles Colbert, Joe Moore And Johnny Coleman Were Not Given Credit)

RPM 429 - Love Me Always / Loop De Loop De Loop* - 1955

Arthur Lee Maye & The Crowns (Members Arthur Lee Maye, Richard Berry, Charles Colbert, Joe Moore And Johnny Coleman)

RPM 438 - Please Don't Leave Me / Do The Bop - 1955
Speciality 573 - Gloria / Oo-Rooba-Lee - 1956 These Tracks First Appeared On RPM 45's And Are Bootlegs!. The Label With Saw Tooth Horizontal Lines Is Scarcer Than The Label Without.

Arthur Lee Maye (born 11-December-1934 in Tuscaloosa, ALA --- died 17-July-2002 in Riverside County, CA --- cause: liver cancer) (group comprising of Arthur Lee Maye, Charles Colbert, Joe Moore, Johnny Coleman and Charles Holmes were not given credit)

Dig 124 - This Is The Night For Love* / Honey Honey* - 1956 *lead Arthur Lee Maye.
Dig 133 - Whispering Wind / A Fool's Prayer - 1956
Dig 146 - Gee / Only You - 1957 (Unissued)
Dig 149 - Sincerely / Sh-Boom - 1957 (Unissued)
Dig 151 - Honey Love / At My Front Door -1957? (Unissued)
Flip 330 - Hey Pretty Girl / Cause You're Mine Alone - 1957

Cry Baby Curtis (Backing Vocals The Crowns Minus Arthur Lee Maye)

Cash 1062 - I Wanna / Did You Think I Care - 1958

Lee Maye Of The Milwaukee Braves (Group Comprising Of Arthur Lee Maye, Eugene Maye, Joe Moore, Johnny Coleman And Charles Holmes Were Not Given Credit)

Cash 1063 - Will You Be Mine / Honey Honey - 1958

Arthur Lee Maye (Group Comprising Of Arthur Lee Maye, Eugene Maye, Joe Moore, Johnny Coleman And Charles Holmes Were Not Given Credit)

Cash 1065 - All I Want Is Someone To Love / Pounding* - 1958 (lead on both tracks Arthur Lee Maye) *session Arthur Wright (bass), James Carmichael (keyboards) and Jesse Sailes (drums))

Henry Strogin (Backing Vocals The Crowns Comprising Of Eugene Maye, Charles Colbert, Joe Moore And Johnny Coleman Group Was Minus Arthur Lee Maye Due To His Baseball Commitments)

Dynamic 1002 - Why Did You Go Away / My Aching Feet - 1960
Dynamic 1002 - Why Did You Go Away / Tutti Frutti - 1960
Amazon 1001 - I'll Tag Along / I Love L.A. - 1961
Ball 1015 - I'll Tag Along / Why Did You Go Away - 1961

Lee Maye Of The Milwaukee Braves (Group Comprising Of Arthur Lee Maye, Eugene Maye,

Joe Moore, Johnny Coleman And Charles Holmes Were Not Given Credit)

Imperial 5790 - Will You Be Mine / Honey Honey - 1961

Arthur Lee Maye

Lenox 5566 - Halfway (Out Of Love With You) / I Can't Please You - 1963
Kent 406 - Love Me Always / Loop De Loop De Loop - 1964
Jamie 1272 - Who Made You What You Are / Loving Fool - 1964
Jamie 1276 - How's The World Treating You / Loving Fool - 1964
Jamie 1284 - Only A Dream / The Breaks Of Life - 1964
Jamie 1287 - Who Made You What You Are / Even A Nobody - 1964 (the above JAMIE 45's were recorded in Muscle Shoals, Alabama)

Lee Maye

Jet **Stream** 735 - Have Love Will Travel / Loving Fool - 1964

The Off-Beats (members Arthur Lee Maye backed by a Nashville studio group)

Guyden 2101 - Have Love Will Travel / Hoodlum - 1964 (flip is an instrumental)

Barbara Lynn & Lee Maye

Jamie 1295 - Careless Hands / (Don't Pretend) Just Lay It On The Line - 1965

Lee Maye

Tower 243 - When My Heart Hurts No More / At The Party* - 1966 *cover of a 1962 record by Big Sambo & The Housewreckers on Eric 7003.

Arthur Lee Maye

Pacemaker 252 - Fools Rush In / Jes' Lookin' – 1967

Lee Mays & The Zonics (members

Gaye 5002 – Nothing Means Nothing To You / Writing This Letter – 1967

Lee Maye

Chess 2000 - Fools Rush In / Jes' Lookin' - 1967
ABC-Paramount 11028 - If You Leave Me / The Greatest Love I've Ever Known - 1968
Buddah 141 - He'll Have To Go / Jes' Lookin' - 1969

Arthur Lee Maye

Pic 1 115 - Today Today / Touch Me On My Shoulder - 196?
Pic 1 120 - Total Disaster / What's Happening - 196?
Pic 1 126 - Stop The World / At The Party - 197?

Country Boys & City Girls (Featuring Lee Maye)

Happy Fox 511 - Forgetting Someone / ? - 1976

Lee Maye (backing vocals by Dave Antrell and Charles Williams)

Antrell 102 - Moonlight / I'm Happy And In Love - 1985 (the yellow label green vinyl release, is scarcer than the gold label release)

Arthur Lee Maye & The Crowns / The Jacks

Collectables Col 039357 - Love Me Always / Why Don't You Write Me* - ? *flip by The Jacks.

The Blue Jays (members Leon Peels, Arthur Lee Maye, Dave Antrell and ?)

Classic Artists 111 - Once Upon A Love / Alice From Above - 1990

Curtis Mayfield

Solo Recordings only.

Curtom (Distributed by Buddah

Curtom 1955 - If There's A Hell Below We're All Gonna Go/ The Makings Of You - 1970
Curtom 1960 - Beautiful Brother Of Mine/ Give It Up - 1971
Curtom 1963 - Mighty Mighty (Spade and Whitey)/ pt.2 - 1971
Curtom 1966 - Get Down/ We're A Winner - 1971
Curtom 1968 - We Got To Have Peace (Mono) / We Got To Have Peace (Stereo) - 1973 (Promo only, clear vinyl)
Curtom 1968 - We Got To Have Peace/ We're A Winner - 1972
Curtom 1972 - Beautiful Brother Of Mine (re)/ Love To Keep You In My Mind - 1972
Curtom 1974 - Move On Up/ Underground - 1972
Curtom 1975 - Freddie's Dead/ Underground from the movie Superfly - 1972
Curtom 1978 - Superfly/ Underground from the movie Superfly - 1972
Curtom 1987 - Future Shock/ The Other Side Of Town - 1973
Curtom 1991 - If I We're Only A Child Again/ Think (instr.) - 1973
Curtom 1993 - Can't Say Nothing/ Future Song - 1973
Curtom 1999 - Kung Fu/ Right On For The Darkness - 1974
Curtom 2005 - Sweet Exorcist/ Suffer - 1974
Curtom 2006 - Mother's Son/ Love Me - 1975
Columbia 10147 - Stash That Butt Sucker / Zanzibar - 1975

Curtom distributed by Warner Bros.

Curtom 0105 - So In Love/ Hard Times - 1975
Curtom 0118 - Only You Babe/ Love To The People - 1976
Curtom 0122 - Party Night/ P.S. I Love You - 1976
Curtom 0125 - Show Me Love/ Just Want To Be With You - 1977
Curtom 0131 - Do Do Wap Is Strong In Here/ Need Someone To Love from the movie Short Eyes - 1977
Curtom 0135 - You Are, You Are/ Get A Little Bit - 1978
Curtom 0141 - Do It All Night/ Party, Party - 1978
Curtom 0142 - In Love, In Love, In Love/ Keeps Me Loving You - 1978

Curtom distributed by RSO

Curtom 0919 - This Year (vocal)/ This Year (instr.) - 1979
Curtom 0941 - You're So Good To Me (#46/-)/ Between You And Me Baby (with Linda Clifford) - 1979
Curtom 1016 - Tell Me / Heartbeat / Over The Hump - 1979 (12" promo issue only)
Curtom 1029 - Love's Sweet Sensation (vocal)/ Love's Sweet Sensation (instr.) (with Linda Clifford) - 1980
Curtom 1036 - Love Me, Love Me Now/ It's Alright - 1980

Curtom 1046 - Tripping Out/ Never Stop Loving Me - 1980
Boardwalk 122 - She Won't Let Nobody/ You Get All My Love - 1981
Boardwalk 132 - Toot An'Toot An'Toot/ Come Free Your People - 1981
Boardwalk 155 - Hey Baby/ Summerhot - 1982
Boardwalk 169 - Dirty Laundry/ Nobody But You - 1983
CRC/ Ichiban 001 - Baby It's You/ Breakin' In The Streets - 1985

Curtom distributed by Ichiban

Curtom 101 - Move On Up/ Little Child, Running Wild UK '12 - 1988
Arista 9806 - He's A Flyguy / Inst - 1989
Curtom 12-PO22 - I Mo Git U Sucka / He's A Fly Guy - 1989 (12" promo issue only)
Curtom 102 - I Mo Git U Sucka/ He's A Fly Guy - 1990
Curtom 106 - Homeless/ People Never Give Up - 1990
Curtom 12-PO52 - Got To Be Real / On And On - 1990 (12" promo issue only)
Curtom 108 - Do Be Down/ Got To Be Real - 1990
Capitol 586 - Superfly 1990/ Superfly 1990 (fly mix edit) – 1990

The Metros

The Metros (members were Alfred "Fred" Mitchell, Percy Williams, Robert Suttles, James Buckman and Gordon Dunn)

RCA Victor 47-8994 - Sweetest One / Time Changes Things – 1966
RCA Victor 47-9159 - Since I Found My Baby / No Baby - 1967 (some copies issued with picture sleeve)
RCA Victor 47-9331 - Let's Groove / The Replacer - 1967

Joe Buckman (James Buckman)

Sepia 3 – Right Now / Till The End Of Time - 1969

The Metros (members were Alfred "Fred" Mitchell, Percy Williams, Robert Suttles, James Buckman and Gordon Dunn)

Soul King 401 - What's Wrong With Your Love (Version #1) / She's Just Not Everybody's Girl* - 1991 (recorded 1970 in Detroit) *originally slated for release in November-1972 on Gold Soul 1027.

Tony Middleton

The Dovers (members Tony Middleton, Richie Davis, Ralph Martin, Joe Martin and John Steele)

The 5 Willows (members Tony Middleton, Richie Davis, Ralph Martin, Joe Martin (born 12-February-1935 in Harlem, New York --- died 19-February-2005 at Presbyterian Hospital, New York City --- cause: ?) and John "Scooter" Steele (died 1997) (Doc Green also sang with the group a short time before joining The 5 Crowns))

Allen 1000 - My Dear, Dearest Darling / Rock Little Francis – 1953
Allen 1002 - Dolores / All Night Long - 1953
Allen 1003 - White Cliffs Of Dover / With These Hands - 1953
Pee Dee 290 - Love Bells / Please Baby - 1953
Herald 433 - Lay Your Head On My Shoulder / Baby, Come A Little Bit Closer -1954

Herald 442 - Look Me In The Eyes / So Help Me - 1954

The Willows

Melba 102 - Church Bells Are Ringing* / Baby Tell Me - 1956 *the songs bass line was sung by Richard Simon a friend of the group as John Steele had missed the session. The chimes used in the recording were played by the yet unknown lead singer of another Melba group The Tokens, whose name was Neil Sedaka
Melba 102 - Church Bells May Ring / Baby Tell Me - 1956 (title was changed and released with same label number)
Melba 106 - Do You Love Me / My Angel - 1956
Melba 115 - My Angel / Little Darlin' - 1957
Club 1014 - This Is The End / Don't Pull, Don't Push, Don't Shove – 1957

Tony Middleton and The Willows

Eldorado Eld 508 - First Taste Of Love / Only My Heart - 1957
Gone 5015 - Let's Fall In Love / Say Yeah – 1957

Tony Middleton

Saxony 104 - I'm On My Way / Lover - 1958

The Willows

Michelle 501 - This Is The End / Dont Push, Don't Pull – 1959

The Willows (members brothers Ralph and Joe Martin, Dottie Martin (Joe's wife --- born 1939 --- died 2000) and Freddie Donovan)

Warwick 524 - You / My Dear, Dearest Darling - 1959

Tony Middleton sings with orchestra and chorus

Triumph 600 - Count Your Blessings (See What Love Has Done) / I Just Want Somebody - 1959
Triumph 605 - The Universe / Blackjack - 1959

Tony Middleton

Alto 2001 - Untouchable / I Need You - 1960
Big Top 3037 - Unchained Melody / Sweet Baby Of Mine - 1960
Roulette 4345 - I'm Gonna Try Love (One More Time) / Is It This Or Is It That - 1961

The 5 Willows

Lost-Nite 174 - My Dear, Dearest Darling / Rock, Little Francis - 1960 ~ 1963
Lost-Nite 183 - Delores / All Night Long - 1960 ~ 1963
Lost-Nite 187 - The White Cliffs Of Dover / With These Hands - 1960 ~ 1963
Lost-Nite 192 - Love Bells / Please Baby - 1960 ~ 1963 (all above reissues, released during these years as there is no zip code on record label)

The Willows

4 - Star 1753 - There's A Dance Goin' On / Now That I Have You – 1961

The Crests (members Tony Middleton, James Ancrum, Gary Lewis, Harold Torres, and Jay Carter)

Selma 311 - Guilty* / Number One With Me - 1962 *has spoken intro --- scarce.
Selma 311 - Guilty* / Number One With Me - 1962 *does not have spoken intro --- common.

Tony Middleton

Alfa 113 - My Home Town / Please Take Me In – 1962
United Artists 410 - Driftin' / Memories Are Made Of This – 1962

The Hollywood Flames (members David Ford, John Berry, Reggie Jackson, Ray Brewster, and Tony Middleton)

Vee-Jay 515 - Drop Me A Line* / Letter To My Love** - 1963 *lead Tony Middleton. **lead John Berry.

Tony Middleton

Philips 40151 - I Need You Tonight / Send Me Away – 1963
Philips 40184 - Too Hot To Handle / I Just Couldn't Help Myself – 1964

The Willows

Heidi 103 - It's Such A Shame / Tears In Your Eyes – 1964
Heidi 107 - Sit By The Fire / Such A Night – 1965

Tony Middleton

ABC - Paramount 10695 - You Spoiled My Reputation / If I Could Write A Song - 1965

Burt Bacharach

Kapp 685 - My Little Red Book / What's New Pussycat -1965 (featuring Tony Middleton)

Tony Middleton

Mala 544 - Paris Blues / Out Of This World - 1966
MGM 13493 - To The Ends Of The Earth / Don't Ever Leave Me - 1966
Mr .G 811 - Let Me Down Easy (Part 1) / Let Me Down Easy (Part 2) – 1968
Mr. G 815 - Good Morning World (Part 1) / Good Morning World (Part 2) – 1968

Tony Middleton with Chuito & The Latin Uniques (members Tony Middleton, ...)

Storm 1005 - Spanish Maiden / Aqui Llego - 1969
Speed 1005 - Spanish Maiden / Aqui Lliego - 1969

Tony Middleton & Bobby Matos

Speed 1016 - Return To Spanish Harlem / Already Satisfied - ?

Tony Middleton

Maggie 715 - I'm Jack And I'm Back / Day's Of Joy - 196?
A & M 1084 - Keep On Dancing / Angela - 1969
A & M 1124 - Harlem Lady / Sound Of Goodbye - 1969
Scepter 12290 - Border Song (Holy Moses) / Silliest People - 1970
Toy 1001 - Ruby Tuesday / Sittin' In The Sunshine - 1971
Toy 3803 - Rock And Roll Lullaby / Sittin' In The Sunshine - 1972
Columbia 45972 - It Would'nt Have Made Any Difference / Lovelight - 1973
Cotton 1 - Rota Roota Grind (Vocal) / Rota Roota Grind (Instrumental) - 197?

Pala 006 - I Need You / Untouchable - 1973

The Willows (members members Tony Middleton, Richie Davis, Ralph Martin, Joe Martin and John Steele)

Goldies 45 2548 - Church Bells May Ring / Baby Tell Me - 1973

Tony Middleton

Royal Flush 102 - Lady Fingers / A Garden In The Ghetto - 1976

Tony Middleton / Barbara English

T. K. Disco Tkd-12 - Lady Fingers / House Of Strangers* - 1976 (12" release) *flip by Barbara English.

Tony Middleton

Eric 5012 - Paris Blues / Out Of This World - 197?

The Jacks / The Willows

Collectables Col 030257 - Why Don't You Write Me / Church Bells May Ring* - ? *flip by The Willows.

Bobby Day / The Willows

Collectables Col 038977 - Rockin Robin / Church Bells May Ring* - ? *flip by The Willows.

Garnet Mimms

The Norfolk Four (members Garrett Mimms, ...) 1953

Savoy ? - 1953

The Harmonizing Four (members Garrett Mimms, ...)

The Deltones (members Garrett Mimms, ...)

The Gainors (members Garnet Mimms, Sam Bell, Howard Tate, Willie Combo and John Jefferson)

Cameo Parkway 151 - The Secret / Gonna Rock Tonite - 1958
Cameo Parkway 156 - You Must Be An Angel / Follow Me – 1958
Red Top 110 - You Must Be An Angel / Follow Me – 1958
Mercury 71466 - She's My Lollipop / Message With Flowers – 1959
Mercury 71630 - Nothing Means More To Me / I'm In Love With You - 1960
Talley-Ho 102 - This Perfect Moment / Where I Want To Be – 1961
Talley-Ho 105 - Tell Him / Darling - 1961

Garnet Mimms & The Enchanters (members Garnet Mimms (former member of The Gainors), Sam Bell (former member of The Gainors), Charles Boyer and Zola Pearnell)

United Artists 629 - Cry Baby* / Don't Change Your Heart - 1963 *song written by Jarry Ragavoy under his pseudonym Norman Meade, and Bert Berns under his pseudonym Bert Russell. The uncredited Gospelaires sang backing vocals on this track and not The Enchanters. The

Gospelaires members were Dionne Warwick, Dee Dee Warwick and Estelle Brown. The Enchanters sang backing vocals on the flip. Song was recorded in May of 1963.
United Artists 658 - For Your Precious Love* / Baby Don't You Weep - 1963 *originally recorded in 1958 by Jerry Butler & The Impressions on Vee-Jay 280.
United Artists 694 - Anytime You Need Me / Tell Me Baby - 1964
United Artists 715 - One Girl / A Quiet Place - 1964

The Enchanters (members William Gilmore, Samuel Bell, Zola Pearnell and Charles Boyer)

Warner Bros. 5460 - I Wanna Thank You* / I'm A Good Man - 1964 *recorded 11-May-1964.
Loma 2012 - I Paid For The Party / I Want To Be Loved - 1965
Loma 2035 - God Bless The Girl And Me / You Were Meant To Be My Baby - 1966
Loma 2054 - I've Lost All Communications / We Got Love - 1966

Garnet Mimms (Born Garrett Mimms On 16-November-1933 In Ashland, West Virginia)

United Artists 773 - Look Away / One Woman Man – 1964
United Artists 796 - A Little Bit Of Soap / I'll Make It Up To You - 1964
United Artists 848 - So Close / It Was Easier To Hurt Her – 1965
United Artists 868 - Adventures Of Moll Flanders / Welcome Home - 1965
United Artists 868 - Every Time / Welcome Home - 1965
United Artists 887 - Everytime / That Goes To Show You – 1965
United Artists 951 - Looking For You / More Than A Miracle – 1965
United Artists 995 - I'll Take Good Care Of You / Prove It To Me – 1966
United Artists 50058 - My Baby / Keep On Smilin' - 1966 (Unreleased)
Veep 1232 - It's Been Such A Long Time / Thinkin' – 1966
Veep 1234 - My Baby / Keep On Smiling – 1966
Veep 1252 - All About Love / The Truth Hurts – 1967
Verve 10596 - I Can Hear My Baby Crying / Stop And Think – 1968
Verve 10624 - We Can Find That Love / Can You Top This – 1968
Verve 10642 - Happy Landing / Take Me – 1969
Verve 10650 - Sad Song / Get It While You Can – 1970
GSF6874 - Stop And Check Yourself / Another Time Another Place – 1972
GSF 6887 - I'll Keep Loving On / Somebody Someplace – 1972

Garnet Mimms & The Enchanters (members Garnet Mimms, Sam Bell, Charles Boyer and Zola Pearnell)

United Artists 0109 - Cry Baby / Don't Change Your Heart - 1973 (Silver Spotlight Series)
Collectables Col 060217 - Cry Baby / A Quiet Place - ?
Stardust 1136 - Cry Baby / A Quiet Place - ? (gold marble vinyl)

Garnet Mimms & The Truckin' Company (Members Garnet Mimms,

Arista 0239 - What It Is (Part 1) / What It Is (Part 2) – 1977
Arists 0289 - Johnny Porter / Tail Snatcher – 1977
Arista 0332 - Right Here In The Palm Of My Hand / Tail Snatcher - 1978

The Miracles

The Five Chimes (Members In 1954 William "Smokey" Robinson, Clarence "Humble Dawson, Pete "Pee Wee" Moore, Ronnie "Whitey" White (Who Replaced A Departed Donald Woker) And James "Rat" Grice)

The Matadors (Members William "Smokey" Robinson, Warren "Pete" Moore, Ronnie White, Bobby Rogers And His Brother Emerson Rogers)

? - Adios, My Desert Love / ? - 1955 (Acetate) An Acappella Cover Demo Of Nolan Strong & The Diablos Song. This Demo Actually Ended Up On A Rare Late 1960's Lp Entitled "Roadhouse Presents The Great Unreleased Group Sounds" The Track Was Billed As Being By Smokey And Group To Avoid Legal Complications.

The Matadors In 1956 Emerson Rogers Joined The Army So The Group Drafted Someone They Knew The Service Could Not Touch, Emerson's Sister Claudette Rogers.

The Miracles

End 1016 - Got A Job / My Mama Done Told Me - 1958
End 1029 - Money / I Cry - 1958 (Mostly Grey White Label, No Mention Of Roulette Records - Scarcer Copy)
End 1029 - Money / I Cry - 1958 (Multi-Coloured Label With "A Division Of Roulette Records Inc" On Label)
Chess 1734 - Bad Girl* / I Love Your Baby - 1959 (Blue Label With Vertical Chess Logo) *Co-Written By Berry Gordy And Smokey Robinson.
Motown G1/G2 - Bad Girl / I Love Your Baby - 1959
Motown Tlx-2207 - Bad Girl / I Love Your Baby - 1959

Ron & Bill (Ronnie White And Bill "Smokey Robinson)

Tamla 54025 - It / Don't Say Bye-Bye - 1959
Argo 5350 - It / Don't Say Bye-Bye - 1959

The Miracles

Chess 1768 - I Need A Change / All I Want (Is You) - 1960
Tamla 54028 - The Feeling Is So Fine / You Can Depend On Me* - 1960 *Alternate Take On Flip Side -- Matrix Number Followed By "A" In Trail Off Wax.
Tamla 54028 - The Feeling Is So Fine / You Can Depend On Me - 1960 (More Common Version)
Tamla 54028 - Way Over There* / Depend On Me - 1960 *No Strings On "A" Side -- Scarcer Version.
Tamla 54028 - Way Over There* / Depend On Me - 1960 *With Over Dubbed Strings On "A" Side.

The Miracles Featuring Bill "Smokey" Robinson

Tamla 54034 - Shop Around / Who's Lovin' You - 1960 Original Take, Withdrawn Shortly After Release. In Trail Off Wax Is H555 18a. -- Scarce.
Tamla 54034 - Shop Around / Who's Lovin' You - 1960 Hit Take. In Trail Off Wax Is L-1 -- Horizontal Lines Label -- Scarcer.
Tamla 54034 - Shop Around* / Who's Lovin You - 1960 Hit Take. In Trail Off Wax Is L-1 -- Globe Label -- More Comon. *Marvin Gaye Plays Drums, Berry Gordy Plays Piano. This Was Motown's First Million Seller.
The Miracles
Tamla 54036 - Ain't It Baby / The Only One I Love - 1961
Tamla 54044 - Mighty Good Lovin' / Broken Hearted - 1961 Both "Stripes" And "Globes" Label Copies Exist. Probably The Last 45 Issued With Old Label Design.
Tamla 54048 - Everybody's Gotta Pay Some Dues / I Can't Believe - 1961
Tamla 54048 - You Gotta Pay Some Dues / I Can't Believe - 1961
Tamla 54053 - What's So Good About Good-By / I've Been Good To You - 1962
Tamla 54059 - I'll Try Something New / You Never Miss A Good Thing - 1962

Marvin Gaye / Supremes / Singin' Sammy Ward / Contours / Marvelettes / Miracles

Promo - Motor Town Special MTS- 1 - Individual Artists - 1962 (Promo issue only from the first

Motown Revue in 1962. It features the artists on tour talking over their latest record to promote the tour. Of interest are the Supremes talking over their minor hit 'Let Me Go The Right Way' on which Diana Ross introduces herself as Diane, her earlier name)

Tamla 54069 - Way Over There / If Your Mother Only Knew - 1962
Tamla 54073 - You've Really Got A Hold On Me* / Happy Landing - 1962 *Can Be Heard In Movies "Nothing But A Man" (1963), "The T.A.M.I. Show" (1964), "The Wanderers" (1979) And "More American Graffiti" (1979). The Beatles Sang The Song In The 1970 Movie "Let It Be".
Tamla 54078 - A Love She Can Count On / I Can Take A Hint - 1963
Tamla 54083 - Mickey's Monkey* / Whatever Makes You Happy - 1963 *Can Be Heard In Movies "Nothing But A Man" (1963), "Mean Streets" (1973) And "Cooley High" (1975).
Chess 1734 - Bad Girl / I Love Your Baby - 1963 (Black Label)

The Marvelettes / Mary Wells / Miracles / Marvin Gaye

Tamla/Motown - Album Excerpts - 1963 (Though From Tamla / Motown, No Label Name Is Shown, Nor Is There A Title. Promo Issue Only)

The Miracles

Tamla 54089 - I Gotta Dance To Keep From Crying / Such Is Love, Such Is Life - 1963
Tamla Ex-009 - The Christmas Song / Christmas Everyday - 1963 (Promo Issue)
Tamla 54092 - (You Can't Let The Boy Overpower) The Man In You / Heartbreak Road - 1964 By The Beginning Of 1964 Claudette, Who Had Married Smokey In 1963, Had Retired From The Group.
Tamla 54098 - I Like It Like That / You're So Fine And Sweet - 1964

Hitsville Usa Dm 097311 - Greetings To The Tamla Motown Appreciation Society - 1964 This American Record Was Limited To 300 Copies For Dispersal Throughout The Various Fan Clubs Within Europe As A Promo For Their First European Tour. Each Act Gives An Individual Greeting Over Its Latest Record. Artists Involved Include The Miracles, Stevie Wonder, Marvin Gaye, The Marvelettes, The Temptations, Martha And The Vandellas, The Contours, Eddie Holland, Kim Weston And The Supremes. The Record Has An Introduction From Publicist Margaret Phelps And Berry Gordy. Please Note This 45 Actually Lists The Miracles As They Were Still Being Called At The Time As Smokey Robinson & The Miracles. Also The Dave Mentioned On Many Of The Greetings Is Dave Godin, Who Ran The Society.

The Miracles

Tamla 54102 - That's What Love Is Made Of / Would I Love You - 1964
Tamla 54109 - Come On Do The Jerk / Baby Don't You Go - 1964
Tamla 54113 - Ooh Baby Baby* / All That's Good - 1965 *Covered By Linda Ronstadt In 1978.
Tamla 54118 - The Tracks Of My Tears / A Fork In The Road - 1965
Tamla 54123 - My Girl Has Gone / Since You Won My Heart - 1965
Tamla 54127 - Going To A-Go-Go / Choosey Beggar - 1965
Jobete Music Company Inc - Beauty Is Only Skin Deep - ? (Unreleased acetate)
Chess 1734 - Bad Girl / I Love Your Baby - 1966 (Blue Label With Chess On Top)
Tamla 54134 - Whole Lot Of Shakin' In My Heart (Since I Met You) / Oh Be My Lover - 1966
Tamla 54140 - Come 'Round Here ------ I'm The One You Need / Save Me - 1966

Motown 2482 - Seasons Greetings From Motown - 1966 (Promo Issue) Various Artists Deliver Very Short "Christmas Greetings" Radio Station Spots. Artists Involved Martha And The Vandellas, The Temptations, The Miracles, Shorty Long, The Velvelettes, The Spinners, The Four Tops, The Elgins And The Supremes.

Topps/Motown 11 - Shop Around - 1967 (Cardboard Record)

Smokey Robinson & The Miracles

Standard Groove 13090 - I Care About Detroit - 1967 (One Sided Promo Issue) Through The Riots Of 1967 ~ 1968 Smokey And The Boys Tried To Promote Love And Unity In The City With This Mellow Disc. Issued To Detroit Radio Stations At The Time Of The Riots. Copies With A Tamla Globe Logo Are Scarcer Than Those Without.
Tamla 54145 - The Love I Saw In You Was Just A Mirage / Come Spy With Me - 1967
Tamla 54152 - More Love* / Swept For You Baby - 1967 *Covered By Kim Carnes In 1980 Went To Number 10 Pop.
Tamla 54159 - I Second That Emotion / You Must Be Love - 1967
Tamla 54162 - If You Can Want / When The Words From Your Heart Get Caught Up In Your Throat - 1968 Tamla In A Box Label, Common
Tamla 54162 - If You Can Want / When The Words From Your Heart Get Caught Up In Your Throat - 1968 Tamla Globe Label, Scarcer.
Tamla 54167 - Yester Love / Much Better Off - 1968
Tamla 54172 - Special Occasion / Give Her Up - 1968
Tamla 54178 - Baby, Baby Don't Cry / Your Mother's Only Daughter - 1968
Tamla 54183 - Here I Go Again / Doggone Right - 1969
Tamla 54184 - Abraham, Martin And John */ Much Better Off - 1969 *Original By Dion.
Tamla 54189 - Point It Out / Darling Dear - 1969
Tamla 54194 - Who's Gonna Take The Blame / I Gotta Thing For You - 1970
Columbia 54199 - Tears Of A Clown / ? - 1970 (Test Pressing)
Tamla 54199 - The Tears Of A Clown / Promise Me - 1970
Tamla 54205 - I Don't Blame You At All / That Girl - 1971
Tamla 54206 - Crazy About The La La La / Oh Baby Baby I Love You - 1971
Tamla 54211 - Satisfaction / Flower Girl - 1971
Tamla 54220 - We've Come Too Far To End It Now / When Sundown Comes - 1972
Tamla 54220 - We've Come Too Far / When Sundowm Comes - 1972 (Some Canadian Copies Have Flip Spelling Error)
Tamla 54225 - I Can't Stand To See You Cry / With Your Love Came - 1972

The Miracles (Members Billy Griffin, Warren "Pete" Moore, Ronnie White And Bobby Rogers)

Tamla 54237 - Don't Let It End (Til You Let It Begin) / Wigs And Lashes - 1973
Tamla 54240 - Give Me Just Another Day / I Wanna Be With You - 1973
Tamla 54248 - Do It Baby / I Wanna Be With You - 1974
Tamla 54256 - Don't Cha Love It / Up Again - 1974
Tamla 54259 - You Are Love / Gemini - 1975
Tamla 54262 - Love Machine (Part 1) / Love Machine (Part 2) - 1975
Tamla 54268 - Night Life / Smog - 1976

The Miracles Featuring Billy Griffin

Columbia As 283 - Sing For The Brotherhood / Sing For The Brotherhood - 1976 (12" Promo Issue) Around This Time The Group Add's Don Griffin Brother Of Billy Griffin To Their Lineup.
Columbia 10464 - Spy For The Brotherhood / The Bird Must Fly Away - 1976
Columbia 10515 - Women (Make The World Go 'Round) / Spy For The Brotherhood - 1977
Columbia 10517 - Women (Make The World Go 'Round) / I Can Touch The Sky - 1977
Columbia 10706 - Mean Machine / The Magic Of Your Eyes (Laura's Eyes) - 1978

In Conversation with Don Mancha

So who was Jack Montgomery ? It's A Question that has been asked again and again in '60s Soul circles. Very little was known about the man when Tim Brown wrote 'The Complete Jack Montgomery' back in 1989 in 'Voices From The Shadows #10, other than the recorded output. There were only four singles released, all on different labels, two of Detroit origin, one New

York, and one Chicago. Until now nothing else has been discovered about the man who made the records.

In fact the answer was there all the time, Jack Montgomery's real name was Marvin Jones, and he's down as the co-writer of both sides of the Scepter single, both sides of the Revue single, and co-producer of the Austons single.

So what incredibly complicated investigative process led me to this conclusion ? Did I don my dirty mac and do a Columbo around the backstreets of Downtown Detroit ? Or run up a huge transatlantic phone bill ? None of these, it was so simple really. I had the pleasure of having Don Mancha (Legendary writer / producer / arranger of Soul records in the late Sixties) as a guest one evening, and I asked Don what he knew of Jack Montgomery. His reply:

"Jack Montgomery ? Well I gave him the name Jack Montgomery for a start."

Whaaaat ! Guess what my next question was !!?

Don's reply ***"He was called Marvin Jones, he came to me as a singer with a good voice and ambitions, he was a draughtsman by trade, a regular guy. My partner at the time was Don Montgomery, so we just changed the name because it sounded better."***

I then asked for a little more information, I'd always assumed that the Austons single was the first. As usual I was wrong.

Don: ***"When he came to me he hadn't recorded anything, so we put him on my label, Barracuda, with a track I wrote, I did the production as well, Empire Productions was me, it's also a name I used when I DJ'ed on the radio."***

The next stage was to move onto the Scepter release, which was of course 'Dearly Beloved / Do You Believe'. How did the tracks end up at Scepter in New York ?

Don: ***"Simple really, Don (Montgomery) and I wanted major label budgets for a couple of songs I'd written, Jack was the guy we wanted to sing them, So I flew out to New York and hooked up with Johnny Terry because of the connections he had in the Music industry in New York (He was a member of The Drifters at one stage). He didn't really have the experience, but he had the connections and the enthusiasm. I went to several labels, RCA I remember, that's where Robert Bateman went when he left Detroit, but they kept me waiting around for about three weeks, and then wouldn't come up with the budget I wanted, then we got in at Scepter through Johnny and recorded three tracks."***

Don actually did the production and arrangement himself even though Johnny Terry's name appears on the labels. This does though totally discount the theory that Terry and Mancha were Mike and Steve.

Don: ***"In fact Steve Mancha was chosen as Clyde's (Wilson) name by Don Davis and me. Steve is not related in anyway, but we decided that the name Steve Mancha sounded real good."***

I also asked Don about the different labels on the Scepter single. The more common issues and the white demos have 'Dearly Beloved' as the title, whereas some issues which are considerably rarer have 'My Dear Beloved' as the title.

Don: ***"I don't know anything about that, the track was registered as 'Dearly Beloved'."*** So that's one mystery I was unable to solve.

That officially ends Don Mancha's involvement with Jack Montgomery. Of course that's not the end of the story. Don had recorded three tracks at Scepter and returned to Detroit to carry on with other projects, leaving Johnny Terry to deal with the finances from the New York end. Apparently Johnny Terry couldn't read or write, but he could certainly add up, especially in his favour. After several acrimonious conversations the partnership was dissolved for want of a better phrase.

Don: ***"My partner, Don Montgomery, was connected in Detroit, if you know what I mean, and he really wanted to whack Johnny Terry, he really did, but I persuaded him not to. Then it turns out that Johnny had absconded with the master tapes to the third track we recorded on Jack in New York."***

This of course turned out to be 'Baby Baby Take A Chance On Me' on Revue 11009. Which also has a rather strange configuration of releases: Demos with the vocal on both sides, the rarer demo with vocal and instrumental, and issues with vocal and instrumental. I played Don the single.

Don: ***"Yeah. That's the third track we cut on Jack in New York. but you won't find my name on it because Johnny (Terry) had taken the masters, but I recognise the drums and piano as one of mine."***

So that does end the Don Mancha involvement in the Jack Montgomery story, and it goes a long way to explaining why there was never a vocal to the other side of 'Baby Baby Take A Chance On Me'.

With regards to the fourth single, 'Beauty Isn't Born' on Auston's 0001, Don has no knowledge of either the company 'Jozelle' of which Austons is a subsidiary, and cannot recall ever coming across anyone called G A Grizzell who is the co-producer with Marvin Jones. It can only be surmised that this single was a last attempt by Jack Montgomery to get a hit. It has to be the last single though because there is no involvement from Don Mancha (Who came up with the name Jack Montgomery) or Johnny Terry (Who disappeared with the master tapes for the third single) unless of course G A Grizzell is a pseudonym for Johnny Terry.

Don's final comment on Jack Montgomery: ***"He passed away several years ago."***

So that really does conclude the Jack Montgomery story.

Jack Montgomery

Barracuda 101- Don't Turn Your Back On Me / Never In A Million Years (Instrumental to 'Never In A Million Years' by The Honey Bees on Garrison 3005)
Scepter 12152 - Dearly Beloved / Do You Believe It
Scepter 12152 - My Dear Beloved / Do You Believe It (Same song just a different title on the label)
Revue 11009 - Baby Baby Take A Chance On Me / Baby Baby Take A Chance On Me (Inst)
Revue 11009 - Baby Baby Take A Chance On Me / Baby Baby Take A Chance On Me (Demo with vocal on both sides. Also exists as a Demo with vocal and Instrumental sides)
Austins 0001 - Beauty Isn't Born / Inst.

Azie Mortimer

Big Top 3041 - Lips / Wrapped Up In A Dream - 1960 (promo issue only - unsure if 45 was released commercially)
Regatta 2002 - Brother Love / Treat Me Like You Love Me - 1961

A. Z. Mortimer

Palette 5097 - When Your Talkin' Love / Mama - What Should I Do? - 1962

Azie Mortimer

Troy 103 - Battle Hymn Of The Republic / Little Soldier – 1963
Troy 104 - Little Playboy / Forever Kind Of Love – 1963
Troy 105 - Untouched By Human Love / Bring Back Your Love – 1963
Troy 106 - Little Old Lady / Cool It - 1963
Swan 4158 - Put Yourself In My Place / Bring Back Your Love - 1963
Epic 9584 - Cry Me A River / Little Boy - 1963
United Artists 826 - The Other Half Of Me / Next Time - 1965
United Artists 838 - (I Get The Feeling) You're Ashamed Of Me / Deeper In My Heart* - 1965 (withdrawn)*also released in 1966 by Sonji Clay on American Music Makers (no #)
United Artists 847 - The Other Half Of Me / (I Get The Feeling) You're Ashamed Of Me - 1965
RCA Victor 47-8985 - Little Miss Everything / The Best Years Of Our Lives - 1966
Number One 7501/2 - Cool It / Haunted -1968
Number One 7503 - Cool It / When I Fall In Love - 1968
Number One 7778 - That's That (Get Off My Back) / Eternally - 1969
Okeh 7336 - You Can't Take It Away* / A One Way Love (Is A Strong Way) - 1969 *also recorded in 1965 by Fred Hughes on Vee-Jay 703.
Okeh 7337 - Prove It / I Don't Care - 1969
Bloomie 101/2 - Telling A Lie / Haunted - ?

Mr Flood's Party

Now (thought to be Mr. Flood's Party)

Embassy 1968 - I Want / Like A Flying Bird - 1967
Cotillion 44005 - Deja Vu / Having A Hard Time - 1968

Mr. Flood's Party (members RM Hyatt, Marc Adam, John Whitman, Dan Conway)

Cotillion 44017 - Deja Vu / Alice Was A Dream - 1969
GM 714 - Compared To What* / Unbreakable Toy - 1971 (also released in Germany on Metronome M25 374) *Gene McDaniels penned this modern day jazz standard for his old friend Les McCann, who along with Eddie Harris had a 1969 hit with it on Atlantic 2694. Roberta Flack also covered "Compared To What" in 1969 on Atlantic 2665

Lp's

Cotillion Sd9003 - Mr. Flood's Party - 1969
Among tracks:- Deja Vu / The Liquid Invasion / Garden Of The Queen / Mind Circus ....

Corbett and Hirsch

Atco Sd 33-361 - Mike Corbett And Jay Hirsch With Hugh McCracken - 1971

Venue Reports - July 2001

The Cellar Bar, Jarvis Heath Hotel, Bewdley, 6th July 2001

A new venture for the original West Midlands Soul Club, and I have to say this is one of the best venues I have ever been in. A very smart, clean, cellar bar, which has just been refurbished from the look of it. Musically nobody knew what to expect until people started to arrive and we saw what attracted them onto the dancefloor. In the end it was a mixture which did the business, a few oldies, a few Seventies, a few R & B, and a few mega rarities, all of which attracted a full dancefloor at varying times. A fairly busy first night as well although it was difficult to say how many were actually in because of all the little rooms and alcoves. Overall a success, and one which makes the next one look even better.

The Corner Café Complex, Scarborough 2nd Anniversary Allnighter 7th July, 2001

I hadn't realised how far North Scarborough was until I realised I was going to have to leave home at 2.30 pm to get there for 8 pm ! Having found the venue I was pleased to say it was another very smart room. Numbers weren't brilliant, but enough attended to make it worthwhile. Music varied, much like Friday night, but he surprising thing to me was how some of the records I expected to be floor fillers didn't attract anyone really, yet some of the Seventies things which I would have said were played out, got the best reaction on the dancefloor. A very enjoyable night though, spent in the company of friends, so what more could you ask for. Thanks again to the guys from York who gave me a lift on the Sunday morning, it saved me about three hours travelling time. Cheers.

The Greatstone Hotel, Stretford, 21st July, 2001.

What a fabulous venue. Another cellar bar with four separate rooms joined by open doorways. Purely by coincidence the line up tonight was that which will be the UK contingent spinning tunes in Nuremberg later in the year. Carl Willingham was the first to go on, and I must admit I was a little disappointed in what he played: A few too many played out tunes (Billy Eckstine and Earl Jackson), too much very early R & B as well. John Mills took over at 11.00 pm, and then we rotated doing half hour sets between John Mills, myself, and John Weston. The dancefloor soon filled up and stayed that way whatever was played. Ross, the promoter was impressed, and has offered the three of us an open invite to return. We happily accepted, so that's one to look out for in the future.

The Beehive, Bradford, 28th July, 2001

Back to Bradford for my second spot there. This is a great venue, very atmospheric, and to quote Derek Pearson, "you're so close to the dancers when you are DJing, you can smell them". Unfortunately a combination of factors, first weeks of the school holidays, Togetherness, and Bishop Auckland both being on, meant that the numbers were the lowest they've had this year. Musically though it was still of the top order. Rarities, obscurities, and quality oldies, all night. Guest DJs for the night were Mick Howard, Ronnie Pedley and me, along with residents Derek Pearson, and my mate Tony Coleby, a strong Lancashire / Yorkshire combination there. So, all I can add now is that I really enjoyed it, as did the others who were there. So why weren't you ? If you can make the first anniversary on October 27th, do it, you won't be disappointed.

Group Line Ups

The Natural 4 (Chris James, Steve Striplin, Del Mos Whitely, Darryl Canady)
The Newcomers (William Summers, Bert Brown, Terry Bartlet, Randy Brown)

The Natural Four

The Natural Four (members Chris James, Al Bowden, Allan Richardson and John January)

Boola Boola 2383 - You Did This For Me / I Thought You Were Mine - 1969
Boola Boola 2383 - You Did This For Me / Why Should We Stop Now - 1969
ABC 11205 - You Did This For Me / Why Should We Stop Now - 1969
ABC 11236 - The Same Thing In Mind / The Situation Needs No Experience - 1969
ABC 11253 - I Thought You Were Mine / Hurt - 1969
ABC 11257 - Stepping On Up / Message From A Black Man - 1970
Boola-Boola 6384 - Why Should We Stop Now / You Did This For Me - 1969
Chess 2119 - Give A Little Love - The Devil Made Me Do It - 1971
Boola Boola 1001 - Twelve Months Of The Year / Hanging Onto A Lie - 1971

The Natural Four (members Chris James, Steve Striplin, Del Mos Whitely and Darryl Canady)

Curtom 1981 - Things Will Be Better Tomorrow / Eddie You Should Know Better - 1972
Curtom 1984 - Eddie You Should Know Better / Try Love Again - 1973
Curtom 1990 - Can This Be Real / Try Love Again - 1973
Curtom 1995 - Love That Really Counts / Love's Society - 1974
Curtom 2000 - You Bring Out The Best Of Me / You Can't Keep Running Away - 1974
Curtom 2000DJ - You Bring Out The Best In Me / You Bring Out The Best In Me (Short Version) - 1974#
Curtom 0101 - Heaven Right Here On Earth / While You're Away - 1975
Curtom 0104 - Love's So Wonderful / What's Happening Here - 1975
Curtom 0114 - It's The Music / It's The Music (Instrumental) – 1976
Curtom 0119 - Free (2:55) / Free (3:08) - 1976 (Promo Issue Only)
Curtom 0119 - Free / Nothing Beats A Failure But A Try - 1976

Northern Soul Is Dead !

I've thought about this for a long time, but more recently the factors involved have altered and swayed the balance. I really do think that 'Northern Soul' is dying, or already dead. The term 'Northern Soul' is commonly accepted to have been originated by Dave Godin when he ran the Soul City Record shop. It was used to describe the type of record that Northerners were buying, as opposed to the type of record that Southerners were buying. No more, no less. Dave had noticed that there was a distinct difference in that the Northerners were buying uptempo, on the fours, Sixties things, whilst the Southerners were buying current releases which tended to be veering towards the just started Funk sound.

Dave Godin then used the term in an article he wrote for Blues & Soul in 1971, called 'The Soul Of The North' about his first visit to The Twisted Wheel in Manchester. That was it, 'Northern Soul' was born. And for the next ten years the term described the music and the scene perfectly. Towards the end of the decade though the term became used with derision by Soul music fans who hated the pop music stompers that were being played under the banner of 'Northern Soul'.......'Theme From Joe 90', 'Hawaii 5-0', 'Under My Thumb', The Sharronettes, the list seems endless these days, but they all filled the floor back in the Seventies and bore as little relationship to Soul as England winning something at football ! It led to two things. An awful lot of 'Northern Soul' fans left the scene, some never to return, and more 'Modern' records began to feature on the playlists of the DJs who cared.

So where are we now ? There is a thriving scene, with music from the Sixties through to the Nineties being played at venues across the country. All well and good you would think.

Well I'm sorry, I don't think all is well and good. In fact, I can see the death of the Northern Soul scene if things continue as they are. I've been to several nights recently where the music has left rather a lot to be desired. I want to hear danceable Soul music when I go out, preferably from the Sixties.

I don't want to hear Modern Soul that is so slow that the dancefloor looks like a field of corn swaying in the wind ! They might be brilliant Soul records that I would really enjoy listening to at home, but they are not records which should be played in a venue with a dancefloor I don't want to hear dance tracks that are more at home in a rave. It's no good people telling me that the vocal is very Soulful when it lasts 30 seconds out of a five minute track. I'm told these are apparently Soulful Garage tracks. That's as may be, but I don't want to listen to this type of record. The only sound I want to hear coming from a garage is one of mechanics fixing cars !

Look how many venues now advertise 'across the board' music policies. How many venues have actually asked what people want. It's all very well saying, if you don't like it, don't go. I would say if you are going to be playing Soulful Garage, don't advertise it as Northern Soul ! The majority of venues do try to keep the balance right though, playing a few Modern things, that are danceable Soul music in amongst a Sixties set, but I've noticed that the trend towards playing shite is increasing.

Crossover is another term that has filtered in on a more regular basis. Sometimes this turns up good records, other times it turns up crap. They are just failed disco records, but I feel the introduction of Crossover signalled the beginning of the rot, and it was a major factor in my own decision to stop playing any Seventies records when I DJ. I'm not the only one who has taken that decision either.

You also have to look at the recent decline in numbers at allnighters. Of all the venues that I attend on a regular basis the only ones that have not suffered are the 100 Club in London, and The Ritz in Manchester. Both of which tend to have a 90% Sixties playlist. All the others have suffered lower attendance's along with their progressive playlists.

There is some hope. There is now a feeling amongst Sixties Soul collectors and DJs that enough is enough, and we must get back to the basic Sixties format. I'm not advocating a return to playing Oldies though, there are still plenty Sixties Newies out there waiting to be played, at Soul nights and Allnighters. I'll give The Dome in Tufnell park as an example here. A playlist that is 95% Sixties, Newies and rarities mixed in with the Oldies, and the attendance's are exceeding that of most allnighters. It's time that promoters realised that it's no good saying they want to take the scene forward, and then play music which is almost unrecognisable as Soul music in the sense of 'Northern Soul'. It's not what is wanted.

So, keep the nightclub and rave sounds off our scene. If people want that fine, let them go to clubs that play that sort of stuff, but keep them away from 'Northern Soul'. These records have nothing to do with 'Northern Soul', and in the majority of cases nothing to do with 'Rare Soul' either. So remember, if you don't like the music being played as 'Northern Soul', complain to the DJ and the promoter, and ask for some 'Northern Soul'

Group Line Ups

The O'Jays (Eddie Levert, Walter Williams, William Powell, Bobby Massey, Bill Isles)
The O'Kaysions (Donnie Weaver, Jim Spidel, Jim Hennant, Ron Turner, Bruce Joyner)
The Ohio Untouchables (Robert Ward, Marshall Jones, Ralph 'Pee Wee'Middlebrook, Leroy 'Sugarfoot' Bonner, Cornelius Johnson)
The Orlons (Rosetta Hightower, Marlena Davis, Steve Caldwell, Shirley Brickley
The Ovations (Louis Williams, Melvin Jones, Nathan 'Pedro' Lewis)

The O'Jays

The Mascots

King 5377 - Story Of My Heart / Do The Wiggle - 1960
King 5435 - Lonely Rain / That's The Way I Feel - 1960

The O'Jays

Daco ? - Miracles / Can't Take It - 1960
Apollo 759 - Miracles / Can't Take It - 1961
Little Star 124 - How Does It Feel / Crack Up Laughing - 1963
Little Star 125 - Dream Girl / Joey St. Vincent - 1963

Jimmy Norman With Vocal Background by The O'Jays

Little Star 126 - Love Is Wonderful / What's The Word Do The Bird- 1963

The O'Jays

Imperial 5942 - How Does It Feel / Crack Up Laughing - 1963
Imperial 5976 - Lonely Drifter / That's Enough - 1963
Imperial 66007 - Stand Tall / The Storm Is Over - 1963
Imperial 66025 - I'll Never Stop Loving You / My Dearest Beloved - 1964
Imperial 66037 - You're On Top / Lovely Dee - 1964
Imperial 66076 - Girl Machine / Oh How You Hurt Me - 1964
Imperial 66102 - Lipstick Traces / Think It Over, Baby - 1965
Imperial 66121 - Whip It On Me Baby / I've Cried My Last Tear - 1965
Imperial 66131 - You're The One (You're The Only One) / Let It All Come Out - 1965
Imperial 66145 - I'll Never Let You Go / It Won't Hurt - 1965
Imperial 66162 - I'll Never Forget You / Pretty Words - 1966
Imperial 66177 - No Time For You / It's A Blowin' Wind - 1966
Imperial 66197 - Friday Night / Stand In For Love - 1966
Imperial 66200 - Lonely Drifter / That's Enough - 1966
Minit 32015 - Working On Your Case / Hold On* - 1967 *also recorded in 19 by The

Soulmasters on Beach 101
Bell 691 - I Dig Your Act / I'll Be Sweeter Tomorrow (Than I Was Today) - 1967
Bell 704 - I'm So Glad I Found You / Look Over Your Shoulder - 1968
Bell 737 - The Choice / Going, Going, Gone - 1968
Bell 749 - I Miss You / Now That I Found You - 1968
Bell 770 - Don't You Know A True Love / That's All Right - 1969
Neptune 12 - One Night Affair / There's Someone (Waiting Back Home) - 1969
Neptune 18 - Branded Bad / You're The Best Thing Since Candy - 1969
Neptune 20 - Christmas Ain't Christmas New Year's Ain't New Year's Without The One You Love / There's Someone Waiting (Back Home) - 1969
Neptune 22 - Deeper (In Love With You) / I've Got The Groove - 1970
Neptune 31 - Looky Looky (Look At Me Girl) / Let Me In Your World - 1970
Neptune 33 - Christmas Ain't Christmas New Year's Ain't New Year's Without The One You Love / Just Can't Get Enough - 1970
Saru 1220 - Shattered Man / La De Da (Mean's I'm Out To Get You) - 1971
Little Star 1401 - Now He's Home / Just To Be With You - 1972
Philadelphia Int'l 3517 - Back Stabbers / Sunshine - 1972
Philadelphia Int'l 3522 - 992 Arguments / Listen To The Clock On The Wall - 1972
Philadelphia Int'l 3524 - Love Train / Who Am I - 1973
Bell 45,378 - Look Over Your Shoulder / Four For The Price Of One - 1973
Trip 3008 - Now He's Home / Shattered Man - 1973
Philadelphia Int'l 3531 - Time To Get Down / Shiftless, Shady, Jealous Kind Of People - 1973
Philadelphia Int'l 3535 - Put Your Hands Together / You Got Your Hooks In Me - 1973
Philadelphia Int'l 3537 - Christmas Ain't Christmas New Year's Ain't New Year's Without The One You Love / Just Can't Get Enough - 1973
Philadelphia Int'l 3544 - For The Love Of Money / People Keep Tellin' Me - 1974
Philadelphia Int'l 3558 - Sunshine (Part 1) / Sunshine (Part 2) - 1974
Astroscope 106 - Wisdom Of A Child / Peace - 1974
Astroscope 110 - Don't You Know A True Love (When You See Her) / Peace - 1974
Test Pressing Mx No. As 112 - Peace / Peace - 1974 (45rpm test pressing has no logo - the label is all white with typewriter / block style printing on a white background - it shows the title, record number: MX AS #112, artist, O Jay's - Peace. Both sides have the same designation no record company name is listed)
All Platinum 112 - Peace / Peace Part 2 - 1974
Philadelphia Int'l 3565 - Give The People What They Want / What Am I Waiting For - 1975
Philadelphia Int'l 3573 - Let Me Make Love To You / Survival - 1975
Philadelphia Int'l 3577 - I Love Music (Part 1) / I Love Music (Part 2) - 1975
Philadelphia Int'l Asz 168 - I Love Music (Special Disco Version - Mono) (6:51) / I Love Music (Special Disco Version - Stereo) (6:51) - 1975 (7" 33 1/3rpm Pre 12" Release)
Philadelphia Int'l 3581 - Christmas Ain't Christmas New Year's Ain't New Year's Without The One You Love / Just Can't Get Enough - 1975
Philadelphia Int'l 3587 - Livin' For The Weekend / Stairway To Heaven - 1976
Philadelphia Int'l 3596 - Family Reunion / Unity - 1976
Philadelphia Int'l 3601 - Message In Our Music / She's Only A Woman - 1976
Philadelphia Int'l 3610 - Darlin' Darlin' Baby (Sweet, Tender, Love) / A Prayer - 1976
Philadelphia Int'l 3631 - Work On Me / Let's Spend Some Time Together - 1977

The Philadelphia International All Stars (Lou Rawls, Billy Paul, Teddy Pendergrass, The O'Jays, Archie Bell and Dee Dee Sharpe) **/ MFSB**

Philadelphia Int'l 3636 - Let's Clean Up The Ghetto / Let's Clean Up The Ghetto* - 1977 *flip by MFSB.

The O'Jays

Philadelphia Int'l 3642 - Use Ta Be My Girl / This Time Baby - 1978
Philadelphia Int'l 3652 - Brandy / Take Me To The Stars - 1978
Philadelphia Int'l 3666 - Cry Together / Strokety Stroke - 1978

Philadelphia Int'l 3707 - Sing A Happy Song / One In A Million (Girl) - 1979
Philadelphia Int'l 3726 - I Want You Here With Me / Get On Out And Party - 1979
Philadelphia Int'l 3727 - Forever Mine / Get On Out And Party - 1979
TSOP 3771 - Christmas Ain't Christmas New Year's Ain't New Year's Without The One You Love / Just Can't
get Enough - 1980
TSOP 4790 - Girl, Don't Let It Get You Down / You're The Girl Of My Dreams - 1980
TSOP 4791 - Once Is Not Enough / To Prove I Love You - 1980
Philadelphia Int'l 02096 - Forever Mine / Girl, Don't Let It Get You Down - 1981
TSOP 70050 - You Won't Fall / You'll Never Know (All There Is To Know ' Bout Love) - 1981

Elvis Costello / Eddie Money / Jaco Pastorius / Larry Gatlin & The Gatlin Brothers / The O'Jays / Paul Robeson / Glenn Gould

Music '80's PV 15786 - (I Don't Want To Go To) Chelsea / Running Back / Donna Lee / I Still Don't Love You Anymore / Survival / Every Time I Feel The Spirit / Hindemith: Sonata Fos Bass Tuba And Piano: Ii Allegro Assai - 1981 (45rpm)

The O'Jays

Philadelphia Int'l 02834 - Don't Walk Away Mad / I Just Want To Satisfy - 1982
Philadelphia Int'l 02982 - One By One / My Favorite Person - 1982
Philadelphia Int'l 03009 - Out In The Real World / Your Body's Here With Me - 1982
Philadelphia Int'l 03892 - A Letter To My Friends / I Can't Stand The Pain - 1983
Philadelphia Int'l 04069 - Put Our Heads Together / Nice And Easy - 1983
Philadelphia Int'l 4z9 04073 - Put Our Heads Together (Vocal) (7:00) / Put Our Heads Together (Instrumental) (5:14) -1983 (12" 33-1/3rpm Release)
Philadelphia Int'l 04437 - I Really Need You Now / Extraordinary Girl - 1984
Philadelphia Int'l 04535 - Let Me Show You (How Much I Really Love You) / Love You Direct - 1984
Philadelphia Int'l 50013 - Just Another Lonely Night / What Good Are These Arms Of Mine - 1985
Philadelphia Int'l 50021 - What A Woman / I Love America - 1985
Philadelphia Int'l 50067 - Don't Take Your Love Away / I Just Want Somebody To Love Me - 1987
Philadelphia Int'l 50104 - Let Me Touch You / Undercover Lover - 1987
Philadelphia Int'l 50122 - I Just Want Someone To Love Me / Lovin' You - 1988
EMI Spro O4305/20 - Have You Had Your Love Today (Two Versions) / Lovin' You - 1989 (12" Promo Issue Only)
EMI 50180 - Have You Had Your Love Today / The Pot Can't Call The Kettle Black - 1989
EMI 50212 - Out Of My Mind (Radio Mix) / Out Of My Mind (Soul 2 Mix) - 1989
EMI 4853/4 - Merry Christmas Baby / The Christmas Song - 1989 (12" Promo Issue Only)
EMI 50230 - Serious Hold On Me / The Track - 1990
Manhattan ? - 1989 ~ 1990
EMI S7-17491 - Somebody Else Will / Decisions - 1993
EMI S7-18914 - Have Yourself A Merry Little Christmas / I Can Hardly Wait ' Til Christmas - 1995

O'Kaysions

The Kays (members Wayne Pittman, Steve Watson, Donne Weaver, Gerald Toler, and Jimmy Hinnant)

JCP 1007 - Hey Girl / Shout - 1964

The O'Kaysions (members Donnie Weaver, Steve Watson, Jimmy Hinnant, Eddie Dement, Wayne Pittman and Gerald Toler)

North State 1001 - Girl Watcher / Deal Me In - 1968 (one thousand copies were issued with a picture sleeve)
ABC 11094 - Girl Watcher / Deal Me In - 1968
Sparton 1676 - Girl Watcher / Deal Me In - 1968 (Canadian release)
ABC 11153 - Love Machine / Dedicated To The One I Love - 1968
ABC 11207 - Colors / Twenty Four Hours From Tulsa - 1969
Cotillion 44089 - Watch Out Girl / Happiness - 1970
Cotillion 44134 - Life And Things / Travelin' Life - 1971

The O'Kaysions

Roulette 130 - Girl Watcher / Deal Me In - 1973

The O'Kaysions / Louis Armstrong

Goldies 45 2423 - Girl Watcher / What A Wonderful World* - 1973 *flip by Louis Armstrong.

The O'Kaysions

I-Katcher 821 - Girl Watcher / Boy Watcher /// Freedom Lady - 1982

The O'Kaysions / The Esquires

Collectables Col 031297 - Girl Watcher / Get On Up* - ? *Flip by The Esquires.

Ep's

ABC 664 - Girl Watcher - 1968 Tracks: How Are You Fixed For Love? / Dedicated To The One I Love / The Soul Clap /// Little Miss Flirt / Sunday Will Never Be The Same / My Baby's Love.

The Olympics

The Ward Brothers (family group comprising of Walter Ward, His Father and three uncles) early 1950's gospel group.

The West Coast Gospel Singers (members Walter Ward, Eddie Lewis, James Lloyd and Jimmy Ward)

The Challengers (members Walter Ward, Eddie Lewis, Marcus Banks, Freddie Lewis and Nathan ?) 1954 group line-up.

The Challengers (members Walter Ward, Eddie Lewis, Marcus Banks, Charles Fizer and Walter Hammond)

Melatone 1002 - I Can Tell / The Mambo Beat - 1958

The Olympics (members Walter Ward (born 28-August-1940 in Jackson, Mississippi --- died after a long illness on 11-December-2006 in Northridge, Los Angeles), Eddie Lewis, Charles Fizer, and Walter Hammond (younger brother of Clay Hammond). Melvin King replaced Charles Fizer in 1958 and remained in group as a replacement Walter Hammond when Charles Fizer returned in 1959. Charles Fizer (born 3-June-1940 --- died 14-August-1965 - cause: was shot during the Watts rioting) replaced by Julius "Mack Starr" McMichael, former member of The Paragons. Melvin King left in 1966. Kenny Sinclair former member of The Six Teens joined in 1970)

Demon 1508 - Western Movies / Well! - 1958

Demon 1512 - (I Wanna) Dance With The Teacher / Ev'rybody Needs Love – 1958
Demon 1514 - Chicken / Your Love – 1959
Arvee 562 - Private Eye / (Baby) Hully Gully – 1959
Arvee 595 - Big Boy Pete* / The Slop -1960 *originally recorded in 1959 by Don & Dewey on Speciality 659.
Arvee 5006 - Shimmy Like Kate / Workin' Hard – 1960
Arvee 5020 - Dance By The Light Of The Moon / Dodge City – 1960

The Olympics / Cappy Lewis

Arvee 5023 - Little Pedro / Bull Fight* - 1961 *Flip By Cappy Lewis.

The Olympics

Arvee 5031 - Stay Where You Are / Dooley – 1961
Titan 1718 - Cool Short / The Chicken – 1961

Jody Reynolds / The Olympics

Titan 1801 - Endless Sleep / Western Movies* - 1961 *flip by The Olympics. (some copies issued with picture sleeve)

The Olympics

Arvee 5044 - The Stomp / Mash Them Taters – 1961
Arvee 5051 - Everybody Likes To Cha Cha Cha / Twist – 1962
Arvee 5056 - Baby, Its Hot / The Scotch – 1962
Arvee 5073 - What'd I Say Part 1 / What'd I Say Part 2 – 1963

Jody Reynolds / The Olympics

Liberty 54514 - Endless Sleep / Western Movies* - 1963 *Flip By The Olympics.

The Olympics

Tri Disc 105 - Return Of Big Boy Pete / Return Of The Watusi – 1962
Tri Disc 106 - The Bounce / Fireworks - 1963
Tri Disc 107 - Dancin' Holiday / Do The Slauson Shuffle – 1963
Tri Disc 110 - Bounce Again / A New Dancin' Partner – 1963
Tri Disc 112 - Broken Hip / So Goodbye – 1963
Zee 103 - Western Movies / Well - 1963
Duo Disc 104 - The Boogler (Part 1) / The Boogler (Part 2) -1964
Duo Disc 105 - Return Of Big Boy Pete / Return Of The Watusi – 1964
Arvee 6501 - Stay Where You Are / Big Boy Pete '65 – 1965
Loma 2010 - Rainin' In My Heart / I'm Comin' Home – 1965
Loma 2013 - Good Lovin'* / Olympic Shuffle (Instrumental) - 1965 *recorded 17-February-1965. (the instrumental tracks to The Blossoms' "Latin Boy Shuffle
Loma 2017 - Baby I'm Yours / No More Will I Cry – 1965
Mirwood 5504 - Secret Agents / We Go Together (Pretty Baby) – 1966
Mirwood 5513 - Secret Agents / Mine Exclusively – 1966
Mirwood 5523 - Baby, Do The Philly Dog / Western Movies - 1966
Mirwood - Baby Do The Philly Dog (Instrumental) (2:25) - 1966 (although unissued on vinyl this was released in the U. K. as by The Fred Smith Orchestra on a 2002 Goldmine Cd "Allnighter 4" GSCD 159)
Mirwood 5525 - The Duck / The Bounce - 1966
Mirwood 5529 - The Same Old Thing / I'll Do A Little Bit More - 1967
Mirwood 5533 - (Baby) Hully Gully / Big Boy Pete – 1967

The Olympics / The Olmpics

Parkway 6003 - Good Things / Lookin' For Love - 1967 (D. J. copies have been found with the group name mis-spelled on flip side)

The Olympics

Parkway 6003 - Good Things / Lookin' For Love – 1967
Jubilee 5674 - The Cartoon Song / Things That Made Me Laugh – 1969

The Olympics (members Walter Ward, Kenny Sinclair (former member of The Bagdads), Mack Starr,)

Warner Brothers 7369 - Please, Please, Please / Girl, You're My Kind Of People – 1970

The Olympics

Songsmith 1 - There Ain't No Way / Three Billion People – 1971
Eric 135 - Big Boy Pete / Dance By The Light Of The Moon – 1973

The Olympics (members Walter Ward, Kenny Sinclair, Mack Starr, ...)

Pride 1024 - The Apartment / Worm In Your Wheatgerm – 1973
MGM 14505 - The Apartment / Worm In Your Wheatgerm – 1973

The Olympics

Mac Winn 102 - I Feel Your Love (Coming On) / Papa Will - ?
Crestview 20010 - The Duck / The Bounce - ?
Lost-Nite 311 - Big Boy Pete / Mine Exclusively - ?
Collectables Col 030407 - Western Movies / Endless Sleep - ?

The Olympics / Jody Reynolds

Era 026 - The Bounce / Endless Sleep* - ? *flip by Jody Reynolds.

Venue Reports August 2001

The Riverbank Hotel, Cardiff, 4th August, 2001

Another nightmare journey courtesy of the railways meant I didn't arrive until 9.45 pm when I should have been there before 8.00 pm. Ah well, I was glad I did get there. What a fabulous venue this is, and underground cellar that is long and narrow with alcoves for the tables and a low ceiling. Attendance was down, but it's that summer holiday time again. So what, we all had a great time, the music from all the DJs was spot on. Special mention must go to Nigel Shaw who did a spot at short notice (and then gave me a lift home in he morning). Musically it varied from Rarities, through R & B, Newies, Oldies, Midtempo, but very little Seventies which is how I like it. Well worth a return visit.

Nantwich Civic Hall, 25th August, 2001

The first allnighter held here promoted by Geoff Richardson. And it was a good one. The venue itself is superb, a good, big dancefloor, slightly raised area for seating and a separate area for record dealers. Music policy is under the control of Roger Banks, so it was a good line up that had a bit of something for everyone. Standout spot of the night though was by Chris Penn. My only complaint was that Rob Smith and Brian Rae had been scheduled to do the last two spots, which meant that the niter finished with two complete hours of oldies. Considering that The Ritz was on in Manchester the next day, a very creditable 200 Souls turned up. The next one is scheduled for the end of October, and there will even be a Modern room at that one.

The Black Horse, Wolverhampton, 31st August, 2001.

An East Midlands special with John Day, Ady Cope, Andy Murfin and others DJing. Numbers were good enough to make this a very enjoyable night, with some good music from all the DJs. Rarities to cheapies and R & B all went across the decks, and it just goes to prove that Sixties Soul is still strong. As a venue, The Black Horse is up there with the best and as long as guests of this quality keep on being booked the venue can only go from strength to strength

Group Line Ups

The Parliaments (George Clinton, Grady Thomas, Calvin Simon, Clarence 'Fuzzy' Haskins, Raymond Davis)
The Peoples Choice (Frankie Brunson, Roger Andrews, Dave Thompson, Leon Lee)
The Poets (Ronnie Lewis, Melvin Bradford, Paul Fulton, Johnny James)
The Poppies (Dorothy Moore, Rosemary Taylor, Pet McCune)
The Precisions (Bobby Brooks, Dennis Gilmore, Michael Morgan, Billy Prince, Arthur Ashford)

Eddie Parker

Eddie Parker (Born in Saginay)

Awake 502 - I'm Gone / Crying Clown - 1966
Ashford 1 - Love You Baby / Instrumental - 1968
Triple B 0001 - I Need A True Love / Crying Clown - 1970
Jay Walking 018 - Can't You See (What You're Doing To Me) / Do The Choo Choo -1971
Prodigal 903 - Body Chains / Instrumental - ?
Prodigal 0617 - Body Chains / Body Chains (Instrumental) - 1975
Miko 803 - But If You Must Go / I Need A True Love - ?
RJ 1 - She / Dreams - 1980

Eddie Parker & The Sunlovers

Aliza 48 - You'll Never Make The Grade / This Love Of Ours - ?

Eddie Parker and Soft Touch

Prodigal 618 - After You Give Your All, What Is There / Say That You Love Me Boy - 1975

Dean Parrish

Dean Parrish (Born 1942 In Brooklyn, New York To Italian Parents)

Warner Bros. 5436 - Come On Down (To The World's Fair) / The Pavillion - 1964
Musicor 1099 - Bricks, Broken Bottles And Sticks / I'm Over Eighteen - 1965
Boom 60012 - Tell Her / Fall On Me - 1966
Boom 60016 - Determination / Turn On Your Lovelight- 1966
Boom 60038 - Skate (Part 1) / Skate (Part 2) - ?
Laurie 3418 - I'm On My Way / Watch Out - 1967

Steeplechase (members Dean Parrish (lead vocals and guitar), Joey Forgione (died October-2003) (drums and backing vocals) a former member of The Soul Survivors on Crimson, Bobby Spinella (keyboards and backing vocals) a former member of The Critters on Musicor, Prancer and Kapp, Tony Radicello (now known as Tony Alexander) (twelve string guitar, organ and backing vocals - former member of The Soul Survivors Band), Kim King (guitar), Paul Fleisher (horn) and Eddie Kramer (piano and vocals))

Polydor 14030 - Lady Bright / Never Coming Back – 1970

Bobby Patterson

The Royal Rockers (members Bobby Patterson, ...) mid 1950's band formed by Bobby Patterson. The group cut a 45 for Liberty but it was never issued.

Robert Patterson And His Combo

Future 2202 - Walkin' The Floor Over You / Beautiful Brown Eyes - 1963
Future 45-2204 - Tell Me How / Dear Debbie - 1963

Bobby Patterson (born 13-March-1944 in Dallas, Texas)

Abnak 112 - You Just Got To Understand / Till You Give In - 1966
Abnak 117 - You've Just Got To Understand / ? - 1966
Jetstar 107 - If I Didn't Have You* / What's Your Problem Baby - 1966 *also recorded in 196? by The Magics on R. F. A. 100
Jetstar 108 - Till You Give In / Long Ago – 1967

Bobby Patterson and The Mustangs (members Bobby Patterson (vocals), Andrew Jones (guitar), Michael Fugett (bass), Timothy McNeely (keyboards and trombone), Bobby Simpson (saxophone), Bill Thompson (trumpet) and Ronald Brewster (drums))

Jetstar 109 - Let Them Talk / Soul Is Our Music - 1967 (promo issues came in coloured vinyl)
Jetstar 110 - I'm Leroy - I'll Take Her / Sock Some Lovin' At Me - 1968 (promo issues came in coloured vinyl)
Jetstar 111 - Broadway Ain't Funky No More / I Met My Match - 1968 (promo issues came in coloured vinyl)
Jetstar 112 - The Good Ol' Days / Don't Be So Mean – 1968

Bobby Patterson

Jetstar 113 - Sweet Taste Of Love / Busy, Busy Bee - 1968 (promo issues came in yellow vinyl)
Jetstar 114 - T. C. B. Or T. Y. A. / What A Wonderful Night For Love – 1969
Jetstar 115 - My Thing Is Your Thing (Come Get It) / Keeping It In The Family - 1969 (promo copies came in yellow vinyl)

Jetstar 116 - My Baby's Coming Back To Me / What A Wonderful Night For Love - 1969 (promo issued came in orange vinyl)
Jetstar 117 - My Baby's Coming Back To Me / Guess Who – 1969
Jetstar 118 - Trial Of Mary Maguire / The Knockout Power Of Love – 1970
Jetstar 119 - If A Man Ever Loved A Woman (Baby I Love You) / You Taught Me How To Love – 1970
Jetstar 121 - I'm In Love With You* / Married Lady - 1970 *also recorded in 1985 by The Entertainers on HMC 3991.
Paula 352 - Right On Jody / If You Took A Survey – 1971
Paula 362 - She Don't Have To See You (To See Right Through You) / How Do You Spell Love (M. O. N. E. Y.) - 1972
Paula 379 - It Takes Two To Do Wrong / Take Time To Know The Truth – 1973
Paula 386 - I Get My Groove From You / What Goes Around, Comes Around – 1973
Paula 388 - If Love Can't Do It (It Can't Be Done) / I'm In The Wrong – 1973
Granite 536 - If He Hadn't Slipped And Got Caught / Same – 1976
Granite 536 - If He Hadn't Slipped And Got Caught / I Got To Get Over It – 1976
All Platinum 2371 - Right Place, Wrong Time / I'll Take Care Of You – 1977
All Platinum 2371 - Right Place, Wrong Time / I Got A Suspicion – 1977
Paula 458 - How Do You Spell Love / Recipe For Peace - 198?
Proud 100 - I Can Help You Get Even With Him / I Got To Get Over - ?

Bobby Story (Bobby Patterson)

Proud 102 - Right Place, Wrong Time / I Got A Suspicion - 1982

Bobby Patterson

Paula 458 - How Do You Spell Love / Recipe For Peace - 1985
Malaco 1210 - Groove Me / Groove Me Some Mo - 1983 12" Single

Unissued on Vinyl

If I Didn't Know Better - appeared in the U. K. on the 1991 Kent Cd "Bobby Patterson - Taking Care Of Business" CDKEND 098
Who Wants To Fall In Love - appeared in the U. K. on the 1991 Kent Cd "Bobby Patterson - Taking Care Of Business" CDKEND 098.

Patti & The Emblems

Patti & The Emblems (Members Pat Russell (died 1998), Eddie Watts, Vance Walker (died 1-February-2008 --- cause: ?) and Alex Wildes)

Herald 590 - Mixed-Up, Shook-Up, Girl / Ordinary Guy - 1964
Herald 593 - The Sound Of Music Makes Me Want To Dance / You Took Advantage Of A Good Thing - 1964
Herald 595 - And We Danced / You Can't Get Away From Me - 1964
Sphere Sound ? - Mixed-Up, Shook-Up, Girl / Ordinary Guy - 1964
Congress 263 - Easy Come, Easy Go / It's The Little Things - 1966
Kapp 791 - Let Him Go Little Heart / Try It, You Won't Forget It - 1966
Kapp 850 - Please Don't Ever Leave Me / All My Tomorrows Are Gone - 1967
Kapp 870 - I'll Cry Later / One Man Woman - 1967
Kapp - Love Will Come - 1968 (recorded 1-February-1968 this unissued track was released in the U. K. on a 1999 Kent Cd "Ben-Lee's Philadelphia Story" CDKEND 164 and again released in the U. K. on a 2000 Goldmine Cd "The Northern Soul Of Philadelphia" GSCD127)
Kapp - He Said, She Said - (this unissued track at the time was released in the U. K. on a 1999 Kent Cd "Ben-Lee's Philadelphia Story" CDKEND 164)

Kapp 897 - I'm Gonna Love You A Long, Long Time / My Heart's So Full Of You - 1968

Freda Payne

Freda Payne (born Freda Charcilia Payne on 19-September-1945 in Detroit, Michigan)

ABC - Paramount 10366 - Slightly Out Of Tune (Desafinado) / He Who Laughs Last - 1962
ABC - Paramount 10437 - Pretty Baby / Grin And Bear It - 1963
Impulse! 221 - It's Time / Sweet September - 1963
MGM 13509 - You've Lost That Lovin' Feelin' / Sad Sad September - 1966
Invictus 9073 - The Unhooked Generation / Easiest Way To Fall - 1969
Invictus 9075 - Band Of Gold / Easiest Way To Fall - 1970
Invictus 9080 - Deeper And Deeper / The Unhooked Generation - 1970
Invictus 9085 - Cherish What Is Dear To You (While It Is Near To You) / They Don't Owe Me A Thing - 1971
Invictus 9092 - Bring The Boys Home */ I Shall Not Be Moved** - 1971 *uncredited male vocals provided by Steve Mancha. **covered by The Barrino Brothers in 1972 on Invictus 9084 and in 1971 on Invictus 9104.
Invictus 9100 - You Brought The Joy / Suddenly It's Yesterday - 1971
Invictus 9109 - I'm Not Getting Any Better / The Road We Did'nt Take - 1972
Invictus 9128 - He's In My Life* / Through The Memory Of My Mind - 1972 *previously issued in 1970 by The Glass House on Invictus 9076.
Invictus 1255 - Two Wrongs Don't Make A Right / We've Gotta Find A Way Back To Love - 1973
Invictus 1257 - For No Reason / Mother Misery's Favorite Child - 1973
ABC Dunhill 15018 - It's Yours To Have / Run For Life - 1974
ABC 12079 - Shadows On The Wall / I Get Carried Away - 1975
ABC 12139 - Lost In Love / You - 1975
Capitol 4383 - I Can't Live On A Memory / I Get High (On Your Memory) - 1976
Capitol 4431 - Baby, You've Got What It Takes / Bring Back The Joy - 1977
Capitol 4494 - Love Magnet / Loving You Means So Much To Me - 1977
Capitol 4537 - Feed Me Your Love / Stares And Whispers - 1978
Capitol 4631 - Happy Days Are Here Again-Happy Music (Dance The Night Away) / Falling In Love - 1978
Capitol Spro-8922/3 - Happy Days Are Here Again-Happy Music (5:52) / I'll Do Anything For You (5:32) - 1978 (12" Promo)
Capitol 8509 - I'll Do Anything For You (7:40) / (Instrumental) - 1978 (12" Release)
Capitol 4695 - I'll Do Anything For You (Part 1) / I'll Do Anything For You (Part 2) - 1979
Capitol 4775 - Red Hot / Longest Night - 1979
Capitol Spro-9219 - Red Hot (7:01) / Red Hot (7:01) - 1979 (12" Promo Issue)
Capitol 4805 - Can't Wait / Longest Night - 1979
Sutra 009 - In Motion (5:35) / (Instrumental) - 1982 (12" Release)
Sutra 117 - In Motion / (Instrumental) - 1982

Scherrie Payne

Airwave Aw7-94979 - I'm Not In Love, Girl, You're In Love (Long Version) / I'm Not In Love, Girl, You're In Love (Short Version) - 1982 (background vocals by Mary Wilson, Edmund Sylvers and Freda Payne)
Airwave Aw12-94979 - Girl, You're In Love / I'm Not In Love (Mix-X-X-Tend Version) (9:47) / I'm Not In Love / Girl, You're In Love (7:47) - 1982 (background vocals by Mary Wilson, Edmund Sylvers and Freda Payne)

Freda Payne / The 8th Day

Ripete R45-144 - Band Of Gold / She's Not Just Another Woman* - **?** *flip by The 8th Day.

Freda Payne

Collectables Col 3328 - Band Of Gold / Bring The Boys Home - ?

Freda Payne / Caldera

Capitol 87 - Love Magnet (6:23) / Sky Islands (6:17)* - ? *Flip By Caldera

Ann Peebles

The Peebles Choir (family gospel group Ann Peebles sang in from age eight)

Big Lucky Carter (born Levester Carter in Wier, Mississippi in 1920, died 24-December-2002)

M. O. C. 670 - Stop Arguing Over Me* / Miss Betty Green - 1969 *Speech By Ann Peebles

Ann Peebles (born on 27-April-1947 in East St. Louis)

Hi 2157 - Walk Away / I Can't Let You Go - 1969
Hi 2165 - Give Me Some Credit / Solid Foundation - 1969
Hi 2173 - Generation Gap (Between Us) / I'll Get Along - 1970
Hi 2178 - Part Time Love / I Still Love You - 1970
Hi 2186 - I Pity The Fool / Heartaches, Heartaches - 1971
Hi 2198 - Slipped, Tripped And Fell In Love / 99 Lbs - 1971
Hi 2205 - Breaking Up Somebody's Home / Trouble, Heartaches And Sadness - 1972
Hi 2219 - Somebody's On Your Case / I've Been There Before - 1972
Hi 2232 - I'm Gonna Tear Your Playhouse Down / One Way Street - 1973
Hi 2248 - I Can't Stand The Rain / I've Been There Before - 1973
Hi 2265 - (You Keep Me) Hangin' On / Heartaches, Heartaches - 1974
Hi 2271 - A Love Vibration / Do I Need You - 1974
Hi 2278 - Until You Came Into My Life / Put Yourself In My Place - 1974
Hi 2284 - Beware / You've Got To Feed The Fire - 1975
Hi 2294 - Come To Mama / I'm Leaving You - 1975
Hi 2302 - Dr. Love Power / I Still Love You - 1976
Hi 2309 - I Needed Somebody / I Don't Lend My Man - 1976
Hi 2320 - Fill This World With Love / It Was Jealousy - 1976
Hi 77502 - If This Is Heaven / When I'm In Your Arms - 1977
Hi 78509 - Old Man With Young Ideas / A Good Day For Lovin' - 1978
Hi 78518 - I Didn't Take Your Man / Being Here With You - 1978
Hi 78519 - I Didn't Take Your Man (Disco Mix) (6:30) / Being Here With You (2:30) - 1978 (12" Release)
Hi 79528 - If You Got The Time (I've Got The Love) / Let Your Lovelight Shine - 1979
Hi 80533 - Heartaches / I'd Rather Leave While I'm In Love - 1980
Hi 81534 - Mon Belle Amour / Waiting - 1981 (With Don Bryant)

The Pentagons

The Shields (members Kenneth Goodloe (died 4-August-1991 --- cause: heart attack), Ted Goodloe, Joe C. Jones, Carl McGinnis (born 13-August-1931 - died ? - June-1985), Bill James and Otis "Odie" Munson)

Fleet Int'l ? - You'll Be Coming Home Soon / ? – 1958

The Pentagons (members Kenneth Goodloe, Ted Goodloe, Joe Jones, Carl McGinnis, Bill James and Otis "Odie" Munson)

Speciality 644 - It's Spring Again / Silly Dilly - 1958

The Shields (members Kenneth Goodloe, Ted Goodloe, Joe Jones, Carl McGinnis, Bill James and Otis "Odie" Munson)

Transcontinental 1013 - The Girl Around The Corner / Fare Thee Well My Love - 1960
Falcon 100 - The Girl Around The Corner / Fare Thee Well My Love - 1960

The Pentagons (members Kenneth Goodloe, Ted Goodloe, Joe Jones, Carl McGinnis, Bill James and Otis "Odie" Munson)

Fleet Int'l 100 - To Be Loved (Forever)* / Down At The Beach - 1960
Donna 1337 - To Be Loved (Forever) / Down At The Beach – 1961
Donna 1344 - For A Love That Is Mine / I Like The Way You Look – 1961
Jamie 1201 - I Wonder (If Your Love Will Ever Belong To Me) / She's Mine – 1961
Jamie 1210 - Until Then / I'm In Love - 1962
Caldwell 411 - Until Then / I'm In Love – 1962

The Chesterfields (members Kenneth Goodloe, Ted Goodloe, Joe Jones, Carl McGinnis, Bill James and Otis "Odie" Munson)

Philips 40060 - You Walked Away / A Dream Is But A Dream - 1962

Joel Scott (Joe C. Jones)

Philles 101 - Here I Stand / You're My Only Love – 1962

The Corduroys (members Floyd Smith (lead), Kenneth Goodloe, Ted Goodloe, Johnny Blakely and Juan Johnson)

Hale 100 - Ain't Gonna Let You Go / Forever Yours – 1964

The Pentagons (members Floyd Smith (lead), Kenneth Goodloe, Ted Goodloe, Johnny Blakely and Juan Johnson)

Sutter 100 - Gonna Wait For You / Forever Yours - 1964

Joe Phillips (Joe C. Jones)

Omen 06 - Just Can't Help Thinking About You / ? – 1965
Omen 18 - Without You / ? – 1966

The Themes (members Floyd Smith, Kenneth Goodloe, Ted Goodloe, ...)

Minit 32009 - No Explanation Needed / Bent Out Of Shape - 1966

21st Century (members Floyd Smith, Kenneth Goodloe, Ted Goodloe, ...)

Noel 1 - Shadow Of A Memory* / Coming Right Back - 1968 *also recorded in 1970 by Minnie Jones and The Minuettes on Sugar 100.
Dot 17190 - Shadow Of A Memory / Coming Right Back – 1968
Dot 17256 - Every Little Heartache / Got No Reason - 1969

Soul Patrol (members Floyd Smith, Kenneth Goodloe, Ted Goodloe, ...)

Highland 1077 - Save Your Love / Need Of Love - 1972

The Pentagons / Earl Phillips

Oldies 45 - To Be Loved (Forever) / Oop-De-Oop* - 1964 *flip by Earl Phillips only.

The Pentagons

Original Sound 4560 - To Be Loved (Forever) / ? - ?
Audio Dynamics 153 - About The Girl I Love / Summer's Over - 1967 (could be different group entirely)

The Jones Brothers (members Joe C. Jones and Otis Munson) half brothers.

Seel 10 - That's All Over Baby / Without Your Love - 1969
Bell 831 - That's All Over Baby / Without Your Love - 1969

The Jones Bros. (members Joe C. Jones and Otis Munson)

Silver 100 - Your Good Lovin' / So Much Love - 1970

The Jones Brothers (members Joe C. Jones and Otis Munson)

Avi 102 - Good Old Days / Lucky Lady - 1976

The Jones Brothers Lead Vocal Joey Jones (members Joe C. Jones and Otis Munson)

Avi 122 - No If's And But's About It / Storyteller - 1977
Avi 122 - No If's And But's About It / The Ice Cream Song - 1977

The Pentagons (members Kenneth Goodloe, Ted Goodloe, Joe Jones, Carl McGinnis, Bill James and Otis "Odie" Munson)

Lost Nite 210 - To Be Loved (Forever) / Down At The Beach - ?

The Pentagons / Little Caesar & The Romans

Eric 0138 - To Be Loved (Forever) / Those Oldies But Goodies (Remind Me Of You)* -1970's *flip by Little Caesar & The Romans only.

The Pentagons / The Shields

Collectables Col 030967 - I Wonder (If Your Love Will Ever Belong To Me) / You Cheated* - ? *flip by The Shields.

The Pentagons / The Jaguars

Collectables Col 033237 - To Be Loved (Forever) / The Way You Look Tonight* - ? *flip by The Jaguars.

The Pentagons

Collectables Col 038057 - Until Then / She's Mine - ?

Oscar Perry

Oscar Perry (born 1943 outside of Houston, Texas --- died 4-August-2004 ---- cause?)

Spinner 501 - Just Above A Whisper / Poor Me – 1957
Lee J. ? - True Confessions / ? – 1957
Lee J. 1901 - Now You've Left Again / ? - ?
Lee J. 1902 - I Found True Love / Goodbye My Love – 1958
Lee J. 1903 - Bow Your Head / He Started No Riots (Voice Of Hope) – 1958
Lee J. 113 - A Thousand Years / Your Direction – 1959
Lee J. ? - Big Sam / ? – 1960
Ivory ? - Do The Duck / ? – 1960
Feron (No #) - Face Reality - 1961 (One-Sided Stock Issue)
Feron 103 - Face Reality / The Rest Of My Life – 1961
Sophie ? - Long Red Cadillac / ? – 1962
Sophie 3834 - It Would Be So Nice / Something To Write Home About – 1965
Back Beat 606 - (Treat Me) Like I Was Your Only Child / (Love Me) Like It Was The Last Time – 1968
Back Beat 614 - Fool From The Sticks / (Love Me) Like It Was The Last Time – 1969
Crazy Cajun ? - I'll Take Care Of You / ? – 1972
Mercury 73363 - Can't Mend A Broken Heart (Same Old Thread) / Once In A While – 1973
Jetstream 833 - Has Anybody Seen Her / People Are Talking – 1973
Jetstream ? - Playboy Side Of Town / ? – 1973
Mercury ? - Anybody See Her / ? - 1973
Mercury 73408 - Mother! Can Your Child Come Home / He Sent Me You - 1973

Lee Williams & Oscar Perry

Black Soul 741 - Do What You Wanna Do / Mother! Can Your Child Come Home - 1974

Oscar Perry

Peri-Tone 1011704 - Your Bionic Man (Part 1) / Your Bionic Man (Part 2) – 1974
Peri-Tone ? - Don't Leave Me For A Stranger / ? – 1974
Peri-Tone ? - Heaven Sent An Angel / ? – 1974
Peri-Tone ? - You Didn't Mean It / ? – 1974
Peri-Tone 101574 - We Came A Long Ways / Lay Your Loving On Me – 1974

Oscar Perry And The Love Generators

Peri-Tone 1001 - Main String / I Was Right – 1975

Oscar Perry And The Love Generators

Peri-Tone 101674 - I Got What You Need / Come On Home To Me – 1975
Peri-Tone 101774 - 4 Corner Get Down / If It Could Be – 1976
Peri-Tone 101874 - Gimme Some / Come On Home To Me - 1976

Oscar Perry

Peri-Tone 101974 - It's Too Late Now / If It Could Be – 1976
Phil L. A. Of Soul 380 - Gimme Some / Come On Home To Me – 1976
Gamma ? - Body Movements / ? – 1978
Yellow Horizon 001 - Just What The Doctor Ordered / (Part 2) – 1978
Yellow Horizon 242 - Let Me Do It (Until You're Satisfied) / Let's Take A Raincheck - 1978

Yellow Horizon 242101 - Wind Me Up / I Didn't Plan It This Way – 1979
Gamma ? - Disco Ruby / ? – 1979
Red Sun ? - Love All Night Long / ? - 1979
Blue Horizon 102412 - Can't Hold A Good Man Down / Changes! When You're In Love - 1980
Jet Stream 900 - Danger Zone / Love Everything About You - 1981
Jet Stream 901 - She Needs Love / (She's An Upsetter) Bad Bad Mother Machine - ?
Red Sun ? - I Didn't Plan It This Way / ? – 1982
Red Sun 10-111 - Merry-Go-Round / You've Got My Nose Open - 1982
Red Sun 10-112 - I Wanna Thank You / Teasin' Me - 1982
Red Sun 10-113 - Rock Me Baby / Then You Can Tell Me Goodbye - 1983
Quazar 102 - Snap Your Fingers / We're Gonna Make It – 1985
Look Out 159 - Merry-Go-Round / Merry-Go-Round (Part 2) - 198?
Fair Play 102 - Merry-Go-Round / Merry-Go-Round (Part 2) - 1986
T. S. O. T. 001 - Do Me Some Cheating / Do Me Some Cheating (Instrumental) - ?
Paradise 5003 - I'm On My Way / I Want To Get Old With You - ?
Lock Key 115 - Big Sam / ? - ?

James Phelps

The Gospel Songbirds (members at one time or another James Phelps, Otis Clay, Cash McCall,.....)

C. H. Brewer (No #) - When They Ring Those Golden Bells / God's Creation - 1955

The Holy Wonders (members at one time or another James Phelps, Lou Rawls, ...)

Jimmy Phelps and The Du-Ettes (members

Mecca 5/6 - Blue Point Drive / Neither You Nor I - 1960 (James Phelps has stated that he has no knowledge of this recording)

The Clefs Of Calvary (members James Phelps (when he left the group in 1964 he was replaced by Roscoe Robinson (former lead of The Five Blind Boys Of Mississippi) , Calvin April, Ezell Wilkins, Willie Harris and Lester Earl

Tru-Sound 9 - Troubles Of This World / ? – 1962
? - Standing Where Jesus Stood / ? - ?

The Clefs Of Calvary (members James Phelps, Richard Smith, Bobby Pointer, "Curley" and ?)

The Soul Stirrers (James Phelps member of group during this period replacing Jimmy Cutler

Sar 154 - Mother Don't Worry About Me / Lead Me To Calvary – 1964

James Phelps (born Shreveport, Louisiana)

Argo 5499 - Love Is A Five-Letter Word / I'll Do The Best I Can - 1965
Argo 5509 - La De Da, I'm A Fool In Love / Wasting Time - 1965
Cadet 5534 - Oh, What A Feeling / Action – 1966
Fontana 1581 - Don't Be A Cry Baby / Walking The Floor Over You – 1967
Fontana 1600 - Fabulous One / The Wrong Number – 1967
Apache 2007 - You Were Made For Love / The Look On Your Face - 1971
Paramount 0136 - My Lover's Prayer* / Check Yourself - 1971 *also recorded in 1966 by Otis Redding on Volt 136.

Wilson Pickett

The Violinaires of Detroit, Michigan (members Robert Gandy (lead vocals), Wilson Pickett (alternate lead) Isaiah Jones (tenor), Calvin Fair (tenor), Wilson DeShields (baritone and guitar) and Leo Conery (bass))

Gotham G 776 - Sign Of The Judgement / My Work Will Be Done - 1957 (According to the sleeve notes of the "Gotham Gospel" album on Krazy Kat, Wilson Pickett was not a member of The Violinaires when the group recorded "Sign Of The Judgement" / "My Work Will Be Done" for Gotham late in 1957, and certainly his voice isn't in evidence on either tracks. Apparently the group didn't record again until the mid 1960's, by which time Pickett had long since departed. The Spiritual Five 45 was released on Peacock in 1963 and Opal Nations has a CD out on his Pewburner label featuring the group's Nashboro / Peacock sides with the Pickett tracks on it.)

The Falcons And Band (Ohio Untouchables) (members Wilson Pickett, Eddie Floyd, Lance Finnie, Willie Schofield and Bonny "Mack" Rice plus Robert Ward, Marshall Jones, Ralph Middlebrooks, Clarence Satchell and Cornelius Johnson)

Lupine 103 - I Found A Love* / Swim* - 1962 *Lead Wilson Pickett.
Lupine 1003 - I Found A Love / Swing - 1962 (Same As The Previous Release But With A Misspelt Title)

The Newports (Members Wilson Pickett, Eddie Floyd, Lance Finnie, Willie Schofield And Bonny "Mack" Rice)

Contour 301 - Hurry Arthur Murray / Chicky Chop Chop - 1962

The Falcons (Members Wilson Pickett, Eddie Floyd, Lance Finnie, Ben Knight And Bonny "Mack" Rice)

Atlantic 2153 - Lah - Tee - Lah - Tah / Darling - 1962

The Falcons (Members Wilson Pickett, Gene "Earl" Martin, Lance Finnie, Ben Knight And Bonny "Mack" Rice)

Atlantic 2179 - Let's Kiss And Make Up* / Take This Love I Got* - 1962 *Lead Wilson Pickett.

Wilson Pickett (Born 18-March-1941 In Prattville, Atlanta- Died 19th January in Reston, Virginia. cause: Heart attack))

Correc-Tone 501 - Let Me Be Your Boy / My Heart Belongs To You - 1962 (Backing Vocals The Supremes)
Cub 9113 - Let Me Be Your Boy / My Heart Belongs To You - 1962 (Backing Vocals The Supremes)

The Spiritual Five (Members Wilson Pickett, ...)

Peacock 3001 - Christ's Blood* / Call Him Up* - 1963 *Lead Wilson Pickett.

Wilson Pickett

Double-L 713 - If You Need Me / Baby Call On Me - 1963
Double-L 717 - It's Too Late / I'm Gonna Love You - 1963
Double-L 724 - I'm Down To My Last Heartbreak / I Can't Stop - 1963

Atlantic 2233 - I'm Gonna Cry / For Better Or Worse - 1964 (Recorded 12th May, 1964)
Atlantic 2271 - Come Home Baby* / Take A Little Love - 1964 *Backing Vocals By Cissy Houston.
Atlantic 2289 - In The Midnight Hour* / I'm Not Tired - 1965 *Recorded 12-May-1965 --- Ann Mason Did An "Answer Song" To This Track Released On Atlantic 2309.

Wilson Pickett And The Falcons (Members Wilson Pickett, Eddie Floyd, Lance Finnie, Willie Schofield And Bonny "Mack" Rice)

Lupine 003 - You're On My Mind / Anna* - 1965 *Lead Wilson Pickett.

Wilson Pickett

Atlantic 2306 - Don't Fight It / It's All Over - 1965
Atlantic 2320 - 634-5789 (Soulsville U.S.A.)* / That's A Man's Way - 1966 *there was an "answer song" to this track released in 1966 titled "I Got Your Number (634-5789)" by Marva Jones on Ski-Hi 4790
Atlantic 2334 - Ninety-Nine And A Half (Won't Do)* / Danger Zone - 1966 *also recorded in 1967 by The Standells on Tower 348 and in 1979 as "99 & ½ Won't Do" by Frankie Diamond and The Motivations on Starr 11279.
Atlantic 2348 - Land Of A 1000 Dances* / You're So Fine - 1966 *recorded 11-May-1966. --- also recorded in 1962 by Chris Kenner on Instant 3252 and in 1964 by Cannibal & The Headhunters on Rampart 642.
Rowe/Ami 1012 - "Play Me" Sales Stimulator - 1966 (Red Vinyl Jukebox Related Item)
Verve 10378 - Let Me Be Your Boy / My Heart Belongs To You - 1966
Atlantic 2365 - Mustang Sally / Three Time Loser* - 1966 *Recorded 14-October-1966.
Atlantic 2381 - Everybody Needs Somebody To Love / Nothing You Can Do* - 1967 *also recorded in 1965 by Bobby Womack on Him 1001.
Atlantic 2394 - I Found A Love - Part 1 / I Found A Love - Part 2 - 1967 (Re-Recording)
Philco-Ford Hp-11 - Land Of 1000 Dances / Midnight Hour - 1967 (4" Plastic "Hip Pocket Record" Came With Colour Sleeve)
Atlantic 2412 - You Can't Stand Alone / Soul Dance Number Three - 1967
Atlantic 2430 - Funky Broadway* / I'm Sorry About That - 1967 *originally recorded in 1966 by Dyke & The Blazers on Artco 45-101 and also recorded in 1967 by Glen Miller on Doctor Bird 1089.
Atlantic 2448 - I'm In Love / Stag-O-Lee - 1967
Atlantic 2484 - I've Come A Long Way / Jealous Love - 1968
Atlantic 2484 - I've Come A Long Way - 1968 (One Sided Stock Issue)
Atlantic 2504 - She's Looking Good* / We've Got To Have Love - 1968 *also recorded in 1967 by Rodger Collins on Galaxy 750.
Atlantic 2528 - I'm A Midnight Mover / Deborah - 1968
Atlantic 2558 - I Found A True Love / For Better Or Worse* - 1968 *Recorded 12-May-1964.
Atlantic 2575 - A Man And A Half / People Make The World (What It Is) - 1968
Atlantic 2591 - Hey Jude / Search Your Heart - 1968
Atlantic 2611 - Mini-Skirt Minnie / Back In Your Arm's - 1969
Atlantic 2631 - Born To Be Wild / Toe Hold - 1969
Atlantic 2648 - Hey Joe* / Night Owl - 1969 *also recorded in 1968 by The Zero End on Garland 2003.
Atlantic 2682 - You Keep Me Hangin' On / Now You See Me, Now You Don't – 1969
Atlantic 2722 - Sugar, Sugar – 1970 (One Sided Release)
Atlantic 2722 - Sugar, Sugar / Cole, Cooke & Redding - 1970
Atlantic 2753 - She Said Yes / It's Still Good - 1970
Atlantic 2765 - Engine Number 9 / International Playboy - 1970
Atlantic 2781 - Don't Let The Green Grass Fool You* / Ain't No Doubt About It - 1971 *also recorded in 1971 by The Angels Of Joy on Gospel Corner 149 and in 1972 by Veda Brown on Stax 0143.
Atlantic 2797 - Don't Knock My Love - Pt. 1 / Don't Knock My Love - Pt. 2 - 1971
Atlantic 2824 - Call My Name, I'll Be There / Woman Let Me Down Home - 1971

Atlantic 2852 - Fire And Water / Pledging My Love - 1971
Atlantic 2878 - Funk Factory / One Step Away - 1972
Atlantic 2909 - Mama Told Me Not To Come / Covering The Same Old Ground - 1972
RCA Victor 74-0908 - Mr. Magic Man / I Sho' Love You - 1973
Atlantic 2961 - Come Right Here / International Playboy - 1973
RCA Victor Apbo-0049 - Take A Closer Look At The Woman You're With / Two Women And A Wife - 1973
RCA Victor Apbo-0174 - Soft Soul Boogie Woogie / Take That Pollution Out Of Your Throat - 1973
RCA Victor Apbo-0309 - Take Your Pleasure Where You Find It / What Good Is A Lie - 1974
RCA Victor Pb-10067 - I Was Too Nice / Isn't That So - 1974
Wicked 8101 - The Best Part Of A Man / How Will I Ever Know - 1975
Wicked 8102 - Love Will Keep Us Together / It's Gonna Be Good - 1976
Erva 318 - Love Dagger / Time To Let The Sun Shine On Me - 1977
Big Tree 16121 - Who Turned You On / Dance You Down - 1978
Big Tree 16129 - Groovin' / Time To Let The Sun Shine In – 1978
Atlantic Dsko 128 – Funky Situation (3:53) / She's So Tight (3:31) – 1978 (12" promo issue only)
EMI America 8027 - I Want You / Love Of My Life - 1979
Emi America 8034 - Live With Me / Granny - 1980
Emi America 8070 - Ain't Gonna Give You No More / Don't Underestimate the Power Of Love - 1981
EMI America 8082 - Back On The Right Track / It's You – 1981

Jackie Moore and Wilson Pickett

Montage 1218 – Precious, Precious / ? – 1982
Catawba Ca 1000 – Seconds (5:11) / Seconds (Instrumental) (4:32) – 1982 (12" release)

Wilson Pickett

Motown 1898 - Don't Turn Away / Can't Stop Now - 1987
Motown 217 - Land Of l000 Dances (Four Versions) / Just Let Her Know - 1987 (12" Single Release)
Motown 1916 - In The Midnight Hour / Just Let Her Know - 1987
Motown 1938 - Love Never Let Me Down / Just Let Her Know - 1988
Motown 53407 - Love Never Let Me Down / Just Let Her Know - 1988

The Falcons & Band (Ohio Untouchables) (members Wilson Pickett, Eddie Floyd, Lance Finnie, Willie Schofield and Bonny "Mack" Rice plus Robert Ward, Marshall Jones, Ralph Middlebrooks, Clarence Satchell and Cornelius Johnson)

Relic 1037 - I Found A Love / Swim - ?

Wilson Pickett

Atlantic Oldies Series 13023 - I'm In Love / Stagger Lee - ?
Atlantic Oldies Series 13024 – In The Midnight Hour / 634-5789 (Soulsville, U. S. A.) - ?
Atlantic Oldies Series 13026 - Don't Knock My Love (Part 1) / Mustang Sally - ?
Atlantic Oldies Series 13029 - Land Of 1000 Dances / Engine Number Nine - ?
Atlantic Oldies Series 13030 - Ninety-Nine And A Half / Don't Let The Green Grass Fool You - ?

The Falcons & Band (Ohio Untouchables) / Chris Kenner

Atlantic Oldies Series 13112 - I Found A Love / Land Of 1000 Dances* - ? *Flip By Chris Kenner.

Wilson Pickett

Atlantic Oldies Series 13124 - Don't Fight It / A Man And A Half - ?
Precision Prc-12-1702 - Mustang Sally (The Boss Is Back) (7:54) / Mustang Sally (The Boss Is Back) (7:54) - ? (12" release)

Elwood Blues Revue featuring Wilson Pickett

Atlantic Dmd 1197 - Land Of A Thousand Dances (Long Version) (5:42) / Land Of A Thousand Dances (Short Version) (3:46) /// Land Of A Thousand Dances (Dance Version) (5:29) / Land Of A Thousand Dances (Short Version) (4:46) – 1988 (12" promo issue only --- plays at 33-1/3rpm)
Atlantic 7-89062 - Land Of A Thousand Dances (Part 1) / Land Of A Thousand Dances (Part 2) - 1988 (from the movie "The Great Outdoors")

The Falcons / The Falcons & Band (Ohio Untouchables)

Collectables Col 3385 - You're So Fine / I Found A Love* - ? *Flip By The Falcons & Band (Ohio Untouchables)

The Plants

The Equadors (members George Jackson, Steve McDowell, James Lawson and Thurmon Thrower) group formed in 1955 in Baltimore. Zell Sanders became their manager and changed their name.

The Plants (members George Jackson (lead), Steve McDowell (first tenor), James Lawson (baritone) and Thurmon Thrower (bass))

J&S 1602 - Dear I Swear / It's You - 1957 (label has company address under logo -- this is the scarcer version)
J&S 1617 / 1618 - From Me / My Girl - 1958

Justine "Baby" Washington

Neptune 107 - Work Out / Let's Love In The Moonlight - 1959 (backing vocals The Plants)

The Plants

J&S 248 / 249 - I Searched The Seven Seas / I Took A Trip Way Over The Sea - 1959 (completely different group)
J&S 1602 - Dear I Swear / It's You - 1961 (no company address on label)

George Jackson

Lescay 3006 - Watching The Rainbow / Miss Frankenstein - 1962 (backing vocals The Unisons)
Double R 248 - When I Stop Lovin' You / That Lonely Night - 1966 (Backing Vocals The Jive Five)
Cameo 460 - When I Stop Lovin' You / That Lonely Night - 1967 (Backing Vocals The Jive Five)
Mercury 72736 - Tossin' And Turnin' / Kiss Me - 1967
Mercury 72782 - I Don't Have The Time To Love You / Don't Use Me - 1968

The Platters

Tony Williams and The Platters (members Tony Williams, David Lynch, Alex Hodge and Herb Reed, manager and song writer of group Buck Ram)

Federal 12153 - Give Thanks / Hey Now - 1953

Shirley Gunter & "The Queens" (Shirley Gunter is sister of Cornell Gunter of The Flairs and Coasters fame)

Flair 1020 - Send Him Back / Since I Fell For You - 1953

Zola Taylor (born Zola Mae Taylor on 18-March-1938 in Los Angeles, California --- died 30-April-2007 in Riverside, California --- cause: complications from pneumonia)

RPM 405 - Make Love To Me / Oh My Dear - 1954

The Platters

Federal 12164 - I'll Cry When You're Gone / I Need You All The Time – 1954
Federal 12181 - Roses Of Picardy / Beer Barrel Polka – 1954
Federal 12188 - Tell The World / Love All Night – 1954
Federal 12198 - Voo-Vee-Ah-Bee / Shake It Up Mambo - 1954

Shirley Gunter & "The Queens" (members Shirley Gunter, Lula Bea Kinney, Lula Mae Suggs and Zola Taylor)

Flair 1027 - Found Some Good Lovin' / Strange Romance – 1954
Flair 1050 - Oop Shoop / It's You – 1955
Flair 1060 - You're Mine / Why – 1955
Flair 1065 - What Difference Does It Make / Baby I Love You So – 1955
Flair 1070 - That's The Way I Like It / Gimme, Gimme, Gimme – 1955

The Platters

Federal 12204 - Maggie Doesn't Work Here Anymore / Take Me Back, Take Me Back - 1955

Linda Hayes and The Platters (Linda Hayes is actually Bertha Williams from R-I-H Records)

King 4773 - Please Have Mercy / Oochi Pachie - 1955 (Zola Taylor joins group around this time also Alex Hodge leaves and Paul Robi joins)

The Platters

Mercury 70633 - Only You (And You Alone) / Bark, Battle And Ball - 1955 (both tracks recorded 26-April-1955)
Mercury 70753 - The Great Pretender* / I'm Just A Dancing Partner - 1955 *also recorded in 1961 by Kathy Young on Indigo 137 and in 1962 by Carol Fran on Lyric 1006
Federal 12244 - Only You (And You Alone) / You Made Me Cry – 1955
Federal 12250 - Tell The World / I Need You All The Time – 1956
Mercury 70819 - (You've Got) The Magic Touch / Winner Take All – 1956
Mercury 70893 - My Prayer / Heaven On Earth – 1956
Mercury 70948 - You'll Never Know / It Isn't Right – 1956
Federal 12271 - Give Thanks / I Need You All The Time – 1956
Mercury 71011 - One In A Million / On My Word Of Honor – 1956
Mercury 71032 - I'm Sorry / He's Mine – 1957
Mercury 71093 - My Dream* / I Wanna** - 1957 *recorded 19-February-1957. **recorded 26-April-1955.

Tony Williams

Mercury 71158 - Let's Start All Over Again* / When You Return - 1957 *also recorded by The Feathers as "Standing Right There" in 1955 on Aladdin 3277.

The Metrotones (members Charles "Sonny" Turner (aka Sonny Dinks), Melvin Smith, James Frierson, Leuvenia Eaton and Leonard Veal (of Hesitations fame)).

Reserve 114 - More And More / ? - 1957 (same number also used for a Tracey Twins release)
Reserve 116 - Please Come Back / Skitter Skatter - 1957

The Platters

Mercury 71184 - Only Because / The Mystery Of You - 1957 (both tracks recorded 6-March-1957)
Mercury 71246 - Helpless / Indiff'rent* - 1957 *recorded 22-October-1957.
Mercury 71289 - Twilight Time / Out Of My Mind – 1958
Mercury 71320 - You're Making A Mistake / My Old Flame - 1958

Patti Page / The Diamonds /// The Danleers / The Platters

Mercury Mep-55 - Fibbin' / Walking Along /// I Really Love You / It's Raining Outside - 1958 (promo issue 45 Shorties : abridged selections for disc jockey programming only)

The Platters

Mercury 71353 - I Wish / It's Raining Outside (Chove La Fora) - 1958
Mercury 71383 - Smoke Gets In Your Eyes* / No Matter What You Are** - 1958 *recorded 24-September-1958. **recorded 4-December-1957.
Mercury - Hula Hop - 1958 (recorded 26-September-1958 this unissued track was released in Canada on a 1991 Mercury 2 CD set "The Platters - The Magic Touch: An Anthology" P2 10314 (disc one))

Eddie Beal

Cass 100 - Noop Noop / The Monkey's Wedding - 1958 (this recently discovered 45 features movie soundtrack vocalist Marni Nixon who sings the "A"-side title, the song is a uptempo word-jazzy duet with bass lead, possibly Herb Reed of the Platters and other members joining in behind Nixon's heavily echoed Betty Boop-styled response ("noop noop" apparently means "nope nope"). Strong male vocal group backing and R&B sax solo. According to the song's writer and producer Skip Carmel, the group was "whatever group Eddie Beal was working with at the time," though he was fairly sure it was Reed with whom Carmel and Beal worked in San Francisco. The flip, "The Monkey's Wedding" uses similar vocal exchange, but has a weaker group presence)

The Platters

Mercury 71427 - Enchanted* / The Sound And The Fury - 1959 *recorded 12-February-1959.
Mercury 71467 - Remember When* / Love Of A Lifetime - 1959 *recorded 25-September-1958.
Mercury 10007 - Remember When / Love Of A Lifetime - 1959
Mercury 71502 - Where / Wish It Were Me - 1959 (both tracks recorded 29-December-1958)

Tony Williams

Mercury 71532 - Charmaine / Peg O' My Heart - 1959

The Platters

Mercury 71538 - My Secret*/ What Does It Matter - 1959 *recorded 27-August-1959.

Mercury 71563 - Harbor Lights / Sleepy Lagoon - 1960 (both tracks recorded 11-August-1959)
Mercury 71624 - Ebb Tide* / (I'll Be With You) In Apple Blossom Time - 1960 *recorded 13-August-1959.
Mercury 71656 - Red Sails In The Sunset* / Sad River - 1960 *recorded 13-August-1959 --- track also recorded in 1960 by Ray Sharpe on Jamie 1128.
Mercury 71697 - To Each His Own* / Down The River Of Golden Dreams - 1960 *recorded 12-February-1959.

Tony Williams (Tony Williams Goes Solo)

Reprise 20,019 - Sleepless Nights / Movin' In – 1961
Reprise 20,030 - My Prayer / Miracle - 1961

Nate Nelson

Prigan 2001 - Once Again / Tell Me Why - 1961

The Platters

Mercury 71749 - If I Didn't Care* / True Lover - 1961 (Sonny Turner lead) *recorded 24-September-1958.
Mercury 71791 - Trees / Immortal Love - 1961
Mercury 71847 - I'll Never Smile Again* / You Don't Say - 1961 *recorded 25-September-1958.
Mercury 71904 - Song For The Lonely / You'll Never Know – 1961
Mercury 71921 - It's Magic / Reaching For A Star - 1962 (Paul Robi and Zola Taylor leave group and replaced with Nate Nelson & Sandra Dawn, around this time Buck Ram sue's Mercury Records because they refused to release anymore Platters material without Tony Williams lead vocals. The year ended in legal; turmoil). Barbara Randolph was briefly a member of the Platters- in 1964, following the exit of Zola Taylor. Barbara is featured on their Mercury Album "The New Soul of the Platters". In 1965, she was replaced by Betty Jackson, who gave way to Sandra Dawn in 1966.

Tony Williams

Reprise 20,056 - It's So Easy To Surrender / That's More Like It - 1962 (Released Only Italy!)
Reprise 20,067 - Come Along Now / That's More Like It – 1962
Reprise 20,073 - Sing, Lover, Sing / Mandalino - 1962 (Released Only In Hong Kong!)
Philips 40069 - Second Best / Chloe - 1962

The Platters

Power 7012 - Only You / Voo Vee Ah Bee - 1962 (some copies came with picture sleeve)
Mercury 71986 - More Than You Know / Every Little Moment – 1962
Mercury 72060 - Memories / Heartbreak – 1962
Mercury 72107 - Once In A While / I'll See You In My Dreams – 1963
Mercury 72129 - Strangers / Here Comes Heaven Again - 1963

Buck Ram (born Samuel Ram on 21-November-1907 in Chicago, Illinois --- died 1-January-1991 of natural causes)

Personality 3507 - Soran Song / Twilight In Tokyo - 1963

Tony Williams

Reprise 20,136 - Loving You / Dream - 1963 (Released Only In Italy!)
Philips 40123 - Save Me / Twenty-Four Lonely Hours – 1963
Philips 40141 - How Come / When I Had You - 1963

The Platters

Mercury 72194 - Viva Ju Joy / Quando Caliente El Sol – 1963
Mercury 72242 - Java Jive / Michael Row The Boat Ashore – 1964
Mercury 72305 - Sincerely / P.S. I Love You – 1964
Mercury 72359 - Love Me Tender / Little Things Mean A Lot - 1964

The Platters 1965

Entree 107 - Run While It's Dark / Won't You Be My Friend - 1965

The Platters (members David Lynch, Herb Reed, Sonny Turner, Nate Nelson and Sandra Dawn)

Musicor 1166 - I Love You 1000 Times */ Don't Hear, Speak, See No Evil** - 1966 *lead Sonny Turner (on backing vocals is George Clinton), **lead Nate Nelson
Musicor 1195 - Devri*/ Alone In The Light (Without You) - 1966 *Lead Sonny Turner
Musicor 1211 - I'll Be Home* / (You've Got) The Magic Touch - 1966 *Lead Nate Nelson
Musicor 1229 - With This Ring* / If I Had A Love - 1967 *Lead Sonny Turner, On Backing Vocals Is George Clinton. (Dave Lynch Leaves Group In 1967)
Musicor 1251 - Washed Ashore (On A Lonely Island In The Sea)* / What Name Shall I Give You, My Love - 1967 *Lead Sonny Turner
Musicor 1251 - Washed Ashore (On A Lonely Island In The Sea)* / One In A Million - 1967 *Lead Sonny Turner
Musicor 1262 - On Top Of My Mind / Shing-A-Ling-A-Loo – 1967
Musicor 1275 - Sweet, Sweet Lovin' */ Sonata - 1967 *Lead Sonny Turner
Musicor 1288 - Love Must Go On / How Beautiful Our Love Is – 1968
Musicor 1302 - So Many Tears / Think Before You Walk Away* - 1968 *also recorded as "You Might Need Me Another Day" in 1966? by Gloria Taylor on King Soul 493-1
Musicor 1322 - Hard To Get A Thing Called Love / Why – 1968
Musicor 1341 - Fear Of Losing You / Sonata - 1968 (last remaining original Platter Herb Reed leaves group in 1969)
Musicor 1443 - Sweet, Sweet Lovin' */ Be My Love - 1971

Buck Ram

United Artists Xw-224 - Sunday With You / If The World Loved - 1973

The Buck Ram Platters (members Monroe Powell, Ella Woods, Chico LaMar, Craig Alexander (Zola Taylor's cousin) and Gene Williams (died 5-August-2008 in Las Vegas, Nevada --- cause: pancreatic cancer))

Avalanche Xw224 - Sunday With You / If The World Loved - 1973**The Platters**

Owl 320 - Are You Sincere / Sixteen Tons – 1973
Ram 1002 - Only You / Here Comes The Boogie Man – 1977
Ram 1004 - My Ship Is Coming In / Guilty – 1977
Ram 1005 - My Ship Is Coming In / Guilty – 1977
Ram 4852 - Personality / Who's Sorry Now - 1978

The Platters / Harry Chapin

W.I.A.A. 592 - What's It All About (Sept 81) Public Service Show - 1981 (radio station promo issue only --- interview with Buck Ram -- flip by Harry Chapin)

The Platters

Gusto 2154 - Tell The World / Love All Night - 1981
Antler 3000 - I Do It All The Time / Shake What Your Mama Gave You - 1982
Antler 3001 - I Do It All The Time / Shake What Your Mama Gave You - 1982

The Platters / Count Basie

W.I.A.A. 640 - What's It All About (Sept 82) Public Service Show - 1982 (radio station promo issue only -- flip by Count Basie)

The Platters

Mercury 76160 - Platterama Medley / Red Sails In The Sunset – 1982
Mercury 76160 - Platterama Medley / Platterama Medley - 1982 (Promo Issue Only)
U.S Dept. Of Agriculture - Only You: Forest Fire Prevention Psa Spots - 1984 (promo issue only -- PSA commercials, eight ads, features The Platters and includes a spot by Ted Nugent)

Dorothy Moore & The Poppies

The New Stranger Baptist Choir (Members Dorothy Moore, ...) Circa 1952.

The Dolletts (Members Dorothy Moore, ...)

ABC 10625 - Small Talk (Doesn't Bother Me) / Free From The Chains Of Love – 1965

Dorothy Moore & The Dollets (Members Dorothy Moore, ...)

ABC 10627 - Believe It Or Not / I'm A Lonely Girl – 1965

The Poppies (Members Dorothy Moore, Rosemary Taylor And Pet McClune)

Epic 9893 - The Lullaby Of Love / I Wonder Why – 1966
Epic 10019 - He's Ready / He's Got Real Love - 1966 (Also Issued With Picture Sleeve)
Epic 10059 - Do It With Soul / He Means So Much To Me – 1966
Epic 510086 - There's A Pain In My Heart / My Love And I – 1966

Dottie Cambridge (Dorothy Moore)

MGM 13846 - Cry Your Eyes Out / Perfect Boy – 1967
MGM 13902 - He's About A Mover / Save Our Love Baby – 1968
Music City Recorders 10" acetate - Shows All Over Your Face / Take To The High Road - ? (Produced by Huey P.Meaux)

Dorothy & The Hesitations (Members Dorothy Moore,...)

Jamie 1358 - Trying To Work A Plan / Don't Set Me Up (For The Kill) - 1968 (Supposedly Dorothy Moore After The Poppies Broke Up)

Dorothy Moore

Avco 4590 - See How They've Done My Love / One Day You're Gonna Hurt Me – 1972
Avco 4599 - Same Old Feeling / One Day You're Gonna Hurt Me – 1972
GSF 6908 - Cry Like A Baby / Just The One I've Been Looking For – 1973
Chimneyville 10204 - Don't Let Go / Two Of A Kind – 1974
Chimneyville 10207 - Making Love / Making Love - 1975 (Duet With King Floyd)
Malaco 1029 - Misty Blue / Here It Is – 1975

Malaco 1033 - Funny How Time Slips Away / Ain't That A Mother's Love – 1976
Malaco 1037 - For Old Times Sake / Daddy's Eyes – 1976

Dorothy Moore / Eddie Floyd

Malaco 1040 - We Really Should Be In Love / I'll Never Be Loved - 1977

Dorothy Moore (Born 13-October-1947 In Jackson, Mississippi)

Malaco 1042 - Love Me / I Believe You – 1977
Malaco 1047 - With Pen In Hand / Too Blind To See – 1977
Malaco 1048 - Let The Music Play / 1 - 2 - 3 (You And Me) – 1978
Malaco 1052 - Special Occasion / Girl Overboard – 1978
Malaco 1054 - (We Need More) Loving Time / Write A Little Prayer – 1978
Malaco 2062 - Talk To Me ---- Every Beat Of My Heart / Lonely – 1980
Malaco 2064 - Angel Of The Morning / Making Love – 1980
Handshake 02879 - I've Been Someone's Lover Before...../ What's Forever For – 1982
Street King 7120 - Just Another Broken Heart / ? – 1984
Street King Skds-1120 - Just Another Broken Heart (Vocal) / Just Another Broken Heart (Instrumental) - 1984 (12" Release)
Street King Skds-11208 - Just Another Broken Heart (Vocal) /// Just Another Broken Heart (Dub Version) / Just Another Broken Heart (Radio Edit) - 1984 (12" Release)
Prelude 8094 - We Just Came Apart At The Dreams / (Instrumental) -1986
Volt 3106 - Don't Hold Your Breath / Can't Get Over You (Once Again I'm Misty Blue) (4:24) - 1988 (12" Release)
Volt 301 - Endless Summer Nights / Walk Through This Pain - 1989
Malaco 2168 - All Night Blue / Talk To Me – 1990
Malaco 2172 - Be Strong Enough To Hold On (Cd Single) – 1991
Malaco 2192 - Stay Close To Home (Cd Single) – 1991
Volt 990 - Can't Get Over You (Once Again I'm Misty Blue) / ? - ?
T. K. Disco Tkd-57 - Let The Music Play / Make It Soon - ? (12"Release)

The Precisions

There are several different groups called The Precisions.

The Precisions (Los Angeles Group)

Highland 300 - Eight Reasons (Why I Love You) / Mama Told Me – 1962
Rayna 1001 - White Christmas / Brenda - ?

The Precisions (New York Group)

Golden Crest 571 - Cleopatra / Someone To Watch Over Me – 1962

The Precisions (Boston Group)

Wild 903 - The Love (I Found In You) / Boston - ? (With Herchel Dwellingham & Orchestra)
Wild 903 - The Love (I Found In You) / What Would You Do - ? (With Herchel Dwellingham & Orchestra)

The Precisions (Scranton, PA)

Strand 25038 - You Can't Play Games / Dream On – 1961
Debra 1001 - Sweet Dreams / Stop Leading Me On - 1963

The Precisions (Detroit Origin) (members Arthur Ashford (died 6-November-2003, cause cancer), Michael Morgan, Billy Prince and Denis Gilmore (one-time member of The Nonchalants)

D-Town 1033 - My Lover Come Back / I Wanna Tell My Baby - 1965
D-Town 1055 - Mexican Love Song / You're Sweet – 1965
Drew 1001 - Such Misery / A Lovers Plea - 1967
Drew 1002 - Sugar Ain't Sweet / What I Want – 1967 (Withdrawn because of a pressing fault, possibly less than a dozen copies survived)
Drew 1002 - Why Girl / What I Want – 1967
Drew 1003 - If This Is Love (I'd Rather Be Lonely)* / You'll Soon Be Gone - 1967 *tambourine player Lou Ragland.
Drew 1004 - Instant Heartbreak (Just Add Tears) / Dream Girl – 1968
Drew 1005 - A Place / Never Let Her Go – 1968
Atco 6643 - Into My Life / Don't Double With Trouble – 1969
Atco 6669 - New York City / You're The Best (That Ever Did It) – 1969

The Precisions (Philadelphia Group)

Hen Mar 4501 - Take A Good Look / My Sense Of Direction - 1972

Group Line Ups

Quiet Elegance (Mildred Vaney, Yvonne Dearing, Lois Reeves)

? And The Mysterians

Pa - Go - Go 102 - 96 Tears / Midnight Hour - 1965
Cameo 428 - 96 Tears / Midnight Hour - 1966
Cameo 441 - I Need Somebody / "8" Teen - 1966
Cameo 467 - Can't Get Enough Of You, Baby / Smokes - 1967
Cameo 479 - Girl (You Captivate Me) / Got To - 1967
Cameo 496 - Do Something To Me / Love Me, Baby (Cherry July) - 1967
Capitol 2162 - Make You Mine / I Love You, Baby (Like Nobody's Business) - 1968
Chickory 410 - Talk Is Cheap / She Goes To Church On Sunday - 1968
Super K 102 - Hang In / Sha La La - 1969
Tangerine 989 - Ain't It A Shame / Turn Around, Baby (Don't Ever Look Back) - 1970
Luv 159 - Funky Lady / Hot 'N' Groovy - 1975
Abkco 4020 - 96 Tears / Can't Get Enough Of You, Baby - 1983
Abkco 4033 - I Need Somebody / Girl (You Captivate Me) - 1983

Q

Peacock ? - You Better Move On / Don't Play That Song (You Lied) - 1987

Peacock ? - Time Is On My Side / Time Is On My Side - Early 1990's Cassette Single.

? And The Mysterians

Collectables 4050 - 96 Tears / Midnight Hour - 1997

Venue Reports - September 20012

The Lea Manor, Albrighton, 1st September, 2001.

My first booking at Albrighton this year, and it was one of the most enjoyable DJ spots I've done this year. The venue has cooled off a little this year, and numbers were still down. I know Tate and Lin refuse to associate the reduced numbers with the change in music policy at the beginning of this year, but I can't think of any other reason. Consequently I was gratified to have a full dancefloor right through my spot which fully supported my feelings that Sixties Soul is still wanted at Albrighton. Butch played an excellent spot, as did Dave Flynn, although the dancefloor was a little quieter for Dave. Having said that, This was certainly one of the better nights at Albrighton this year.

The Aquarius, Hednesford, 7th September, 2001.

After all the problems with the Council threatening to knock the building down, this was my second DJ spot at the Aqua this year. The club has now been sold and the new owners have spent some money doing the place up again, so this is now a really top class venue. Musically on the night it was right across the board, and by that I mean Oldies, Newies, and Seventies. The full dance floor was testimony that the DJs got it right on the night. Nige Shaw played another good spot and should really be getting more bookings than he does. My spot was well accepted which goes to show that people will dance to things they haven't heard before, even at venues that are more Oldies biased. All in all, a really good night. Thanks to Phil Richards for the lift as well.

Lea Manor, Albrighton, 14th September, 2001.

The wrong night really, only a fortnight after the allnighter, and the night before the 100 Club anniversary. There were only about thirty people in attendance, and even one of the DJs didn't bother turning up (Len Cook). Musically, Chic played a good across the board set early on and then did a second set of Nineties, Ted Massey played mostly Sixties, and Gareth Donovan, who apparently works at the Crazy Beat record shop in London, quite happily agreed to play an hour and three quarters of Modern, In fact I think he'd have carried on right through to the end if asked. Rather than carry on until two though, Lin decided to finish the night early at half one.

100 Club Anniversary, 15th September, 2001.

Hot, sweaty, Oldies, Newies, Rarities, friends, regulars, tourists, free single, Ady Croasdell take a bow, still the number one !

Loughborough University Students Union, Loughbourough, 22nd September 2001

This venue really does have the potential to go huge. It's layout is good, the numbers are increasing with every one, and the music is evolving from purely oldies to include a few more rarities. Two rooms as well, although from where I was sitting it did appear that the smaller room (Which was billed as a 'mixed' music policy) was mostly Sixties as well. All credit to the lads running the venue because it's a big place to fill but I reckon there must have been well over 200 in attendance, perhaps even 300. My playlist for the 12:00 till 1:00 spot was:

Lonnie Lester - You Can't Go - Nu-Tone

Bud Harper - Wherever You Were - Peacock
Ted Taylor - Somebody's Always Trying - Okeh
Patience Valentine - If You Don't Come - SAR
Fuller Brothers - Time's A Wasting - Soul Clock
Bobby Freeman - I'll Never Fall In Love Again - Autumn
Doni Burdick - Bari Track - Sound Impression
Gordon Keith - Look Ahead - Calumet
Vondells - Hey Girl - Airtown Custom
Major Harris - Call Me Tomorrow - Okeh
Seven Souls - I Still Love You - Okeh
Willie Mitchell - That Driving Beat - Hi
Jr Walker - Tune Up - Soul
Marjorie Black - One More Hurt - Sue
Brice Coefield - Ain't That Right - Omen
Joanne Courcy - I Got The Power - Twirl
Magnetics - I Have A Girl - Ra Sel
TC Lee & The Bricklayers - Up And Down the Hill - King
David & Reubin - I Love Her So Much It Hurts Me - Warner Brothers
Doug Banks - I Just Kept On Dancing - Argo
Tommy Navarro - I Cried My Life Away - De Jac

The next one is set for Christmas sometime but they haven't arranged the date yet, and I know that the promoters are looking to run allnighters at the venue. One to watch out for.

The Black Horse, Wolverhampton, 28th September, 2001.

So I book half a day off from work to go to a leaving do, arrive at the pub at 12:30, and leave at 6:00 pm. Straight home, shower, shave, sh.., something to eat and straight back out to arrive at The Black Horse at 8:30 pm. Then I discover I'm DJing at 12:30 am ! I have very little recollection of what I played, but I know at one stage everybody in the room was dancing bar five people so I must have done ok. The rest of the night's music was good as well, and all I can do now is recommend that you go to the next Black horse..

Roar Nightclub, Bilston, 29th September, 2001.

This was the first promotion at Roar Nightclub in Bilston. And what a good night it turned out to be. This venue is going to establish itself very quickly as the top two room event in the Midlands.

Upstairs was the Modern room, and although I didn't spend much time in there I did pop up a couple of times to see how it was going on. Music was provided by John Pugh, Blue Max, Jordi, Gary Holyman, and the irrepressible Gavin Page (Who greeted me over the mic the first time I went up by saying "Rimmer, you're in the wrong room, piss off !"). Trouble is, the bloke does have such immaculate taste in Soul music. Numbers in the Modern room varied all night, as they did in the Sixties room with people going from one room to the other and back. Because of that it's going to be hard to put a figure on how many there were through the door, but I'd guess at over 150.

Downstairs, my territory (It's where the bar was, and a pint of bitter was only £1.40, in a nightclub for God's sake !). Des Parker started proceedings off with a well thought out set of unknowns, rarities and cheapies whilst people started to come in, get drinks, and find seats. Kenny Onions was next up, and Ken went straight for the jugular with a set of storming Oldies mixed in wth a few Newies. As expected, people started to dance at this point. I took over at 11.00 pm and played a set which contained more Oldies than I usually play, but I still managed to slip things like The Magnetics and The Vondells in there mixed in with some uptempo R & B.

John Pugh took over from me and the floor almost caught fire, whilst there were a lot of regulars off the scene there, the night had also pulled a lot of locals in as well, so Oldies were the order of the day. Blue Max joined John downstairs as well, so The Catacombs lived again for a while.

Guy Hennigan was next up, half of the original Sixties Mafia, in full force, to a great dance floor reaction. Starting off with the 'Back Street' instrumental it just got better and better. Full respect to Guy, he doesn't get any where near the number of bookings he should these days. Fortunately he's one of the residents at Bilston, so he'll be back next time as well

The last spot should have been Little Scotty, but for whatever reason, he didn't arrive, so the last hour was covered by Rob Haigh for quarter of a hour, and then Guy Hennigan went back on to finish the night off.

To sum it up, the venue's good, the dance floor's good, the bar prices are good, the fact it's two rooms is good, the DJ line up's good, and with room for a few more bodies this will turn into a top night. The next one is on November the 24th. Get yourself along.

Group Line Ups

The Radiants (Mauric McAllister, Wallace Sampson, Elzie Butler, Green 'Mac' McLauren)
The Reflections (Tony Micale (Aka Tony Michaels), John Dean, Phil Castrodale, Dan Bennie, Ray Steinberg)
The Ringleaders (Willie Hawkins, Edgar Donahue, Vandy Lane, Brent Anderson)
Ruby & The Romantics (Ruby Nash Curtis, Ed Roberts, George Lee, Ron Moseley, Leroy Faun)
The Royal Jokers (Willie Jones, Noah Howell, Billy Lyons, Raymond Dorsey)

Jimmy Radcliffe

The Fascinators (Members Jimmy Radcliffe, ...)

Jimmy Radcliffe (Born James Radcliffe on 18-November-1936 in Harlem, New York City - Died 27-July-1973 in the Veterans Administration Hospital in The Bronx, New York City - Cause: - Suffering from kidney failure, died of natural causes while waiting for a transplant)

Musicor 1016 - Twist Calypso / Don't Look My Way – 1962
Musicor 1024 - (There Goes) The Forgotten Man / An Awful Lot Of Cryin' - 1962
Musicor 1033 - Through A Long And Sleepless Night / Moment Of Weakness – 1963
Musicor 1042 - Long After Tonight Is All Over / What I Want I Can Never Have – 1964
Aurora 154 - My Ship Is Comin' In / Goin' Where The Lovin' Is – 1965
Shout 202 - Lucky Old Sun / So Deep – 1966

The Steve Karmen Big Band Featuring Jimmy Radclife

United Artists 50451 - Breakaway Part 1 / Breakaway Part 2 - 1968 (Spanish Copies Came With

Picture Sleeve)

Jimmy Radcliffe

RCA 74-0138 - Funky Bottom Congregation / Lay A Little Lovin' On Me – 1969
Jaysina - The Thrill Of Loving You - ? (Acetate)

Della Reese

Toured with **Mahalia Jackson** from 1945 to 1950.

The Meditation Singers (original members Della Reese, Earnestine Rundless, Lillian Mitchell and Marie Waters (Della Reeses' sister) Della Reese left group in 1953 and was replaced by Laura Lee)

Erskine Hawkins Orchestra 1953 to 1954

Della Reese (born Delloreese Patricia Early on 6-July-1931 in Detroit, Michigan)

Great Lakes 1203 - Yes Indeed / Blue And Orange Birds – 1954
Jubilee 5198 - In The Still Of The Night / Kiss My Love Goodbye – 1955
Jubilee 5214 - Time After Time / Fine Sugar – 1955
Jubilee 5233 - I've Got My Love To Keep Me Warm / Years From Now – 1956
Jubilee 5247 - Headin' Home / Daybreak Serenade – 1956
Jubilee 5251 - My Melancholy Baby / One For My Baby – 1956
Jubilee 5263 - In The Meantime / The More I See You – 1956
Jubilee 5278 - How About You / How Can You Not Believe – 1957
Jubilee 5292 - And That Reminds Me / I Cried For You - 1957 (With The Honey Dreamers)
Jubilee 5307 - I Only Want To Love You / By Love Possessed – 1957
Jubilee 5317 - How Can You Lose (What You Never Had) / If Not For You – 1958
Jubilee 5323 - I've Got A Feelin' You're Foolin' / C'mon, C'mon – 1958
Jubilee 5332 - I Wish / You Gotta Love Everybody – 1958
Jubilee 5345 - Sermonette / Dreams End At Dawn - 1958

Della Reese & Kirk Stuart

Jubilee 5346 - When I Grow Too Old To Dream / You're Just In Love – 1958
Jubilee 9000 - When I Grow Too Old To Dream / You're Just In Love - 1958 (Stereosonic Release)

Della Reese

Jubilee 9007 - Stormy Weather / Lover Man - 1958 (Stereo Release)
Jubilee 5369 - Time Was / Once Upon A Dream – 1959
Jubilee 5375 - I Don't Want To Walk Without You / I'm Nobody's Baby – 1959
RCA Victor 47-7591 - Don't You Know / Soldier Won't You Marry Me – 1959
RCA Victor 47-7644 - Not One Minute More / You're My Love – 1959
RCA Victor Epa-4349 - Don't You Know / Soldier, Won't You Marry Me /// Not One Minute More / You're My Love - 1959 (Ep Release Some Copies Issued With Picture Sleeve)
RCA Victor 47-7683 - Someday / The Lady Is A Tramp – 1960
RCAVictor 47-7706 - Someday You'll Want Me To Want You / Faraway Boy – 1960
RCA Victor 47-7750 - Everyday / There's No Two Ways About It - 1960 (Some Copies Issued With Picture Sleeve)
RCA Victor 47-7784 - And Now / There's Nothin' Like A Boy - 1960 (Some Copies Issued With

Picture Sleeve)
RCA Victor 47-7833 - The Most Beautiful Words / You Mean All The World To Me - 1961

The Limeliters / Della Reese / Mario Lanza / Norman Luboff Choir

RCA Victor 33-150 - Headline Hits - 1961 (promo issue only Ep made for "Nestle's")

Della Reese

RCA Victor 47-7867 - The Touch Of Your Lips / Won'cha Come Home, Bill Bailey – 1961
RCA Victor 47-7884 - I Possess / A Far, Far Better Thing - 1961 (Some Copies Issued With Picture Sleeve)
RCA Victor 47-7961 - One / What Do You Think, Joe – 1961
RCA Victor 47-7996 - Ninety-Nine And A Half Won't Do / You Don't Know How Blessed You Are – 1962
RCA Victor 47-8021 - Rome Adventure / Here's That Rainy Day – 1962
RCA Victor 47-8070 - I Love You So Much It Hurts / Blow Out The Sun – 1962
RCA Victor 47-8093 - As Long As He Needs Me / It Makes No Difference Now - 1962 (Some Copies Issued With Picture Sleeve)
RCA Victor 47-8145 - Be My Love / I Behold You – 1963
Jubilee 5453 - Sermonette / You Gotta Love Somebody – 1963
RCA Victor 47-8187 - More / Serenade – 1963
RCA Victor 47-8260 - Angel D'amore / Forbidden Games – 1963
RCA Victor 47-8337 - A Clock That That's Got No Hands / The Bottom Of Old Smokey – 1964
RCA Victor 47-8394 - If I Didn't Care / Wind In The Willows – 1964
ABC Paramount 10691 - After Loving You / How Do You Keep From Crying – 1965
ABC Paramount 10721 - And That Reminds Me / I Only Want A Buddy, Not A Sweetheart - 1965 (Some Copies Issued With Picture Sleeve)
ABC Paramount 10759 - 'T'ain't Nobody's Bizness If I Do / I Ain't Ready For That – 1965
ABC 10815 - Stranger On Earth / If It's The Last Thing I Do – 1966
ABC 10841 - It Was A Very Good Year / Solitary Woman – 1966
ABC 10876 - Sunny / That's Life – 1966
ABC 10931 - Soon / Every Other Day – 1967
ABC 10962 - I Heard You Cried Last Night / On The South Side Of Chicago – 1967
ABC 11017 - Let's Make The Most Of A Beautiful Thing / Sorry Baby – 1967
ABC 11051 - I Gotta Be Me / Never My Love – 1968
Avco Embassy 4515 - Games People Play / Compared To What – 1969
Avco Embassy 4545 - Billy My Love / ? – 1970
Avco Embassy 4566 - The Trouble Maker / The Love I've Been Looking For – 1971
RCA Victor 48-1018 - Ninety-Nine And A Half Won't Do / And Now – 1971
RCA Victor 74-0558 - You Came A Long Way From St. Louis / Nobody's Sweetheart – 1971
Avco 4586 - If It Feels Good Do It / Good Lovin' (Makes It Right) – 1972
Virgo 6002 - In The Still Of The Night / And That Reminds Me - 1972 (Golden Memories Series)
LMI 1002 - I Don't Want To Be Right (If Loving You Is Wrong) / Let Me – 1973
Chi Sound Xw978 - I'll Be Your Sunshine / Nothing But A True Love – 1977
Collectables Col 045577 - Don't You Know / Not One Minute More - ?

Martha Reeves & The Vandellas

The Sabre-Ettes (members Martha Reeves, Shirley Walker (later member of The Fascinations on Mayfield), ? and ?)

The Sabre-Ettes (members Martha Reeves, Shirley Walker, Bernadine Boswell, Joanne Levell and Fern Bledsoe (a former secretary at MOTOWN)) group survived for roughly one year (roughly 1960) singing at The Broadway Sportman Club)

Mike Hanks & The Del-Phis (members Mike Hanks, Gloria Williams, Rosalind Ashford and Annette Sterling)

Mah's 1003 - When True Love Comes To Be / The Hawk - 1960

The Del-Phis (members Martha Reeves, Gloria Williams, Rosalind Ashford and Annette Sterling - group also backed Detroit artists J.J. Barnes, Leon Peterson and Mike Hanks)

Checkmate 1005 - I'll Let You Know / It Takes Two - 1961

The Vels

Mel-O-Dy 103 - There He Is At My Door / You'll Never Cherish A Love So True - 1962 (lead Gloria Williams)

Saundra Mallett & The Vandellas (members Saundra Mallett --- later of The Downbeats who became The Elgins on V.I.P fame, Martha Reeves, Rosalind Ashford and Annette Sterling)

Tamla 54067 - Camel Walk / It's Gonna Be Hard Times* - * exact same song issued on The Elgins album on V.I.P. "DARLING BABY"- VS-400

LaBrenda Ben

Motown 1033 - Camel Walk* / Chaperone - 1962 * First Issued As By Saundra Mallett & The Vandellas

Marvin Gaye

Tamla 54068 - Stubborn Kind Of Fellow / It Hurts Me Too - 1962 (Martha Reeves, Rosalind Ashford and Annette Sterling on backing vocals)

Martha & The Vandellas (members Martha Reeves, Rosalind Ashford and Annette Sterling)

Gordy 7011 - I'll Have To Let Him Go / My Baby Won't Come Back - 1962
Gordy 7014 - Come And Get These Memories / Jealous Love - 1963
Gordy 7022 - Heat Wave / A Love Like Yours (Don't Come Knocking Everyday) - 1963
Gordy 7025 - Quicksand / Darling, I Hum Our Song - 1963

Lee Alan and The Vendellas

YMCA/WXYZ 94472 - Set Me Free - 1963 ~1964 (local DJ. Lee Alan is backed by The Vandellas trying to recreate the backing vocals they used on "Stubborn Kind Of Fellow" by Marvin Gaye. Proceeds from this record went to a YMCA summer camp)

Martha & The Vandellas

Gordy 7027 - Live Wire / Old Love (Let's Try Again) - 1964 (Annette Sterling leaves group and is replaced by Betty Kelley)
Gordy 7031 - In My Lonely Room / A Tear For The Girl - 1964
Gordy 7033 - Dancing In The Street / There He Is (At My Door) - 1964
Gordy 7036 - Wild One / Dancing Slow - 1964

Hitsville U.S.A. DM 097311 - GREETINGS TO TAMLA MOTOWN APPRECIATION SOCIETY - 1964 (this American record was limited to 300 copies for dispersal throughout various fan clubs within Europe as a promo for their first European tour. Each act gives an individual greeting over it's latest record. Artists involved The Miracles, Stevie Wonder, Marvin Gaye, The Marvelettes,

The_Temptations, Martha and The Vandellas, The Contours, Eddie Holland, Kim Weston and The Supremes. The record has an introduction from publicist Margaret Phelps and Berry Gordy)

Martha & The Vandellas

Gordy 7039 - Nowhere To Run / Motoring -
Gordy 7045 - You've Been In Love Too Long / Love (Makes You Do Foolish Things) - 1965
Gordy 7048 - My Baby Loves Me / Never Leave Your Baby's Side - 1965 (Betty Kelley leaves group and is replaced by Lois Reeves -- Martha's sister ---- formerly of The Orlons)
Gordy 7053 - What Am I Gonna Do Without Your Love / Go Ahead And Laugh - 1966
Gordy 7056 - I'm Ready For Love / He Doesn't Love Her Anymore - 1966

The Hondells / Del Shannon / Martha and The Vandellas

Pepsi-Cola 8256 - Pepsi-Cola Ad Radio Youth Market - 1966 (Promo Only - Extolling The Virtues of drinking Pepsi-Cola)

Various Artists

Motown 2482 - Seasons Greetings From Motown - 1966 (promo issue only - very short "Christmas Greetings" radio station spots are delivered by Martha and The Vandellas, The Temptations, The Miracles, Shorty Long, The Velvelettes, The Spinners, The Four Tops, The Elgins and The Supremes ----- it was pressed in red vinyl)

Martha and The Vandellas

Gordy 7058 - Jimmy Mack / Third Finger, Left Hand - 1967
Gordy 7062 - Love Bug Leave My Heart Alone / One Way Out - 1967 (Rosalind Ashford leaves group and is replaced by Sandra Tilley from The Velvelettes)

Vandellas

CDX ?? 7-Bill (+6.0) - Honey Chile - 1967 (one sided acetate has time 2:47 and date (10-18-67) typed on label plus RECOAT handwritten across label in thick black felt pen obscuring other label details)

Martha and The Vandellas

Gordy 7067 - Honey Chile / Show Me The Way - 1967
Topps/Motown 7 - Dancing In The Street - 1967 (Cardboard Record)
Topps/Motown 14 - Love Is Like A Heat Wave - 1967 (Cardboard Record)

Martha Reeves & The Vandellas

Gordy 7070 - I Promise To Wait My Love / Forget Me Not - 1968
Gordy 7075 - I Can't Dance To That Music You're Playin' / I Tried - 1968

Gladys Knight & The Pips / The Four Tops / Martha Reeves & The Vandellas / The Voices Of Tabernacle

Motown W4kb-4900-1a - Excerpts From Album M 642 "In Loving Memory" (Tribute To Mrs. Loucye G. Wakefield) - 1968 (Promo Issue Only)

Martha Reeves & The Vandellas

Gordy 7080 - Sweet Darlin' / Without You - 1968
Gordy 7085 - (We've Got) Honey Love / I'm In Love (And I Know It) - 1969

Gordy 7094 - Taking My Love (And Leaving Me) / Heartless - 1969
Gordy 7098 - I Should Be Proud / Love, Guess Who - 1970
Gordy 7103 - I Gotta Let You Go / You're The Loser Now - 1970
Gordy 7110 - Bless You / Hope I Don't Get My Heart Broke - 1971
Gordy 7113 - In And Out Of My Life / Your Love Makes It All Worthwhile - 1972
Gordy 7118 - Tear It On Down / I Want You Back - 1972
Gordy 7127 - Baby Don't Leave Me / I Won't Be The Fool I've Been Again - 1973

Martha & The Vandellas / James Brown

A & M 3022 - Nowhere To Run* / I Got You (I Feel Good)** - 1988 * "A" side by Martha and The Vandellas. **flip by James Brown.

The Reflections

Larados With The Band Of Lucky Lee (Members Ronnie Morris, Don Davenport (Born 21-April-1938 In Dickson County, Tennessee - Died 1-January-2003 In Trenton, Michigan. Cause: ?), Tom Hust (Born 30-August-1940 - Died 13-January-1943 In Wayne County, Michigan. Cause ?), Bernie Turnbull (Born 31-August-1936 --Died Wednesday-5-February-2003 In Wayne County, Michigan. Cause:?), Bob Broderick, Tony Micale, Gary Banovitz, Rick Benko And John Dean)

Fox 962/3 - Bad Bad Guitar Man / Now The Parting Begins - 1958

The Reflections (Members Tony Micale (Aka Tony Michaels), John Dean, Phil Castrodale, Dan Bennie And Ray Steinberg)

Crossroads 401 - Maybe Tomorrow / I Really Must Know - 1961
Crossroads 402 - Because Of You / Rocket To The Moon - 1962
Tigre 602 - (I Remember) In The Still Of The Night / Tic Toc - 1962
Kay-Ko 1003 - Helpless / You Said Goodbye - 1963
Golden World 9 - (Just Like) Romeo And Juliet / Can't You Tell By The Look In His Eyes - 1964
Golden World 12 - Like Columbus Did / Lonely Girl - 1964
Golden World 15 - Oowee Now / Talkin' Bout My Girl - 1964
Golden World 16 - Henpecked Guy / Don't Do That To Me - 1964
Golden World 19 - You're My Baby / Shabby Little Hut - 1964
Golden World 20 - Poor Man's Son / Comin' At You - 1965
Golden World 22 - Wheelin' And Dealin' / Deborah Ann - 1965
Golden World 24 - June Bride / Out Of The Picture - 1965 ~
Golden World 29 - Girl In The Candy Store / Your Kind Of Love - 1965
Lana 140 - (Just Like) Romeo And Juliet / ? - 196?
ABC 10794 - Like Adam And Eve / Vito's House - 1966
(Tony Micale Had Left The Group By The Time This 45 Was Recorded)
ABC 10822 - You're Gonna Find Out (You Love Me) / Long Cigarette - 1966

The High And Mighty (The Reflections)

ABC 10821 - Escape From Cuba / Tryin' To Stop From Cryin' - 1966

Tony Michaels

Golden World 41 - I Love The Life I Live (And Live The Life I Love)* / Picture Me And You - 1966 *Vocal Version Of "Hungry For Love" By The San Remo Golden Strings.

The Reflections / Dobie Gray

Eric 277 - (Just Like) Romeo And Juliet */ The "In" Crowd** - 1979 * "A"Side The Reflections. **Flip Side Dobie Gray.

The Reflections

Adam & Eve 1 - Helpless / ? - 1980's (Only 500 Copies Made)

Diane Renay

Diane Renay (Renee Diane Kushner)
Atco 6240 - Falling Star / Little White Lies – 1962
Atco 6262 - Dime A Dozen / Tender – 1963
20th Century Fox 456 - Navy Blue / Unbelievable Guy* - 1964 *co-written by Bob Crewe and Larry Santos.
20th Century Fox 477 - Kiss Me Sailor / Soft Spoken Guy – 1964
20th Century Fox 514 - Growin' Up Too Fast / Waitin' For Joey – 1964
20th Century Fox 533 - It's In Your Tears / Present From Eddie – 1964
MGM 13296 - Billy Blue Eyes / Watch Out Sally – 1964
MGM 13335 - I Had A Dream* / Troublemaker - 1965 *backing vocals The Charlettes
New Voice 800 - Words / The Company You Keep – 1965
New Voice 803 - Cross My Heart, Hope To Die / Happy Birthday, Broken Heart - 1965
New Voice 813 - Soldier Boy / Words - 1966 (recently found 45)
United Artists 50048 - Dynamite / Please Gypsy – 1966
D Man 101 - Can't Help Lovin' That Man / It's A Good Day For A Parade - ?
Fontana 1679 - Hold Me, Thrill Me, Kiss Me / Yesterday – 1969
Eric 175 - Navy Blue / Kiss Me Sailor – 1973

Diane Renay / The Cavaliers

Oldies 45 108 - Navy Blue / Dance, Dance, Dance* - **?** *flip by Diane Renay.

Diane Renay

Rex 293 - Maybe / Together Again – 1981
Dice Tgr 8018 - Navy Blue / Navy Blue – 1987

The Rivingtons

The Emanons (members Al Frazier, ...)

The Mellomoods (members Al Frazier, ...)

The Canaan Crusaders (members Thurston Harris, ...)

The Indiana Wonders (members Thurston Harris, ...)
(members Leon Hughes, Willie Ray Rockton, Matthew Nelson, Thurston Harris and Al Frazier) group was without name went they were signed to Federal records.

The Lamplighters (members Willie Ray Rockton, Matthew Nelson, Thurston Harris and Al Frazier)

Federal 12149 - Turn Me Loose / Part Of Me – 1953
Federal 12152 - Be-Bop Wino / Give Me – 1953

Jimmy Witherspoon and The Lamplighters (members Jimmy Witherspoon, Willie Ray Rockton, Matthew Nelson, Thurston Harris and Al Frazier)

Federal 12156 - Move Me Baby / Sad Life – 1953

The Lamplighters (members Willie Ray Rockton, Matthew Nelson, Thurston Harris and Al Frazier)

Federal 12166 - Smootchie / I Can't Stand It – 1954
Federal 12176 - I Used To Cry Mercy, Mercy / Tell Me You Care – 1954
Federal 12182 - Salty Dog / Ride Jockey Ride – 1954
Federal 12192 - Five Minutes Longer / You Hear – 1954
Federal 12197 - Goody Good Things / Yum Yum – 1954
Federal 12206 - Believe In Me / I Wanna Know – 1954

The Sharps (members Al Frazier, Carl White, John "Sonny" Harris, and Turner "Rocky" Wilson Jr.)

Mikes 101 - Love Me My Darling / Heaven Only Knows – 1954

The Lamplighters (members Willie Ray Rockton, Matthew Nelson, Thurston Harris and Al Frazier)

Federal 12212 - Love, Rock And Thrill / Roll On – 1955

The Tenderfoots (members Al Frazier, Carl White, Sonny Harris and Matthew Nelson)

Federal 12214 - Kissing Bug / Watussi Wussi Wo – 1955
Federal 12219 - Save Me Some Kisses / My Confession – 1955
Federal 12225 - Those Golden Bells / I'm Yours Anyhow – 1955
Federal 12228 - Cindy / Sugar Ways - 1955

The Lamplighters (members Al Frazier, Carl White, Sonny Harris, Matthew Nelson and Thurston Harris)

Federal 12242 - Don't Make It So Good / Hug A Little, Kiss A Little – 1956
Federal 12255 - Bo Peep / You Were Sent Down From Heaven – 1956
Federal 12261 - It Ain't Right / Everything's All Right – 1956

Paul Anka & The Jacks (members Paul Anka, Al Frazier, Carl White, John "Sonny" Harris, and Turner "Rocky" Wilson Jr.)

RPM 472 - I Confess / Clau - Wile - Deveest - Fontaine - 1956

The Sharps

Tag 2200 - Six Months, Three Weeks (Two Days And An Hour) / Cha - Cho Hop - 1956 (with Jack McVea Orchestra)
Jamie 1040 - Come On / Sweet Sweetheart – 1957
Vik 0264 - Come On / Sweet Sweetheart – 1957
Lamp 2007 - Our Love Is Here To Stay / Lock My Heart – 1957

Thurston Harris (background vocals The Sharps)

Aladdin 3398 - Little Bitty Pretty One / I Hope You Won't Hold It Against Me - 1957

Thurston Harris and The Sharps

Intro 6099 - Little Bitty Pretty One / I Hope You Won't Hold It Against Me – 1957

The Sharps

Aladdin 4301 - What Will I Gain / Shugglin' – 1957
Chess 1690 - Six Months, Three Weeks, Two Days, Two Hours / Cha - Cho Hop – 1958
Combo 146 - All My Love */ Look What You've Done To Me - 1958 *Non Member Joe Green on lead vocals

Duane Eddy (handclaps and rebel yells by The Sharps)

Jamie 1104 - Rebel Rouser / Stalkin' - 1958

The Sharps

Dot 15806 - All My Love / Look What You've Done To Me – 1958
Jamie 1108 - Look At Me / Have Love, Will Travel – 1958
Jamie 1114 - Here's A Heart / Gig - A - Lene – 1958

The Crenshaws (members Al Frazier, Carl White, John Harris and Turner Wilson)

Warner Brothers 5505 - Off Shore / Let The Good Times Roll – 1961
Warner Brothers 5254 - Moonlight In Vermont / He's Got The Whole World In His Hand's – 1961

Carl Lester & The Showstoppers (members

Brent 7021 - When You See Me Hurt / Don't You Know What I Believe – 1961

The Rivingtons

Liberty 55427 - Papa - Oom - Mow - Mow / Deep Water – 1962
Liberty 55513 - Kickapoo Joy Juice / My Reward – 1962
Liberty 55528 - Mama - Oom - Mow - Mow / Waiting – 1962
Liberty 55553 - The Bird's The Word / I'm Losing My Grip - 1963 (Some Copies Issued With Picture Sleeve)
Liberty 55585 - The Shaky Bird (Part 1) / The Shaky Bird (Part 2) – 1963
Liberty 55610 - Cherry / Little Sally Walker - 1963
Liberty 55671 - Wee Jee Walk / Fairy Tales – 1964
Reprise 0293 - I Tried / One Monkey – 1964
A. R. E. 100 - All That Glitters / You Move Me Baby (Am I Moving You) – 1964
Vee Jay 634 - You Move Me Baby / All That Glitters – 1964
Vee Jay 649 - I Love You Always / Years Of Tears – 1964
Vee Jay 677 - The Willy / Just Got To Be More - 1965 (Al Frazier Becomes Group's New Manager And Is Replaced By Darryl White)
Columbia 43581 - A Rose Growing In The Ruins / Tend To Business – 1966
Columbia 43772 - Yadi - Yadi - Dum - Dum / Yadi - Yadi Revisited – 1966
Columbia (No #) - Little Sally Walker - 1967 (One Sided Acetate)
Quan 1379 - You're Gonna Pay / I Don't Want A New Baby – 1967

Carlos And The Rivingtons (members

Baton Master 202 - Teach Me Tonight / Reach Our Goal – 1967
AGC 5 - I Lost The Love (That I Found) / Mind Your Man - 1968

The Rivingtons

RCA 74-0301 - Pop Your Corn (Part 1) / Pop Your Corn (Part 2) – 1969
Wand 11253 - Papa - Oom - Mow - Mow / I Don't Want A New Baby - 1973

The Rivingtons ((late 1970's members) Carl White, Madero White, Rocky Wilson Jr. and Sonny Harris)

Jd 122 - Don't Hate Your Father (Part 1) / Don't Hate Your Father (Part 2) – 1976
Liberty 1484 - Papa Oom Mow Mow / Papa Oom Mow Mow - 1982 (Promo Issue Only)
United Artists 54543 - Papa Oom Mow Mow / Papa Oom Mow Mow - ?

Danny Williams / The Rivingtons

Underground 1048 - White On White / Papa-Oom-Mow-Mow* - ? *Flip By The Rivingtons.

George Clinton / The Rivingtons

Collectables Col 061897 - Atomic Dog / Papa-Oom-Mow-Mow* - ? *Flip By The Rivingtons.

The Rivingtons

Collectables Col 062187 - The Weejee Walk / Papa-Oom-Mow-Mow - ?

Alvin Robinson

Al Robinson

Imperial 5727 - Pain In My Heart / I'm Leaving You Today – 1961
Imperial 5762 - Woke Up / I Wanna Know –1961
Imperial 5824 - Oh Red / The Blues – 1962
Post 10001 - Oh Red / The Blues - 1962

Alvin Robinson (born 22-December-1937 in New Orleons, Louisiana --- died 24-January-1989 in New Orleons, Louisiana --- cause: ?)

Red Bird 010 - Down Home Girl* / Fever - 1964 *covered by The Rolling Stones and included on their second UK album - this 45 was successful enough to spark the reply in 1966 by The Ad Libs on Blue Cat 123.
Tiger 104 - Something You Got / Searchin' - 1964.
Blue Cat 104 - Something You Got / Searchin' – 1965
Blue Cat 108 - How Can I Get Over You / I'm Gonna Put Some Hurt On You – 1965
Blue Cat 113 - Let The Good Times Roll* / Bottom Of My Soul - 1965
Joe Jones 1 - You Brought My Heart Right Down To My Knees / Whatever You Had, You Ain't Got It No More - 1966
Atco 45-6581 - Let Me Down Easy / Baby Don't You Do It - 1968

Shine (Al Robinson)

Pulsar 2408 - Empty Talk / Sho' 'Bout To Drive Me Wild - 1969

Al Robinson

Pulsar 2417 - Soulful Woman / Give Her Up - 1969

Robert Parker / Alvin Robinson

Trip 147 - Barefootin' / Something You Got - ?

Roscoe Robinson

The Southern Sons Quartet (members Roscoe Robinson, David Smith, Earl Ratliff and Cliff Givens)

Trumpet 118 - Search Me Lord / New, Born Again - 1950
Trumpet 119 - Peace In The Valley / Nearer My God To Thee – 1950

Joiner's Five Trumpets (members Roscoe Robinson (lead), Walter Ford (lead), Lonnie B. Ford (tenor), George Anthony (baritone) and John Ford (bass))

Job 121 – Where Can I Go / This Changing World – 1952

The Silver Quintette (Members Roscoe Robinson, ...)

Vee-Jay 223 – Father Don't Leave Me / Sinner's Crossroads - 1956

The Fairfield Four (Members Roscoe Robinson, ...)

Old Town 1081 - Memories / Don't Let Nobody – 1960

The Original Five Blind Boys (Jackson Harmoneers) Lead: Robinson (Members Roscoe Robinson, ...)

Peacock 1811 – Time To Think About The Lord / I Call On Jesus – 1960

Original Five Blind Boys - Lead: Robinson (Members Roscoe Robinson, Wilmer Broadnax, ...)

Peacock 1824 – Sending Up My Timber / Lord, Lord, You've Been Good To Me – 1961

The Five Blind Boys (Members Roscoe Robinson,Wilmer Broadnax, ...)

Peacock 1838 – Can't Serve The Lord / Constantly Abiding – 1961

The Original Five Blind Boys (Jackson Harmoneers) (members Roscoe Robinson,Wilmer Broadnax, ...)

Peacock 1855 – I Got It Within Me / The Tide Of Life – 1962

The Five Blind Boys (members Roscoe Robinson,Wilmer Broadnax, ...)

Peacock 1868 – Father I Stretched My Hands To Thee / Lord Remember Me – 1962
Peacock 1881 – You Done What The Doctor Couldn't Do / Speak For Jesus - 1963

Roscoe Robinson / Roscoe Robinson And The The Blind Boys Of Ohio

Constellation 600 - Sell Out To The Master / I'm A Child Of The King* - 1963 *flip by Roscoe Robinson And The Blind Boys Of Ohio.

Roscoe Robinson (Born 1933 In Pine Bluff, Arkansas)

Tuff 405 - What Makes A Man Do Wrong / Too Many Lies - 1963

Rosco Robinson

Gerri 001 - That's Enough / One More Time - 1965
Wand 1125 - That's Enough / One More Time - 1966

Roscoe Robinson

Wand 1143 - How Much Pressure (Do You Think I Can Stand) / Do It Right Now - 1966
Wand 1149 - What You're Doing To Me / A Thousand Rivers - 1967
Wand 1161 - Just A Little Bit* / I Gotta Keep Tryin' - 1967 *also recorded in 1963 by Jerry Butler on VEE-JAY 556 an in 1965 by Roy Head & The Traits on Scepter 12116.
Sound Stage 7 2595 - Darling, Please Tell Me / Why Are You Afraid - 1967
Sound Stage 7 2603 - Let Me Know / One Bo-Dillion Years* - 1968 *also recorded in 1966 by Little Richie on Sound Stage 7 2567.
Sound Stage 7 2610 - Fox Hunting On The Weekend / You Don't Move Me No More - 1968
Sound Stage 7 2618 - Why Must It End / How Many Times Must I Knock - 1968
Sound Stage 7 2639 - I'm Burning And Yearning (For You) / Standing In The Safety Zone - 1969
Gerri 002 - Don't Forget The Soldiers (Fighting In Vietnam) / Tis Yuletide - 1969
Gerri 77 - That's It / In Time You'll See - 1969
Gerri ? - Oo Wee Baby I Love You* / Leave You In The Arms (Of Your Other Man) - 1969 *also recorded in 1965 by Fred Hughes on Vee-Jay 684.
Atlantic 2637 - Oo Wee Baby I Love You / Leave You In The Arms (Of Your Other Man)* - 1969 *recorded 2-May-1969.
Sound Of Birmingham Recording Studios - Let Me Be Myself - 1969 (unissued at the time this alternate version of the Paula 45 was released in 2006 in the U. S. A. on a Rabbit Factory Inc. Cd "The Birmingham Sound : The Soul Of Neal Hemphill Vol. 1")
Sound Of Birmingham Recording Studios - Two Heart Accident - 1969 (unissued at the time released in 2006 in the U. S. A. on a Rabbit Factory Inc. Cd "The Birmingham Sound : The Soul Of Neal Hemphill Vol. 1")
Fame 1469 - Don't Pretend (Just Be Yourself) / What Color Is Love - 1970
Paula 350 - Yesterday Is Gone (Tomorrow Is Too Late) / Let Me Be Myself - 1971
Paula 357 - Prove It / I'm Satisfied - 1972
Paula 365 - Don't Set Me Free / I'm Satisfied - 1972
Paula 373 - Trust Me* / You And Me - 1972 *written and recorded by Bobby Womack in 1967 on Minit 32024.
Paula 378 - We're Losing It Baby / We Got A Good Thing Going - 1973
Paula 384 - Standing In The Safety Zone / You Qualify - 1973

The Royal Jokers

The Serenaders (Members Noah Howell, Norman Thrasher, Isaac "Ike" Reese, Henry Booth And Thearon "T-Man" Hill)

J-V-B 2001 - Tomorrow Night* / Why Don't You Do Right** - 1952 *Lead Thearon Hill. **Lead Noah Howell. (The "A" Side Is A Cover Of Lonnie Johnson's 1948 Hit. While The Flip Song More Recently Showed Up Sung By Jessica Rabbit, In The Cartoon Movie "Who Framed Roger Rabbit?")

The Caverliers (Members Noah Howell, Norman Thrasher, Isaac Reese, Henry Booth And Thearon Hill)

No Known Recordings.

The Musketeers (Members Noah Howell, Norman Thrasher, Isaac Reese, Henry Booth And Thearon Hill)

Roxy 801 - Goodbye My Love* / Love Me Till My Dying Day** - 1952 *Leads Thearon Hill & Norman Thrasher. **Lead Thearon Hill. (The Flip Side Title Was Misprinted And Should Have Been "Love Me Till Your Dying Day")

The Serenaders (Members Noah Howell, Norman Thrasher, Isaac Reese, Henry Booth And Thearon Hill)

Coral 60720 - It's Funny* / Confession Is Good For The Soul** - 1952 *Lead Thearon Hill. **Lead Noah Howell.
Coral 65093 - Misery* / But I Forgive You** - 1952 *Lead Thearon Hill. **Leads Noah Howell & Thearon Hill.

The Muskateers (Members Noah Howell, Norman Thrasher, Isaac Reese, Henry Booth And Thearon Hill) (Note Mispelling Of Group Name By Record Label)

Swing Time 331 - Deep In My Heart* / Love Me Til Your Dying Day** - 1953 *Same Song As "Goodbye My Love" On Roxy 801, Leads Thearon Hill & Norman Thrasher. **Lead Thearon Hill.

The Serenaders (Members Noah Howell, Norman Thrasher, Isaac Reese, Henry Booth And Thearon Hill)

Red Robin 115 - Will She Know?* / I Want To Love You Baby** - 1953 *Lead Thearon Hill. **Leads Thearon Hill & Isaac Reese.
Deluxe 6022 - Please, Please Forgive Me* / Baby** - 1953 *Leads Noah Howell & Thearon Hill. **Lead Noah Howell.
Swing Time 347 - Ain't Goin' To Cry No More* / M-Ay-B-E-L-L** - 1954 *Lead Norman Thrasher. **Group Sings In Unison. (On The Flip The Group Actually Sings "M-A-B-E-L")

The Royals (Members Noah Howell, Norman Thrasher, Isaac Reese, Henry Booth And Thearon Hill)

Venus 103 - Someday We'll Meet Again* / I Want You To Be My Baby - Mambo** - 1954 *Lead Thearon Hill. **Group Sings In Unison. (Both Sides Of This Recording Were Written By Maurice King Who Later Became A Musical Director For Motown. In The Early 1950's Bea Baker (Better Known As Lavern Baker) Was A Vocalist In Maurice King's Band)

The Royal Jokers (Members Noah Howell, Norman Thrasher, Ted Green, Willie Jones And Thearon Hill)

Atco 6052 - You Tickle Me Baby* / Stay Here* - 1955 *Lead Willie Jones.
Atco 6062 - Don't Leave Me Fanny* / Rocks In My Pillow** - 1956 *Lead Willie Jones. **Leads Noah Howell & Norman Thrasher. (The Flip Is A Re-Recording Of Their Coral 65093 Release "But I Forgive You")
Atco 6077 - She's Mine All Mine* / Ride On Little Girl* - 1956 *Lead Willie Jones.

The Scooters (Members Noah Howell, Norman Thrasher, Isaac Reese, Henry Booth And Thearon Hill)
Dawn 224 - Someday We'll Meet Again* / Really** - 1957 *Lead Thearon Hill. **Not Them. (This Is A Very Bizarre Recording As The Group Never Recorded Or Named Themselves The Scooters. The "A" Side Is The Royals Recording From Venus 103, While The Flip Is A Totally Different Group Altogether. Also Someone At The Pressing Plant Must Have Made A Mistake Because If You Play The Record At 45rpm It Sounds Like The Chipmunks Singing R&B, But If You Play It At 33 1/3 Rpm The Record Is Clearly The Royals)

The Royal Jokers (Members Noah Howell, Ted Green, Willie Jones And Billy Lyons A Former Member Of The 5 Jets)

Fortune 840 - Sweet Little Angel* / I Don't Like You That Much** - 1958 *Lead Ted Green.

**Lead Noah Howell.
Hi-Q 5004 - September In The Rain* / Spring** - 1958 *Lead Billy Lyons. **Lead Willie Jones. (After This Release Raymond Dorsey Former Member Of The Thrillers, The 5 Jets, The 5 Stars And The Early Voice Masters Joins The Group)
Metro 20032 - Sam's Back* / Grabitis** - 1960 *Lead Ted Green. **Lead Noah Howell.
Keldon 322 - Lovey Dovey* / Nickel, 3 Dimes And 5 Quarters* - 1960 *Lead Billy Lyons. (The "A" Side Is A Cover Of The Clovers 1954 Release On Atlantic 1022)
Big Top 3064 - Hard Times* / Red Hot* - 1961 *Lead Ted Green. (After This Release Ted Green Leaves The Group)
Fortune 560 - You Tickle Me Baby* / You Came Along** - 1963 *Lead Willie Jones. **Lead Billy Lyons.
Wingate 020 - Love Game (From A To Z)* / Love Game (From A To Z) (Instrumental Version) - 1966 *Lead Willie Jones. (After This Release Willie Jones And Billie Lyons Leave The Group And Are Replaced By Bobby Ruffin And Stanley Mitchell A Former Member Of The Tornados On Chess And Bumble Bee)

Ruby & The Romantics

The Supremes (members Edward Roberts, Ronald Mosely, Leroy Fann and George Lee)

Ruby & The Romantics (members Ruby Nash, Edward Roberts, Ronald Mosely, Leroy Fann (born 9-November-1936 - died ?-November-1973 - cause: heart attack) and George Lee (born 24-March-1936 --- died 25-October-1994 in the Bronx, New York --- cause: cancer))

Kapp 501 - Our Day Will Come* / Moonlight And Music - 1963 *the demo to this track was originally sung by Pearl Woods.
Kapp 525 - My Summer Love / Sweet Love And Sweet Forgiveness - 1963
Kapp 544 - Hey There Lonely Boy* / Not A Moment Too Soon - 1963 *covered in 1969 by Eddie Holman as "Hey There Lonely Girl" on ABC 11240.
Kapp 557 - Young Wings Can Fly (Higher Than You Know) / Day Dreaming - 1963
Kapp 564 - Much Better Off Than I've Ever Been / ? - 1963
Kapp 578 - Our Everlasting Love / Much Better Off Than I've Ever Been - 1964
Kapp 646 - Does He Really Care For Me / Nevertheless (I'm In Love With You) - 1965
Kapp 665 - Your Baby Doesn't Love You Anymore / We'll Meet Again - 1965
Kapp 702 - Imagination / Nobody But My Baby - 1965
Kapp 759 - Remember Me / We Can Make It - 1966
Kapp 773 - Hey There Lonely Boy / Think - 1966
Kapp 839 - I Know / We'll Love Again - 1967
ABC 10911 - Twilight Time / Una Bella Brazilian Melody - 1967
ABC 10941 - Twilight Time / Una Bella Brazilian Melody - 1967
ABC 11065 - More Than Yesterday Less Than Tomorrow / On A Clear Day You Can See Forever - 1968
A & M 1042 - Hurting Each Other* / Baby I Could Be So Good At Lovin' You - 1969 *also recorded in 1965 by Jimmy Clanton on Mala 500.
MCA 60052 - Our Day Will Come / Young Wings Can Fly - 1973
MCA 60127 - Hey There Lonely Boy / When You're Young And In Love – 1973

Jimmy Ruffin

Jimmy Ruffin (born 7-May-1939 in Collinsville, Mississippi)

Miracle 1 - Don't Feel Sorry For Me / Heart - 1961

The Four Hollidays (member Jimmy Ruffin)

Master 3001 - Deep Down In My Heart / ? - ?
Markie 109 - Grandma Bird / Step By Step - 1963
Markie 115 - I'll Walk Right Out Of The Door / ? - 1963

Jimmy Ruffin

Soul 35002 - Since I've Lost You / I Want Her Love - 1964
Soul 35016 - As Long As There Is L-O-V-E / (Love) How Can I Say I'm Sorry - 1965
Soul 35022 - What Becomes Of The Brokenhearted / Baby I've Got It - 1966
Soul 35027 - I've Passed This Way Before / Tomorrow's Tears - 1966
Soul 35032 - Gonna Give Her All The Love I've Got* / World So Wide (Nowhere To Hide From Your Heart) - 1967
Soul 35035 - Don't You Miss Me A Little Bit / I Want Her Love - 1967
Soul 35043 - I'll Say Forever My Love / Everybody Needs Love - 1968
Soul 35046 - Don't Let Him Take Your Love From Me / Lonely, Lonely Man Am I - 1968
Soul 35053 - Sad And Lonesome Feeling / Gonna Keep On Tryin' Till I Win Your Love - 1968
Soul 35060 - Farewell Is A Lonely Sound / If You Will Let Me, I Know I Can - 1969

David & Jimmy Ruffin

Soul 35076 - Stand By Me / Your Love Was Worth Waiting For - 1970

Jimmy Ruffin

Soul 35077 - Maria (You Were The Only One) / Living In A World I Created For Myself - 1970

David & Jimmy Ruffin

Soul 35082 - When My Love Hand Comes Do Down / Steppin' On A Dream - 1971
Soul 35086 - Lo And Behold / The Things We Have To Do - 1971

Jimmy Ruffin

Soul 35092 - Our Favorite Melody / You Gave Me Love - 1972
Chess 2160 - Tell Me What You Want / Do You Know Me - 1974
Atco 45-6926 - Tears Of Joy / Goin' Home - 1974
Motown 1329 - What Becomes Of The Brokenhearted / Baby I've Got It - 1974
Chess 2168 - What You See (Ain't Always What You Get) / Boy From Mississippi - 1975
Epic 50339 - Fallin' In Love With You / Fallin' In Love With You - 1977
Epic 50384 - Fallin' In Love With You / Fallin' In Love With You - 1977
RSO 1021 - Hold On To My Love / (Instrumental) - 1980 written and produced by Robin Gibb.
RSO 1042 - Night Of Love / Searchin' - 1980

Maxine Nightingale featuring Jimmy Ruffin

Highrise 2004 - Turn To Me / Give A Little Love (To Me) - 1982

Jimmy Ruffin with Jackson Moore

ERC/L 109 - I'm Gonna Love You Forever (Vocal) / I'm Gonna Love You Forever (High N-R-G MiX) - 1984 (12" single)

Group Line Ups

The Sapphires (Carol Jackson, George Gainer, Joe Livingstone)
The Shirelles (Shirley Owens Alston, Addie "Miki" Harris, Beverly Lee, Doris Coley Kenner)
The Showstoppers (Earl Smith, Timmie Smith, Alec Burke, Laddie Burke)
The Silhouettes (Bill Horton, Richard "Rick" Lewis, Earl Beal, Ray Edwards)
The Skyliners (Jimmy Beaumont, Janet Vogel, Wally Lester, Joe Verscharen, Jackie Taylor)
Sly, Slick, & Wicked (John 'Sly' Wilson, Charles 'Slick' Still, Marc 'Wicked' Sexton (who was replaced by DeFrantz Forrest))

Evie Sands

Evie Sands

ABC 10458 - The Roll / My Dog – 1963
Gold 215 - Danny Boy, I Love You So / I Was Moved – 1964
Blue Cat 118 - Take Me For A Little While */ Run Home To Your Mama - 1965 (Evie signed with Blue Cat at age seventeen) *also recorded in 1965 by Jackie Ross on Chess 1938.
Blue Cat 122 - I Can't Let Go / Uptight – 1965
Cameo 413 - Picture Me Gone* / It Makes Me Laugh - 1966 *also recorded in 1967 by Madeline Bell on Mod 1007.
Cameo 436 - Love Of A Boy / We Know Better – 1966
Cameo 475 - Angel Of The Morning / Dear John – 1967
Cameo 2002 - Billy Sunshine / Don't Make Me Laugh - 1967
A & M 0980 - Until It's Time For You To Go / Shadow Of The Evening – 1968
A & M 1026 - One Fine Summer Morning / I'll Hold Out My Hand – 1969
A & M 1090 - Anyway That U Want Me / I'll Never Be Alone Again – 1969
A & M 1157 - Maybe Tomorrow / Crazy Annie – 1969
A & M 1175 - Maybe Tomorrow / But You Know I Love You – 1970
A & M 1192 - It's This I Am, I Find / Take Me For A Little While – 1970
Capitol / Haven 7010 - You Brought The Woman Out Of Me / Early Morning Sunshine – 1975
Capitol / Haven 7013 - I Love Making Love To You / One Thing On My Mind – 1975
Capitol / Haven 7020 - Yesterday Can't Hurt Me / (Am I) Crazy 'Cause I Believe – 1975
Arista / Haven 806 - The Way You Do The Things You Do / Love In The Afternoon – 1976
Big Tree 16104 - You Can Do It (Mono) / You Can Do It (Stereo) - 1977 (promo issue only)
RCA 11549 - Keep My Love Light Burnin' / I Can't Wait For You - 1979
RCA 11653 - You Sho' Look Good To Me / Brain Damage – 1979

Janie Grant / Evie Sands

Trip 10 - Triangle / Take Me For A Little While* - ? *flip by Evie Sands.

Larry Santos

The Tones (members Larry Santos, ...)

Baton 265 - We (Belong Together) / Three Little Loves - 1959 (with The Al Caiola Orchestra)

Larry & The Legends (members Larry Santos, ...)

Atlantic 2220 - Creep / Don't Pick On My Baby - 1964 (with The Four Seasons on back up vocals)

Larry Santos

Atlantic 2250 - Someday (When I'm Gone) / True - 1964 (with The Four Seasons on back up vocals)

The Madisons (members Larry Santos, ...)

Lawn 240 - Can You Imagine It / The Wind And The Rain – 1964
Limelight 3018 - Because I Got You / Bad Baboon – 1964
Jomada 601 - Only A Fool / Stagger – 1965
MGM 13312 - Cheryl Anne / Looking For True Love – 1965

The Madisons / The Montereys

Twin Hit 2685 - Valerie / ?* - 1965 *flip by The Montereys.

Larry Santos

Evolution 1007 - You Got Me Where You Want Me / Tomorrow Without Love - 1969
Evolution 1010 - Subway Man / Woman-Child – 1970
Evolution 1018 - Great Divide / Paper Chase – 1970
Evolution 1024 - Mornin' Sun / Wandering Man – 1970
Evolution 1029 - Now That I Have Found You / Wandering Man – 1970
Evolution 1039 - Let It End / Little Bit Of You – 1971
Evolution 1043 - I Love You More Than Everything / Let It End – 1971
Big Tree 136 - Life Is Beautiful / Touchin' You – 1972

Dandelion Wine (members Larry Santos, Thelma Hopkins, Joyce Vincent, ...)

Sussex 502 - Some Kind Of Summer / Hot Dog* - 1973 *same song as the 1969 release "I'd Be Nowhere Today" by The Nu People on Venture 638. Dandelion Wine was a manufactured group put together for this release.

Larry Santos

Casablanca 844 - Can't Get You Off My Mind* / We Can't Hide It Anymore - 1975 *Listed As "A" Side.
Casablanca 844 - We Can't Hide It Anymore* / Can't Get You Off My Mind - 1975 *Listed As "A" Side.
Casablanca 869 - You Are Everything I Need / Long, Long Time – 1976
Casablanca 881 - Magic Mountain / Don't Let The Music Stop - 1977 (both sides written by Larry Santos)
Casablanca 2357 - I'll Come Back To You / W ..... Laura - ?
Overture 7 - I'll Come Back To You / ? - ?
Overture Ov1201 - Interplay / We Can't Hide It Anymore - 1980 (12" release)

Larry Santos / Larry Santos & Laura Santos

Overture 702 - We Can't Hide It Anymore / I'll Come Back To You* - 1981 *flip by Larry Santos & Laura Santos.

Larry Santos

Warlock 1002 - Beg, Buy, Borrow Or Steal Your Love / Someone's Gotta Start Today - ?

The Seven Souls

Ivory Hudson & The Harlequins (members Ivory Hudson, Bob Welch (later member of Fleetwood Mac), ...) an Oregon based integrated soul band which moved to Los Angeles and played the black club circuit around the time of the Watts riots. After touring Europe the group returned to Los Angeles where they changed their name to The Seven Souls and lost a battle of the bands competition to Sly & The Family Stone. Bob Welch left the group soon after.

The Seven Souls (members at various times Ivory Hudson, Henry Moore, Bob Welch who replaced Ray Tusken , Fred Murphy (drummer - died 2003), Henry Thompson (died 26-May-2004), Anthony Lytle, Wayne Purnell (piano), Bobby Watson, David T. Walker, Tony Maiden, Billy Diez (bass) and Ron Edge (drums))

Okeh 7289 - I Still Love You / I'm No Stranger - 1967 Also released in France & Italy
Venture_614 - Groove On / Got To Find A Way - 1968

Dee Dee Sharp

Chubby Checker featuring Dee Dee Sharp / Chubby Checker

Parkway 835 - Slow Twistin' / La Paloma Twist* - 1962 *flip by Chubby Checker only.

Chubby Checker & Dee Dee Sharp

Cameo 105 - Do You Love Me / One More Time - 1962 (promo issue only)

Dee Dee Sharp (born Dione LaRue on 9-September-1945 in Philadelphia - married record producer Kenny Gamble in 1967)

Cameo 212 - Mashed Potato Time / Set My Heart At Ease - 1962
Cameo 219 - Gravy (For My Mashed Potatoes) / Baby Cakes - 1962 (some copies issued with picture sleeve)
Cameo 230 - Ride! / The Night - 1962 (some copies issued with picture sleeve)
Cameo 244 - Do The Bird / Lover Boy - 1963 (some copies issued with picture sleeve)
Cameo 260 - Rock Me In The Cradle Of Love / You'll Never Be Mine - 1963 (some copies issued with picture sleeve)
Cameo 274 - Wild / Why Doncha Ask Me - 1963 (some copies issued with picture sleeve)
Cameo 296 - Where Did I Go Wrong / Willyam, Willyam - 1964 (some copies issued with picture sleeve)
Fairmount 1004 - (It's Wonderful) The Love I Feel For You / Willyam, Willyam - 1964

Cameo 329 - Never Pick A Pretty Boy / He's No Ordinary Guy - 1964
Cameo 335 - Good / Deep Dark Secret - 1964

Dee Dee Sharp

Cameo 347 - To Know Him Is To Love Him / There Ain't Nothin' I Wouldn't Do For You - 1965
Cameo 357 - Let's Twine / (That's What) My Mama Said - 1965

Dee Dee Sharp Gamble

Cameo 375 - I Really Love You* / Standing In The Need Of Love - 1965 (some copies issued with picture sleeve) *also recorded in 1968 by The Ambassadors on Arctic 147.
Cameo 382 - It's A Funny Situation / There Ain't Nothing I Wouldn't Do For You - 1966
Atco 6445 - My Best Friend's Man / Bye Bye Baby - 1966
Atco 6502 - What Am I Gonna Do / (Heart And Soul) Baby I Love You - 1967

Ben E. King & Dee Dee Sharp

Atco 6557 - We Got A Good Thing Going On / What'cha Gonna Do About It - 1968

Dee Dee Sharp

Atco 6576 - A Woman Will Do Wrong* / You're Just A Fool In Love - 1968 *also recorded in 1966 by Helene Smith with The Rocketeers on Deep City 2368 and in 1967 by Irma Thomas on Chess 2017.
Atco 6587 - Help Me Find My Groove / This Love Won't Run Out - 1968
Gamble 219 - What Kind Of Lady* / You're Gonna Miss Me (When I'm Gone) - 1968 *the instrumental to this track was recorded in 1968 by The Producers on Huff Puff 1003.
Gamble 4005 - The Bottle Or Me / You're Gonna Miss Me (When I'm Gone) - 1970

Dee Dee Sharp Gamble with David "Bunny" Sigler

Philadelphia International 3512 - Conquer The World / We Got A Thing Going On - 1971

Chubby Checker

Abkco 4017 - Slow Twistin' */ Birdland - 1973 *re-release of Parkway 835 no mention of Dee Dee Sharp.

Dee Dee Sharp

Abkco 4018 - Mashed Potato Time / Ride - 1973

Dee Dee Sharp Gamble

T. S. O. P. 4776 - Happy 'Bout The Whole Thing / Touch My Life - 1975
T. S. O. P. 4778 - I'm Not In Love / Make It Till Tomorrow - 1976
Philadelphia International 3625 - Nobody Could Take Your Place / Flashback - 1977

Philadelphia International All Stars (members Lou Rawls, Billy Paul, Teddy Pendergrass, The O'Jays, Archie Bell and Dee Dee Sharp) **/ MFSB**

Philadelphia International 3627 - Let's Clean Clean Up The Ghetto / Let's Clean Up The Ghetto* - 1977 (all profits from this release were committed to a five-year charity project) *flip by MFSB.

Dee Dee Sharp

Philadelphia International 3636 - What Colour Is Love / I'd Really Love To See You Tonight - 1977

Dee Dee Sharp Gamble

Philadelphia International 3638 - Just As Long As I Know You're Mine / I Believe In Love - 1978
Philadelphia International 3644 - I Wanna Be Your Woman / Trying To Get The Feeling Again - 1978
Philadelphia International 70058 - Easy Money / I Love You Anyway - 1981
Philadelphia International 02041 - Breaking And Entering / I Love You Anyway - 1981

Dee Dee Sharp

Gusto 2079 - Mashed Potato Time / Do The Bird - ?

Jean Carn / Dee Dee Sharp Gamble

Columbia 4zh 07834 - Was That All It Was (6:30) / Breaking And Entering (6:59)* - 1987 *flip by Dee Dee Sharp Gamble. (12" release)

The Sharpees

Little Herbert & The Arabians (members Herbert Reeves, Stacy Johnson,............................)

Teek 4824 - Bouncing Ball / Condition Your Heart - 1961
Teek 4824 - Pray Tell Me / ? - 1961 (Same Teek Number Used Twice)

Little Miss Jessie (Jessie Smith)

Mel-O 101 - My Baby's Gone / St. Louis Twist (Instrumental - By Benny Sharp & His Band) - 1961 (vocal backing by The Sharpees formerly known as The New Breed, members at this time were Benny Sharp, Stacy Johnson, Vernon Guy and Horise O'Toole. In 1962 Stacy Johnson and Guy Vernon left the group and joined The Ike & Tina Turner Revue whilst with Ike Turner the pair recorded two singles apiece with Ike Turner these are listed below.)

Vernon Guy (born 21-March-1945 in St. Louis -- a former member of The Seven Gospel Singers, who later changed their name to The Cool Sounds)

Teena 1703 - They Ain't Lovin' You / You've Got Me - 1963
Sonja 2007 - Anything --- To Make It With You / (Instrumental Version) - 1963

Stacy Johnson (born 13-April-1945 in St. Louis.)

Sony 113 - Remove My Doubts / Don't Believe Him - 1963
Modern 1001 - Consider Yourself / Don't Believe Him - 1964

The Sharpees (members Herbert Reeves, Benny Sharp, Horise O'Toole and Guy Vernon)

One - Derful 4835 - Do The 45* / Make Up Your Mind** - 1965 *lead Herbert Reeves. **lead Guy Vernon. (shortly after this record was released Horise O'Toole caught TB he had to leave the group for health reasons, he was replaced by Stacy Johnson)
One - Derful 4839 - Tired Of Being Lonely / Just To Please You - 1965
One - Derful 4842/4843 - I've Got A Secret / Make Up Your Mind - 1965
One - Derful 4845 - The Sock / My Girl Jean - 1966

Stacy Johnson

M - Pac 7230 - I Stand Alone / Don't Try To Fool Me - 1966

Benny Sharp & The Sharpees (members Benny Sharp, Stacy Johnson, Herbert Reeves and Guy Vernon)

Midas 303 - Music (I Like It) / Part 2 - 1969 (The Sharpees stayed together as a group while various members were working as solo artists on the road or in the studio, until 1972 when Herbert Reeves was shot and killed)

Stacie Johnson

Mowest 5047 - Woman In My Eyes / A Carbon Copy - 1973 (Unissued)

Vernon Guy

Electric Land 3 - Ooh Vernon / My Brand New Woman - 1980

The Sharpees (members Herbert Reeves, Benny Sharp, Horise O'Toole and Guy Vernon)

Knockout 4 - Do The 45 / Make Up Your Mind - ?

The Sharpees (Guy Vernon, Stacy Johnson, Bobby Williams and Paul Grady (Guy's nephew)) this was the lineup around a new set of The Sharpees formed in 1981 by Guy Vernon and Stacy Johnson)

The Shirelles

The Poquellos (members Shirley Owens, Addie "Miki" Harris, Beverly Lee and Doris Coley)

The Shirelles (members Shirley Owens, Addie "Miki" Harris, Beverly Lee and Doris Coley)

Tiara 6112 - I Met Him On A Sunday / I Want You To Be My Boyfriend - 1958
Decca 30588 - I Met Him On A Sunday / I Want You To Be My Boyfriend - 1958
Decca 30669 - My Love Ia A Charm / Slop Time - 1958
Decca 30761 - Stop Me / I Got The Message - 1958
Scepter 1203 - Dedicated To The One I Love / Look A Here Baby - 1958 (issued on white and red labels -- white label scarcer)
Scepter 1205 - A Teardrop And A Lollipop / Doin' The Ronde - 1959 (issued on white and red labels -- white label scarcer)
Scepter 1207 - Please Be My Boyfriend / I Saw A Tear - 1960 (issued on white and red labels -- white label scarcer)
Scepter 1208 - Tonight's The Night / The Dance Is Over - 1960 (issued on white, pink and red labels -- white label scarcest followed by pink then red)
Scepter 1211 - Tomorrow / Boys - 1960 (Original Title)
Scepter 1211 - Will You Love Me Tomorrow / Boys - 1960
Scepter 1203 - Dedicated To The One I Love / Look Here Baby - 1961
Decca 25506 - I Met Him On A Sunday / My Love Is A Charm - 1961
Scepter 1217 - Mama Said / Blue Holiday - 1961
Scepter 1220 - A Thing Of The Past / What A Sweet Thing That Was - 1961
Scepter 1223 - Big John / Twenty-One - 1961
Scepter 1227 - Baby It's You / Things I Want To Hear (Pretty Words) - 1961
Scepter 1228 - Soldier Boy / Love Is A Swingin' Thing - 1962

Valli

Scepter 1233 - Hurry Home To Me (Soldier Boy) / Jimmy's In A Hurry - 1962 ("answer" record, The Shirelles "Soldier Boy" is the background vocal)

The Shirelles

Scepter 1234 - Welcome Home Baby / Mama, Here Comes The Bride - 1962
Scepter 1237 - Stop The Music / It's Love That Really Counts - 1962
Scepter 1243 - Everybody Loves A Lover / I Don't Think So - 1962
Scepter 1248 - Foolish Little Girl / Not For All The Money In The World - 1963
Scepter 1255 - Don't Say Goodnight And Mean Goodbye / I Didn't Mean To Hurt You - 1963
Scepter 1259 - What Does A Girl Do? / Don't Let It Happen To You - 1963
Scepter 1260 - It's A Mad, Mad, Mad, Mad World / 31 Flavors - 1963 (From The Film "It's A Mad, Mad, Mad, Mad World)
Scepter 1264 - Tonight You're Gonna Fall In Love With Me / 20th Century Rock And Roll - 1963
Scepter 1267 - Sha-La-La / His Lips Get In The Way - 1964
Scepter 1278 - Thank You Baby / Doomsday - 1964
Scepter 1284 - Maybe Tonight / Lost Love - 1964
Scepter 1292 - Are You Still My Baby / I Saw A Tear - 1964
Scepter 1296 - Shh, I'm Watching The Movies / A Plus B - 1965

Jan & Dean / Roy Orbison / The Four Seasons / The Shirelles

Coke - Let's Swing The Jingle For Coca-Cola - 1965 (issued to radio stations only - Coca-Cola radio spots)

The Shirelles

Scepter 12101 - March (You'll Be Sorry) / Everybody's Goin' Mad - 1965
Scepter 12114 - My Heart Belongs To You / Love That Man - 1965
Scepter 12123 - (Mama) My Soldier Boy Is Coming Home / Soldier Boy - 1965
Scepter 12132 - I Met Him On A Sunday -- ' 66 / Love That Man - 1966
Scepter 12150 - Till My Baby Comes Home / Que Sera, Sera - 1966
Scepter 12162 - Look Away / After Midnight - 1966
Scepter 12162 - Shades Of Blue / Looking Away - 1966
Scepter 12178 - Teasin' Me - Look Away - 1966
Scepter 12185 - Don't Go Home (My Little Baby) / Nobody Baby After You - 1967
Scepter 12192 - Too Much Of A Good Thing / Bright Shiny Colors - 1967
Scepter 12198 - Last Minute Miracle / No Doubt About It - 1967
Scepter 12209 - Wild And Sweet / Wait Till I Give The Signal - 1968
Scepter 12217 - Hippie Walk (Part 1) / Hippie Walk (Part 2) - 1968
Blue Rock 4051 - Don't Mess With Cupid / Sweet Sweet Lovin' - 1968
Blue Rock 4066 - Call Me / There's A Storm Goin' On In My Heart - 1968 (Doris Coley leaves group -- they carry on as a trio - returns in 1975)

Shirley & The Shirelles

Bell 760 - A Most Unusual Boy / Look What You've Done To My Heart - 1969
Bell 787 - Looking Glass / Playthings - 1969
Bell 815 - Never Give You Up / Go Away And Find Yourself - 1969

The Shirelles

United Artists 50648 - There Goes My Baby - Be My Baby / Strange, I Still Love You - 1970
United Artists 50693 - It's Gonna Take A Miracle / Lost - 1970
United Artists 50740 - Take Me For A Little While / Dedicated To The One I Love - 1971

RCA Victor 48-1019 - No Sugar Tonight / Strange, I Still Love You - 1971
RCA Victor 48-1032 - Brother, Brother / Sunday Dreaming - 1972
RCA Victor 47-0902 - Let's Give Each Other Love / Deep In The Night - 1973
RCA Victor APBO-0192 - Touch The Wind (Eres Tu) / Do What You've A Mind To - 1973

Shirley (Shirley Owens - goes solo in 1975)

Prodigal 611 - I Hear Those Church Bells Ringing - Chapel Of Love / I Do Love You - 1974

Shirley Alston (Shirley Owens)

Prodigal 616 - I'd Rather Not Be Loving You / Can't Stop Singin' ('Bout The Boy I Love) - 1975

The Shirelles / Don Julian & The Larks

Original Sound 4514 - Soldier Boy */ I Want You Back** - 198? * "A" side The Shirelles. **flip Don Julian & The Larks.

The Shirelles / Adam-Wade

Grand 0032 - Boys / Take Good Care Of Her* **- ?** *flip by Adam-Wade

The Shirelles / Adam-Wade

Grand 0032 - Boys / Take Good Care Of Her - ? (same 45 as above but when you play it, it's Bobby Vee singing "Devil Or Angel" on one side and "I'm Sorry" on the other)

The Shirelles

Collectables Col 030017 - Tonight's The Night / Mama Said - ?
Collectables Col 030027 - Dedicated To The One I Love / Soldier Boy - ?
Collectables Col 030037 - Will You Love Me Tomorrow / A Teardrop And A Lollipop - ?
Collectables Col 030047 - Foolish Little Girl / Baby It's You - ?
Collectables Col 033777 - Blue Holiday / A Long Story Short - ?
Collectables Col 035627 - A Thing Of The Past / What A Sweet Thing That Was - ?

The Shirelles / The Fontaine Sisters

Collectables Col 901427 - I Met Him On A Sunday (Ronde-Ronde) / Chanson D'amour* - ? *flip by The Fontaine Sisters.

The Showmen

The Israelites (members General Johnson Sr., General Johnson Jr. (born General Norman Johnson on 23-May-1943 in Norfolk, Virginia), ...) 1949

The Humdingers (members Norman Johnson (lead), Gene "Cheater" Knight (first tenor), Dorsey "Chops" Knight (second tenor), Leslie "Fat Boy" Felton (baritone) and Milton "Smokes" Wells (bass))

Atlantic – How Could You Forget – 1956 (unissued --- recorded 12-September-1956)
Atlantic – One More Kiss – 1956 (unissued --- recorded 12-September-1956)
Atlantic – Ride Alone – 1956 (unissued --- recorded 12-September-1956)
Atlantic – Papa Lollipop – 1956 (unissued --- recorded 12-September-1956)

The Showmen (members Norman Johnson, Gene Knight (died 1992 in Norfolk, Virginia --- cause: ?), Dorsey Knight, Leslie Felton and Milton Wells)

Minit 632 - It Will Stand / Country Fool – 1961 (recorded 10-June-1961)
Minit 643 - The Wrong Girl / Fate Planned It This Way - 1962
Minit 647 - I'm Coming Home / I Love You Can't You See - 1962
Minit 654 - True Fine Mama / The Owl See's You - 1962
Minit 662 - 39 - 21 - 46* / Swish Fish - 1963 *also recorded in ? by Willie Tee Walker & The Magnificents on Red Coach 633

Carl Frost and The Showmen (members Carl Frost, Gene Knight, Dorsey Knight, Leslie Felton and Milton Wells)

Lawn 223 – Mind Your Mama / I'm Still In Love With You – 1963 According To Goldmine July-1998 article page 120

The Showmen (members Norman Johnson, Gene Knight, Dorsey Knight, Leslie Felton and Milton Wells)

Imperial 66033 - It Will Stand / Country Fool - 1964
Imperial 66071 - Somebody Help Me / Country Fool - 1964

Norman Johnson (Joe Banashak one of the co-founders of Minit Records held onto a few Showmen recordings when he sold Minit to Imperial. He later released the 45 as by Norman Johnson).

Instant 66033 - Valley Of Love / Let Her Feel It In Your Kiss - 1965

The In-Crowd (members Fayette Pickney, Helen Scott and Janet Jones with members of The Showmen)

Swan 4204 - Let's Shindig / You're Gonna Miss Me – 1965

The Showmen (members Norman Johnson, Gene Knight, Dorsey Knight, Leslie Felton and Milton Wells)

Swan 4213 - In Paradise / Take It Baby - 1965
Swan 4219 - Our Love Will Grow / You're Everything - 1965

Norman Johnson

Swan 4241 - The Honey House / Please Try And Understand – 1965

The Showmen

Airecords 334 - Valley Of Love / Let Her Feel It In Your Kiss - 1965
Minit 32007 - 39 - 21 - 46 / Swish Fish - 1966
Jokers Three 4809 - A Little Bit (Of Your Love) / Need Love - 1967
B B 4015 - In Paradise / Take It Baby – 1967

The Showmen (members Gene Knight, Dorsey Knight, Leslie Felton and Milton Wells)

Amy 11036 - Action / What Would It Take – 1968

The Showmen (members Norman Johnson, Gene Knight, Dorsey Knight, Leslie Felton and Milton Wells)

Liberty 56166 - It Will Stand / Fate Planned It This Way - 1970

The Jive Five / The Showmen

United Artists 1001 - I'm A Happy Man / It Will Stand* - 1973 *flip By The Showmen.

The Showmen (members Leslie Felton, Milton Wells, Randall Wilkins (died 13-August-1979 --- cause: automobile accident) and Pearly White Jr.) 1977

The Showmen (members Reggie Sands, ...)1981

The Showmen (members Leslie Felton, Hank Rush and Greg Gallashaw)

The Showmen / The Psalms

Surfside 830115 - No Trespassing / I Love You Can't You See /// Give Some Love* / Some Love* - 1983 *flip by The Psalms.

The Showmen (members Leslie Felton, Hank Rush and Greg Gallashaw)

Surfside 850426 - Sweet Beach Music / Sweet Beach Music – 1985

Ruth Brown / Sammy Turner /// The Showmen / Sonny Boy Williamson

Ripete 1030 - Sugar Babe / Always /// In Paradise* / Don't Start Me To Talking - 1988 *track by The Showmen.

The Showmen (members Leslie Felton, Hank Rush and Greg Gallashaw)

Surfside 071690 - Shaggin' The Night Away / ? – 1990

The Showmen (members Norman Johnson, Gene Knight, Dorsey Knight, Leslie Felton and Milton Wells)

Ripete 161 – It Will Stand / 39–21–46 - 1990
Collectables Col 033127 - It Will Stand / 39–21–46 - ?

The Silhouettes

The Soulettes (members Bill Horton, ...) 1940's all female gospel group with the exception of Bill Horton.

The Dicky Howard's Quintet (members Ray Edwards, ...)

Nestor ? - Going Down The River / Rolling Down The Highway – 1954

The Balladeers (members Clarence Basil, Earl Beal, Raymond Edwards,..) group formed in Philadelphia.

The Gospel Tornados (members Bill Horton, Richard "Rick" Lewis (born 2-September-1933 --- died 19-April-2005 in Philadelphia, PA --- cause: kidney failure), Earl Beal and Ray Edwards) group formed in Philadelphia.

The Thunderbirds (members Bill Horton, Richard "Rick" Lewis, Earl Beal and Ray Edwards)

The Silhouettes (members Bill Horton, Richard "Rick" Lewis, Earl Beal and Ray Edwards)

Junior 391 - Get A Job* / I Am Lonely - 1957 (Brown Label -- First Pressing) *Also Recorded In 1964 By Vito & The Salutations On Regina 1320.
Junior 391 - Get A Job / I Am Lonely - 1957 (Blue Label -- Second Pressing)
Junior 396 - I Sold My Heart To The Junkman* / What Would You Do - 1958 *Also Recorded In 1962 By The Blue Belles On Newtown 5000.
Ace 552 - I Sold My Heart To The Junkman / What Would You Do - 1958
Ember 1029 - Get A Job / I Am Lonely - 1958 (Red Label)
Ember 1032 - Headin' For The Poorhouse / Miss Thing - 1958
Ember 1037 - Bing Bong / Voodoo Eyes - 1958 (Glossy Red Label -- First Pressing)
Ember 1037 - Bing Bong / Voodoo Eyes - 1958 (Flat Red Label -- Second Pressing)
United Artists 147 - I Sold My Heart To The Junkman / What Would You Do - 1958 (cancelled)
Junior 400 - Evelyn / Never Will Part - 1959

The Invictors (members Barry Boswell, Ray Edwards, Bill Yuhas, Gene Yuhas and Robert Rohrbach)

Bee 1117 - I'll Always Care For You / I Don't Wanna Go - 1959

Bill Horton and The Silhouettes

Ace 562 - Evelyn / Never Will Part - 1959

The Silhouettes

20th Century 240 - Never / Bull Frog – 1959
Ember 1029 - Get A Job / I Am Lonely - 1960 (Black Label)
Grand 142 - I Wish I Could Be There / Move On Over (To Another Land) – 1961
Imperial 5899 - The Push* / Which Way Did She Go - 1962 *Written By Van Mccoy.
Junior 993 - Your Love / Rent Man - 1963 (Bill Horton and Ray Edwards leave group -- replaced by John Wilson and Cornelius Brown)

Bill Harton and The Dawns (members Bill Horton -- name mis-spelt on label, Joe Moody, Robert Byrd and George Willis)

Lawn 241 - Like To See You In That Mood / Shadow – 1964

The Termites (members Barry Boswell, Ray Edwards, Bill Yuhas, Gene Yuhas and Robert Rohrbach)

Bee B-1825 - Carrie Lou / Give Me Your Heart* - 1964 *flip is by a totally different group named The Termites.

The Silhouettes (members Bill Horton, Richard "Rick" Lewis, Earl Beal and Ray Edwards)

Flashback 13 - Get A Job / I Am Lonely – 1965

The New Silhouettes

Good Way 101 - Not Me Baby / Gaucho Serenade – 1966
Jamie 13330 - Climb Every Mountain / We Belong Together – 1967

Bill Horton

Kayden 403 - I Wanna Know / No One Can Take Your Place – 1967

The Termites

Bee Bgx-1825 - Carrie Lou / Give Me Your Heart – 1998

The Silhouettes

Lana 108 - Get A Job / I Am Lonely - ?
Lost-Nite 418 - Bing Bong / Voodoo Eyes - ?
Hi-Oldies 439 - Get A Job / I Am Lonely - ?
Collectables Col 011877 - I Sold My Heart To The Junkman / What Would You Do - 1980's
Collectables Col 014877 - Bing Bong / Voodoo Eyes - 1980's
Collectables Col 014957 - Get A Job / I Am Lonely - 1980's
Bye George 1000 - Monday Monday / St. Thomas - ?

The Silhouettes / The Diamonds / Jimmy Clanton / Huey (Piano) Smith & The Clowns / The Rays / Timmie Rogers

All Time Hits Mx:SI-102 - Get A Job / Little Darlin' / Just A Dream / Don't You Just Know It / Silhouettes / Back To School Again - ? (45rpm single)

Benny Spellman

Benny Spellman (born 11-December-1931in Pensacola, Florida - was a member of Huey Smith & The Clowns for a short period - left music in 1968 to work on beer promotions)

Minit 606 - Life Is Too Short / Ammerette - 1960
Minit 613 - Darling No Matter Where / I Didn't Know - 1960

Ernie K-Doe

Minit 623 - Mother-In-Law* / Wanted, $10,000 Reward - 1961 (*bass vocal by Benny Spellman - "A" side is at the correct speed - trail off number is SO-738-2 - common copies)
Minit 623 - Mother-In-Law* / Wanted, $10,000 Reward - 1961 (*bass vocal by Benny Spellman - "A" side was accidentally mis-mastered at 33 1/3 rpm - trail off number is 45-SO-738 - scarce copies)

Benny Spellman

Ace 630 - That's All I Ask Of You / Roll On Big Wheel - 1961
Minit 644 - Lipstick Traces (On A Cigarette) / Fortune Teller
Imperial 040 - Lipstick Traces (On A Cigarette) / Fortune Teller
Minit 652 - Every Now And Then / I'm In Love - 1962
Minit 659 - Stickin' Whicha' Baby / You Got To Get It - 1963
Minit 664 - Talk About Love / Ammerette - 1963
Watch 6332 - Walk On, Don't Cry / Please Mister Genie - 1964
Watch 6336 - Slow Down Baby (You Drive Too Fast) / Someday They'll Understand - 1964
Alon 9018 - Tain't The Truth / No Don't Stop - 1965
Alon 9024 - The Word Game / I Feel Good - 1965
Atlantic 2291 - The Word Game / I Feel Good - 1965
Alon 9027 - It Must Be Love / Spirit Of Loneliness - 1965
Alon 9031 - It's For You / This Is My Love - 1966
Sansu 462 - But If You Love Her / Sinner Girl - 1967

Skyliners

The Skyliners (members Jimmy Beaumont, Janet Vogel, Wally Lester, Joe VerScharen and Jackie Taylor)

Calico 103 - Since I Don't Have You / One Night, One Night - 1959
Calico 104 - Since I Don't Have You / One Night, One Night - 1959
Calico 106 - This I Swear* / Tomorrow - 1959 *Released In Canada On Barrel 610
Calico 109 - It Happened Today / Lonely Way - 1959
Calico 114 - How Much / Lorraine From Spain - 1960
Calico 117 - Pennies From Heaven / I'll Be Seeing You - 1960
Calico 120 - Believe Me / Happy Time - 1960
Colpix 188 - I'll Close My Eyes / The Door Is Still Open - 1961

Jimmy Beaumont and The Skyliners

Colpix 607 - Ba ' lon Rhythms / The End Of A Story - 1961

The Skyliners

Colpix 613 - Close Your Eyes / Our Love Will Last - 1961
Cameo 215 - Three Coins In The Fountain / Everyone But You - 1962 (Joe Verscharen Had Left Group At Time Of This Release)
Viscount 104 - Comes Love / Tell Me - 1962
Motown 1046 - Since I Fell For You / I'd Die - 1963 (Record Never Got Beyond Test Pressing Stage --- 2 Known Copies)
Atco 6270 - Since I Fell For You / I'd Die - 1963 (The Group Disbands After This Release)
Original Sound 35 - Since I Don't Have You / One Night, One Night - 1963
Original Sound 36 - Pennies From Heaven / I'll Be Seeing You - 1963
Original Sound 37 - This I Swear / It Happened Today - 1963
Jubilee 5506 - Everything Is Fine / The Loser* - 1965 (Jackie Taylor Forms A New Version Of The Group) *Released In Canada On Jubilee 5506.
Jubilee 5512 - Who Do You Love / Get Yourself A Baby - 1965
Jubilee 5520 - I Run To You / Don't Hurt Me Baby - 1965

The Skyliners / Wade Flemons

Oldies 45 - 123 - Pennies From Heaven / Her I Stand* - 1960's *flip by Wade Flemmons

The Skyliners / Preston Epps

OLDIES 45 - ?

Jimmy Beaumont and The Skyliners

Capitol 3979 - Where Have They Gone / I Could Have Loved You So Well - 1974 (group reforms in 1970, members Jimmy Beaumont, Janet Vogel Rapp (now married) Wally Lester and Joe VerScharen)
Drive 6250 - Our Day Is Here / The Day The Clown Cried - 1976

The Skyliners

Tortoise Int'l Pb-11243 - Oh How Happy / We've Got Love On Our Side - 1978 (members Jimmy Beaumont, Janet Vogel Rapp, Bobby Sholes and Jimmie Ross)

Tortoise Int'l Pb-11312 - Love Bug (Done Bit Me Again) / Smile On Me - 1978
Tortoise Int'l 11345 - Love Bug (Done Bit Me Again) / ? - 1978 (12" promo issue only)

The Skyliners / The Echoes

Collectables Col 002517 - Close Your Eyes / Baby Blue* - ? flip by The Echoes

The Skyliners

Collectables Col 040577 - Pennies From Heaven / It Happened Today - ?
Collectables Col 040587 - Since I Don't Have You / One Night, One Night - ?
Collectables Col 040607 - This I Swear / Lonely Way - ?

Skyliners / Tune Weavers

Classic Artists 116 - What Are You Doing New Years Eve* / ** ? - 1989 (promo copy only 1000 copies made) *sung only by The Skyliners. **sung only by The Tune Weavers.

The Skyliners

Classic Artists 123 - You're My Christmas Present / Another Lonely New Years Eve - 1990 (red vinyl --- only 1000 copies made --- members Jimmy Beaumont, Bobby Sholes, Rick Morris and Donna Groom)
Classic Artists 123 - You're My Christmas Present / Another Lonely New Years Eve - 1990 (black vinyl --- only 1000 copies made)
Double AA - 122 - Rock 'N' Roll Ruby / I Do All Right - ?

Sly, Slick & Wicked

Paramount Paa-0165 - Stay My Love / Surely [1972]
Paramount Paa-0186 - It's Not Easy / Your Love Was Meant For Me [1973]
People Pe-625 - Sho Nuff / I'm Ready For You [1973]
Shaker Records 102 - Turn On Your Lovelight/ We Don't Have To Be Lovers - 1974
Epic 9-50758 - All I Want Is Your / The Prophet - 1978

Sly & The Family Stone

The Stewart Four (Members Sylvester Stewart, Freddie Stewart, Rose Stewart And Vaetta Stewart)

Church Of God In Christ, Northern Sunday School Department 78-101 - On The Battlefield For My Lord / Walking In Jesus' Name - 1952 (78rpm Format Only)

The Stewart Brothers (Members Sylvester Stewart ....)

Ensign 4032 - The Rat / Ra Ra Roo - 1959
Keen 2113 - Sleep On The Porch / Yum Yum Yum - 1959 (Some Copies Issued With A Picture Sleeve)

Joey Piazza & The Continentals (Members In A High School Rock And Roll Group Joey Piazza, Sylvester Stewart..........................)

The Biscanes (Members Sylvester Stewart,...........................)

VPM 1006 - Yellow Moon / Heavenly Angel - 1961

The Viscaynes (Members Sylvester Stewart,.........................)

VPM 1006 - Yellow Moon / Uncle Sam Needs You (My Friend)* - 1961 *Written By H. B. Barnum.

Danny Stewart (Sylvester Stewart)

Luke 1008 - A Long Time Away / I'm Just A Fool - 1961

Sylvester Stewart (Born 15-March-1944, In Denton,Texas)

G & P 901 - A Long Time Away* / Help Me With My Broken Heart - 1961 *Dubbed-In Re-Issue Of The Luke 108 Track.

Danny Stewart (Sylvester Stewart)

Luke 1009 - Are You My Girlfriend* / You've Forgotten Me - 1961 *Used "A Long Time Away" Backing Track.
Luke 1009 - Are You My Girlfriend / Do You Remember - 1961 (? Unissued)

The Viscaynes & The Ramblers (Members Sylvester Stewart,..)

Trop 101 - Stop What You Are Doing / I Guess I'll Be - 1961

The Viscaynes (Members Sylvester Stewart...)

Trop 101 - Stop What You Are Doing / I Guess I'll Be - 1961

Sly Stewart

Autumn 3 - I Just Learned How To Swim / Scat Swim - 1964

Sly

Autumn 14 - Buttermilk Pt. 1 / Buttermilk Pt. 2 - 1965
Autumn 26 - Temptation Walk Pt. 1 / Temptation Walk Pt. 2 - 1965

The Stoners (Members Sylvester Stewart, Cynthia Robinson ....)

Freddie & The Stone Souls (Freddie Stewart , Greg "Handsfeet" Enrico....................) These Two Non-Recorded Groups Would Become The Nucleus For Sly & The Family Stone.

Billy Preston

Capitol 5660 - In The Midnight Hour / Advice - 1966 (With Sylvester Stewart)
Capitol 5797 - Phoney Friends / Can't She Tell - 1967 (With Sylvester Stewart)

Sly & The Family Stone (Members Sylvester Stewart (Born 15-March-1944), Fred Stewart (Born 5-June-1946), Larry Graham Jr. (Born 14-August-1946), Cynthia Robinson (Born 12-January-1946), Rosie Stone (21-March-1945) Who Joined The Group In 1968, Gregg Errico (Born 1-September-1946) And Jerry Martini (1-October-1943)) The Group's First Gig Was At A Club Called Winchester Cathedral.

Epic 10229 - Higher / Underdog - 1967
Epic ? - Bad Risk / ? - 1967
Epic 10256 - Dance To The Music / Let Me Hear It From You - 1967
Loadstone 3951 - I Ain't Got Nobody / I Can't Turn You Loose - 196?

The French Fries (Sly & The Family Stone)

Epic 10313 - Dance A La Musique / Small Fries - 1968 (Unissued In The Name Of Sly & The Family Stone, This Was A French Language Version Of "Dance To The Music" With The Bands

Vocals Sped Up Chipmunk's Style)

Sly & The Family Stone

Epic 10353 - Life / M'lady - 1968
Epic 10407 - Everyday People / Sing A Simple Song - 1968 (Some Copies Issued With A Picture Cover)
Epic 10450 - Stand! / I Want To Take You Higher* - 1969 (Some Copies Issued With Picture Sleeeve) Epic 10497 - Hot Fun In The Summertime / Fun - 1969
Epic 10555 - Thank You (Falettinme Be Mice Elf Agin) / Everybody Is A Star - 1969 (Some Copies Issued With A Picture Cover)

Joe Hicks

Scepter 1226 - I'm Goin' Home / Home, Sweet Home - 1969 (Sly & The Family Stone Involvement In 45)

Abaco Dream (New York City Group, Members Paul Douglas, Dave Williams, Dennis Williams, Frank Maid And Mike Sassano)

A & M 1081 - Life & Death In G & A / Cat Woman - 1969 (Rumoured That Sylvester Stewart Played On This 45)

Little Sister (Rosie Stone)

Stone Flower 9000 - You're The One (Part 1) / You're The One (Part 2) - 1970 (Produced By Sylvester Stewart)
Stone Flower 9001 - Somebody's Watching You / Stanga - 1970

Sly & The Family Stone

Epic 10805 - Family Affair / Luv N' Haight - 1971

Sly Stone

Woodcock 001 - Rock Dirge Pt. 1 / Rock Dirge Pt. 2 - 1971

Sly & The Family Stone (Members Sylvester Stewart, Fred Stewart, Rusty Allen, Cynthia Robinson, Rosie Stone, Andy Newmark And Jerry Martini This Became The Group Line-Up Sometime In 1972)

Epic 10829 - Runnin' Away / Brave & Strong - 1972
Epic 10850 - Smilin' / Luv N' Haight - 1972
Epic 11017 - If You Want Me To Stay / Babies Makin' Babies - 1973
Epic 11017 - If You Want Me To Stay / Thankful N' Thoughtful - 1973
Epic 11060 - Frisky - If It Were Left Up To Me - 1973
Epic 11140 - Time For Livin' / Small Talk - 1974
Epic 50035 - Loose Booty / Can't Strain My Brain - 1974
Epic 50119 - Hot Fun In The Summertime / Fun - 1975
Epic 50135 - I Get High On You / That's Lovin You - 1975
Epic 50175 - Li Lo Li / Who Do You Love - 1975
Epic 50201 - Greed / Crossword Puzzle - 1976

Sly Stone & The Biscaynes

Subarro 489 - Oh What A Nite* / You've Forgotten Me - 1976

Sly & The Family Stone

Epic 50331 - Family Again / Nothing Less Than Happiness - 1977

Sly Stone

Epic 50794 - Dance To The Music / Sing A Simple Song - 1979 (12" Release)
Epic 50795 - Dance To The Music / Sing A Simple Song - 1979

Sly & The Family Stone

Warner Bros. 49062 - Sheer Energy / Remember Who You Are - 1979
Warner Bros. 49132 - Who's To Say / Same Thing - 1979
Warner Bros. 29682 - High Y'all / Ha Ha He He - 1983

Jesse Johnson Featuring Sly Stone

A & M 2878 - Crazay / Drive 'Yo Cadillac - 1986 (Some Copies Issued With Picture Cover)

Sly Stewart / Rae Dawn Chong

A & M 2890 - Eek-Ah-Bo-Static Automatic / Black Girls* - 1986 *Flip By Rae Dawn Chong.

Sly Stone & Martha Davis / Rae Dawn Chong

A & M 2896 - Love And Affection* / Black Girls** - 1986 * From The Movie"Soul Man". **Flip By Rae Dawn Chong.

Sly & The Family Stone

Direction 4471 - Hot Fun In The Summertime / Fun - ?

The Soul Brothers Six

The Soul Brothers Five (members Sam Armstrong, Charles Armstrong, Moses Armstrong, Harry Armstrong and Gene Armstrong)

The Soul Brothers Six (members Willie John Ellison, Sam Armstrong, Charles Armstrong, Moses Armstrong, Harry Armstrong and Gene Armstrong)

Fine ? - Stop Hurting Me / ? - 1965
Fine 25661 - I Don't Want To Cry / Move Girl - 1965

The Soul Brothers Six (members Willie John Ellison, Sam Armstrong, Charles Armstrong, Moses Armstrong, Vonn Elle Benjamin and Lester Peleman)

Lyndell 746/7 - Don't Neglect Your Baby / Oh I Need You Yes I Do - 1966

The Soul Brothers Six (members Willie John Ellison, Joe Johnson, Charles Armstrong, Harry Armstrong, Vonn Elle Benjamin and Lester Peleman)

Atlantic 2406 - Some Kind Of Wonderful* / I'll Be Loving You - 1967 (both tracks recorded 30-March-1967 at Atlantic Studios, NYC) *written by John Ellison and covered in 1974 by Grand Funk Railroad on Capitol 4002.
Atlantic 2456 - You Better Check Yourself* / What Can You Do When You Ain't Got Nobody - 1967 *recorded 26-October-1967.

Atlantic 2535 - Your Love Is Such A Wonderful Love / I Can't Live Without You* - 1968
*recorded 18-April-1968.
Atlantic 2592 - Thank You Baby For Loving Me* / Someone Else Is Loving My Baby - 1969
*recorded 5-February-1968 at Atlantic Studios, New York City.
Atlantic 2645 - Drive / What You Got (Is So Good For Me) - 1969

Willie John Ellison (born 11-August-1941 in Montgomery, West Virginia)

Phil L. A. Of Soul 337 - You've Got To Have Rhythm / Giving Up On Love - 1970

John Ellison

Phil L. A. Of Soul 341 - All I Want Is Your Love / Doggone Good Feeling - 1971

John Ellison and The Soul Brothers Six (members John Ellison, Joe Johnson, James Johnson, Charles Pevy and Eddie Reno)

Phil L. A. Of Soul 355 - Funky Funky Way Of Making Love / Let Me Be The One - 1972

The Soul Brothers Six (members John Ellison, Joe Johnson, James Johnson, Charles Pevy and Eddie Reno)

Phil L. A. Of Soul 360 - You're My World / You Gotta Come A Little Closer - 1973
Phil L. A. Of Soul 365 - Lost The Will To Live / Let Me Do What We Ain't Doin' - 1974
GRT 116 - Can You Feel The Vibrations / Short Version - 1976 (Canadian 45)
GRT 1230-128 - Dazz / Dazz (Disco Version) - 1976 (Canadian 45)
GRT 3230-01 - I Think I'm Falling In Love / I Think I'm Falling In Love (Disco Version) - 1976 (Canadian 45)

The Spinners

The Domingoes (members Crathman Plato, Pervis Jackson (born 17-May-1938 in New Orleons, Louisina --- died 18-August-2008 --- cause: cancer),..........)

The Spinners (members Bobby Smith, George Dixon, Billy Henderson, Henry Fambrough and Pervis Jackson)

Tri-Phi 1001 - That's What Girls Are Made For / Heebie Jeebies - 1961 *lead vocal Bobby Smith.
Tri-Phi 1004 - Love (I'm So Glad)* / Sudbuster - 1961 *Lead Vocal Harvey Fuqua.
Tri-Phi 1007 - Itching For My Baby, But I Don't Know Where To Scratch / What Did She Use - 1962 *Lead Vocal Bobby Smith.
Tri-Phi 1010 - She Loves Me So / Whistling About You - 1962

Harvey & The Spinners

Tri-Phi 1010 - She Loves Me So / Whistling About You - 1962

The Spinners

Tri-Phi 1013 - I've Been Hurt / I Got Your Water Boiling Baby - 1962

Bobby Smith And The Spinners

Tri-Phi 1018 - She Don't Love Me / Too Young, Too Much, Too Soon - 1962

Loe And Joe (With The Spinners)

Harvey 112 - Little Ole Boy, Little Ole Girl / That's How I Am Without You - 1962

The Spinners

Motown 1067 - Sweet Thing / How Can I - 1964
Motown 1078 - I'll Always Love You / Tomorrow May Never Come - 1965
Motown 1093 - Truly Yours / Where Is That Girl - 1966

Various Artists

Motown 2482 - Seasons Greetings From Motown - 1966 (very short "Christmas greetings" radio station spots are delivered by Martha & The Vandellas, The Temptations, The Miracles, Shorty Long, The Velvelettes, The Spinners, The Four Tops, The Elgins and The Supremes ---- it was pressed in red vinyl)

The Spinners

Motown 1109 - For All We Know / Cross My Heart - 1967
Motown 1136 - Bad Bad Weather / I Just Can't Help But Feel The Pain - 1968
Motown 1155 - (She's Gonna Love Me) At Sundown / In My Diary - 1969
VIP 25050 - (She's Gonna Love Me) At Sundown / In My Diary - 1969
VIP 25054 - (She's Gonna Love Me) At Sundown / Message From A Black Man - 1970
VIP 25057 - It's A Shame / Together We Can Make Such Sweet Music - 1970
VIP 25060 - My Whole World Ended (The Moment You Left Me) / We'll Have It Made - 1971(Promo Copies Came Out In Red Vinyl)

The Spinners (members Bobby Smith, Phillipe Wynne (died 13-July-1984 --- cause: heart attack), Henry Fainbrough, Billy Henderson and Pervis Jackson)

Atlantic 2904 - I'll Be Around* / How Could I Let You Get Away - 1972 *also released in Australia by Doug Parkinson & The Southern Star Band on ATA K7339.
Atlantic 2927 - Could It Be I'm Falling In Love / Just You And Me Baby - 1972
Atlantic 2962 - One Of A Kind (Love Affair) / Don't Let The Green Grass Fool You - 1973
Motown 1235 - Together We Can Make Such Sweet Sweet Music* / Bad, Bad Weather - 1973 *this version has strings and runs nine seconds longer than the version on V.I.P. 25057.
Atlantic 2973 - Ghetto Child / We Belong Together - 1973
Atlantic 3006 - Mighty Love - Part 1 / Mighty Love- Part 2 - 1973
Atlantic 3027 - He'll Never Love You Like I Do / I'm Coming Home - 1974

Dionne Warwick & Spinners

Atlantic 3029 - Then Came You / Just As Long As We Have Love - 1974
Atlantic 3202 - Then Came You / Just As Long As We Have Love - 1974

The Spinners

Atlantic 3206 - Love Don't Love Nobody (Part 1) / Love Don't Love Nobody (Part 2) - 1974
Atlantic 3252 - Living A Little, Laughing A Little / Smile, We Have Each Other - 1975
Atlantic 3268 - Lazy Susan / Sadie - 1975
Atlantic 3284 - I Don't Want To Lose You / Games People Play - 1975
Atlantic 3284 - I Don't Want To Lose You / They Just Can't Stop It The (Games People Play) - 1975 (Altered Title)
Atlantic 3309 - You Made A Promise To Me / Love Or Leave* - 1975 *recorded ?-May-1975.
Atlantic 3341 - Wake Up Susan / If You Can't Be In Love - 1976 (John Edwards becomes a full time member of the group some time in early 1976)

Atlantic 3355 - The Rubberband Man / Now That We're Together - 1976
Atlantic 3382 - You're All I Need In Life / You're Throwing A Good Love Away - 1977

The Spinners / Johnny Mathis

W. I. A. A. 375 - What's It All About - 1977 (June 1977 Public Service Show --- flip side features Johnny Mathis)

The Spinners

Atlantic 3400 - Me And My Music / I'm Riding Your Shadow - 1977
Atlantic 3425 - Heaven On Earth (So Fine) / I'm Tired Of Giving - 1977
Atlantic 3462 - Easy Come, Easy Go / One Step Away - 1978
Atlantic 3483 - If You Wanna Do A Dance / Once In A Life Proposal - 1978

Abba / Spinners / Firefall / England Dan & John Ford Coley

Warner Bros. Special Products - 1978 (promo issue - Coca-Cola / Burger King promotion issued with paper sleeve)

The Spinners

Atlantic 3546 - Are You Ready For Love / Once You Fall In Love - 1979
Atlantic 3590 - I Love The Music / Don't Let The Man Get You - 1979
Atlantic 3619 - Body Language / With My Eyes - 1979
Atlantic 3637 - Working My Way Back To You / Disco Ride - 1979 (Original Disc Has Shorter Title)
Atlantic 3637 - Working My Way Back To You - Forgive Me, Girl / Disco Ride - 1979
Atlantic 3664 - Cupid - I've Loved You For A Long Time / Pipedreams - 1980
Atlantic 3757 - Love Trippin' / Now That You're Mine Again - 1980
Atlantic 3765 - I Just Want To Fall In Love / Heavy On The Sunshine - 1980
Atlantic 3798 - Yesterday Once More - Nothing Remains The Same / Be My Love - 1981
Atlantic Os-13220 - Cupid - I've Loved You For A Long Time / Working My Way Back To You - Forgive Me, Girl - 1981 (Oldies Series)
Atlantic 3814 - Long Live Soul Music / Give Your Lady What She Wants - 1981
Atlantic 3827 - Winter Of Our Love / The Deacon - 1981

Gino Soccio With The Spinners

Atlantic 3865 - What You Feel Is Real / Street Talk - 1981

The Spinners

Atlantic 3865 - You Go Your Way (I'll Go Mine) / Got To Be Love - 1981
Atlantic 3882 - Love Connection / Love Connection - 1981 (Promo Only)
Atlantic 3882 - Love Connection (Raise The Window Down) / Love Is Such A Crazy Feeling - 1981
Atlantic 4007 - Never Thought I'd Fall In Love / Send A Little Love - 1982
Atlantic 89922 - Funny How Time Slips Away* / I'm Calling You Now - 1982 *also recorded in 1961 by Jimmy Elledge on RCA-Victor 47-7946.
Atlantic 89962 - So Far Away / Magic In The Moonlight - 1982
Atlantic Os-13170 - Mighty Love (Part 1) / Mighty Love (Part 2) - 1982 (Oldies Series)
Atlantic Os-13171 - He'll Never Love You Like I Do / I'm Coming Home - 1982 (Oldies Series)
Atlantic 89862 - City Full Of Memories / No Other Love - 1983
Atlantic 89648 - All Your Love / (We Have Come Into) Our Time For Love - 1984
Atlantic 89689 - Right Or Wrong / Love Is In Season - 1984
Atlantic 84982 - Love Don't Love Nobody (Part 1) / Love Don't Love Nobody (Part 2) - 1985
Mirage 99580 - The Witness / She Does - 1985

Mirage 99604 - Put Us Together Again / Show Me Your Magic - 1985
Atlantic 89226 - Spaceballs / Spaceballs (Dub Version) - 1987

Dionne Warwick & The Spinners / Dionne Warwick

Arista 9940 - I Don't Need Another Love / Heartbreaker* - 1990 *Flip By Dionne Warwick (Some Copies Issued With Picture Sleeve)

The Spinners

Atlantic Os-13206 - The Rubberband Man / If You Wanna Do A Dance - ? (Oldies Series)
Motown Yesteryear 483 - We'll Have It Made / It's A Shame - ?

Edwin Starr

Futuretones (members Edwin Hatcher, John Berry, Parnell Burks, Richard Isom and Roosevelt Harris with musicians Russel Evans (guitar), Pinhead (trumpet), Julias Robertson (bass), Brownie (drummer) and Gus Hawkins (sax))

Reserve 121 - Please Come Back / Skitter Skatter* - 1957 *originally recorded in 1956 by The Metrotones on Reserve 116.
Tress 2 - I Know / Roll On - 1957 (shortly after this release Edwin Hatcher was drafted into the armed forces)

Bill Doggett Combo from 1963 ~ 1965 (Edwin Starr member -- unsure of what recordings he was on during this period)

Edwin Starr (born Charles Edwin Hatcher on 21-January-1942 in Nashville, Tennessee. Raised in Cleveland, Ohio. Died 2-April-2003 at his home in Chilwell near Nottingham, England. Cause: heart attack)

Ric-Tic 103 - Agent Double-O-Soul / (Instrumental) - 1965 (red label)
Ric-Tic 103 - Agent OO-Soul (Agent Double-O-Soul) / (INSTRUMENTAL) - 1965 (yellow label)
Ric-Tic 107 - Back Street* / (Instrumental) - 1965
Ric-Tic 109 - Stop Her On Sight (S.O.S.) / I Have Faith In You -
Ric-Tic 109-X - Scott's On Swingers (S.O.S.) / Scott's On Swingers (S.O.S) - 1966 (this was a white label promo release for Detroit disc jockey Scott Regan of WKNR-AM. The red label copies are all English bootlegs)

The Holidays (members Eddie Anderson, Steve Mancha and J.J. Barnes, Edwin Starr's vocal overdubbed on recording - not actual member)
Golden World 36 - I'll Love You Forever / Makin' Up Time - 1966 (produced by Don Davis)

Edwin Starr

Ric-Tic 114 - Headline News / Harlem – 1966
Ric-Tic 118 - It's My Turn Now / Girls Are Getting Prettier – 1967
Ric-Tic 120 - You're My Mellow / My Kind Of Woman – 1967
Gordy 7066 - Gonna Keep On Tryin' Til I Win Your Love / I Want My Baby Back - 1967
Gordy 7071 - I Am The Man For You Baby / My Weakness Is You – 1968
Gordy 7078 - Way Over There / If My Heart Could Tell The Story - 1968
Gordy 7083 - Twenty-Five Miles / Love Is The Destination - 1969 (also issued on red vinyl)
Gordy 7087 - I'm Still A Struggling Man / Pretty Little Angel - 1969

Edwin Starr & Blinky (Sandra "Blinky" Williams)

Gordy 7090 - Oh How Happy* / Ooh Baby Baby - 1969 *written by Edwin Starr while in the service in Germany. Was a number 12 pop hit for Edwin Starr discovered group Shades Of Blue in June of 1966 on IMPACT 1007.

Edwin Starr

Gordy 7097 - Time / Running Back And Forth – 1970
Gordy 7101 - War / He Who Picks A Rose – 1970
Gordy 7104 - Stop The War Now / Gonna Keep On Tryin' Til I Win Your Love – 1970
Gordy 7107 - Funky Music Sho Nuff Turns Me On / Cloud Nine - 1971
Soul 35096 - Take Me Clear From Here / Ball Of Confusion (That's What The World Is Today) - 1972
Soul 35100 - Who Is The Leader Of The People / Don't Tell Me I'm Crazy - 1972 (Promo Copies Issued In Blue Vinyl)
Soul 35103 - There You Go (Vocal) / There You Go (Instrumental) – 1973
Soul 35112 - Ain't It Hell Up In Harlem / Don't It Feel Good To Be Free - 1974 (Release Transferred To Motown 1284)
Motown 1276 - You've Got My Soul On Fire / Love (The Lonely People's Prayer) - 1973
Motown 1284 - Ain't It Hell Up In Harlem / Don't It Feel Good To Be Free - 1973 (Originally Scheduled For Release On Soul 35112)
Motown 1300 - Big Papa / Like We Used To Do – 1974
Motown 1326 - Who's Right Or Wrong / Lonely Rainy Days In San Diego – 1974
Granite 522 - Pain / I'll Never Forget You – 1975
Granite 528 - Stay With Me / Party – 1975
Granite 532 - Abyssinia Jones / Beginning – 1975
20th Century 2338 - I Just Wanna Do My Thing / Mr. Davenport And Mr. James – 1977
20th Century Tcd-62 - I Just Wanna Do My Thing / Mr. Davenport And Mr. James - 1977 (12" Release)
20th Century 2389 - I'm So Into You / Don't Waste Your Time – 1978
20th Century 2396 - Contact / Don't Waste Your Time – 1978
20th Century Tcd-0024 - Contact (7:21) / Don't Waste Your Time (4:01) - 1978 (12" Release)
20th Century Tcd-069 - Contact (Intro - 1:36) (Song - 7:21) / Working Song (Intro - 2:22) (Song - 7:38) - 1978 (12" Release) (Some Promo Copies Issued In Pink Vinyl)

Edwin Starr / Gene Chandler

Casablanca 874 117-1 - Contact (7:17) / Get Down (8:14) - 1978 (12" Release) *Flip By Gene Chandler.
20th Century Tcd-073 - Contact (7:21) / Get Down (8:14) - 1979 (12" Release) *Flip By Gene Chandler.

Edwin Starr

20th Century Tcd-074 - Contact / ? - 1979 (12" Release)
20th Century 2408 - H.A.P.P.Y. Radio / My Friend – 1979
20th Century Tcd-076 - H.A.P.P.Y. Radio (Extendended Disco Version) (6:45) / My Friend (3:56) - 1979 (12" Release)
20th Century Tcd-077 - H.A.P.P.Y. Radio (Vocal) (6:45) / H. A. P. P. Y. Radio (Instrumental) (6:45) - 1979 (12" Promo Issue Only)
20th Century 2420 - It's Called The Rock / Patiently – 1979
20th Century Tcd-093 - It's Called The Rock (7:24) / Patiently (4:34) - 1979 (12" Release)
20th Century 2423 - It's Called The Rock / H.A.P.P.Y. Radio – 1979
20th Century Tcd-095 - It's Called The Rock (7:24) / H.A.P.P.Y. Radio (6:45) - 1979 (12" Release) 20th Century 2441 - It's Called The Rock / H.A.P.P.Y. Radio – 1980
20th Century 2445 - Stronger Than You Think I Am / (Instrumental) – 1980
20th Century 2450 - Tell-A-Star / Boop Boop Song – 1980
20th Century Tcd-107 - Tell A Star / Tell A Star - 1980 (12" Promo Issue)
20th Century Tcd-107 - Tell-A-Star (5:20) / Boop Boop Song (6:05) - 1980 (12" Release)
20th Century 2455 - Get Up-Whirlpool / Better And Better – 1980

20th Century 2462 - Get Up...Whirlpool / ? – 1980
20th Century Tcd-109 - Get Up...Whirlpool (8:20) / Bigger And Better (3:10) - 1980 (12" Release)
20th Century 2477 - Twenty-Five Miles / Never Turn My Back On You – 1980
20th Century Tcd-119 - Twenty-Five Miles / Never Turn My Back On You - 1980 (12" Release)
20th Century Tcd-120 - Twenty-Five Miles (5:12) / (Instrumental) - 1980 (12" Promo Issue)
20th Century 2496 - Real Live #10 / Sweat – 1981
20th Century Tcd-128 - Real Live #10 (Stereo) / Real Live #10 (Mono) - 1981 (12" Promo Issue)
Montage 1216 - Tired Of It / ? – 1982
Montage 7908 - Tired Of It / Double Or Nothing - 1982 (12" Release)
A.S.K. Sh-29116 - Hit Me With Your Love (2-4-6-8-10) (5:23) / Over And Over (5:11) - 1982 (12" Release)
A.S.K. L111155 - You Hit The Nail On The Head (Rick Gianatos Mix) (5:31) / Sweetest Thing (2:56) - ? (12" Release)
Casablanca Timepieces 424 677-7 - Contact / H. A. P. P. Y. Radio - 1984
Hippodrome 12-Hippo-1 - Missiles We Don't Want To Die / ? - 1985 (12" Release)
Motown Zt41966 - Twenty-Five Miles (Remix '89) / (Single Version '89) /// (Instrumental) / (Dub '89) - 1989 (12" Release)
Collectables Col 043297 - Contact / H. A. P. P. Y. Radio - ?

Edwin Starr / The Soul Patrol

Ripete 454005 - Release This Love / Shake, Rattle And Roll* - ? *Flip By The Soul Patrol.

Edwin Starr / Ashan Putli

Jazz Funk Jf004 - I Wanna Do My Thing / Space Talk* - ? (12" Release) *Flip By Ashan Putli.

Edwin Starr

J. S. 6003 - Mind Games Medley : ? - ?

The Supremes

The Primettes

Lu Pine 120 - Tears Of Sorrow / Pretty - 1960 (Lu-Pine 120 Hyphenated Is Also A Joe Stubbs 45)

The Supremes

Tamla 54038 - I Want A Guy / Never Again - 1961
Tamla 54045 - Buttered Popcorn / Who's Lovin' You - 1961
Motown 1008 - I Want A Guy / Never Again - 1961
Motown 1027 - Your Heart Belongs To Me / (He's) Seventeen - 1962
Motown 1034 - Let Me Go The Right Way / Time Changes Things - 1962

Marvin Gaye / Supremes / Singin' Sammy Ward / Contours / Marvelettes / Miracles

Promo - Motor Town Special MTS- 1 - Individual Artists - 1962 (Promo issue only from the first Motown Revue in 1962. It features the artists on tour talking over their latest record to promote the tour. Of interest are the Supremes talking over their minor hit 'Let Me Go The Right Way' on which Diana Ross introduces herself as Diane, her earlier name)

The Supremes

Motown 1040 - My Heart Can't Take It No More / You Bring Back Memories - 1963
Motown 1044 - A Breath Taking, First Sight Soul Shaking, One Night Love Making, Next Day Heart Breaking Guy / Rock And Roll Banjo Band - 1963
Motown 1044 - A Breath Taking Guy / Rock And Roll Band - 1963
Motown 1051 - When The Lovelight Starts Shining Through His Eyes / Standing At The Crossroads Of Love - 1963
Motown 1054 - Run, Run, Run / I'm Giving You Your Freedom - 1964
Motown 1060 - Where Did Our Love Go / He Means The World To Me - 1964
Motown 1066 - Baby Love / Ask Any Girl - 1964
Motown 1068 - Come See About Me / Always In My Heart - 1964

Hitsville U.S.A. Dm 097311 - Greetings To The Tamla Motown Appreciation Society - 1964 This American Record Was Limited To 300 Copies For Dispersal Throughout Various European Fan Clubs As A Promo For Their First European Tour. Each Act Gives An Individual Greeting Over It's Latest Record. Artists Involved Are The Miracles, Stevie Wonder, Marvin Gaye, The Marvelettes, The Temptations, Martha And The Vandellas, The Contours, Eddie Holland, Kim Weston And The Supremes. The Record Has An Introduction From Publicist Margaret Phelps And Berry Gordy.

The Supremes

Eeoc Sl4m 3114 - Things Are Changing / Things Are Changing - 1965 (Promo - For The Equal Employment Opportunity Commission)
Motown 1074 - Stop! In The Name Of Love / I'm In Love Again - 1965
Motown 1075 - Back In My Arms Again / Whisper You Love Me Boy - 1965
George Alexander Inc. 1079 - Supremes' Interview / The Only Time I'm Happy - 1965 (Special Premium 45 - Designated Motown 1079)
Motown 1080 - Nothing But Heartaches / He Holds His Own - 1965
Motown 1083 - I Hear A Symphony / Who Could Ever Doubt My Love - 1965
Motown 1085 - Children's Christmas Song / Twinkle, Twinkle, Little Me - 1965 (Promo Copies Are On Red Vinyl)
Motown 1089 - My World Is Empty Without You / Everything Is Good About You - 1966
American Int'l Pictures ? - Dr. Goldfoot And The Bikini Machine - 1966 (Single Sided 45 Used To Promote The Film Of The Same Name)

Christine Schumacher With The Supremes

Motown L-294m05 - Mother You, Smother Me / Mother You, Smother Me - 1966 (Winner Of Record A Record With The Supremes Contest, Diana Ross Does Not Sing On 45)

The Supremes

Motown 1094 - Love Is Like An Itching In My Heart / He's All I Got - 1966
Motown 1097 - You Can't Hurry Love / Put Yourself In My Place - 1966
Motown 1101 - You Keep Me Hangin' On / Remove This Doubt - 1966

Various Artists

Seasons Greetings From Motown 2482 - 1966 (Very Short Christmas Greetings Radio Station Spots Are Delivered By Martha Reeves And The Vandellas, The Temptations, The Miracles, Shorty Long, The Velvelettes, The Spinners, The Four Tops, The Elgins And The Supremes)

The Supremes

Motown 1103 - Love Is Here And Now You're Gone / There's No Stopping Us Now - 1967

Snatches From The Soundtrack (Featuring The Supremes

Colgems Music Corp - The Happening - 1967 (Promo issue only, no number, this 45 contains snatches from the film 'The Happening', including the title track by the Supremes which was made unique by them ending with the word etcetera)

The Supremes

Motown 1107 - The Happening / All I Know About You - 1967
PDMN 0375 FHLL - We Couldn't Make It Without You - 1967 (One sided acetate made especially for Berry Gordy)

Willie Horton

City Of Detroit M 1900 7568e1 - Detroit Is Happening / ? -1967 (The Supremes Minus Diana Sing An Altered Version Of Their Hit "The Happening")

The Supremes

Colgems - "Snatches From The Soundtrack: The Happening" - 1967 (Promo - No Selection Number Used)
Topps/Motown 1 - Baby Love - 1967 (Cardboard Record)
Topps/Motown 2 - Stop! In The Name Of Love - 1967 (Cardboard Record)
Topps/Motown 3 - Where Did Our Love Go - 1967 (Cardboard Record)
Topps/Motown 15 - Come See About Me - 1967 (Cardboard Record)
Topps/Motown 16 - My World Is Empty Without You - 1967 (Cardboard Record)

Diana Ross & The Supremes

Motown 1111 - Reflections / Going Down For The Third Time - 1967
(No name or label number) - In And Out Of Love - 1967 (Unreleased 10" acetate featuring three alternative versions of the song)
Motown 1116 - In And Out Of Love / Guess I'll Always Love You - 1967
Motown 1122 - Forever Came Today / Time Changes Things - 1968
Motown 1125 - What The World Needs Now / Your Kiss Of Fire - 1968 (Unreleased)
Motown 1126 - Some Things You Never Get Used To / You've Been So Wonderful To Me - 1968
Motown 1135 - Love Child / Will This Be The Day - 1968

Diana Ross & The Supremes & The Temptations

Motown 1137 - I'm Gonna Make You Love Me / A Place In The Sun - 1968

Diana Ross & The Supremes

American Pressing - I'm Living In Shame / ? - 1969 (test Pressing)
Motown 1139 - I'm Livin' In Shame / I'm So Glad I Got Somebody - 1969

Diana Ross & The Supremes & The Temptations

Motown 1142 - I'll Try Something New / The Way You Do The Things You Do - 1969

Diana Ross & The Supremes

Motown 1146 - The Composer / The Beginning Of The End - 1969
Motown 1148 - No Matter What Sign You Are / The Young Folks - 1969

Diana Ross & The Supremes & Temptations

Motown 1150 - Stubborn Kind Of Fellow / Try It Baby - 1969

Motown 1153 - The Weight / For Better Or Worse - 1969

Diana Ross & The Supremes

No name or number - Someday We'll Be Together - 1969 (Unreleased 10" acetate featuring an alternative take of the song)
Motown 1156 - Someday We'll Be Together */ He's My Sunny Boy - 1969 *Sung By Diana Ross, Julia Waters And Maxine Waters

The Supremes

Motown 1162 - Up The Ladder To The Roof / Bill, When Are You Coming Home - 1970
Motown 1167 - Everybody's Got The Right To Love / But I Love You More - 1970
Motown 1172 - Stoned Love / Shine On Me - 1970

The Supremes & Four Tops

Motown 1173 - River Deep-Mountain High / Together We Can Make Such Sweet Music - 1970
Motown 1181 - You Gotta Have Love In Your Heart / I'm Glad About It - 1971

The Supremes

Motown 1182 - Nathan Jones / Happy (Is A Bumpy Road) - 1971
Motown 1190 - Touch / It's So Hard For Me To Say Goodbye - 1971
Motown 1195 - Floy Joy / This Is The Story - 1972
Motown 1200 - Automatically Sunshine / Precious Little Things - 1972
Motown 1206 - Your Wonderful, Sweet Sweet Love / The Wisdom Of Time - 1972
Motown 1213 - I Guess I'll Miss The Man / Over And Over - 1972
Motown 1225 - Bad Weather / Oh Be My Love - 1973
Motown 1350 - It's All Been Said Before / ("B"- Side Unassigned) - 1975 (Unreleased)
Motown 1357 - He's My Man / Give Out But Don't Give Up - 1975
Motown 1374 - Where Do I Go From Here / Give Out But Don't Give Up - 1975
Motown 1391 - I'm Gonna Let My Heart Do The Walking / Early Morning Love - 1976
Motown 1407 - You're My Driving Wheel / You're What's Missing In My Life - 1976
Motown 1415 - Let Yourself Go / You Are The Heart Of Me - 1977

Diana Ross & The Supremes

Motown 1488 - Medley Of Hits / Where Did We Go Wrong - 1980
Motown 1523 - Medley Of Hits / Where Did We Go Wrong - 1981

Venue Reports - October 2001

The Whitehouse, Cannock, 6th October, 2001.

Quite a few people have tried running Soul nights at this pub out in the middle of Cannock Chase. Chic and Kiddo ran a charity night here a few months ago, and it was so successful they decided to try a monthly night here as well. And it's a great room as well. Numbers were quite respectable for a first night, and the music policy was across the board, with the Sixties provided by all of us, and the more Modern stuff by Chic, Kiddo, and Nige Mayfield.

The Pavillion, Huddersfield, 12th October, 2001.

Thanks to our glorious railway system I arrived at Bolton over an hour late, but John Mills was there to pick me up within a couple of minutes, a quick meal and we were on our way to Huddersfield. Directions had been provided by Colin Wood, one of the promoters, and they led us there perfectly. A really nice venue, dance floor at one end, bar and seating in the middle, with some tables for dealers at the door end. Music policy was 'Play what you want' so John Purvis, Colin, and Eddie Engle set the tone for the night. In fact Eddie played an absolute blinder of a set. John Mills followed him and came up with a good mixture of Sixties and Seventies. Although this was only the fourth event at this venue, the numbers have been increasing every time, so I was pleased to hear that the attendance tonight was the highest yet.

!00 Club, London, 13th October, 2001.

Considering this was October, it was bloody hot downstairs at 100 Oxford Street ! Guests this month were Roger Banks and Bob Hinsley, so the combination with Butch, Mick, and Ady meant a good night was had by all. As I tend to attend the 100 Club every month, and have a great time every month I'm running out of words to describe the night, and make it sound different to the previous month, so I'll finish by saying, if you haven't been before, why not ?

Nantwich Civic Hall, Nantwich, 20th October, 2001.

Another good night at Nantwich. To start with Bolton had beaten Manchester United at Old Trafford in the afternoon, and then an allnighter in a nice venue with a good D line up. Over the 200 mark again through the door, and although people danced all night the sheer size of the dancefloor always made them look a little sparse. That didn't matter though because I didn't hear a bad spot all night, and thoroughly enjoyed myself.

The Jarvis Heath, Hotel, Bewdley, 26th October, 2001.

John Weston rang me up and offered me a lift, so that was that. Paul Cross and Kiddo were the guest DJs, Basil and Stuart Russell the residents. Mel and Pat, Chic, John Farrell and a couple of others were also there. But unfortunately that was about it. So the numbers were dreadful. However, because there are several large settees in the foyer bit we had a good time, it was like sitting in a mate's front room, listening to good music, with a bar ! This is the last night here on a Friday, but in the New Year the venue is being re-launched on a Saturday night instead, so that is something to look forward to.

The Queen Mary Ballroom, Dudley, 27th October, 2001.

So last night I was supposed to go to a 40th Birthday party, but my wife was ill, so I went to the zoo instead. It was oldies, oldies, oldies, oldies, and then a few more oldies. Then the star of screen and books, duss binstanley arrived and played a few more oldies. Seriously though, this was a gamble by Phil, because Russ charges an outrageous amount. The gamble paid off though. Over 200 in, the dancefloor full, and a cracking atmosphere. I must admit that Phil and Mark Freeman did the business, mixing known and forgotten oldies in with the odd post Wigan thing. Russ' spot was rather predictable, but what the hell, Phil hired him to play those records, so who am I to complain. Little Scotty finished the night off in his own inimitable style. It's a great venue, with a good dancefloor, and a well staffed bar. A really successful night that was enjoyed by everyone I spoke to. Congratulations to Phil and all involved.

Group Line Ups

The Tams (Joseph Pope, Charles Pope, Floyd Ashton, Horace Key, Robert Lee Smith)
The Temprees (Jasper Phillips, Harold H Scott, Del Juan Calvin)

The Trammps (Earl D Young, Jimmy Ellis, Barrington McDonald, Horold 'Doc' Wade, Stanley Wade, John Hart, Michael Thompson)
The Trends (Eddie Dunn, Emmett Garner, ralph O'Neill, Jerome Jackson)
The Tymes (George Williamson, Albert 'Ceasar' Berry III, George Hilliard, Norman Burnett, Donald Banks)

Booker T. & The MG's

Volt 102 - Green Onions / Behave Yourself - 1962
Stax 127 - Green Onions / Behave Yourself - 1962
Atlantic 1600 - Green Onions / Behave Yourself - 1962
Stax 131 - Jelly Bread / Aw' Mercy - 1963
Stax 134 - Home Grown / Burnt Biscuits - 1963
Stax 134 - Big Train / Burnt Biscuits - 1963
Stax 137 - Chinese Checkers / Plum Nellie - 1963
Stax 142 - Mo' Onions / Fannie Mae - 1963
Stax 142 - Tic Tac Toe / Fannie Mae - 1963
Stax 153 - Soul Dressing / M. G. Party - 1964
Stax 161 - Can't Be Still / Terrible Thing - 1964
Stax 169 - Boot-Leg / Outrage - 1965
Stax 182 - Red Beans And Rice / Be My Lady - 1965
Stax 196 - Booker-Loo / My Sweet Potato - 1966
Atlantic 584044 - Booker-Loo / My Sweet Potato - 1966
Stax 203 - Jingle Bells / Winter Wonderland - 1966
Stax 211 - Hip Hug-Her / Summertime (Edited Version) - 1967
Stax 224 - Groovin' / Slim Jenkin's Place - 1967
Stax 236 - Silver Bells / Winter Snow - 1967
Stax 0001 - Soul-Limbo / Heads Or Tails - 1968
Stax 0013 - Hang 'Em High* / Over Easy - 1968 *From The Film Of The Same Name.
Stax 0028 - Time Is Tight* / Johnny, I Love You - 1969 *From The Soundtrack "Uptight"
Stax 0037 - Mrs. Robinson* / Soul Clap '69 - 1969 *From The Film The Graduate.
Stax 0049 - Slum Baby / Meditation - 1969
Stax 0073 - Something (Edited Version) / Sunday Sermon - 1970
Stax 0082 - Melting Pot (Edited Version) / Kinda Easy Like (Edited Version) - 1970

Booker T. & The MG'S / The MG's

Stax 0108 - Fuquawi / Jamaica This Morning* - 1971 *Flip By The MGs Only.

The M. G. 's

Stax 0169 - Sugarcane / Blackslide - 1973
Stax 0200 - Neckbone / Breezy - 1974

Booker T. Jones

Epic 50031 - Evergreen / Song For Casey - 1974
Epic 50078 - Front Street Rag / Mama Stewart - 1975
Epic 50149 - Life Is Funny / Tennessee Voodoo - 1975

Booker T. & The MG's

Stax/Fantasy 1001 - Soul Limbo / Hang 'Em High - 1977 (Double Hitters Series)
Stax/Fantasy 1002 - Time Is Tight / Mrs. Robinson - 1977 (Double Hitters Series)
Stax/Fantasy 1003 - Melting Pot / Slum Baby - 1977 (Double Hitters Series)

Elektra 45392 - Stick Stuff / Tie Stick - 1977
Elektra 45424 - Grab Bag / Reincarnation - 1977

Booker T. & Priscilla

A & M 1298 - The Wedding Song / She - 1977
A & M 1487 - Crippled Crow / Wild Fox - 1977

Booker T.

Asylum 45392 - Stick Stuff / Tie Stick - 1977
Asylum 45424 - Grab Bag / Reincarnation - 1977
A & M 2100 - Knockin' On Heaven's Door / Let's Go Dancin' - 1978
A & M 2234 - The Best Of You / Let's Go Dancin' - 1980
A & M 2279 - Will You Be The One / Cookie - 1980
A & M 2374 - I Want You / You're The Best - 1981
A & M 2394 - Don't Stop Your Love / I Came To Love You - 1982

Booker T. & The MG's

Collectables Col 710017 - Soul Limbo / Hang 'Em High - ?
Collectables Col 710027 - Time Is Tight / Mrs. Robinson - ?
Collectables Col 710037 - Melting Pot / Slum Baby - ?

Booker T.

Columbia 77526 - Cruisin' / Just My Imagination - 1994

The Tams

The Tams (Members - Brothers Joseph Pope And Charles Pope, Floyd "Little Floyd" Ashton, Robert Smith And Willie "Frog" Rutherford (Who Bought The Trademark Tam-O-Shanter Hats For Performances And Named The Group The Tams. In The Late 1950's Willie Rutherford Was Caught And Sent To Prison For Stealing A Tv.) Willie Rutherford Was Replaced By Horace "Sonny" Key.

Heritage 101 - Vacation Time / If Love Were Like Rivers - 1961
Arlen 711 - Untie Me* / Disillusioned - 1962 *Written By Tommy And Joe South. 45 Produced By Ray Stevens Who Also Played Piano On Recording.
Arlen 716 - Here I Am / My Baby Loves Me - 1962
Arlen 717 - Deep Inside Me / If You're So Smart (Why Do You Have A Broken Heart) - 1962

The Tams With Little Floyd

General American 714 - My Baby Loves Me / Find Another Love - 1962

The Tams

Arlen 720 - Blue Shadows / You'll Never Know - 1963
Arlen 729 - Find Another Love / Don't Ever Go - 1963
ABC-Paramount 10502 - What Kind Of Fool (Do You Think I Am?) / Laugh It Off - 1963 (45 Cut At Rick Hall's Fame Studio - Muscle Shoals, Alabama)
ABC-Paramount 10533 - You Lied To Your Daddy / It's All Right (You're Just In Love) - 1964
ABC-Paramount 10573 - Hey Girl Don't Bother Me / Take Away - 1964
ABC-Paramount 10601 - Silly Little Girl / Weep Little Girl - 1964
ABC-Paramount 10614 - The Truth Hurts / Why Did My Little Girl Cry - 1964(Increasing

Problems With Alcohol And Sporadic Live Performances Led To The Halt Of Floyd Ashton Recording With The Group Sometime In 1964, Although His Picture Still Appeared On Album Covers. He Was Replaced With Albert Cottle Jr.)
King 6012 - Untie Me / Find Another Love - 1965
ABC-Paramount 10635 - What Do You Do / Unlove You - 1965
ABC-Paramount 10702 - Concrete Jungle / Till The End Of Time - 1965
ABC-Paramount 10741 - I've Been Hurt* / Carrying On - 1965 *A Later Interpretation Of This Song Was By Bill Deal & The Rhondells On Heritage 812.
ABC-Paramount 10779 - Riding For Fall / Got To Get Used To A Broken Heart - 1966
ABC 10825 - Holding On / It's Better To Have Loved A Little - 1966
ABC 10885 - Get Away (Leave Me Alone) / Shelter - 1966
ABC 10929 - Breaking Up / How 'Bout It - 1967
ABC 10956 - Everything Else Is Gone / Mary, Mary, Row Your Boat - 1967
ABC 11019 - All My Hard Times / A Little More Soul - 1967
ABC 11066 - Be Young Be Foolish Be Happy* / That Same Old Song - 1968 *First Recorded By The Sensational Epics, With Joe Morris (Of The Swingin' Medallions) As Producer.
ABC 11128 - Trouble Maker / Laugh At The World - 1968
ABC 11183 - Sunshine, Rainbow, Blue Sky, Brown Eyed Girl / There's A Great Big Change In Me - 1969
ABC 11228 - Love, Love, Love / Love Maker - 1969
1-2-3 1726 - Too Much Foolin' Around / How Long Love - 1970
Capitol 3050 - Tams Medley / Wire Help - 1971
ABC Dunhill - Hey Girl Don't Bother Me / Weep Little Girl -1971 (Some Copies Issued With "#1 In England" Sleeve)
Apt 26010 - Numbers / Long Distance Operator - 1972
ABC 11358 - Don't You Just Know It / Making Music - 1973
MGM South 7023 - Alley Oop / What Did He Do For You - 1973
R & B (no #) - Laugh It Off / I've Been Hurt - 1977 (came in a plain white label with red logo lettering with "A '77 Lori Production" and "Dynatone Recording" typed on label - these are alternate versions of earlier charted tracks)
Sounds South 14098 - This Precious Moment / Hey Girl (Disco Version) - 1978
Passion 123 - Tell You For The Last Time / Hideaway - 1978
Wonder 1001 - Tams Tune Medley / I've Been Hurt (New) - 1982
Compleat 109 - Making True Love / My Baby Sure Can Shag - 1983
Collectables Col 012187 - Untie Me / Disillusioned - 1980's

The Tams / The Marvelows

Collectables Col 037107 - Be Young, Be Foolish, Be Happy / In The Morning - 1980's

The Tams

Collectables Col 902247 - What Kind Of Fool / Be Young, Be Foolish, Be Happy - ?
Ripete 1014 - Jesus Is Your Ticket To Heaven* / It Happens Everytime - 1988 *originally written for Ronnie Milsap.
Ripete 2005 - There Ain't Nothing Like Shaggin' / Showtime - 1989

Joe Pope Sans Tams

Surfside 910214a - If This Ain't Love, Keep On Foolin' Me / If This Ain't Love, Keep On Foolin' Me - 1991
Surfside 920401a - Down And Dirty Love / Down And Dirty Love - 1991
(Above Two Surfside Releases Were Written And Produced By General Johnson, Who Along With Ken Knox From Chairmen Of The Board And Local Musician Willie Walker Provided Background Vocals, Rather Than The Actual Tams (The Record Label Is Misleading))

Howard Tate

The Evening Star (members Little Joe Cook, Garnett Mimms and Sam Bell)

The Belairs (members Garnett Mimms, Sam Bell and Howard Tate)

Mercury? - mid 1950's

The Gainors (members Garnet Mimms, Sam Bell, Howard Tate, Willie Combo, John Jefferson)

Cameo Parkway 151 - The Secret / Gonna Rock Tonite - 1958
Cameo Parkway 156 - You Must Be An Angel / Follow Me - 1958
Red Top 110 - You Must Be An Angel / Follow Me - 1958
Mercury 71466 - She's My Lollipop / Message With Flowers - 1959
Mercury 71569 - Please Consider / She's Gone - 1959
Mercury 71630 - Nothing Means More To Me / I'm In Love With You - 1960
Talley-Ho 102 - This Perfect Moment / Where I Want To Be - 1961
Talley-Ho 105 - Tell Him / Darling - 1961

Bill Doggett (Howard Tate was his vocalist for a few years)

Howard Tate (born 1943 in Macon, Georgia)

Utopia 510/511 - Half A Man / You're Lookin' Good - 1964
Verve 10464 - Half A Man / You're **Lookin'** Good - 1964
Verve 10420 - How Come My Bulldog Don't Bark / Ain't Nobody Home - 1966
Verve 10464 - Look At Granny Run Run / Half A Man - 1966
Verve 10496 - Glad I Knew Better / Get It While You Can* - 1966 *also recorded in 1971 by Janis Joplin on Columbia 45433.
Verve 10525 - Baby, I Love You / How Blue Can You Get - 1967
Verve 10547 - I Learned It All The Hard Way / Part Time Love - 1967
Verve 10573 - Stop* / Shoot 'Em All Down - 1967 *also recorded in 1971 by Sam Moore on Atlantic 2799.
Verve 10604 - Everyday I Have The Blues / Night Owl - 1967
Verve 10625 - Sweet Love Child / I'm Your Servant - 1968
Turntable 505 - That's What Happens / These Are The Things That Make Me Know You're Gone - 1969
Turntable 507 - Have You Ever Had The Blues / Plenty Of Love - 1969

Turntable 508 - My Soul's Got A Hole In It / It's Too Late - 1969
Atlantic 2836 - Strugglin' / Keep Cool (Don't Be A Fool) - 1971
Atlantic 2860 - She's A Burglar / You Don't Know Nothing About Love - 1971
Atlantic 2894 - 8 Days On The Road / Girl Of The North Country - 1971
Epic 11118 - Ain't Got Nobody To Give It To / Can You Top This - 1974
HT 001 - Brand New Me / Pride - 1976
TBF 101 - Sweetness / One Armed Bandit - 1986

Lloyd Price / Howard Tate

Turntable 5005 - Bad Conditions / That's What Happens* - ? *flip by Howard Tate.

Bobby Taylor

The Columbus Pharaohs with Tommy Wills Orch. (members Morris Wade, Bobby Taylor, Ronald Wilson and Bernard Wilson)

Esta 290 - Give Me Your Love / China Girl - 1958

4 Pharaohs (members Morris Wade, Bobby Taylor, Ronald Wilson and Bernard Wilson)

Ransom 101 - Give Me Your Love / China Doll - 1958

The Four Pharoahs (members Morris Wade, George Smith, Ronald Wilson and Robert Lowery)

Ranson 100 - Pray For Me / The Move Around - 1958

Introducing Morris Wade With Music By The Manhattans

Ransom 102 - It Was A Nite Like This / Is It To Late - 1958
Ransom 103 - Is It Too Late / It Was A Night Like This - 1958 (Backed By Sonny Til)

The Four Pharoahs (members Morris Wade, Bobby Taylor, Ronald Wilson and Bernard Wilson)

Paradise 109 - Give Me Your Love / China Doll – 1958

The Four Pharoahs (members Morris Wade, Bobby Taylor and Ronald Wilson) 1959

King Pharoah & The Egyptians (members Harold "King Pharoah" Smith, Morris Wade, Ronald Wilson and Robert Lowrey)

Federal 12413 - By The Candlelight / Shimmy Sham - 1961

King Pharoah & The Egyptians (members Harold Smith, Morris Wade, Ronald Wilson, Leo Blakely and Paul Moore)

King Pharoah & The Egyptians (members Morris Wade, Pete Oden, Leo Blakely, Paul Moore and Sylvester Moore) 1963

The Egyptian Kings (members Morris Wade, Pete Oden, Leo Blakely, Paul Moore and Sylvester Moore)

Nanc 1120 - Give Me Your Love / I Need Your Love - 1963 (has company address under label name - scarcer copies)
Nanc 1120 - Give Me Your Love / I Need Your Love - 1963 (has "Dist. By Swingin' Records" under name - common copies)

The Egyptian Kings (members Harold Smith, Morris Wade, Pete Oden, Leo Blakely, Paul Moore and Sylvester Moore) 1963

The Egyptian Kings (members Harold Smith, Morris Wade, Forest Porter, Leo Blakely, Paul Moore and Sylvester Moore) 1963

The Egyptian Kings (members Harold Smith, Morris Wade, William Suber, Leo Blakely, Paul Moore and Sylvester Moore) 1965

The Shades (members Tommy Melton (vocals), Tommy Chong (guitar), Wes Henderson (bass) and Floyd Sneed (drums)) Canadian multi racial group (hence the name)

Little Daddy & The Bachelors (members Bobby Taylor, Wes Henderson, Ted Lewis, Eddie Patterson, Robbie King and Tommy Chong)

? - Too Much Monkey Business / Come On Home - ? Canadian released 45 (the group was known to have recorded at least two tracks - unsure but suspect that they are on the same 45 - does anyone know?)

Four Niggers and a Chink (members Bobby Taylor, Wes Henderson, Ted Lewis, Eddie Patterson, Robbie King and Tommy Chong)

Bobby Taylor & The Vancouvers (members Bobby Taylor, Wes Henderson, Ted Lewis, Eddie Patterson, Robbie King (born ? - died 17-September-2003 in Vancouver, Canada - cause throat cancer) and Tommy Chong (later to have fame as one half of the well documented comedy / recording duo Cheech & Chong)) an interracial sextet based in Vancouver, Canada. Jimi Hendrix working as an R & B sideman joined the group in December-1962 until he met up with and left with Little Richard. Bobby Taylor "discovered" The Jackson Five.

Gordy 7069 - Does Your Mama Know About Me* / Fading Away** - 1968 (Some copies released in red vinyl) *covered in 1973 by Jermaine Jackson on Motown 1244. **cover of the 1966 release by The Temptations on Gordy 7049.
Gordy 7073 - I Am Your Man / If You Love Her – 1968
Gordy 7079 - Malinda / It's Growing* - 1968 *cover of the 1965 release by The Temptations on Gordy 7040.
Integra 103 - This Is My Woman / A Stop Along The Way – 1968

Bobby Taylor

Gordy 7088 - Oh I've Been Bless'd / It Should Have Been Me Loving Her - 1969 (Unissued)
V. I. P. 25053 - Oh I've Been Bless'd / Blackmail – 1969
V. I. P. 25053 - Blackmail / Blackmail - 1969 (Promo Issue Only)
Gordy 7092 - My Girl Has Gone* / It Should Have Been Me Loving Her - 1969 *cover of the 1965 release by The Miracles on Tamla 54123.

Wes Henderson

Rare Earth 5007 - In Bed / Reality – 1969

Bobby Taylor

Mowest 5006 - Hey Lordy / Just A Little Bit Closer – 1971
Sunflower 126 - There Are Roses Somewhere In The World / It Was A Good Time (Rosy's Theme) - 1972
Tommy Zs7 1751 - I Can't Quit Your Love (Mono) / I Can't Quit Your Love (Stereo) - 1973 (promo issue only)
Tommy Zs7 1751 - I Can't Quit Your Love / Queen Of The Ghetto – 1973
Playboy 6046 - Why Play Games / Don't Wonder Why – 1975

Bt & Tb (Bobby Taylor and Thom Bell)

Philadelphia International 3571 - I Can't Quit Your Love / Queen Of The Ghetto - 1973 (same instrumental tracks as the Tommy ZS7 1751 release)

Bobby Taylor & The Vancouvers (members Bobby Taylor, Wes Henderson, Ted Lewis, Eddie Patterson, Robbie King and Tommy Chong)

Motown Yesteryear 540 - Does Your Mama Know About Me / I Am Your Man - ?

Evil Twang (members Robbie King, Chris Houston, Brian Goble, Adam Drake, Luke Doucet, Jerry Doucette and Steven Drake) - unsure of any group recordings.

Felice Taylor

The Sweets (members Florian Taylor, Darlene Taylor and Norma Taylor) sister group.

Valiant 711 - The Richest Girl / Mama Saw Me With The Guy - 1965

Florian Taylor (Felice Taylor)

Groovy 103 - Think About Me / Knowing (That You Want Her) – 1966
Cadet 2246 - Think About Me / Knowing (That You Want Her) – 1966

Felice Taylor

Mustang 3024 - It May Be Winter Outside (But In My Heart It's Spring)* / Winter Again - 1966 *covered by Love Unlimited in 1973 on 20TH Century 2062
Mustang 3026 - I'm Under The Influence Of Love* / Love Theme (Instrumental) - 1967 *also recorded in 1967 by The Apollas on Warner Bros. 7060 and in 1974 by Love Unlimited on 20th Century 2082.
Kent 483 - I Can Feel Your Love / Good Luck* - 1968 *this flip and the flip on Kent 488 are the same song, just different titles.
Kent 488 - Captured By Your Love / New Love* - 1968 *this flip and the flip on Kent 483 are the same song, just different titles.

R Dean Taylor

R. Dean Taylor (Richard Dean Taylor born 1939 in Toronto, Ontario, Canada)

Audio Master 1 - At The High School Dance / How Wrong Can You Be? - 1960
Barry 3023 - At The High School Dance / How Wrong Can You Be? - 1960 (Canadian Release)
Mala 444 - I'll Remember / It's A Long Way To St. Louis - 1962
Barry 3099 - I'll Remember / It's A Long Wat To St Louis - 1962 (Canadian Release
Barry 3140 - We Fell In Love As We Tangoed / Beautiful Dreamer - 1962 (Canadian Release)
V. I. P. 25027 - Let's Go Somewhere / Poor Girl - 1965
V.I.P. 25042 - There's A Ghost In My House / There's A Ghost In My House - 1966 (Promo Issue).
V.I.P. 25042 - There's A Ghost In My House / Don't Fool Around - 1966
V.I.P. 25045 - Gotta See Jane / Don't Fool Around - 1967
Classic 6728 - At The High School Dance / ? - 196?
Rare Earth 5013 - Indiana Wants Me / Love's Your Name - 1970 (Some Copies Issued On Red Vinyl)
Rare Earth 5023 - Ain't It A Sad Thing / Back Street - 1970 (Some Copies Issued With A Picture Sleeve)
Rare Earth 5026 - Gotta See Jane / Back Street - 1971 (Some Copies Issued On Red Vinyl)
Rare Earth 5030 - Candy Apple Red / Woman Alive - 1971 (Some Copies Issued On Red Vinyl)
Rare Earth 5041 - Taos New Mexico / Shadow - 1972
Farr 001 - We'll Show Them All / Magdalena - 1976
Motown Yesteryear 459 - Indiana Wants Me / Gotta See Jane - ?
Jane ? - 1977
Ragamuffin ? - 1979

20th Century 2510 - Let's Talk It Over / Add Up The Score - 1981
Strummer 3747 - Out In The Alley / Bonnie - 1982
Strummer 3748 - Let's Talk It Over / ? - 1982

Ted Taylor

The Glory Bound Travellers (Among It's One Time Members Ted Taylor,)

The Mighty Clouds Of Joy (among it's one time members Ted Taylor, ...)

The Santa Monica Soul Seekers (among it's one time members Lou Rawls, Ted Taylor, Aaron Collins, Willie Davis, Will "Dub" Jones, Glendon Kingsby, Lloyd McCraw,....)

The Jacks (members Aaron Collins (lead and second tenor), Will "Dub" Jones (lead and bass), Willie Davis (first tenor), Lloyd McCraw (baritone and group manager) and Ted Taylor (first tenor)

The Cadets (Members Aaron Collins (Lead And Second Tenor), Will "Dub" Jones (Lead And Bass), Willie Davis (First Tenor), Lloyd Mccraw (Baritone And Group Manager) And Ted Taylor (First Tenor) When Group Signed To Modern Records In 1955 Joe Bihari Changed Their Name Because Upon Hearing The Group's Potential And Adaptability He Conceived The Idea Of Creating Two Groups Out Of One, Giving The Jacks A New Additional Name The Cadets.

Modern 956 - I Cried / Don't Be Angry* - 1955 *Cover Of 1955 Record By Nappy Brown On Savoy 1155.

The Jacks (Members Aaron Collins (Lead And Second Tenor), Will "Dub" Jones (Lead And Bass), Willie Davis (First Tenor), Lloyd Mccraw (Baritone And Group Manager) And Ted Taylor (First Tenor)

RPM 428 - Smack Dab In The Middle / Why Don't You Write Me - 1955
RPM 428 - My Darling / Why Don't You Write Me – 1955

Donna Hightower

RPM 432 - Love Me Again / Dog Gone It - 1955 (Backed By The Jacks)

The Jacks

RPM 433 - I'm Confessin' / Since My Baby's Been Gone – 1955

The Cadets

Modern 960 - Rollin' Stone* / Fine Lookin' Baby - 1955 *cover of 1955 record by The Marigolds on Excello 2057.

Young Jesse

Modern 961 - Mary Lou / Don't Think I Will - 1955 (Backed By The Cadets)

The Cadets

Modern 963 - I Cried / Fine Lookin' Baby – 1955

Donna Hightower

RPM 439 - Bob-O-Link / Since You - 1955 (Backed By The Jacks)

Dolly Cooper

Modern 965 - Ay La Ba / My Man - 1955 (Backed By The Cadets)

The Jacks

RPM 444 - This Empty Heart / My Clumsy Heart – 1955

The Cadets

Modern 969 - So Will I / Annie Met Henry - 1955
Modern 971 - Do You Wanna Rock* / If It Is Wrong - 1956 *a reworked version of The Drifters song from 1955 "What'chs Gonna Do" on Atlantic 1055

The Jacks

RPM 454 - So Wrong / How Soon – 1956

The Cadets

Modern 985 - Church Bells May Ring* / Heartbreak Hotel - 1956 *cover of 1956 record by The Willows on Melba 102. **cover of 1956 record by Elvis Presley on RCA 6420. (after this recording Prentice Moreland replaced Ted Taylor)

Ted Taylor (born Theodore Austin Taylor on 16-February-1937 at Okmulgee, near Tulsa, Oklahoma. Died 22-October-1987 in Louisiana, cause: automobile accident)

Ebb 113 - Everywhere I Go / Days Are Dark - 1957

Bob Reed & His Band, Vocal By "Ivory Lucky" (Ted Taylor)

Melatone 1003 - I'm Leaving You / I'm Gonna Change My Way Of Living - 1957
Melatone 1004 - Malibu / Barrel House - 1957
Melatone 1021 - I'm Leaving You / I'm Going To Change My Way Of Living – 1957

Ted Taylor

Ebb 132 - If I Don't See You Again / Keep Walking On - 1958
Ebb 151 - Wrapped Up In A Dream / Very Truly Yours - 1958
Duke 304 - Be Ever Wonderful / Since You're Home - 1959
Duke 308 - Count The Starts / Hold Me Tight - 1959
Top Rank International 2010 - Fallin' In Love / ? - 1959
Top Rank International 2011 - I'm Saving My Love / Chanta-Lula - 1959
Top Rank International 2048 - Has My Love Grown Cold / I Need You So - 1960
Top Rank International 2076 - Darling Take Me Back / Look Out - 1960
Top Rank International 3001 - Someday (I Know, I Know) / You Know I Do - 1961

Austin Taylor

Laurie 3067 - A Heart That's True / Push Push - 1961

Ted Taylor

Laurie 3076 - You've Been Crying / Little Boy How Old Are You – 1961

Austin Taylor

Laurie 3082 - I Don't Want To Love You / Lovin' Hands - 1961
Laurie 3095 - I Love Being Loved By You / Together Forever - 1961

Ted Taylor

Warwick 628 - Someday / You Know I Do - 1961

Bob Reed And His Band (Members Ted Taylor .....)

Melatone 1003 - I'm Leaving You / I'm Going To Change My Way Of Living - 1961
Melatone 1004 - Malibu / Barrel House - 1961

Ted Taylor

Gold Eagle 1805 - My Darling / She's A Winner - 1961
Gold Eagle 1810 - Tat Happy Day / I Don't Care - 1961
Gold Eagle 1812 - No Matter What You Do / Never In My Life – 1961

Ted Taylor's Combo Featuring Wiley Terry

Gold Eagle 1818 - Bandstand Drag / Rockin' Horse - 1961 (Instrumentals)

Ted Taylor

Soncraft 400 - Anytime, Anyplace, Anywhere / I Lost The Best Things I Ever Had - 1961
Dade 5000 - Darling If You Must Leave / I Lost The Best Things I Ever Had - 1962
Apt 25063 - Little Things Mean A Lot / My Days And Nights Are So Blue - 1962
United Artists 452 - Pretending Love / Can't Take No More - 1962
Okeh 7154 - Pretending Love / Don't Lie - 1962
Okeh 7159 - You Must Have Been Meant For Me / Time Has A Way - 1962
Okeh 7165 - Can't Take No More / I'll Release You* - 1962 *an "answer record" to the 1962 release by Esther Phillips "Little Esther" on Lenox 5555.
Okeh 7171 - Be Ever Wonderful* / That's Life I Guess - 1962 *also recorded in 1968 by Joe Hinton on Back Beat 589.
Okeh 7176 - You Give Me Nothing To Go On / Him Instead Of Me - 1963
Okeh 7179 - I'll Make It Up To You / It Ain't Like That No More - 1963
Okeh 7190 - So Hard / Need You Home - 1964
Okeh 7198 - Somebody's Always Trying / Top Of The World - 1964 (some promo copies were issued in purple vinyl)
Okeh 7206 - If It Wasn't For You / Don't Deceive Me (Please Don't Go) - 1964
Okeh 7214 - So Long, Bye Bye Baby / I Love You Yes I Do* - 1965 *also recorded in 1961 by James Brown on King 5547
Okeh 7222 - I'm So Satisfied / (Love Is Like A) Ramblin' Rose - 1965

Ted Taylor / The Artistics

Okeh Jzsp 111745 / Jzsp 111809 - Stay Away From My Baby / This Heart Of Mine* - 1965 (demo copies issued in purple vinyl) *flip by The Artistics.

Ted Taylor

Okeh 7231 - Stay Away From My Baby / Walking Out Of You Life – 1965
Okeh 7240 - Daddy's Baby / Mercy Have Pity – 1966
Okeh 7252 - Big Wheel / No One But You – 1966
Epic 2241 - Be So Wonderful / (Love Is Like A) Ramblin' Rose - ? (Re-Issue)
Epic 2249 - Stay Away From My Baby / Daddy's Baby - ? (Re-Issue)

Atco 6388 - Dancing Annie / Try Me Again – 1965
Jewel 135 - Strange Things Keep Happening / Little Boy (How Old Are You?) – 1965
Atco 6408 - River's Invitation / Long Distance Call – 1966
Atco 6434 - Thank You For Helpng Me See The Light / Help The Bear – 1966
Jewel 748 - Very Truly Yours / Days Are Dark – 1966
Jewel 759 - You've Been Crying / Close Your Eyes – 1966
Jewel 774 - Everywhere I Go / Keep Walking On – 1966
Atco 6481 - Feed The Flame* / Baby Come Back To Me - 1967 *Recorded 10-April-1967.
Ronn 15 - Miss You So / I'm Gonna Get Tough – 1968
Ronn 21 - I Need Your Love So Bad / Ollie-Mae – 1968
Ronn 25 - Without A Woman / Honey Lou – 1968
Ronn 29 - You Got To Feel It / Strangest Feeling – 1969
Ronn 33 - Long Ago / I'm Gonna Send You Back To Oklahoma – 1969
Ronn 34 - It's Too Late / The Road Of Love – 1969
Ronn 37 - I'm Lonely Tonight / If I Thought You Needed Me – 1969
Ronn 40 - I Feel A Chill / Loving Physician – 1970
Ronn 44 - Something Strange Is Goin' On In My House / Funky Thing - 1970
Ronn 46 - It's A Funky Situation / I'm So Glad You're Home – 1970
Ronn 49 - Can't Take No More / Singing Man – 1971
Ronn 52 - How's Your Love Life Baby / This Is A Troubled World – 1971
Ronn 57 - How Do You Walk Away From Fear / Only The Lonely Knows – 1972
Ronn 63 - I'm Just A Crumb In Your Bread Box Of Love / Houston Town – 1972
Ronn 65 - I Want To Be Part Of You Girl / Going In The Hole – 1972
Ronn 72 - Make Up For Lost Time / What A Fool – 1973
Ronn 74 - Break Of Day / Fair Weather Woman – 1973

Little Johnny Taylor & Ted Taylor

Ronn 75 - Cry It Out Baby / Walking The Floor – 1973

Ted Taylor

Ronn 77 - She Loves To Do It As Well As You / Ready For The Heartbreak – 1974
Ronn 82 - I've Got To Find Somebody New / For All The Days In My Life – 1974
Ronn - Friendship Only Goes So Far - ? (although unissued on vinyl this was released in the U. K. on a 2001 Westside Cd "Soul Jewels Volume 2 - I Wake Up Crying" WESA 913)
Ronn - Let's Call The Whole Thing Off - ? (although unissued on vinyl this was released in the U. K. on a 2001 Westside Cd "Soul Jewels Volume 2 - I Wake Up Crying" WESA 913)
Ronn - Fair Warning - unissued as a 45 but released in the U. K. on a 2003 Kent Cd "Masterpieces Of Modern Soul" CDKEND 222.
Alarm 110 - Everybody's Stealing / Caught Up In A Good Woman's Love – 1975
Alarm 2112 - Somebody's Getting It / Steal Away – 1975

Little Johnny Taylor & Ted Taylor

Ronn 89 - Pretending Love / Funky Ghetto – 1976

Ted Taylor

Ronn 106 - Houston Town / Cummin's Prison - 1976
Ronn 112 - Be Ever Wonderful / I Love You Just The Same - 1976
Ronn 114 - Little Red Rooster / Stay Away From My Baby - 1976
Ronn 116 - Steal Away / My Key Jumped Back In My Hand - 1976
Alarm 110 - Everybody's Stealin' / Caught Up - 1976
Alarm 112 - Somebody's Getting It / Steal Away - 1976
Alarm 2114 - Gonna Hate Myself / Stick By Me – 1976
Alarm 2117 - Ghetto Disco / You Can Make It If You Try – 1977
T. K. 31 - Ghetto Disco / ? - 1977 (12" Release)

Alarm 2119 - Two Minute Warning / Paying For My Love Mistakes – 1977
Alarm 2123 - You Make Loving You So Easy / Talk To Me - ?

The Taylors featuring Ted Taylor

Alarm 2124 - Paying For My Love Mistakes / Spanish Harlem - ?
Alarm 2125 - Spanish Harlem / ?

Ted Taylor

MCA 1985 - Keepin' My Head Above Water (6:58) / Keepin' My Head Above Water (3:17) - 1978 (12" promo issue)
MCA 40937 - Keepin' My Head Above Water / I Can't Fake It Anymore – 1978
MCA 40977 - Chase The World Away / Double My Money Bag –

Solpugits 101 - I Let You Hurt Me Too Long / Pleading For Love* - ? *also recorded in 1955 by Larry Birdsong with Louis Brooks & His Hi-Toppers on Excello 2076 and in 1959 by Roscoe Shelton on Excello 2167.

Bob Reed & His Band, Vocal by "Ivory Lucky" (Ted Taylor)

Watts City 1003 - I'm Leaving You / I'm Going To Change My Way Of Living - 1983 (Re-issue of Melatone 1003 disc)

Ted Taylor

Solpugits 102 - You're Tippin' She's Rippin' / Little Red Rooster - 1987
Solpugits 2313 - Children Of The Light / Loving You Till The Break Of Day - 1987

The Temptations

Otis Williams & The Siberians (Members Otis Williams, Elbridge Bryant, James "Pee Wee" Crawford, Arthur Walton And Vernard Plain -- Lead)

? - Pecos Kid / All Of My Life - 1958 Only reference to this release is Otis Williams in his book The Temptations.

The El Domingoes (Members Otis Williams, Elbridge Bryant, James "Pee Wee" Crawford, Arthur Walton And Vernard Plain -- Lead)

Little David Bush (David Ruffin)

Vega 1002 - Believe Me / You And I - 1958

Eddie Bush (David Ruffin)

? - Statue Of A Fool / ? - ? (78 Rpm Format)

The Voice Masters (Members Ty Hunter, C.P. Spencer, Lamont Dozier, David Ruffin And Freddie Gorman)

Anna 101 - Hope And Pray / Oop's I'm Sorry - 1959 (This was the first release on the Anna Label)
Anna 102 - Needed / Needed (For Lovers Only) - 1959

Ty Hunter & The Voice Masters

Anna 1114 - Everything About You / Orphan Boy - 1960
Anna 1123 - Every Time / I'm Free - 1960

David Ruffin

Anna 1127 - I'm In Love / One Of These Days - 1960

The Voice Masters

Frisco 15235 - In Love In Vain / Two Lovers - 1960 (Identification Number shown since no selection number is used)

The Distants (Members Richard Street (Strick) (Former singer with High School group The Swallows), Otis Williams, Melvin Franklin, Eldrige Bryant And James Crawford)

Northern 3732 - Come On* / Always** - 1960 *Co-Written by Johnnie Mae Matthews. **Written by Ex-Member Vernard Plain. (This label number was also assigned to Johnnie Mae Matthews with "So Lonely / Help Me" and also Pop Corn & His Mohawks with "Pretty Girl / You're The One")

The Distants Vocal By Richard Strick

Warwick 546 - Come On / Always - 1960

The Distants

Northern ? - Alright / Open Your Heart - 1960 (Backing Vocals The Andantes) - Reference to this release is Otis Wiliams in his book The Temptations.
Warwick 577 - Always / Open Up Your Heart -1960

The Temptations (Members Otis Williams, Melvin Franklin, Eddie Kendricks, Paul Williams And Elbrige Bryant)

Miracle 5 - Oh, Mother Of Mine / Romance Without Finance - 1961
Miracle 12 - Check Yourself / Your Wonderful Love* - 1961 *Covered In 1969 by Chuck Jackson on Motown 1144. This was the last release on the Miracle Label.

Richard Street & The Distants (Members Richard Street, Eddie Kendricks And Paul Williams)

Thelma 82335/6 - Answer Me / Save Me From This Misery - 1961
Harmon 1002 - Answer Me / Save Me From This Misery - 1962

David Ruffin

Check-Mate 1003 - Actions Speak Louder Than Words / You Can Get What I Got - 1961
Check-Mate 1010 - Knock You Out (With Love) / Mr. Bus Driver (Hurry) - 1962

The Temptations

Gordy 7001 - Dream Come True / Isn't She Pretty - 1962 (The first issue on the Gordy Label)
Gordy 7010 - Paradise / Slow Down Heart - 1962

The Pirates

Mel-O-Dy 105 - Mind Over Matter (I'm Gonna Make You Mine)* / I'll Love You Till I Die - 1962 (The Group Was The Temptations) *Written by Nolan Strong who also released it in 1962 on Fortune 546.

The Temptations

Gordy 7015 - I Want A Love I Can See / The Further You Look, The Less You See - 1963
Gordy 7020 - May I Have This Dance? / Farewell, My Love - 1963 (Elbrige Bryant leaves group and is replaced by David Ruffin after this release)
Gordy 7028 - The Way You Do The Things You Do* / Just Let Me Know - 1964 *Lead Eddie Kendricks - Song also covered In 1969 by Diana Ross & The Supremes & The Temptations on Motown 1142.

Liz Lands & The Temptations

Gordy 7030 - Keep Me / Midnight Johnny - 1964

The Temptations

Gordy 7032 - I'll Be In Trouble / The Girl's Alright With Me* - 1964 *Also released in 1974 by The Undisputed Truth on Gordy 7139.
Gordy 7035 - Girl (Why you Wanna Make Me Blue) / Baby, Baby I Need You - 1964

Hitsville U.S.A. Dm 097311 - Greetings To The Tamla Motown Appreciation Society - 1964 This American record was limited to 300 copies for dispersal throughout various European Fan Clubs as a Promo for their first European tour. Each act gives an individual greeting over it's latest Record. Artists involved are The Miracles, Stevie Wonder, Marvin Gaye, The Marvelettes, The Temptations, Martha And The Vandellas, The Contours, Eddie Holland, Kim Weston And The Supremes. The record has an introduction from Publicist Margaret Phelps and Berry Gordy.

The Temptations

Gordy 7038 - My Girl* / (Talking 'Bout) Nobody But My Baby - 1965 *Lead David Ruffin - Song also released in 1968 by Stevie Wonder on Tamla 54168.
Gordy 7040 - It's Growing* / What Love Has Joined Together** - 1965 *Song also released in 1968 by Bobby Taylor & The Vancouvers on Gordy 7079. **Originally released in 1963 by Mary Wells on Motown 1042.
Gordy 7043 - Since I Lost My Baby / You've Got To Earn It - 1965
Gordy 7047 - My Baby / Don't Look Back - 1965
Gordy 7049 - Get Ready* / Fading Away** - 1966 *Also released in 1970 by Rare Earth on Rare Earth 5012 And In 1979 by Smokey Robinson on Tamla 54301. **Covered in 1968 by Bobby Taylor & The Vancouvers on Gordy 7069.
Gordy 7054 - Ain't Too Proud To Beg - 1966 (One Sided Disc)
Gordy 7054 - Ain't To Proud To Beg / You'll Lose A Precious Love - 1966 (Issued with Picture Sleeve)
Gordy 7055 - Beauty Is Only Skin Deep / You're Not An Ordinary Girl - 1966 (Issued with Picture Sleeve)
Gordy 7057 - (I Know) I'm Losing You* / I Couldn't Cry If I Wanted To** - 1966 *Also released In 1970 by Rare Earth on Rare Earth 5017. **Originally released in 1963 by Eddie Holland on Motown 1049.

Various Artists

Motown 2482 - Seasons Greetings From Motown - 1966 very short "Christmas Greetings" Radio Station spots are delivered By Martha And The Vandellas, The Temptations, The Miracles, Shorty Long, The Velvelettes, The Spinners, The Four Tops, The Elgins and The Supremes ---- Issued in red vinyl.

The Temptations

Gordy 7061 - All I Need / Sorry Is A Sorry Word* - 1967 *Also released in 1970 By Ivy Jo on V.I.P. 25055.
Topps/Motown 4 - My Girl - 1967 (Cardboard Record)
Topps/Motown 13 - The Way You Do The Things You Do - 1967 (Cardboard Record)
Gordy 7063 - You're My Everything* / I've Been Good To You - 1967 (Has Gordy on top of label) *Also released in 1970 by Gladys Knight & The Pips on Soul 35071.
Gordy 7063 - You're My Everything / I've Been Good To You* - 1967 (Has Gordy on left side of label) *Originally released in 1961 by The Miracles on Tamla 54053.
Gordy 7065 - (Loneliness Made Me Realize) It's You That I Need / Don't Send Me Away - 1967
Gordy 7067 - All I Need / All I Need - 1967 (White Label Promo Issue Only)
Gordy 7068 - I Wish It Would Rain / I Truly, Truly Believe - 1967
Gordy 7072 - I Could Never Love Another (After Loving You) / Gonna Give Her All The Love I've Got* - 1968 *Originally released in 1967 by Jimmy Ruffin on Soul 35032.
Gordy 7074 - Please Return Your Love To Me / How Can I Forget* - 1968 David Ruffin leaves and is replaced by Dennis Edwards after this release. *Also released in 1969 by Marvin Gaye on Tamla 54190.
Gordy 7081 - Cloud Nine* / Why Did She Have To Leave Me (Why Did She Have To Go) - 1968 (This 45 became Motown's first Grammy Winner - For Best Group R & B Performance) *Also released in 1969 by Gladys Knight & The Pips on Soul 35068 and in 1971 by Edwin Starr on Gordy 7107

Diana Ross & The Supremes & The Temptations

Motown 1137 - I'm Gonna Make You Love Me / A Place In The Sun - 1968

The Temptations

Gordy 7082 - Silent Night / Rudolph, The Red-Nosed Reindeer - 1968
Gordy 7084 - Run Away Child, Running Wild* / I Need Your Love - 1969 *Also released in 1969 by Earl Van Dyke on Soul 35059.

Diana Ross & The Supremes & The Temptations

Motown 1142 - I'll Try Something New / The Way You Do The Things You Do - 1969

The Temptations

Gordy 7086 - Don't Let The Joneses Get You Down / Since I've Lost You* - 1969 *Originally released in 1964 by Jimmy Ruffin on Soul 35002.
Gordy 7093 - I Can't Get Next To You / Running Away (Ain't Gonna Help You) - 1969

Diana Ross & The Supremes & The Temptations

Motown 1150 - Stubborn Kind Of Fellow / Try It Baby - 1969
Motown 1153 - The Weight / For Better Or Worse - 1969

The Temptations

Gordy 7096 - Psychedelic Shack / That's The Way Love Is* - 1970 *Originally released in 1967 by The Isley Brothers On Tamla 54154.
Gordy 7099 - Ball Of Confusion (That's What The World Is Today)* / It's Summer - 1970 *Also released in 1971 by The Undisputed Truth on Gordy 7112 and in 1972 by Edwin Starr on Soul 35096. (Issued With Picture Sleeve and some copies came in red vinyl)
Gordy 7102 - Ungena Za Ulimwengu (Unite The World) / Hum Along And Dance* - 1970 *Covered in 1973 by Rare Earth on Rare Earth 5054. (Some copies issued in red vinyl)

Gordy 7105 - Just My Imagination (Running Away With Me) / Just My Imagination (Running Away With Me)* - 1971 (White Label Promo Issue Only) *Also released in 1973 by The Undisputed Truth on Gordy 7130.
Gordy 7105 - Just My Imagination (Running Away With Me) */ You Make Your Own Heaven And Hell Right Here On Earth** - 1971* Lead Eddie Kendricks -- He leaves group shortly after this release to start a solo career at Motown. Also Paul Williams leaves due to ill health. Both are replaced by Damon Harris (From The Vandals And T-Neck) and Richard Street (From The Distants And The Monitors) Also at this time Ricky Owens (Of The Vibrations) sang with the group for a short time. **Also released in 1971 by The Undisputed Truth on Gordy 7112.
Gordy 7109 - It's Summer / I'm The Exception To The Rule* - 1971 Members Otis Williams, Paul Williams, Melvin Franklin And Dennis Edwards. *Originally released in 1965 by The Velvelettes on V.I.P. 25017.
Gordy 7111 - Superstar (Remember How You Got Where You Are) / Gonna Keep On Tryin' Till I Win Your Love* - 1971 Members Otis Williams, Melvin Franklin, Richard Street, Damon Harris And Dennis Edwards. *Also released in 1975 by David Ruffin on Motown 1336.**Also released in 1967 by Edwin Starr on Gordy 7066 and also in 1970 on Gordy 7104. In 1968 by Jimmy Ruffin on Soul 35053. In 1969 by Marvin Gaye on Tamla 54185. In 1973 by The Undisputed Truth on Gordy 7124.
Gordy 7115 - Take A Look Around / Smooth Sailing (From Now On) - 1972
Gordy 7119 - Mother Nature / Funky Music Sho Nuff Turns Me On* - 1972 *Originally released in 1971 by Edwin Starr on Gordy 7107.
Gordy 7121 - Papa Was A Rollin' Stone / (Instrumental)* - 1972 (Originally released In 1972 by The Undisputed Truth on Gordy 7117) *Flip won a Grammy as Best Instrumental.
Gordy 7126 - Masterpiece (Vocal) / Masterpiece (Instrumental) - 1972
Gordy 7129 - Plastic Man / Hurry Tomorrow - 1973
Gordy 7131 - Hey Girl (I Like Your Style) / Ma* - 1973 *Also released in 1973 by Rare Earth on Rare Earth 5053 and on Rare Earth 5056.
Gordy 7133 - Let Your Hair Down / Ain't No Justice - 1973
Gordy 7135 - Heavenly / Zoom - 1974
Gordy 7136 - You've Got My Soul On Fire* / I Need You - 1974 *Originally released in 1973 by Edwin Starr on Motown 1276.

The Temptations / The Temptations Band

Gordy 7138 - Happy People / Happy People (Instrumental) - 1974 *Flip By The Temptations Band.

The Temptations

Gordy 7142 - Shakey Ground / I'm A Bachelor - 1975
Gordy 7144 - Glasshouse / The Prophet - 1975 Around this time Damon Harris is replaced by Glenn Leonard (From The Unifics)
Gordy 7146 - Keep Holding On / What You Need Most (I Do Best Of All) - 1975 Members Otis Williams, Melvin Franklin, Richard Street, Glenn Leonard And Dennis Edwards.
Gordy 7150 - Up The Creek (Without A Paddle) / Darling Stand By Me (Song For A Woman) - 1976
Gordy 7151 - Who Are You (And What Are You Doing The Rest Of Your Life) - 1976 (Single Sided Disc -Promo Issue Only)
Gordy 7151 - Who Are You (And What Are You Doing The Rest Of Your Life) / Darling Stand By Me (Song For A Woman) - 1976 (Unreleased)
Gordy 7152 - Let Me Count The Ways (I Love You) / Who Are You (And What Are You Doing The Rest Of Your Life) - 1976
Atlantic 3436 - In A Lifetime / I Could Never Stop Loving You - 1977 Members Otis Williams, Melvin Franklin, Richard Street, Glenn Leonard And Louis Price.
Atlantic 3461 - Think For Yourself / Let's Live In Peace - 1978
Atlantic 3517 - Bare Back / I See My Child - 1978
Atlantic 3538 - Ever Ready Love / Touch Me Again - 1978
Atlantic 3567 - Mystic Woman / I Just Don't Know How To Let You Go - 1979

Gordy 7182 - Power / Power - 1980 (Promo Copy -- Red Vinyl -- Same Version Both Sides)
Gordy 7183 - Power / Power (Part 2) - 1980 Lineup now consists of a returned Dennis Edwards, Otis Williams, Melvin Franklin, Richard Street And Glenn Leonard.
Gordy 7188 - Struck By Lightning Twice / I'm Coming Home - 1980
Gordy 7208 - Aiming At Your Heart / The Life Of A Cowboy - 1981
Gordy 7213 - Oh What A Night / Isn't The Night Fantastic - 1981

The Temptations Featuring Rick James

Gordy 1616 - Standing On The Top - Part 1 / Standing On The Top - Part 2 - 1982 (Rick James Is Melvin Franklin's Nephew) Members On This 45 Eddie Kendricks, David Ruffin, Dennis Edwards, Richard Street, Otis Williams, Melvin Franklin And Glenn Leonard.

The Temptations

Gordy 1631 - More On The Inside / Money's Hard To Get - 1982
Gordy 1654 - Silent Night / Everything For Christmas - 1982 Members Otis Williams, Melvin Franklin, Richard Street, Glenn Leonard And Dennis Edwards.
Gordy 1666 - Love On My Mind Tonight / Bring Your Body (Exercise Chant) - 1983
Gordy 1683 - Made In America / Surface Thrills - 1983

The Temptations / Finis Henderson

Motown 119 - Surface Thrill* / ** ? - 1983 (12" Promo Issue Only) *The Temptations Only. **Finis Henderson Only.

The Temptations

Gordy 1707 - Miss Busy Body (Get Your Body Busy) (Part 1) (Vocal) / Miss Busy Body (Get Your Body Busy) (Part 2) (Instrumental) - 1983 Members Otis Williams, Melvin Franklin, Richard Street, Ron Tyson And Dennis Edwards.
Gordy 1713 - Silent Night / Everything For Christmas - 1983
Gordy 1720 - Sail Away / Isn't The Night Fantastic - 1984
Gordy 1765 - Treat Her Like A Lady / Isn't The Night Fantastic - 1984 Members Otis Williams, Melvin Franklin, Richard Street, Ron Tyson And Ali-Ollie Woodson.
Gordy 1781 - My Love Is True (Truly For You) / Set Your Love Right - 1985
Gordy 1789 - How Can You Say That It's Over / I'll Keep My Light In My Window - 1985
Gordy 1818 - Do You Really Love Your Baby / I'll Keep My Light In My Window - 1985
Motown 4550 - Do You Really Love Your Baby (3 Versions) / I'll Keep My Light In Your Window - 1985 (12" Release)
Gordy 1834 - Touch Me / Set Your Love Right - 1986

The Temptations / Smokey Robinson

Motown 1837 - A Fine Mess */ Wishful Thinking - 1986 * From The Film Of Same Title. Flip Is By Smokey Robinson

The Temptations / Jackson 5 / De Barge / The Commodores

Quaker - Motown Sound - 1986 (45rpm Cardboard Picture Disc Issued With Box Of "Quaker Granola Dipp Bars". No Selection Number Used)

The Temptations

Motown 180 - A Fine Mess / A Fine Mess - 1986 (12" Promo Issue)
Gordy 1856 - Lady Soul / Put Us Together Again - 1986
Gordy 1871 - To Be Continued / You're The One - 1986

Motown 1908 - I Wonder Who She's Seeing Now* / Girls (They Like It) - 1987 * Harmonica Solo By Stevie Wonder -- Members Otis Williams, Melvin Franklin, Richard Street, Ron Tyson And Dennis Edwards.
Gordy 1881 - Someone / Love Me Right - 1987 (Last Issue On The Gordy Label)
Motown 1920 - Look What You Started / More Love, Your Love - 1987
Motown 4598 - Look What You Started (4 Versions) / More Love, Your Love - 1987 (12" Release)
Motown Yesteryear 690 - Silent Night / Everything For Christmas - 198?
Motown 1933 - Do You Wanna Go With Me / Put Your Foot Down - 1988
Motown 1974 - All I Want From You / (Instrumental) - 1989
Motown 4649 - All I Want From You / (Instrumental) - 1989 (12" Release)
Motown L33-17880 - All I Want From You (Club Mix) / (Debbie Favorite Mix) - 1989 (12" Promo Issue)
Motown 2023 - Soul To Soul / (Instrumental) - 1990
Motown L33-18149 - Soul To Soul (3 Versions) - 1990 (12" Promo Issue)
Motown L33-18206 - One Step At A Time (3 Versions) - 1990 (12" Promo Issue)#
Motown 53954 - Get Ready 1990 (4 Versions) - 1990 (12" Release)
Motown 1132 - Get Ready 1990 (4 Versions) - 1990 (12" Promo Issue)

The 1991 **Temptations** Lineup Includes Ali-Ollie Woodson, Damon Harris, Richard Street, Ron Tyson, And Louis Price.

Motown 1604 - The Jones (4 Versions) - 1991 (12" Promo Issue)
Motown 37463 1025 1 - Hoops On Fire (3 Versions) - 1992 (12" Promo Issue)
Motown 860862-7 - Stay* / My Girl - 1998 *Produced By Narada Michael Walden.

The 2001 **Temptations** lineup includes Harry McGilberry (the 17th Temptation replacing Melvin Franklin), Otis Williams, Ron Tyson, Terry Weeks (in group since 1997) and Barrington "Bo" Henderson (in group since 1998)

Tammi Terrell

Tammi Montgomery (born Thomasina Montgomery 29-April-1945, died 16-March-1970, cause: brain cancer. Buried at Mt. Lawn Cemetry, Sharon Hill (suburb of Philly))

Scepter 1224 - If You See Bill / It's Mine - 1961
Wand 123 - Voice Of Experience */ I Wancha To Be Sure - 1962 *Backing Vocals By **The Shirelles**. .

Tana Montgomery

Try Me 28001 - I Cried / If You Don't Think - 1963 (Both Sides Written By James Brown)

Tammi Montgomery

Checker 1072 - If I Would Marry You / This Time Tomorrow - 1964

Tammi Terrell

Motown 1086 - I Can't Believe You Love Me / Hold Me Oh My Darling - 1965
Motown 1095 - Come On And See Me / Baby Don'cha Worry* - 1966 *Cover Of 1963 Song By Johnny & Jackey (Johnny Bristol And Jackey Beavers) On Tri-Phi 1019.

Marvin Gaye & Tammi Terrell

Tamla 54149 - Ain't No Mountain High Enough / Give A Little Love - 1967
Tamla 54156 - Your Precious Love / Hold Me Oh My Darling - 1967

Tammi Terrell

Motown 1115 - What A Good Man He Is / There Are Things - 1967

Marvin Gaye & Tammi Terrell

Tamla 54161 - If I Could Build My Whole World Around You / If This World Were Mine - 1967

Tammi Terrell

Jobete (No #) Cdmn-0639-Fhll (+8.0) - Oh What A Good Man He Is - 1968 (10"acetate plays at 45rpm - has date (9 - 12 - 67) on label plus also in type # 9 - 12 - 67 - V - 4 (BJS:) 2:51 written on label plus some markings in ball point and felt pen)

Marvin Gaye & Tammi Terrell

Tamla 54163 - Ain't Nothing Like The Real Thing / Little Ole Boy, Little Ole Girl* - 1968 *Cover Of 1961 Record By Loe & Joe (Lorrie Rudolph And Joe Charles) On Harvey 112.
Tamla 54169 - You're All I Need To Get By / Two Can Have A Party - 1968
Tamla 54173 - Keep On Lovin' Me Honey / You Ain't Livin' Till You're Lovin' - 1968

Tammi Terrell

Motown 1138 - This Old Heart Of Mine (Is Weak For You) / Just Too Much To Hope For - 1968

Marvin Gaye & Tammi Terrell

Tamla 54179 - Good Lovin' Ain't Easy To Come By / Satisfied Feelin - 1969
Tamla 54187 - What You Gave Me / How You Gonna Keep It (After You Get It) - 1969
Tamla 54192 - California Soul / The Onion Song - 1970

Joe Tex

The Sunbeams (members John Cumbo, Bobby Lee Hollis, Bobby Coleman, James Davis, William Edwards and Joe Tex) early 1955

Joe Tex (born Joseph Arrington Jr. on 8-Aug-1933 in Rogers, Texas: died of heart attack 13-Aug-1982. Changed name to Yusuf Hazziez in July 1972)

King 4840 - Come In This House / Davy, You Upset My Home – 1955
King 4884 - My Biggest Mistake / Right Back To My Arms – 1956
King 4911 - She's Mine / I Had To Come Back To You – 1956
King 4980 - Get Way Back / Pneumonia – 1956
King 5064 - I Want To Have A Talk With You / Ain't Nobody's Business - 1957 (all the King material was recorded in New York at Belltone Studios)
Ace 544 - Cut It Out / Just For You And Me – 1958

Little Booker (James Booker born ?-December-1939 in New Orleons - died ?)

Ace 547 - Teenage Rock (Instrumental) / Open The Door* - 1958 *lead vocal Joe Tex.

Joe Tex

Ace 550 - You Little Baby Face Thing / Mother's Advice – 1958

Joe Tex & his X Class Mates

Ace 559 - Charlie Brown Got Expelled / Blessed Are These Tears – 1959

Joe Tex

Ace 572 - Don't Hold It Against Me / Yum, Yum, Yum – 1959
Ace 591 - Boys Will Be Boys / Grannie Stole The Show - 1960 (all the Ace material was recorded at Cosmo's studio New Orleons. Using the same band Little Richard and Fats Domino used. Allen Toussaint was on organ)
Anna 1119 - All I Could Do Was Cry (Part 1) / All I Could Do Was Cry (Part 2) - 1960 (cover of Etta James original)

Joe Tex & The Vibrators

Anna 1124 - I'll Never Break Your Heart (Part 1) / I'll Never Break Your Heart (Part 2) – 1960

Joe Tex

Jalynne 105 - Goodbye My Love / Wicked Woman - 1960
Anna 1128 - Baby, You're Right / Ain't It A Mess - 1961 (the last release on the Anna label)
Dial 3000 - What Should I Do / The Only Girl I've Ever Loved – 1961
Dial 3002 - One Giant Step / The Rib – 1961
Dial 3003 - Popeye Johnny / Hand Shakin', Love Makin', Girl Talkin', Son-Of-A-Gun From Next Door – 1962
Dial 3007 - Meet Me In Church* / Be Your Own Judge - 1962 *also recorded in 1967 by Don Varner and scheduled to be released on Veep 1296 but unissued.
Dial 3009 - I Let Her Get Away / The Peck – 1963
Dial 3013 - Someone To Take Your Place* / I Should Have Kissed You More - 1963 *recorded in Beaumont, Texas, at Big Bopper's studio, session financed by Joe Tex.
Checker 1055 - You Keep Her / Don't Play – 1963
Michelle Mx 934 - I've Got A Song / The Next Time She's Mine - **?**
Soul Sound 009 - I Should Have Kissed Her More / Someone To Take Your Place - ?
Ace 674 - Boys Will Be Boys / Baby You're Right (I'm Gonna Hold What I Got) – 1963
Dial 3016 - I Wanna Be Free / Blood's Thicker Than Water - 1963
Dial 3019 - Looking For My Pig / Say Thank You – 1964
Dial 3020 - I'd Rather Have You / Old Time Lover – 1964
Dial 3023 - I Had A Good Thing But I Left (Part 1) / I Had A Good Thing But I Left (Part 2) – 1964
Checker 1087 - Sit Yourself Down / Get Closer Together – 1964
Dial 4001 - Hold What You've Got / Fresh Out Of Tears – 1964
Dial 4003 - You Better Get It / You Got What It Takes – 1965
Dial 4006 - A Woman Can Change A Man / Don't Let Your Left Hand Know – 1965
Dial 4011 - One Monkey Don't Stop No Show / Build Your Love On A Solid Foundation – 1965
Checker 1104 - Baby, You're Right / All I Could Do Was Cry (Part 2) - 1965
King 5981 - Come In This House / I Want To Have A Talk With You – 1965
Dial 4016 - I Want To (Do Everything For You) / Funny Bone – 1965
Dial 4022 - A Sweet Woman Like You / Close The Door – 1965
Dial 4026 - The Love You Save (May Be Your Own) / If Sugar Was As Sweet As You – 1966
Atlantic 78124 - The Love You Save - 1966 (a Compact 33 7" release with six tracks "The Love You Save (May Be Your Own) / Build Your Love (On A Solid Foundation) / Heartbreak Hotel /// I'm A Man / Funny Bone / Don't Let Your Left Hand Know (What Your Right Hand Is Doing)") (issued with a picture sleeve)
Dial 4028 - S.Y.S.L.J.F.M. (Letter Song) / I'm A Man - 1966 ("S.Y.S.L.J.F.M." stood for "Save Your Sweet Love Just For Me")

Dial 4033 - I Believe I'm Gonna Make It / You Better Believe It, Baby – 1966
Dial 4045 - I've Got To Do A Little Bit Better / What In The World – 1966
Dial 4051 - Papa Was Too / The Truest Woman In The World – 1966
Dial 4055 - Show Me */ A Woman Sees A Hard Time (When Her Man Is Gone) - 1967 *Joe Tex claimed he wrote song in 3 ~ 4 minutes! the song was also recorded in 1969 by Ketty Lester on Pete 714.
Dial 4059 - Woman Like That, Yeah / I'm Going And Get It – 1967
Dial 4061 - A Woman's Hands / See See Rider – 1967
Dial 4063 - Skinny Legs And All / Watch The One – 1967
Dial 4068 - I'll Make Everyday Christmas (For My Woman) / Don't Give Up – 1967
Dial 4069 - Men Are Gettin' Scarce / You're Gonna Thank Me, Woman – 1968
Dial 4076 - I'll Never Do You Wrong / Wooden Spoon – 1968
Dial 4079 - Chocolate Cherry / Betwixt And Between – 1968

The Soul Clan (Members Solomon Burke, Arthur Conley, Don Covay, Ben E. King And Joe Tex)

Atlantic 2530 - Soul Meeting / That's How It Feels – 1968

Joe Tex

Dial 4083 - Keep The One You Got / Go Home And Do It – 1968
Dial 4086 - You Need Me, Baby / Baby, Be Good – 1968
Dial 4089 - That's Your Baby / Sweet, Sweet Woman – 1968
Dial 4090 - Buying A Book / Chicken Crazy – 1969
Parrot 45012 - Say Thank You / Looking For My Pig – 1969
Dial 4093 - That's The Way / Anything You Wanna Know – 1969
Dial 4094 - We Can't Sit Down Now / It Ain't Sanitary – 1969
Dial 4095 - I Can't See You No More (When Johnny Comes Marching Home) / Sure Is Good - 1969
Dial 4096 - Everything Happens On Time / You're Right, Ray Charles – 1970
Dial 4098 - I'll Never Fall In Love Again / The Only Way I Know To Love You – 1970
Dial 1001 - Bad Feet / I Know Him – 1971
Dial 1003 - Papa's Dream / I'm Comin' Home – 1971
Dial 1006 - King Thaddeus (Mono) / King Thaddeus (Stereo) - 1971 (Possible Promo Issue Only)
Dial 1008 - Give The Baby Anything The Baby Wants / Takin' A Chance - 1971
Dial 1010 - I Gotcha / A Mother's Prayer – 1972
Dial 1012 - You Said A Bad Word / It Ain't Gonna Work Baby – 1972
Atlantic 2874 - I'll Never Fall In Love Again (Part 1) / I'll Never Fall In Love Again (Part 2) – 1972
Dial 1018 - Rain Go Away / King Thaddeus – 1973
Dial 1020 - Woman Stealer / Cat's Got Her Tongue – 1973
Dial 1021 - All The Heaven A Man Really Needs / Let's Go Somewhere And Talk – 1973
Dial 1024 - Trying To Win Your Love / I've Seen Enough – 1973
Dial 1154 - Sassy Sexy Wiggle / Under Your Powerful Love – 1975
Dial 1155 - I'm Goin' Back Again / My Body Wants You – 1975
Dial 1156 - Baby, It's Rainin' / Have You Ever – 1975
Dial 1157 - Mama Red / Love Shortage – 1975
Epic 50313 - Ain't Gonna Bump No More (With No Big Fat Woman) / I Mess Up Everything I Get My Hands On – 1976
Epic 50352 - Ain't Gonna Bump No More (With No Big Fat Woman) / Be Cool (Willie Is Dancing With A Sissy) - 1977 (12" Release)
Epic 50426 - Hungry For Your Love / I Almost Got To Heaven Once – 1977
Epic 50494 - Rub Down / Be Kind To Old People – 1977
Epic 50530 - Get Back, Leroy / You Can Be My Star – 1978
Dial 2800 - Loose Caboose / Music Ain't Got No Color – 1979
Dial 2801 - Who Gave Birth To The Funk / If You Don't Want The Man – 1979
Dial 2802 - Discomania / Fat People – 1979

T. K. 410 - Discomania / ? - 1979 (12" Release)
Polydor 2109 - Stick Your Key In (And Start Your Car) / Lady J. (I Love You) – 1980
Columbia 02565 - Don't Do Da Do / Here Comes No. 34 (Do The Earl Campbell) – 1981
Handshake 02565 - Don't Do Da Do / Here Comes No. 34 (Do The Earl Campbell) - 1981 (Earl Campbell was a star for the University of Texas Longhorns and later the ill-fated Houston Oilers. He hailed from Tyler Texas which is in Northeast Texas and close to Joe Tex's home town. He did a commercial for chewing tobacco proclaiming "I'm A Skoal Man" and now pushes his own brand of sausage)
Handshake 02565 - Don't Do Da Do / Loose Caboose – 1981
Handshake 4w9 02566 - Don't Do Da Do / Loose Caboose - 1981 (12" Release)
Handshake 4w9 02566 - Don't Do Da Do / Loose Caboose - 1981 (12" Release)
Collectables Col 033837 - Hold On To What You Got / Show Me - ?
Collectables Col 033847 - Skinny Legs And All / I Gotcha - ?
Collectables Col 039547 - Ain't Gonna Bump No More / A Woman Can Change A Man - ?
Collectables Col 039557 - Men Are Getting Scarce / I Want To Do Everything For You - ?

Carla Thomas

The Teen-Town Singers (member at age ten Carla Thomas (four years younger than the specified Teen-Town minimum age - stayed with group till she was eighteen)

Rufus & Carla (Rufus Thomas with his daughter Carla Thomas)

Satellite 102 - Cause I Love You / Deep Down Inside - 1960 (this was actually the eighth Satellite release but the numbering system was begun again when Estelle Axton came into the company and Fred Byler and Neil Herbert left)

Carla Thomas (born 21-December-1942

Satellite 104 - Gee Whiz (Look At His Eyes)* / For You - 1960 *written By Carla Thomas when she was sixteen, this record had actually been turned down by Vee-Jay records of Chicago.

Rufus & Carla Thomas

Atco 6177 - Cause I Love You / Deep Down Inside – 1960

Rufus & Friend (Rufus Thomas with his daughter Carla Thomas)

Atco 6199 - I Didn't Believe / Yeah, Yea-Ah – 1961

Carla Thomas

Atlantic 2086 - Gee Whiz (Look At His Eyes) / For You – 1960
Atlantic 2101 - A Love Of My Own / Promises – 1961
Atlantic 2113 - (Mama, Mama) Wish Me Good Luck / In Your Spare Time (Please Think Of Me) – 1961
Atlantic 2132 - The Masquerade Is Over / I Kinda Think He Does – 1962
Atlantic 2163 - I'll Bring It On Home To You* / I Can't Take It - 1962 *an "answer" song to Sam Cooke's 1962 recording "Bring It On Home To Me" on RCA Victor 47-8036.
Atlantic 2189 - What A Fool I've Been / The Life I Live – 1963
Atlantic 2212 - Gee Whiz, It's Christmas / All I Want For Christmas Is You* - 1963 *written by A. C. "Moonhah" Williams (died 2-December-2004 --- cause: heart attack)
Atlantic 2238 - I've Got No Time To Lose / A Boy Named Tom – 1964
Atlantic 2258 - A Woman's Love / Don't Let The Love Light Leave - 1964
Atlantic 2272 - How Do You Quit (Someone You Love) / The Puppet – 1965

Rufus & Carla

Stax 151 - That's Really Some Good / Night Time Is The Right Time* - 1964 *cover of the 1959 recording by Ray Charles on Atlantic 2010.

Carla Thomas

Stax 172 - Stop! Look What You're Doin' / Every Ounce Of Strength – 1965

Rufus & Carla

Stax 176 - When You Move You Lose / We're Tight – 1965

Carla Thomas

Stax 183 - Comfort Me* / I'm For You - 1966 *background vocals by Gladys Knight & The Pips.

Rufus & Carla

Stax 184 - Birds And Bees* / Never Let You Go - 1966 *cover of Jewel Akens 1964 recording "The Birds And Bees" on **Era** 3141. Stax shortened the title.

Carla Thomas

Stax 188 - Let Me Be Good To You / Another Night Without My Man – 1966
Stax 195 - B-A-B-Y / What Have You Got To Offer Me – 1966
Stax 206 - All I Want For Christmas Is You / Winter Snow* - 1966 *covered in 1967 by Booker T. & The MG's on Stax 236.
Stax 207 - Something Good (Is Going To Happen To You)* / It's Starting To Grow - 1967 *recorded 19-December-1966.
Stax 214 - Unchanging Love / When Tomorrow Comes* - 1967 *covered in 1970 by The Emotions on Volt 4031.

Otis & Carla (Otis Redding and Carla Thomas)

Stax 216 - Tramp* / Tell It Like It Is- 1967 *cover of 1966 recording by Lowell Fulson on Kent 456.

Carla Thomas

Stax 222 - I'll Always Have Faith In You* / Stop Thief - 1967 *backing vocals by Eddie Floyd.

Otis & Carla

Stax 228 - Knock On Wood* / Let Me Be Good To You - 1967 *cover of 1966 recording by Eddie Floyd on Stax 194.

Carla Thomas

Stax 239 - Pick Up The Pieces / Separation - 1967

Otis & Carla

Stax 244 - Lovey Dovey* / New Year's Resolution - 1968 *cover of a 1954 recording by The Clovers on Atlantic 1022.
Atco 6665 - When Something Is Wrong With My Baby* / Ooh Carla, Ooh Otis - 1968 *cover of 1967 recording by Sam & Dave on Stax 210.

Carla Thomas

Stax 251 - A Dime A Dozen / I Want You Back – 1968
Stax 0011 - I've Fallen In Love (With You) / Where Do I Go* - 1968 *cover of song used in the musical "Hair".
Stax 0024 - I Like What You're Doing (To Me) / Strung Out – 1969

Johnnie Taylor / Johnnie Taylor, Eddie Floyd, William Bell, Pervis Staples, Carla Thomas, Mavis Staples & Cleotha Staples

Stax 0040 - Soul-A-Lujah (Part 1) / Soul-A-Lujah (Part 2)* - 1969 *flip by Johnnie Taylor, Eddie Floyd, William Bell, Pervis Staples, Carla Thomas, Mavis Staples & Cleotha Staples

Johnnie Taylor & Carla Thomas

Stax 0042 - Just Keep On Loving Me / My Love – 1969

William Bell & Carla Thomas

Stax 0044 - I Can't Stop / I Need You Woman – 1969

Carla Thomas

Stax 0056 - Guide Me Well* / Some Other Man (Is Beating Your Time) - 1970 *track cut in Detroit with Melvin Davis on drums.
Stax 0061 - The Time For Love Is Anytime / Living In The City - 1970 (from the movie "Cactus Flower")

William Bell & Mavis Staples / William Bell, Carla Thomas

Stax 0067 - Leave The Girl Alone / All I Have To Do Is Dream* - 1970 *flip by William Bell, Carla Thomas --- a cover of 1958 recording by The Everly Brothers on Cadence 1348.

Carla Thomas

Stax 0080 - Hi De Ho (That Old Sweet Roll) / I Loved You Like I Love My Very Life – 1970
Stax (No #) - Love Means (You Never Have To Say You're Sorry) / Daughter You're Still You're Daddy's Child - 1971 (promo issue only)
Stax 0113 - You've Got A Cushion To Fall On* / Love Means (You Never Have To Say You're Sorry) - 1972 *backing vocals by The Emotions.
Stax 0133 - Sugar / You've Got A Cushion To Fall On - 1972
Stax 0149 - I May Not Be All You Want / Sugar – 1972
Stax 0173 - I Have A God Who Loves / Love Among People – 1973
Gusto 816 - All I Want For Christmas Is You / Gee Whiz, It's Christmas – 1979
Collectables Col 710417 - I Like What You're Doing (To Me) / Guide Me Well - ?

Irma Thomas

Irma Thomas (born Irma Lee on 18-February-1941 in Ponchatoula, Louisiana discovered by Tommy Ridgley while working as a waitress)

Ronn 328 - You Can Have My Husband (But Please Don't Mess With My Man) / Set Me Free - 1960
Ronn 330 - A Good Man / I May Be Wrong - 1960
Bumpa 711 - Foolish Girl / When I Met You - ?

Bandy 368 - Look Up (When Ever) / For Goodnss Sake - 1961
Minit 625 - Girl Needs Boy - 1961
Minit 633 - It's Too Soon To Know / That's All I Ask - 1961
Minit 642 - I Done Gone Over It / Gone - 1962
Minit 653 - It's Raining / I Did My Part - 1962
Minit 660 - Somebody Told Me / Two Winters Long - 1963
Minit 666 - Ruler Of My Heart / Hittin' On Nothing - 1963
Imperial 66013 - Wish Someone Would Care / Break-A-Way - 1964
Imperial 66041 - Anyone Who Knows What Love Is (Will Understand) / Time Is On My Side - 1964
Imperial 66069 - Times Have Changed / Moments To Remember - 1964
Imperial 66080 - He's My Guy / (I Want A) True True Love - 1964
Imperial 66095 - Some Things You Never Get Used To / You Don't Miss A Good Thing - 1965
Imperial 66106 - I'm Gonna Cry Till My Tears Run Dry / Nobody Want's To Hear Nobody's Trouble - 1965
Imperial 66120 - The Hurt's All Gone / It's Starting To Get To Me Now - 1965
Imperial 66137 - Take A Look / What Are You Trying To Do - 1965
Imperial 66178 - It's A Man's-Woman's World (Part 1) / It's A Man's-Woman's World (Part Two) - 1966
Chess 2010 - Cheater Man* / Somewhere Crying - 1967 *also recorded in 1967 by Esther Phillips on Atlantic 2417.
Chess 2017 - A Woman Will Do Wrong* / I Gave You Enough - 1967 *also recorded in 1966 by Helene Smith with The Rocketeers on Deep City 2368 and in 1968 by Dee Dee Sharp on Atco 6576.
Chess 2036 - Good To Me / We Got Something Good - 1968
Cotillion 44144 - Full Time Woman / She's Taken My Part - 1971
Canyon 21 - Save A Little Bit / That's How I Feel About You - 1971
Canyon 31 - I'd Do It All Over You / We Won't Be In Your Way Anymore - 1972
Roker 502 - These Four Walls / Woman's Viewpoint - 1973
Jin 1028 - Wish Someone Would Care / It's Raining - ?
United Artists 0088 - Wish Someone Would Care / Take A Look - 1973 (silver spotlight series)
Fungus 15119 - You're The Dog (I Do The Barking Myself) / She'll Never Be Your Wife - 1973
Fungus 15141 - In Between Tears / ? - 1973
Fungus 15353 - Coming From Behind / Part 2 - Wish Someone Would Care (Monologue) – 1974
Maison De Soul 1012 - Break-A-Way / Don't Blame Him - ?
Maison De Soul 1058 - Hittin' On Nothin' / Hip Shakin' Mama – 1977
Maison De Soul 1072 - Break-A-Way / I Don't Blame Him - 1977
RCS 1006 - Safe With Me / Zero Will Power - 1979
RCS 1008 - Take What You Find / I Can't Help Her - 1980
RCS 1010 - Woman Left Lonely / Dance Me Down Easy - 1980
RCS 1013 - Looking Back / Don't Stop - 1981

Irma Thomas / The Winstons

Collectables Col 033147 - I Wish Someone Would Care / Color Him Father* - ? *flip by The Winstons.

Irma Thomas

Rounder 4555 - The New Rules / The Love Of My Man - 1986
Sound Of New Orleans 10311 - I Believe Saints Go All The Way / Mardi Gras Mambo - 1988

George Tindley

The Royal Flames (members George Tindley (died 1996 --- cause: ?), Bernard Harris, Wesley

Hayes (born John Wesley Hayes on ? --- died 26-November-2009 --- cause: ?) , Robert Henderson and Stephen Presbery)

The Dreams (members George Tindley, Bernard Harris, Wesley Hayes, Robert Henderson and Stephen Presbery)

Savoy 1130 - Darlene* / A Letter To My Girl - 1954 *recorded 1-April-1954.
Savoy 1140 - Under The Willow / I'm Losing My Mind - 1954
Savoy 1157 - I'll Be Faithful / My Little Honeybun - 1955

Kenny Esquire & The Starlites (members George Tindley, Bernard Harris, Wesley Hayes, Stephen Presbery and Billy Taylor from The Castelles)

Ember 1011 - They Call Me A Dreamer / Pretty Brown Eyes - 1956
Ember 1021 - Tears Are Just For Fools / Boom Chica Boom - 1957

Steve Gibson & The Red Caps (members Steve Gibson, Emmett Mathews, Jimmy Springs, Henry Tucker Green, Bobby Gregg, Damita Jo, Romaine Brown and George Tindley)

Rose 5534 - Bless You / I Miss You So - 1959

Steve Gibson & The Original Red Caps (members Steve Gibson, Emmett Mathews, Jimmy Springs, Henry Tucker Green, Bobby Gregg, Damita Jo, Romaine Brown and George Tindley)

Casa Blanca 5505 - Where Are You / San Antone Rose - 1959

Steve Gibson & The Red Caps (members Steve Gibson, George Tindley.......................from here group lineups are sketchy. Damita Jo left in 1960 and was replaced by a Gloria Smith)

Hunt 326 - Bless You / Cheryl Lee - 1959
Hunt 330 - Where Are You / San Antone Rose - 1959
ABC-Paramount 10105 - I Went To Your Wedding / Together - 1960

George Tindley

Ember 1058 - The Gypsy / I Wish - 1960
Ember 1060 - Wedding Bells / No Lonely Nights - 1960

Steve Gibson & The Red Caps

Stage 3001 - Blueberry Hill / Poor Poor Me* - 1960 *vocals by George Tindley.

George Tindley

Herald 558 - Close Your Eyes / Heart Of Gold - 1961
Parkway 834 - Fairy Tales / Just For You - 1962

Steve Gibson & The Red Caps

Band Box 325 - No More / Peppermint Baby - 1962

George Tindley and The Modern Red Caps (members George Tindley, George Grant (formerly with The Castelles on Grand) and during the mid 1960's a Tammy Montgomery -- later known as Tammi Terrell.

Smash 1768 - I Couldn't Care Less / Done Being Lonely – 1962
Rowax 801 - Don't You Here Them Laughing / They Can Dream – 1963

George Tinley & The Modern Red Caps (members George Tindley, George Grant, ...)

Doo-Wopp 101 - Ain't Gonna Worry About You / Since I Met Cindy - 196?

The Modern Red Caps (members George Tindley, George Grant.....................)

Lawn 254 - Empty World / Our Love Will Never Be The Same – 1965
Lawn - No Sign Of You - 1965 (although unissued on vinyl this was released in the U. K. on a 1996 Kent Cd "Swan's Soul Sides - Dance The Philly" CDKEND 120)
Lawn - Annie - 1965 (Unissued)
Penntowne 101 - Free / Never Kiss A Good Man Good-Bye – 1965
Swan 4243 - Never Too Young (To Fall In Love) / Golden Teardrops - 1966

George Tindley

Wand 11205 - Ain't That Peculiar / It's All Over But The Shouting - 1969
Wand 11208 - Honky Tonk Women / So Help Me Woman - 1969
Wand 11215 - Wan-Tu-Wah-Zuree / Pity The Poor Man - 1970

Oscar Toney Jnr

The Sensational Melodies Of Joy (members Oscar Toney, Jr. , ...)

The Searchers (members Oscar Toney Jr. and his brothers Roosevelt Toney and Willie James Toney (who used to gig with Bobby Moore & The Rhythm Aces))

Mac 351 - Yvonne / Little Wanda - 1960 (backed by The Kayos)

The Kayos (members Donald "Cement" MacNally (owner of the MAC record label), Oscar Toney, Jr..............................) resident house band for over seven years at Donald MacNally's club C'estbon in Columbus, Georgia.

Oscar Toney, Jr. (born 26-May-1939 in Selma, Alabama. Raised in Columbus Georgia from age three)

King 5906 - Can It All Be Love / You're Gonna Need Me - 1964

The Dothan Sextet (members Oscar Toney, Jr. , .previous vocalists with this group were Mighty Sam and James Purify.

Oscar Toney, Jr.

Bell 672 - For Your Precious Love / Ain't That True Love -1967
King 6108 - I've Found A True Love / Keep On Loving Me - 1967
Bell 681 - Turn On Your Lovelight / Any Day Now (My Wild Beautiful Bird) - 1967
Bell 688 - You Can Lead Your Woman To The Altar* / Unlucky Guy - 1967 (arranged by Moses Dillard, flip also co-written by Moses Dillard) *cover of 1967 record by William Bollinger on Chess 1994
Bell 699 - Without Love (There Is Nothing) / A Love That Never Grows Cold - 1968
Bell 714 - Never Get Enough Of Your Love / A Love That Never Grows Cold - 1968
Bell 744 - Just For You / Until We Meet Again - 1969
Bell 776 - Down In Texas / Ain't That True Love
Capricorn 8005 - Down On My Knees / Seven Days Tomorrow - 1970
Capricorn 8010 - I Wouldn't Be A Poor Boy / Person To Person - 1970
Capricorn 8018 - Workin' Together / Baby Is Mine - 1971
Capricorn 0005 - I Do What You Wish / Thank You, Honey Chile - 1972
Atco 6933 - Everything I Own* / Everybody's Needed - 1974 *also recorded in 1972 by Bread on

Elektra 45765
Contempo 7702 - Is It Because I'm Black* / Make It Easy On Yourself** - 1974 *also recorded in 1969 by Syl Johnson on Twinight 125. **also released in 1962 by Jerry Butler on Vee-Jay 451.
Contempo 7702 - Is It Because I'm Black / The Thrill Is Gone* - 1974 *also recorded in 1951 by Roy Hawkins on Modern 826.
Flashback 36 - For Your Precious Love / Ain't That True Love -

The Top Notes

The Five Pearls (members Howard Guyton, Derek Martin, David Cortez Clowney (aka Dave "Baby" Cortez), Coley Washington and Geo Torrance)

Aladdin 3265 - Please Let Me Know / Real Humdinger – 1954

The Sheiks (members: Derek Martin, Howard Guyton, Coley Washington, Dave 'Baby' Cortez)

Cat 116 - Walk That Walk / The Kissing Song - 1954

The Pearls (Members: Derek Martin, Howard Guyton, Coley Washington, George Torrance, Dave 'Baby' Cortez (Who was a cousin of Howard Guyton))

Atco 6057 - The Pearls - Shadows Of Love / Yum Yummy - 1956
Atco 6066 - The Pearls - Bells Of Love / Come On Home - 1956

Howie & The Sapphires (Members Howard Guyton, ...)

Okeh 7112 - More Than The Day Before / Rockin' Horse – 1959

The Top Notes (Members Derek Ray, Guy Howard)

Atlantic 2066 - A Wonderful Time / Walkin' With Love – 1960
Atlantic 2080 - Say Man / Warm Your Heart – 1960
Atlantic 2097 - Hearts Of Stone* / The Basic Things - 1961(produced by Phil Spector - arranger conductor Teddy Randazzo) * King Curtis on sax.
Atlantic 2115 - Twist And Shout / Always Late (Why Lead Me On) - 1961 (produced by Phil Spector - arranger / conductor Teddy Randazzo)
Festival 1021 - Wait For Me Baby / Come Back Cleopatra – 1962

Jimmy Ricks & The Raves (members Jimmy Ricks and Leonard Puzey -- both former members of The Ravens plus Howard Guyton and Derek Martin)

Atco 6220 - Daddy Rolling Stone / Homesick – 1962
Festival 25004 - Daddy Rolling Stone / Um Gowa – 1962

Derek & Howard

Festival 25005 - Wait For Me Baby / I Love You So Much - 1963

The Top Notes

ABC - Paramount 10399 - I Love You So Much / It's Alright – 1963

Derek Martin

Crackerjack 4013 - Daddy Rollin' Stone / Don't Put Me Down Like This - 1963 (issued in the U. K. on Suel-308 as being by Derak Martin (Vocal Accompaniment C. Foxx))
Sue 118 - Cha Cha Skate / Too Soon To Know – 1965
Roulette 4631 - You Better Go - 1965 (One Sided Promo Issue)
Roulette 4631 - You Better Go / You Know – 1965
Roulette 4647 - I Won't Cry Anymore / Your Daddy Want's His Baby Back – 1965
Sue 143 - Count To Ten / If You Go – 1966
Roulette 4670 - Don't Resist / Bumper To Bumper – 1966

Howard Guyton

Verve 10386 - I Watched You Slowly Slip Away* / I Got My Own Thing Going - 1966 *also released in 1965 by Lou Courtney on Philips 40287.

Derek Martin

Roulette 4743 - Breakaway / Take Me Like I Am - 1967
Tuba 2010 - Soul Power / Sly Girl – 1967
Roulette 7017 - You Know / You Better Know – 1968
Volt 160 - Soul Power / Sly Girl – 1968
Buttercup 009 - You Blew It Baby / The Moving Hands Of Time – 1970
Buttercup 011 - Your Love Made A Man Out Of Me / I Got To Chase That Dream – 1970
Vibration 522 - Falling Out Of Love / That's What I'll Do – 1973
Vibration 526 - How Can I Get Away / That's What I'll Do – 1973
All Platinum 2358 - Beautiful Woman / Beautiful Woman (Instrumental) – 1975
Arctic 201/202 - Don't Leave Me / Stoned Out Of My Mind - ?

Derek Martin / Ben Aiken

Collectables Col 002607 - You Better Go / Stay Together Young Lovers* - ? *Flip by Ben Aiken.

The Toys

The Charlettes (members Barbara Harris, Barbara Parritt, June Monteiro and Dottie Berry)

Angie 1002 - The Fight's Not Over / Whatever Happened To Our Love - 1963

Barbara Chandler

Kapp 542 - It Hurts To Be Sixteen / Running Running Johnny - 1964 (background vocals by The Charlettes --- Vince Marc, Barbara Chandler's husband becomes group manager and Dottie Berry leaves group in 1964)

Diane Renay

MGM 13335 - I Had A Dream */ Troublemaker - 1965 *backing vocals The Charlettes

The Toys (members Barbara Harris, June Monteiro and Barbara Parritt)

Dyno Voice 209 - A Lover's Concerto* / This Night - 1965 *adapted from Bach: Minuet in G.
Dyno Voice 214 - Attack* / See How They Run - 1965 *The Toys had a cameo spot singing this in the beach movie "It's A Bikini World" starring Tommy Kirk and Deborah Walley, along with The Castaways, The Animals and The Gentrys.
Dyno Voice 218 - May My Heart Be Cast Into Stone / On Backstreet - 1966
Dyno Voice 219 - Can't Get Enough Of You Baby* / Silver Spoon - 1966

Dyno Voice 222 - Baby Toys / Happy Birthday Broken Heart - 1966
Philips 40432 - Ciao Baby / I Got Carried Away - 1967
Philips 40456 - My Love Sonata / I Close My Eyes - 1967
Musicor 1300 - You Got It Baby / You've Got To Give Her Love - 1968
Musicor 1319 - Sealed With A Kiss / I Got My Heart Set On You - 1968
Virgo 6022 - A Lover's Concerto / Attack - 1972

The Toys / The Bob Crewe Generation

Eric 185 - A Lover's Concerto / Music To Watch Girls By* - 197? *flip side by The Bob Crewe Generation.

The Toys

Gusto 2117 - A Lovers Concerto / Attack - ?
Collectables Col 003057 - A Lovers Concerto / Attack - ?

The Toys

Collectables COL 003057 - A Lovers Concerta / Attack - ?

Allen Toussaint

The Flamingos (members Snooks Eaglin, Allen Toussaint, ...)

Al Tousan

RCA Victor 47-7192 - Whirlaway / Happy Times - 1958

Allen & Allen (Allen Toussaint and Allen Orange)

Minit 609 - Heavenly Baby / Tiddle Winks - 1960

Al Tousan

Seville 103 - Chico / Sweetie-Pie - 1960
Seville 110 - Back Home In Indiana / Naomi - 1960
Seville 113 - A Blue Mood / Moo Moo - 1961
Seville 124 - Twenty Years Later / Real Churchy - 1962

The Stokes (members Allen Toussaint, Billy Fayard and Al Fayard)

Alon 9019 - Whipped Cream* / Piecrust - 1965 *covered in 1965 by Herb Alpert & The Tijuana Brass on A & M 760.

Allen Toussaint (born 14-January-1938 in the Gert Town district of New Orleans)

Alon 9021 - Go Back Home / Poor Boy, Got To Move - 1965

The Stokes (members Allen Toussaint, Billy Fayard and Al Fayard)

Alon 9023 - Fat Cat / Banana Split - 1965

The Young Ones (members Allen Toussaint, Billy Fayard and Al Fayard)

Alon 9025 - Sawdust Floor / Two Cents - 1965

The Stokes (members Allen Toussaint, Billy Fayard and Al Fayard)

Alon 9026 - Bump Bump / We Did It Again - 1965
Alon 9029 - One Mint Julep / Young Man - Old Man - 1966
Alon 9032 - Crystal Ball / Lock Stock And Barrell - 1966

The Rubaiyats (members Willie Harper, Allen Toussaint, ...) session group made up with members of The Meters.

Sansu 456 - Omar Khayyam / Tomorrow - 1966

Willie & Allen (Willie Harper and Allen Toussaint)

Sansu 464 – I Don't Need No One / Baby Do Little – 1967

Allen Toussaint

Bell 732 - Get Out Of My Life, Woman / Gotta Travel On - 1968 *also recorded in 1968 by The Noblemen 4 on Recap 291.
Bell 748 - I've Got That Feelin' Now / Hans Christianderson - 1968
Bell 782 - We The People / Tequila - 1969
Tiffany 9015 - From A Whisper To A Scream / Sweet Touch Of Love - 1970
Scepter 12317 - From A Whisper To A Scream / **Sweet** Touch Of Love - 1971
Scepter 12334 - Working In A Coal Mine* / What Is Success - 1971 *also recorded in 1966 by Lee Dorsey on Amy 958.
Reprise 1109 - She Once Belonged To Me / Soul Sister - 1972
Reprise 1132 - Out Of The City / Am I Expecting Too Much - 1972
Reprise 1334 - When The Party's Over / Country John - 1975
Sansu 1001 - Dancin' Lady / Headwinds - 1975 (also released on this number was Tommy Ridgely with "Sometimes You Get It")
Warner Bros. 8561 - Night People / Optimism Blues - 1978
Warner Bros. 8609 - Happiness / Lover Of Mine - 1978
WB - Just A Kiss Away - 1970's (10" acetate - song is arranged by Nick Decaro)
Crystal Fire 2201 - It's Time For A Change (Let's Do It) / It's A Stand Off - 1986 (12" release)
Cayenne 1000 - Mr. Mardi Gras / I Love A Carnival Ball - 1987

Doris Troy

The Halos (members John "Gregory" Carroll, Al Showell (both former members of The Dappers on Rainbow), Doc Wheeler and Doris Higgenson) 1960 line-up.

The Halos (members John "Gregory" Carroll, Al Showell (both former members of The Dappers on Rainbow), Doc Wheeler and Doris Higgenson) 1960 line-up.

The Halos (members John "Gregory" Carroll, Doris Higgenson and Leonard Puzey (a sometime member of The Cues))

Doris Payne (Doris Higgenson - took her grandmothers name)

Everest 19327 - I Want To Be Loved (But Only By You) / What A Wonderful Lover – 1960

Doc Bagby & Doris Payne

Shirley 101 - Foolish Decision / You Better Mind - 1960 (Backing Vocals By The Gospelaires)

Jay & Dee (the Dee is rumoured to be Doris Troy)

Arliss 1008 - Dream Talk / What A Night, Night, Night – 1961

Pearl Woods & The Gems (members Pearl Woods, Fred Johnson (Pearl Woods' then husband), Doris Troy and Gilbert Monk)

Wall 552 - Sloppin' / One More Time - 1962

Doris Troy (born Doris Higgensen on 6-January-1937 in New York City. Died 16-February-2004 in Las Vegas - cause: Emphysema)

Atlantic 2188 - Just One Look* / Bossa Nova Blues - 1963 *produced by John "Gregory" Carroll. Originally released in 1963 by Andy & The Marglows on Imperial 55570.
Atlantic 2206 - Tomorrow Is Another Day* / What'cha Gonna Do About It - 1963 *also recorded in 1965 by Joey Heatherton Coral 62459.
Atlantic 2222 - One More Chance / Please Little Angel - 1964
Cameo 392 - I'll Do Anything (He Wants Me To Do) / Heartaches - 1965
Atlantic 2269 - Hurry / He Don't Belong To Me - 1965
Calla 114 - I'll Do Anything (He Wants Me To) / Heartaches - 1966
Capitol 2043 - Face Up To The Truth / He's Qualified - 1967 (both tracks written by Doris Troy)
Apple 1820 - Ain't That Cute* / Vaya Con Dios - 1970 *written by George Harrison and Doris Troy.
Apple 1824 - Get Back* / Jacob's Ladder - 1970 *this version came out before The Beatles - Apple 2490.
People Peo112 - Stretchin' Out / Don't Tell Your Mama - 1974
Midland International Mb-10806 - Lyin' Eyes / Give God Glory - 1976
Midland Int'l Mb-11082 - Can't Hold On / Another Look - 1977
Midsong 11083 - Can't Hold On (5:28) / Another Look (4:36) - 1977 (12"release)

Doris Troy / Jackie Moore

Atlantic Oldies Series 13067 - Just One Look / Precious Precious* - ? *flip by Jackie Moore.

Ike & Tina Turner

Jackie Brenston Productions!

Memphis Recordings And Sound Service - "Rocket 88" / Track # 1 "Come Back Where You Belong" track # 2 **Ike Turner** I'm Lonesome Baby - 1951 (16" acetate plays at 78 rpm.) Found in 1995, minimum bid at a 1998 auction $20,000.00. The "A" side has a 40 second unknown alternate take on Rocket 88, which follows the released take of the song.

Jackie Brenston and His Delta Cats (members Jackie Brenston, Ike Turner, Willie Kizart, Raymond Hill and Willie Sims)

Chess 1458 - Rocket "88" / Come Back Where You Belong - 1951 (band was The Kings Of Rhythm)

Ike Turner with The Kings Of Rhythm

Chess 1459 - I'm Lonesome Baby / Heartbroken And Worried - 1951

Jackie Brenston and His Delta Cats

Chess 1469 - My Real Gone Rocket / Tuckered Out - 1951(Band Was Kings Of Rhythm)
Chess 1472 - Juiced / Independant Woman - 1951 (Flip Side Ike Turner On Piano)

Howlin' Wolf (Chester Arthur Burnett)

Chess 1479 - How Many More Years* / Moanin' At Midnight - 1951 *Ike Turner On Piano.

Robert Bland (Bobby Bland)

Modern 848 - Dry Up Baby / Crying All Night Long - 1951 (Ike turner on piano)

The Howlin' Wolf

RPM 333 - Riding In The Moonlight* / Moaning At Midnight - 1951 *Ike Turner on piano.
RPM 340 - Passing By Blues / Crying At Daybreak - 1951 (Ike Turner on piano)
RPM 347 - My Baby Stole Off / I Want Your Picture - 1951 (Ike Turner on piano)

Ike Turner and His Kings Of Rhythm (members Ike Turner, Jackie Brenston,Willie Kizart, Raymond Hill and Willie Sims)

Chess 1496 - Heartbroken And Worried / I'm Lonesome Baby - 1951

Sonny Blair (Sullivan Jackson)

Meteor 5006 - Please Send My Baby Back / Gonna Let You Go - 1952 ("A"side Ike Turner on piano. Flip side Ike Turner on guitar and actually sung by Baby Face Turner, but credited to Sonny Blair, who plays harmonica)

Ike Turner Singing with Ben Burton and his Orchestra

RPM 356 - You're Driving Me Insane / Trouble And Heartaches - 1952

Bonnie and Ike Turner With Orchestral Acc.

RPM 362 - My Heart Belongs To You / Looking For My Baby - 1952

Houston Boines

RPM 364 - Superintendent Blues / Monkey Motion - 1952 (Ike Turner on piano)

Drifting Slim (Elmon Mickle)

RPM 370 - Good Morning Baby / My Sweet Woman - 1952 (Ike Turner on piano)

Houston Baines (Houston Boines)

Blues & Rhythm 7001 - Going Home / Relation Blues - 1952 (Ike Turner on piano)

Brother Bell (Johnny O'Neal)

Blues & Rhythm 7002 - Whole Heap Of Mama / If You Feel Froggish - 1952 (Ike Turner on piano)

Charley Booker

Blues & Rhythm 7003 - Rabbit Blues / No Ridin' Blues - 1952 (Ike Turner On Piano)

Little Junior Parker

Modern 864 - Bad Women, Bad Whiskey / You're My Angel - 1952 (Ike Turner On Piano)

Bobby "Blue" Bland With Ike Turner Orchestra

Modern 868 - Good Lovin' (Love You Baby-Love You Yes I Do) / Drifting From Town To Town - 1952 (Ike Turner On Piano & Guitar)

Ben Burton

Modern 871 - Bee Hive Boogie / Blues And Jam - 1952 (Ike Turner On Piano)

Charley Booker

Modern 878 - Moonrise Blues / Charley's Boogie Woogie - 1952 (Ike Turner On Piano)

Mary Sue

Modern 880 - Everybody's Talking / Love Is A Gamble - 1952 (Ike Turner On Piano)

Baby Face Turner

Modern 882 - Blue Serenade / Gonna Let You Go - 1952 (Ike Turner On Guitar)

B.B. King

Rpm 374 - Story From My Heart And Soul / Boogie Woogie Woman - 1952 With Ike Turner On Piano.

Ben Burton

Modern 894 - Lover's Blues / Cherokee Boogie - 1953 (Ike Turner On Piano)

Royal Brent

Rockin' 521 - Sugar Bun / Danny Boy - 1953 (Ike Turner Session?)

Elmore James with The Broom Dusters

Flair 1022 - Please Find My Baby* / Strange Kinda Feeling - 1953 *Ike Turner on guitar

The Prisonaires (members Johnny Bragg (lead), Edward Lee Thurman (tenor), John Edward Drue Jr. (tenor), Marcel Sanders (bass) and William Stewart (baritone))

Sun 189 - My God Is Real* / Softly And Tenderly** - 1953 *Clara Ward gave Johnny Bragg the idea to record this old spiritual song. **with Ike Turner on piano.
Sun 191 - A Prisoner's Prayer* / I Know - 1953 *Ike Turner on guitar.

Little Milton

Sun 194 - Beggin' My Baby / Somebody Told Me - 1953 (Ike Turner on piano)
Billy "The Kid" Emerson

Sun 195 - No Teasing Around / If Lovin' Is Believing - 1954 (Ike Turner On Guitar)

Little Milton

Sun 200 - Alone And Blue / If You Love Me Baby - 1954 (Ike Turner On Piano)

Billy "The Kid" Emerson

Sun 203 - I'm Not Going Home / The Woodchuck - 1954 (Ike Turner On Guitar)

Raymond Hill

Sun 204 - The Snuggle / Bourbon Street Jump - 1954 (Ike Turner On Guitar)

Elmore James With The Broom Dusters

Flair 1031 - Hand In Hand / Make My Dreams Come True - 1954 (Ike Turner On Piano)

Eugene Fox (With Ike Turner)

Checker 792 - Stay At Home / Sinners Dream - 1954

Jesse Knight & His Combo (With Ike Turner)

Checker 797 - Nobody Seems To Want Me / Nothing But Money - 1954

Lover Boy

RPM 409 - The Way You Used To Treat Me / Love Is Scarce - 1954 (Ike Turner vocal and guitar on "A" side, vocal and piano on flip side)

Lonnie "The Cat" with Bobby Hines Band (and members of The Kings of Rhythm)

RPM 410 - I Ain't Drunk / The Road I Travel - 1954 (Ike Turner and Bobby Hines share the same piano)

The Fox (Eugene Fox with Ike Turner)

RPM 420 - The Dream Pt. 1 / The Dream Pt. 2 - 1954

Johnny Wright with the Ike Turner Orchestra (members Johnny Wright (vocals), Ike Turner (guitar), Jesse Knight Jr. (bass), Raymond Hill (saxophone), Eddie Jones (saxophone) and Eugene Washington (drums))

Deluxe 6029 - I Stayed Down / I Was In St. Louis - 1954

Clayton Love

Modern 929 - Why Don't You Believe In Me / Wicked Little Baby - 1954 (Ike Turner on guitar)

Denis Binder & His Orchestra (members Dennis Binder, Ike Turner, Jesse Knight Jr., Eugene Fox, Bobby Fields, ...)

Modern 930 - I Miss You So / Early Times - 1954

Matt Cockrell

Flair 1037 - Baby Please / Gypsy Blues - 1954 (Ike Turner on piano)

Billy Gale and His Orchestra (members William James Gayles (vocals), Ike Turner (guitar), Jesse Knight Jr. (bass), Bobby Field (tenor saxophone), Eugene Fox (tenor saxophone), ...)

Flair 1038 - Night Howler / My Heart Is In Your Hands - 1954

Elmore James and His Broom Dusters

Flair 1039 - Sho Nuff I Do / 1839 Blues - 1954 (Ike Turner on piano)

Ike Turner & His Orchestra

Flair 1040 - Cubano Jump / Loosely - 1954

The Flairs (with Ike Turner)

Flair 1041 - Baby Wants / You Were Untrue - 1954

The Sly Fox (Eugene Fox)

Spark 108 - Hoo-Doo Say / I'm Tired Of Beggin' -1954 with Ike Turner vocal & guitar.
Spark 112 - My Four Women / Alley Music - 1954

Little Milton

Sun 220 - Looking For My Baby / Homesick For My Baby - 1955 (Ike Turner on piano)

Ike Turner & His Orchestra

Flair 1059 - Cuban Getaway / Go To It - 1955

Johnny Wright - Ike Turner & Orchestra (members Johnny Wright (vocals), Ike Turner (guitar), Jesse Knight Jr. (bass), Raymond Hill (saxophone), Eddie Jones (saxophone) and Eugene Washington (drums))

RPM 443 - Suffocate / The World Is Yours - 1955

The Trojans (vocal group with Ike Turners Orchestra)

RPM 446 - As Long As I Have You / I Wanna Make Love To You - 1955

Richard Berry with the Ike Turner Orchestra

RPM 448 - Rockin' Man / Big John - 1955

Willie King with The Ike Turner Band featuring Billy Gayles

Vita 123 - Peg Leg Woman / Mistreating Me - 1956

Billy Gales with Ike Turner's Rhythm Rockers (members William James Gayles (vocals), Ike Turner (guitar), Jesse Knight Jr. (bass), Raymond Hill (tenor saxophone), Eddie Jones (tenor saxophone), Jackie Brenston (baritone saxophone), Fred Sample (piano) and Eugene Washington (drums))

Federal 12265 - I'm Tore Up* / If I Had Never Known You - 1956 *also recorded in 1962 by Lee Williams on Federal 12502.

The Rockers (vocal group with Ike Turner)

Federal 12267 - What Am I To Do / I"l Die In Love With You - 1956

Billy Gales with Ike Turners Rhythm Rockers (members William James Gayles (vocals), Ike Turner (guitar), Jesse Knight Jr. (bass), Raymond Hill (tenor saxophone), Eddie Jones (tenor saxophone), Jackie Brenston (baritone saxophone), Fred Sample (piano) and Eugene Washington (drums))

Federal 12272 - Let's Call It A Day* / Take Your Fine Frame Home - 1956 *session: The Rockers (backing vocals)

The Rockers

Federal 12273 - Why Don't You Believe / Down In The Bottom - 1956

Billy Gales with Ike Turners Kings Of Rhythm (members William James Gayles (vocals), Ike Turner (guitar), Jesse Knight Jr. (bass), Raymond Hill (tenor saxophone), Eddie Jones (tenor saxophone), Jackie Brenston (baritone saxophone), Fred Sample (piano) and Eugene Washington (drums))

Federal 12282 - Do Right Baby / No Coming Back - 1956

Jackie Brenston with Ike Turners Kings Of Rhythm

Federal 12283 - What Can It Be / Gonna Wait For My Chance - 1956

The Gardenias (members Luther Ingram, ...)

Federal 12284 - Flaming Love / My Baby's Tops - 1956 (Ike Turner on guitar)

Billy Gales with Ike Turners Kings Of Rhythm

Federal 12287 - Just One More Time / Sad As A Man Can Be - 1957

Jackie Brenston with Ike Turners Kings Of Rhythm (members Jackie Brenston (vocals), Ike Turner (guitar), Jesse Knight Jr. (bass),.....................)

Federal 12291 - Much Later / The Mistreater - 1957

Ike Turner & His Orchestra

Federal 12297 - Do You Mean It / She Made My Blood Run Cold - 1957 (vocals by Clayton Love)
Federal 12304 - Rock A Bucket */ The Big Question - 1957 *vocal by Clayton Love.
Federal 12307 - You've Changed My Love * / Trail Blazer - 1957 *vocal by Clayton Love.

Ike Turner, Carson Oliver & Little Ann

Tune Town 501 - Boxtop / Chalypso Love Cry - 1958 one of the backing vocalists was Annie Mae Bullock (Tina Turner) and possibly Robbie Montgomery.

Kenneth Churchill & The Lyrics with The Ike Turner Orchestra

Joyce 304 - Would You Rather / Fate Of Rock And Roll - 1958

Otis Rush and His Band (members Otis Rush (vocals and guitar), Ike Turner (guitar), Willie Dixon (bass), Eddie Jones (tenor saxophone), Carlson Oliver (tenor saxophone), Jackie Brenston (baritone saxophone), Harold Burrage or Little Brother Montgomery (piano) and Odie Payne (drums))
Cobra 5030 - Double Trouble / Keep On Loving Me Baby - 1958

Betty Everett & The Willie Dixon Band

Cobra 5031 - I'll Weep No More / Tell Me Darling - 1958 (Ike Turner on piano on "A" side, guitar on flip side)

Otis Rush and His Band (members Otis Rush (vocals and guitar), Ike Turner (guitar), Willie Dixon (bass), Eddie Jones (tenor saxophone), Carlson Oliver (tenor saxophone), Jackie Brenston (baritone saxophone), Harold Burrage or Little Brother Montgomery (piano) and Odie Payne (drums))

Cobra 5032 - All Your Love (I Miss Loving) / My Baby Is A Good 'Un - 1958

Ike Turner's Kings Of Rhythm

Cobra 5033 - Box Top* / Walking Down The Aisle** - 1959 *Vocals Tommy Hodge And Carson Oliver. **Vocals Billy Gayles

Buddy Guy

Artistic 1503 - You Sure Can't Do / This Is The End - 1959 (Ike Turner On Guitar)

Ike Turner's Kings Of Rhythm Vocal By Tommy Hodge

Artistic 1504 - Down & Out / (I Know) You Don't Love Me -1959

Icky Renrut

Stevens 104 - Jack Rabbit / In Your Eyes Baby - 1959 *Vocal Jimmy Thomas (Icky Renrut Was Ike Turner)

Little Cooper & The Drifters

Stevens 105 - Moving Slow / Evening Train - 1959 (Ike Turner On Guitar)

Icky Renrut

Stevens 107 - Ho --- Ho / Hey --- Hey* - 1959 * Vocal:Jimmy Thomas (Icky Renrut Was Ike Turner)

Ike Turner & The Kings Of Rhythm

Sue 722 - My Love* / That's All I Need** - 1959 *Vocals Ike Turner, **Vocals Tommy Hodge

Ike & Tina Turner

Sue 730 - A Fool In Love / The Way You Love Me - 1960
Sue 734 - You're My Baby / A Fool Too Long - 1960
Sue 735 - I Idolize You* / Letter From Tina - 1960 *also recorded in 1964 by The Charmaines on Fraternity 921 but release of the 45 was cancelled.

Jackie Brenston With Ike Turner & His Kings Of Rhythm

Sue 736 - Trouble Up The Road / You Ain't The One - 1960

Ike & Tina Turner

Sue 740 - I'm Jealous / You're My Baby - 1961

Eloise Hestor (With Ike Turner)

Sue 742 - My Man Rock Head / I Need You - 1961

Jimmy & Jean With Ike Turner's Orchestra

Sue 743 - I Wanta Marry You / I Can't Believe - 1961

Ernest Lane

M. J. C. 1 - What Kind Of Love / Sliced Apples - 1961 Ike Turner band member.

Ike Turner

Sue 749 - It's Gonna Work Out Fine / Won't You Forgive Me - 1961

Ike & Tina Turner

Sue 749 - It's Gonna Work Out Fine* / Won't You Forgive Me - 1961 *male spoken parts are by Mickey "Guitar" Baker.
Sue 735 - Poor Fool / You Can't Blame Me - 1961

Ike Turner & His Orchestra

King 5553 - The Big Question / She Made My Blood Run Cold - 1961

Billy Gayles

Shock 200 - I'm Hurting / I'm Dreaming Of You - 1961 (Ike Turner On Piano)

Mickey & Sylvia

Willow 23000 - Baby You're So Fine / Love Drops - 1961 (Ike Turner On Piano)

Albert King

Bobbin 131 - Don't Throw Your Love On Me So Strong* / This Morning - 1961 (*Ike Turner On Piano)

Dolores Johnson With Ike Turner's Band

Bobbin 132 - Give Me Your Love / Gotta Find My Baby - 1962

Tina Turner With The Ikettes

Teena 1702 - Prisoner In Love (No Bail In This Jail) / Those Words - 1962

Ike & Tina Turner

Sue 757 - Tra La La / Puppy Love - 1962
Sue 760 - Prancing / It's Gonna Work Out Fine - 1962

Bobby "Blue" Bland & Ike Turner And His Orchestra

Kent 378 - Love You Baby / Drifting - 1962

Ike & Tina Turner

Sue 765 - You Shoulda Treated Me Right / Sleepless - 1962
Sue 768 - Tina's Dilemma / I Idolize You - 1962
Sue 772 - The Arguement / Mind In A Whirl - 1962
Sue 774 - Please Don't Hurt Me / Worried And Hurtin' Inside - 1962

Jimmy Thomas (With Ike Turner)

Sue 778 - You Can Go / Hurry And Come Home - 1962

The Ikettes (With Tina Turner)

Atco 6212 - I'm Blue (The Gong-Gong Show) / Find My Baby - 1962

Vernon Guy With Ike Turner's Band & The Ikettes

Teena 1703 - You've Got Me / They Ain't Lovin' Ya - 1963

Flora Williams (With Ike Turner)

Teena 170? - Love Me Or Leave Me / I'll Wait For You - 1963

Ike & Tina Turner

Sue 784 - Don't Play Me Cheap / Wake Up - 1963
Sonja 2001 - If I Can't Be First / I'm Going Back Home - 1963

Jimmy Thomas With The Ike & Tina Revue

Sonja 2004 - You've Tasted Another's Lips / I Love Nobody But You - 1963

Ike & Tina Turner

Sonja 2005 - You Can't Miss Nothing That You Never Had / God Gave Me You - 1963

Fontella Bass & Tina Turner

Sonja 2006 - Poor Little Fool / This Would Make Me Happy - 1963
Vesuvias 1002 - Poor Little Fool / This Would Make Me Happy - 1963

Vernon Guy (With Ike Turner)

Sonja 2007 - Anything To Make It With You / Anything To Make It With You (Instrumental) - 1963

Little Bones (The World's Greatest Singing Cricket) (Aka Ike Turner)

Prann 5001 - What'd I Say / Ya-Ya - 1963

The Turnabouts

Prann 5002 - Gettin' Away / Cotton Pickin' - 1963 (Ike Turner Member Of Group)

Little Bones (The World's Greatest Singing Cricket)

Prann 5006 - Going To The River / I Know - 1963

The Nasty Minds (Featuring Ike Turner)

Sonja 5001 - Getting Nasty / Nutting Up - 1963

Bobby John (With Ike Turner)

Sony 111 - Lonely Soldier / The Bad Man - 1963

Venetta Fields With Ike Turner's Band

Sony 112 - You're Still My Baby / I'm Leaving You - 1963

Stacy Johnson (With Ike Turner)

Sony 113 - Remove My Doubts / Don't Believe 'Em - 1963

Ike & Tina Turner Revue With The Ikettes

Innis 3000 - Here's Your Heart / Here's Your Heart (Instrumental) - 1964

Gloria Garcia With The Ike & Tina Revue

Innis 3001 - No Puedes Extranar / Koonkie Cookie - 1964

Ike Johnson & Dee Dee

Innis 3002 - You Can't Have Your Cake (And Eat It Too) / The Drag - 1964 (Ike Johnson Is Reportably Ike Turner)

Ike & Tina Turner

Warner Bros. 5433 - A Fool For A Fool / No Tears To Cry - 1964 (some copies issued with picture sleeve)
Warner Bros. 5461 - It's All Over / Finger Poppin' - 1964
Warner Bros. 5493 - Ooh Poo Pah Doo / / Merry Christmas Baby - 1964
Kent 402 - I Can't Believe What You Say (For Seeing What You Do) / My Baby Now - 1964
Kent 409 - Am I A Fool In Love / Please, Please, Please - 1964

Stacy Johnson With Ike Turner's Band

Modern 1001 - Consider Yourself / Don't Blame Him - 1964 With Ike Turner On Guitar

Ike Turner And His Orchestra

Royal American 105 - I Know You Don't Love Me / I'm On Your Trail - 1965 Vocal: Tommy Hodge

Ike & Tina Turner

Loma 2011 - Tell Her I'm Not Home / I'm Thru With Love - 1965
Loma 2015 - Somebody Somewhere Needs You / Just To Be With You - 1965
Modern 1007 - Goodbye, So Long / Hurt Is All You Gave Me - 1965

Modern 1012 - I Don't Need / Gonna Have Fun - 1965
Kent 418 - Chicken Shack / He's The One - 1965
Sue 135 - Two Is A Couple / Tin Top House - 1965

Ike Turner & His Kings Of Rhythm

Sue 138 - The New Breed (Part 1) / The New Breed (Part 2) - 1965

Ike & Tina Turner

Sue 139 - Stagger Lee And Billy / Can't Chance A Breakup - 1965
Sue 146 - Dear John / I Made A Promise Up Above - 1966
Kent 457 - Flee Flu Fla / I Wish My Dreams Would Come True - 1966
Tangerine 963 - Beauty Is Just Skin Deep / Anything You Wasn't Born With - 1966
Tangerine 967 - Dust My Broom / I'm Hooked - 1966
Philles 131 - River Deep -- Mountain High* / I'll Keep You Happy - 1966 *also recorded in 1967 by The 2 Of Clubs (members Linda Parrish and Patti Valentine) on Fraternity 994 and in 1973 by Ellie Greenwich on Verve 10724.
Associated Recording Studios - Everything Under The Sun - 1966 (one sided acetate with track title and Saturday Music typed on label. Ike + Tina Turner and numbers 1231 hand written on label)

Ika and Tina - Turner

Bell Sound Studios - Everything Under The Sun / Two To Tango - 1966 (acetate - more polished version - has time 4:00 scribbled out and 3:56 added with name Ika and Tina Turner typed on label)

Ike & Tina Turner

Philles 134 - Two To Tango / A Man Is A Man Is A Man - 1966
Philles 135 - I'll Never Need More Than This / The Cash Box Blues Or (Oops We Printed The Wrong Story Again) - 1967
Philles 136 - I Idolize You / A Love Like Yours (Don't Come Knocking Every Day) - 1967
Cenco 112 - Get It-Get It / You Weren't Ready (For My Love) - 1967

Ike & Tina & The Ikettes

Innis 6666 - Betcha Can't Kiss Me / Don't Lie To Me - 1968
Innis 6667 - So Fine / So Blue Over You - 1968
Innis 6668 - I Better Get Ta' Steppen' / Poor Sam - 1968
Innis ? - I Made A Promise Up Above / Dear John - 1968

Ike & Tina Turner

Pompeii 66675 - It Sho' Ain't Me / We Need An Understanding - 1968

Tina Turner With Ike Turner & The Kings Of Rhythm

Pompeii 66682 - Too Hot To Hold / You Got What You Wanted - 1968

Ike & Tina Turner

Pompeii 66700 - Shake A Tail Feather / Cussin', Cryin', And Carryin' On - 1969

Ike Turner

Sterling Award 100 - Thinking Black / Black Angel - ?

Ike Turner And The Soul Seven (Members Of The Soul Seven William Sneed (Drums), Charles Hunt (Trombone), Bishop Berry (Baritone Sax), Larry Blake (Tenor Sax), Mike Mckinney (Bass), Eugene Goff (Guitar) And Harold Carrol (Trumpet))

Pompeii 7001 - Everythings Everything (Part 1) / Everythings Everything (Part 2) - 1969

Ike & Tina Turner

Pompeii 7003 - Betcha Can't Kiss Me / Cussin', Cryin', And Carryin' On - 1969
Minit 32060 - I'm Gonna Do All I Can (To Do Right By My Man) / You've Got Too Many Ties That Bind - 1969
Minit 32068 - I Wish It Would Rain / With A Little Help From My Friends - 1969
Minit 32077 - I Wanna Jump / Treating Us (Women) Funky - 1969
A & M 1118 - River Deep -- Mountain High / I'll Keep You Happy - 1969
Blue Thumb 101 - I've Been Loving You Too Long / Grumbling - 1969
Blue Thumb 102 - The Hunter / Crazy ' Bout You Baby - 1969
Blue Thumb 104 - Bold Soul Sister / I Know - 1969
A & M 1170 - A Love Like Yours (Don't Come Knocking Every Day) / Save The Last Dance For Me - 1970

Ike & Tina Turner & The Ikettes

Minit 32087 - Come Together / Honky Tonk Women - 1970

Ike & Tina Turner

Kent 4514 - Please, Please, Please (Part 1) / Please, Please, Please (Part 2) - 1970

Ike & Tina Turner & The Ikettes

Liberty 56177 - I Want To Take You Higher / Contact High - 1970

Ike & Tina Turner

Sonja 2005 - God Gave Me You / ? -1970

Fontella Bass

Sonja 2006 - Poor Little Fool / This Would Make Me Happy - 1970 (Reissue Of 45 Only Credits Fontella Bass Omitting Tina Turner)

Ike Turner (born Izear Luster Turner Jr. on 5-November-1931, Clarksdale, Mississippi --- died 12-December-2007 in San Diego, California --- cause: ?)

Liberty 56194 - Takin' Back My Name / Love Is A Game - 1970

Ike & Tina Turner

Liberty 56207 - Workin' Together / The Way You Love Me - 1970
Liberty 56216 - Proud Mary / Funkier Than A Mosquito's Tweeter - 1970
Tangerine 1019 - Dust My Broom / Anything You Wasn't Born With - 1971
Blue Thumb 202 - I've Been Loving You Too Long / Crazy ' Bout You Baby - 1971
United Artists Sp-48 - I Want To Take You Higher / Ooh Poo Pah Doo - 1971 (Dj Copy)
United Artists 50782 - Ooh Poo Pah Doo / I Wanna Jump - 1971

United Artists 50837 - I'm Yours (Use Me Anyway You Wanna) / Doin' It - 1971
Special Radio Spot Sp-53 - Live At Carnegie Hall - ? (One Sided Promo Issue Only)

Ike Turner

United Artists 50865 - River Deep -- Mountain High / Na Na - 1971

Ike & Tina Turner

Trc ? - 1971
United Artists 0 - City Girl, Country Boy - 1972 (10", 45 Rpm One Sided Stereo Acetate)
United Artists 0 - Unhappy Birthday - 1972 (10", 45rpm One Sided Stereo Acetate)
United Artists 50881 - Do Wah Ditty (Got To Get Ya) / Up In Heah - 1972

Tina Turner

Audio Disc - You Can't Do Without - ? (Acetate -- Unreleased Single -- Recently Sold For $100.00 Usa)

Ike Turner

United Artists 50900 - Right On / Tacks In My Shoes - 1972

Ike Turner & The Family Vibes

United Artists 50901 - Bootie Lip / Soppin' Molasses - 1972

Ike & Tina Turner

United Artists 50913 - Outrageous / Feel Good - 1972

Ike Turner

United Artists 50930 - Lawdy Miss Clawdy (Mono) / Lawdy Miss Clawdy (Stereo) - 1972 (Promo Issue)
United Artists 50930 - Lawdy Miss Clawdy / Tacks In My Shoes - 1972

Ike & Tina Turner

United Artists 50939 - Games People Play / Pick Me Up (Take Me Where Your Home Is) - 1972
United Artists 50955 - Let Me Touch Your Mind / Chopper - 1972
United Artists Un 1972 78 Rpm - Something In The Way He Moves - 197? (10", 45rpm One Sided Stereo Acetate)
United Artists Un 1972 78 Rpm - Every Little Bit Hurts - 197? (10". 45rpm One Sided Stereo Acetate)

Ike Turner

United Artists 51102 - Dust My Broom / You Won't Let Me Go - 1973

Ike & Tina Turner

United Artists 0119 - A Fool In Love / I Idolize You - 1973
United Artists 0120 - It's Gonna Work Out Fine / Poor Fool - 1973
United Artists 0121 - I Want To Take You Higher / Come Together - 1973
United Artists 0122 - Proud Mary / Tra La La - 1973

United Artists Xw 174 - With A Little Help From My Friends / Early One Morning - 1973
United Artists Xw 257 - Work On Me / Born Free - 1973

Ike Turner

United Artists Xw 278 - El-Burrito / Garbage Man - 1973

Ike & Tina Turner

United Artists Xw 298 - Nutbush City Limits / Help Him - 1973
United Artists Xw 409 - Sweet Rhode Island Red / Get It Out Of Your Mind - 1974

Ike Turner

United Artists Xw 460 - Take My Hand, Precious Lord / Father Alone - 1974

Ike & Tina Turner

United Artists Xw 524 - Nutbush City Limits / Ooh Poo Pa Doo - 1974
United Artists Xw 528 - Sexy Ida (Part 1) / Sexy Ida (Part 2) - 1974
United Artists Xw 598x - Baby, Get It On / Baby, Get It On (Disco Version) - 1975
United Artists Xw 598 - Baby, Get It On / Help Me Make It Through The Night - 1975

Tina Turner

United Artists Xw 724 - Whole Lotta Love / Rockin' `N' Rollin' - 1975

Ike & Tina Turner

United Artists Xw 730 - Delilah's Power / That's My Power - 1975

Tina Turner

Poldor Pro-002 - Acid Queen / Pinball Wizard* - 1975* Flip By Elton John (Promo Only)
United Artists Xw 920 - Come Together / I Want To Take You Higher - 1977
United Artists Xw 1265 - Fire Down Below / Viva La Money - 1979
Wagner Irda 567 - If This Is The Last Time / We Had It All - 1979
Interfusion K-8075 - Hold On / Are You Breaking My Heart - 1980

Ike Turner Featuring Tina Turner & Home Grown Funk

Fantasy D-161 Party Vibes / Shame, Shame, Shame - 1980 (12" Promo Issue)

Ike Turner & Kings Of Rhythm

Fleetville Fv-303 - New Breed (Pt. 1) / New Breed (Pt. 2) - 198?

Tina Turner

Fantasy 948 - Lean On Me / Shame, Shame, Shame - 1984
Capitol B-5332 - Let's Stay Together / I Wrote A Letter - 1984
Capitol B-5354 - What's Love Got To Do With It / Rock `N' Roll Widow - 1984
Capitol Spro 9196 - What's Love Got To Do With It (Extended 5:34) / What's Love Got To Do With It (Extended 5:34) - 1984 (12" Promo Issue Only -- White Label)
Capitol B-5387 - Better Be Good To Me / When I Was Young - 1984

Capitol B-5433 - Private Dancer / Nutbush City Limits - 1984
Capitol B-5461- Show Some Respect / Let's Pretend We're Married - 1984

David Bowie

Emi America 8246 - Tonight* / Tumble And Twirl - 1984 *Tina Turner Backing Vocals.

Bryan Adams & Tina Turner

A & M 2791 - It's Only Love / The Only One - 1985

Ike and Tina Turner

Striped Horse 7001 - Living For The City / Chicken - 1985
Striped Horse 1201 - Living For The City / Bootsy Whitelaw - 1985 (12" Release)

Tina Turner

Capitol B-5491 - We Don't Need Another Hero (Thunderdome) / (Instrumental) - 1985
Capitol B-5510 - One Of The Living / One Of The Living (Dub) - 1985
Capitol B-5518 - One Of The Living / One Of The Living (Dub) - 1985

Bryan Adams / Bryan Adams & Tina Turner

A & M 8654 - One Night Love Affair / It's Only Love* - 1986 *Flip By Bryan Adams & Tina Turner.

Tina Turner

Capitol B-5615 - Typical Male / Don't Turn Around - 1986
Capitol B-5644 - Two People / Havin' A Party - 1986
Capitol B-5668 - What You Get Is What You See / What You Get Is What You See (Live) - 1987
Capitol 9826 - Back Where You Started / Back Where You Started - ? (12" Promo Issue Only -- White Label)
Capitol B-44003 - Break Every Rule / Take Me To The River - 1987
Capitol Cl 452 - Girls / Break Every Rule - 1987

Eric Clapton & Tina Turner / Eric Clapton

Duck 28279 - Tearing Us Apart / Hold On* - 1987 *Flip By Eric Clapton.

Tina Turner

Capitol B-44111 - Afterglow / Afterglow - 1987
Capitol 79192-68 - Afterglow (4 Versions) - 1987 (12"Release)
Capitol B-44442 - The Best (Edit) / Undercover Agent For The Blues - 1989
Capitol B-44473 - Steamy Windows / The Best (Edit) - 1989
Capitol Nr-44510 - Look Me In The Heart / Stronger Than The Wind - 1990
Capitol S7-57702 - Way Of The World / You Know Who - 1992
Virgin S7-17401 - I Don't Wanna Fight / Tina's Wish - 1993
Virgin S7-17498 - Why Must We Wait Until Tomorrow / Shake A Tail Feather - 1993
Virgin S7-18047 - Proud Mary (Edit Live Version) / The Best (Live) - 1994
Virgin S7-19217 - Missing You / Do Something - 1996

The Tymes

The Latineers (members Donald Banks, Albert Berry, Norman Burnett and George Hilliard) 1956 group

The Tymes (members George Williams (born George Reginald Williams Jr. on the 6-December-1935 in Philadelphia, Pennsylavania --- died 28-July-2004 - cause: cancer) , George Hilliard, Donald Banks, Albert Berry and Norman Burnett. First called The Latineers. Albert Berry and George Hilliard were replaced by female singers Terri Gonzales and Melanie Moore in the early 1970's)

Parkway 871 A - So In Love / Roscoe James McClain - 1963
Parkway 871 C - So Much In Love* / Roscoe James McClain - 1963 *female voice on this track is Marlena Davis of The Orlons.
Parkway 884 - Wonderful! Wonderful! / Come With Me To The Sea – 1963
Parkway 891 - Somewhere / View From My Window – 1963
Parkway 908 - To Each His Own / Wonderland Of Love - 1964 (some copies issued with picture sleeve)
Parkway 919 - The Magic Of Our Summer Love / With All My Heart – 1964
Parkway 924 - Here She Comes / Malibu - 1964
Parkway 933 - The Twelfth Of Never / Here She Comes* - 1964 *misspressing plays "I Won't Cry."
Parkway 933 - The Twelfth Of Never / Here She Comes – 1964
MGM 13536 - Street Talk / Pretend - 1966
MGM 13631 - What Would I Do / A Touch Of Baby - 1966
Winchester 1002 - These Foolish Things / This Time It's Love - 1967
Columbia 44630 - People / For Love Of Ivy - 1968
Columbia 44799 - The Love That You're Looking For (Ain't Gonna Find It Here) / God Bless The Child - 1969
Columbia 44917 - If You Love Me Baby / Find My Way - 1969
Columbia 45078 - "Love Child / Most Beautiful Married Lady- 1970
Columbia 45336 - "She's Gone / Someone To Watch Over Me" - 1971
RCA 10022 - "You Little Trustmaker / The North Hills" - 1974
RCA 10128 - "Ms. Grace / The Crutch" - 1974
RCA 10244 - "Interloop / Someway Somehow I'm Keepin' You" - 1975
RCA 10422 - "If I Can't Make You Smile / God's Gonna Punish You" - 1975
RCA 10493 - "You Little Trustmaker / The North Hills" - 1975
RCA 10561 - "Good Morning Dear Lord / It's Cool" - 1976
RCA 10713 - "Goin' Through The Motions / Only Your Love" - 1976
RCA 10862 - "Love's Illusion / Savannah Sunny Sunday" - 1976
RCA 11136 - "How Am I To Know / I'll Take You There" - 1977
RCA 12082 - You Little Trust Maker / Ms Grace - 1980 (Unreleased)
Hammer ? - Brothers And Sisters / ? – 1980
Ripete 268 - So Much In Love / Misty - 1989 (new recording)
Collectables Col 045437 - You Little Trustmaker / Ms. Grace - ?

The Tymes (members Donald Banks, Albert Berry, Norman Burnett, Lafayette Gamble and Jimmy Wells) 2003

Group Line Ups

The Ulti-Mations (Bobby L Davis, Vaughan Clemens, Alan C BennettGerald Jones, Brandon Smith)
The Unifics (Al Johnson, Gregory Cook, Michael Ward, Hal Worthington, Glenn Leonard)

The Ultimations

Mar-V-Lus 6020 - Would I Do It Over / With Out You - 1967

Venue Reports - November 2001

The Aquarius, Hednesford, 2nd November, 2001.

I can never work this place out, it's mostly full of Oldies fans, who dance to the records you would least expect them to dance to ! A very enjoyable night though. Nige Shaw, Nige Brown, and Spook provided the music, with Neil Rushton as the guest DJ, so you got a mixture that ran right through Oldies to rarities to Modern to R & B. Probably the most successful night in the Midlands now, and well worth a visit if you haven't been before.

Lowton Civic Hall, 9th November, 2001

I very rarely get to Lowton because it always used to clash with Albrighton, but that will change in the coming year. The Capitol Soul Club boys had come in north to play a few records, and combine Tim Brown, and Ian Cunliffe into the DJ line up and you've got the makings of a good night out. I'm told numbers were down, but it was still busy enough to make it a good night, so I enjoyed myself, chatted to a few people who I don't see regularly enough and had fun listening to the top quality tunes being played.

Valatone Soul Club, London 10th November, 2001.

Johnny Timlin has persevered with this venue, and the numbers are now quite respectable. I travelled down with John Weston to meet up with the York crew, and a few beers were drunk. Overall the music was a little bit too much on the Modern side for me, but Shifty played a good last hour set so that made up for it.

100 Club, London, 10th November, 2001.

Numbers were down at the 100 Club, but I'll tell you what, those that went to Stoke missed the best set I'd heard all year from Butch. His second set was superb, and just re-affirmed his position as the number one DJ on the scene. Carl Willingham was the guest and with the exception of that turgid late Fifties thing he plays (which now jumps when he plays it !) he also played two excellent sets and went down much better than he did on his previous visit, despite bringing less supporters with him. I must of course mention John Weston's meeting with the nutter on the train. He does it every time ! this very strange guy was writing lots of things down in a notebook and then got about thirty used train tickets out of his pocket and starts copying the details down as well. He eventually looks up and starts talking to John about being a bus driver in North London. What made it funnier was John actually joined in the discussion and talked about areas like Walthamstow. It was so funny I had to go to the toilet to stop myself laughing out loud.. How does he do it !

Group Line Ups

The Valentinos (Bobby Womack, Cecil Womack, Harry Womack, Friendly Womack, Curtis Womack)
The Van Dykes (Rondalis L Tandy, Wenzon Mosely, James Mays)
The Vibrations (Ricky Owens, Carl Fisher, James Johnson, David Govan, Donald Bradley)
The Volcanos (Harold Wade, Stanley Wade, Eugene Jones)
The Vontastics (Jose Holmes, Kenneth Golar, Raymond Penn, Bobby Newsom)

Patience Valentine

Sar 111 - In The Dark / Dance And Let Your Hair Down - 1961
Sar 119 - I Miss You So / If You Don't Come - 1961
Sar 142 - Ernestine / Unlucky Girl - 1963
Sar 157 - Lost And Lookin' / Woman In A Man's World - 1964
Thrush 102 - Waking Up To A Dream / Longing - ?

The Velours

The Velours (members Jerome "Romeo" Ramos, John Cheetom, Donald Heywood, Kenneth Walker and Marvin Holland)

Onyx 501 - My Love Come Back / Honey Drop – 1956

The Velours Sammy Lews Orch. (members Jerome "Romeo" Ramos, John Cheetom, Donald Heywood, Kenneth Walker and Marvin Holland)

Onyx 508 - Romeo / What You Do To Me - 1957 (after this release Kenneth Walker and Marvin Holland leave group and are replaced by Charles Moffitt and John Pearson --- this is the most valuable of all their recordings)

The Velours (members Jerome "Romeo" Ramos, John Cheetom, Donald Heywood, Kenneth Walker and Marvin Holland)

Onyx 512 - Can I Come Over Tonight / Where There's A Will (There's A Way) – 1957
Onyx 515 - This Could Be The Night / Hands Across The Table – 1957
Onyx 520 - Remember / Can I Walk You Home - 1958
Orbit 9001 - Remember / Can I Walk You Home – 1958
Cub 9014 - I'll Never Smile Again / Crazy Love - 1958 (on this release the group added another tenor - Troy Keyes (who in 1963 recorded on the Atco record label as a member of The High Keys and went on to make a number of solo recordings such as "Love Explosions" on ABC 11027 in 1967 plus a 1968 duet with Norma Jenkins "A Good Love Gone Bad" on ABC 11116). Troy Keyes sings lead on this release. Troy Keyes then leaves group and Keith Williams joins)
Cub 9029 - Blue Velvet* / Tired Of Your Rock And Rollin' - 1958 *originally recorded in 1955 by The Clovers on Atlantic 1052.
Studio 9902 - Little Sweetheart / I Promise – 1959
Gone 5092 - Can I Come Over Tonight / Where There's A Will – 1960
Goldisc 3012 - Sweet Sixteen / Daddy Warbucks - 1960
End 1090 - The Lonely One / Lover Come Back - 1961(after this release Charles Moffitt (died ?-December-1986), Keith Williams and John Pearson leave group -- John Pearson becoming road manager for The Flamingos ---- Richard Pitts formerly from The Newtones (who had a 1958 release on Baton 260 "Remember The Night") joins the group)
Relic 502 - Romeo / What You Do To Me - 1964
Relic 503 - My Love Come Back / Honeydrop - 1964
Relic 504 - Can I Come Over Tonight / Where There's A Will – 1964
Relic 516 - This Could Be The Night / Hands Across The Table - 1964
Rona 010 - Woman For Me / She's My Girl - 1966

The Velours (members Jerome "Romeo" Ramos, John Cheetom, Donald Heywood and Richard Pitts)

MGM 13780 - I'm Gonna Change* / Don't Pity Me - 1967 *originally recorded by The Four Seasons as an Lp track.

The Fantastics (in 1968 the group decided to change their name and take their chances as part of a Soul explosion in England, members Jerome "Romeo" Ramos, John Cheetom, Donald Heywood and Richard Pitts)

MGM 1434 - Baby Make Your Own Sweet Music / Who Could Be Loving You – 1968
Deram 264 - Face To Face With Heartache / This Must Be My Rainy Day – 1969
Deram 283 - Ask The Lonely / Waiting Round For The Heartaches - 1970
Deram 334 - For The Old Times Sake / Exodus Main Theme – 1971
Deram 7528 - Face To Face With Heartache / This Must Be My Rainy Day - 197?
Bell 977 - Something Old, Something New / High And Dry – 1971
Bell 1141 - Something Old, Something New / High And Dry – 1971
Bell 1162 - Something Wonderful / Man Made The World – 1971
Bell 45,157 - (Love Me) Love The Life I Lead / Old Rags And Tatters – 1971
Polydor 2027004 - Baby Make Your Own Sweet Music / Who Could Be Loving You - 1971
Bell 45,279 - Best Of Strangers Now / Something To Remember You By - 1972

The Velours (members Jerome "Romeo" Ramos, John Cheetom, Donald Heywood, Kenneth Walker and Marvin Holland)

Lost-Nite 391 - My Love Come Back / Honey Drop - ?
Lost-Nite 394 - Where There's A Will / Can I Come Over Tonight - ?
Lost-Nite 400 - This Could Be The Night / Hands Across The Table - ?

The Velours (members

Lost-Nite 402 - Romeo / What You Do To Me - ?
Clifton 75 - C'est La Vie / Good Loving - 197?
Clifton 75 - C'est La Vie / Good Loving - 197?
Clifton 82 - Old Fashioned Christmas / I Wish You Love - 197?

The Velours / Buddy Knox

Roulette Gg-43 - Can I Come Over Tonight / Hula Love* - ? *flip by Buddy Knox. (Golden Goodies Series)

The Velours

Starlight 19 - This Could Be The Night / Mio Amore – 1984

Charles Moffitt & The Velours / James Myers Quintet

Clifton 100 - C'est La Vie / World Of Fantasy* - 1985 *flip by James Myers Quintet.
Artists 136 - I Apologize / We Are Made As One - 1994 (1000 red vinyl copies made total - 100 were promo issue only)

The Velvelettes

The Barbee's (members Carolyne Gill, Sandra Tilley and Betty Kelly)

Stepp 236 - The Wind / Que Pasa? (What's Happening) - 1962

The Velvelettes (members Millie Gill, Carolyn "Cal" Gill, Bertha Barbee, Norma Barbee and Betty Kelly)

I.P.G. 1002 - There He Goes* / That's The Reason Why - 1963 (produced by William "Mickey" Stevenson and reputedly features Stevie Wonder on harmonica) *also recorded in 1964 by The Royalettes on Warner Bros. 5439.
V.I.P. 25007 - Needle In A Haystack / Should I Tell Them – 1964
V.I.P. 25013 - He Was Really Sayin' Somthin' / Throw A Farewell Kiss - 1964 (promo copy - mis-spelt title)
V.I.P. 25013 - He Was Really Sayin' Somethin' / Throw A Farewell Kiss – 1964
V.I.P. 25017 - Lonely Lonely Girl Am I* / I'm The Exception To The Rule** - 1965 *also released in 1968 by Jimmy Ruffin as "Lonely Lonely Man Am I" on Soul 35046. **also released by The Temptations in 1971 on Gordy 7109.
V.I.P. 25021 - A Bird In The Hand (Is Worth Two In The Bush)* / Since You've Been Loving Me - 1965 *also released in 1975 by The Allens on Motown 1340.
V.I.P. 25030 - A Bird In The Hand (Is Worth Two In The Bush) / Since You've Been Loving Me – 1965
V.I.P 25034 - These Things Will Keep Me Loving You / Since You've Been Loving Me - 1966 (this 45 has the same record number as a test pressing by Chris Clark of her unissued version of "Do I Love You (Indeed I Do)")
Soul 35025 - These Things Will Keep Me Loving You / Since You've Been Loving Me – 1966

Various Artists

Motown 2482 - Christmas Greetings From Motown - 1966 (very short "Christmas Greetings" radio station spots are delivered by Martha & The Vandellas, The Temptations, The Miracles,

Shorty Long, The Velvelettes, The Spinners, The Four Tops, The Elgins and The Supremes. It was pressed in red vinyl.)

The Velvelettes

Motown Yesteryear 481 - Needle In A Haystack / Lonely Lonely Girl Am I - ?

The Vibrations

The Heart Thrills (members Carl Fisher (born Carlton Fisher on 27-December-1939 in Quardon, Texas) David Govan (born 2-August-1940 in Los Angeles, California), Cleo White (brother of Carl White)..)1955 line-up.

The Jayhawks (members Jimmy Johnson, Cleo White, Carl Fisher, Rene Beard and Carver Bunkum)

Flash 105 - Counting My Teardrops / The Devil's Cousin - 1956

The Jayhawks (members Jimmy Johnson, Carl Fisher, Dave Govan and Carver Bunkum)

Flash 109 - Stranded In The Jungle* / My Only Darling - 1956 *covered by The Cadets in 1956 on Modern 994.

The Jayhawks (members Jimmy Johnson, Carl Fisher, Richard Owens, Dave Govan and Don Bradley)

Flash 111 - Love Train / Don't Mind Dyin' - 1956

Earl Palmer and The Jayhawks (members Earl Palmer, Jimmy Johnson, Carl Fisher, Richard Owens, Dave Govan and Don Bradley)

Aladdin 3379 - Johnny's House Party (Part 1) / Johnny's House Party (Part 2) - 1957

The Jayhawks (members Jimmy Johnson, Carl Fisher, Richard Owens, Dave Govan and Don Bradley)

Aladdin 3393 - The Creature / Everyone Should Know - 1957

The Vibes (members members Jimmy Johnson, Carl Fisher, Dave Govan, Richard Owens and Don Bradley (born Donald Bradley on 7-August-1936 in Los Angeles, California))

Allied 10006 - What's Her Name / You Are - 1958

Danny Tyrell with The Cleeshays (members Danny Tyrell, Jimmy Johnson, Carl Fisher, Dave Govan, Richard Owens and Don Bradley)

Eastman 784 - Let's Walk, Let's Talk / You're Only Seventeen - 1958

Sonny Knight with The Cleeshays (members Sonny Knight, Jimmy Johnson, Carl Fisher, Dave Govan, Richard Owens and Don Bradley)

Eastman 784 - Eat Your Mush And Hush / You're Only Seventeen - 1958
Eastman 787 - Eat Your Mush And Hush / Lipstick Kisses - 1958

The Vibes (members Jimmy Johnson, Carl Fisher, Dave Govan, Richard Owens and Don

Bradley)

Allied 10007 - Misunderstood / Let The Old Folks Talk - 1959

The Jayhawks (members Jimmy Johnson, Carl Fisher, Dave Govan, Richard Owens and Don Bradley)

Eastman 792 - I Wish The World Owed Me A Living / Start The Fire - 1959
Eastman 798 - New Love / Betty Brown - 1959

The Vibrations (members Jimmy Johnson, Carl Fisher, Dave Gowan, Don Bradley and Ricky Owens from The Six Teens on FLIP)

Bet 001 - So Blue / Love Me Like You Should - 1960
Checker 954 - So Blue / Love Me Like You Should - 1960
Checker 961 - Cave Man / Feel So Bad - 1960
Checker 967 - Doing The Slop / So Little Time - 1960
Checker 969 - The Watusi / Wallflower - 1961
Checker 974 - The Junkaroo / Continental - 1961

The Marathons (members Jimmy Johnson, Carl Fisher, Dave Gowan, Don Bradley and Ricky Owens) The name change came about when H.B. Barnum convinced The Vibrations to do a little "moonlighting" as he needed an Olympics styled novelty act to cut a single immediately and his "hot" act The Olympics were away on an East Coast tour.

Arvee 5027 - Peanut Butter / Talkin' Trash - 1961 (Checker filed a lawsuit against Arvee records and ended up keeping the Arvee record but Arvee kept the name for use with another unknown group to complete a Marathons Lp)
Argo 5027 - Peanut Butter / Down In New Orleons - 1961
Chess 1790 - Peanut Butter / Down In New Orleons - 1961

The Vibrations (members Jimmy Johnson, Carl Fisher, Dave Gowan, Don Bradley and Ricky Owens (born Richard Edgar Owens on 24-April-1939 in St. Louis, Missourri --- died 6-December-1995 in Los Angeles County, California --- cause: ?))

Checker 982 - Stranded In The Jungle / Don't Say Goodbye - 1961
Checker 987 - All My Love Belongs To You / Stop Right Now - 1961
Checker 990 - Let's Pony Again / What Made You Change Your Mind - 1961
Checker 1002 - Over The Rainbow / Oh Cindy - 1961
Checker 1011 - The New Hully Gully / Anytime - 1962
Checker 1022 - If He Don't / Hamburgers On A Bun - 1962
Checker 1038 - Since I Fell For You / May The Best Man Win - 1963
Atlantic 2204 - Lonesome Little Lonely Girl / Between Hello And Goodbye - 1963
Checker 1061 - Dancing Danny / Dancing Danny - 1963
Atlantic 2221 - My Girl Sloopy* / Daddy Woo - Woo - 1964 *Track Recorded 7-January-1964.

The Jayhawks (members Jimmy Johnson, Carl Fisher, Dave Govan and Carver Bunkum)

Oldies 45 49 - My Only Darling / Stranded In The Jungle - 1964

The Vibrations (members Jimmy Johnson, Carl Fisher, Dave Gowan, Don Bradley and Ricky Owens)

Okeh - Don't Let It Hide - 1964 (previously unissued track which was released in the U. K. on a 2008 Kent Cd "The Vibrating Vibrations The Okeh And Epic Singles 1963 - 1968" CDKEND 304)
Okeh - I Peeped Your Hole Card - 1964 (previously unissued track which was released in the U. K. on a 2008 Kent Cd "The Vibrating Vibrations The Okeh And Epic Singles 1963 - 1968"

CDKEND 304)
Okeh - Follow Your Heart - 1964 (previously unissued track which was released in the U. K. on a 2008 Kent Cd "The Vibrating Vibrations The Okeh And Epic Singles 1963 - 1968" CDKEND 304)
Okeh 7205 - Watusi Time / Sloop Dance - 1964
Okeh 7212 - Hello Happiness / Keep On Keeping On - 1964
Okeh 7220 - Ain't Love That Way / End Up Crying - 1965
Okeh - The Searching Is Over - 1965 (previously unissued track which was released in the U. K. on a 2008 Kent Cd "The Vibrating Vibrations The Okeh And Epic Singles 1963 - 1968" CDKEND 304)
Okeh 7228 - Talkin' About Love / If You Only Knew - 1965
Okeh 7230 - Misty* / Finding Out The Hard Way - 1965 *Recorded 19-November-1964.
Okeh 7238 - Gina / The Story Of A Starry Night - 1966 (Unreleased)
Okeh 7241 - Canadian Sunset / The Story Of A Starry Night - 1966
Okeh 7249 - Gonna Get Along Without You Now* / Forgive And Forget** - 1966 *recorded 29-March-1966 --- Track was also released as "Can't Do Without You" in 1968 by Lee Andrews & The Hearts on Lost Nite 1004. **recorded 5/6-November-1965.
Okeh 7257 - Soul A Go - Go* / And I Love Her** - 1966 *recorded 29-March-1966. **recorded 10-May-1966 --- also recorded in 1964 by The Beatles on Capitol 5235
Okeh 7276 - You Better Beware / Pick Me - 1967
Okeh - Pick Me - 1967 (unissued at the time unedited stereo mix which was released in the U. K. on a 2008 Kent Cd "The Vibrating Vibrations The Okeh And Epic Singles 1963 - 1968" CDKEND 304)
Okeh - Always Had Your Way - 1967 (previously unissued track which was released in the U. K. on a 2008 Kent Cd "The Vibrating Vibrations The Okeh And Epic Singles 1963 - 1968" CDKEND 304)
Okeh 7297 - Together / Come To Yourself - 1967
Okeh 7311 - Love In Them There Hills / Remember The Rain - 1968 (Recorded 1-March-1968)
Amy 11006 - A Shot Of Love / Tra La La La La - 1968
Epic 10418 - 'Cause You're Mine / I Took An Overdose* - 1968 (recorded 1-March-1968)
Epic - 'Cause You're Mine - 1968 (recorded 1-March-1968 --- unissued at the time unedited stereo mix which was released in the U. K. on a 2008 Kent Cd "The Vibrating Vibrations The Okeh And Epic Singles 1963 - 1968" CDKEND 304)
Neptune 19 - Expressway To Your Heart / Who's Gonna Help Me Now - 1969
Neptune 21 - Smoke Signals / Who's Gonna Help Me Now - 1970

The Vibrating Vibrations (members Carl Fisher (lead), Jimmy Johnson (tenor), Dave Govan (baritone) and Don Bradley (bass))

Neptune 28 - Right On Brother - Right On / Surprise Party For Baby - 1970

The Vibrations (members Carl Fisher (lead), Jimmy Johnson (tenor), Dave Govan (baritone) and Don Bradley (bass))

Mandala 2511 - Ain't No Greens In Harlem / Wind Up Toy - 1972
Mandala 2514 - Man Overboard / The Man - 1972
North Bay 307 - Sneakin' / When Will My Turn Come - 1973
Chess 2151 - Make It Last / Shake It Up - 1974

The Vibrations (members Jimmy Johnson, Carl Fisher, Dave Gowan, Don Bradley and Ricky Owens)

Goldies 45 2643 - The Watusi / Wallflower - 1974

The Vibrations / Walter Jackson

Okeh 4-7205 - Sloop Dance / It's All Over* - ? *flip by Walter Jackson (some copies came in purple vinyl)

The Vibrations / Andre Williams

Chess 140 - Watusi / Cadillac Jack - ?

The Bobbettes / The Vibrations

Atlantic Oldies Series 13044 - Mr. Lee / My Girl Sloopy - ? (Back To Back Hits)

The Dells / The Vibrations

Collectables Col 034547 - The Love We Had (Stays On My Mind) / The Watusi* - ? *flip by The Vibrations.

The Ocapellos / The Vibrations

Collectables Col 034667 - The Stars / Oh Cindy* - ? *Flip By The Vibrations.

The Volumes

The Valumes (members Eddie Union, Elijah "Teenie" Davies, Larry Wright, Joe Truvillion and Ernest Newson)

Chex 1002 - I Love You / Dreams - 1962 (The Most Expensive Version Going For $300.00 Usa)
Richard "Popcorn" Wylie playing rhythm on a suitcase -- record took 12 takes.

The Volumes (members Eddie Union, Elijah "Teenie" Davies, Larry Wright, Joe Truvillion and Ernest Newson)

Chex 1002 - I Love You / Dreams - 1962 (Has No Reference To Jay-Gee Records On The Label, This Goes For About $30.00 Usa)
Chex 1002 - I Love You / Dreams - 1962 (Has "Nationally Dist. By Jay-Gee Rec. Co. Inc." Written On The Label, This Goes For About $25.00 Usa)
Chex 1005 - Come Back Into My Heart / The Bell - 1962 (Lamont Dozier On Drums)

The Volumes

Jubilee 5446 - Sandra / Teenage Paradise - 1963
Jubilee 5454 - Our Song / Oh My Mother In Law - 1963
Old Town 1154 - Why / Monkey Hop - 1964
American Arts 6 - Gotta Give Her Love* / I Can't Live Without You - 1964 *Backing Vocals By The Royaltones.
American Arts 18 - I Just Can't Help Myself / One Way Lover - 1965 (Eddie Union leaves in 1965)

The Magnetics (Members: Gerald Mathis (lead singer), Bobby Peterson (the same singer who was in the Magnetics on Allrite), Elijah Davis, Ernest Newsome & William 'Pete' Crawford)

Bonnie 107374 - Lady In Green / Heart You're Made Of Stone - 1965

The Volumes

Astra 1020 - Gotta Give Her Love / I Can't Live Without You - 1965 (Some Copies Issued In Red Vinyl)
Twirl 2016 - I Got Love / Maintain Your Cool - 1966
Impact 1017 - The Trouble I've Seen / That Same Old Feeling - 1966 (Gerald Mathis On Lead Vocal)
Inferno 2001 - You Got It Baby / A Way To Love You - 1967 (Jimmy Burger On Lead Vocal)

Inferno 2004 - My Kind Of Girl / My Road Is The Right Road - 1967
Inferno 5001 - Ain't That Loving You / I Love You Baby - 1968
Karen 1551 - Ain't Gonna Give You Up / Am I Losing You - 1970
Karen 101 - Ain't Gonna Give You Up / Am I Losing You - ?
Virgo ? - 1973
ABC ? - 1973
Collectables Col 038047 - I Love You / Come Back Into My Heart -

The Volumes (Possibly not the same group as above releases)

Garu 107 - I've Never Been So In Love / I'm Gonna Miss You - ?

Group Line Ups

The Whatnauts (Carlos 'Billy' Herndon, Garnett Jones, Gerald 'Chunky' Pickney)
The Whispers (Walter Scott, Wallace Scott, Nicholas Caldwell, Gordy 'Snake' Harmon, Marcus Hudson)

Junior Walker

The Jumping Jacks (members Billy "Sticks" Nicks, Autrey DeWalt III, Willie Woods, ...)

The All Stars (In essence this was a very early form of Jr Walker and the All Stars although the name on the label was Joe Van Battle)

Von 704 - 2-2-5 Special (Part 1) / 2-2-5 Special (Part 2) - ?

Jr. Walker All Stars (members Jr. Walker (saxophone -- born 1931 -- died 23-November-1995 at his home in Battle Creek, Michigan. Cause: diagnosed with cancer in 1993) , Vic Thomas (organ), Willie Woods (guitar - born 5-September-1936, died 27-May-1997 in Kalamazoo, Michigan. Cause: lung cancer) and James Graves (drums -- born 1938 -- died 1967 cause: car crash))

Harvey 113 - Twist Lackawanna / Willie's Blues – 1962
Harvey 117 - Cleo's Mood / Brainwasher – 1962
Harvey 119 - Good Rockin' / Brainwasher - 1963

Jr. Walker & The All Stars (members

Soul 35003 - Monkey Jump / Satan's Blues - 1964

Jr. Walker & All The Stars (members

Soul 35008 - Shot Gun / Hot Cha – 1965

Jr. Walker & The All Stars (members

Soul 35008 - Shotgun / Hot Cha – 1965
Soul 35012 - Do The Boomerang / Tune Up - 1965
Soul 35013 - Shake And Fingerpop / Cleo's Back – 1965
Soul 35013 - Shake And Fingerpop / Leo's Back - 1965 (Mis-Spelt "B" Side)
Soul 35015 - (I'm A) Roadrunner / Shoot Your Shot – 1966
Soul 35017 - Cleo's Mood / Baby You Know You Ain't Right – 1965
Soul 35024 - How Sweet It Is (To Be Loved By You) / Nothin' But Soul - 1966
Soul 35026 - Money (That's What I Want) (Part 1) / Money (That's What I Want) (Part 2) – 1966
Soul 35030 - Pucker Up Buttercup / Anyway You Wannta – 1967
Soul 35036 - Shoot Your Shot / Ain't That The Truth – 1967
Soul 35041 - Come See About Me / Sweet Soul – 1967
Soul 35048 - Hip City (Part 1) / Hip City (Part 2) – 1968
Soul 35055 - Home Cookin' / Mutiny – 1968
Soul 35062 - What Does It Take (To Win Your Love) / Brainwasher (Part 1) – 1969
Soul 35067 - These Eyes / I've Got To Find A Way To Win Maria Back – 1969
Soul 35070 - Gotta Hold On To This Feeling / Clinging To The Thought That She's Coming Back – 1970
Soul 35073 - Do You See My Love (For You Growing) / Groove And Move – 1970
Soul 35081 - Holly Holy / Carry Your Own Load – 1970
Soul 35084 - Take Me Girl, I'm Ready / Right On Brothers And Sisters – 1971
Soul 35090 - Way Back Home (Vocal) / Way Back Home (Instrumental) – 1971
Soul 35095 - Walk In The Night / I Don't Want To Do Wrong – 1972
Soul 35097 - Groove Thang / Me And My Family – 1972
Soul 35104 - Gimme That Beat (Part 1) / Gimme That Beat (Part 2) – 1973
Soul 35106 - I Don't Need No Reason / Country Boy – 1973
Soul 35108 - Peace And Understanding (Is Hard To Find) / Soul Clappin' – 1973
Soul 35110 - Dancin' Like They Do On Soul Train / I Ain't That Easy To Love - 1974

Jr. Walker

Soul 35114 - You Are The Sunshine Of My Life / Until You Come Back To Me (That's What I'm Gonna Do) - 1974 (Unreleased)

Jr. Walker & The All Stars (members

Motown 1352 - What Does It Take (To Win Your Love) / Country Boy - 1975

Jr. Walker (born Oscar G. Mixon (later his name was changed to Autry DeWalt III) in Blytheville, Arkansas)

Motown 1380 - I'm So Glad / Hot Shot - 1976 (Unreleased)
Soul 35116 - I'm So Glad / Soul Clappin' - 1976 (Unreleased)
Soul 35118 - You Ain't No Ordinary Woman / Hot Shot - 1976
Soul 35122 - Hard Love / Whopper Bopper Show Stopper – 1977
Whitfield 8861 - Back Street Boogie / Don't Let Me Go Astray – 1979
Whitfield 49052 - Wishing On A Star / Hole In The Wall - 1979

Foreigner

Atlantic 3831 - Urgent* / Girl On The Moon - 1981 *Saxophone Jr. Walker.

Jr. Walker

Motown 1689 - Blow The House Down / Ball Baby (Instrumental) – 1983
Motown 1708 - Rise And Shine / Closer Than Close - 1983 (Unissued)

Jr. Walker & The All Stars

Washington Hit Makers 1007 - I'll Go Where Your Music Takes Me / I'll Go Where Your Music Takes Me (Radio Version) / I'll Go Where Your Music Takes Me (Long Version) - 1989 (12" Release)
Washington Hit Makers 1007 - I'll Go Where Your Music Takes Me / I'll Go Where Your Music Takes Me - 1989 (7" Release)

Jr. Walker & The All Stars (members

Collectables Col 466 - Shotgun / Do The Boomerang - ?

Ep's

SOUL 60701 - SHOTGUN - 1965 Tracks: Shotgun / Roadrunner / Shake And Fingerpop /// Cleo's Mood / Do The Boomerang / Cleo's Back.

SOUL 60702 - SOUL SESSIONS - 1966 Tracks: Good Rockin' / Shake Everything / Mark Anthony (Speaks) /// Decidedly / Brainwasher / Three Four Three.

SOUL 60703 - ROAD RUNNER - 1967: Tracks: (I'm A) Road Runner / How Sweet It Is (To Be Loved By You) / Last Call /// Pucker Up Buttercup / Baby You Know You Ain't Right / Twist Lackawanna.

Justine 'Baby' Washington

The Hearts Vocal Quartet Dave McRae Orch. (members Justine Washington, Anna Barnhill, Joyce Peterson and Theresa Chatman)

Baton 222 - Going Home To Stay / Disappointed Bride - 1956 (with Rex Garvin on piano)

The Jaynetts (Members Justine Washington, Anna Barnhill, Joyce Peterson And Theresa Chatman)

J&S 1765/1766 - I Wanted To Be Free / Where Are You Tonight - 1956

Baby Washington / The Shytone Five Orchestra

J&S 1655/1656 - Everyday / Smitty's Rock (Instrumental)* - 1957 *Flip By The Shytone Five Orchestra.

The Hearts (Members Justine Washington, Anna Barnhill, Joyce Peterson And Theresa Chatman)

J&S 1660 - You Say You Love Me / So Long Baby - 1957
J&S 1657 - Dancing In A Dream World / You Needn't Tell Me, I Know - 1957

Baby Washington (Born Justine Washington On 13-October-1940 In Bamberg, South Carolina)

J&S 1604 - Congratulations Honey / There Must Be A Reason - 1957

Baby Washington With Orchestra

J&S 1607/1608 - Ah-Ha / Been A Long Time Baby - 1958

Baby Washington / The Jaynetts

J&S 1619/1620 - Hard Way To Go / Be My Boyfriend* - 1958 *Flip By The Jaynetts.

The Jaynetts

J&S 1765/1766 - I Wanted To Be Free / Where Are You Tonight - 1958 (this 45 is actually "Baby" Washington singing lead on two songs for The Hearts, that had been recorded in 1957. This set of The Jaynetts was Zell Sanders (the president of J &S records) way of keeping all The Hearts various members together and also of having enough members to form two groups. Zell Sanders would not use this name again for another five years)

Baby Washington with Orchestra

Neptune 101 - The Time* / You Never Could Be Mine - 1958 *covered in 1961 by The Del Pris on Varbee 2003 and in 1973 by Inez Foxx on Volt 4093.

Baby Washington

J&S 1632/33 - I Hate To See You Go / Knock Yourself Out - 1959
Checker 918 - I Hate To See You Go / Knock Yourself Out – 1959
Neptune 104 - The Bells (On Our Wedding Day) / Why Did My Baby Put Me Down - 1959 (background vocals by The De Vaurs)
Neptune 107 - Workout / Let's Love In The Moonlight - 1959 (backing vocals The Plants and background vocals by The De Vaurs)
Neptune 116 - Deep Down Love / Your Mama Knows What's Right - circa 1960

Jeanette B. Washington

Neptune 120 - Medicine Man / Tears Fall - 1960 (background vocals by The De Vaurs)

Jeanette (Baby) Washington

Neptune 121 - Too Late / Move On – 1960
Neptune 122 - Nobody Cares (About Me) / Money's Funny - 1961 (background vocals by The De Vaurs)

Jeanette "Baby" Washington

ABC Paramount 10223 - Let Love Go By / My Time To Cry – 1961
ABC Paramount 10245 - There You Go Again / Don't Cry, Foolish Heart – 1961

Baby Washington

Sue 764 - Go On / No Tears – 1962
Sue 767 - A Handful Of Memories* / Careless Hands - 1962 *also recorded by Tutti Hill but unissued until released in the U. K. on a 2002 Kent CD "The Arock & Sylvia Story" CDKEND 212.
Sue 769 - Hush Heart / I've Got A Feeling – 1962
Sue 783 - That's How Heartaches Are Made* / There He Is** - 1963 *also recorded in 1968 by Bobby Hutton on Blue Rock 4055. **also recorded in 1964 as "There She Is" by Roy Hamilton on M-G-M 13217.
J&S 1001 - (Love Me) Or Leave Me Alone / It's Been A Long Time – 1963

Sue 790 - Leave Me Alone / You And The Night And The Music – 1963
Sue 794 - Hey Lonely / Doodlin' – 1963

Justine Washington

Sue 797 - I Can't Wait Until I See My Baby's Face* / Who's Going To Take Care Of Me - 1963 *also recorded in 1964 by Pat Thomas on Verve 10333 and in 1967 by The Monticellos on Red Cap 102 plus in 1969 by Sonji Clay on Songee 1002.

Baby Washington

Sue 104 - The Clock / Standing On The Pier - 1964
Sue 114 - It'll Never Be Over For Me* / Move On Drifter - 1964 *also released in the U. K. in 1968 by Timi Yuro on Liberty 15182
Sue 119 - Run My Heart / Your Fool – 1964

Justine Washington

Sue 124 - I Can't Wait Until I See My Baby's Face / Who's Going To Take Care Of Me – 1965

Baby Washington

Sue 129 - Only Those In Love / The Ballad Of Bobby Dawn – 1965
Sue 137 - No Time For Pity / There He Is – 1965
Sue 149 - White Christmas / Silent Night - 1966
Sue 150 - You Are What You Are / Either You're With Me (Or Either You're Not) – 1967
Veep 1274 - White Christmas / Silent Night- 1967
Sue 4 - I Know* / It'll Change (Instrumental) - 1968 *also recorded in 1961 by Barbara George on A. F. O. 302.
Veep 1297 - Think About The Good Times* / Hold Back The Dawn - 1969 *written by Sidney Barnes & J. J. Jackson.
Cotillion 44047 - I Don't Know / I Can't Afford To Lose Him* -1969 *also recorded in 1967 by Ella Washington on Sound Stage 7 2597.
Cotillion 44055 - Breakfast In Bed* / What Becomes Of A Broken Heart** - 1969 *also recorded in 1969 by Dusty Springfield on Atlantic 2606. **also recorded as "What Becomes Of The Brokenhearted" in 1966 by Jimmy Ruffin on Soul 35022
Trip 6 - That's How Heartaches Are Made / Only Those In Love - 1970
Cotillion 44065 - I Love You Brother / Let Them Talk – 1970
Cotillion 44086 - Don't Let Me Lose This Dream / I'm Good Enough For You – 1970
Chess 2099 - Is It Worth It / Happy Birthday – 1970
Master 5 901 - Baby Let Me Get Close To You / I Just Wanna Be Near To You - 1972
Master 5 9102 - Tell Me A Lie / Just Can't Get You Off My Mind - 1972
Trip 100 - The Time / Nobody Cares (About Me) - 1972
Trip 101 - The Bells (On Our Wedding Day) / Work Out - 1972

Baby Washington & Don Gardner

Master 5 9103 - Forever* / Baby Let Me Get Close To You - 1973 *originally recorded in 1957 as "Darling Forever" by The Four Chevelles on Delft 357

Baby Washington

Master 5 9104 - Just Can't Get You Out Of My Mind / You (Just A Dream) - 1973
Master 5 9107 - I've Got To Break Away From You / You (Just A Dream) - 1973
Master 5 9109 - Can't Get Over Losing You* / Just Can't Get You Out Of My Mind - 1974 *also recorded in 1972 by Donnie Elbert on All Platinum 2336.

Baby Washington & Don Gardner

Master 5 9110 - Lay A Little Lovin' On Me / Baby Let Me Get Closer To You - 1974

People 101 - Forever* / Baby Let Me Get Close To You - 1974? *also recorded in 1963 by The Marvelettes on Tamla 54077.

Baby Washington

Master 5 3500 - Care Free / Can't Get Over Losing You* - 1975 *written by Donnie Elbert.
Master 5 3502 - Tell Me A Lie / Just Can't Get You Out Of My Mind – 1975

Jeanette (Baby) Washington

Sixth Avenue 10816 - Either You Love Me Or Leave Me (3:40) / Either You Love Me Or Leave Me (4:27) - 1976 (promo issue only)
Sixth Avenue 10816 - Either You Love Me Or Leave Me / Cup (Runneth Over) - 1976

Baby Washington

Master 5 545 - Tear After Tear / I've Got To Break Away – 1978

Jeanette "Baby" Washington

Avi 253 - I Wanna Dance / I Can't Get Over Losing You – 1978

Baby Washington

7I 3000 - Turn Your Boogie Loose / Turn, Turn, Turn – 1979
Law-Ton 1660 - Come See About Me / You Are Just A Dream – 1980

Baby Washington / Charles Brown

Liberty 1393 - Silent Night / Merry Christmas Baby* - 1980 *Flip By Charles Brown Only.

Baby Washington

Collectables Col 013097 - That's How Heartaches Are Made / There He Is - 1980's
Collectables Col 014107 - The Bells / Why Did My Baby Put Me Down - 1980's

The Soul Sisters / Baby Washington

Collectables Col 031497 - I Can't Stand It / Only Those In Love* - 1980's (flip by Baby Washington)

Baby Washington

Master Five 1001 - Crying In The Midnight Hour / Pedestal – 1988

Mary Wells

Mary Wells (born Mary Esther Wells on the 13-May-1943 in Detroit, Michigan ---- died 26-July-1992 at UCLA's Kenneth Norris Jr. Cancer Center in Los Angeles --- cause: cancer of the larynx)

Motown 1003 - Bye, Bye Baby* / Please Forgive Me - 1960 *also recorded in 1967 by Betty Everett on ABC 10861.

Motown 1011 - I Don't Want To Take A Chance / I'm Sorry - 1961 (pink "lines" label scarcer than blue "map" label)
Motown 1016 - Strange Love / Come To Me* - 1961 (some copies issued with picture sleeve) *also released in 1959 by Marv Johnson Vocal Accompaniment by the Rayber Voices on Tamla 101
Motown 1024 - The One Who Really Loves You / I'm Gonna Stay – 1962
Motown 1032 - You Beat Me To The Punch / Old Love (Let's Try It Again)* - 1962 *covered in 1964 by Martha & The Vandellas on Motown 1032.
Motown 1035 - Two Lovers / Operator – 1962
Motown 1039 - Laughing Boy / Two Wrongs Don't Make A Right – 1963
Acetate Jd-109 - Second Time Around / I'll Never Stop Loving You - 1963 (Unissued)
Acetate Jd-122 - I Wanna Be Around / ? - 1963 (Unissued)
Acetate Jd-150 - Drop In The Bucket / ? - 1963 (Unissued)

The Marvelettes / Mary Wells / Miracles / Marvin Gaye

Tamla/Motown - Album Excerpts - 1963 (though from Tamla / Motown, no label name is shown, nor is there a title -- promo issue only)

Mary Wells

Motown 1042 - Your Old Stand By / What Love Has Joined Together* - 1963 *covered in 1965 by The Temptations on Gordy 7040.
Motown 1048 - You Lost The Sweetest Boy / What's Easy For Two Is So Hard For One - 1963 (some copies issued with picture sleeve)
Motown 1056 - My Guy* / Oh Little Boy (What Did You Do To Me)** - 1964 *the track was recorded 2-March-1964. The session lineup was Earl Van Dyke (organ), Johnny Griffith (piano), Eddie Wills (guitar), Robert White (guitars), James Jamerson (bass), Benny Benjamin (drums), Dave Hamilton (vibes), Herbert Williams (trumpet), Russ Conway (trumpet), Paul Riser (trombone) and George Bohannon (trombone). There was an "answer" record to this track recorded in 1964 titled "Your Guy" by Bobby Wells on Mercury 72272. **backing vocals by Liz Lands.

Marvin Gaye & Mary Wells

Motown 1057 - Once Upon A Time / What's The Matter With You Baby – 1964

Mary Wells

Motown 1061 - When I'm Gone / Guarantee For A Lifetime – 1964
Motown 1065 - Whisper You Love Me / I'll Be Available – 1964
20th Century Fox 544 - Ain't It The Truth / Stop Takin' Me For Granted – 1964
20th Century Fox 555 - Use Your Head / Everlovin' Boy – 1965
20th Century Fox 570 - Never, Never Leave Me / Why Don't You Let Yourself Go – 1965
20th Century Fox 590 - He's A Lover / I'm Learnin' – 1965
20th Century Fox 6606 - Me Without You / I'm Sorry – 1965
20th Century Fox 6619 - I Should Have Known Better / Please Please Me – 1965
Atco 6392 - Dear Lover / Can't You See (You're Losing Me) * - 1965 *Recorded 26-November-1965 in Chicago.
Atco 6423 - Keep Me In Suspense* / Such A Sweet Thing - 1966 *Recorded 10-May-1966.
Atco 6436 - Fancy Free / Me And My Baby – 1966
Atco 6469 - Coming Home / Hey You Set My Soul On Fire – 1967
Jubilee 5621 - The Doctor / Two Lovers' History – 1968
Jubilee 5629 - Can't Get Away From Your Love / A Woman In Love – 1968
Jubilee 5639 - Don't Look Back / 500 Miles – 1968
Jubilee 5676 - Mind Reader / Never Give A Man The World – 1969
Jubilee 5684 - Dig The Way I Feel / Love Shooting Bandit – 1969
Jubilee 5695 - Sweet Love / It Must Be – 1970

Jubilee 5718 - Mr. Tough / Never Give A Man The World – 1971
Reprise 1031 - I Found What I Wanted / I See A Future In You – 1971
Reprise 1308 - If You Can't Give Her Love (Give Her Up) / Cancel My Subscription – 1974
Epic 49-02663 - Gigolo (6:15) / Let's Mix It Up - 1981 (12" Release)
Epic 14-02664 - Gigolo (3:15) / I'm Changing My Ways – 1982~
Epic 14-02855 - These Arms (4:09) / Spend The Nights With Me – 1982
Epic 49-02873 - These Arms (5:30) / Spend The Nights With Me - 1982 (12" Release)

Marvin Gaye / Marvin Gaye & Mary Wells

Motown Mots7-2083 - My Last Chance / Once Upon A Time - 1990

Rudy West & The Five Keys

The Sentimental Four (members Rudy West (born 25-July-1933 in Newport News, Virginia --- died 14-May-1988 --- cause: heart attack following cancer treatment), Bernie West, Ripley Ingram (born 21-January-1930 --- died 23-March-1995 --- cause: ?) and Raphael Ingram) 1945 gospel group from which The Five Keys originated -- no known recordings.

The Sentimental Four (members Rudy West, Bernie West, Ripley Ingram, Raphael Ingram and Edwin Hall) 1949 lineup. Mid 1949 Raphael Ingram gets drafted as is replaced by James "Dickie" Smith, former member of local group The Virginia Brown Dots.

The 5 Keys (members Rudy West, Bernie West, Ripley Ingram, Dickie Smith and Edwin Hall) 1950 group lineup.

The 5 Keys (members Rudy West, Bernie West, Ripley Ingram, Dickie Smith and Maryland Pierce)

Aladdin 3085 - With A Broken Heart / Too Late - 1951 (Due To A Pressing Plant Error Some Copies Of This Single Had A Floyd Dixon Song In Place Of "With A Broken Heart").
Aladdin 3099 - Hucklebuck With Jimmy / The Glory Of Love - 1951
Aladdin 3113 - Old Mcdonald / It's Christmas Time - 1951
Aladdin 3118 - Old McDonald* / Yes Sir, That's My Baby** - 1952 *lead Maryland Pierce. **leads Rudy West & Dickie Smith.
Aladdin 3118 - Old McDonald* / Yes Sir, That's My Baby - 1952 *two known copies play "Teardrops From My Eyes" instead of "Old McDonald".
Aladdin 3127 - Red Sails In The Sunset* / Be Anything But Be Mine* - 1952 *leads Rudy West & Dickie Smith. ("Red Sails In The Sunset" was a 1935 hit for Bing Crosby, while the flip was a hit for Eddie Howard).
Aladdin 3131 - Mistakes / How Long - 1952
Aladdin 3136 - I Hadn't Told Anyone Till You / Hold Me - 1952
Aladdin 3158 - I Cried For You / Serve Another Round - 1952
Aladdin 3167 - Come Go My Bail Louise / Can't Keep From Crying - 1953
Aladdin 3175 - Mama (Your Daughter Told A Lie On Me) / There Ought To Be A Law - 1953
Aladdin 3190 - These Foolish Things / Lonesome Old Story - 1953
Aladdin 3204 - Teardrops In Your Eyes / I'm So High - 1953
Aladdin 3214 - My Saddest Hour / Oh! Babe - 1953 (Flat Blue Label Is Scarcer Than Glossy Blue Label Release.)
Aladdin 3228 - Love My Loving / Someday Sweetheart - 1954

Dickie Smith with Don Gardner & His Sonotones

Bruce 103 - New Kind Of Love / When You're Gone - 1954 (with Don Gardner & His Sonotones -- having some time before entering the services, Willie Winfield, Dickie's cousin sets him up a recording session with Bruce records)

The 5 Keys

Aladdin 3245 - Deep In My Heart / How Do You Expect Me To Get It - 1954
Groove 0031 - I'll Follow You / Lawdy Miss Mary - 1954 (Promo Issues Only)
Capitol 2945 - Ling, Ting, Tong* / I'm Alone* - 1954 *lead Maryland Pierce --- this track was also recorded in 1954 by The Charms on Deluxe 6076. (Rudy West is discharged from the army and rejoins the group -- Ulysses Hicks is kept on with the intention of phasing him out, all this is done with his knowledge)
Capitol 3032 - Close Your Eyes* / Doggone It, You Did It** - 1955 *leads Maryland Pierce & Rudy West --- also recorded in 1967 by Peaches and Herb on Date 1549. **lead Maryland Pierce. (1st - February - 1955 Ulysses Hicks dies of a heart attack at age 25 while still touring with the group)
Aladdin 3263 - My Love / Why, Oh Why - 1955
Capitol 3127 - The Verdict / Me Make Um Pow Wow - 1955
Capitol 3185 - Don't You Know I Love You /' I Wish I'd Never Learned To Read - 1955
Capitol 3267 - Cause You're My Lover / Gee Whittakers - 1955
Aladdin 3312 - Story Of Love / Serve Another Round - 1956
Capitol 3318 - What Goes On / You Broke The Rules Of Love - 1956
Capitol 3392 - I Dreamt I Dwelt In Heaven / She's The Most -1955 (Small Hole Release Is Scarcer Than Large Hole Release)
Capitol 3455 - Peace And Love / My Pigeon's Gone - 1956
Capitol 3502 - Out Of Sight, Out Of Mind / That's Right - 1956
Capitol 3597 - Wisdom Of A Fool / Now Don't That Prove I Love You - 1956
Capitol T-828 - Just For A Thrill / The Gypsy - 1957 (Promo Issue Only)
Capitol 3660 - Let There Be You / Tiger Lily - 1957
Capitol 3710 - It's A Groove / Four Walls - 1957
Capitol 3738 - This I Promise You / The Blues Don't Care - 1957
Capitol 3786 - Boom-Boom / The Face Of An Angel - 1957
Capitol 3830 - Do Anything / It's A Crying Shame - 1957
Capitol 3861 - From Me To You / Whippety Whirl - 1957
Capitol 3948 - With All My Love / You're For Me - 1958
Capitol 4009 - Handy Andy / Emily Please - 1958
Capitol 4092 - One Great Love / Really-O Truly-O - 1958 (Rudy West Leaves The Group)
King 5251 - I Took Your Love For A Toy / Ziggus - 1959
King 5273 - Dream On / Dancing Senorita - 1959

Rudy West (backed by studio group)

King 5276 - Just To Be With You / You Were Mine - 1959
King 5385 - My Mother's Prayers / As Sure As I Live - 1959

The 5 Keys

King 5302 - How Can I Forget You / I Burned Your Letter - 1959

Rudy West (backed by studio group)

King 5305 - The Measure Of My Love / This Is Something Else - 1959

The 5 Keys

King 5330 - Gonna Be Too Late / Rosetta - 1960
King 5358 - I Didn't Know / No Says My Heart - 1960
King 5398 - Valley Of Love / Bimbo -1960 (infighting leads to the breakup of the group, Maryland

Pierce decided to keep The Five Keys going with a new lineup consisting of himself, Gene Moore, Raymond Haskiss, Daytill "Pepper" Jones and Ramon Loper rejoins group -- group stayed together a few months then Maryland Pierce left)
King 5446 - You Broke The Only Heart / That's What You're Doing To Me - 1961
King 5496 - Stop Your Crying / Do Something For Me - 1961

Rudy West & The Five Keys (members Rudy West, Bernie West, Ripley Ingram, James "Saggy" Boyd and Willie Friday)

Seg-Way 1008 - Out Of Sight, Out Of Mind / You're The One - 1961

The Five Keys

Imperial 016 - The Glory Of Love / My Saddest Hour - 1962

The Fantastic Five Keys

Capitol 4828 - From The Bottom Of My Heart* / Out Of Sight Out Of Mind** - 1962 *lead Maryland Pierce. **lead Rudy West --- also recorded in 1967 by Carol Fran on Roulette 4719

Jesse Belvin & The Five Keys / Feathers

Candlelite 427 - Love Song* / Why Don't You Write Me** - 1963 *the group was actually Bobby Relf & The Laurels. **flip by The Feathers the Aladdin group.

The Five Keys

Capitol 6049 - Close Your Eyes / The Verdict - 1964
King 5877 - I'll Never Stop Loving You / I Can't Escape From You - 1964
Bangar 661 - Run-Around / I Tell My Heart - 1965

Rudy West & The Five Keys (members Rudy West, Bernie West, Ripley Ingram, James "Saggy" Boyd and Willie Friday)

Inferno 4500 - No Matter / Hey Girl - 1967 (This 45 Was Recorded At The Seg-Way Session)

The Five Keys

Capitol 6186 - Out Of Sight Out Of Mind / The Verdict - 1972
Capitol 6192 - Ling, Ting, Tong / Wisdom Of A Fool - 1972

The Five Keys / The Marylanders

Roadhouse 1003 - Sweetheart / Sittin' Here Wondering - Flip Side By The Marylanders.

The 5 Keys

United Artists Xw150 - The Glory Of Love / My Saddest Hour - 1972 (Silver Spotlight Series)

The Five Keys featuring Rudy West

Ram Landmark 101 - Goddess Of Love / Stop What You're Doing To Me - 1973

The Five Keys

Owl 321 - A Dreamer / Your Teeth And Your Tongue - 1973
Bim Bam Boom 116 - Out Of Sight Out Of Mind / Close Your Eyes - 1973 (An A Capella 45)

The Five Keys / Marvin & Johnny

Liberty 1394 - It's Christmas Time / It's Christmas** - 1980 *lead Rudy West. **flip by Marvin & Johnny

The Five Keys

Gusto 2141 - Gonna Be Too Late* / Your Teeth And Tongue* - ? *Lead Maryland Pierce.

Rudy West of The Five Keys with Rhythm Accompaniment

Classic Artists 112 - Miracle Moment Of Love* / When Was The Last Time* - 1989 *lead Rudy West. (1000 copies made in red vinyl and 1000 copies made in black vinyl)
Classic Artists 115 - I Want You For Christmas / Express Yourself Back Home - 1989 (1000 copies made in red vinyl and 1000 copies made in black vinyl)

The Five Keys / Fats Domino

The Right Stuff S7-19768 - Every Heart Is Home At Christmas / Frosty The Snowman - 1997 flip by Fats Domino.

The Five Keys

Collectables Col 060127 - Out Of Sight, Out Of Mind / Ling Ting Tong - ?
Collectables Col 061717 - It's Christmas Time / Red Sails In The Sunset - ?

Kim Weston

The Wright Specials (member Kim Weston, ...) although a member of the group Kim Weston has stated that she never recorded with the group

Kim Weston (born ? - December-1939 in Detroit, Michigan)

Tamla 54076 - It Should Have Been Me* / Love Me All The Way - 1963 *also recorded in 1968 by Gladys Knight & The Pips on SOUL 35045 and in 1974 by Yvonne Fair on Motown 1323.
Tamla 54085 - Just Loving You / Another Train Coming - 1963
Tamla 54100 - Looking For The Right Guy - 1964 (one sided promo disc)

Marvin Gaye & Kim Weston

Tamla 54104 - What Good Am I Without You / I Want You 'Round - 1964

Hitsville U.S.A. Dm 097311 - Greetings To Tamla Motown Appreciation Society - 1964 (This American 45 Was Limited To 300 Copies For Dispersal Throughout The Various Fan Clubs Within Europe As A Promo For Their First European Tour. Each Act Gives An Individual Greeting Over It's Latest Record. Artists Involved Include, The Miracles, Stevie Wonder, Marvin Gaye, The Marvelettes, The Temptations, Martha And The Vandellas, The Contours, Eddie Holland, Kim Weston And The Supremes. The Record Has An Introduction From Publicist Margaret Phelps And Berry Gordy.

Kim Weston

Tamla 54106 - A Little More Love / Go Ahead And Laugh - 1964
Tamla 54110 - I'm Still Loving You / Go Ahead And Laugh - 1964
Gordy 7041 - I'll Never See My Love Again / A Thrill A Moment - 1965
Gordy 7046 - Take Me In Your Arms (Rock Me A Little While) / Don't Compare Me To Her - 1965
Gordy 7050 - Helpless / A Love Like Yours (Don't Come Knocking Every Day) - 1966

Marvin Gaye & Kim Weston

Tamla 54141 - It Takes Two / It's Got To Be A Miracle (This Thing Called Love) - 1966

Kim Weston

Mgm 13720 - I Got What I Need / Someone Like You - 1967
Mgm 13804 - That's Groovy / Land Of Tomorrow - 1967
Mgm 13881 - Nobody / You're Just The Kind Of Guy - 1967
Mgm 13927 - Lift Every Voice And Sing / This Is America - 1968
Mgm 13928 - The Impossible Dream / When Johnny Comes Marching Home - 1968
Mgm 13992 - I Will Understand / Thankful - 1968

Johnny Nash & Kim Weston

Banyan Tree 1001 - We Try Harder / My Time - 1969

Kim Weston

Banyan Tree 1002 - Changes / Both Sides Now - 1969
People 1001 - Danger-Heartbreak Ahead / I'll Be Thinkin' - 1970
Pride 1 - Lift Ev ' Ry Voice And Sing / This Is America - 1970
Volt 1502 - If I Had My Way / Gonna Be Alright - 1971
Volt 1503 - Little By Little, Bit By Bit / (I Wanna Be A) Hang-Up To You - 1971
Mikim 1502 - If I Had My Way / If I Had My Way - 1971 (Promo Issue Only)
Mikim 1502 - If I Had It My Way / Gonna Be Alright - 1971
Mikim 1503 - Little By Little And Bit By Bit / (I Wanna Be A) Hang Up To You - 1971
Mikim 1504 - The Choice Is Up To You / Buy Myself A Man - 1972
Enterprise 9101 - Beautiful People / Goodness Gracious - 1974
Rahkim 101 - Detroit (That's My Home Town) / (Instrumental) - 1975

Danny White

Danny White (born Joseph Daniel White on 6-July-1931 in New Orleans, Louisiana one time member of Huey Smith & the Clowns --- Died 5-January-1996 in Capitol Heights, Maryland --- cause: stroke)

Dot 16188 - Give A Take / Somebody Please Help Me - 1961
Frisco 104 - Kiss Tomorrow Goodbye* / The Little Bitty Things - 1963 *also recorded in 1977 by Reuben Bell on Alarm 2118.
Frisco 106 - Never Tell Your Friend / Make Her Mine - 1963
Frisco 109 - The Twitch / Why Must I Be Blue - 1963
Frisco 110 - One Little Lie / Loan Me A Hankerchief - 1963
ABC-Paramount 10525 - One Little Lie / Loan Me A Hankerchief - 1964
ABC-Paramount 10569 - Hold What You Got / I've Surrendered - 1964
ABC-Paramount 10589 - Moonbeam / Love Is A Way Of Life - 1964
Frisco 110 - Miss Fine, Miss Fine / Can't Do Nothing Without You - 1965
Frisco 112 - Miss Fine Miss Fine / Can't Do Nothing Without You - 1965

Frisco 114 - My Living Doll / Note On The Table - 1965
Kashe 443 - Never Like This / King For A Day - 1965
Atlas 1257 - I'm Dedicating My Life / Keep My Woman Home - 1965
Atteru 2000 - I'm Dedicating My Life / Keep My Woman Home - 1966 (much higher quality than Atlas pressing)
Unity 1257-1/2 - I'm Dedicating My Life / Keep My Woman Home - ?
Decca 32048 - Taking Inventory* / Cracked Up Over You** - 1966 *also recorded in 19 by Vic Waters & The Entertainers on Capitol 2406. **also recorded in 19 by Lee Rogers on Wheelsville 118.
Decca 32106 - You Can Never Keep A Good Man Down / Kiss Tomorrow Goodbye - 1967
SSS International 754 - Natural Soul Brother / One Way Love Affair - 1968
Rocky Coast 19765 - Dance Little Lady Dance / Dance Little Lady Dance (Instrumental) - 1977
Rocky Coast 19767 - Now That I Found You / (You Gotta) Help Me Girl - 1977

Spencer Wiggins

The New Rival Gospel Singers (members Maxine Wiggins, Spencer Wiggins, Percy Wiggins,.)

The Four Stars (members Spencer Wiggins, Percy Wiggins, David Porter and Tyrone ?)

The Southern Wonder Juniors (members Spencer Wiggins, Percy Wiggins,..)

Spencer Wiggins (born 1942 in Memphis, Tennessee)

Bandstand USA 1004 - Lover's Crime / What Do You Think About My Baby - 1965
Goldwax_118 - Love Works That Way / I'll Be True To You - ? (bootleg which came out years after Goldwax ceased to exist --- all boots skip)
Goldwax 308 - Take Me Just As I Am / The Kind Of Woman That's Got No Heart – 1966
Goldwax 312 - Old Friend (You Asked Me If I Miss Her) / Walking Out On You – 1966
Goldwax 321 - Uptight Good Woman* / Anything You Do Is Alright – 1967 *also recorded in 1967 as "Uptight Good Man" by Laura Lee on Chess 2030.
Goldwax 330 - Lonely Man / The Power Of A Woman - 1967
Goldwax - Let's Talk It Over - 1967 (recorded 27-July-1967 --- although unissued on vinyl at the time this was originally released on a Japanese P-VINE Cd, and in the U. K. on 1998 Goldmine Cd "Northern Soul Satisfaction" GSCD88. It was also released on Torch 001 a somewhat dubious 7" single in the U. K. It has now been released in the U. K. on a 2009 Kent Cd "Goldwax Northern Soul" CDKEND 313 plus released 2010 in the U. K. on a Kent Cd "Spencer Wiggins Feed The Flame The Fame And XL Recordings" CDKEND 340)
Goldwax – Love Attack – (recorded 27-July-1967 --- also recorded in 1966 by James Carr on Goldwax 309. This unissued at the time track was recorded at Goldwax and sold to Fame but not released. It can be found on a 2009 Kent Cd released in the U. K. titled "Goldwax Northern Soul" CDKEND 313 and released 2010 in the U. K. on a Kent Cd "Spencer Wiggins Feed The Flame The Fame And XL Recordings" CDKEND 340)
Goldwax – We Gotta Make Up Baby – 1967 (recorded 27-July-1967 --- unissued at the time this was released 2010 in the U. K. on a Kent Cd "Spencer Wiggins Feed The Flame The Fame And XL Recordings" CDKEND 340)
Goldwax – Love Works That Way – 1967 (recorded 27-July-1967 --- unissued at the time this was released 2010 in the U. K. on a Kent Cd "Spencer Wiggins Feed The Flame The Fame And XL Recordings" CDKEND 340)
Goldwax – Water - 1967 (recorded 27-July-1967 --- unissued at the time this was released 2010 in the U. K. on a Kent Cd "Spencer Wiggins Feed The Flame The Fame And XL Recordings" CDKEND 340)
Goldwax – Cry To Me - 1967 (recorded 27-July-1967 --- unissued at the time this was released 2010 in the U. K. on a Kent Cd "Spencer Wiggins Feed The Flame The Fame And XL Recordings" CDKEND 340. Song was also recorded in 1961 by Solomon Burke on Atlantic 2147

and in 1963 by Betty Harris on Jubilee 5456)
Goldwax - Let's Talk It Over - 1967 (although unissued on vinyl at the time this was originally released on a Japanese P-VINE Cd, and in the U. K. on a 1998 Goldmine Cd "Northern Soul Satisfaction" GSCD88. It was also released on Torch 001 a somewhat dubious 7" single in the U. K.)
Goldwax 333 - That's How Much I Love You / I'm A Poor Man's Son - 1968
Goldwax - That's How Much I Love You - (unissued alternate version which was released in 2006 in the U. K. on a Kent Cd "Spencer Wiggins The Goldwax Years" CDKEND 262)
Goldwax - I'm A Poor Man's Son - (unissued alternate version which was released in 2006 in the U. K. on a Kent Cd "Spencer Wiggins The Goldwax Years" CDKEND 262)
Goldwax 337 - Once In A While (Is Better Than Never At All) / He's Too Old - 1968
Goldwax - Once In A While (Is Better Than Never At All) - (unissued extended version (3:33 minutes) which was released in 2006 in the U. K. on a Kent Cd "Spencer Wiggins The Goldwax Years" CDKEND 262)
Goldwax 339 - I Never Loved A Woman (The Way I Love You)* / Soul City U. S. A. - 1969 *on slide guitar Duane "Skydog" Allman. Song was originally recorded in 1967 as "I Never Loved A Man (The Way I Love You)" by Aretha Franklin on Atlantic 2386.
Fame 1463 - Love Machine / Love Me Tonight* - 1969 *recorded 27-July-1967. Song was also recorded in 1967 by Carmol Taylor on Timmy 40,008
Fame 1470 - Double Lovin'* / I'd Rather Go Blind** – 1970 *also recorded in 1971 by The Osmonds on M-G-M K 14259. **also recorded in 1967 by Etta James on Cadet 5578.
Fame – I'm At The Breaking Point - ? (unissued at the time this was released 2010 in the U. K. on a Kent Cd "Spencer Wiggins Feed The Flame The Fame And XL Recordings" CDKEND 340)
Fame – This Love Is Gonna Be True - ? (unissued at the time this was released 2010 in the U. K. on a Kent Cd "Spencer Wiggins Feed The Flame The Fame And XL Recordings" CDKEND 340)
Fame – Holding On To A Dying Love - ? (unissued at the time this was released 2010 in the U. K. on a Kent Cd "Spencer Wiggins Feed The Flame The Fame And XL Recordings" CDKEND 340)
Fame – Make Me Yours - ? (unissued at the time this was released 2010 in the U. K. on a Kent Cd "Spencer Wiggins Feed The Flame The Fame And XL Recordings" CDKEND 340. Song was also recorded in 1967 by Bettye Swann on Money 126 and in 1977 by Jackie Moore on Kayvette 5129 and in 1980 by Bobby Montgomery on Highland 078.
Fame – Ooh-Be Ooh-Be-Doo - ? (unissued at the time this was released 2010 in the U. K. on a Kent Cd "Spencer Wiggins Feed The Flame The Fame And XL Recordings" CDKEND 340)
Fame – Hit And Run - ? (unissued at the time this was released 2010 in the U. K. on a Kent Cd "Spencer Wiggins Feed The Flame The Fame And XL Recordings" CDKEND 340)
Sounds Of Memphis 716 - I Can't Be Satisfied (With A Piece Of Your Love) / Take Time To Love Your Woman - 1973
XL - Best Thing I Ever Had - (unissued track which was released in the U. K. on a 2007 KENT Cd "Can't Be Satisfied: The XL And Sounds Of Memphis Story" CDKEND 283 and released 2010 in the U. K. on a Kent Cd "Spencer Wiggins Feed The Flame The Fame And XL Recordings" CDKEND 340)
XL 1345 - I Can't Get Enough Of You Baby / You're My Kind Of Woman – 1973
XL 1347 - Feed The Flame* / El Paso – 1973 *also recorded in 1967 by Ted Taylor on Atco 6481.

Charles Sheffield / Spencer Wiggins

Southern Artists 666 - It's Your Voodoo Working / Let's Talk It Over* - ? *flip by Spencer Wiggins.

Jerry Williams

Little Jerry (Jerry Williams)

Mechanic ? - Htd Blues (Hardsick Troublesome Downout Blues) / Nats Wailing - 1954 (78 rpm format) (Session: Step-Father Nat Cross (guitar) and Step-Mother Vera Cross (drums))
Mechanic ? - Sweet Sue / Nat's Wailing - 1955 (78 rpm format)
Ember 1081 - There Ain't Enough Love / Don't You Feel - 1960
Aldo 502 - I'll Always Remember (Chapel On The Hill) / I'm So Mad - 1961

Jerry Williams (born 1942 in Portsmouth, Virginia)

V-Tone 501 - Let's Do The Wobble (Before Chubby Gets It) / You Call It Love - 1963

Little Jerry

Academy 5858 - Hum Baby / She's So Divine - 1963

Little Jerry Williams

Southern Sound 118 - I'm The Lover Man / The Push, Push, Push - 1964
Loma 2005 - I'm The Lover Man / The Push, Push, Push - 1964

Jerry Williams

Southern Sound 123 - Detroit / The 1965 Kingsize Nicotine Blues - 1965

Little Jerry Williams

Calla - Baby You're My Everything (Take 3) - 1965 (this unissued version was released in 2000 in the U. K. on a Westside CD "Jerry Williams Jr. A. K. A. Swamp Dogg - Swamp's Things ..." WESM 500)
Calla 105 - Baby You're My Everything / Just What Do You Plan To Do About It - 1965
Academy 113 - Hum Baby / She's So Divine - 1965
Calla 109 - Baby, Bunny (Sugar, Honey) / Philly Duck - 1966

Jerry Williams

Calla 116 - If You Ask Me (Because I Love You) / Yvonne - 1966
Calla 121 - What's The Matter With You Baby / Just What Do You Plan To Do About It - 1967
Calla 124 - Your Man / Kiss Me - 1967 (Withdrawn)
87-30 Records 102 - Your Man / Give The Disc Jockey Some - 1967
Musicor 1285 - Run Run Roadrunner* / I'm In The Danger Zone - 1967 *also recorded in 1973 by Gene Pitney on Musicor 1474.

Brooks & Jerry (Brooks O'Dell and Jerry Williams)

Dynamo 114 - I Got What It Takes (Part 1) / I Got What It Takes (Part 2) - 1968

Jerry Williams

Cotillion 44022 - Shipwrecked / Sock It To Yourself - 1968
Cotillion 44039 - It's Still Good / Come And Get It - 1969

Swamp Dogg (Jerry Williams)

Canyon 30 - Mama's Baby, Daddy's Maybe / Salafaster - 1970
Canyon 53 - Synthetic World / Total Destruction To Your Mind - 1970
Roker 505 - These Are Not My People / I Was Born Blue - 1971

Slick 'n' The Family Brick (members Gary U. S. Bonds, Jerry Williams, Kenny Carter, Charlie

Whitehead and Johnny Northern)

Swamp Dogg Presents 500 - Don't Trust A Woman / The Pelican - 1971

Swamp Dogg

Swamp Dogg Presents 501 - Straight From My Heart / Don't Throw Your Love To The Wind - 1971
Elektra 45721 - Creeping Away / Do You Believe - 1972
Cream 1021 - Sam Stone / Knowing I'm Pleasing Me And You - 1973
Brut 806 - Buzzard Luck / Ebony And Jet - 1973
Brut 818 - Buzzard Luck / Ebony And Jet - 1973
Stone Dogg 804 - Wifesitter / Please Let Me Kiss You Goodbye - 1973
Stone Dogg 805 - Mighty Mighty Dollar Bill / Choking To Death (From The Ties That Bind) - 1973
Island 028 - I Wanna Lifetime Of Loving You / Did I Come Backtoo Soon Or Stay Away Too Long - 1974
Wizard 1306 - I Sure Love To Ball / I Did It All - 1977

Swamp Dogg & The Riders Of The New Funk (members Jerry Williams, ...)

Musicor 6306 - My Heart Just Can't Stop Dancing / Silly Silly Silly Me - 1977

Swamp Dogg

Atomic Art 301 - Come On And Dance With Me / Sally Dog - 1979
Warner Bros. Pro-S-793 - Gone / This Song /// Philosophizer - 1979 (Promo Issue Only)
Ala 112 - Right Arm For Your Love / Come And Get It - 1982
Rare Bullet 102-12 - This Is It / All She Wants Is Reggae Music - 1983
Rare Bullet 12-2021 - Shut Your Mouth / Mouth Music - 1983

Miss Vera's Boys (Jerry Williams)

Rare Bullet 12-2022 - Kiss Me, Hit Me, Touch Me / Moon Mixture - 1985 (12" Release)

Jackie Wilson

The Ever Ready Gospel Singers (members Jackie Wilson,.....)

The 4 Falcons (members Jackie Wilson, Levi Stubbs, Lawson Smith and Sonny Woods)

Sonny Wilson

Dee Gee 4000 - Rainy Day Blues / Rockaway Rock - 1952
Dee Gee 4001 - Danny Boy / Bulldozer Blues - 1952

Billy Ward & The Dominoes (Jackie Wilson singing lead)

Federal 12139 - Where Now, Little Heart / You Can't Keep A Good Man Down - 1953
King 1280 - Rags To Riches / Don't Thank Me - 1953
King 1281 - Christmas In Heaven / Ring In A Brand New Year - 1953
Federal 12162 - Until The Real Thing Comes Along / My Baby's 3-D - 1953
Federal 12178 - Tootsie Roll / I'm Gonna Move To The Outskirts Of Town - 1954
King 1342 - Tenderly / A Little Lie - 1954

King 1364 - Three Coins In The Fountain / Lonesome Road - 1954
King 1368 - Little Things Mean A Lot / I Really Don't Want To Know - 1954
Jubilee 5163 - Come To Me Baby / Gimme, Gimme, Gimme - 1954
Federal 12193 - Above Jacob's Ladder / Little Black Train - 1954
Federal 12209 - If I Never Get To Heaven / Can't Do Sixty No More - 1955
Federal 12218 - Love Me Now Or Let Me Go / Caveman - 1955
King 1492 - May I Never Love Again / Learnin' The Blues - 1955
Jubilee 5213 - Sweetheart's On Parade / Take Me Back To Heaven - 1955
King 1502 - Give Me You / Over The Rainbow - 1955
Federal 12263 - Bobby Sox Baby / How Long, How Long Blues - 1956
Decca 29933 - St. Therese Of The Roses / Home Is Where You Hang Your Heart - 1956
Decca 30043 - Will You Remember / Come On Snake Let's Crawl - 1956
Decca 30149 - Half A Love / Evermore - 1956
Decca 30199 - Rock, Plymouth Rock / 'Til Kingdom Come - 1957
Federal 12301 - One Moment With You / St. Louis Blues - 1957
Decca 30420 - To Each His Own / I Don't Stand A Ghost Of A Chance - 1957
Decca 30514 - September Song / When The Saints Go Marching In - 1957

Jackie Wilson (born Jack Leroy Wilson 9-June-1934 in Detroit, Michigan - died 20-January-1984 in Mount Holly, New Jersey, at Burlington County Memorial Hospital.- the exact cause of death was not revealed)

Brunswick 55024 - Reet Petite / By The Light Of The Silvery Moon - 1957
Brunswick 55052 - To Be Loved / Come Back To Me - 1958
Brunswick 55070 - As Long As I Live / I'm Wanderin' - 1958
Brunswick 55086 - We Have Love / Singing A Song - 1958
Brunswick 55105 - Lonely Teardrops / In The Blue Of The Evening - 1958
Demo (No #) - Let George Do It - 1958 (promo issue only label markings only show title, vocalist as being Jackie Wilson and words and music by Roquel "Billy" Davis and Berry Gordy Jr.) Record was pressed as a 78 & 45 to support the 1958 campaign of George Edwards (husband of Berry Gordy's sister Esther) for state representative)
Brunswick 55121 - That's Why (I Love You So) / Love Is All - 1959 (Some Copies Also Issued With A Picture Sleeve)
Brunswick 55136 - I'll Be Satisfied / Ask – 1959
Brunswick 55149 - You Better Know It / Never Go Away - 1959
Brunswick 55165 - Talk That Talk / Only You And Only Me - 1959
Brunswick 0 - One Kiss - 1960 (One Sided Test Pressing)
Brunswick 55166 - Night / Doggin' Around – 1960
Brunswick 55167 - (You Were Made For) All My Love / A Woman, A Lover, A Friend – 1960
Brunswick 55170 - Alone At Last / Am I The Man – 1960
Brunswick 55201 - My Empty Arms / The Tear Of The Year – 1961
Brunswick 55208 - Please Tell Me Why / Your One And Only Love – 1961
Brunswick 55216 - I'm Comin' On Back To You / Lonely Life – 1961
Brunswick 55219 - Years From Now / You Don't Know What It Means – 1961
King 5463 - Lay It On The Line / That's When You Know You're Growing Old – 1961
Brunswick 55220 - The Way I Am / My Heart Belongs To Only You – 1961
Brunswick 55221 - The Greatest Hurt / There'll Be No Next Time – 1962

Jackie Wilson & Linda Hopkins

Brunswick 55224 - I Found Love / There's Nothing Like Love – 1962

Jackie Wilson

Brunswick 55225 - Hearts / Sing (And Tell The Blues So Long) – 1962
Brunswick 55229 - I Just Can't Help It / My Tale Of Woe – 1962
Brunswick 55233 - Forever And A Day / Baby That's All – 1962

Brunswick 55236 - What Good Am I Without You / A Girl Named Tamiko – 1962
Brunswick 55239 - Baby Workout / I'm Going Crazy – 1963

Jackie Wilson & Linda Hopkins

Brunswick 55243 - Shake A Hand / Say I Do – 1963

Jackie Wilson

Brunswick 55246 - Shake! Shake! Shake! / He's A Fool - 1963
Brunswick 55250 - Baby Get It (And Don't Quit It) / The New Breed – 1963
Brunswick 55254 - Silent Night / Oh Holy Night – 1963
Brunswick 55260 - Haunted House / I'm Travelin' On – 1964
Brunswick 55263 - Call Her Up / The Kickapoo – 1964
Brunswick 55266 - Big Boss Line / Be My Girl – 1964
Brunswick 55269 - Squeeze Her-Tease Her (But Love Her) / Give Me Back My Heart – 1964
Brunswick 55273 - Watch Out / She's Alright – 1964
Brunswick 55277 - Danny Boy / Soul Time – 1965

Jackie Wilson & Linda Hopkins

Brunswick 55278 - Yes Indeed / When The Saints Go Marching In – 1965

Jackie Wilson

Brunswick 55280 - No Pity (In The Naked City) / I'm So Lonely – 1965
Brunswick 55283 - I Believe I'll Love On / Lonely Teardrops (Slow Version) – 1965

Jackie Wilson & Lavern Baker

Brunswick 55287 - Think Twice / Please Don't Hurt Me – 1965

Jackie Wilson

Brunswick 55289 - I've Got To Get Back (Country Boy) / Three Days, One Hour, Thirty Minutes – 1966
Brunswick 55290 - Soul Galore / Brand New Thing – 1966
Brunswick 55294 - I Believe / Be My Love – 1966
Brunswick 55300 - Whispers (Gettin' Louder)* / The Fairest Of Them All - 1966 *Covered In 1971 By Erma Franklin On Brunswick 55430.
Brunswick 55309 - I Don't Want To Lose You / Just Be Sincere – 1967
Brunswick 55321 - I've Lost You / Those Heartaches – 1967
Brunswick 55336 - (Your Love Keeps Lifting Me) Higher And Higher / I'm The One To Do It - 1967(This session was actually done at COLUMBIA Recording which was located in the CBS Building at 630 N. McClurg Ct. on the Near North side. The CBS affiliated WBBM TV & radio stations were (and still are) located there. The date was July 6, 1967 and The Funk Brothers and The Andantes were on the session)
Brunswick 55354 - Since You Showed Me How To Be Happy / The Who Who Song – 1967

Jackie Wilson & Count Basie

Brunswick 55365 - For Your Precious Love / Uptight (Everything's Alright) – 1968
Brunswick 55373 - Chain Gang / Funky Broadway - 1968

Jackie Wilson

Brunswick 55381 - (I Get The) Sweetest Feeling* / Nothing But Heartaches (Keep Haunting Me) - 1968 *Covered In 1971 By Erma Franklin On Brunswick 55430.

Brunswick 55392 - For Once In My Life / You Brought About A Change In Me - 1968
Brunswick 55402 - I Still Love You / Hum De Dum De Do - 1969
Brunswick 55418 - Helpless / Do It The Right Way - 1969
Brunswick 55423 - With These Hands / Why Don't You (Do Your Thing) - 1969
Brunswick 55435 - Let This Be A Letter (To My Baby) / Didn't I - 1970
Brunswick 55443 - (I Can Feel The Vibrations) This Love Is Real / Love Uprising - 1970
Brunswick 55449 - This Guy's In Love With You / Say You Will - 1971
Brunswick 55454 - Say You Will / ? - 1971
Brunswick 55461 - Love Is Funny That Way / Try It Again - 1971
Brunswick 55467 - You Got Me Walking / The Mountain - 1972
Brunswick 55475 - The Girl Turned Me On / Forever And A Day - 1972
Brunswick 55480 - What A Lovely Way / You Left The Fire Burning - 1972
Brunswick 55490 - Beautiful Day / What 'Cha Gonna Do About Love - 1973
Brunswick 55495 - Because Of You / Go Away - 1973
Brunswick 55499 - Sing A Little Song / No More Goodbyes - 1973
Brunswick 55504 - It's All Over / Shake A Leg - 1973

Jackie Wilson & The Chi-Lites

Brunswick 55522 - Don't Burn No Bridges / Don't Burn No Bridges (Instrumental) - 1975

Jackie Wilson

Brunswick 55536 - Nobody But You / I've Learned About Life - 1977
Brunswick 1013 - For Your Precious Love / ? - ?
Gusto ? - (Yes I Can See) The Handwriting On The Wall / ? - 1977
Gusto ? - I Need Someone In My Arms / ? - 1977
Gusto ? - Deed I Do / ? - 1977
Eric 4504 - Lonely Teardrops / Night - 1983
Eric 4505 - Baby Workout / Baby Workout - 1983
Eric 4506 - (Your Love Keeps Lifting Me) Higher And Higher / Whispers (Gettin' Louder) - 1983
Columbia 07329 - Reet Petite / You Better Know It - 1987
Collectables Col 030487 - Whispers / Night - ?
Collectables Col 030507 - Danny Boy / All My Love - ?
Collectables Col 030517 - Talk That Talk / Alone At Last - ?

The Dominoes

Collectables Col 036187 - Pedal Pushin' Papa / Can't Do Sixty No More - ?

Jackie Wilson

Collectables Col 039247 - Squeeze Her, Tease Her / Your One And Only Love - ?
Collectables Col 039267 - I'm Coming On Back To You / The Tear Of The Year - ?
Wax Musuem 4619 - Because Of You / She Did Me Wrong - ?

Stevie Wonder

Little Stevie Wonder

Tamla 54061 - (I Call It Pretty Music, But ...) The Old People Call It The Blues (Part 1) - 1962 (One Sided Promo Issue Only)
Tamla 54061 - (I Call It Pretty Music, But ...) The Old People Call It The Blues (Part 1) / (I Call It Pretty Music, But ...) The Old People Call It The Blues (Part 2) - 1962 (Some Copies Issued With Picture Sleeve)

Little Stevie Wonder & Clarence Paul / Little Stevie Wonder On Vocal & Drums

Tamla 54070 - Little Water Boy / La La La La La* - 1962 *also recorded in 1964 by The Blendells on Reprise 0291.

Little Stevie Wonder

Tamla 54074 - Contract On Love / Sunset – 1963
Tamla 54080 - Fingertips -- Pt. 1 / Fingertips -- Pt. 2 – 1963
Tamla 54086 - Workout Stevie, Workout / Monkey Talk – 1963
Tamla 54090 - Castles In The Sand / Thank You (For Loving Me All The Way) – 1964

Stevie Wonder

Tamla 54096 - Hey Harmonica Man / This Little Girl – 1964
Tamla 54103 - Sad Boy / Happy Street – 1964

Hitsville U.S.A. Greetings To Tamla Motown Appreciation Society Dm 097311 - 1964 (this American record was limited to 300 copies for dispersal throughout the various fan clubs within Europe as a promo for their first European tour. Each act gives an individual greeting over its latest record. Artists involved include The Miracles, Stevie Wonder, Marvin Gaye, The Marvelettes, The Temptations, Martha And The Vandellas, The Contours, Eddie Holland, Kim Weston And The Supremes. The 45 has an introduction from Publicist Margaret Phelps and Berry Gordy)

Stevie Wonder & Clarence Paul (Clarence Paul's Name Handwritten On Label)

Dub # 6699 - I Dont Want Nobody's Gonna Make Me Cry - 1964 (One Sided Acetate Has Time 2:30 Typed And Date Aug 3 1964 Stamped On Label Plus Also Typed On Label Is Dm-Ply-095205 And (Cx 5)

Stevie Wonder

Tamla 54108 - Pretty Little Angel / Tears In Vain - 1964 (Unreleased)
Tamla 54114 - Kiss Me Baby / Tears In Vain – 1965
Tamla 54119 - High Heel Sneakers / Funny How Time Slips Away* - 1965 *also recorded in 1961 by Jimmy Elledge on RCA-Victor 47-7946
Tamla 54119 - High Heel Sneakers / Music Talk – 1965
Tamla 54124 - Uptight (Everything's Alright) / Purple Rain Drops – 1965
Tamla 54124 - Uptight (Everything's Alright) / Stevie Info: Meet Stevie Wonder - ? (Picture Disc)
Tamla 54130 - Nothing's Too Good For My Baby / With A Child's Heart* - 1966 *Covered In 1973 By Michael
Jackson On Motown 1218.
Tamla 54136 - Blowin' In The Wind* / Ain't That Asking For Trouble - 1966 *also recorded in 1963 by Bob Dylan on Columbia 42856 and in 1963 by The Staple Singers on Riverside 4568
Tamla 54139 - A Place In The Sun / Sylvia – 1966
Tamla 54142 - Someday At Christmas / The Miracle Of Christmas – 1966
Topps/Motown 8 - Fingertips Part 2 - 1967 (Cardboard Record)
Topps/Motown 10 - Uptight (Everything's Alright) - 1967 (Cardboard Record)
Tamla 54147 - Travlin' Man / Hey Love – 1967
Tamla 54151 - I Was Made To Love Her / Hold Me – 1967
Tamla 54157 - I'm Wondering / Every Time I See You I Go Wild – 1967
Tamla 54165 - Shoo-Be-Doo-Be-Doo-Da-Day / Why Don't You Lead Me To Love – 1968
Tamla 54168 - You Met Your Match / My Girl - 1968

Eivets Rednow

Gordy 7076 - Alfie / More Than A Dream* - 1968 *The Opening Melody On "More Than A Dream" Is Identical To The Opening Melody Of The 1965 Release By Gerry And The Pacemakers "Ferry Cross The Mersey" On Laurie 3284.

Stevie Wonder

Tamla 54174 - For Once In My Life* / Angie Girl - 1968 *originaly recorded in 1966 by Jean Du Shon on Cadet 5545.
Tamla 54180 - I Don't Know Why / My Cherie Amour – 1969
Tamla 54180 - My Cherie Amour / Don't Know Why I Love You - 1969 (Re-Released)
Tamla 54188 - Yester-Me, Yester-You, Yester-Day / I'd Be A Fool Right Now - 1969
Tamla 54191 - Never Had A Dream Come True / Somebody Knows, Somebody Cares – 1970
Tamla 54196 - Signed, Sealed, Delivered, I'm Yours* / I'm More Than Happy - 1970 *covered in 1978 by The Soul Children on Stax 3206.
Tamla 54200 - Heaven Help Us All / I Gotta Have A Song – 1970
Tamla 54202 - We Can Work It Out / Never Dreamed You'd Leave In Summer – 1971
Tamla 54208 - If You Really Love Me / Think Of Me As Your Soldier – 1971
Tamla 54214 - What Christmas Means To Me / Bedtime For Toys – 1971
Tamla 54216 - Superwoman (Where Were You When I Needed You) / I Love Every Little Thing About You* - 1972 *Covered In 1972 By Syreeta On Mowest 5016.
Tamla 54223 - Keep On Running / Evil – 1972
Tamla 54226 - Superstition / You've Got It Bad Girl – 1972
Tamla 54232 - You Are The Sunshine Of My Life / Tuesday Heartbreak - 1973
Tamla 54235 - Higher Ground / Too High – 1973
Tamla 54242 - Living For The City / Visions – 1973
Tamla 54245 - Don't You Worry 'Bout A Thing / Blame It On The Sun – 1974
Tamla 54252 - You Haven't Done Nothin' */ Big Brother - 1974 *Background Vocals By The Jackson 5.
Tamla 54254 - Boogie On Raggae Woman / Seems So Long - 1974 (Mispelled Title)
Tamla 54254 - Boogie On Reggae Woman / Seems So Long – 1974
Tamla 54274 - I Wish / You And I – 1976
Tamla T 340ep - Saturn / Ebony Eyes /// All Day Sucker / Easy Goin' Evening - 1976 (Called "A Something's Extra For Songs In The Key Of Life," This was issued with the 2-lp set of the same name and is sometimes found separately, though it was never sold separately)
Tamla 54281 - Sir Duke* / He's Misstra Know-It-All - 1977 *Tribute To Duke Ellington.
Tamla 54286 - Another Star / Creepin' – 1977
Tamla 54291 - As / Contusion - 1977
Motown Yesteryear Y 620f - I Wish / Sir Duke – 1978
Motown Yesteryear Y 621f - Another Star / As – 1978

Diana Ross, Marvin Gaye, Smokey Robinson & Stevie Wonder

Motown 1455 - Pops, We Love You (A Tribute To Father) / (Instrumental) - 1979 Song Written For Berry Gordy Sr.'S 90th Birthday.

Stevie Wonder

Tamla 54303 - Send One Your Love / (Instrumental) – 1979
Tamla Pr 61 - A Seed's A Star-Tree (Medley) / Power Flower / Black Orchid / Outside My Window - 1979 (12" Promo Issue)
Tamla 54308 - Outside My Window / Same Old Story – 1980

Stevie Wonder / John Denver

What's It All About - 1980 (Public Service - Radio Station Issue 45)

Stevie Wonder

Motown K052z-64076 - Master Blaster (Jammin') (4:49) / Master Blaster (Dub) - 1980 (12" Release)
Tamla Pr-76 - Master Blaster (Vocal) / (Dub) – 1980
Tamla 54317 - Master Blaster (Jammin') / (Instrumental) – 1980
Tamla Pr-77 - I Ain't Gonna Stand For It / Did I Hear You Say You Love Me // All I Do / Do Like You – 1980
Tamla 54320 - I Ain't Gonna Stand For It / Knocks Me Off My Feet – 1980

Stevie Wonder / Rev. Martin Luther King

Motown 4517 - Happy Birthday / Rev. Martin Luther King (Greatest Excerpts From His Speeches)* - 1980 *Flip By Rev. Martin Luther King.

Stevie Wonder / Judy Collins

W.I.A.A. 574 - What's It All About (May 81) Public Service Show - 1981 (Radio Station Spots -- Promo Issue Only -- Flip By Judy Collins)

Stevie Wonder

Tamla 54323 - Lately / If It's Magic – 1981
Tamla 54328 - Did I Hear You Say You Love Me / As If You Read My Mind – 1981
Tamla 54331 - Happy Birthday / (Instrumental) - 1981 (Unreleased)
Tamla 1602 - That Girl / All I Do – 1982

Paul Mccartney With Stevie Wonder

Columbia 02860 - Ebony And Ivory / Rainclouds* - 1982 *Flip Side Is Paul Mccartney Solo
Columbia 02878 - Ebony And Ivory / Rainclouds* / Ebony And Ivory* - 1982 *Two Tracks Paul Mccartney Only.
12" Release)

Stevie Wonder

Tamla 1612 - Do I Do / Rocket Love – 1982
Tamla 98/99 - Do I Do (Lp) / Instrumental / Front Line (Lp) (Instrumental) - 1982 (12" -Two Record Promo Set With Picture Sleeve)
Tamla 1639 - Ribbon In The Sky / Black Orchid – 1982
Motown Yesteryear Y 646f - Master Blaster (Jammin') / Master Blaster (Dub) – 1982
Motown Yesteryear Y 647f - I Ain't Gonna Stand For It / Lately – 1982

Donna Summer

Geffen 29895 - State Of Independence / Love Is Just A Breath Away - 1982 (All-Star Choir Includes James Ingram, Michael Jackson, Kenny Loggins, Lionel Richie, Dionne Warwick And Stevie Wonder)

Charlene & Stevie Wonder / Charlene

Motown 1650 - Used To Be / I Want To Come Back As A Song* - 1982 *Flip Side Is Charlene Solo, Promo Copies Issued In A Lyric Sheet Cover.

Stevie Wonder

Motown Yesteryear Y 657f - That Girl / Do I Do – 1983
Motown 1745 - I Just Called To Say I Love You / (Instrumental) - 1984 From The Film "Woman In Red"
Motown 4527 - Don't Drive Drunk (12" Version) (Instrumental) / Did I Hear You Say You Love

Me - 1984 (12" Release)
Motown 1769 - Love Light In Flight / It's More Than You - 1984 From The Film "Woman In Red"
Motown Pr 161 - Love Light In Flight (Remix) / (Instrumental) - 1984 (12" Promo Issue)
Motown Yesteryear Y 684f - I Just Called To Say I Love You / Love Light In Flight – 1985
Motown Yesteryear Y 685f - Don't Drive Drunk / (Instrumental) - 1985
Motown 1774 - Don't Drive Drunk / (Instrumental) - 1985 (Unreleased)

Steveland Morris (Stevie Wonder)

Funhouse 07fa-1068 - Remember My Love (English Version) / Remember My Love (Japanese Version) - 1985 (Japanese Lyrics By Hiroe & Satsuya Kanzawa)

U.S.A. For Africa (United Support Of Artists - A Collection Of 46 Major Artists Formed To Help The Suffering Of People Of Africa And The U.S.A. - Soloists: Lionel Richie, Stevie Wonder, Paul Simon, Kenny Rogers, James Ingram, Tina Turner, Billy Joel, Michael Jackson, Diana Ross, Dionne Warwick, Willie Nelson, Al Jarreau, Bruce Springsteen, Kenny Loggins, Steve Perry, Daryl Hall, Huey Lewis, Cyndi Lauper, Kim Carnes, Bob Dylan And Ray Charles)

Columbia 04839 - We Are The World / Grace* - 1985 *Flip By Quincy Jones.

Stevie Wonder / Smokey Robinson & Syreeta

Tamla Pr-168 - Upset Stomach / First Time On A Ferris Wheel* - 1985 *Flip By Smokey Robinson And Syreeta. (From Berry Gordy's The Last Dragon Soundtrack)

Stevie Wonder

1808tf - Part Time Lover / Part Time Lover - 1985 (White Test Pressing - Same Both Sides, That Has Stevie Wonder "Part Time Lover" Written In Ball Point Pen With Time (3:43) On Label)
Tamla 1808 - Part-Time Lover / (Instrumental) - 1985 (Some Copies Also Issued With Picture Sleeve)
Tamla 4548 - Part-Time Lover (8:20) / (Instrumental) - 1985 (12"Release)

Dionne & Friends (Dionne Warwick, Elton John, Gladys Knight And Stevie Wonder)

Arista 9422 - That's What Friends Are For / Two Ships Passing In The Night* - 1985 *Flip Is Dionne Warwick Solo.

Stevie Wonder

Tamla 1817 - Go Home / (Instrumental) – 1985
Tamla 4553 - Go Home (3 Versions) (9:22) (6:26) (8:36) - 1985 (12"Release)
Tamla 1832 - Overjoyed / (Instrumental) – 1986
Tamla 1846 - Land Of La La / (Instrumental) – 1986
Tamla Pr 186 - Land Of La La (8:40) / (Instrumental) - 1986 (12" Promo Issue)

Julian Lennon & Stevie Wonder

Capitol B-5618 - Time Will Teach Us / (Instrumental) – 1986

Stevie Wonder

Motown 1907 - Skeletons / (Instrumental) – 1987
Motown 4593 - Skeletons (6:43) / (Instrumental) - 1987 (12" Release)
Motown L33-17755 - With Each Beat Of My Heart (Lp) (Edit) (Instrumental) - 1987 (12" Promo Issue)

Stevie Wonder & Michael Jackson

Motown 1930 - Get It / (Instrumental) – 1988
Motown 4604 - Get It (6:47) / (Instrumental) - 1988 (12"Release)

Julio Iglesias Featuring Stevie Wonder

Columbia 07781 - My Love / Words And Music* - 1988 *Flip Side Julio Iglesias Solo.

Stevie Wonder

Motown 1919 - You Will Know / (Instrumental) – 1988
Motown 1919 - You Will Know / You Will Know & Stevie Wonder Interview - 1988 (Promo Issue Only)
Motown Pr 222 Md - You Will Know (Lp) / (Instrumental) / Interview - 1988 (3" Promo Issue Only Cd. Single)
Motown 1946 - My Eye's Don't Cry / (Instrumental) - 1988 (Some Copies Issued With Picture Sleeve)
Motown 4616 - My Eyes Don't Cry (3 Versions) - 1988 (12" Release)
Motown 4826 - With Each Beat Of My Heart (Lp) (Edit) (Instrumental) - 1988 (12"Release)
Motown L33-17755 - With Each Beat Of My Heart (Lp) (Edit) (Instrumental) - 1988 (12" Promo Issue Only)
Motown 1953 - With Each Beat Of My Heart / (Instrumental) – 1989
Motown 1990 - Keep Our Love Alive / (Instrumental) – 1990
Motown 1065 - Keep Our Love Alive / (Instrumental) - 1990 (12" Promo Issue)
Motown 4665 - Keep Our Love Alive / (Instrumental) - 1990 (12" Release)
Motown 2081 - Gotta Have You / Feeding Off The Love Of The Land – 1991
Motown 1093 - Gotta Have You (Three Versions) - 1991 (12" Promo Issue)
Motown 1145 - Gotta Have You (Three Versions) - 1991 (Cd. Single Promo Issue Only)
Motown 4759 - Gotta Have You (4 Versions) - 1991 (12" Release)
Motown 1591 - Gotta Have You (4 Versions) - 1991 (Cd. Single Promo Issue Only)
Motown 2127 - Fun Day / (Instrumental) – 1991
Motown 1602 - Fun Day (Edit) (Lp) (Instrumental) - 1991 (12" Promo Issue)
Motown 1690 - Fun Day (Eight Versions) - 1991 (12"Promo Issue)
Motown 2143 - These Three Words / These Three Words – 1991
Motown P12-1007 - These Three Words (3 Versions) - 1991 (12" Promo Issue Only)
Motown 860310-7 - For Your Love / (Instrumental) – 1995
Motown 374631215 - Tomorrow Robins Will Sing (7 Versions) - 1995 (12" Promo Issue Only)
Motown 37463 1261 - For Your Love (Four Versions) - 1995 (12" Promo Issue Only)
Motown 376431261 - For Your Love (Four Versions) - 1995 (Cd. Single Promo Issue Only)
Motown 860418-7 - Tomorrow Robins Will Sing / For Your Love – 1995
Motown 860 357-2 - Tomorrow Robins Will Sing - 1996 (Cd. Single)
Motown 374631482 - Kiss Lonely Goodbye (6 Versions) - 1996 (12" Promo Issue Only)
Motown 860 476-2 - Kiss Lonely Goodbye (3 Versions) - 1996 (Cd. Single)

98° & Stevie Wonder

Walt Disney 32800 - True To Your Heart - 1998 (Cd. Single Promo Issue Only)

Stevie Wonder

Motown ? - I Wish - 1999 (Cd. Single Promo Issue Only)

Richard 'Popcorn' Wylie

Northern 3732 - Pretty Girl / You're The One - 1960 (Three 45's on the Northern label carry this record number Northern 3732 - "Come On / Always" - 1960 is by The Distants And Northern

3732 - "So Lonely / Help Me" -1960 is by Johnnie Mae Matthews)
Motown 1002 - Shimmy Gully / Custer's Last Stand - 1960

Richard Wylie & His Band / Popcorn Wylie & The Mohawks

Motown 1009 - Money (That's What I Want) / I'll Still Be Around - 1961

Popcorn & The Mohawks

Motown 1019 - Real Good Lovin' / Have I The Right - 1961

Richard "Popcorn" Wylie (born Richard Wayne Wylie on 6-June-1939 in Detroit, Michigan --- found dead 7-September-2008)

Epic 9543 - Come To Me / Weddin' Bells - 1962
Epic 9575 - Brand New Man / So Much Love In My Heart - 1963
Epic 9611 - Head Over Heels In Love / Greater Than Anything - 1963
Epic 9663 - Do You Still Care For Me / Marlene - 1964

Stewart Ames (With Richard Wylie)

J & W 1000 - King For A Day / Angelina Oh Angelina - 1966

Richard "Popcorn" Wylie

Karen 1542 - Rosemary, What Happened / (Instrumental) - 1968
Carla 715 - Move Over Babe (Here Comes Henry) / Move Over Baby (Here Comes Henry) - 1968
Soul 35087 - Funky Rubber Band (Vocal) / Funky Rubber Band (Inst) - 1971
ABC 12067 - Lost Time (Mono) / Lost Time (Stereo) - 1975 (Promo Issue)
ABC 12067 - Lost Time / Trust In Me - 1975
ABC 12124 - Georgia's After Hours / E. S. P. - 1975

Sandy Wynns

The Crystals (members Darlene Wright (lead vocals), Fanita James, Edna Wright and Gracia Nitsche)

Philles 106 - He's A Rebel* / I Love You Eddie** - 1962 *also recorded in 1963 was an "answer" song to this track titled "He's A Yankee" by The Sweethearts on Brunswick 55240. **also cut as "I Love You Betty" by Terry Day on Columbia 4-427678.

The Girlfriends (members Nanette Williams, Gloria Jones and Carolyn Willis who also sang with Bob B. Soxx & The Blue Jeans and back up for O.C. Smith and Lou Rawls)

Colpix 712 - My One And Only Jimmy Boy / For My Sake - 1963 (produced by David Gates)

The Cogic Singers (member Edna Wright - sister of Darlene Love -- group name stands for Church Of God In Christ) Other members included: Frankie Karl, Gloria Jones, Billy Preston, Sandra "Blinky" Williams and Andrea and Sandra Crouch)

Simpson 273 - It's A Blessing / Since I Found Him - 1964

Hale & The Hushabyes (a fictitious group made out of session singers, among members Brian Wilson, Sonny & Cher, Jack Nitzsche, The Blossoms, Jackie DeShannon, Darlene Love, Edna Wright and Albert Stone)

Apogee 104 - Yes Sir, That's My Baby* / Nine Hundred Quetzals - 1964 *lead Edna Wright, who also sang backup for The Righteous Brothers, Johnny Rivers and Ray Charles' Raelettes)
Reprise 0299 - Yes Sir, That's My Baby / Jack's Theme - 1964

Sandy Wynns (Edna Wright)

Doc 103 - A Touch Of Venus / A Lover's Quarrel - 1964
Champion 14001 - A Touch Of Venus / A Lover's Quarrel - 1965
Champion 14002 - Yes, I Really Love You / Love Belongs To Everyone - 1965
Simco 30,001 - I'll Give That To You / You Turned Your Back On Me - 1966
Canterbury 520 - Love's Like Quicksand / How Can Something Be So Wrong - 1967

Arthur & Mary (Arthur Adams and Edna Wright)

Modern 1042 - Let's Get Together / Is That You - 1967 (a quote from Arthur Adams - "Modern Records had an idea for me to do it with Mary Love, but that's Edna Wright")

A Date With Soul

York 408 - Yes Sir, That's My Baby / Bee Side Soul - 1967

The Brothers and Sisters of Los Angeles (members (The Brothers) Josephy Green, Andrew Herd, Jesse Kirkland, Chester Pipkin, Billy Storm, Ed Wallace, Fred Willis and Don Wyatt. (The Sisters) Shirley Allen, Sherrell Atwood, Ginger Blake, Hazel Carmichael, Merry Clayton, Marjorie Cranford, Oma Drake, Georgette Finchess, Brenda Fitz, Patrice Holloway, Gwen Johnson, Ruby S. Johnson, Gloria Jones, Clydie King, Sherlie Matthews, Barbara Perrault, Julia A. Tilman, Lolietha White, Carolyn Willis and Edna Wright (a.k.a. Sandy Wynns))

Ode 121 - Mighty Quinn / The Chimes Of Freedom - 1969
Ode 123 - The Times They Are A Changin' / Mr. Tambourine Man - 1969

The Honey Cone (members Carolyn Willis, Edna Wright and Shelly Clark a former (unrecorded) Ikette who also sang backing vocals for Dusty Springfield and Little Richard. Group was spotted by Holland / Dozier / Holland on The Andy Williams show backing Burt Bacharach and asked to join the Invictus / Hot Wax set up)

Hot Wax 6901 - While You're Out Looking For Sugar / The Feeling's Gone - 1969
Hot Wax 6903 - Girl's, It Ain't Easy / The Feeling's Gone - 1969
Hot Wax 7001 - Take Me With You / Take My Love - 1970
Hot Wax 7005 - Take Me With You / When Will It End – 1970

Moose & The Pelicans (members Darlene Love, Fanita James and Edna Wright)

Vanguard 35110 - We Rockin' / The Ballad Of Davy Crockett - 1970
Vanguard 35129 - He's A Rebel / We Rockin' - 1971
Vanguard 35129 - He's A Rebel (Mono) / He's A Rebel (Stereo) - 1971 (promo issue only)

The Honey Cone (members Carolyn Willis, Edna Wright and Shelly Clark)

Hot Wax 7011 - Want Ads* / We Belong Together - 1971 *General Johnson and Greg Perry tune, originally cut by Scherrie Payne and Glass House, then by Freda Payne.
Hot Wax 7106 - Stick-Up / V.I.P.* - 1971 *also issued in 1971 by Scherrie Payne on Invictus 9114.
Hot Wax 7110 - One Monkey Don't Stop No Show (Part 1) / One Monkey Don't Stop No Show (Part 2) - 1971
Hot Wax 7113 - The Day I Found Myself / When Will It End - 1972

Hot Wax 7205 - Sittin' On A Time Bomb (Waitin' For The Hurt To Come) / It's Better To Have Loved And Lost - 1972
Hot Wax 7208 - Innocent 'Til Proven Guilty / Don't Send Me An Invitation - 1972
Hot Wax 7212 - Ooh, Baby Baby* / Ace In The Hole - 1972
Hot Wax 7301 - Women Can't Live By Bread Alone / If I Can't Fly - 1973

The Honey Cone

Collectables Col 033317 - Want Ads / Stick Up - ?

The Honey Cone / 100 Proof (Aged In Soul)

Collectables Col 033337 - One Monkey Don't Stop The Show / Somebody's Been Sleeping* - ?
*Flip By 100 Proof (Aged In Soul).

Venue Reports 2001

The Lea Manor, Albrighton, 1st December, 2001

The last allnighter to be held at Albrighton, and it appears that the Soul nights are going to be quarterly next year. Numbers have been falling all through this year, and although it is a shame, the venue has lived it's life. Sixties fans have, in the main, abandoned the venue because of the change in music policy in January, and that meant that it was no longer viable to run on a monthly basis.

Over the past seven years this venue became one of the most respected Soul nights in the country. Virtually every top DJ has guested there, but what made the venue special was that the core of the DJ line up was drawn from local West Midland collectors. Around twenty people were rotated round on a monthly basis, and if people weren't DJing, they attended as punters. Due to some astute advertising by Tate and Lin this group of DJs became known as the Albrighton Allstars. The original music policy was Quality Oldies, Sixties Newies, Crossover, and the best of '80s and '90s, and the mixture of DJs worked so well that the reputation of the venue grew until it was recognised as one of the most forward thinking venues in the country.

For the last allnighter the line up was Neil Felton, Chic, Dave Rimmer, Ted Massey, Ginger Taylor, Soul Sam, Butch, Bob Hinsley, John Weston, and Chic again for the last hour. So over half the music was provided by Albrighton DJs, Butch and Sam are regulars, Bob Hinsley has worked there on a number of occasions, and there was only Ginger Taylor who had never DJ'ed there before. (I think this was reflected in the fact that he was the DJ who repeated most tracks)

It was, quite simply, a superb night. The music played was exemplary throughout the night, the room was busy and the atmosphere was back. I would say without doubt that this was the most enjoyable allnighter I have attended throughout 2001. A fitting tribute on the closure of an important chapter in Soul music in the West Midlands. My thanks to Tate and Lin, and Martyn Bradley. As promoters they worked the hardest of all.

Rob Haigh also worked hard on the night, he sat behind the decks and wrote down every record that was played over the full ten hours. That list is reproduced here to show just how good the music was.

Neil Felton 9pm – 10pm

The Gents – Such A Beautiful Thing – Paramount
The Ballads – Butterfly – Baija
Johnny Johnson – I Don't Know Why – UK Stateside
Jimmy Beaumont & The Skyliners – Our Day Is Here – Drive
Nancy Butts – I Want To Hold Your Hand Baby – Flaming Arrow

Pat & The Blenders – Just Because – Fast Eddie
The Embers – Aware Of Love – EEE
The Experts – My Love Is Real – Tag
The Holidays – I Lost You – Groove City
The Ideals – The Mighty Lover – Boogaloo
Brooks Odell – Standing Tall – Columbia
Nancy Wilson – That Special Way – Capitol
Clydene Jackson – I Need Your Love – UK Soul HQ
Mickey Lenay – I'm Gonna Walk – Vulcan
Jean Wells – With Your Love & What You've Got – Calla
September Jones – I'm Coming Home – Kapp
Lonnie Russ – Say Girl – Music House
Esquires – Woman – Bunky LP
Vanguards – Good Times Bad Times – Lamp
Round Robin Monopoly – People Do Change – Truth
Rotations – I Can't Find Her- Debrossard
Beverley & The Del Capris – Mama I Think I'm In Love – Columbia

Chic 10pm – 11pm

Liz Verdi – Think It Over – Columbia
Betty Llooyd – I'm Catching On – BSC
Lloraine Rudolph – Keep Coming Back For More – Jetstream
Rhonda Davies – Can You remember – Duke
Skip Jackson & The Chantons – I'm Onto You Girl – Dot-Mar
Larry Davies – I've Been Hurt So Many Times – Kent
The Shadows – My Love Is Gone – USA
The Cashmeres – Showstopper – Hem
Archie Bell & The Drells – 1,000 Wonders – Atlantic
Jimmy Ruffin – He Who Picks A Rose – Soul
Brothers Of Soul – I'd Be Grateful – Boo
Claude Huey – Why Would You Blow It – Galaxy
Little Tommy – Baby Can't You See – Sound Of Soul
The Winstons – Ain't Nothin' Like A Little Lovin' – Curtom
Ruby Winters – I Don't Want To Hurt Nobody – Diamond
Patrice Holloway – Stolen Hours - Capitol
C P Love – Trickbag – Unissued Acetate
Celest Hardie – You're Gone – Reynolds
Dusty Wilson – Can't Live Without You – Bronse
Cookie Jackson – Do You Still Love Me – Congress
Diplomats – Cards On The Table – Arock
Ann Byers – I'm Happy Without You – Academy
Keni Lewis – I'm Not The Marrying Kind – White Label
The Jive Five – You're A Puzzle – UA
Barbara Lynn – I'm A Good Woman = Tribe

Dave Rimmer – 11pm – 12pm

The Swans – Nitty Gritty City – Unreleased Dore
Frank Dell – He Broke Your Game Wide Open – Valise
Joanne Courcy – I Got The Power – Twirl
Enchantments – I'm In Love With Your Daughter – Faro
Rose St John – And If I Had My Way – UA
T C Lee & The Bricklayers – Up & Down The Hill – King
Lonnie Lester – You Can't Go – Nu-Tone
Dorothy Williams – The Well's Gone Dry – Goldwax
The Gilettes – Same Identical Thing – J & S
Don Gardner – My Baby Likes To Boogaloo – Tru-Glo-Town

Delcos – Arabia – Ebony
Lee Shot Williams – I Hurt Myself – Sharma
Patience Valentine – If You Don't Come – SAR
Tommy Navarro – I Cried My Life Away – De Jac
Garland Green – Girl I Love You – Revue
Sparkles – Try Love – Old Town
Joe Douglas – Crazy Things – Playhouse
Sam Fletcher – I'd Think It Over – Tollie
Troy Dodds Try My Love – El Camino
Magnetics – I Have A Girl – Ra-Sel
Caressors – I Can't Stay Away – Ru Jac
Doc & The Interns – Baby I Know – Now
Gordon Keith – Look Ahead – Calumet
Vondells – Hey Girl You've Changed – Airtown

Ted Massey – 12pm – 1am

Brooks Brothers – Lookin' For A Woman – Tay
John & The Wierdest – Can't Get Over These Memories – Tie
Gene Toones – What More Do You Want – Simco
The Soul Set – Will You Ever Learn – Bi Me
Bernie Williams – Ever Again – Bell
Jackie Beavers – I Need My Baby – Revilot
Imperial C's – Someone Tell Her – Phil LA Of Soul
Sam Williams – Love Slipped Through My Fingers – Tower
Candi Statan – Upper Hand – Unity
The Poets – Wrapped Around Your Finger – J2
Empires – You're On Top Girl – Candi
Ty Karim – You Really Made It Good To Me – Romark
Johnny Rogers – Make A Change – Amon
Bob & Fred – I'll Be On My Way – Big Mac
Tearra – Just Lovin' You – Midtown
Tommy Ridgeley – My Love Gets Stronger Every Day – International
The Montclairs – Hey You – Arch
Magnetics – Count The Days – Sable
Lee McKinley & The Magnetics – I'll Keep Holding On – Sable
Cashmeres – Showstopper – Hem
Chuck Holiday – Just Can't Trust Nobody – Gloria
Cashmeres – Don't Let The Door Hit Your back – Hem
Otis Lee – Hard Roe To Hoe – Quaint
Phonetics – Just A Boy's Dream – Trudel
Ultimates – Girl I've Been Trying To Tell You – Bri Roma

Ginger Taylor 1am – 2am

The Four Tracks – Like My Love For You – Mandingo
Mark IV – If You Can't Tell Me Something Good – Britelite
Timmy Williams – Competition – Mala
Walter & The Admerations – Man O Man – La Cindy
The Swans – Nitty Gritty City – Unreleased Dore
Patience Valentine – If You Don't Come – SAR
Larry Trider – Carbon Copy – Coral
Jimmy Andrews – Big City Playboy – Bluejay
Admirations – You Left Me – Peaches
Joey De Lorenzo – Wake Up To The Sunshine Girl – Di-Val
Utopias – Girls Are Against Me – La Salle
Johnny Hunnicut – I'm Comin' Over – Triode
Inspirations – Your Wish Is My Command – Midas

Little Eddie Taylor – I Had A Good Time – Peacock
Gene Barber – I Need A Love – Hit
Jimmy Ruffin – Lucky Lucky Me – Jobete Acetate
Bobby Day – Pretty Little Girl – Next Door – RCA
Leon Peterson – Now You're On Your Own – Sky Lark
C P Love – Trickbag – Unissued acetate
Joanne Courcey – I've Got The Power – Twirl
Allan Sisters – I'm With The Downtown Crowd - Quality

Soul Sam – 2am – 3am

Unique Blend – Yes I'm In Love – Eastbound
Essex IV – My Reaction To You – Wind Mill
Richard Caiton – I'd Like To Get Near You – Uptight
Treasure Mind – Trace Of Smoke – JB
Timeless Legend – Baby Don't Do This To Me – Black Forest
Ace Spectrum – Don't Send Nobody Else – Atlantic
Tab Walton – Love Me – Oeiole
Tolbert – I've Got It – Rojac
Beres Hammond – Do This World A Favour – Rocky One
Al Hudson & The Soul Partners – I'm About Lovin' You – Atco
Willie T – I'm Having So Much Fun – Gatur
Herbie Brown – One More Broken Heart – Ba
4 Dynamics – Things A Lady Ain't Supposed To Do – Peachtree
Eula Cooper – Let Our Love Grow Higher – Super Sound
Margaret Little – Love Finds A Way – C/U
Imperial C's – Someone Tell Her – Phil LA Of Soul
Mr Soul – What Happened To Yesterday – Genuine
Clarence Carter – I Can't Fight This Feeling – Dyco
Eddie Billups – Shake Off That Dream – Sound Stage 7
Jimmy Bo Horne –I Can't Speak – Dade
New Wanderers – Ain't Gonna Do You No Harm - Ready
John & The Wierdest – Can't Get Over These Memories

Butch – 3am – 4am

The Themes – Does She Love You Like I Did – C/U
The Antellects – Love Slave – Flodavieur
Mayfield Singers – Don't Say No – Mayfield Acetate
Nat Hall – Why – Loop
Jean Carter – I Wanna Know – Decca Acetate
Ronnie McNeir – Isn't She A Pretty Thing – De-To
Little Tommy – Baby Can't You See – Sound Of Soul
Patrinelle Staton – Little Love Affair – Sepia
Vanguards – Good Times Bad Times – Lamp
Connie Laverne – Can't Live Without You – GSF
4 Dynamics – Things A Lady Ain't Supposed To Do – Peachtree
Just Brothers – Go On And Laugh – Acetate
The Butlers – Think It Over – Acetate
Del Larks – Just You And I – C/U
The Themes – Does She Love You Like I Did – C/U
Sound Of Philadelphia – Love Keeps Me Trying – C/U
The Saints – I'll Let Slide – Wig Wam
The Parisans – Twinkle Little Star – Demon
The Denures – It's Raining Teardrops – Coral
Martha Jean Love – He's My Old Time Lover – Acetate
Doris troy – Face Up To The Truth – Capitol

Bob Hinsley - 4am – 5am

Trends – Not Too Old To Cry – ABC
Gambrells – You Better Move – Carla
Tranells – Blessed With A Love – Flo Jo
Jesse Johnson – Left Out – Old Town
Vivian Carroll – Oh Yeah Yeah Yeah – Merben
John Bowie – You're Gonna Miss A Good Thing – Merben
Tobi Lark – Sweep It Out In The Shed – Topper
T C Lee & The Bricklayers – Up And Down The Hill – King
Mac Staten – There She Goes – Prelude
Bobby Rich – There's A Girl Somewhere – Sam Bea
Charisma Band – Ain't Nothin' Like Your Love – Buddha
Buddy Miles – I'm Just A Kiss Away – Columbia
Luther – Don't Wanna Be A Fool – Cotilion
Karmello Brooks – Tell Me baby – Milestone
Joan Baker – Everybody's Talking – Diamond
Impacts – Jerkin' In Your Seat – Counsel
Executive Four – I Gotta Good Thing Going – Lu Mai
John Wesley – Love Is Such A Funny Thing – Melic
Betty Wilson – I'm Yours – Dayco
Clyde McPhatter – Give Me One More Chance – Decca
Terry Callier – Look At Me Now – Cadet
Joe Douglas – Crazy Things – Playhouse
Don & Ron – I'm So So Sorry – White Cliff

John Weston - 5am – 6am

D C Blossoms – Hey Girl – Shrine
Patti Austin – All My Love – Coral
Vicki Labatt – Got To Keep Hanging On – Shagg
Cynthia – That's What I Am – Big Hit
Ronnie Micnair – Good Side Of Your Love – Tortoise
Gino Washington – I'm So In Love – Atak
Clydene Jackson – I Need Your Love – Crossover
Maxine Brown – Just Give Me One Good Reason – Epic
Supremes – Stormy – Acetate
Annabelle Fox – Lonely Girl – Satin
The Sweets – Something For My Baby – Soultown
Monique – If You Love Me – Maurci
Debbie Curtis – I Check My Mailbox – Jabro
Shirley Edwards – Dream My Heart – Shrine
Amanda Love – You Keep Calling Mr By Her Name – Starville
Jeanette Williams – I Can't Wait – Terry
Suger & The Spices – I Have Faith In Me – Swan
Sandpipers – Lonely To Long – Giant
The Honeybees – Never In A Million Years – Garrison
Sharon McMahon – Gotta Find Another Guy – Karen
Gambrells – You Gotta Move – Carla
The Capitols – Hello Stranger - Karen
J T Rhythm – My Sweet Baby – Palmer
Magnificent 7 – Never Will I Make My Baby Cry – Dial

Chic – 6am – 7am

Dynells – Call On Me – Atco
Stoppers – Come Back Baby – Jubilee
Bonnie Herman – Hush Don't Cry – Columbia

Rose St John – Fool Don't Laugh – Veep
Johnny Bartel – If This Isn't Love – Solid State
Cashmeres – Don't Let The Door Hit Your Back – Hem
The Strides – I Can Get Along – M-S
The Masquaders – That's The Same Thing - Acetate
Kenny Carter – What's That On Your Finger – Acetate
Constellations – I Don't Know About You – Gemini
Ultimates – Girl I've Been Trying To Tell You – Br Roma
Jan Jones – Independent Woman – Day Wood
Betty Wright – Man Of Mine – Alston
John Edwards – How Can I Make It – Acetate
R B Hudmon – Holdin' On – Atlantic
Rivage – Strung Out On Your Love – Tempus J
Fabulous Playmates – Don't Turn Your Back On Love – Select
The Minits – Still A Part Of Me – MGM (Sound Of Memphis)
Almeta Lattimore – These Memories – Mainstream
Darrow Fletcher – It's No Mistake – Crossover
Supremes – You've Been So Wonderful – Tamla
George Smith – I've Had It – Turntable
Walter Jackson – It's An Uphill Climb – Okeh
Al Wilson – I've Got A Feeling

The 100 Club, 8th December, 2001.

It was guest night tonight, and Butch, Mick Smith, and Shifty were not in evidence. Guests for the night were Ginger Taylor, Arthur Fenn, Jo Wallace and PTP from 'These Old Shoes'. Sometimes these nights work, others they don't. This time it did, and it was a really good night. Enough said.

'Turning Your Heartbeat Up' Weekender, Nuremburg, 14th / 15th December 2001.

Why is it that travelling to Europe is such a pain ? Once we get there we have a great time. This year the bag containing all the train tickets for John Weston, John Mills, Paddy and myself was stolen in Belgium. We ended up having to buy new tickets ! However, having travelled overnight on Wednesday we arrived in Nuremburg in good time to have a beer at Finnegans on the Thursday evening. So the weekend started in true style. Friady morning was taken up in trying to but a Junior Hacksaw because the keys to the padlocks on my DJ box were also stolen. Can you imagine how difficult it is trying to explain in English that you want a saw to cut some padlocks off ! I managed it though, and met the others in Finnegans at midday.

John Mills and I then went back to the hotel to saw the padlocks off. Now I know it was a cheap saw, and the padlocks were good quality Yale security locks, but within minutes it had stripped all the teeth off the saw, and not marked the lock. Back to Finnegans for a re-think. In the end, Martin, the bar manager used his grinder to cut the locks off.

That brings us to Friday night, Michael and Silke had arrived bringing Liz and Graham with them, we were all ready to go. With the exception of Paddy who had overindulged with the falling down water and had to be helped back to the hotel where he slept all night !

Carl and Maria Willingham rang up to say their plane had been diverted to Munich and all their luggage had gone missing, with the exception of Carl's records. They were in a taxi and would arrive two hours later. Then the music started.

The line up was Carl Willingham, John Mills, John Weston, Michael Fuchs, Ralf Mehnert, and yours truly. Each year we have been there have been more and more people into the music rather than just standing around drinking. This year was no exception. Over 600 turned up and the night was buzzing. The dancefloor filled up early on and stayed that way right until the last record at 6.00 am. Then back to the hotel for a cup of tea !

Saturday morning was spent wandering around the town, and then into Finnegans for a good English breakfast, with a pint of Kilkenny ! The others arrived around midday so we moved onto O'Sheas Bar and had a few more pints.

The alldayer was due to start at 3.00 pm and run through till 9.00 pm. I don't know whether it was by design or just how people felt but the next six hours were probably the best six hours of mid-tempo Soul I have ever heard in one session. Not many bodies through the door, but at least Paddy managed to join us !

Saturday night started at 10.00 pm and my spots were scheduled for later on, so I sat and chatted and sold records and tapes. Sales were nowhere near as good this year as previous years, but that just meant that I could pack up earlier and chat more. Again the dancefloor was full, again right up to the last record I played at 6.00 am 'The Drifter' by Ray Pollard. That was it, another weekender over. Well not quite !

On Sunday night the two Johns and I were asked if we would be guests on the Nuremburg Radio Z's Soul Show. Of course we said yes, so Osi, the host for the show, picked us up at 7.30 pm and we did a two hour show. At the time of writing I haven't got copies of the show but they should be on their way, so if anyone is interested give me a ring.

Overall, despite the hassle of having a bag stolen, it was another great weekend. My thanks go to Michael and Silke for inviting us, and for the wonderful Christmas present all the DJs received.

The Star Hotel, Worcester, 28th December, 2001.

What a nice friendly venue this is. I'd never been before, and wondered what the music policy would be when I got there. I needn't have worried though, I did an hour and a half, started with a few midtempo, then a few R & B, then some uptempo oldies, then a bit more R & B, and finished off with some current niter sounds, and people danced all the way through. Pete Richardson finished the night off for the last hour with a Motown and Club classics spot, which filled the dancefloor nicely, so everyone went home happy.

Bretby Allnighter, Bretby Country Club, 29th December, 2001.

Being my usual pessimistic self I was a bit worried about the numbers at this allnighter. Trentham Gardens was also on, and the weather reports from the North were of terrible snow. Of course I was totally wrong. Trentham was on, and busy I'm told, the snow fell at Bretby as well, but the numbers were well up. It was a great way to end the year, a good variety of music, lots of punters, and a busy dancefloor. Special mention amongst the DJs must go to Dude, who I know was very nervous about his spot, but I thought he did really well. Finally a mention for Sam Moore the promoter, who paid the bar staff extra to run for an extra hour.

So that's it for 2001, a busy year with some successful venues, some disasters, and some mediocre.In total I attended 61 venues, and DJ'ed at 38 of them. Overall though it's been another great year. Thanks to all the Promoters for having the nerve to put venues on (It's a thankless task a lot of the time, I know, I've been there !), Thanks to all the dancers wherever and whenever I've DJ'ed, and thanks to anyone who just spent time chatting to me.

Group Line Ups

The Younghearts (James Moore, Charles Ingersol, Ronnie Preyer, Earl Carter)
Maurice Williams & The Zodiacs (Maurice Williams, Henry Gaston, Wiley Bennett, Charles Thomas, Albert Hill, Willie Morrow)

The X-Cellents

The Original Playboys (members Roger Sayre (guitar and vocals), Jerry "Moon" Ditmer (bass), Barry Allenbaugh (keyboards and vocals) and Jerry Thomas (drums and vocals))

Leisure Time 1206 - I'll Always Be On Your Side / Hey Little Willie - 1965

The X-Cellents (members Roger Sayre, Jerry Ditmer, Ray Bushbaum and Jerry Thomas)

Smash 1996 - I'll Always Be On Your Side / Hey Little Willie – 1965

The E-Cellents (members Roger Sayre, Jerry Ditmer, Ray Bushbaum and Jerry Thomas)

Sure Play 0002 - And I'm Cryin' / The Slide – 1966

The X-Cellents (members Roger Sayre, Jerry Ditmer, Ray Bushbaum and Jerry Thomas)

Sure Play 1206-45-0003 - Little Wooden House / Hang It Up! - 1966

R. Sayre The Vacant Lot (members Roger Sayre, Jerry Ditmer, Ray Bushbaum and Jerry Thomas)

Ltd 0004 - Don't You Just Know It / This Little Feelin' - 1966 (some copies issued with picture sleeve)

The Younghearts

The Vows (members James Moore, Bob Solomon, ...)

V. I. P. 25016 - Buttered Popcorn* / Tell Me - 1965 *cover of 1961 recording by The Supremes on Tamla 54045.

The Younghearts (members James Moore, Charles Ingersol, Ronnie Preyer, Earl Carter and Bob Solomon who replaced Earl Carter in 1970 (died 30-May-1975 at age 31 - cause: cancer))

Canterbury 506 - A Little Togetherness / Beginning Of The End - 1967

The Young Hearts (members James Moore, Charles Ingersol, Ronnie Preyer and Earl Carter)

Pick-A-Hit 102 - Oh, I'll Never Be The Same Again / Get Yourself Together – 1967

The Younghearts (members James Moore, Charles Ingersol, Ronnie Preyer and Earl Carter)

Minit 32039 - Oh, I'll Never Be The Same Again / Get Yourself Together - 1969
Minit 32049 – I've Got Love For My Baby / Takin' Care Of Business – 1968
Minit 32057 – Sweet Soul Shakin' / Girls – 1969
Minit 32066 – Misty / Count Down – 1969
Minit 32084 – The Young Hearts Get Lonely Too (Live) / Little Togetherness – 1969

The Standards

Amos 134 – When You Wish Upon A Star / Inst – 1970

The New Young Hearts (Members Broughan Williams, Mark Putney, Peter Wayne, Shad Miller)

Soultown 10 – Young Hearts Get Lonely Too / A Little Togetherness – 1970
Zea 50001 – The Young Hearts Get Lonely Too / Why Do You Have To Go – 1970
Zea 50004 – When You Wish Upon A Star / A Little Togetherness – 1971

The Kings Of Hearts

Zea 50004 When You Wish Upon A Star / A Little Togetherness – 1971 (Same release as above)

The Younghearts

Avco Embassy 4554 – Oo-La-Wee / Change Of Mind – 1971
20th Century 2008 – Don't Crush My World / I'm Still Gonna Need You – 1971
20th Century 2054 – All The Love In The World / Do You Have The Time – 1973
20th Century 2080 – Stop What You're Doing Girl / Me And You – 1973
20th Century 2130 – Dedicate (My Life To You) / Wake Up And Start Standing – 1974
20th Century 2190 – We've Got Love / I Said To Myself – 1975
20th Century 2267 – Candy / My Love Grows Stronger – 1976
ABC 12036 – Sho 'Nuff Must Be Love / Let's Fall In Love Again – 1977
Soultown 3000 - I've Got Dancing Fever / Hey Love - 1980
Good Old Gold 067 - Oh, I'll Never Be The Same Again / Take Out - ?
Good Old Gold 068 - I've Got Love For My Baby / Honest I Do - ?

www.soulfulkindamusic.net

CPSIA information can be obtained
at www.ICGtesting.com
Printed in the USA
LVHW081619211122
733717LV00006B/629

9 781533 143259